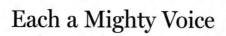

Each a Mighty Voice

Each a Mighty Voice

A Century of Speeches from
The Commonwealth Club of California

Edited by Steven Boyd Saum
Foreword by Kevin Starr
Afterword by Gloria C. Duffy

COMMONWEALTH CLUB OF CALIFORNIA
SAN FRANCISCO, CALIFORNIA

HEYDAY BOOKS
BERKELEY, CALIFORNIA

Library of Congress Cataloging-in-Publication Data

Each a mighty voice : a century of speeches from the
Commonwealth Club of California / [edited by]
Steven Boyd Saum ; foreword by Kevin Starr.
    p. cm.
  Includes index.
  ISBN 1-890771-87-2 (hardback : alk. paper)
  1. Speeches, addresses, etc., American--California. I.
Saum, Steven Boyd. II. Commonwealth Club of
California.
  PS572.C2E15 2004
  815'.50809794--dc22
                                     2004013157

Book design by Rebecca LeGates
Printed by Banta Book Group, Harrisonburg, VA

Orders, inquiries, and correspondence should be
addressed to:
Heyday Books
P.O. Box 9145, Berkeley, CA 94709
(510) 549-3564, fax (510) 549-1889
www.heydaybooks.com

Printed in the United States of America

10 9 8 7 6 5 4 3 2 1

*For the members of The Commonwealth Club of California,
out of respect for the commitment they have shown for over
a century to the notion that words and ideas matter*

The Commonwealth Club of California

Founded in 1903 as a public service organization, The Commonwealth Club of California is the nation's oldest and largest public affairs forum, with membership open to all. A nonpartisan nonprofit organization with eighteen thousand members, The Club hosts speeches, debates, and discussions throughout the San Francisco Bay Area on topics of regional, national, and international interest, as part of its mission of informing the public. The Club pays no honoraria to its speakers and is consistently rated one of the most prestigious speaking venues in the country.

The Club's founders had one major goal: to "get the facts" through in-depth study of current affairs. That is still The Club's goal today—to ensure that members and the general public hear all sides of important issues from the people who know the most about them. One hundred years ago, The Club established "study sections" to examine particular issues in depth, and this tradition is carried on today by Member-Led Forums that include international affairs, health and medicine, and environment and natural resources.

More than two hundred radio stations across the country broadcast Commonwealth Club programs each week. Started in 1924, this is the longest-running radio program in the United States. Select Club programs are also televised nationally on C-Span.

Excerpts and full transcripts of Club speeches, as well as detailed program listings, appear in The Club's publication, *The Commonwealth*. Published since 1925, *The Commonwealth* is distributed to the entire membership, as well as to schools, universities, and libraries nationwide.

The Commonwealth Club brings members closer to the people and events shaping the world around you. With over four hundred events every year—ranging from politics to the arts, media, literature, and even sports—The Commonwealth Club brings you face-to-face access to some of the most interesting people in the world.

The Commonwealth Club of California
595 Market Street, San Francisco, CA 94105
111 North Market Street, 6th Floor, San Jose, CA 95113
telephone: (415) 597-6700
fax: (415) 597-6729
www.commonwealthclub.org

Contents

Acknowledgments xi
Foreword by Kevin Starr xiii
Introduction: Loose Truth, by Steven Boyd Saum xvii

Section One: The Progressive Era and the New Deal

1911 Theodore Roosevelt, *The Doubtful Zone of Authority
Between State and Federal Authority* 3
1919 Woodrow Wilson, *The Peace Treaty and the
Covenant of the League of Nations* 15
1932 Franklin D. Roosevelt, *Present Public Problems* 24
1941 Chaim Weizmann, *The Jew and the World Today* 38

Section Two: The Cold War and Vietnam

1947 Cecil B. De Mille, *The Motion Pictures
and International Relations* 45
1951 Joseph R. McCarthy, *Communism in Our Government* 54
1959 Nikita Khrushchev, *The San Francisco Speech* 65
1960 Dwight D. Eisenhower, *Presidential Reflections* 76
1961 Edward Teller, *Peace through Civil Defense* 85
1967 Martin Luther King Jr., *The Future of Integration* 93
1967 George C. Wallace, *States' Rights and Constitutional
Government* 100
1967 Barry Goldwater, *The United States and the World Today* . . . 105
1968 Robert F. Kennedy, *What Do We Stand For? The Liberation
of the Human Spirit,* and *May 1968 Speech to The
Commonwealth Club of California* 112
1969 Tom Smothers, *Censorship and the New Freedoms* 126
1970 Abba Eban, *The Middle East: Its Past Agony and
Its Future Hope* 131
1971 Ronald V. Dellums, *A Radical Perspective on Life* 143
1972 Shirley Chisholm, *Democratic Party Presidential
Candidate Speaks* 148
1972 Katharine Graham, *Fairness and Freedom of the Press* 154

1973 Bella Abzug, *Every Issue Is a Woman's Issue* 167

1974 Jesse Jackson, *Rebirth of a Nation* 178

1976 Henry A. Kissinger, *The Permanent Challenge of Peace:*
U.S. Policy toward the Soviet Union 184

1976 George H. W. Bush, *The CIA and the*
Intelligence Community 198

1976 William Westmoreland, *Vietnam in Perspective* 204

1977 Morton Halperin, *The Crimes of the Intelligence Agencies* . . . 214

Section Three: Morning in America and the New World Order

1981 Joan Baez, *Human Rights in the Eighties: Seeing through*
Both Eyes 223

1983 Walter Cronkite, *Hear America Singing* 232

1983 Ronald Reagan, *Address to The Commonwealth Club* 242

1984 Prince Bandar bin Sultan, *Peace in the Middle East* 253

1984 Daniel Ortega Saavedra, *Peace in Central America* 260

1986 Desmond Tutu, *Freedom and Tolerance* 266

1986 Corazón Aquino, *People Power* 275

1987 Randy Shilts, *The Politics of AIDS* 281

1991 Richard B. Cheney, *U.S. Defense Policy: The Gulf War*
and Beyond 286

1991 Maxine Hong Kingston, *Writing in a Time of War* 293

1991 George Shultz and Don Oberdorfer, *U.S.–Soviet*
Relations on the Eve of Revolution 298

1991 Jacques Yves Cousteau, *The Rights of Future Generations* . . . 307

1992 Audrey Hepburn, *Children First: Building a Global Agenda* . . 313

1992 William Greider, *The Betrayal of American Democracy* 318

1992 Dan Quayle, *The Vice President Speaks* 324

1992 Amory Lovins, *Abating Global Warming for Fun and Profit* . . 331

1992 Mikhail Gorbachev, *A Special Presentation by*
His Excellency Mikhail Gorbachev 340

1994 Václav Havel, *From Prisoner to President* 349

Section Four: America Y2K and the Jihad

1993 Madeleine Albright, *What You Need to Know about
the UN and Foreign Policy Today* 359
1998 Kofi Annan, *The United Nations in Our Daily Lives* 367
1999 William Jefferson Clinton, *A State of the Union
for Foreign Policy* 374
1999 Mavis Leno, *Buried Alive* 392
2000 David Broder, *Democracy Derailed* 401
2001 John McCain and Russ Feingold,
Campaign Finance Reform 408
2001 Bill O'Reilly, *No Spin Zone* 416
2001 Hanan Mikhail-Ashrawi, *Peacemaking in the Middle East* . . . 423
2002 Patrick J. Buchanan, *Death of the West* 430
2002 Ralph Nader, *Crashing the Party* 436
2002 Lowell Bergman, *The Media and the War on Terrorism* 445
2002 Benjamin Barber, *Confronting Terrorism:
Smart Bombs or Smart Concepts?* 454

Afterword: On Context, by Gloria C. Duffy, Ph.D. 463

Sources of Speeches 469
Index 473

Acknowledgments

A book like this would not be possible without the work and dedication of many individuals who have both contributed their own efforts and mustered the resources of their organizations to assist with the task. Were it not for the efforts of Commonwealth Club members over the past hundred years, none of this material would be available in the first place. A century into The Club's work, thanks to the generous financial support of ChevronTexaco and the James Irvine Foundation, The Commonwealth Club and Heyday Books are able to bring to a new audience this remarkable collection of speeches on politics and the media. Our personal thanks go to Skip Rhodes (Corporate Community Engagement Manager, ChevronTexaco) and Mary Bitterman (former President and CEO, James Irvine Foundation) for believing in the project.

As for the exhilarating and exhausting chore of assembling the contents of this book itself: Justin Gerdes conducted a great deal of background research and can count among his credits tracking down a long-hidden copy of FDR's prepared remarks. Justin brought intelligence, a sense of critical inquiry, and a rare thoughtfulness and care to his work—which also included a fair amount of photo sleuthing. Helping assemble the contents from the earliest stages were also members of the editorial team at The Commonwealth Club, who over several years pulled together the thousands of pages of material we considered: interns Jamie Olsen, Alexandra Davidson, Carolyn Churchill, Clifford Agocs, and Kristen Stevens, and assistant editor Sonya Abrams. Thanks also go to the Club staffers and interns (including Kym Zielinski, Kristen Wright, and Kristina Reid) who were pressed into emptying out The Club's storage space in Alameda; to historians Diane North and William Issell for ideas and advice early on, as well as Linda Norton, Jim Quay, Patricia Wakida, Richard Walker, and Charles Wollenberg; and to Ralph Lewin and Alden Mudge at the California Council for the Humanities for suggestions and encouragement. Serving as guide on the editor's first foray into the Club archives (when they were still teetering towers of crumbling boxes), as well as moral support on the project in its nascent stage, was James Coplan Jr., who worked with The Club for a quarter of a century himself. Jeanne Wong worked with The Club for more than forty years and earned the appreciation and admiration of thousands of members over the years. She began here just before the Cuban missile crisis, and for this book she shared stories that hadn't been written down anywhere. (You might have seen her on television in August 2002, though, at a Commonwealth Club talk by Vice President Cheney, leading protestors out by the hand.) She retired in May 2004, and her meticulousness and warmth will be remembered by all of us for years to come.

Thanks to the direction of Elena Danielson, Director of the Hoover Institution Library and Archives, and support of Associate Archivist Lisa Miller, and particularly thanks to archival acumen (as well as physical labor) of Archival Specialist Natasha Porfirenko, all those crumbling boxes of Commonwealth Club materials are being sorted and catalogued. Without their assistance, this project would not include some of the gems it does. Likewise, without the work of the team that initiated The Commonwealth Club's Twentieth Century Audio Archive project to begin digitizing recordings of Club speeches going back to the 1940s, some of these gems would not have had the sparkle they do. Headphones off to Judson True, Catherine Mitchell, Gene Herson, and Rolando Esteverena, as well as to the David and Lucile Packard Foundation; for hands-on audio production, give credit to Ricardo Esway, Scott Shafer, Gregory Dalton, and Josh Coley; and thanks to Heather Wagner, Audio-Visual Specialist at Hoover, for ongoing work on The Club's audio archives.

For help in providing photographs worth thousands of words, we owe a great deal of gratitude to Richard Geiger and Gary Fong at the *San Francisco Chronicle* and to Laura Perkins, who brought her expertise in navigating the paper's archive. Edward F. Adams would be proud of the collaboration. Pat Akre at the San Francisco History Center of the San Francisco Public Library helped us track down a wealth of historical photographs. Susan Snyder and Linda Norton at The Bancroft Library offered their guidance and encouragement as well, and Susan Schendel of Hoover searched the Shultz archives. Longtime Club photographer Paul Eric Felder helped us plumb recent material and offered support for a book project from the beginning.

Thanks go to William F. Adams (great-grandson of The Club's founder) for underwriting our efforts to put together a helpful index. And last but not least, for getting our book from a collection of computer code to the page, I offer humble appreciation to the marvelous team at Heyday Books, particularly publisher Malcolm Margolin, editor Jeannine Gendar, editorial assistant Sarah Neidhardt, and art director Rebecca LeGates. They do beautiful work.

Steven Boyd Saum, May 2004

This book was made possible thanks to the generous support of ChevronTexaco and the James Irvine Foundation.

Foreword

Kevin Starr

One hundred years ago, three forces—pre-Progressivism, the developing maturity of the San Francisco Bay Area, and the power of the spoken word—converged to energize the founding of The Commonwealth Club of California. True, individual personalities were involved, especially *San Francisco Chronicle* editorial and features writer Edward F. Adams, who first convened The Club; but Adams and the founding members were taking their direction from the threefold convergence of reform, urbanism, and personal testimony that were defining public life in the early years of the twentieth century.

Notice the distinction that is being made between pre-Progressivism and Progressivism in its ascendancy. As of 1903, the Lincoln-Roosevelt League that spearheaded Progressivism in California was four years in the future. Hiram Johnson's victory at the polls would be another seven years hence. High Progressivism, in point of fact—meaning the great reform legislatures of 1911 to 1917—would be almost impossible to imagine as of 1903, so captive was California to special interests and machine politics. Still, reform—more correctly, pre-Progressive reform—was in the air. Everywhere one looked in California during this period, a growing cadre of men and women were trying to make California a better place. In San Francisco the pioneering female physician Charlotte Amanda Blake Brown had recently established Children's Hospital in an effort to bring comprehensive care to a neglected portion of the population. A San Francisco banker by the name of Amadeo Peter

Giannini was thinking very carefully about the reform of American banking practices, specifically the extension of banking privileges to ordinary men and women. Another Bay Area resident, Phoebe Apperson Hearst, was thinking with equal creativity about the early education of children, the education of women in the professions, and the need to improve the University of California. In Southern California, reformers such as John Randolph Haynes, H. Gaylord Wilshire, Kate Crane Gartz, and others were thinking comparably regarding the public ownership of utilities, the need to reform municipal government, and the right of women to vote. At the newly established Leland Stanford Junior University in Palo Alto, founding President David Starr Jordan was equally concerned with the rights of women as he sought to align his new university with the pre-Progressive forces that were coalescing.

Jordan was also calling for the upgrading of architecture and urban design—in San Francisco especially. His architectural challenge to San Francisco, made in an 1899 essay, was part of an outpouring in this period calling for an architecture, a city plan, and a civic administration worthy of San Francisco's newly achieved status as a metropolitan capital. Former Mayor James Duval Phelan, another great reformer of this period, had said as much—innumerable times—while serving as mayor from 1897 through 1901. San Francisco, Phelan urged, had come of age. It was no longer a frontier outpost and was hardly even a provincial capital. It was, rather, the capital of the Far West and a leading city on the Asia Pacific Basin, and it should conduct itself accordingly. That is why Phelan filed claim on the waters of the Tuolumne River, which eventually led to the Hetch Hetchy project: so that San Francisco might have the water and the hydroelectricity with which to fulfill the role being assigned to the city by the dawning twentieth century. Phelan and others had already formed the Association for the Improvement and Adornment of San Francisco, and in May 1904 that group extended an invitation to the famed planner-architect Daniel Hudson Burnham of Chicago to come to San Francisco and create for the city a new master plan. A new generation of architects, meanwhile—among them Walter Bliss, William Faville, Willis Polk, Albert Pissis, and Bernard Maybeck—were responding to Jordan's and Phelan's challenge with a series of buildings fully worthy of San Francisco's developing identity.

Such aspiration and ferment, such civic ambition, such an outpouring of creativity and reform—building great buildings, launching the reform of politics, re-planning cities, taking higher education to a new level—involved ideas, a multitude of ideas, some congruent, others contradictory. Here was an era, in fact, in which existing institutions—newspapers, magazines, literature, the pulpit—were straining to keep up with the pace of ideas. Without radio, television, or the Internet, such ideas had to be either written and read, or they could come in speech alone, whether such speech be the prepared utterances of the pulpit or university classroom or the more spontaneous speech of political debate. Not surprisingly, the printed word was gaining strength in this era. In such figures as Frank Norris, Jack London, Mary Austin, John Muir, Edwin Markham, and others, the literary tradition of California was being re-founded. Academic scholarship had arrived in Berkeley and Palo Alto, and professors such as Joseph LeConte, Henry Morse Stephens, and Edward Wickson were respected public figures, as was horticulturalist Luther Burbank of Santa Rosa. The pulpit itself was entering a golden age. And newspaper writers such as Fremont Older, Chester Rowell, and Ambrose Bierce were at the top of their game.

But words conveying vital ideas could not merely be written or read or recited from prepared manuscripts. For the era to reach its highest intensity and creativity, there must also be speech, discussion, debate, the spoken word. At some dawn time in our development, language made its appearance; indeed, the very emergence of speech was perhaps the pivotal moment in human evolution. Not surprisingly, then, human beings—no matter how sophisticated or diverse our media—have always adhered to the spoken word as the primary mode of communication. Speaking, we become more human.

Since classical times, the spoken word has held its own in public discourse. Nor has the invention of printing overwhelmed it. Indeed, it might even be claimed that the more information finds its way into print, the more valuable—the more respected, the more necessary—becomes the spoken word. The spoken word constitutes living testimony. Someone is speaking to someone else, even if that someone else is in a larger audience. Even if the speech is prepared, the very utterance of it, coming from the very physical self of the speaker, confers an authenticity almost anthropological in its subliminal power. If an idea is true, runs an ancient human assumption, or even if it seeks to be considered as true, it has to first pass through the crucible of speech. For the ancient Hebrews, a word, once uttered, possessed a life of its own. In Hellenic philosophy, the word, the logos, was the only way that an idea could know itself. All traditions—whatever their religious and philosophical orientation—bear a special reverence for sworn testimony: the truth, the whole truth, and nothing but the truth, coming from one individual, communicated to another, as honestly as possible.

And so the founders of The Commonwealth Club, poised on the brink of an era of technological development—the radio within a few years, film even then appearing, the invention of television a quarter of a century off, popular use of the Internet nearly a century into the future—reaffirmed the spoken word as being essential to civic discourse. And so the speaking began, voices of every sort, and the speaking continued down through the century, addressing the great public issues of the time in the belief that such public utterance constituted a high and very necessary forum for democracy. Soon, the radio—the medium that bears the most intimate relationship to the spoken word—would take these speeches to innumerable other places; but the authenticity of such broadcasts came from the fact that the words being heard were words being spoken, living words to a living audience in pursuit of a living truth.

In time as well, the pre-Progressivism of 1903 would become the full-fledged reform movement of the following decade. The city of San Francisco would become the nucleus of the fourth largest urban concentration in the United States. And The Commonwealth Club of California, which took its origins in a city struggling to reform itself, would become a respected international forum for that one necessary crucible—the spoken word—through which all ideas must pass if they are to enter history energized by authenticity and moral force.

Introduction: Loose Truth

But failure is not an American habit; and in the strength of great hope we must all shoulder our common load.—Franklin Delano Roosevelt

---

September 1932. At the end of a golden day of Indian summer, one hundred thousand people line the sidewalks between San Francisco's Ferry Building and the Palace Hotel. The occasion: the arrival of the governor of New York and Democratic candidate for president of the United States, Franklin Delano Roosevelt. He has come in by train from Sacramento to Oakland, and the ferry carries him across the water to the city where he'll spend the night. The city's Republican mayor turns out to accompany Governor Roosevelt on the ride from the wharf down Market Street to the Palace, where a thousand more people are jammed between the columns of the lobby.

"Happy Days are Here Again" is his campaign song. And this greeting will be the highlight of his tour of the West. In return, at a luncheon the next day, Roosevelt will deliver one of the most stirring addresses of his career, monumental in the way it challenges Americans to rethink the social, political and economic structure of the nation—a talk that will be judged by journalists and FDR himself to be the best of his campaign, and by scholars as one of the greatest American speeches of the twentieth century. It will be referred to as "New Conditions Impose New Requirements upon Government and Those Who Conduct Government" or, later, in a nod to Edward Bellamy, the "Looking Forward" speech. It will also be known simply as "The Commonwealth Club Speech."

Not quite thirty years old in 1932, The Commonwealth Club of California has invited Roosevelt to speak on "Present Public Problems," which is how the speech is titled in his prepared remarks. Roosevelt knows Club members are some of the most influential men in California business and politics, and that The Club itself, as Roosevelt says, "has stood in the life of this city and state, and, it is perhaps accurate to add, the nation, as a group of citizen leaders interested in fundamental problems of government, and chiefly concerned with achievement of progress in government through nonpartisan means." His cousin Teddy spoke to the group more than twenty years earlier and, at a black-tie dinner, verbally scrapped with a couple of members over whether the federal government should be involved in conserving the nation's natural resources. The next year, Theodore Roosevelt enlisted one of The Club's charter members, Hiram Johnson (then governor of California), as his running mate on the Progressive "Bull Moose" ticket. The day before FDR arrives in San Francisco, he publicly praises Johnson, now a U.S. senator, for being "long a warrior in the ranks of American progress."

Those who occupied the White House after Theodore Roosevelt vacated it made their own pilgrimages to speak to this club. William Howard Taft addressed the group twice, once discussing the Philippines and once the League of Nations. Knowing that The Commonwealth Club had helped shape important legislation and policy in the Golden State, Woodrow Wilson came to the group as part of his final, heroic effort to enlist American support for ratification of the League of Nations treaty. Calvin Coolidge came to give an update on dealing with Congress. Warren G. Harding made the journey as well but never had the chance to deliver his address: the night before his talk, he died in his sleep. By the time FDR gives his address, Republican rival Herbert Hoover, a *member* of The Commonwealth Club, has already spoken to the group four times; before his death, he'd address The Club more than a dozen times.

From his suite in the Palace, Roosevelt travels down the main floor in a freight elevator. His son James assists him up the fifteen-foot-long ramp to the speaker's platform. Photographers squeeze forward, flash bulbs popping nonstop. Ten minutes later, Club staffers herd them away. The hotel has furnished a massive, carved oak chair upholstered in red as a throne for the guest of honor. Roosevelt stands to address the audience of more than seventeen hundred men. He works his way around the chair and grips the top of the back with one hand, clasps a sheaf of papers in the other. "My friends," he says, "I want to speak not of politics but of government. I want to speak not of parties, but of universal principles. They are not political, except in that larger sense in which a great American once expressed a definition of politics, that nothing in all of human life is foreign to the science of politics."

September again, and the California sun is shining brilliantly on a Monday morning in 1959. A visitor staying at the Hotel Mark Hopkins takes the elevator down from his suite on the fourteenth floor and heads out for an early morning stroll on California Street. This pudgy fellow with quick eyes and a jaunty step—journalist William Randolph Hearst Jr. once described him to The Commonwealth Club as a "strong, rugged, tough guy, as bald as Yul Brynner; there's a wart on his nose and another on his forehead, not the most attractive guy you've ever seen"—admires the view from Nob Hill: the sparkling bay, the hills of Berkeley and Oakland, Angel Island, the fortress-like Alcatraz. He waves at a passing cable car. He stops while a woman fiddles with her camera, fumbling as she tries to take his picture. Snipers are on the rooftops of the surrounding buildings, but the visitor has told his bodyguards to stay back. Averell Harriman once hosted this fellow at his New York residence and told him—a man who had herded sheep and worked in coal mines as a pipefitter—that had he emigrated to the U.S., as so many of his countrymen had, he would have likely risen to be a great union leader. Instead, he's here at President Eisenhower's invitation, first among equals in the council of ministers of the Union of Soviet Socialist Republics. His name: Nikita Sergeyevich Khrushchev.

At a dinner cohosted by The Commonwealth Club, Khrushchev tells the crowd of nearly three thousand people who have filled the ballrooms at the Sheraton Palace (and a thousand more watching on closed-circuit television in another room) that the sun today shone as brightly in California as it had in Crimea, where he had rested before he embarked on his tour of America. The clouds seem to be clearing, too, in the perpetually gray skies over U.S.-Soviet relations, thanks in no small part to Khrushchev's visit to San Francisco. "You have charmed my heart," he tells the crowd—adding, "but in my head I still think that our system is a good system."

The *New York Times* will carry news of the dinner on page one, beneath a triple-decker headline, reporting that according to Henry Cabot Lodge Jr., Khrushchev's official escort, the visit has done more than any other stopover on the tour to cement American-Soviet goodwill. That report is especially welcome, coming in the wake of a disastrous visit to Los Angeles where the head of Twentieth Century Fox traded jibes with the premier at a star-studded luncheon, the mayor insulted Khrushchev at an official dinner, and Khrushchev was denied a visit to Disneyland after someone threw a tomato at the police.

Before The Commonwealth Club, Khrushchev rambles and jokes—he's not fond of being bound by the "scraps of paper" that contain his prepared texts—and he invites the whole city to visit the Soviet Union. He gets a standing ovation. But even in San Francisco, some are not happy The Club is hosting the man who earned the sobriquet "Butcher of Budapest" for putting down the 1956 Hungarian uprising. A spate of angry letters and resignations from Club membership arrive before the dinner, though they're far outnumbered by members who are irate because there are not enough tickets to go around. San Francisco Mayor George Christopher presents Khrushchev with a redwood gavel; its three raps have become synonymous with the opening and closing of Commonwealth Club meetings. For his part, Khrushchev gushes, "I would like to put this gavel to good use in the Soviet Union and to strike it after the signature of a treaty of friendship, nonaggression, and eternal love between the peoples of the Soviet Union and of the United States of America."

May 1967. LBJ is in the White House, and before the year is out, nearly half a million U.S. troops will be in Vietnam. In the Hotel St. Francis on San Francisco's Union Square, a Baptist preacher has been invited to address The Commonwealth Club on civil rights and Vietnam. "Many are now thinking of the long hot summer ahead," he observes—hot because of the riots and "urban disorder" that are bearing down on the nation—"and have forgotten the long cold winter behind." In San Francisco, the year will be recorded as the "summer of love." Across the rest of the country, the anger and poverty and despair that fueled the violence in Omaha, Brooklyn, Jacksonville, and Cleveland the summer before are still unassuaged. Riots have already occurred that spring in Nashville and Omaha; Mississippi has called in the National Guard.

"The job of the Civil Rights Movement is to make America one nation, with liberty and justice for all," the minister says. He has a gentle Georgia drawl and speaks with an intellectual and moral authority, with a sense of tradition and higher purpose that one expects from a recipient of the Nobel Peace Prize. "The future of integration," he says, "will be determined by the speed with which we truly become one." He is Dr. Martin Luther King Jr., and his warnings about the summer to come are sadly prescient. Newark and Detroit will see the worst of the violence, with dozens killed, millions of dollars in property destroyed, and thousands of federal troops called in to quell the violence.

As for integration, King says, "Achievements of the last twelve years have been obtained at bargain rates. It didn't cost the nation a thing. But to move forward will cost billions."

November 1972. Four months since the *Washington Post* carried the headline "5 Held in Plot to Bug Democrats' Office Here," and four months since it was revealed that James W. McCord Jr., the salaried security coordinator for President Nixon's Committee to Re-elect the President (CREEP), was among those arrested for the break-in. Thus began *Post* coverage of Watergate—which in October included the FBI's revelation that "the Watergate bugging incident stemmed from a massive campaign of political spying and sabotage conducted on behalf of President Nixon's reelection." That reelection comes by landslide in November 1972, just a week before *Post* publisher Katharine Graham speaks at The Commonwealth Club, laying out what is at stake in the attacks the paper now faces from the administration: "What it really comes down to," she says, "is nothing less than the state of the First Amendment; our freedom to gather the news and to publish it, and your freedom to read it." Also at stake, of course, is the office of the president, from which this scandal will cause Richard Nixon to resign.

May 1992. A quarter of a century after Martin Luther King Jr.'s talk, the vice president of the United States speaks to The Commonwealth Club on family values. Three weeks before, network television carried live the verdict of the trial of four white Los Angeles police officers accused of beating motorist Rodney King, who is black. One officer was found guilty of use of excessive force; the others were acquitted of all charges. The outrage many African Americans felt at the injustice exploded, and in the mayhem that followed in LA, businesses were looted, bystanders assaulted, and fires set throughout the city. Four thousand National Guard troops were called out, and three days passed before the violence subsided.

The vice president speaks of the failed War on Poverty and the creation of a self-perpetuating welfare system in America. He speaks of the problem of children born out of wedlock and declares, "Bearing babies irresponsibly is simply wrong. Failing to support children one has fathered is wrong, and we must be unequivocal about this." The sentence that follows will be carried across the country and becomes a defining moment in Quayle's tenure as vice president: "It doesn't help matters when prime-time TV has Murphy Brown, a character who supposedly epitomizes today's intelligent, highly paid professional woman, mocking the importance of fathers by bearing a child alone and calling it"—and he pauses for emphasis—"just another lifestyle choice." Those whom Quayle has dubbed the "media elites" will mock the correlation. For that one line, his 1992 Commonwealth Club address, billed as "The Vice President Speaks," is instead recorded in the annals of politics and media as "The Murphy Brown Speech."

Franklin Roosevelt, Nikita Khrushchev, Martin Luther King Jr., Katharine Graham, and Dan Quayle are just a few of the men and women who appear in this book, and whose ideas and character are brought to life in their own words. Odds are you've picked up this volume because, among the names of political leaders and media luminaries included, you saw a few you recognized. Scroll through the table of contents from 1967 to 1968 and alongside Martin Luther King Jr., you'll find George Wallace, Barry Goldwater, and Robert F. Kennedy—who gave one of the last speeches of his life to The Commonwealth Club in May '68. And while the book is put together chronologically, we might instead have undertaken the interesting exercise of juxtaposing Joseph McCarthy and Bella Abzug, Nikita Khrushchev and Bill O'Reilly, Ronald Reagan and Joan Baez, Henry Kissinger and Corazón Aquino, Desmond Tutu and Richard Cheney, Maxine Hong Kingston and Edward Teller, Václav Havel and Cecil B. De Mille, Lowell Bergman and Audrey Hepburn.

So how did all these speakers get here? Well, that's a good story, too: one about an institution that holds claim to being the premier public affairs forum in the U.S. and happens to host the longest-running radio show in the country as well. It is an institution that Grateful Dead drummer Mickey Hart has called "a jewel set deep in the heart of San Francisco" and that Madeleine Albright says "is to free speech what the Golden Gate is to bridges, and fireworks are to the Fourth of July." It's an organization of which Richard Nixon and Ronald Reagan were members, yet one which led Ralph Nader to wonder aloud, "I wonder why there aren't more Commonwealth Clubs in other cities to develop civic forums the way your club has done. I like the word 'commonwealth' because it involves what we own in common in the United States....I think that word is going to come back into vogue."

An Agora for San Francisco

Set the Wayback Machine for February 1903. The population of California is seven hundred and fifty thousand—about the same number of people who will inhabit the forty-nine square miles of San Francisco one hundred years later. It's just over a month before the Senate will ratify the treaty granting the U.S. the right to build the Panama Canal, and three months before President Theodore Roosevelt (namesake of the newly introduced teddy bear) will arrive in the great American port city on the Pacific to dedicate the new Manila Bay Monument in Union Square—a monument erected in recognition of Admiral Dewey's defeat of the Spanish in the Philippines just a few years before. That summer, the Ford Motor Company will incorporate, William S. Harley and Walter Davidson will make their first motorcycle, and in December, the Wright brothers will get *The Flyer* airborne above the dunes of North Carolina.

It's a cold, clear night in San Francisco. A Tuesday. An editorial and features writer for the *San Francisco Chronicle*, Edward F. Adams, has arranged a dinner at Marchand's Restaurant, overlooking Union Square. The sixty-three-year-old Adams has spent months "ringing doorbells," trying to drum up interest in a new project, a "public service club," because, as this newspaper-man has acknowledged, the press and the universities do not provide people with all the facts they need to make informed decisions. Out of the dozens invited, only a handful agree to attend. Yet what a handful: Benjamin Ide Wheeler, president of the University of California; Superior Court Justice William P. Lawlor; and Dr. Frederic Burk, president of San Francisco State Normal School, later known as San Francisco State University. Strolling up Geary Street with Adams is John P. Young, managing editor of the *Chronicle*.

Following dinner, reading from a prepared text, Adams announces that "California suffers greatly because the best elements of the population fail to cooperate for the common good as effectively as the bad elements cooperate for evil purposes." The state needs more help than editorials can provide. "The good elements which compose the vast majority of our population," he says, "lack only good leadership to unite them for good purposes. I propose that we lead. I have no fear of lack of following so long as it is self-evident that we only propose to find truth and turn it loose in the world."

That audacious mission, Adams says, will be accomplished by a "fact-finding forum," not another "boosters' club." We might call the institution that took shape a think tank, one in which its members study in depth the vital problems of the day and dine together to discuss them and their solutions. For a name, renowned classicist Wheeler suggests *Agora*—taking inspiration from the marketplace of ancient Athens, where members of the polis would gather to discuss politics and philosophy. (Or, as Adams put it years later, "where Socrates loafed and gabbed, leaving his poor wife, Xanthippe, to bring in the wood and hustle for something to eat.") The name doesn't quite stick. To some it sounds a little too close to *angora;* given the mature age of the founders and their abundant facial hair, it is suggested their forum might become known as the Old Goats' Club. Meeting again a few months later, they land on a name that drops the classical allusion and sets out a vision for what it is they're trying to forge: The Commonwealth Club of California.

The Club was founded amid the reforms building toward the Progressive era, when there were efforts to curb the power and influence wielded by special interests in the state—especially the railroad giants, such as the Southern Pacific, which virtually ran the state of California as its own fiefdom. Out of the reform movements also came an age, as a writer for the *Los Angeles Times* opined a few years later, that "might be aptly named the age of clubs." But, that writer noted, unlike so many others, this club was not "disposed to waste its wind on dreamy, impracticable notions." Despite being headquartered in San Francisco, it was "composed of level-headed, practical business men....It is an added pleasure to think that that fad-ridden city has one institution of real merit."

The Club was meant to be a forum where, Adams said, men could engage in full-throated discussions about shaping policies with "absolute intellectual honesty in the perfect assurance that what any man may say in the privacy of The Club will never be made use of to his injury or discredit." Their concerns were local, statewide, and, very soon, national and international, though addressed from a California perspective. The man they asked to serve as the first president was not from San Francisco but Sacramento: Colonel Harris Weinstock, "six feet high and broad as humanity," a businessman known throughout the state as a square dealer. Adams speculated that membership, which was by invitation, might one day reach one hundred men. Five years later, membership in The Club had grown to four hundred and its reputation was known statewide, from Eureka to El Centro.

Beginning with a look at labor relations, The Club issued reports known for their thoroughness and objectivity. One study looked at "Regulation of Water Rights" in 1905, just five years after the first irrigation water poured into the Imperial Valley, and assessed, "California has absolutely no state administrative system for assuming the equitable distribution of water in accordance with the rights of each user and the public." The Club actively debated the proposed Hetch Hetchy dam—still a live wire nearly a century later. The agenda also included serious social concerns: child labor (1906), Indian rights (1909), air pollution (1913). A "powerful engine for educational and political reform," as the *Chronicle* put it, The Club shaped new legislation: a civil service system to replace the spoils system (1904); the direct primary law, which took selection of primary candidates out of smoke-filled rooms and put it in the hands of voters (1907); California banking laws (1908); jury selection (1920); public defender's offices (1932). The Club helped to enact permanent voter registration and absentee voting, and to establish small claims courts. A 1935 study of migrant labor shocked readers with its description of the conditions in which laborers lived. In 1909 alone, The Club urged sixty-two bills and three constitutional amendments on the state legislature. Adams traveled to Sacramento fight for their passage. "The bills went into the legislative wastebasket," lamented Earle Ashley Walcott, The Club's first executive secretary, in a talk nearly two decades later—"from which nine following legislatures have slowly fished them out and put them on the statute books....So much for being ahead of your time." One boost to reformist efforts came in 1910, when charter member Hiram Johnson was elected governor on a Progressive platform of "initiative, referendum, and recall." In the form of amendments to the state constitution, that trinity has profoundly shaped California politics ever since—not necessarily, some would argue, as journalist David Broder does in this book, for the better.

The recall amendment of 1911 was written by Club member John Randolph Haynes and debated at length by The Club. During the 2003 gubernatorial recall campaign, Arnold Schwarzenegger, appearing in the California State Railroad Museum in Sacramento, invoked Hiram Johnson's crusade against the power of the railroad barons. Ballot initiatives now blossom like poppies after the rainy season, but they were once more scarce: it is this process that begat a Club-sponsored reform of the state budget system in the early 1920s that California Governor C. C. Young esteemed "the greatest achievement in governmental administration in California's history."

As universities and well-heeled think tanks expanded the breadth and depth of their research, The Club evolved from advocacy organization to speaker's forum. Tax-exempt status put an end to lobbying efforts in the 1970s. But The Club still engages in special projects that fit within the parameters of a nonpartisan forum: a survey in 2000 of political candidates' health-care policies; an award-winning television documentary, *Final Choice,* looking at right-to-die issues; and, most recently, a multi-year project studying governance issues in the Golden State.

Not By Bread Alone

Every Saturday until 1917, and thereafter every Friday at noon, Club members would pack the Gold Ballroom of the Sheraton Palace to hear from royalty and religious leaders, cabinet officers and diplomats, inventors and educators, journalists and heroes, industrialists and labor leaders, travelers and scientists, generals and admirals, presidents and would-be presidents. (Shortly after FDR's speech to The Club, Socialist Norman Thomas spoke. More recently, Ralph Nader and Pat Buchanan took to The Club's podium in the same month.) It was not until 1910 that The Club invited women to speak, with Dr. Caroline Rosenberg, president of Mills College, leading the way. The Club studied the issue of women's suffrage and for decades hosted Ladies Day events (which women were allowed to attend!), and in 1971, a mere sixty-eight years after its founding, The Club admitted its first women members. (That was two years after Yale and Princeton first admitted female undergraduates.) When Bella Abzug spoke to The Club in 1973, she noted that the list of prominent past speakers only included seven women. "So I understand you left a few off," she said. What she probably didn't know was that as late as the sixties, the executive secretary would station a female office manager at the door and charge her with scouting for women who were trying to sneak in by dressing up in men's business suits.

To list all the men and women who have spoken at The Club would fill more than a hundred pages. Among names immediately recognizable to us nearly a century later are labor leader Samuel Gompers and William Jennings

Bryan, who spoke on "The Causeless War" in 1916, as well as Polish composer and politician Ignace Paderewski and arctic explorer Admiral Robert E. Peary.

The year 1924, *The Nation* editorialized at the time, was destined to be known as "the radio year." It was also the year The Commonwealth Club took to the airwaves with its Friday luncheon addresses carried live via the California Farm Bureau's radio network. The three raps of the gavel on the podium echoed across the airwaves, and The Club became the first organization of its kind to host a weekly radio show. Speakers could now be heard by thousands of people—and later, with national broadcasts, hundreds of thousands. Naturally, The Club hosted radio pioneer Guglielmo Marconi (in 1933), though it would not begin to record its programs for another decade.

The 1920s also saw The Club ramping up its work in publishing with the inauguration of a weeky bulletin, *The Commonwealth,* carrying news of upcoming speakers and meetings, as well as "Friday Flashes": edited transcriptions of luncheon addresses from, over the next two decades, the likes of muckraking journalist Lincoln Steffens, lawyer Clarence Darrow, educator Robert Gordon Sproul, writer Upton Sinclair, architect Bernard Maybeck, California Governor Earl Warren, Secretary of Labor Frances Perkins, journalists Clare Booth Luce and husband Henry, Supreme Court Justice William O. Douglas, Vice President Harry S. Truman, and singer and actor Paul Robeson. World leaders who spoke to The Club included Manuel Quezón, first president of the Philippine Commonwealth, and Chaim Weizmann—whose 1941 address about the plight of the Jews is included in this anthology, and who would go on to become the first president of an independent Israel.

Commonwealth Club 101

Folks not already acquainted with The Commonwealth Club might associate the name with some wood-paneled watering hole where British expats drink brandy and savor cigars. Fifty years ago, The Club was headquartered in the Hotel St. Francis and it did in fact boast a "spacious replica of a famed study in England" replete with "dark, hand-carved and paneled oak. Comfortable chairs and chesterfields for reading or study—and 'Silence Please' signs [to] assure your freedom to concentrate." And it is true that founder Edward F. Adams was fond of pungent cigars. But look up *commonwealth* in the OED, and the first definition you see is "public welfare; general good or advantage." Working for the common good—noble democratic aspirations indeed. But the OED then notes this definition is obsolete in ordinary use. Which raises a larger question: Has the notion of working for the common good become obsolete, too? As we round the corner into the twenty-first century, do we see a disinvestment in community, both in the literal and metaphoric sense? That, in fact, is one of the questions that some of the more recent speeches in this book try to answer. And, as you might imagine, though they spoke only weeks apart in 1992, Vice President Dan Quayle and *Rolling Stone* National Editor William Greider may have noted similar symptoms ailing the body politic—but not causes and solutions.

Since its inception, at times with more diligence than at others, The Club has addressed the breadth and diversity of the state and the nation. Negro Labor News Service Editor Frank Cross spoke on "The Negro at the Crossroads" in the 1930s, and NAACP Secretary Dr. Walter White spoke on "The Negro and the Crisis" in 1942—discussing some of the same issues that scholar Ron Takaki would address sixty years later, taking a historic view of the World War II fight for freedom abroad and equal rights at home. The 1960s saw African American speakers taking on broader political issues: Louis E. Lomax on worldwide nonwhite unrest (1964) and UN Undersecretary for Special Political Affairs Ralph Bunche on UN activities (1966). In recent years, The Club has made an effort to get out the message that its work is to look at issues that affect people young and old, no matter their race, class, or gender. It once had the reputation of being a "predominantly white, affluent, male" stronghold, as one journalist put it in his coverage of Jesse Jackson's 1984 talk. For several decades, though, membership has been open to all; invitations are no longer required. The most rapidly growing demographic of The Club these days is the under-thirty-five set, thanks to the work of Inforum, a division of The Club that looks at edgier issues, such as gay marriage, partial birth abortion, and online music.

This leads back to the question of The Club's politics. The simple answer, for those of us who take seriously The Club's mission: nonpartisan. Really. Conservative newspapers have mocked The Club for inviting union leaders, yet it has also been described as "a forum before which liberal Democrats usually receive little more than cold stares." Hundreds have come to demonstrate outside during talks by Mohammed Zia Ul-Haq and Madame Nhu; talks by Henry Kissinger, Richard Cheney, and Paul Wolfowitz have been interrupted by protestors. Joseph McCarthy elicited one shout of "Libel!" from the back of the room during his talk. And Enron president Jeffrey Skilling was hit with a pie—which was smuggled past the security checkpoint at the door. (For the record, it was blueberry—which *Wall Street Journal* reporters got right—not chocolate, as the *New York Times* claimed.)

The eighteen thousand members are now pretty evenly split between women and men, donkeys and elephants, with a few fierce independents. Audiences differ radically, depending on who's speaking. In March '02, Michael Moore had 'em packed in so tight we were pushing fire code violations. In May '02, George W. Bush received a standing ovation. In September '02, so did Al Gore.

One of The Club's most important contributions has been the California Book Awards, created in 1931 to bring recognition to writers and a West Coast literary scene badly neglected by the East Coast publishing establishment. Among the recipients of the more than three hundred and fifty medals awarded: Ray Bradbury, Michael Chabon, Czeslaw Milosz, Richard Rodriguez, William Saroyan, Wallace Stegner, John Steinbeck, and Amy Tan.

And Speaking of Books

What about this one? Some thirty thousand speeches have been delivered at The Commonwealth Club, so an omnibus anthology of the famous and infamous would be about the size of a cable car. We wanted a book you could pick up without a forklift. So back to The Club's roots we went, to politics and the media and where the two intersect. Even so, an exhaustive anthology of presidents, pundits, world leaders, and journalists would fill a few shelves, unless their remarks were edited down to sound bites. Instead, all of us involved in this project hope you will find that this book illuminates (in brilliant flashes, naturally) some of the pivotal moments and fundamental issues of the twentieth century and the beginning of the twenty-first. With a title courtesy of William Wordsworth, *Each a Mighty Voice* includes important people with something valuable to say in their historical moment—and, ideally, delivering a message that resonates across the years: Woodrow Wilson arguing passionately for the ratification of the League of Nations treaty; Corazón Aquino leading the People Power Revolution to victory in the Philippines; Desmond Tutu gauging, in 1986, the numbered days of apartheid against the willingness of the system's defenders to let it go. It is a collection of spoken words that bring together past and present, with arguments from decades ago that resonate today, from the Middle East to the UN to the environment. There are calls to action—Randy Shilts sketching out the obstructionist politics of AIDS; Audrey Hepburn making a plea on behalf of UNICEF. Ghostly voices echo from a time and place that hardly seem real today: Edward Teller evoking the palpable fear of nuclear annihilation in 1961 (a year before the Cuban missile crisis), or, only twenty years ago, Nicraguan leader Daniel Ortega Saavedra pleading for peace (a popular theme among world leaders and diplomats) in Central America. George Wallace's conjuring up of segregation as a matter of states' rights under the Constitution is still unsettling; and, in its discussion of where the authority of the federal government ends and that of states begins, you'll find it picks up some of the arguments that Teddy Roosevelt raised decades before.

You don't have to be a policy wonk or political junkie to find something provoking or downright inspiring in this volume. Asking Americans to tap their finest qualities, the breadth and the depth of the ideal of the nation, Walter Cronkite takes his text from another Walter—Whitman—and says, "Shut up and listen...you can still hear America singing." Before announcing his bid for the presidency in 1968, Bobby Kennedy does some soul-searching and asks, "What do we stand for?" His answer: "The liberation of the human spirit." Ron Dellums jettisons his planned topic—Congress—at the last minute and heads for the more broadly philosophical: "A Radical Perspective on Life." And closing the curtain on the collection is scholar Benjamin Barber, who, in "Confronting Terrorism: Smart Bombs or Smart Concepts," looks at the forces of tribalism and transglobal capitalism undermining democracy and actually offers a solution.

The speeches themselves have arrived here via several different channels: full transcripts, prepared remarks, and edited versions from *The Commonwealth*. We've had the benefit of some brand-new transcripts made from digitized versions of archival recordings, thanks to an audio archive project launched several years ago, the first fruits of which can be harvested online. The list in the back of this book includes more details on the written form from which individual speeches have been reproduced.

As part of its centennial year, 2003, The Commonwealth Club undertook the mother of all spring cleanings and moved its audio and print archives to the Hoover Institution Library and Archives at Stanford University, where the materials could be properly catalogued and preserved. Papers that were stacked ceiling-high inside a self-storage unit, a teetering forest of disintegrating cardboard boxes, have already been through an initial sorting. Thanks to archivist Natasha Porfirenko's work, Justin Gerdes, who assisted with much of the research for this book, was able to lay his hands on FDR's prepared remarks. There are certainly more gems to be found in those archives. And you won't need to wear a dust mask to find them.

The Commonwealth Club has an amazing story to tell, and we hope this book is just the beginning of that effort. Ultimately, this is not just the story of a club of social reformers who set out to wrest power from the big bad railroads and make democracy work in California. (Though that's not a bad story, is it?) It's a story of who we are, as Californians and Americans and global citizens. It's about the ongoing work of building for the common good. And it's about finding this elusive creature called the truth and setting it loose upon the world. Now, as for the meaning of truth...

Section One

The Progressive Era and the New Deal

March 27, 1911

Theodore Roosevelt

Former President of the United States of America

"Whiskey is for drinkin'," Mark Twain reputedly said. "Water is for fightin' over." And the story of California and the settling of the American West can't be told without the fight over water, or "liquid gold," being a part of it. Even during the gold rush, California miners were pitted against farmers over water. Then it was the populations of growing cities—particularly San Francisco and Los Angeles—whose thirst had to be slaked with water transported over hundreds of miles. In the case of Los Angeles, it was at the expense of farmers in the Owens Valley. (Roman Polanski's 1970s film noir, *Chinatown*, vividly dramatizes the intrigue—and the violence—which were a part of the battle for water in Southern California.) For San Francisco, building the dam that for nearly a century has provided a majority of its water meant flooding the Hetch Hetchy Valley in Yosemite National Park, a travesty that elicited from preservationist John Muir this response: "Dam Hetch Hetchy! As well dam for water tanks the people's cathedrals and churches, for no holier temple has ever been consecrated by the heart of man."

Muir is one of the icons of the environmental movement. Alongside him and, one could say, battling with him over the soul of how we should conserve natural resources, was Theodore Roosevelt, the twenty-sixth president of the United States. While in office, Roosevelt set aside some 230 million acres of land as national parks, national forests, game and bird preserves, and other federal reservations—more than any president before or since. True, Roosevelt traveled to Yosemite in 1903 to meet with Muir and together they laid the foundation for the president's conservation programs. But Roosevelt sought a balance between the preservation and use of natural resources. Sierra Club founder Muir was ready, in the words of fierce critics such as industrialist Andrew Carnegie, to thwart "the imperative needs of a city to full and pure water supply...for the sake of a few trees."

In March 1911, Theodore Roosevelt stood atop the newly completed Roosevelt Dam and pushed the switch opening the sluice gates. The dam would provide irrigation water for the Salt River Valley in the Arizona Territory (Arizona would not become a state until the following year). It was a project made possible by the Reclamation Act, passed nearly a decade before, which used funds from the sale of federal lands to finance water projects. Roosevelt declared the Reclamation Act, along with the creation of the Panama Canal, his greatest achievements as president. Today, those who have enlisted in the environmental movement are more likely to oppose the construction of dams than support them; even the World Bank no longer supports dams on the scale of the Three Gorges Dam in China.

But step back to the beginning of the twentieth century, when California and national leaders had to grapple with the need to supply water for the burgeoning populations of the state's cities while continuing to supply water to a once arid land that was becoming the most productive agricultural region in the country. In March 1911, nearly seven hundred Commonwealth Club members and their guests donned black ties and tails for a dinner in honor of Roosevelt at the Fairmont Hotel atop San Francisco's Nob Hill, with the issue of conservation of natural resources the intellectual fare for the evening. Roosevelt's speech came after supporters and opponents aired their opinions on the topic and Club founder and *San Francisco Chronicle* editorial writer Edward F. Adams noted, "The Commonwealth Club does not hold love fests; it holds scraps; and I think I see the signs in the next few months of the most interesting scrap we have ever had." As for Roosevelt, Adams noted of the man who built a reputation for trust-busting when in the White House, "Those of us who are radicals love Colonel Roosevelt for what we once thought his radicalism; those of us who are conservatives feel our souls warming to him as we think of some of his disciples." Roosevelt's response?

"Mr. Chairman, when you said that the conservatives present would welcome me, I could not but regret the inability of Wall Street to hear you." Seen one way, the language in the banter and in the speech that follows seems antiquated in its formality; seen another, it's an amazing impromptu display of rhetorical flourishes and oratory.

Leading the argument against Roosevelt that March night was Judge Frank H. Short, an opponent of what he saw as radical conservation efforts who had represented various corporations and argued water issues before the U.S. Supreme Court. Looking at the bountiful natural resources that the West held, particularly timber and mineral wealth, Short shared a parable of Uncle Sam and his four sons: "East, North, South, and West. Uncle Sam, being liberal to a fault and mindful of a trust, transferred to his three eldest sons—East, North, and South—all of their share in his estate....After their industrious younger brother began to show the real value of his, the leftover, portion of their father's estate, East, North, and South began to look with covetous eyes upon the younger brother's inheritance." At least one account notes that Judge Short's remarks caused "the former president to be visibly disconcerted."

Roosevelt was further disconcerted the following year, when he once again sought the Republican Party nomination for president. The party machinery had other plans, and incumbent William Howard Taft was renominated. Roosevelt bolted for the Progressive Party, renamed the Bull Moose Party in his honor, and chose as his vice presidential running mate California governor Hiram Johnson—a longtime Commonwealth Club member and the leading Progressive politician in the state. Roosevelt and Johnson polled a strong second, but they split the Republican vote with Taft, opening the way to victory by Democrat Woodrow Wilson. The following year was an even worse defeat for many conservationists, when Congress passed the Raker Act, authorizing construction of the Hetch Hetchy Dam. Controversy still surrounds the dam, both over its ownership by a corporation versus the people of San Francisco and over whether it ought to be demolished.

The argument Roosevelt presents in its broadest sense—states' rights versus the responsibility and power of the federal government, and where the rights of the people fit into the picture—is one that even predates the Constitution of the United States. And it's an argument you'll see resurface in other speeches in this book, whether the topic is civil rights in the 1960s or terrorism in the twenty-first century. As for water and its scarcity: in California today, more than 90 percent of the state's water is piped over two hundred and fifty miles to users, over half of it from the Colorado River—and in 2003, after a seven-year battle, California finally brokered a deal with six other states over the amount of water it could continue pulling from the river. The BBC began a series in 2000 on world water wars; and a 2001 UN report estimates that by 2025 one in three people in the world will not have access to fresh drinking water. Even the U.S. House of Representatives set up a subcommittee in 2003 to try to answer the question, Will water be the "oil" of the twenty-first century?

"The Doubtful Zone of Authority Between State and Federal Authority"

When we note the wisdom of the fathers as binding upon conditions which the fathers could by no possibility have foreseen, I want to recall the statement of that wise and witty philosopher, Mr. Dooley, when Thomas Jefferson was quoted on some policy essential to our well-being: "Thomas Jefferson was a great man, but he lived before the days of open plumbing."[1]

In speaking of the proper attitude which we ought to take in reference to a conservation of our forests and other natural resources, and irrigation, and to the use of electricity in connection with water power, you spoke of a decision of the Supreme Court rendered eighty years ago[2], at a time before

1. Martin Dooley was a creation of humorist Finley Peter Dunne, whose satires of Chicago and later the national and international scene made Mr. Dooley the most popular figure in American journalism at the turn of the century. Naturally, among Dunne's targets was Theodore Roosevelt, whose account of fighting with the Rough Riders he retitled *Alone in Cuba*.
2. Judge Frank H. Short, speaking before Teddy Roosevelt, argued that the Supreme Court had held "some seventy-five or eighty years ago" that public lands were to be held by the federal government in trust for the states, to be passed to private ownership "as rapidly as could reasonably be done." Short's claim rested on language in *Pollard v. Hagan* (1845), in which the court ruled that Article IV of the Constitution provides the federal government only temporary authority to manage federal lands. Pamela Baldwin, an attorney with the Congressional Research Service, has noted, however, that the Short-*Pollard* argument is "offset by other holdings of the Supreme Court before and after *Pollard* and it has been commonly accepted that the federal government may own and hold property as Congress directs."

any human being knew that electricity could be used in connection with water power, or that irrigation was thought of or could have been applied to a single acre under cultivation in the United States—at a time before it had entered the head of any American, or almost any man in the civilized world, that it was necessary to conserve the forests of the country.

No man, no member of the bar, or judge, can have a more profound respect than I have for a decision of the Supreme Court. I do not, however, include in the functions which I attribute to the members of that august tribunal the function of prophecy. If we treated the Constitution as a straightjacket instead of what the great Chief Justice Marshall declared it to be, an instrument to aid in our growth, we utterly misunderstand the function of the instrument. It would be impossible for this country to grow if it declined to go into any policy rendered necessary by the creation of conditions, not merely new, but conditions which could not possibly have been foreseen when the Supreme Court decided on some totally different question. The dictum that you quoted, if it was rendered eighty years ago, was rendered even before the Homestead Act was passed. It was rendered at a time when men like Daniel Webster, men like Rufus Choate and Edward Everett still believed that the wise course for the nation to follow was to sell all its public land in great masses to the highest bidder, take the proceeds and turn everything over to the states in which the public lands were situated. It was rendered before our people had grasped the truth that it was to our interests not to treat those lands merely from the standpoint of revenue, but in the interest of all the people. And when I say all the people, I do not mean that each man got fifty cents worth out of it; I mean in the interests of the people, because it is the interest of all our people that we shall have a free, self-supporting democracy on the largest scale throughout this Union. That decision was rendered before our people, grasping the wisdom of the proper policy to pursue, had decreed that the land should be sold to actual settlers in 160-acre quarter sections on condition that they should be actual residents on that soil.

If the nation had power to sell its lands in small parcels on condition that those who bought it should actually reside thereon and till the land, then the nation has power to sell the land on the condition that the waters running over that land shall be so used that the use shall be in the interest of the whole people and not in the interest of any small monopoly composed of a few people only. *(Applause)*

If the nation had the right to pass the Homestead law and to protect the actual settler against the land speculator, the land monopolist, then the nation has the right to dispose of the remaining lands in such fashion as to guarantee our people in the future against seeing the most valuable power lying in any portion of these lands from becoming the property in perpetuity of some monopoly.

I listened with very great interest to the parable of Uncle Sam and his four sons, and how Brothers East, North, and South united to do wrong to poor Brother West. I was the instrument of that wrongdoing in the case of the Reclamation Service, and as you have listened to the poetry of it, I will tell you the facts.

We passed the Reclamation Service Act, providing that the waters of the West should be used not for a few speculators, but for the men of the West. We passed that law providing that the nation should make the initial expenditure—that Uncle Sam should pay them out of the portions of the four brothers contributed mostly by the three who were robbers—and then should be reimbursed as far as possible by the proceeds of sale to the men who benefited from it. Not one dollar comes to the easterner, the northerner, or the southerner; every dollar is spent in the West, every dollar is spent to build up the small man of the West and prevent the big man East or West coming in and monopolizing the water and the land.

I will give you an illustration of what I saw last week myself in Arizona. The bad Brothers East, North, and South, as typified by me, provided that in Arizona, which had no senators, no congressmen, not a particle of political influence (they could not give me or anyone else any support, political or otherwise, for what we did)—I say we provided that the biggest expenditure in irrigation should be in the Salt River of Arizona, should be in the form of spending about $2.5 million of the money of the four brothers, and that it should be spent solely in the territory of the poor brother. I did that after careful consultation with the head of the Reclamation Service because it had become evident after three decades of experiment that the settlers could not store and use that water for themselves, and that Arizona did not have the means to build a dam for itself, and that either we had to let the water be developed by a great and rich company and be turned into a monopoly of the very worst and most undesirable type, or else the government had to come in and develop the water power in the interest of the small man, in the interest of the twenty-acre irrigation farmer. We appropriated the money, we built the dam, I dedicated it and turned the water on the other day, and we shall see in that valley—that valley of the West—a population of seventy-five thousand farmers, and townspeople dependent upon farmers, who will owe their existence and their well-being to the fact that the bad brothers—East, North, and South—turned in and committed the frightful iniquity of paying to the western brother the money which he could not afford to pay.

The appeal is made that in the name of states' rights the national government shall not do the duty it is bidden to do under the Constitution. I believe in the fact and not the word; I care for the fact and not for the word. I am for the people's rights. Where the people's rights mean the rights of the nation, I am for the rights of the nation; where the people's rights mean states' rights, I am for the states' rights.

We are asked in the interest of states' rights to have the national government surrender its control over the lands. Surrender it to whom? To the people of the states? Not at all. Surrender the Alaska lands to whom? To those magnificent Alaskans, the Guggenheim syndicate of Colorado, and the Morgan syndicate of New York? And in the name of states' rights, of local self-government, I am asked to agree to turn over the greatest assets that Alaska has to capitalists in Denver and in New York.

Take your own state. While I was president, a break occurred in the Colorado River, and it began to make what was called the Salton Sea in California. The Californian representatives came at once to me, not to protest against the three bad brothers interfering in local self-government in California; they came to ask me if I would not see if the national government wouldn't interfere and have the break stopped. I had to get hold of the railroad people and see that the dam was repaired. We had to take action in connection with one company, one corporation down there in Southern California. We had to interfere with local self-government in California by acting against that corporation which was located in California. What do you think the corporation was? It was a New Jersey corporation. Local self-government had managed to give its powers over to a New Jersey corporation; a corporation created in New Jersey, incidentally of New York capital. We had to interfere with that corporation. And the plea is made that we are not to interfere for the sake of the people of California with a New Jersey corporation, because it is against the doctrine of states' rights.

I will give you another instance, and I could multiply them indefinitely. Out in Denver last year I struck this same question as to whether the United States had any moral or legal right to interfere with the acquirement in perpetuity by great private corporations of the right to use power generated by streams flowing across the national domain. And I heard precisely the argument that I have heard tonight, the argument that we must not interfere with the local self-government of Colorado, that we must leave Colorado citizens alone. But who do you think the Colorado citizens were? One man was from Ohio and two from New York.

Great organized capital nowadays never has a merely state location. Organized capital goes into all the different states. Where the state can deal with it best I want the state to do it; where, in the interests of the people of the state, the nation can deal with it best, I want the nation to do it. And whereas in California I believe that the situation can be satisfactorily dealt with only by the heartiest and fullest cooperation between nation and state, I wish to see that cooperation secured, and I wish to see them act in unison.

But I have not yet quite finished with the three bad brothers. (I had expected to enjoy this dinner, but not as much as I am enjoying it.) As I understand, the chief point of iniquity in the act of the aforesaid brothers was that in their corporate capacity they had asked Uncle Sam to help preserve his heritage for the fourth brother—not for the other three, but for the poor fourth brother. Now, I want to call your attention to this fact: unfortunately, when the nation was called into being, our people knew so little of the usefulness of the national function they did not provide a power in the nation to control any of the lands in the old states. The chief concern of the East and South for the last eight or ten years has been not to force this policy on the West but to persuade Uncle Sam to do in the East what he is doing in the West. Now, let me explain that to you. We have finally succeeded in partially realizing that ideal. The chief concern of the East has been to get Uncle Sam to take possession of the Appalachian forests, and the forests in the White Mountains and along the Alleghenies, so that Uncle Sam may be able to do there what he is now doing in the West. In other words, two or three bad brothers are begging Uncle Sam to do to them what he has done to the fourth virtuous brother. I am speaking of the attempt to extend to the East, in the Alleghenies and in the White Mountains, the system of national control of forests, of national control of the states' resources that obtain in the West.

The improvement of the rivers and harbors from the standpoint of navigation has been applied in the West precisely as in the East. It has been applied to the Sacramento just as it has been applied to the Ohio. It has been applied to San Francisco just as it has been applied to New York. It has been applied to the Columbia just as it has been applied to the Mississippi. There has been absolute equity of treatment of all sections of the Union in dealing with the improvement of our rivers and harbors.

Irrigation stood on a totally different footing from the improvement of rivers and harbors. Personally, I very strongly believe that rivers and harbors should be improved, somewhat as we make new streets in cities; that is, that the people to be immediately benefited should share the expense with the national government. But that has never been done—no more in the Sacramento and the Columbia than in the Mississippi and the Ohio. When the irrigation service stood on a totally different footing, the rivers were improved on the theory that the commerce that goes upward flows throughout the country; the harbors are improved on the theory that the commerce that comes to them is distributed throughout the country. In the irrigation service we were making a totally new departure. I was trying to get that scheme of the irrigation service put through. No western congressman or senator dreamed for a moment that it would be possible to get it put through on the idea of making the national government pay for it all. And I can give you the exact reason for it. We improved the river—the Oregon or the Sacramento; we improved it for the boats carrying commerce that would go up and down the stream. No section of the improved water is given to any one man. No steamboat captain or steamboat owner used any one section of water. On the contrary, when we built the dam of which I have spoken in Arizona, we distributed the water in the irrigation ditches by what is called so many miner's inches to each acre of land; the man owning twenty acres of land gets so many miner's inches of water from his irrigation ditch; water which he only can use; water which is of such enormous benefit to him that he is only too eager to pay for getting it. I come from short grass country and I know what they need. Every community of water users strains every nerve to have an irrigation project such as that of the Salt River put among them, and of course, expect to pay, for they know that in paying they are getting from the national government tenfold the value of what they pay. It is turning the arid regions and semiarid regions of this country into the most productive portions of the country, acre for acre; they are being turned into the most fertile and productive portions of this country because of that irrigation.

And since when have they been thus turned in? Since the national government took charge of the works. No state government was taking any effective steps, because it could not take any effective steps, to develop the irrigable land. Just as with the forests: New Hampshire wants its forests preserved but the state has never preserved them. The nation can step in and do it because the nation can act, not only for New Hampshire, but for the states in the watershed of the rivers in New Hampshire. South Carolina, North Carolina, Georgia, Tennessee have not preserved their forests as they should preserve them. The nation can step in and can preserve them because—and this seems to be an elemental fact—water hasn't any objection to flowing out of one state and into another. The Colorado flows out of Colorado and into Arizona and California. The Mississippi River drains half the states of this country. Kansas is dependent for its water supply upon the national government seeing that reasonable equity is done, as between it and Colorado, from which the water supply comes.

Not only does the national government have to step in as between the states, but during my administration it twice had to step in and deal with foreign powers, once with Canada in connection with the St. Mary's and Milk River irrigation projects, and once with Mexico in connection with the irrigation projects of the Rio Grande in New Mexico. We had to step in and deal with foreign governments, because the water does not stay normally in any one state. It runs out of that state into another, or into a foreign country, and may then return, as the Milk River does, into our own country. Here in California that is true only of the southern part of the state, the part affected by the Colorado River. Most of your rivers are intrastate rivers. And let me point out this fact: that I have never heard the most rigid defender of states' rights insist that the federal government should not improve the Sacramento because it was an intrastate stream.

If we had a right to dispose of the land—not absolute but on condition that certain requisites are complied with, doing that in the interest of the democracy as a whole—we have the right to dispose of the land with a proviso as to the use of the water running over it, designed to secure that use for the people as a whole and to prevent it from ever being absorbed by a small monopoly. The details of the grant are not necessary for me to discuss. Personally, gentlemen, I have believed in disposing of those waters for a longer period and on easier terms than some of my more advanced fellow reformers have. I have been willing to assent to it and I think I am right in this matter. My object is to keep that great power from passing out of the hands of the people in perpetuity.

This century is bound to see an astounding development of the use of electrical power generated by running water. The development I believe will be extraordinary. We cannot foresee what the social conditions will be half a century hence. We cannot foresee how our people will feel, and what their needs will be fifty years hence, any more than the Supreme Court eighty years ago could see our needs of today. My aim is to hand over to our children and to our grandchildren the public property so unimpaired that they may then do whatever their needs then dictate. I realize absolutely that we must have that power developed in the present. For that reason I would allow the corporation leasing the power to lease it for any length of time necessary to ensure them an ample return upon their money. Personally, I would be delighted to see it made fifty years instead of twenty-five. Personally, I should be glad to see the terms made as easy as possible, because the thing that concerns me is what I regard as the vital principle, the principle of not parting with the property, the principle of keeping it in the public hands, so that at the end of the next forty or fifty years of national development the people shall have it in their possession, and shall not find that they have developed a small number of wealthy men who own something that the public can no longer get except by revolution.

Now I have struck the crux of my appeal. I wish to save the very wealthy men of this country, and their advocates and upholders, from the ruin that they would bring upon themselves if they were permitted to have their way. It is because I am against revolution; it is because I am against the doctrines of the extremists, of the socialists; it is because I wish to see this country of ours continued as a genuine democracy; it is because I distrust violence and disbelieve in it; it is because I wish to secure this country against ever seeing a time when the "have-nots" shall rise against the "haves"; it is because I wish to secure for our children and our grandchildren and for their children's children the same freedom of opportunity, the same peace and order and justice that we have had in the past; it is because of that, that I wish to see the state—wherever the state has the power and the duty—and the nation—wherever the nation has the power and the duty—step in and conserve our national resources, and to part with them only on such terms as will secure, so far as it is possible to secure, a general participation by all of the people in the benefits arising from them, and to prevent their being monopolized by a few men of enormous wealth who would use them for their own selfish gratification in the present and to build up their power in the present, and who in doing so would create a spirit of unrest and anger and murderous discontent which in the end might result in an upheaval that would not only bring them down but bring down the whole fabric of the Republic in an unjust effort to undo the effects of past injustice.

September 18, 1919

Woodrow Wilson

President of the United States of America

In January 1918, with the armies of the Allies and the Central Powers still battling one another in the seemingly endless slaughter known as the Great War, Woodrow Wilson laid out the ideals on which the postwar world should be built. Among those ideals, enumerated as the "Fourteen Points," were a peace of reconciliation, based on democracy; self-determination; and a League of Nations. An armistice in November 1918 ended the war—but in the U.S., elections swept a Republican majority into Congress that would thwart Wilson's desire to have the Senate ratify the League of Nations treaty. In the summer of 1919, facing opposition in the Senate to the treaty, Wilson took his plea on behalf of the league straight to the American people. Citing concern over Article X of the treaty, the so-called "collective security" provision that obliged member nations to protect one another, Senator Henry Cabot Lodge demanded amendments to the treaty that Wilson refused to consider. Instead, Wilson hoped an eight-thousand-mile railway journey that included forty speeches—among them a September address before The Commonwealth Club of California—would rally citizens to his side. Some sixteen hundred people filled the room in San Francisco's Palace Hotel for the Thursday luncheon to discuss what businessman and Club chairman for the day R. B. Hale (the original proponent of the Panama-Pacific Exposition in 1915) called the "most vital question before the American people today....It transcends in importance party affiliations, personal friendships, or private interests." It was not through war, but through an arbitration process and ultimately economic pressure that the league would enforce the new international order. At the end of Wilson's speech, the crowd gave him a standing ovation.

A week later, Wilson nearly collapsed after giving a speech in Pueblo, Colorado. He traveled back to Washington and on October 2 suffered a severe stroke that paralyzed his left side. The Senate voted on the treaty in November, but Wilson urged Democrats to vote against it rather than back the changes Senator Lodge insisted be made. The showdown was repeated in March, and once again ratification failed. Wilson urged that the 1920 elections be seen as a referendum on the treaty. The Democrats lost, and Warren G. Harding went on to sign a separate peace with Germany. A month after the 1920 elections, Wilson was awarded the Nobel Peace Prize.

"The Peace Treaty and the Covenant of the League of Nations"

Our thought must be of the present and the future. The men who do not look forward now are of no other service to the nation. But the immediate need of this country and of the world is peace, not only a settled peace, peace upon a definite and well-understood foundation supported by such covenants as men can depend upon, but supported by such purposes as will permit of a concert of action throughout all the free peoples of the world. I don't believe that we even now stop to consider how remarkable the peace conference in Paris has been. It is the first great international conference which did not meet to consider the interests and advantages of the strong nations. It is the first international conference that did not convene in order to make the arrangements which would establish the control of the strong.

Now the peace of the world is absolutely indispensable to us, and immediately indispensable to us. There is not a single domestic trouble that can be worked out in the right temper or opportunely and in time unless we have conditions that we can count on.

I don't need to tell businessmen that they cannot conduct their business if they don't know what is going to happen tomorrow. You cannot make plans unless you have certain elements in the future upon which you can depend. You cannot seek markets unless you know whether you are going to seek them among people who suspect you or people who believe in you. If the United States is going to stand off and play truant in this great enterprise of justice and right, then you must expect to be looked upon with suspicion and hostile rivalry everywhere in the world. They will say, "These men are not intending to assist us, they are intending to exploit us."

You know that there was a conference just a few months before we went into the war, of the principal allied powers, held in Paris for the purpose of concerting a sort of economic league in which they would manage their purchasing as well as their selling in a way which would redound to their advantage and make use of the rest of the world. That was because they then thought, what they will be obliged to think again if we do not continue our partnership with them, that we were standing off to get what we could out of them. And they were making a defensive economic arrangement.

Very well. They will do that again. Almost by instinct they will do it again; not out of a deliberate hostility to the United States, but by an instinctive impulse of their own business interests. And, therefore, we cannot arrange a single element of our business until we have settled peace, and know whether we are going to deal with a friendly world or an unfriendly world.

We cannot determine our own economic reforms until then, and there must be some very fundamental economic reforms in this country. There must be a reconsideration of the structure of our economic society. Whether we will or not, the majority of mankind demand it, in America as well as elsewhere. We have got to sit down in time of quiet, in time that will permit of consideration, and determine what we are going to do. We cannot do it until we have peace. We cannot release the great industrial and economic power of America and let it run free until there are right channels in which it can run; and the channels of business are mental channels as well as physical channels.

In an open market, men's minds must be open. It has been said so often that it is a very trite saying, but it remains nevertheless true, that a financial panic is a mere state of mind. There are no fewer resources in the country at the time of a panic than there were on the day before the panic. But something has frightened everybody and caused them to draw in their credits, and everybody builds a fence around himself and is careful to keep behind the fence, and waits to see what is going to happen. So a panic is a waiting in fear of something that is going to happen. It doesn't usually happen.

Slowly they draw their breath and see that the world looks just the same as it did, and say to each other, "We had better go to work again." As a friend of mine described it at the time of one of our panics some twenty-five years ago, he met a man and in talking asked him if business was not looking up. The reply was, "Yes, it is so flat on its back it can't look any other way." But even if it is flat on its back it can see the world. It is not lying on its face.

But while the whole world is in doubt about what to expect, the whole world is under the special apprehension that is characteristic of a panic. You do not know what is safe to do with your money now. You have got to know what the world of tomorrow is going to be. You won't know until we settle this great matter of peace.

And I want to remind you how the permanency of peace is at the heart of this treaty. This is not merely a treaty of peace with Germany. It is a world settlement; not affecting those parts of the world, of course, which were not involved in the war, because the conference had no jurisdiction over them. But the war did extend to most parts of the world, and the scattered, dismembered assets of the central empires and of Turkey gave us plenty to do, and cover the greater part of the distressed populations of the world. So that it is nothing less than a world settlement. And at the center of it stands this covenant for the future which we call the Covenant of the League of Nations. Without it the treaty cannot be worked; without it, it is a mere temporary arrangement with Germany. The Covenant of the League of Nations is the instrumentality for the maintenance of peace.

And how does it propose to maintain it? By the means that all forward-looking and thoughtful men have desired for generations together, by substituting arbitration and discussion for war.

To hear some gentlemen talk, you would think that the council of the League of Nations is to spend its time considering when to advise other people to fight. That is what comes of a constant concentration of attention upon Article X. Article X ought to have been somewhere further down in the covenant, because it is in the background, it is not in the foreground.

At the heart of the covenant, every fighting nation solemnly agrees that they will never go to war without first having done one or the other of two things—without either submitting the matter of dispute to arbitration, in which case they promise absolutely to abide by the verdict, or if they do not agree to submit it to arbitration, submit it to discussion by the council of the League of Nations, in which case they promise to lay all the documents and all the pertinent facts before that council.

They consent that the council shall publish all the documents and all the pertinent facts so that all the world shall know them; that it shall be allowed six months in which to consider the matter; and that even at the end of six months if the conclusions they come to are not unanimously arrived at, or not accepted, they will still not go to war for three months following the rendering of the decision. So that even allowing no time for the preliminaries, there are nine months of cooling off, nine months of discussion, and not of private discussion, not of discussion between those who are heated, but of discussion between those who are disinterested except in the main events of the peace of the world—when the whole purifying and rectifying influence of the public opinion of mankind is brought to bear upon the conference.

If anything approaching that had been the arrangement of the world in 1914, the war would have been impossible. And I confidently predict that there is not an aggressive people in the world who would dare bring a wrongful purpose to that jury. It is the most formidable jury in the world.

The only effective force in the world is the force of opinion. And if any member of the league ignores these promises with regard to arbitration and discussion, what happens? War? No, not war, but something more tremendous, I take leave to say, than war. An absolute isolation and boycott.

It is provided in the covenant that any nation that disregards these solemn promises with regard to arbitration and discussion shall be thereby deemed ipso facto to have committed an act of war against the other members of the league, and that there shall thereupon follow an absolute exclusion of that nation from communication of any kind with the members of the league.

No goods can be shipped in or out. No telegraphic messages can be obtained, except through the elusive wireless, perhaps. There would be no communication of any kind between the peoples of that nation and the peoples of other nations. And there isn't a nation in Europe that can stand that for six months. Germany could have faced the armies of the world more readily than she faced the boycott of the world. Germany felt the pinch of the blockade more than she felt the stress of the blow.

There is not, so far as I know, a single European country—and I say European because I think our own country is exceptional—which is not dependent upon some other part of the world for some of the necessaries of its life. Some of them are absolutely dependent. Some of them are without raw materials, practically, of any kind. Some of them are absolutely without fuel of any kind, either coal or oil. Almost all of them are without that variety of supplies of war which are necessary to modern industry and necessary to the manufacture of the munitions of war. When you apply that boycott, you have got your hand upon the throat of the offending nation, and it is a proper punishment—it is an exclusion from civilized society.

Germany committed several acts of war against us before we accepted the inevitable and took up her challenge. And it was only because of a sort of accumulation of evidence that Germany's design was not merely to sink American ships and injure American citizens but that that was incidental to her design, her design being to destroy every free political society, that war was finally determined to exist. I remember saying to Congress before we went into war that if Germany committed some act of war against us that was intolerable I might have to give Congress different advice. And I remember a newspaper correspondent asked me what I thought would con- stitute such an act. I said, "I don't know, but I am perfectly certain I will know it when I see it. I cannot hypothetically define it, but it will be perfectly obvious when it occurs."

And if Congress regards this act by some other member of the league as such an act of war against it as necessitates the maintenance of the honor of the United States, then it may, in those circumstances, declare war. But it is not bound to declare war, under the engagement of the covenant.

So that what I am emphasizing, my fellow citizens, is this: that the heart of this covenant is arbitration and discussion, and that that is the only possible basis for peace in the future.

It is a basis for something better than peace. Really, civilization pro- ceeds on the principle of understanding one another. You know how peace between those who employ labor and those who labor depends upon con- ference and mutual understanding. If you don't get together with the other side it will be hostility to the end. And after you have heard the case of the other fellow it sometimes becomes a little awkward for you to insist upon the whole of your case. Because the human mind does have this fine quality, that it finds it embarrassing to face the truth and deny it. Moreover, the basis of friendship is intercourse.

I know I am very fond of a large number of men whom I know to be crooks. They are engaging fellows. When I form a judgment against them I have to be in another room—that's all there is about it. I cannot, because of my personal attitude toward them, form a harsh judgment. Indeed, I suppose the very thing that gives some men a chance to be crooks is their fascinating personality—they put it over on one. It is mighty hard to hate a fellow you know. And it is mighty hard to hate a nation you know.

If you intermingle, as I have had the good fortune to mingle, with scores of people of other nations in recent months, you would have the same feeling that I do, that after you get over the superficial differences of language and some differences of manner, they are the same kinds of folks. As I have said to a number of audiences on this trip, the most thrilling thing that happened to me over there was the constant intercourse I was having with delegations of people representing nations from all over the globe, some of which I had, shamefacedly, to admit I never heard of.

Do you know where Azerbaijan is? Well, one day there came in a very dignified and interesting group of gentlemen who were from Azerbaijan. I didn't have time, until they were gone, to find out where they came from. But I did find this out immediately: that I was talking to men who talked the same language that I did in respect of ideas, in respect of conceptions of liberty, in respect of conceptions of right and justice.

And I did find this out: that they, with all of the other delegations that came to see me were, metaphorically speaking, holding their hands out to America, saying, "You are the disciples and leaders of the free peoples of the world. Can't you come and help us?"

Until we went into this war, my fellow citizens, it was the almost universal impression of the world that our idealism was a mere matter of words, that what we were interested in was getting on in the world and making as much as we could out of it. That was the sum and substance of the usual opinion of us outside of America. In the short space that we were in this war that opinion was absolutely reversed.

Consider what they saw. The flower of our youth sent three and four thousand miles away from their homes, homes which could not be directly touched by the flames of that war, sent to foreign fields to mix with foreign and alien armies, to fight for the cause which they recognized as the common cause of mankind and not the peculiar cause of America. It caused a revulsion of feeling, a revulsion of attitude, which I dare say has never been paralleled in history. And at this moment, unless the cynical counsels of some of our acquaintances should prevail (which God forbid!), they are expecting us to lead the civilized world, because they trust us, they really and truly trust us.

They would not believe, no matter where we sent an army to be of assistance to them, that we would ever use that army for any purpose but to assist them. They know that when we say, as we said when we sent men to Siberia, we are sending them to assist in the distribution of food and clothing and shoes, so that brigands won't seize them, and that for the rest we are ready to render any assistance which they want us to render and will interfere in absolutely nothing that concerns their affairs, they believe us. There isn't a place in this world now, unless we wait a little longer, where America's political ambitions are looked upon with suspicion.

In order that we may not forget, I have brought with me the figures as to what this war meant to the world. This is a body of businessmen, and you will understand these figures. They are too big for the imagination of men who do not handle big things. Here is the cost of the war in money, exclusive of what we loaned one another, the direct cost of the war:

Great Britain and her dominions, $38 billion; France, $26 billion; the United States, $22 billion—this is the direct cost of our operations; Russia, $18 billion; Italy, $13 billion. And the total, including Belgium, Japan, and other countries, $123 billion. This is what it cost the Central Powers: Germany, $39 billion, the biggest single item; Austria-Hungary, $21 billion; Turkey and Bulgaria, $3 billion; a total of $63 billion. And the grand total of direct war cost is thus $186 billion—almost the capital of the world. The expenditures of the United States were at the rate of $1 million an hour for two years—including nighttime with daytime. That is the biggest advertising item I have ever heard of.

The record of dead during the war is as follows: Russia lost in dead 1,700,000 men—poor Russia that got nothing but terror and despair out of it all; Germany lost 1,600,000 men; France, 1,385,000 men; Great Britain, 900,000 men; Austria, 800,000 men; Italy, 364,000 men; the United States, 50,300 in dead—a total for all the belligerents of 7,450,300 men, just about seven and a half million men killed, because we could not have arbitration and discussion; because the world had never had the courage to propose the conciliatory methods which some of us are now doubting whether we ought to accept.

The totals for the wounded are not obtainable, except our own. Our own wounded were 230,000, excluding those who were killed. The total of all battle deaths in all the war in the world, from the year 1793 to the year 1914, was something under 6,000,000 men. So that about a million and a half more men were killed in this war than in all the wars of something more than one hundred preceding years.

We can hardly realize that. Those of us who lost sons or brothers can realize it—we know what it meant. The women who have little children crowding about their knees know what it means. They know that the world has hitherto been devoted to brutal methods of settlement.

Every time a war occurs it is the flower of the manhood of the belligerents that is destroyed; it is not so much the present generation as the next generation that goes maimed off the stage, or is laid away in obscure graves upon some battlefield. And the great nations are impaired in their vitality for two generations to come and all their lives are embittered by a method of settlement for which we could find and have now found a substitute.

My fellow citizens, I believe in Divine Providence. If I did not, I would go crazy. If I thought the direction of the disordered affairs of this world depended upon our finite endeavor, I should not know how to reason my way to sanity. But I do not believe there is any body of men, however they concert their power or their influence, that can defeat this great enterprise, which is the enterprise of divine mercy and peace and good will.

September 23, 1932

Franklin D. Roosevelt

Governor of New York; 1932 Democratic Presidential Candidate

One hundred thousand people lined the streets for Franklin Delano Roosevelt's arrival in San Francisco on September 22, 1932. The governor of New York and Democratic candidate for president trekked from the ferry to the Palace Hotel, where a thousand more people were packed into the lobbies. It was the most enthusiastic response FDR had received on his September tour of the West. And Roosevelt did not disappoint the throngs. The following day, he offered an address at a luncheon hosted by The Commonwealth Club on the "New Deal in Government." (The topic of the talk had been billed as "Present Public Problems.") Reflecting on the principles that have shaped, and should shape, our vision of America, that speech has come to be regarded as one of the greatest American speeches of the twentieth century.

By September 1932, FDR's presidential campaign was going gangbusters. Polls showed the Democrats had every state west of the Mississippi locked up—including Herbert Hoover's home turf of Iowa. California, which had left the Republican fold only twice in the previous three decades, was likely to give FDR its electoral votes. In San Francisco, Republican Mayor Angelo J. Rossi accompanied FDR from the wharf down Market Street to his hotel.

Former (Republican) governor of the Golden State and now U.S. Senator Hiram Johnson gave Roosevelt his tacit endorsement, and Roosevelt publicly praised Johnson as "a warrior in the ranks of American progress."

In accepting the Democratic Party nomination, Roosevelt had called on progressives from all parties to back him. *Literary Digest* polls showed voters prepared to cross party lines by the millions. FDR's running mate, John Nance Garner, advised this astute strategy for the campaign against Hoover: Do nothing. The people were ready to oust Hoover. The Commonwealth Club address stands out in a campaign that *The New Republic* characterized as exemplifying "pussyfooting policy." *Time* said the candidate "emerged from the campaign fog as a vigorous well-intentioned gentleman of good birth and breeding" minus any "crusading convictions." Elsewhere on his western tour, FDR had been taken to task by some less-than-enthusiastic observers of populist politics as "uttering platitudes" on regulation of railroads and utilities. (The collapse of the holding company Insull, a wheeler-dealer in the utilities field, was grist for the campaign mill in 1932, much as the exploits of energy giant Enron provoked outrage at the beginning of the twenty-first century.) The Commonwealth Club address, too, is often short on specifics; but it is long on reflection, and through Roosevelt's victory, the new vision of America he offers here began to come into being. In fact, the members of FDR's "Brains Trust"—a term coined by *New York Times* reporter James Kieran (and now used without the *s*) to denote the group of academic advisors Roosevelt assembled for the campaign—were the ones behind the speech. So this is not simply populist rhetoric; this is also a soon-to-be president offering the analysis that the U.S. has all the industrial capacity it needs and now must concentrate on "the soberer, less dramatic business of administering resources already at hand."

"Present Public Problems"

My friends:

I count it a privilege to be invited to address The Commonwealth Club. It has stood in the life of this city and state, and it is perhaps accurate to add, the nation, as a group of citizen leaders interested in fundamental problems of government, and chiefly concerned with achievement of progress in government through nonpartisan means. The privilege of addressing you, therefore, in the heat of a political campaign, is great. I want to respond to your courtesy in terms consistent with your policy.

I want to speak not of politics but of government. I want to speak not of parties, but of universal principles. They are not political, except in that larger sense in which a great American once expressed a definition of politics, that nothing in all of human life is foreign to the science of politics.

I do want to give you, however, a recollection of a long life spent for a large part in public office. Some of my conclusions and observations have been deeply accentuated in these past few weeks. I have traveled far—from Albany to the Golden Gate. I have seen many people and heard many things, and today, when in a sense my journey has reached the halfway mark, I am glad of the opportunity to discuss with you what it all means to me.

Sometimes, my friends, particularly in years such as these, the hand of discouragement falls upon us. It seems that things are in a rut, fixed, settled, that the world has grown old and tired and very much out of joint. This is the mood of depression, of dire and weary depression.

But then we look around us in America, and everything tells us that we are wrong. America is new. It is in the process of change and development. It has the great potentialities of youth, and particularly is this true of the great West, and of this coast, and of California.

I would not have you feel that I regard this as in any sense a new community. I have traveled in many parts of the world, but never have I felt more the arresting thought of the change and development more than here, where the old, mystic East would seem to be near to us, where the currents of life and thought and commerce of the whole world meet us. This factor alone is sufficient to cause man to stop and think of the deeper meaning of things, when he stands in this community.

But more than that, I appreciate that the membership of this club consists of men who are thinking in terms beyond the immediate present, beyond their own immediate tasks, beyond their own individual interests. I want to invite you, therefore, to consider with me in the large, some of the relationships of government and economic life that go deeply into our daily lives, our happiness, our future, and our security.

The issue of government has always been whether individual men and women will have to serve some system of government or economics, or whether a system of government and economics exists to serve individual men and women. This question has persistently dominated the discussions of government for many generations. On questions relating to these things men have differed, and for time immemorial it is probable that honest men will continue to differ.

The final word belongs to no man; yet we can still believe in change and in progress. Democracy, as a dear old friend of mine in Indiana, Meredith Nicholson, has called it, is a quest, a never ending seeking for better things, and in the seeking for these things and the striving for them, there are many roads to follow. But if we map the course of these roads, we find that there are only two general directions.

When we look about us, we are likely to forget how hard people have worked to win the privilege of government. The growth of the national governments of Europe was a struggle for the development of a centralized force in the nation, strong enough to impose peace upon ruling barons. In many instances the victory of the central government, the creation of a strong central government, was a haven of refuge to the individual. The people preferred the master far away to the exploitation and cruelty of the smaller master near at hand.

But the creators of national government were perforce ruthless men. They were often cruel in their methods, but they did strive steadily toward something that society needed and very much wanted, a strong central state, able to keep the peace, to stamp out civil war, to put the unruly nobleman in his place, and to permit the bulk of individuals to live safely. The man of ruthless force had his place in developing a pioneer country, just as he did in fixing the power of the central government in the development of nations. Society paid him well for his services and its development. When the development among the nations of Europe, however, had been completed, ambition and ruthlessness, having served their term, tended to overstep their mark.

There came a growing feeling that government was conducted for the benefit of a few who thrived unduly at the expense of all. The people sought a balancing—a limiting force. There came gradually, through town councils, trade guilds, national parliaments, by constitution and by popular participation and control, limitations on arbitrary power.

Another factor that tended to limit the power of those who ruled was the rise of the ethical conception that a ruler bore a responsibility for the welfare of his subjects.

The American colonies were born in this struggle. The American Revolution was a turning point in it. After the revolution, the struggle continued and shaped itself in the public life of the country. There were those who because they had seen the confusion which attended the years of war for American independence surrendered to the belief that popular government was essentially dangerous and essentially unworkable. They were honest people, my friends, and we cannot deny that their experience had warranted some measure of fear. The most brilliant, honest, and able exponent of this point of view was Hamilton. He was too impatient of slow moving methods. Fundamentally, he believed that the safety of the republic lay in the autocratic strength of its government, that the destiny of individuals was to serve that government, and that fundamentally a great and strong group of central institutions, guided by a small group of able and public-spirited citizens could best direct all government.

But Mr. Jefferson, in the summer of 1776, after drafting the Declaration of Independence, turned his mind to the same problem and took a different view. He did not deceive himself with outward forms. Government to him was a means to an end, not an end in itself; it might be either a refuge and a help or a threat and a danger, depending on the circumstances. We find him carefully analyzing the society for which he was to organize a government. "We have no paupers. The great mass of our population is of laborers, our rich who cannot live without labor, either manual or professional, being few and of moderate wealth. Most of the laboring class possess property, cultivate their own lands, have families, and, from the demand for their labor, are enabled to exact from the rich and the competent such prices as enable them to feed abundantly, clothe above mere decency, to labor moderately and raise their families."

These people, he considered, had two sets of rights, those of "personal competency" and those involved in acquiring and possessing property. By "personal competency" he meant the right of free thinking, freedom of forming and expressing opinions, and freedom of personal living, each man according to his own lights. To ensure the first set of rights, a government must so order its functions as not to interfere with the individual. But even Jefferson realized that the exercise of the property rights might so interfere with the rights of the individual that the government, without whose assistance the property rights could not exist, must intervene, not to destroy individualism but to protect it.

You are familiar with the great political duel which followed; and how Hamilton and his friends, building toward a dominant centralized power, were at length defeated in the great election of 1800 by Mr. Jefferson's party. Out of that duel came the two parties, Republican and Democratic, as we know them today.

So began, in American political life, the new day, the day of the individual against the system, the day in which individualism was made the great watchword of American life. The happiest of economic conditions made that day long and splendid. On the western frontier, land was substantially free. No one who did not shirk the task of earning a living was entirely without opportunity to do so. Depressions could, and did, come and go; but they could not alter the fundamental fact that most of the people lived partly by selling their labor and partly by extracting their livelihood from the soil, so that starvation and dislocation were practically impossible. At the very worst there was always the possibility of climbing into a covered wagon and moving West, where the untilled prairies afforded a haven for men to whom the East did not provide a place. So great were our natural resources that we could offer this relief not only to our own people, but to the distressed of all the world; we could invite immigration from Europe and welcome it with open arms. Traditionally, when a depression came, a new section of land was opened in the West; and even our temporary misfortune served our manifest destiny.

It was in the middle of the nineteenth century that a new force was released and a new dream created. The force was what is called the Industrial Revolution, the advance of steam and machinery and the rise of the forerunners of the modern industrial plant. The dream was the dream of an economic machine, able to raise the standard of living for everyone; to bring luxury within the reach of the humblest; to annihilate distance by steam power and later by electricity; and to release everyone from the drudgery of the heaviest manual toil. It was to be expected that this would necessarily affect government. Heretofore, government had merely been called upon to produce conditions within which people could live happily, labor peacefully, and rest secure. Now it was called upon to aid in the consummation of this new dream. There was, however, a shadow over the dream. To be made real, it required use of the talents of men of tremendous will, and tremendous ambition, since by no other force could the problems of financing and engineering and new developments be brought to a consummation.

So manifest were the advantages of the machine age, however, that the United States fearlessly, cheerfully, and, I think, rightly accepted the bitter with the sweet. It was thought that no price was too high to pay for the advantages which we could draw from a finished industrial system. The history of the last half-century is accordingly in large measure a history of a group of financial titans whose methods were not scrutinized with too much care, and who were honored in proportion as they produced the results, irrespective of the means they used. The financiers who pushed the railroads to the Pacific were always ruthless, often wasteful, and frequently corrupt; but they did build railroads, and we have them today. It has been estimated that the American investor paid for the American railway system more than three times over in the process; but despite this fact the net advantage was to the United States. As long as we had free land; as long as population was growing by leaps and bounds; as long as our industrial plants were insufficient to supply our own needs; society chose to give the ambitious man free play and unlimited reward, provided only that he produced the economic plant so much desired.

During this period of expansion, there was equal opportunity for all, and the business of government was not to interfere but to assist in the development of industry. This was done at the request of businessmen themselves. The tariff was originally imposed for the purpose of "fostering our infant industry," a phrase I think the older among you will remember as a political issue not so long ago. The railroads were subsidized, sometimes by grants of money, oftener by grants of land; some of the most valuable oil lands in the United States were granted to assist the financing of the railroad which pushed through the Southwest. A nascent merchant marine was assisted by grants of money, or by mail subsidies, so that our steam shipping might ply the seven seas. Some of my friends tell me that they do not want the government in business. With this I agree; but I wonder whether they realize the implications of the past. For while it has been American doctrine that the government must not go into business in competition with private enterprises, still it has been traditional, particularly in Republican administrations, for business urgently to ask the government to put at private disposal all kinds of government assistance. The same man who tells you that he does not want to see the government interfere in business—and he means it, and has plenty of good reasons for saying so— is the first to go to Washington and ask the government for a prohibitory tariff on his product. When things get just bad enough—as they did two years ago—he will go with equal speed to the United States government and ask for a loan; and the Reconstruction Finance Corporation is the outcome of it. Each group has sought protection from the government for its own special interests, without realizing that the function of government must be to favor no small group at the expense of its duty to protect the rights of personal freedom and of private property of all its citizens.

In retrospect we can now see that the turn of the tide came with the turn of the century. We were reaching our last frontier; there was no more free land and our industrial combinations had become great uncontrolled and irresponsible units of power within the state. Clear-sighted men saw with fear the danger that opportunity would no longer be equal; that the growing corporation, like the feudal baron of old, might threaten the economic freedom of individuals to earn a living. In that hour, our antitrust laws were born. The cry was raised against the great corporations. Theodore Roosevelt, the first great Republican progressive, fought a presidential campaign on the issue of "trust busting" and talked freely about malefactors of great wealth. If the government had a policy, it was rather to turn the clock back, to destroy the large combinations and to return to the time when every man owned his individual small business.

This was impossible; Theodore Roosevelt, abandoning the idea of "trust busting," was forced to work out a difference between "good" trusts and "bad" trusts. The Supreme Court set forth the famous "rule of reason" by which it seems to have meant that a concentration of industrial power was permissible if the method by which it got its power, and the use it made of that power, was reasonable.

Woodrow Wilson, elected in 1912, saw the situation more clearly. Where Jefferson had feared the encroachment of political power on the lives of individuals, Wilson knew that the new power was financial. He saw, in the highly centralized economic system, the despot of the twentieth century, on whom great masses of individuals relied for their safety and their livelihood, and whose irresponsibility and greed (if it were not controlled) would reduce them to starvation and penury. The concentration of financial power had not proceeded so far in 1912 as it has today; but it had grown far enough for Mr. Wilson to realize fully its implications. It is interesting, now, to read his speeches. What is called "radical" today (and I have reason to know whereof I speak) is mild compared to the campaign of Mr. Wilson. "No man can deny," he said, "that the lines of endeavor have more and more narrowed and stiffened; no man who knows anything about the development of industry in this country can have failed to observe that the larger kinds of credit are more and more difficult to obtain unless you obtain them upon terms of uniting your efforts with those who already control the industry of the country, and nobody can fail to observe that every man who tries to set himself up in competition with any process of manufacture which has taken place under the control of large combinations of capital will presently find himself either squeezed out or obliged to sell and allow himself to be absorbed." Had there been no World War—had Mr. Wilson been able to devote eight years to domestic instead of to international affairs—we might have had a wholly different situation at the present time. However, the then distant roar of European cannon, growing ever louder, forced him to abandon the study of this issue. The problem he saw so clearly is left with us as a legacy; and no one of us on either side of the political controversy can deny that it is a matter of grave concern to the government.

A glance at the situation today only too clearly indicates that equality of opportunity as we have known it no longer exists. Our industrial plant is built; the problem just now is whether under existing conditions it is not overbuilt. Our last frontier has long since been reached, and there is practically no more free land. More than half of our people do not live on the farms or on lands and cannot derive a living by cultivating their own property. There is no safety valve in the form of a western prairie to which those thrown out of work by the eastern economic machines can go for a new start. We are not able to invite the immigration from Europe to share our endless plenty. We are now providing a drab living for our own people.

Our system of constantly rising tariffs has at last reacted against us to the point of closing our Canadian frontier on the north, our European markets on the east, many of our Latin American markets to the south, and a goodly proportion of our Pacific markets on the west, through the retaliatory tariffs of those countries. It has forced many of our great industrial institutions which exported their surplus production to such countries to establish plants in such countries, within the tariff walls. This has resulted in the reduction of the operation of their American plants, and opportunity for employment.

Right: Commonwealth Club founder and *San Francisco Chronicle* editorial writer Edward F. Adams. *Commonwealth Club Collection, Hoover Institution Library and Archives*

Below: San Francisco's Union Square in 1903—the year The Commonwealth Club was founded, and the year the city erected a new statue to commemorate the U.S. victory in the Spanish-American War. *Courtesy of the San Francisco History Center, San Francisco Public Library*

Left: Finger-wagging oratory from Theodore Roosevelt. *Commonwealth Club Collection, Hoover Institution Library and Archives*

Below: President Theodore Roosevelt in San Francisco in 1903. *Courtesy of the San Francisco History Center, San Francisco Public Library*

To supply San Francisco with water and electricity, the Hetch Hetchy Valley was trans-
formed into the Hetch Hetchy Reservoir. Here are views of Surprise Point in 1908 and
1948. *Courtesy of Taber Photo/the Sierra Club and the Frasher Foto Postcard Collection,
Pomona Public Library, Online Archive of California*

Above: American troops depart San Francisco to fight the Great War in Europe (1917). *Courtesy of the San Francisco History Center, San Francisco Public Library*

Right: To support the war, The Commonwealth Club distributed this card to members. *Commonwealth Club Collection, Hoover Institution Library and Archives*

Manufacturer: Before you fix that price—
Dealer: Before you add that extra profit—
Workman Before you strike— *Ask yourself—*

"Is this MY boy?"

Above: Woodrow Wilson speaks at the Palace Hotel in 1919, making an impassioned plea for the U.S. to sign the League of Nations treaty. *Commonwealth Club Collection, Hoover Institution Library and Archives*

Left: Delivering the most important speech of his campaign, FDR outlines for a Commonwealth Club audience at the Palace Hotel the "new deal in government" he can offer the American people. *Commonwealth Club Collection, Hoover Institution Library and Archives*

Right: Food bartering programs like this one in Alameda County, California, helped feed Americans during the Great Depression. *Courtesy of the San Francisco History Center, San Francisco Public Library*

Below: During the Great Depression, these men found shelter in a pipe city in California (1932). *Courtesy of the San Francisco History Center, San Francisco Public Library*

Presidential candidate Franklin Roosevelt parades down San Francisco's Market Street in September 1932. *Commonwealth Club Collection, Hoover Institution Library and Archives*

Above: An unemployment line in 1937—five years after FDR was first elected. *Courtesy of the San Francisco History Center, San Francisco Public Library*

Right: A tent city built within view of the U.S. Capitol (1937). *Courtesy of ACME Newspictures, the San Francisco History Center, San Francisco Public Library*

Itinerant workers bound for the hop fields in Sonoma County, California (September 1935). *Courtesy of the San Francisco History Center, San Francisco Public Library*

Right: Several months after President Roosevelt signed the Lend-Lease Act, a Canadian billboard makes the case for Anglo-American solidarity. *Courtesy of ACME Newspictures, the San Francisco History Center, San Francisco Public Library*

Below: With the Nazis advancing in Europe and Japanese conquests in the Pacific, Americans against involvement in the war hold a rally in Los Angeles in September 1940. *Courtesy of the Associated Press, the San Francisco History Center, San Francisco Public Library*

The provisional president of the new state of Israel, Chaim Weizmann, holds a press conference in Washington in 1948—after meeting with President Truman to discuss an embargo on arms sales to the Middle East. *Bettmann/CORBIS*

Right: In spring 1948, raids on food convoys from Tel Aviv reduce food supplies in Jerusalem to a bare minimum. Here men, women, and children line up for their daily vegetable ration. *Bettmann/CORBIS*

Below: With safe conduct provided by the International Red Cross, Palestinian refugees flee fighting in July 1948 and trek through no-man's land to the Arab lines in Tulkarem. *Bettmann/CORBIS*

Just as freedom to farm has ceased, so also the opportunity in business has narrowed. It still is true that men can start small enterprises, trusting to native shrewdness and ability to keep abreast of competitors; but area after area has been preempted altogether by the great corporations, and even in the fields which still have no great concerns, the small man starts under a handicap. The unfeeling statistics of the past three decades show that the independent businessman is running a losing race. Perhaps he is forced to the wall; perhaps he cannot command credit; perhaps he is "squeezed out," in Mr. Wilson's words, by highly organized corporate competitors, as your corner grocery man can tell you. Recently a careful study was made of the concentration of business in the United States. It showed that our economic life was dominated by some six hundred-odd corporations who controlled two-thirds of American industry. Ten million small businessmen divided the other third. More striking still, it appeared that if the process of concentration goes on at the same rate, at the end of another century we shall have all American industry controlled by a dozen corporations, and run by perhaps a hundred men. Put plainly, we are steering a steady course toward economic oligarchy, if we are not there already.

Clearly, all this calls for a reappraisal of values. A mere builder of more industrial plants, a creator of more railroad systems, an organizer of more corporations, is as likely to be a danger as a help. The day of the great promoter or the financial titan to whom we granted anything if only he would build, or develop, is over. Our task now is not discovery or exploitation of natural resources, or necessarily producing more goods. It is the soberer, less dramatic business of administering resources and plants already in hand, of seeking to reestablish foreign markets for our surplus production, of meeting the problem of underconsumption, of adjusting production to consumption, of distributing wealth and products more equitably, of adapting existing economic organizations to the service of the people. The day of enlightened administration has come.

Just as in older times the central government was first a haven of refuge, and then a threat, so now in a closer economic system the central and ambitious financial unit is no longer a servant of national desire, but a danger. I would draw the parallel one step farther. We did not think because national government had become a threat in the eighteenth century that therefore we should abandon the principle of national government. Nor today should we abandon the principle of strong economic units called corporations merely because their power is susceptible of easy abuse. In other times we dealt with the problem of an unduly ambitious central government by modifying it gradually into a constitutional democratic government. So today we are modifying and controlling our economic units.

As I see it, the task of government in its relation to business is to assist the development of an economic declaration of rights, an economic constitutional order. This is the common task of statesman and businessman. It is the minimum requirement of a more permanently safe order of things.

Happily, the times indicate that to create such an order not only is the proper policy of government, but it is the only line of safety for our economic structures as well. We know, now, that these economic units cannot exist unless prosperity is uniform—that is, unless purchasing power is well distributed throughout every group in the nation. That is why even the most selfish of corporations for its own interest would be glad to see wages restored and unemployment ended and to bring the western farmer back to his accustomed level of prosperity and to assure a permanent safety to both groups. That is why some enlightened industries themselves endeavor to limit the freedom of action of each man and business group within the industry in the common interest of all; why businessmen everywhere are asking a form of organization which will bring the scheme of things into balance, even though it may in some measure qualify the freedom of action of individual units within the business.

The exposition need not further be elaborated. It is brief and incomplete, but you will be able to expand it in terms of your own business or occupation without difficulty. I think everyone who has actually entered the economic struggle—which means everyone who was not born to safe wealth—knows in his own experience and his own life that we have now to apply the earlier concepts of American government to the conditions of today.

The Declaration of Independence discusses the problem of government in terms of a contract. Government is a relation of give and take, a contract, perforce, if we would follow the thinking out of which it grew. Under such a contract rulers were accorded power, and the people consented to that power on consideration that they be accorded certain rights. The task of statesmanship has always been the redefinition of these rights in terms of a changing and growing social order. New conditions impose new requirements upon government and those who conduct government.

I held, for example, in proceedings before me as governor, the purpose of which was the removal of the sheriff of New York, that under modern conditions it was not enough for a public official merely to evade the legal terms of official wrongdoing. He owed a positive duty as well. I said in substance that if he had acquired large sums of money, he was when accused required to explain the sources of such wealth. To that extent this wealth was colored with a public interest. I said that public servants should, even beyond private citizens, in financial matters be held to a stern and uncompromising rectitude.

I feel that we are coming to a view through the drift of our legislation and our public thinking in the past quarter century that private economic power is, to enlarge an old phrase, a public trust as well. I hold that continued enjoyment of that power by any individual or group must depend upon the fulfillment of that trust. The men who have reached the summit of American business life know this best; happily, many of these urge the binding quality of this greater social contract.

The terms of that contract are as old as the Republic, and as new as the new economic order.

Every man has a right to life; and this means that he has also a right to make a comfortable living. He may by sloth or crime decline to exercise that right; but it may not be denied him. We have no actual famine or dearth; our industrial and agricultural mechanism can produce enough and to spare. Our government, formal and informal, political and economic, owes to everyone an avenue to possess himself of a portion of that plenty sufficient for his needs, through his own work.

Every man has a right to his own property; which means a right to be assured, to the fullest extent attainable, in the safety of his savings. By no other means can men carry the burdens of those parts of life which, in the nature of things, afford no chance of labor; childhood, sickness, old age. In all thought of property, this right is paramount; all other property rights must yield to it. If, in accord with this principle, we must restrict the operations of the speculator, the manipulator, even the financier, I believe we must accept the restriction as needful, not to hamper individualism but to protect it.

These two requirements must be satisfied, in the main, by the individuals who claim and hold control of the great industrial and financial combinations which dominate so large a part of our industrial life. They have undertaken to be not businessmen, but princes—princes of property. I am not prepared to say that the system which produces them is wrong. I am very clear that they must fearlessly and competently assume the responsibility which goes with the power. So many enlightened businessmen know this that the statement would be little more than a platitude, were it not for an added implication.

This implication is, briefly, that the responsible heads of finance and industry, instead of acting each for himself, must work together to achieve the common end. They must, where necessary, sacrifice this or that private advantage, and in reciprocal self-denial must seek a general advantage. It is here that formal government—political government, if you choose—comes in. Whenever, in the pursuit of this objective, the lone wolf, the unethical competitor, the reckless promoter, the Ishmael or Insull whose hand is against every man's declines to join in achieving an end recognized as being for the public welfare and threatens to drag the industry back to a state of anarchy, the government may properly be asked to apply restraint. Likewise, should the group ever use its collective power contrary to the public welfare, the government must be swift to enter and protect the public interest.

The government should assume the function of economic regulation only as a last resort, to be tried only when private initiative, inspired by high responsibility, with such assistance and balance as government can give, has finally failed. As yet there has been no final failure, because there has been no attempt; and I decline to assume that this nation is unable to meet the situation.

The final term of the high contract was for liberty and the pursuit of happiness. We have learned a great deal of both in the past century. We know that individual liberty and individual happiness mean nothing unless both are ordered in the sense that one man's meat is not another man's poison. We know that the old "rights of personal competency"—the right to read, to think, to speak, to choose and live a mode of life, must be respected at all hazards. We know that liberty to do anything which deprives others of those elemental rights is outside the protection of any compact; and that government in this regard is the maintenance of a balance within which every individual may have a place if he will take it; in which every individual may find safety if he wishes it; in which every individual may attain such power as his ability permits, consistent with his assuming the accompanying responsibility.

All this is a long, slow talk. Nothing is more striking than the simple innocence of the men who insist, whenever an objective is present, on the prompt production of a patent scheme guaranteed to produce a result. Human endeavor is not so simple as that. Government includes the art of formulating a policy and using the political technique to attain so much of that policy as will receive general support; persuading, leading, sacrificing, teaching always, because the greatest duty of a statesman is to educate. But in the matters of which I have spoken, we are learning rapidly, in a severe school. The lessons so learned must not be forgotten, even in the mental lethargy of a speculative upturn. We must build toward the time when a major depression cannot occur again; and if this means sacrificing the easy profits of inflationist booms, then let them go; and good riddance.

Faith in America, faith in our tradition of personal responsibility, faith in our institutions, faith in ourselves demand that we recognize the new terms of the old social contract. We shall fulfill them, as we fulfilled the obligation of the apparent Utopia which Jefferson imagined for us in 1776, and which Jefferson, Roosevelt, and Wilson sought to bring to realization. We must do so lest a rising tide of misery engendered by our common failure engulf us all. But failure is not an American habit; and in the strength of great hope we must all shoulder our common load.

June 13, 1941

Chaim Weizmann

President, Zionist Federation; President, Hebrew University

President of the Zionist Federation and of the Jewish Agency for Palestine, Chaim Weizmann had labored for decades for the Zionist cause before speaking at The Commonwealth Club in the summer of 1941. He had played a role in 1917 in pushing forward the Balfour Declaration calling for the establishment of a Jewish homeland in Palestine. But as president of the Zionist Federation, he was unable to prevent the British from presenting, in November 1939, what became known as the White Paper. Looking to ameliorate the concerns of independent Arab nations, the paper in effect called for a halt of Jewish emigration to Palestine. Nevertheless, between 1934 and 1938, over one hundred thousand Jews migrated to Palestine (including some with brutal encouragement from the Nazis); some fifty-one thousand were detained by the British as illegal immigrants.

When Weizmann spoke at The Commonwealth Club, the Nazi empire was reaching its apex: conquests stretched from France in the west to Poland in the east, from Norway in the north to Greece and Yugoslavia in the south. Erwin Rommel's Afrika Korps were battling the British in North Africa. (The day after Weizmann's speech, British forces would be defeated in their attempt to lift the siege on the city of Tobruk.) In Poland, the Nazis had set up ghettos in Lodz and Warsaw and Krakow, though far worse was yet to come for Europe's Jews.

Weizmann's speech tries to rally Americans to his cause. It was Friday the thirteenth, but he had reason to take heart: the Lend-Lease Act had been passed in March, allowing the president to transfer arms, without payment, to any country whose defense was vital to the U.S.; and at the end of May, President Roosevelt had given a speech (which Weizmann mentions here) that recognized the Nazi aim was world domination, targeting those who "think that we are not attacked until bombs actually drop on New York or San Francisco or New Orleans or Chicago...simply shutting their eyes to the lesson we must learn from the fate of every nation that the Nazis have conquered." Six months would pass before the U.S. and Germany were at war, following the Japanese attack on Pearl Harbor in December. Much sooner— just a week after Weizmann's speech—Hitler launched Operation Barbarossa and began his attempted conquest of the Soviet Union. That October, Nazi leaders convened and discussed what eventually took shape as the "final solution": the systematic mass murder of millions of Jews in Europe. In the wake of the war, in 1948, Israel as a country was created and Chaim Weizmann was elected its first president.

"The Jew and the World Today"

The Jews of the world are used to persecution. But today's persecution is different. It is cannibalism. The Nazis have singled out the Jews to stigmatize them as different from the rest of the community. The actions taken against the Jews are similar to the military measures by which Germany is trying to annihilate or subjugate any free people.

The Jews are blamed for all the ills that beset the world. It is a crusade of defamation to make the world Jew-conscious, to draw the attention of the world to a group in their midst against whom are made the most fantastic accusations. Hitler repeats them again and again, until the ordinary person begins to think there is never smoke without fire. The moral and spiritual Nazification of Europe, and I think in part, of America (although I am not informed on this point), has been making progress in a way unbelievable ten years ago.

Among these accusations there is one great one, that the Jews are engaged in a world conspiracy—and I myself have been named as one of the conspirators. For some reason or other the Jews got together, it is said, and hatched out all sorts of plans to gain world domination. But a judicial tribunal probably would not find a shred to justify these terrible accusations. And meanwhile Hitler is doing exactly the thing of which he has accused the Jews.

Only when the physical danger involved in execution of Hitler's plan for world dominion became patent to the Christian world—only then did the slow awakening of the Christian world take place. Until Munich, the world believed that what Germany did to the Jews was merely an internal affair. It was a sort of neutrality which gradually degraded to something in which there was no distinction between right and wrong. It undermined the fundamental spiritual values of humanity.

The collapse of France came not primarily from lack of arms or the inferiority of the French army, but because France was already hollowed out from within. When the spirit of France was gone, then the circumvention of the Maginot Line was merely a military victory.

This country is not immune to ideas that undermined the spiritual values of the great community of Europe. Perhaps bombers will have difficulty in reaching these shores, but ideas can cross over three thousand miles of water. You—we—believe in certain fundamentals laid down in the Bible and further elaborated in the New Testament. Today's battle is definitely a fight between *Mein Kampf* and the Sermon on the Mount.

Through their suffering and their history, the Jews have come to embody the fundamental principles of the Ten Commandments. To dominate the world and to eliminate the spiritual principles that alone will defeat the armored chariots of Hitler, the Jews had to be removed.

Today everything you see in Palestine has been built by Jewish hands—and not merely Jewish brains, but Jewish labor. Our immigrants are still coming—through mined waters, in leaky boats, on journeys sometimes of from nine to ten months, facing every possible danger—but the leaky, uncomfortable boat on which these people come who are the builders of Zion, that boat is their *Mayflower*.

Once the Jew lands on the shores of Palestine, he ceases to be an immigrant or a refugee; he comes home. The Jew in Palestine does not speak English, he speaks Hebrew, and British officials in dealing with them speak

Hebrew. Today, at this great tragic moment, the whole manhood of Palestine stands shoulder to shoulder with the Army of the Nile—they are defending their patrimony and they know well they may expect no quarter from the enemy. They would rather die fighting than be caught like rats in a trap. Believe we shall win, because this spirit, the essential prerequisite to victory, lives in Palestine just as it lives in England, among the ordinary men and women.

Section Two

The Cold War and Vietnam

November 7, 1947

Cecil B. De Mille

Film Director and Producer

In October 1947, under the glare of klieg lights in the white marble caucus room of the Old House Office Building in Washington, D.C., the luminaries of Hollywood began appearing before the House Un-American Activities Committee (HUAC). Among those testifying: Gary Cooper, Walt Disney, and Ronald Reagan. In mid-November, Reagan would be elected president of the Screen Actors Guild. Meanwhile, film giant Cecil B. De Mille took to the podium before The Commonwealth Club to lay out Hollywood's responsibility in representing American ideals, not just at home but to the world. This was, after all, the year in which the Marshall Plan was announced and containment of the USSR became U.S. government policy.

De Mille had cofounded Paramount Studios more than thirty years before, and he was known worldwide as master of the spectacle. His *Ten Commandments* (1923) and *King of Kings* (1927) were believed to have been seen by eight hundred million people. And as he makes clear in this talk, he understood the power of movies to shape perceptions. He also had experienced firsthand what he felt was the unjust intrusion of politics into the media, through labor unions. For nearly a decade, he had hosted the Lux Radio Theater, which dramatized popular films for the radio. When the California ballot had carried, in 1944, a proposition to abolish the "closed shop" in California, the American Federation of Radio Artists had required members to contribute a dollar to fight the measure. De Mille refused to ante up and forbade his sponsor, Lever Brothers, from paying on his behalf. The result: De Mille's contract was revoked and he went off the air.

Here De Mille notes that the hunt for Communists in Hollywood is often cast in terms that are too simple: "Whenever there is a debate on the topic 'Is There a Red Menace in Hollywood?,'" he says, "one side smears Hollywood with mud, and the other side smears it with whitewash." Less than a week after De Mille's Club address, the "Hollywood Ten," including Ring Lardner and Dalton Trumbo, were cited for contempt of Congress by HUAC for refusing to cooperate with the investigation. Just over a week later, they were blacklisted by the studios.

"The Motion Pictures and International Relations"

There are two pictures that hang on the wall at my office. One is the picture of the little barn which I rented in Hollywood for twenty-five dollars a month, thirty-five years ago. That was our first studio. The other picture is of a plant so vast, covering so many acres, that it can only be photographed from the air. That is the Paramount Studios of today. Together, these two pictures tell the story of the motion picture industry's growth in thirty-five short years. It's as though Aladdin had rubbed his lamp and changed an orange grove into an empire. But they tell more than a story of material growth.

The influence of motion pictures has grown by the same leaps and bounds in the same short period of time. Thirty-five years ago, the movies were the stepchild of the entertainment world. No self-respecting citizen would be seen going into a nickelodeon on a back street if he could help it. Nobody except a few dreamers imagined that you could hold an audience with a picture running longer than fifteen or twenty minutes. The movies were just a toy.

Today, motion pictures have a weekly audience in the United States of between seventy and ninety million people. Think for a moment what that means: ninety million men, women, and children spending at least two hours a week taking in, through their eyes and ears, the stories and situations, the ideas and the ideals, and the standards of living and conduct that Hollywood puts before them.

You know the old Chinese saying that one picture's worth a thousand words. Well, during the war, the Army found that it could teach raw recruits several times faster by pictures than by lectures. I sometimes wonder if even the church or the school has as much real influence in molding the minds and desires and standards of the population as Hollywood has. What thirty-five years ago was the business of a few dreamers and experimenters is now the concern of everyone who is concerned about America, or about humanity. The movies are very definitely your business, too.

Look at it for just a moment from the businessman's standpoint. Suppose you're a manufacturer or a salesman of, let's say, bathtubs. If our picture audience sees on the screen gleaming, spotless creations of porcelain and white tile more comfortable and more beautiful and more luxurious than the dingy tin and wooden tubs that I used to be dumped in when I was a kid, he's going to want your product. If a picture-goer in Egypt or Australia or Belgium sees his heroes and heroines arriving in an American-made car, smoking American cigarettes, eating American breakfast foods, he's going to want those products.

We used to say that trade followed the flag. Well, today it follows the film. And that applies to trade and ideas and ideals as much as it applies to manufactured goods. Every can of film that we ship from Hollywood is a teacher of our children and an ambassador of America to the entire world. Former President Hoover said to me only three weeks ago that motion pictures must be the voice of America. Now, what is that voice saying? You have a right to ask that question, because you have a stake in America and in the future.

Is America being well represented at home and abroad by this ambassador? Where does Hollywood stand in the worldwide struggle between collectivism and individualism, between communism and liberty? Hollywood is a convenient target for so-called "witch hunters." I sometimes think that those hunters are actually hunting headlines, while the real witch sits in her little red tent and laughs at them. Whenever there is a debate on the topic "Is There a Red Menace in Hollywood?," one side smears Hollywood with mud, and the other side smears it with whitewash.

Motion pictures belong to the American people, and the people are entitled to the unvarnished facts. Yet there are Communists in Hollywood and some very dangerous ones, because they're very brainy ones. Like all

Communists everywhere, they have one single purpose: to serve the Soviet dictatorship by every means at their command. The pattern of Soviet conquest is the same the world over. Destroy both free enterprise and free government and substitute for them a police state based on slavery. That is Russia and that is each one of the countries that has fallen to Russia. And that will be America, too, if the Communists have their way. And that is the objective of our American Communists: in Hollywood, in industry, in the schools, in the churches, and wherever else they may be—and there are many other places where they are.

The Communists recognize the power of motion pictures, the immense influence of the screen upon the minds of those who watch it. As well as I can judge the Reds' operations, I believe that their design is either to control the motion picture industry or to destroy it, certainly to destroy those who do not follow the Red path. And, in any industry, the Communists can destroy anyone if they can get control of his right to work. They do not now control Hollywood. They do not control motion pictures. Their influence is subtle and indirect. They have to be subtle, but I believe there's not one major producer in Hollywood who would tolerate outright Communist propaganda on the screen.

The American people know that with all its faults, capitalism has given them the highest standard of living and the greatest personal freedom ever known in the world. The Communists cannot deny that, but they can and do make a banker or a successful businessman their villain. They can and do pick out the sordid and degraded parts of American life and picture them as though they were typical of all America, leading the audience—especially the foreign audience—to infer that all America is one vast Tobacco Road and all its successful people Little Foxes.[1]

The Communist governments and Communist trade unions abroad are quick to play the same game, with the added trump of political censorship. The Hungarian film trade union has served notice on the Hungarian government that it will go out on strike against theaters which screen pictures with actors serving what the union called fascist, imperialist capitalism. In

1. The John Ford–directed film *Tobacco Road* (based on a stage adaptation of Erskine Caldwell's novel of the same name) tells the tale of a clan of shiftless "poor whites" in rural Georgia—inbred, indigent, and amoral. William Wyler's film version of Lillian Hellman's play *The Little Foxes* tells the tale of conniving aristocrats in the turn-of-the-century South who marry for wealth, engage in blackmail, and commit murder. Both films were released in 1941.

Romania, the Communist government has barred from the screen eleven American stars a few days after most of them had testified against communism at the hearings in Washington.

It seems to me the motion picture industry has a choice: either to withdraw all of its product from those countries or furnish them only with pictures starring players thought to be un-American in sympathy. While the Communists over here decry political censorship, their comrades abroad are practicing political censorship in one of its most vicious forms, denying good Americans the right to work on their screens. There could be no clearer example of what Communists mean when they talk about freedom. Or, again, the Communists attach themselves like leeches to good and worthy causes, not to help the cause of others, but to help their own cause, which thrives on hatred—the hatred of race for race and class for class. Some of them can even talk about the First Amendment as though they really believed in freedom. And, I'm sorry to say that there are in Hollywood, just as there are in San Francisco and in every other city, a certain number of self-styled liberals perhaps confused and innocent enough to be taken in by this line of propaganda.

Communism is always a real danger wherever it is. Hollywood has no monopoly of it. The Communists are active here on the whole West Coast. They, and their equally dangerous fellow travelers and their innocent dupes, are apt to be in either political party or both political parties, whether you're Democrat or Republican. You may even find them in your church. You may find them in your factories and in your schools and on your newspapers and radio. And one of the biggest victories they could win would be to divert all of our Red-baiting energy toward Hollywood, so you wouldn't see them planting the seeds of chaos in your own backyards.

They want to rot away the economic structure in every great city and every great industry until the national structure of free government falls. Europe is an object lesson written large for us to see and heed. Penetration is the Communist method and chaos their goal. And their blindfolded dupes dance around the crumbling ruins shouting, "Look, this is the new era!" Well, Hollywood has its Communist problems, but I wish the rest of the country were as alert to communism as an element as Hollywood is. In every Hollywood studio and guild and union where the Communists or their sympathizers are active, the Americans are active in opposition. I wish

I could say the same thing about every industry, union, political party, church, and school system in the rest of the country.

Hollywood will welcome investigation and help from any government source or any government agency or any other source, provided the same investigation and the same help are extended to the other parts of the country that need it just as much or more. But Hollywood will not welcome being made a whipping boy for the benefit of headline hunters and sensation seekers or irresponsible mudsmearers. Let the pot wash its own face before it calls the kettle black. The great majority of Hollywood, of course, is anti-Communist and is organizing and working to turn back the Red tide. People in Hollywood are taking sides as they must take sides in San Francisco and everywhere else. They're going to have to say, "I am for America and things American," or "I am for a foreign ideology and the destruction of spiritual values, the destruction of the American form of government." You can't mix these two ideologies, because nothing will mix with communism.

Well, I'm wrong when I say that; there is one thing. Poison will mix with communism. If you shoot one drop of cobra venom into your veins, your whole system will be poisoned. There are only a handful of Communist Party members in the whole nation, but this little minority is infecting a much greater number. In many places, they control a vast number of American workmen through control of his right to work. How many of us have seen our own sons waiver and wonder? I was talking just recently to a fine American who said to me, "My boy has a different ideology. I don't know what happened, I don't know where he got it, but he's got it." Well, that's the insidious poison you've got to fight and destroy wherever it shows itself. If you don't, it will destroy you and your children and your children's children. But anticommunism alone is not the whole answer. You can be anti-pneumonia and still die of pneumonia.

We have a more positive job to do, you and I and all Americans. We must stand up and defend the system that made this country great. Capitalism is not perfect, but there's nothing wrong with it that communism can cure. This is a capitalist country, it was built on capitalism, it succeeded on capitalism. And capitalism is Joe Brown's right to own his own grocery store. Every American—not just the rich men on Wall Street—every American has a stake in capitalism. Every worker has a stake in capitalism, because an employer that doesn't make a profit is not a safe employer. There are no jobs in closed factories. Don't be ashamed of capitalism, as too many of us have been. How many businessmen have come out in defense of their own side? Too many of them have hidden their light under the nearest bushel while a few people have borne the brunt of the whole attack.

If America goes under, the shortsighted timidity of many American businessmen will be as much to blame for it as anything else. If you're on the right side, come out and be on it. It's really a very curious spectacle. America is the envy of the rest of the world today. Why? Because capitalism has kept the doors of freedom and opportunity open, because private enterprise has fostered the determination and courage and creative power that make a country great. And instead of standing up for the system that has kept us free and strong, we're in danger of letting it fall before an ideology born of despotism, cruelty, viciousness, and dishonor, unless we're willing now to stand up and be counted.

Hollywood's part is to put America, the real America, on the screens of the world and into the minds and hearts of our own people. It's a challenging job to put on a few thousand feet of film all that has gone into the making of that new and extraordinary figure that appeared on the world's stage less than two hundred years ago: the American. People sometimes ask me where we get the ideas for pictures. Believe me, they don't just happen. That Aladdin's lamp I mentioned a few minutes ago burns midnight oil. No one walked into a producer's office with a finished manuscript ready to shoot. I got the idea for *Unconquered* one Sunday afternoon when I was reading a history of the American colonies and came across the fact that less than two hundred years ago, you could buy a white man here in America, buy him and own him for fifty pounds and a white woman for twenty. I saw drama there, for drama is conflict, and in that simple bill of sale was a germ of the conflict between Old World oppression and New World liberty.

I saw the story taking shape of how this bartering of human flesh would strike an American. For already, in 1763, though European flags were still flying here, the new American was taking shape, and a new answer was being wrought to the age-old question, "What is a human being worth?" That's what we show in *Unconquered*: the brewing of the American; the brewing of the American spirit; the brewing of American freedom and independence that mankind had only dreamed of until this strange new creature, the American, made it real. Already, in 1763, the melting pot was simmering. Fifteen years later, it would boil, and boil over. Out of the weary stews of the Old World, men and women were coming here and being made into something new. A man might have been a Frenchman, an Englishman, a German, a Swede, a Pole, an Irishman, or a Scotsman or a Swiss. He might have been a titled gentleman or a felon from Old Bailey—our ancestry is very mixed, you know. But none of that counted in the New World. A man's worth was in himself. Here, the old bloodstreams of Europe mixed to produce a new man, just as the Liberty Bell had to be recast before it could ring out its message of freedom.

The Old World has often looked down and laughed at this new creature, the American. They said he was crude, brash, uncouth, the clumsy braggart who played too many games and saw too many movies. But twice in our lifetime that young American—that gum-chewing, wisecracking, sentimental, tough young American from Brooklyn or Texas or San Francisco—has gone back to the Old World to fight for freedom. He may not be able to twist his tongue around "the unalienable rights of man," but let them be threatened and he's in there fighting with both fists. And tomorrow's tyrants will feel his fists again if they delude themselves into thinking that he's too tired or too fat or too rich or too poor to care anymore about freedom.

The Communists and their sympathizers call this "American imperialism." Well, if American imperialism means keeping free nations on their feet; if it means feeding millions of men, women, and children, and countries that can never pay us back except by friendship; if it means the American schools and missions strung around the world from Egypt to China; if it means letting people know that American free enterprise has produced the world's highest standards of living, highest production, highest wages, and the greatest personal freedom; if it means spreading to other countries the ideas of free speech, a free press, freedom of religions, free elections, and the right to work; if American imperialism means these things, then it's bred in the bone of every real American, and he can be very proud of it.

It's Hollywood's job to tell that American his own story, and to tell the world what he's really like and why. It's your job to keep that story true. Hollywood will reflect the America that you make. For one hundred and sixty years, America has been unconquered by any foreign foe. Our greatest weakness, perhaps our only weakness, is from within: from the termites in government; from the Communist minorities in labor; from the little groups in certain churches who put the spirit of Lenin ahead of the spirit of truth; from the misleaders of youth who teach the principles of Karl Marx instead of the principles of Jefferson, Franklin, and Lincoln. And your action, pro-American and pro-freedom, must be as intensive and as broad as the anti-American action of our enemies. In their strategy—and I beg you to listen to these two or three little words—in their strategy, every move, from the swallowing of a nation to the electing of a fellow traveler to some village school board, is a deliberate, planned step toward a Soviet Empire of the world. We must oppose every such move without exception and without compromise. This means more than sitting down like King Canute and bidding the tide go back. It means a vigorous outthrust of all the power we possess, to push ever forward the frontiers of man's freedom, both abroad and here at home.

Fight communism as hard as you can, but fight just as hard to plague spots that breed communism out of injustice and oppression. The world is hungry for what we have, not only for wealth like ours but for the freedom and enterprise that produce that wealth. God has sown the hunger for freedom in every human heart, and then he planted the wheat of freedom here in America, and gave us hands to reap it and make it bread for all mankind. And our work is not done, nor may we take our rest, so long as anywhere in the world one human being asks for liberty and is not fed.

December 14, 1951

Joseph R. McCarthy

Member, U.S. Senate (R–WI)

Wisconsin Senator Joe McCarthy drew national headlines when, speaking to a gathering of Republican women in Wheeling, West Virginia, in February 1950, he cast aspersions on the State Department and declared, "I have in my hand fifty-seven individuals who would appear to be either card-carrying members or certainly loyal to the Communist Party." Only a week before McCarthy's speech, scientist Klaus Fuchs had been arrested for espionage. And less than two weeks before that, attorney and former government official Alger Hiss had been convicted of perjury in what was billed as "the trial of the century." The actual number of Communists McCarthy mentioned is in dispute. What's not in dispute is that for the next three years, in the atomically charged atmosphere of the early 1950s, he pursued Communist foes real and imagined in the American government.

In some quarters, the term "McCarthyism" quickly became synonymous with demagoguery and the "witch hunt" for Communists in the American government, but McCarthy was seen by others as having the courage to stand up to an insidious enemy. In March 1950, the Senate convened the Tydings committee to investigate McCarthy's charges and found that none were substantiated. By the end of 1951, when McCarthy spoke to Commonwealth

Club members at the Palace Hotel, he was billed as "Outspoken Foe of Communism Whose Heavy-Hitting Charges of Red Infiltration in Our State and Other Departments Have Shaken the Nation." While the speech may not illuminate and inspire, it's a remarkable window on the times and an indication of what fueled McCarthy's crusade.

Some background: In 1949, Mao Tse-tung had led the Communists to victory over Chiang Kai-shek's Nationalists in the civil war. The Soviets exploded their first atomic bomb—their progress helped by espionage. European nations liberated by the Red Army had gone Communist, perhaps with FDR's consent (with advisement from Alger Hiss) given at Yalta. North Korea invaded South Korea in the summer of 1950, six months after Truman's secretary of state, Dean Acheson, had given a speech demarcating the American defense perimeter in the Pacific, a perimeter that notably excluded Korea and Formosa (where Chiang Kai-shek was then holed up). And instead of letting General Douglas MacArthur win the war in Korea the way he wanted to—using atomic bombs on the Chinese—Truman had fired him in April 1951. The general returned home to a hero's welcome, complete with ticker-tape parade.

When McCarthy spoke to The Commonwealth Club six months later, he had fixed his guns on another old soldier, George C. Marshall, whom he blamed for "losing China." Truman had sent Marshall to China in autumn 1945, replacing the staunchly anti-Communist Patrick Hurley as mediator of the Chinese civil war. The cease-fire Marshall brokered soon unraveled, and Chiang Kai-shek was left to battle it out with the Communists himself. Marshall later went on to serve as both secretary of state and secretary of defense under Truman.

The cast of characters in McCarthy's Commonwealth Club speech also includes James Forrestal, who had served as secretary of the Navy under FDR and Truman and assisted with creating the Department of Defense in 1947, then became the first secretary of defense. He is one of McCarthy's heroes here, and he had led the Defense Department through the months that Czechoslovakia succumbed to a Communist coup and the Soviets blockaded Berlin. He resigned in 1949 after a mental breakdown, and that March he jumped to his death from a hospital window. (Conspiracy theorists surmised that Soviet agents were to blame.)

Also earning acclaim from McCarthy here are Arthur Bliss Lane, who resigned from his position as U.S. ambassador to Poland after what he saw as the betrayal of Poland by the U.S., and who first spoke at The Commonwealth Club in October 1948 on "The Folly of Appeasement"; and diplomat Joseph Grew, who resigned after insisting that another State Department official, John Stewart Service—at the time undersecretary of state—be prosecuted for passing secret documents to the Communist-affiliated journal *Amerasia* in the mid-1940s. An "old China hand," Service wasn't prosecuted. He was, however, one of McCarthy's villains, and the *Amerasia* case was revived half a decade later by McCarthy.

Another player in that case was Philip Jaffe, editor of *Amerasia*, who was convicted of unauthorized possession of government documents. The fact that this was a case of the government going after a publication for espionage raised, as political scientists Harvey Klehr and Ronald Radosh put it decades later, "important questions about the conflict between freedom of the press and the government's need to keep sensitive information secret, especially during wartime." The lead prosecutor agreed that the defendants were guilty primarily of "an excess of journalistic zeal."

A lesser villain for McCarthy was Henry Julian Wadleigh, who is mentioned in passing. A State Department official who admitted handing over hundreds of documents to Whittaker Chambers during his days as a Communist spy, he was not charged with espionage, because the statute of limitations had expired. After he'd left the State Department he wrote a piece entitled "Why I Spied for the Communists" for the *New York Post Home-News.*

Coming under fire from McCarthy directly was Philip C. Jessup, who had been appointed by Truman to serve as special ambassador in 1949. He had been deputy chief of the U.S. mission to the UN and helped negotiate an end to the blockade of Berlin. McCarthy believed him unfit for the post; William F. Buckley Jr. later quoted McCarthy as having said that even if Jessup wasn't a Communist, he was "on the other side." The State Department's Loyalty and Security Board eventually found "reasonable doubt" as to Jessup's loyalty, and he was removed.

Earning McCarthy's designation in 1950 as "Moscow's top spy" was Johns Hopkins professor Owen Lattimore, who had worked in China in the 1920s and 1930s. When McCarthy spoke at The Commonwealth Club, Lattimore had been acquitted of charges leveled in 1950—though he and McCarthy continued to do battle. In 1952 he would be indicted for having perjured himself in his 1950 testimony; three years later he would be cleared of all charges.

In 1953, McCarthy was appointed chairman of the Permanent Investigating Subcommittee of the Senate Committee on Government Operations. McCarthy's hearings were televised, and the audience was enormous—as was public support for McCarthy. His first target was the Voice of America administration; then the committee forced American embassies' libraries to discard what was determined to be "pro-Communist" literature. The following year McCarthy began his inquiry into Communists in the U.S. Army. Truman was no longer in the White House, but fellow Republican Dwight Eisenhower was no friend of McCarthy. And in the Army hearings, despite locking onto a dentist who took the Fifth Amendment over thirty times, McCarthy finally bit off more than he could chew. The Army's chief attorney, Joseph Welch, memorably responded to McCarthy's attack by asking, "Have you no sense of decency, sir, at long last? Have you no sense of decency?" Public support for McCarthy plummeted. The U.S. Senate voted to censure him at the end of 1954. His heavy drinking dove into full-blown alcoholism, and he died of hepatitis in May 1957.

As for McCarthy's legacy, it's taken a couple of remarkable turns in the past few years. In 1995, the U.S. government began declassifying messages related to VENONA, the code-name for a U.S. and British project to decode Soviet messages from 1940s. The U.S. had begun decoding material as early as 1947, and in the decoded material was information on Soviet espionage in the U.S. Over two hundred sources were named and code names matched up with real people. The consensus among scholars now is that VENONA is authentic and McCarthy actually underestimated the extent of Soviet espionage. What if the material from VENONA had been available to Congress during McCarthy's tenure? Alger Hiss would have been identified as having spied for the Soviets beginning in 1935; Julius Rosenberg would have been confirmed as spying too. But there was no mention in the messages of Owen Lattimore. So would anti-Communist efforts have been more effective and on-target? Or would the net have been cast even more broadly?

The speech that follows has something of a desperate tone. It is literally all over the map, because that's where the Cold War was being waged. For those convinced that McCarthy was a force for evil, it's a warning, especially in the wake of U.S. government security precautions following September 11, 2001. For those who think McCarthy was on target all along and has gotten short shrift by a biased liberal media, this is McCarthy at full volume. Asked several years ago why McCarthy is "pilloried and his motive to root communism from American government universally ridiculed," Harvey Klehr—author of one study of the VENONA transcripts—answered, "Because McCarthy was a demagogue. He accused innocent people, misused evidence, and couldn't tell a Communist spy from a fellow traveler. He gave anti-Communism a bad name." Klehr also notes that the VENONA transcripts have caused some conservative triumphalism, "some of it justified." In that category might be conservative pundit Ann Coulter, whose 2003 book *Treason: Liberal Treachery from the Cold War to the War on Terrorism* exhumes and lionizes McCarthy.

"Communism in Our Government"

Foreign policy doesn't just grow, it is created by men, men with faces and with names. This is not a Democratic fight nor a Republican fight. There is no reason the two parties should be on opposite sides of the battle against communism.

There is nothing more secret or mysterious about international communism than there was about *Mein Kampf*. One of the aims the Communists publicly proclaimed was creation of a Red Poland and of a Red China. The Communists knew they had to have a Red Poland before they could conquer Europe; they knew they had to have a Red China before they could have a Red Pacific. We are all aware how $90 million was lent the Communists in Poland when the situation was touch-and-go there. Acheson's law firm received a $50,000 fee in that deal. Ambassador Arthur Bliss Lane resigned when that loan was granted. Lane was a New Dealer—but he was an American. He has told the story in his book *I Saw Poland Betrayed*.

We are all aware of the Marshall mission to China under State Department orders, which he (either willingly, or as a good soldier) meticulously followed. Two weeks before that mission, William Z. Poster, then head of the Communist Party in the U. S., now in jail, wrote that the key to conquest of America was a Red China. Lenin wrote, "He who controls China controls the world." Marshall said, "As chief of staff I armed thirty-nine Chinese anti-Communist divisions; now with a stroke of the pen I disarm them."

Admiral Cook was questioned: "Did the State Department know that the Chinese Communists were being armed from the mountains of captured

Japanese equipment in Manchuria? Do the Communists control China today because we cut off arms to our friends?" Admiral Cook's reply was, "No, that is *one* reason. The other is that on four occasions when the Communists were losing in China, we forced a truce. Each time they built up strength, then struck again, with initial success. And we did nothing. But when they started to lose, we sought another truce period. After the fourth truce, broken by the Communists, their army had been built from three hundred thousand to two and a half million. Our friends had no arms—we'd cut them off—and the State Department said, 'We'll stand back and wait.'"

John Stewart Service has a long history. When Pat Hurley was in China he despaired of the problem of secrecy. Our secret dispatches within two days were showing up at Communist headquarters in Yenan. Hurley told Roosevelt he could not stop the Communists from getting this information with the motley crew Roosevelt had given him—they were not loyal to America but to the Communists. He said one of the worst was John Stewart Service. When Service came back to the United States, he was picked up in the *Amerasia* case. J. Edgar Hoover said this was an airtight case of Soviet espionage. There was a great cry that we should not try the individuals accused of being Soviet spies, because it might make Russia angry. But Joseph Grew said, "I don't care a tinker's dam who you make mad—I want everyone connected with this spy case to be arrested!"

Then Grew resigned (he was sick or something) and Acheson took over and Service was not convicted but reinstated by Acheson on a board controlling promotion and placement of State Department personnel in the Far East. The Department said in substance, "The hearts of all State Department employees go out to John Stewart Service. McCarthy's irresponsible smearing of John Stewart Service is making it extremely difficult to get others like him into the State Department."

The FBI testified before the Tydings committee that it had trailed Service—with large brown envelopes under his arm—to the hotel room of Philip Jaffe, known to the FBI as a member of the Communist Party, and fined in the *Amerasia* case for stealing some seventeen hundred classified documents! The FBI heard Service discuss with Jaffe top secret military information. The State Department's Loyalty Board held a hearing and said, "Isn't this McCarthyism a nasty thing! Look at all the grief it caused poor John!"

Today a Senate committee is spending tens of thousands of dollars under a resolution to kick McCarthy out of the Senate because he is smearing good

State Department men like John Service. The president's own board has now proclaimed this man unfit to hold public office on the basis of evidence Acheson had had for two years. Is there one reason why Dean Gooderharn Acheson should stay in that job?

Today we are in a war not of our choosing; the Kremlin has proclaimed this war cannot stop short of destruction either of Western civilization or of communism. Since the shooting part of World War II ended, we have been losing this war at the rate of one hundred million people a year! At the time of Dumbarton Oaks there were about one hundred and eighty million behind the Iron Curtain: now there are over eight hundred million. Unless this course is checked, in another eight or twelve years communism will have accomplished its aim: a Red world. Can the trend be checked with the same men doing the planning? Why have we been losing this war at a rate no nation ever lost a war before? It is either because of stumbling, bumbling idiocy of those in power—or because we *planned* it that way. One of the things your representatives in Washington must do is find why we are losing and see if we can't call a halt.

They said, after Hiss and Wadleigh were gone, the State Department is clean! It can't be clean until the course of action changes. If robbery continues after two or three arrests, it is evident more criminals are still at large. We haven't scratched the surface in the State Department.

It's perfectly safe to wave your arms and condemn communism and Russia. But when you start to dig out the sacred cows, then all the bleeding hearts for the Reds in press and radio take after you. Their first target was Chiang, then Jimmy Forrestal at Truman's elbow (they killed Forrestal just as if they had shoved him out of that sixteenth-story window). Their next target was Douglas MacArthur, but what they found here was a giant among men that they cannot destroy.

How was the "sellout of 1951" accomplished? The method of operation is disclosed in an article written by that "great American," Owen Lattimore, in the New York *Compass* for July 17, 1949: "The problem in China was how to allow them to fall without making it look as if the United States had pushed them...." About South Korea also, he wrote, "The thing to do, therefore, is to let South Korea fall—but not to let it look as though we pushed it." Hence his parting recommendation for $150 million economic aid to Korea—enough aid to please the American suckers who are paying for it but not enough to stop the Communists. A month later Lattimore was asked to give his secret advice to Roving Ambassador Jessup just before he started to roam.

When I brought this matter up, the State Department held a press conference. They had never heard of Lattimore. Who was he? I was ill at the time but I phoned the State Department that if this information were not made public within two hours, I would make it public along with another document having nothing to do with communism. The document was made public; it was the Communist Party line all the way down.[1]

Dean Acheson dutifully came before Congress and asked for $150 million of American aid for Korea—no military aid of course. Congress also voted $10 million so South Koreans could have a few guns and tanks to combat the guns and tanks of North Korea. But every time we asked how many were being sent, we got the same answer: this information could not be given because it would endanger the re-armament and security of South Korea.

After the Korean War started, Senator Knowland put the entire record into the *Congressional Record*. How much of the $10 million had been spent when the war started? Not one ounce of gunpowder, not one tank, not one bullet—only $200 to load some wire on the West Coast—but the State Department could not tell us over a nine-month period "without endangering the security of Korea"!

As of this moment there exists the most treasonable order ever issued by this nation in war or peace: an order to the Seventh Fleet to protect the long, exposed, Communist coastline of China from the six hundred thousand free troops of China; that if Chiang's planes attack or sink Communist ships, our Seventh Fleet must shoot those planes down. MacArthur testified that prior to that order, vast numbers of Communist troops had been held on the China coast. After that presidential order, these hundreds of thousands of

---

1. On March 13, 1950, the *Baltimore Evening Sun*, Owen Lattimore's hometown paper, carried the headline "McCarthy Cites Lattimore, Three Others as 'Pro-Red.'" Lattimore was not there to read it. Traveling in Afghanistan, he did not learn of Joseph McCarthy's allegations until receiving a cable from the Associated Press (AP) on the 24th. In the intervening days, McCarthy escalated his attack by leaking Lattimore's name to reporters in off-the-record comments and stating that his entire anti-Communist enterprise rested on the veracity of the Lattimore claims. Confronted with the AP cable, Lattimore sent back a blunt reply: "McCarthy's off record ranting pure moonshine." Upon his return to the U.S., Lattimore continued to fight back, labeling McCarthy a "base and miserable creature," and decrying the way he and others had been caught in "the machine gun of irresponsible publicity in Joseph McCarthy's hands."

Red troops moved north to Korea to kill American boys. He said we had identified in Korea two Communist armies released by the Seventh Fleet. Under presidential orders, our Navy is fighting against the U.S.

Acheson said before Congress that we had won a great victory in Korea. Yes, we have won a great victory, *a victory for Communist Russia*. We have done everything in Korea that Communist Russia hoped we would do. We have rolled back and forth across the unfortunate land and destroyed an entire race of people, every city and town, every farmhouse. We have notified every other nation in range of the Communist aggressors that if they dare to oppose international communism, we will do the fighting on the land of our friends and not that of our enemies.

The head of our air forces says China is now becoming an air power; our estimates give our air losses as nine hundred planes; Red losses, three hundred. Can any of you give a single reason why we should not bomb the bases from which these planes come? Bomb the bridges and the tunnels to keep the Communists back where they belong! But there it is: *"Let them fall, but don't let the American sucker know we pushed them!"*

We are doing the same thing in Europe. We engaged in the "great debate" in the Senate, whether two, four, six, or ten divisions should go to Western Europe and whether the president should get consent of Congress for the first division or the fifth. We wouldn't allow the twenty million of Spain or the fifty million of Germany to defend their own lands. The Communists know we are poor in manpower and rich in weapons of war. Congress finally did act. It passed a resolution calling upon the secretary of state and the secretary of defense to make plans for full utilization of the manpower of Germany and Spain. That meant about as much to our planners as the $10 million for South Korea. As of today they have done nothing, and when we ask what is being done, we get the same answer: "The matter is still under discussion." Unless we use all Western Europe's manpower to defend that very important area when the Russian army starts to move, every American boy we send over there will be condemned to death or slave camps.

MacArthur said we should use the forces on Formosa. General Bradley said yes, that was true. But months have passed, and we have done nothing. Can anyone think of one reason why as of today we should not start using the troops of Chiang Kai-shek to replace American soldiers? Is there any reason why only American boys should fight and die in Korea?

Acheson knows we haven't enough American manpower to fight in every sector of the globe. So the Acheson-Lattimore plan: *"Let them fall, but don't let them know we pushed them."* Time is running out. We are buying time all right, not for America, but for Communist Russia.

When I opposed the nomination of Philip C. Jessup, ambassador-at-large and now delegate to the UN, on grounds he had too great an affinity for Communist causes, that was the greatest understatement McCarthy ever made! I said, "Let's make the stakes high—let's bring him before a jury and if the jury doesn't agree Jessup is bad for America, good for Communist Russia, I'll resign from Congress on condition that the whole motley Yalta crowd leave the State Department!"

Well, the president took me up on this—not directly, but he sent the appointment of Jessup to Congress. Press reports said the committee was stacked four to one in Jessup's favor. It looked like a good safe bet, but they forgot these men were Americans first and Democrats second, and the "jury" stacked in Jessup's favor found him unfit to represent this nation. The president waited for Congress to adjourn and gave Jessup an interim appointment. When I see photos of Jessup talking with Vyshinsky, I think of Alger Hiss....[1]

I'm often asked why McCarthy doesn't talk off the Senate floor where he hasn't got immunity. I've discussed these things on the floor and off the floor, and I intend to continue to do so. I've ordered a recording of this talk, and it will be available to the State Department and Mr. Jessup. If what I have said is libelous, I will accept service.

I have evidence here; I didn't expect a crowd this large, so I have only eight hundred copies of this document.[2] In this document are photostats showing Jessup's association with six organizations officially cited as Communist fronts. Here is sworn testimony before various congressional

1. Andrey Vyshinsky served as prosecutor during the infamous show trials in the Soviet Union in the late 1930s. By 1940 he had risen to become Stalin's deputy commissar of foreign affairs and held that post at the time of the 1945 Yalta conference, where he met with a spy who is believed to have been Hiss. He went on to serve as commissar of foreign affairs (1949–1953) and permanent delegate to the United Nations.
2. When McCarthy's speech was reproduced in *The Commonwealth*, Editor Stuart Ward included the following note: "Copies of 'The Case of Ambassador-at-Large Philip C. Jessup' may be obtained by writing Senator Joseph R. McCarthy, Washington, D.C." A copy of the report exists in The Club archives.

committees identifying as members of the Communist Party and as espionage agents a sizeable number of individuals on Jessup's staff and writers hired by the Institute of Pacific Relations while Jessup was chairman of the Pacific and American Councils of the Institute of Pacific Relations. Here is testimony given under oath by Jessup from the second Hiss trial showing his continued support of Hiss after the facts on his Communist activities were made known in the first trial, together with Jessup's sworn testimony before the Tydings committee, 1950, in which he continues to support Hiss after his conviction.

I don't think President Truman is disloyal, or even remotely part of the Jessup-Acheson crowd. I think he wants to fight communism. I asked the president: "Can't you find, among our 150 million people, one American who has not been playing around with this Communist crowd?" The next morning he gave Jessup access to top secret atomic and hydrogen bomb information.

September 21, 1959

Nikita Khrushchev

Premier of the Soviet Union

In the summer of 1959, President Eisenhower took what he called a bold step to break the Cold War deadlock with the Soviet Union and to preempt worsening of an ongoing crisis with Berlin: he invited Soviet leader Nikita Khrushchev to visit the United States. (Some Republicans called inviting the man who was known in some circles as the Butcher of Budapest, for crushing the 1956 Hungarian uprising, "insane" rather than bold. The sharp-tongued William F. Buckley Jr. suggested filling the Hudson River with red dye so that it resembled a river of blood, which he said would make Khrushchev feel right at home.) Americans had been transfixed by television images of Khrushchev debating Richard Nixon when the vice president visited Moscow in July. The visit by the pipefitter-turned-premier let Americans at long last see him in person. After a turkey dinner at the White House and a meeting at the National Press Club, where he explained once more that the "we will bury you" remark he had made a few years before at a Moscow reception—not at the UN, as many remember it—meant simply that the laws of history dictated that communism must bury capitalism, and several days in New York, Khrushchev flew to Los Angeles. At a luncheon hosted by Twentieth Century Fox, he tussled over a microphone with the head of the studio, squeezed Marilyn Monroe's hand, and visited the set of the movie *Can-Can* (whose stars included Frank Sinatra and Shirley MacLaine). At an official dinner, Los Angeles Mayor Norris Poulson went out of his way to offend Khrushchev with Cold War tough talk. Infuriated, Khrushchev threatened to cancel his trip and fly home the next morning.

But after a calming talk by his escort, American representative to the UN Henry Cabot Lodge Jr., and after a train trip in the style of American politicians up the coast of the Golden State, complete with baby kissing and handshakes at the stations, Khrushchev alighted in San Francisco. There he was charmed by the people and a more genial host, Mayor George Christopher. Khrushchev took a boat ride on the bay, toured the IBM plant, and spoke to The Commonwealth Club—where he averred that he was not trying to entice San Franciscans over to the kingdom of communism, but he was offering his personal invitation to visit the Soviet Union. "It is not sunlight alone that warms our hearts in this land so distant from our country," he told the audience seated before him—and before televisions in an adjoining ballroom. "We have been cordially welcomed and received by the Californians, and I would like the friendship between our peoples to be as inextinguishable and bright as is your southern sun." Rarely content with confining himself to prepared remarks (or "scraps of paper," as he called them), Khrushchev thoroughly enjoyed himself at the dinner. Rambling and filled with these extemporaneous remarks, populated by black cats, magicians, Pushkin, and reflections on the similarities between the teachings of communism and Christianity, the speech reveals the jolly side of the premier's personality.

After a stopover in Iowa (Khrushchev had a special fondness for corn) and Pittsburgh (to visit a steel mill), Khrushchev and Eisenhower met once again and, after a tense weekend at Camp David and at Eisenhower's farm in Gettysburg, ironed out enough differences between the U.S. and USSR for the visit to end with a new sense of hope for peace in the world, which was dubbed the Spirit of Camp David. A summit where the Soviets and Americans would be joined by their French and British counterparts was scheduled in Paris for May 1960; in June President Eisenhower was slated to begin his grand tour of the Soviet Union, complete with a round of golf on the course that Khrushchev was having constructed especially for the visit. Eisenhower had hopes of signing a nuclear test ban with Khrushchev, the crowning achievement to his second term as president. Those hopes were shot out of the sky along with a U-2 spy plane on May Day 1960.

The San Francisco Speech

It is a pleasure to see a rich and beautiful country. It is an even greater pleasure to see the fine use you make of California's wealth. When the pioneer explorer Juan Rodríguez Cabrillo stepped upon the soil of California in 1542, the first European to do so, the land lay virgin and unexplored. There were giant sequoias, redwoods, many of which were already nearly a thousand years old. And somewhere deep in the earth there lay incalculable and still undiscovered riches...oil and gold. But is it only in gold and oil that California is rich? You have everything, trout and salmon, cotton—this priceless gold—oranges, grapes, and redwoods, minerals and vast resources of blue coal. Your land is excellent, ladies and gentlemen, and your city, San Francisco, is magnificent. Its shores are washed by the waves of the Pacific, which also washes the shores of the Soviet far east.

Though I did not come to your city by sea, I know that it starts at the Golden Gate, and I should like to express confidence that the day is not far off when this Golden Gate will open hospitably to Soviet ships bearing the goods you need, while American merchant ships will pass through this gate on their way to Soviet ports. It was across the Pacific that Russian people reached California a long time ago—you know that settlements and towns with Russian names still exist in these parts. For many years the American West maintained trade relations with our country, and it is only recently that Soviet-American trade has been reduced virtually to naught.

I have already said on more than one occasion that we have come to the United States with an open heart and the best of intentions. We want but one thing and that is to live in peace and friendship with you and with other peoples. It is my opinion that the distinguished Californians present here tonight share these sentiments and aspirations with us.

Americans who have visited the Soviet Union returned with different opinions about our country and its life, but they will all confirm that the words "peace" and "friendship" are to be heard everywhere in our country. They are to be seen in the white stone on the slopes of railway tracks. They are to be seen written in flowers in our parks and gardens. They are to be seen traced on house walls. They are in the heart of every Soviet citizen, and this is because all Soviet people are seeking by their peaceful labor to safeguard themselves and the entire world against the horrors of war.

We know well what war means, and though we are strong, we do not want war with its consequences and its destruction ever again to be visited upon mankind. It goes without saying that the best way to prevent war is to nip it in the bud, and that is to destroy the means of conducting war. A few days ago the Soviet government submitted to the United Nations a proposal for general and complete disarmament, with the establishment of unlimited control. A little earlier, at the end of August, the Soviet government decided not to resume nuclear tests in the Soviet Union unless such tests were resumed by the Western powers. The Soviet Union will continue to struggle for a complete cessation of nuclear tests, regarding this as an important step toward the termination of the nuclear arms race and elimination of the threat to the life and health of millions of people.

It is well understood everywhere that these are not the only problems that are of cardinal importance if peace is to be preserved. The existence of remnants of World War II is likewise fraught with the danger of a new war, and therefore this problem, too, must be solved. We do not seek any unilateral advantages or benefits in proposing the conclusion of a peace treaty with Germany and proceeding from the existence of two German states. Who can think of advantages when it is a matter of putting out the still-glowing embers of an old fire? The Soviet government has often stated that it wants to normalize the situation in Germany, which would also eliminate the abnormal situation in Berlin.

I will not go into details. We have already had frank discussions on many questions with the president of the United States, Mr. Eisenhower, and we shall have more. It is to be hoped that as a result of our talks, the two sides will come substantially closer to the solution of urgent international problems, which, in the final count, would ensure the strengthening of universal peace and the security of the people.

All prejudice and ill will must be discarded if we are to achieve an early correct solution of the urgent problems. This is the position from which the Soviet people approach the questions dividing us. We want better to understand you and your motives, but there must be reciprocity. You also should better understand us and our motives. The Soviet Union does not seek any advantages. We want only one thing: that war should never again menace people anywhere on Earth.

Well, that actually brings me to the close of my prepared speech to this responsible gathering, but if you have no objections I would like to share with you some of the impressions that I gained after this text was prepared. I spent a very pleasant day today traveling by car and by ship, I saw your bay, and I would say that I didn't look to see what was insecurely lying about. I looked with the friendliest, the most sincere sentiments, at what you have achieved and at this beautiful bay of yours.

I am very grateful for the invitation accorded to me to visit the longshoremen's union, where I talked to the president of the union and also to a representative of the employers. This was an exceedingly pleasant meeting for me, and the day was particularly memorable because I also was lucky enough to have acquired something here in San Francisco. One of the longshoremen presented me with his longshoreman's cap and I responded by presenting him with my Russian hat. That to me will certainly be a very memorable souvenir of San Francisco. And when I was driving with Mr. Lodge in the car along your wonderful roadways—I don't know how many miles we covered—I was very happy to see the people on the roadside. Some of them had perhaps just come out by accident at the time I was driving by, and some may have come out on purpose to see what sort of a man had come to them from across the sea. All the more so that this man is a Communist and a premier of a great country, and I was happy to see the friendly smiles written on the faces of those people that we passed in the streets.

My visit to the IBM computer plant was also a source of great satisfaction, and I am especially grateful too for the kindness of the director, as you would say in the Soviet Union—you call him the president of the company. He is indeed a very charming man. All the more charming that it is only just a month has passed that he has returned from a visit to the Soviet Union, where he familiarized himself with our factories, with our industry. The plant we saw was making computers. I'm no specialist in the matter, and any assessment that I would give of that plant would be insignificant; but I suppose we also produce machines like that. I don't know who makes the better machines; that, of course, is a question. I saw the machines, but of course I don't understand the actual substance or the matter. Perhaps ours are better; I don't know.

For the time being, we're keeping them a secret, but certainly—both sides are actually keeping them a secret for the time being. They can show me, a man who doesn't understand anything about them, any such machines. It will be to no avail; I won't understand what they are anyway.

But I am sure that the time will very soon come when there will be no such secrets and people will be able to see all such machines and benefit by them.

This brings back to mind the story of when we were about to launch our first rocket. The scientists invited us members of the government to see the rocket. Well, we went and looked at it. We looked at it from this side, from that side, we looked down upon it, we looked up at it. It must have been—we thought it was all very interesting indeed. But what the thing was, none of us knew. In this case, we could look at anything at all and it wouldn't help anyone, because nobody would understand.

I am profoundly grateful to the engineers, the employees, and the workers of that plant for their best hospitality and for the warmth of the welcome accorded to me. I am especially grateful to the cooks for the wonderful meal they prepared for us. It was with great pleasure that I tried a sample of their culinary art. Now, this is a question that all of us are specialists in, and we all know what is good in the matter of food.

I profoundly regret that I was not able today to visit the Scientific Research Institute at Stanford, where the president is the very esteemed scientist Finley Carter. Our scientist Professor Yemelyanov visited the institute today. Well, I would certainly have liked to have been there personally. Unfortunately, I was not able to do so, because one, after all, cannot embrace the all-embraceable, as was said—this was a saying attributed to a man called Kuz.[1] You don't know him, but we certainly do. Although, even the fact of his physical existence is sometimes questioned. But I don't know, he may have existed, he may not, but his sayings are certainly very good.

I would like to say that I have enjoyed your beautiful city of San Francisco. After the end of World War II the Russian soldiers came back from the front and brought back with them a popular song about Bulgaria. Now, the Russians, the Russian people, hold especially dear the people of Bulgaria. For one thing, they have the same religion, the orthodox religion. The language is very similar. And then in the olden days, when the Bulgarians were under the yoke of the Turks, the Russian people deeply sympathized with them. And when the time came, the Russian soldiers

1. While the name Khrushchev mentions was transcribed as "Kuz," he was referring to Kozma Prutkov, who, as Khrushchev notes, did not really exist as a person. "Kozma Prutkov" was a pseudonym under which Russian satirist Aleksei Tolstoy, in collaboration with two cousins, published comic verse and folk proverbs in the nineteenth century.

shed their blood to assist the liberation of the Bulgarians from the Turkish yoke. (By the way, Mr. Mayor, we also helped to liberate the Greeks.) Well, this song I was telling you about has the words—contains the words that Bulgaria is certainly a very fine country, but Russia is best of all. I want to rephrase the words of that song and I want to say that all the cities that I visited in the United States are good, but San Francisco is best of all!

I want to extend my most sincere gratitude to all today's speakers. I want to say that all their speeches were gratifying to me. I don't know who the conductor was who organized such a very cordial, a very warm meeting, such a fine dinner and such pleasant speeches, but I want to extend my heartfelt gratitude. The people of San Francisco positively charmed us. I felt as if I were among true friends who were thinking the same thoughts that our people in the Soviet Union are thinking, and in confirmation of this I can tell you that today, for instance, we stopped our car at random, just in one of the streets, and I asked an ordinary housewife that I met on the street, I asked her what she wanted most of all in life, and her reply was "peace," and that there should be no war. Those are the sentiments, the same sentiments, that agitate the minds of all men, women, and children in the Soviet Union, too, the word they hold dear, the word "peace," which is in their hearts and which is on the tip of their tongues.

The main thing is not to touch upon questions that divide us. We're all, I believe, sick and tired of discussing—of fruitless discussion on such issues, but the main thing is to speak of those points that unite us, that bring us together, to seek out those points where we can find agreement without touching upon the cardinal issues between us. After all, it is, of course, inconceivable that you could persuade me that the capitalist system was better, just as it is inconceivable that I could convince you that the communist system was better. We will evidently all remain with our own convictions, but that should in no way hinder us from going ahead, from living together in peace and caring for the welfare of our respective people. I want to assure you, ladies and gentlemen, that I am not trying to entice you over into the Communist kingdom when I say this, but you will perhaps one day remember my words, and I want to say that when you get to know better us Communists, when you better get to know the thoughts and aspirations that guide us—this will not happen today, I realize—but you will see how noble are these aspirations of Communists when we seek to build a Communist society.

This is not a thing of today. It is a thing of tomorrow, but we conceive this aspiration of ours as most sacred, as something that is most sacred for us. We want to build a society under which every man will be a brother of his neighbor, where there will be no enmity, there will be complete equality; as, by the way, was preached by Christ. And if you do look into our philosophy you will see that we have taken a lot of Christ's precepts regarding, for instance, love for one's neighbor and others. Such is our aim. You should not judge by the civil war in our country, because the civil war was, after all, something that was imposed upon us contrary to our will. After all, you too had a civil war in your country, a civil war which was very cruel, a war in which you killed your fellow men, but you fought that war because you were fighting for a noble goal. You were fighting for liberty. You were fighting for the ideals inscribed on Lincoln's banners, and you won that war. You may not agree with us, but we are guided by noble aspirations in our struggle for communism, and we are going to wage this struggle not by force of arms but by our words. He who does not want to take up this teaching will evidently remain with his own opinions, and we will always respect these opinions.

Mr. Mayor Christopher, I am your guest in this city. I am very gratified by our meeting and by your speech today, but I am a little bit afraid of lavishing too much praise upon you because you are in the midst of an election campaign. I don't want anyone to think that I'm trying to interfere in your elections, especially because if your opponent is present here today, he may think, why am I so one-sided as to lavish praise upon you and not upon him. So I'll try and be neutral. We were talking with Mayor Christopher and I told him at the start of this dinner that I had not as yet made up my mind who I would vote for if I had the right to vote in this city, and I told him that I would think the matter over and perhaps by the end of the dinner I would tell him what opinion I had come to, depending on the quality of the dinner to some extent; but I must say at the close that in this respect, also, you have won my heart in your favor. The meal that was so excellently served here today was certainly a very excellent one. So I do believe that I would vote for you, but I'm reserving my final say. I still want to think it over.

I want also, from this lofty dais, to greet the manager of the store, the supermarket that we visited today; I am truly filled with admiration over what I saw. It was, I believe, excellently organized. It was a wonderful visit.

Well, you are, of course, rich Americans. We're not trying to encroach upon that. We're just a little bit envious. But I want to assure you that we will not remain in debt; we will do our best and we will certainly produce as much as you are producing now, and this will bring about no harm for you. This can only lead to—this can only further the benefit of both our countries. It can but further the cause of peace.

And I consider it also my duty here in San Francisco to say a few words about your neighbor city, the city of Los Angeles. I trust you will manifest patience and hear me out. I want to say some good things about the people of Los Angeles. Now, you—if I were to use a somewhat poetic word, you have virtually charmed us here. You really are charmers, magicians, you have managed to charm me, a representative of a socialist state. You have charmed my heart, but in my head I still think that our system is a good system. You evidently think that your system is a good one. Well, God be with you! Live under it. I am very pleased with my meetings with the population of Los Angeles, but something—something unforeseen happened there. Well, such things do happen. I was told that when we were driving along the streets of the city, the chief of local police was in the car driving ahead of us, and someone, whether from too many or too few brains I don't know, threw a tomato. It may have been a very good tomato, but the fact is that it hit this car in which the chief of police was driving, so he decided to show his power and deprived us of the pleasure of visiting the city of fantasy, Disneyland, which we were scheduled to visit. I am grateful to the chief of police for his care for my welfare, but I don't think—nothing but good would have come out of our visit all the same.

There are superstitious people in the world. Even that very famous poet, Pushkin, was a superstitious man who once drove out of his house when a black cat crossed his path, which in Russia is a sign of bad luck, and so he turned around and went back home. But that was a long, long time ago. I don't believe we should be superstitious in these modern times when we let a black cat cross our path and frighten us and prevent us from carrying out the schedule. And I do want to say a few words in favor of the mayor of Los Angeles. It was—the incident was perhaps a little bit unpleasant. The mayor, all the more so—we met his family, he has really a very charming wife. I might say that you, Mr. Mayor, also have a very charming wife; she is very beautiful indeed. But the mayor of Los Angeles, he introduced us to—he was very cordial before the dinner. He introduced us to his family, to his wonderful daughters, but at the dinner, well, something happened. When things like that do happen—perhaps he just got out on the wrong side of the bed and that's why he delivered that unlucky speech, unfortunate speech of his. But you here present, you are used to speech-making and just recall how often it happens that you are not pleased with the speeches you make. At least I know that sometimes I make a speech and I am later discontent with the speech that I made. So I believe the same thing happened with the mayor of Los Angeles, but let us after all be condescending. Even the Christian teaching tells us to forgive the trespasses of others if they understand that they have trespassed. We must follow this Christian precept and consider that he spoke not from his heart nor from his mind, but it was just an unhappy incident, and let us consider the question to have been closed.

Let us consider that we are in peace with all the people of America, with the people of Los Angeles, and with the people of San Francisco too. (I'm laying more emphasis, as you see, on San Francisco than I am on Los Angeles.) When we were talking before the dinner, I invited the mayor to visit the Soviet Union, to visit Moscow, and I wish to say from this lofty platform that the invitation still stands. If and when he does come, we will not drop the slightest hint of the difference that we had during that dinner, all the more so—it has been intimated to me that he, too, regrets the unfortunate incident. After all, things happen, and a man can sometimes drop an inadvertent phrase. I would gladly extend the same sort of invitation to Mayor Christopher to come to Moscow, but truly I'm a little afraid of doing this, because I don't know whether this would serve him well or go against him in the election. This really is a very difficult question for me to solve, so I would like to address all of you present here and all the citizens of this wonderful, this flourishing and sunny city of San Francisco: welcome to the Soviet Union, come and see us in Moscow. We will be happy to welcome you there. We in Russia have a saying that he who has not seen Russia has not seen the light of day. Come and look at this light.

Permit me to express the hope that our stay in the United States, our meetings with representatives of the business world and the American public will be of undeniable benefit, and will help bring our countries closer together and consequently will help us sooner to reach mutually acceptable decisions. Thank you, ladies and gentlemen, for your kind attention.

[Mayor Christopher then presented Khrushchev with a redwood gavel. Khrushchev took the microphone again.]

We don't use this symbol in our practice *[waving the gavel]*, so I would like to ask Mr. Christopher what do I have to knock this against? Supposed to do that with some use. But I would like to put this gavel to good use in the Soviet Union and to strike it after the signature of a treaty of friendship, nonaggression, and eternal love between the peoples of the Soviet Union and of the United States of America. I would like for the first time to use this gavel, also, after the signature of a treaty between our countries and between all the countries of the world on disarmament, for this is the main weight that is bearing down upon the people and preventing them from living in peace. If I'm able to do so, I shall be truly happy. And I lay great hopes in the fact that during our meetings with your president, Dwight Eisenhower, our hearts should prompt us to reach agreement and to open the way towards solving this question and thus establishing conditions of peace and friendship between our nations. Thank you, Mr. Mayor. Thank you, dear friends.

October 20, 1960

Dwight D. Eisenhower

President of the United States of America

For several years before Nikita Khrushchev visited the U.S., the Americans had been flying U-2 spy planes over the Soviet Union. Khrushchev didn't bring up the spy planes with Eisenhower, and in the Spirit of Camp David which followed his visit, the U.S. halted U-2 flights over the USSR—until spring 1960. As a prelude to the Paris summit, which Eisenhower hoped would lead to a nuclear test ban, the president's advisors convinced him to approve two more flights—since the outcome of the summit would likely prohibit such means of gathering of intelligence. The first flew in April, and several days later General Curtis LeMay, vice chief of staff for the U.S. Air Force and former head of the Strategic Air Command, gave a talk at The Commonwealth Club. Though he did not mention the U-2 flights, he did say, "Just and honest plans for peace can only be made from a position of strength. Our government cannot enter into negotiations in a second-best position."

The second U-2 flight in 1960 flew on May Day. That Sunday morning, as Moscow was preparing for the annual parade past Lenin's Tomb, a spy plane piloted by Francis Gary Powers took off from Peshawar, Pakistan. On its course across the heart of the USSR, the plane was shot out of the sky near the city of Sverdlovsk. The new spirit of Soviet-American friendship crashed along with the pieces of black aircraft tumbling to earth. Eisenhower had called Khrushchev "friend" and taught him the word in English; now Khrushchev was humiliated. He went to Paris but refused to allow the summit proper to begin until Eisenhower apologized. The apology never came, and Eisenhower's invitation to visit the Soviet Union was withdrawn. Khrushchev, however, came back to New York in the autumn for the meeting of the United Nations General Assembly. He banged his shoe and his name was once more on everyone's lips; in the first-ever televised presidential debate, John F. Kennedy and Richard Nixon together invoked his name seven times.

A few weeks later, on the eve of the election, President Eisenhower strode to The Commonwealth Club podium to deliver a talk on disarmament. He emphasized that agreeing to a system of verification would be necessary before any test ban or disarmament treaty could be signed. Since the mid-1950s, Eisenhower had promoted an idea he called Open Skies, which the Soviets rejected. The Soviets feared that would just legitimize American overflights, and they had no aircraft or bases surrounding the United States that would allow them to reciprocate. In 1962, Khrushchev would set out to change that geographical disadvantage and install Soviet missiles and bombers in Cuba—an action that ultimately brought the world as close as it's ever been to nuclear Armageddon. Not until 1963 would the U.S. and USSR sign a partial test ban—though by then it was Kennedy's administration, not Eisenhower's, that could claim the achievement.

From a distance of forty years or more, this speech doesn't carry the partisan political charge that it did at the time. But in the heat of the 1960 Nixon/Kennedy contest, it was taken as an oblique attack on Democratic candidate Kennedy—oblique only in that it failed to mention him by name. Kennedy had lambasted the Eisenhower Administration for allowing the development of a "missile gap," with the Soviets in the lead. (Kennedy's secretary of defense, Robert S. McNamara, would later acknowledge that there was no gap. Rather, U.S. nuclear forces far outnumbered the Soviet arsenal.) The Democratic National Committee successfully argued that this speech, which was broadcast over radio, was a plug for Nixon and that the Democrats should be awarded equal air time. Kennedy, however, never used it.

"Presidential Reflections"

I'm glad to be here this evening to sustain your perfect score as having as a speaker every president of the United States since this club was founded at the beginning of the century. I sincerely hope that my appearance gives you no reason to abandon the practice.

Moved by a wisdom developed out of experience, the organizers of this club devised for their new creation a noble and necessary purpose: better government in their state. Its energizing spark was the belief that—and I take these words from the documents of the time—"California suffers greatly because the best elements of the population fail to cooperate for the common good as effectively as the bad elements cooperate for evil purposes." The dedication of that group and the unremitting efforts of its membership to pursue the course of sound government have remained undimmed for the almost six decades of The Club's existence.

The word "commonwealth" signifies a group united by common interests. But equally significant is the fact that in the political realm a commonwealth, as Mr. Webster defines it, has come to mean generally, if not always, an association based upon free choice. Tonight, I shall try to apply to some aspects of the world of international affairs the founding principle of this organization, that this state suffered because of the failure of some elements to cooperate as effectively for good as others did for evil.

No group, no matter how well intentioned, can cooperate fruitfully unless there is first established a firm basis of common understanding. This the founders of your club recognized by noting that one of the great difficulties was that different groups in California did not know each other. They were separated at that time by wide areas, and they also distrusted each other. Just as the California of 1903, the year your club was founded, was a far cry from the commonwealth of California today, so the world, as we turned into the twentieth century, is scarcely recognizable as the one we know in 1960.

The multiplication of differences and problems before the international community recalled an old alumnus who returned to visit his college after a half-century absence. Delighted to find one of his old physical science professors still teaching, he was amazed to find him still using the same old questions on examinations that he employed fifty years ago. "Why is this?" the alumnus wanted to know. "Very simple," answered his former teacher. "The questions are the same, but the answers always become different." So today, instead of fifty-three members in the family of nations, we have one hundred and six. Instead of one and a half billion people in the world, we have two and a half billion. Instead of weaponry whose maximum range was a few thousand yards, we have nuclear-tipped missiles that can hurtle nine thousand miles to bring wholesale death and destruction.

Parenthetically, in this particular field our marvelous progress is not measured in decades. Our scientists and government have brought us in a few years from a position of former neglect and indifference to a level of extraordinary efficiency and strength. Here is an example of the absurdity of the allegation that America and its economy and its progress are stagnant. I point out that now we spend on long-range ballistic missiles $10 million a day, every day—more than the entire aggregate of all the expenditures for this purpose in all the years from 1945 to 1952. This example could be repeated in a dozen fields.

In 1903, man was still earthbound except for the exploits of a few adventurous balloonists and the Wright brothers, who made their historic flight in December of that year. Today man-made objects whirl around the sun independent of the earth's movement. And the same ones will continue to do so for a future measured in millennia. Nineteen hundred and three was the year of the first automobile crossing from San Francisco to New York. It took sixty-four days, just seven less than it took Columbus to sail from Spain to America. Now it is not uncommon for air travelers to cross the country twice in a single day.

In the early years of this century, the only impression most voters ever received of a presidential candidate came to them from a printed page. Now an electronic miracle brings his voice and his face into forty million living rooms across the land. On all fronts, there have been wrought on the earth great changes that are in themselves important, some almost miraculous. Similar changes are now extending into the celestial regions as well.

Now, in contemplating these great changes and the problems that have followed in their wake, it is essential that we recognize two important truths. First, almost no problem arising between nations today is strictly bilateral. Whether we consider the difficulties arising out of the relationships between Israel and the Arab states or the necessity for our recent embargo on most exports to Cuba, inevitably other nations are affected. We cannot conceive today of an international community operating as a system of bilateral partnerships traveling in unordered and reckless orbit.

Every arrangement we effect with another nation, whether political, commercial, or even cultural, seems inevitably to have an impact on other societies. Some degree of world coordination and cooperation obviously becomes necessary. The recognized need for a cooperative international community was responsible for the founding, here in this city, of the United Nations in 1945. It has been in some areas remarkably successful. Yet, as in the early days of California, we have found that the mere existence of an appropriate organizational mechanism cannot maintain the law, order, and progress so much desired. In the United Nations, we have a charter and agreements supposed to ensure order and avoidance of conflict. But these can be successful only as the understanding and dedication of the members become equal to the task.

A second important truth is that the dimensions of the tasks that lie before us in helping to straighten out this poor old world are so vast and complex as to make its accomplishment beyond the capacity of leaders, governments, and peoples, except those of experience, inexhaustible strength, patience, understanding, and faith. The supreme need of this century is to find a way to produce an effective international order. And the most obvious way to do this is through improvement of the United Nations. Certainly the way is not through domineering empires, the rise and fall of which the world has witnessed for the past five thousand years, but through a free and mutually beneficial association of nations. To realize such an international order, of course, great leadership is required. It must be a leadership that can see nations as partners and equals. It must be leadership that accepts responsibility of power, but one that exercises it in a spirit of trusteeship, through just and patient processes of mutual adjustment. It must always base policies upon a clear identification of long-range common interests. Now upon America has fallen the heavy responsibility of providing this kind of leadership. Unmistakably, we are called upon at this precise moment and in the course of human events to renew and revitalize our efforts to ensure the health and strength of a mighty international commonwealth. Our own conception of an ordered international community conforms roughly to our own political system. The American system presupposes full information and active participation by every citizen in the processes of both local and federal government. The more nearly universal this informed participation, the healthier and stronger is our government, our nation's policy, and our entire social structure.

In our complex industrial society, no thoughtful person would contend that every citizen can become truly informed on so many and such perplexing problems of domestic policy as those involving defense, social services, taxation, employment, public debt, budget, and inflation. Yet on each of these subjects there is firsthand information and personal experience available in almost every section of our nation, and as a consequence, the average of general understanding is reasonably high, but achievement of a satisfactory level of understanding is far more difficult in the field of foreign affairs.

Consider, for example, Korea, Indochina, the Suez Canal, Quemoy and Matsu, the Middle East, the turmoil in the Caribbean, the Berlin difficulty, the economic development of India, or the fifteen newly developing nations in Africa.[1] To extend the range and fullness of understanding on foreign affairs, heroic efforts are made here at home by news-gathering and news-distributing agencies, and by great numbers of private foundations, as well as by study, research, and educational institutions. But because no substantial segment of our population has had firsthand experience in international affairs, these particular problems are far more likely to excite our emotions and prejudices rather than to inspire a painstaking search for all the facts pertaining to a problem and their relation to each other.

Yet every citizen is becoming more and more vitally affected by the issues of foreign policy, and his need for knowledge grows correspondingly greater. We cannot anticipate any hasty or simple solutions to such a large and complicated problem. But no matter is more urgent than the establishment of an effective working relationship between the American people and their government for the conduct of foreign affairs and assuring the nation's security. This problem completely overshadows, at this period of

1. Quemoy and Matsu are islands located between Taiwan (then known as Formosa) and mainland China. Chiang Kai-shek's Nationalist troops fortified the islands in the early 1950s and later used Quemoy to launch raids on the mainland. The People's Republic of China (PRC) began shelling the islands in 1954; the U.S. signed a mutual defense pact with Taiwan and considered using atomic weapons in the islands' defense. The crisis passed the following year when it was clear the USSR would not back China in a larger war over the islands. The PRC resumed shelling the islands in August 1958 and threatened invasion of Formosa. The U.S. deployed the Seventh Fleet in the area, Eisenhower warned the U.S. would not retreat "in the face of armed aggression," and the U.S. began drawing up plans for nuclear strikes on mainland China. But the shelling stopped that fall. During the 1960 presidential debates, Vice President Richard Nixon attacked Senator John F. Kennedy for not being willing to defend the islands.

our history, any other we face. As we push ahead to strengthen the partnership of the citizen with his government, there are, as I see it, some pitfalls to be avoided. First, we must not be afraid to look at ourselves honestly. We must steadily maintain critical self-examination. Our nation must always concern itself with any failure to realize our national and legitimate aspirations. But while maintaining a healthy critical insight, let us not be misled by those who, inexplicably, seem so fond of deprecating the standing, condition, and performance of the entire nation.

Surely we must avoid smugness and complacency, but when in the face of a bright record of progress and development we hear some misguided people wail that the United States is stumbling into a status of a second-class power and that our prestige has sunk to an all-time low, we are simply listening to debasement of the truth. Now, related to this irresponsible practice of defacing the true American portrait is the development of an almost compulsive desire to make counterfeit comparisons, especially between our nation and others. Because of different backgrounds and cultures, such comparisons rarely contain any validity whatsoever. The economic and social statistics of a nation cannot be conveniently compared like Olympic track records. Consider a country, the Soviets, for example, rich in natural resources and abundantly stocked with manpower, which through a violent upheaval suddenly emerges from a feudal, agrarian society into a nation with an expanding and centrally controlled industrialism. What about its growth, its rate of economic growth? Obviously, the tempo of its economic growth can, for a time, leap ahead at a rate faster than a nation which has long since become highly industrialized. If a village has a single telephone, which in many cases in the world it does (or even less), the acquisition of another in a single year is a 100-percent increase in growth. In a mature society such increases are necessarily measured in fractions of the whole. Now, in a broader sense, any attempt at comparison between national patterns of economic organization leads to unfortunate and widespread misunderstandings.

The issue today in the supreme effort to build a thriving international community that can live in peace with justice is not merely capitalism versus socialism. We believe that our free and socially responsible enterprise has demonstrated definite advantages over an economy based upon a socialistic pattern of organization. But we do recognize that those nations whose particular problems lead them to adopt a socialist economy should not be condemned for doing so. What we do contend is that the issue today is not capitalism versus socialism, but rather democracy versus dictatorship, the open society against the closed and secret society. Recognition of this fact compels us to warn newly developing nations of the perils of authoritarianism lest they gravitate toward communist control because of the seductive promises of immediate benefits.

So we see the vital importance of having a free world understand the true basis of the world struggle. To return to our own country, the problems before us in the conduct of foreign affairs involve an endless flow of concrete decisions upon specific issues. The difficulties involved are infinite. They arise hour by hour in some instances, day by day or week to week in others. Each problem, of course, will have to be met by those charged with the particular sphere of responsibility. But though this work is one of the duties of government, the citizenry cannot abandon its inherent function of critical self-examination of performance. All of us must see that the policy decisions of our government officials are responsive to the needs, objectives, values, and historic tendency of the American people. One vital purpose is to see that while meeting the requirements of foreign affairs, we simultaneously sustain our domestic institutions and traditional liberties.

For example, to support progress in our country and, indeed, throughout the free world, we must make certain that there is no cheapening, no debasement of our currency. Tasks like this impose a heavy but necessary strain upon our citizenry. It calls for experienced and mature leadership. This is not a task for a leadership that insists upon agitating small points to the neglect of the nation's true good. This is not a task for a leadership that sees the nation as a giant supermarket for the distribution of special favor. This is not a task for any leadership that scorns fiscal integrity and sees no national disadvantage in deficit spending. Nor is it a task for leadership that, falsely trumpeting an incompetence within the body politic, assigns to a centralized government the responsibility for all progress. It is a task for leadership which understands that our job today is to intensify the beliefs that made America great, leadership which recognizes that sound policy arises out of the inner wisdom and experience of countless communities and people throughout America, fully capable, as always before, of responding to a summons to greatness.

To return now to the theme of your organization, which I have borrowed tonight, the importance of cooperating effectively for good: I repeat that the central need in all international affairs today is to forge a commonwealth of nations, a United Nations that will steadily strengthen the bonds and build the structure of a true world community that can live in peace with justice. Before us still is the opportunity to take, by firm, steady steps, practicable action toward the disarmament. The position of the United States remains, as I have often stated, that our appropriate representatives are willing to meet immediately with those of other countries to consider any feasible and enforceable proposal that will lead mankind to outlaw, for all time, the terrifying tools of war.

We have repeatedly made fair and specific proposals to this end. As yet, the Soviets have refused to negotiate seriously on them. In declaring ourselves ever ready to negotiate the problems of disarmament, we ask only that any program advance shall not give military advantage to any particular country and that it assures the right to inspect the armaments of other nations. A disarmament program failing to offer such assurance is a devious device that could only result in raising rather than decreasing the probability of war. Many other serious international disagreements await resolution. We must never retreat from these purposes, even in the face of discouragement by the wrecking-crew antics of those who want to demolish the United Nations.

We know that peace with justice is not just a matter of bringing about the absence of war. Peace is rather a world living its human ideals and aspirations. Moreover, there is one kind of righteous war, one we must all wage. It is against poverty, illiteracy, and disease. This we shall do, this we propose to do, as we take up our individual tasks without subordinating the national character of our individual societies, because progress will not be found in a superstate run by superpowers. We believe that cooperation and freedom is the way to build the necessary structure for permanent peace.

As I reflect upon the course of American history, I have full confidence that the political genius and wisdom of the American people are equal to their vital responsibility that the world has now conferred upon them. The search for solutions will be a long one, but fortified by a conviction borne with spirit and with a national strength unmatched by any other. I know the American people will lead the way on the greatest mission upon which we have ever embarked: the establishment of a durable peace with justice.

December 13, 1961

Edward Teller

Physicist, the Manhattan Project; Founder of Lawrence Livermore National Laboratory

---

Edward Teller became known as "Father of the H-bomb"—a moniker he despised—when his ten-megaton brainchild was detonated over the Enewetak Atoll in 1952. That same year, he founded the nation's second nuclear weapons laboratory, the Lawrence Livermore National Laboratory. To those who mocked and feared him, with his Hungarian accent and beetle brows, Teller was the real-life Dr. Strangelove. To those who admired him, he was a brilliant scientist—and a Jew who had fled Hitler's Germany—who both helped develop the atomic weapons that helped end World War II and sought to create a hydrogen bomb that was part of an American arsenal to ensure peace through strength. Part of that strength, for Teller, was proactive civil defense, something Congress had put its weight behind in 1950 through creation of the Civil Defense Administration, which oversaw construction of public fallout shelters, stockpiling of food, establishment of the Emergency Broadcast System, and an animated production of Bert the Turtle, who sang a tune reminding kids that, when they saw the flash, it was time to "duck and cover."

Teller's speech to The Commonwealth Club in 1961, asking his audience to be pragmatic about civil defense, closed out the year in which the Soviets had given the go-ahead for construction of the Berlin Wall, American and Soviet tanks had faced off in East Berlin, and the skies over the Pacific and in the Soviet plains of Central Asia were illuminated by nuclear fireballs from test after test. In fact, the year was closing with an almost audible sigh, because that June it had looked like the Cold War might turn hot. Khrushchev had issued Kennedy an ultimatum on Berlin: sign a peace treaty recognizing the divided Germany, or else in December the Soviets would sign one unilaterally. "If that's true," Kennedy had said, "it's going to be a cold winter." Kennedy didn't take the ultimatum public; in private he referred to Khrushchev as a bastard and a son of a bitch. The American press reported frank discussions. But Khrushchev took the ultimatum public, then announced that he was scrapping plans to reduce the Red Army by over a million men. Kennedy went on television and announced he was asking Congress for funds to "identify and mark space" for fallout shelters and for food, water, first aid kits, and other minimum essentials for survival. "The lives of those families which are not hit in a nuclear blast and fire," he said, "can still be saved—if they can be warned to take shelter, and if that shelter is available." Which was precisely Teller's point in discussing civil defense. His talk also came several weeks after one by Gerard Piel, editor of *Scientific American*, who had declared civil defense a hoax and an illusion.

Edward Teller continued advising presidents through the 1970s and was instrumental in assisting the Reagan Administration with developing its Strategic Defense Initiative (AKA Star Wars) program. He died in 2003 at his home in California.

"Peace through Civil Defense"

It is probable that recently the Soviet Union has passed the United States in military strength and, in particular, in the power and effectiveness of their nuclear weapons. This means that we are faced with a most serious situation.

About a month ago, Gerard Piel has made an important contribution in this place to civil defense, which, in turn, is a very significant phase of our preparedness. He said a few things that needed to be said. He said that civil defense is not, and cannot, be simply the building of fallout shelters; that there are other dangers, dangers from blast and from fire, which are as great, or greater, than the danger from fallout. He is right; I am glad that he made this statement. He also said that the two alternatives, "Red or dead," cannot be and must not be the only ones, and that we should look for other alternatives. He certainly is correct.

Now, my purpose in my main day-to-day work, and my purpose in talking to you, is to make a little contribution toward finding and developing an other and a reasonable alternative. My main purpose is to find a way in which we can have peace and in which we can preserve our freedom.

This will not be easy, and I do not know the answer, but I have strong feelings about the direction in which we have to look for an answer. I also have the strong conviction, the complete conviction, that any simple answer is not the right one. I disagree with Mr. Piel, when he put the problem to you in an exaggerated and simplified form. He said that real civil defense will mean that the nation will have to go underground and the down payment on the cost of taking the nation underground would be $150 billion. But that is only the fiscal cost. The social cost of going underground would not fall short of the total transformation of our way of life, the suspension of our civil institutions, the habituation of our people to violence, and ultimate militarization of our society.

The figure $150 billion is grossly and improperly exaggerated. The following statements are even more wrong. Mr. Piel considers civil defense as a form of violence. He says that it is a step in this ever growing danger, the escalation of military force; and he says the civil defense program of our federal government, however as intended, must be regarded as a step in the escalation process. This is a sinister development, because it works as psychological subversion of both government and citizenry.

Gentlemen, these are strong words to use. If civil defense is violence, what is active defense? What is our whole military establishment, together with the development of missiles and of nuclear explosives? Knowing that Mr. Piel is a reasonable and logical person, I know he must be opposed to all of these.

I will try to put to you the dilemma in a fair and simple way. That we are in danger, that we have to try and preserve peace: on that we are all agreed. There is a disagreement as to the question from what quarter our main danger arises. There are those, and Mr. Piel is one of them, who believe that the main danger comes from the military men throughout the world, in Russia as well as in the United States, and the peace-loving people on both sides of the Iron Curtain can develop this dreadful trend which may carry us toward all-out war.

There are others who believe differently, and I am one of them. I believe that we are peace-loving, that with the exception of a small and insignificant minority, a completely insignificant minority, we are all peace-loving. And this includes our military men, many of whom I know, and many of whom I respect very highly.

I also believe, with Mr. Piel, that there are a great majority of peace-loving people behind the Iron Curtain. But I believe, in fact I think I know, that these peace-loving people behind the Iron Curtain have no voice, and the minority in Russia is determined to conquer the world. This is not the same as loving peace, and there are some leaders who love peace only to the extent that they would rather conquer us without bloodshed and without risk. In fact, I believe that they are cautious; I do not believe that they are adventurous; and I do not believe that they will attack us, as long as we are strong.

I believe, for this reason, that we must be both strong and patient; that we must never strike first, but we must be able to retaliate in case we are attacked; and furthermore, we must be able to survive an attack, so that it should become clear to the Russian leaders that by attacking us they cannot win. If we accomplish this, we shall be safe. But it will take a lot to accomplish this.

I do not believe that civil defense is a panacea. I do not believe that civil defense will come easy. It will be hard to have a good civil defense; but it is necessary, and it is possible. The past expenditures on civil defense, amounting to less than one-tenth of a cent out of every tax dollar, has indeed been insignificant. At present, this amount has been stepped up to three-tenths of a cent of each tax dollar. This is a good beginning, but it is still not sufficient. I believe that what we need is, perhaps, 10 percent of our military budget: $4 billion a year, spent reasonably over a series of years.

I believe that the Russians today are not strong enough to attack us. I believe that if we start to work on civil defense today, then they never will be in the position of attacking us; but if we neglect civil defense, we are exposing ourselves to a deadly danger.

Mr. Piel has told you that there are grave dangers in the neighborhood of a nuclear bomb, about which he said that there is no defense against them. These dangers are blast and fire. That these dangers are great is certainly true. That there is no defense against them is incorrect. The defense is expensive, but not very expensive. If you do your best with appropriately constructed mass shelters, you can buy reasonable defense for approximately two hundred dollars per person. This can be done by excavation underground, by building into this little tunnel that you have made underground a Quonset hut-like structure; this has been worked out by the Naval Radiological Defense people here in San Francisco. It is believed, and I think correctly, that such a shelter will stand up under a mighty megaton explosion if that explosion is farther away than approximately one mile.

There will not be much warning. A missile takes only twenty minutes to get here, if it starts from Russia. It is highly desirable, it is necessary, that to everyone a mass shelter should be available in a walking distance of five minutes. In heavily built-up areas, this is possible.

Nor is this Quonset hut structure the only possibility. In places where you have limestone or other soft-rock formations, one can dig straight into the rock and have an even more adequate shelter, for approximately the same amount per person which I have mentioned, or, at any rate, not much more. In many places, in places distant from the actual target area, less complete shelter will be adequate.

The fire hazard may very well be the greatest of our hazards. The danger of fallout has somehow been exaggerated out of all proportion, and the statement which has been often repeated, that there will be a danger to future generations, is in itself grossly distorted. I have estimated that a really terrible attack, the kind of attack that we are fearing in our worst dreams, will have, among other things, the effect of increasing the normal mutation rate for one generation by a factor of two. There will be twice as many stillbirths and twice as many changes than under normal conditions. Mutations have also contributed to the development of the living world, and if a natural process is speeded up by a factor of two for one generation, it's not something you would want to do, but it's certainly not a catastrophe compared to this horrible possibility of an all-out war. Let's *please*, see things in proportion.

The fire danger, however, is a very real one. The Russian mighty megaton bombs, fifty megatons, one hundred megatons, could, in fact, be exploded in such a way to produce a great amount of fire. How much fire will depend, to a great extent, on the question, how much combustible material is around. Fires can be fought. Against fires there *is* a defense, in well-constructed underground shelters, in the shelters of the kind which I have described to you, if to the shelters there is added the relatively small cost of putting in chemicals to absorb the carbon dioxide, and putting in bottled oxygen, which for mass shelters is not very expensive, to supply the people in the shelter with air for the probable duration, the probable maximum duration of the fire, which may be as long as twenty-four hours. This is a minor additional cost, and will make the defense complete not only against nuclear attack but against chemical and biological attack as well.

The civil defense program is a program of enormous complexity, which so far we have not taken seriously enough. If you use your imagination not only to outline the dangers to which you may be subject, but also, in a positive way, to find every reasonable avenue to combat these dangers, I believe that solutions can be found, and I believe that we can even discern the beginnings of a solution.

When we come out of the shelters, then what? How much of the nation's wealth, how much of the nation's livelihood will have been destroyed? Mr. Piel says maybe half or two-thirds. I will admit this is quite possible. I will say that in many essential areas *all* our wealth may be destroyed. Some of you may know that all our wealth amounts to the national income of only three years. If we keep a sensible organization under attack, and if we store some goods against this dreadful rainy day, so that we won't starve, and so that we won't have to start the rebuilding process with our ten bare fingers, we can, after a number of austere, but not necessarily terrible years, rebuild our country to its old strength, and to a better strength.

How to do this won't be easy; it will be even more difficult than planning the shelters. But we have an important asset, which can give us a good start. We have food surpluses which can last for two years. These food surpluses will be destroyed, or may be destroyed, if they are left in an insecure place. If they are put into safe places, which will not be very expensive, and if they are distributed throughout the country, near processing facilities or in a semi-processed spot, we can be sure that we at least will eat while we rebuild the country. And if we have built the shelters, the great majority of our population can be saved, even under the most savage and sudden attack.

We are a rich country. We throw away our machines when we can think of something better. Some of these machines should be mothballed, so that we should have something to start from, in case we are attacked. Civil defense and recovery and planning for recovery is possible in a rich country with surpluses like the United States. This same thing is infinitely more difficult in a country like Russia, which is vigorously and valiantly struggling to establish its first-generation industry. They have no surpluses. They run their machines until the machines fall apart. The Russians can be made quite certain that in case of an all-out war, we shall survive, our country will survive, and we can recover faster than they can recover. Under these conditions we can be sure that they will not attack first.

Now, this is not enough. This is only the negative part of a program. How to make ourselves safe for the next few years? We have bought time. The value of this time depends on what we do with it. The right plan for a peaceful world will not help us if we have no strength to defend ourselves. Our military strength will, on the other hand, be of no avail if we do not know how to construct a peaceful, stable world on this globe which, decade by decade, becomes smaller, more closely interrelated, and therefore, in an anarchic world, more dangerous.

We have made, recently, a very important step toward the construction of a more stable world. We have announced publicly that we shall never strike first. We must say this; we must know it; we must act accordingly. We must behave in such a way that an all-out war will *never* be, and need never be, started by the United States. If we are strong, an all-out war will *not* be started by the other side either.

This does not mean that we shall take every Russian aggression without resistance. We must develop a force, and we can, which will resist Russian aggression in every place, at any time, on the same scale on which this aggression is committed. To do that, we need the most flexible weapons. We need nuclear weapons, among other things, to be used in limited war, but at the same time we must *never* spread such a war beyond the territory in which the Russian aggression has been committed.

If we can act according to these principles, we will have made another important step toward lasting peace. But even that is not enough. The real question is how to construct a lawful, peaceful family of nations. We can be quite sure that the Russians, who are bent on world conquest, will not sit down with us at the negotiating table and will not give up their plan to conquer the world merely because we ask them to do so. We must first develop the strength and develop the unity in the free world, and this will take a decade or two at the very least. If the Russians are convinced, if they will be convinced in the future, that they cannot conquer the world without a devastating war, then may be the time, in a different situation from the present one, to see how, in a gradual and reasonable way, we can begin to agree with them.

We first have to stop them, and in order to do that we need unity. We need unity in the free world. We must begin to build a supranational authority which has moral strength and physical strength to maintain peace, and which has the power to help the backward nations in their struggle for a better existence. We can, with the help of peaceful uses of nuclear explosives, with the help of great projects, like influencing weather—like multiplying the food resources of the world by exploiting the ocean better—in many big ways which can be undertaken only by many nations together. If we do that, if we take the full responsibility for a developing world, for a world in which the Industrial Revolution and a better way of living is spreading from continent to continent; if in this world we can become leaders; if we can make good on our old statement that all men are created equal, whether in North or South America, or Africa or Asia; if we can make good on these magnificent ideas, and these magnificent promises; and if we have the strength to safeguard ourselves and our friends while we are developing our world—then there will be real peace in our time. And a very important part of this real safety and this real peace is this little, gentle contribution of civilian defense.

May 17, 1967

Martin Luther King Jr.

Nobel Peace Prize–Winner, 1964; Civil Rights Advocate

"Many are now thinking of the long hot summer ahead," Martin Luther King Jr. told The Commonwealth Club audience at the Hotel St. Francis in May 1967, "and have forgotten the long cold winter behind." Indeed it was to be a long hot summer, with riots and "urban disorder" in dozens of cities across the U.S. In San Francisco, it might have been the "summer of love"—kicked off with the January Human Be-In, Gathering of the Tribes at Golden Gate Park, featuring Allen Ginsberg, Timothy Leary, and twenty thousand of their closest friends. But for Newark, July featured a riot that killed twenty-three and caused $10 million in property damage. A week later, riots began in Detroit, and five days of mayhem killed more than forty people and destroyed thousands of homes. Even while fires were still burning in Detroit, President Johnson would appoint a special commission, chaired by the governor of Illinois, to investigate the causes of the violence. He also sent nearly five thousand paratroopers to the Motor City to quell the violence.

At the beginning of May, UPI was quoting "big city youth-workers" who predicted a decade of violent summers to come. For his part, Reverend King sketched out a path that included jobs and integration and could bring the violence to an end. Given the violence of the previous two summers, the prediction of riots in 1967 seemed a safe one. August 1965 had brought the Watts riots in Los Angeles, just five days after Johnson signed the Voting Rights Act. In July 1966, racial tension had fueled riots in Omaha, Brooklyn, Jacksonville, and Cleveland. And as King noted, in May the violence of the summer of '67 had already begun, though the calendar showed summer still over a month away. On April 1, there were store windows smashed and fires set in Omaha. A week later, riots at Nashville's Fisk University followed a visit by Black Power advocate Stokely Carmichael. A month later, one week before King's Commonwealth Club speech, Jackson State College, a historically black college in Mississippi, was the site of two days of rioting. National Guard armored transports were called in. The very night that King spoke to his San Francisco audience, Texas Southern University was convulsed with violence. Two students were shot and so were three police, one fatally.

King described the Civil Rights movement as entering a new phase in 1967, one that included eliminating poverty. Unlike voting rights legislation, this would cost billions—billions that were now going to fight a war in Vietnam. Two months before, in Chicago, King had attacked U.S. policy on Vietnam; in New York, he and Benjamin Spock had led an antiwar protest march that drew one hundred thousand. King and Spock were even being touted as potential third-party peace candidates for president. Even if he couldn't win, perhaps King's running could help bring peace to Vietnam—or at least defeat to Lyndon Johnson. The counterargument, though, was that if he ran he'd likely help elect Richard Nixon.

King didn't run, though Spock did in 1972. Meanwhile, in 1967, Johnson continued trying to win the War on Poverty and the war in Vietnam. He appointed Thurgood Marshall to the U.S. Supreme Court, making Marshall the first African American on the court. A month later all hell broke loose in Newark and Detroit.

March 1968 opened with the release of the report by the eleven-person National Advisory Commission on Civil Disorders (AKA the Kerner Commission) that Johnson appointed to look at the causes of the violence and what could be done to prevent it. One chapter of the report focused on "The News Media and the Disorders," noting some attempts at balance but taking newspapers to task for giant headlines that screamed calamity and only threw fuel on the fire, and arguing that the media didn't get to the causes and consequences. Among the commission's prescriptions for the fourth estate: exercise more care with this issue, and more blacks are needed in journalism.

The month ended with Johnson giving a televised address on the war in Vietnam and efforts to negotiate a peace with North Vietnam. At the end of the speech he stunned the nation by declaring, by way of explanation that he wanted to devote himself fully to the duties of office rather than having his presidency become mired in partisan politics, "I shall not seek, and I will not accept, the nomination of my party for another term as your president."

Four days later, Martin Luther King Jr. was assassinated in Memphis. Johnson called thousands of National Guard troops into the capital. Rioting and looting roared across more than one hundred American cities, with some fifty people killed (most of them black), twenty-six hundred injured, twenty-one thousand arrested, and property damage upwards of $60 million.

"The Future of Integration"

There can be no gainsaying the fact that we have two Americas. One is beautiful—with people who have food and material for their bodies, culture for their minds. Their young people grow up in the sunlight of opportunity.

The other America has an ugliness that transforms hope into despair. Hundreds of thousands of men walk the streets for jobs that don't exist. Millions live in rat-infested slums, on an island of poverty. The great tragedy is what it does to their little children. Clouds of inferiority form in their mental skies. These are Mexican Americans, Puerto Ricans, Indians, Appalachian whites in this other America. The vast majority is the American Negro. He finds himself living in a triple ghetto—a ghetto of power, a ghetto of race, a ghetto of human misery.

The job of the Civil Rights movement is to make America one nation, with liberty and justice for all. The future of integration will be determined by the speed with which we truly become one. We've made some strides here and there. There have been legislative and judicial decrees. We've restructured southern society. It's difficult now to find public accommodations segregated anywhere in the South. But the plant of freedom has grown only a bud and not a flower. We've been working ten to twelve years to advance civil rights. There is a new phase; now we're working to make genuine equality a reality. This really means getting rid of poverty; of slums; really achieving good schools.

Achievements of the last twelve years have been obtained at bargain rates. It didn't cost the nation a thing. But to move forward will cost billions. The gains of the past several years against the long-standing evils of the South did little to change conditions in the ghettos of the North. It did little to penetrate the lower depths of Negro degradation. We now have worse slums than twenty years ago. More segregated schools are in the North now than in 1954. The plight of the Negro economically is worse than fifteen years ago. The masses of Negroes have moved backward economically rather than forward. This makes for a great deal of despair in the Negro community.

We've had riots already—before summer has started. I will continue to condemn riots. My philosophy is one of nonviolence. The most potent weapon for the Negro in achieving human dignity is nonviolent resistance. If our programmatic strategy becomes violent, our legacy to the future will be chaos. Black riots can be black suicide. But it is necessary to condemn conditions which cause people to feel there is no alternative to riots in order to eliminate what is intolerable. Riots are the language of the unheard.

What is it American society has failed to hear? The plight of the Negro poor that is worse today; the promises of justice not met; the large segments of the white society more concerned about tranquility and status quo than justice.

Many are now thinking of the long hot summer ahead—and have forgotten the long cold winter behind, when time should have been used to build programs to provide jobs that would do away with long hot summers. It's necessary to move toward a truly integrated society, a truly just society—to develop massive progress that will do this.

The extreme right in our nation is devoted to negative ends; there is an appalling silence and indifference on the part of good people. There are others who maintain that there should be projected a change of heart—that attitudes can't be changed through legislation. If we are to develop real brotherhood, whites must treat the Negro as a real brother.

It's also necessary to point out the other side. Laws may not change the hearts of man, but they can change his habits, if enforced. Brotherhood can't be legislated, but laws can restrain someone from lynching me. And that's important too. More civil rights legislation is needed. But what we have must be enforced. Otherwise it just increases despair.

Another myth is overreliance on the bootstrap philosophy. The problem is a real and deep one. It doesn't help to say, "Other minorities uplifted themselves." It only deepens the frustration of the Negro. People who ask this question are too insensitive to realize that no other ethnic group were slaves on the American soil; even the word *black* was made a stigma. The Negro was freed in 1863, but he wasn't given land, as was the practice for most others. So it is necessary to work out mass programs to aid the Negro because of the long years of denial.

It's cruel to tell a bootless man that he should lift himself up by his own bootstraps. We must deal with the problem of poverty, and poverty generally, possibly with a guaranteed annual income for all American families. It would take only three percent of our gross national product over the next ten years to rid the country of poverty.

We must recognize the mutuality of our society. There is something of self-interest in our becoming one nation. Our destinies are tied together. The Negro needs the white man to save him from his fear; the white man needs the Negro to save him from his guilt. There is no separate black path to fulfillment nor is there a separate white path. We're caught in an inescapable network of mutuality. In the days ahead there will be enough good will to solve our problems. We will gain our freedom. It is tied up with the destiny of America.

We were here before the *Mayflower* arrived at Plymouth Rock, before the Declaration of Independence, before the words of the *Star-Spangled Banner*. The opposition we now face shall be overcome. We are going to achieve a just society. We are able to make a stone of hope out of a mountain of despair. Then the country will truly become the "home of the brave and the land of the free."

[from the question-and-answer session]

Q. *Vietnam is totally unrelated to the Negro dilemma in the U.S. Aren't you hurting your cause by tying the two together?*

A. The war in Vietnam is doing much more damage to civil rights than my taking a stand against that war. Vietnam is playing havoc with our domestic destinies. Just the other day, an important committee of the House cut back almost half of the model cities program and the rent supplement program—things that will deal with problems of the poor. As long as the war in Vietnam is on, it's going to affect the Civil Rights movement. In war the forces of reaction are strengthened, the military industrial complex is strengthened.

I have fought against segregation with all my nonviolent might. And now I'm being told I must segregate my moral concern. It would be absurd to preach about integration and not be concerned about the world in which to integrate. From a content point of view the issues are interrelated—ultimately there can be no peace without justice and no justice without peace. I've preached about nonviolence for a long time, now I say our nation should be nonviolent toward little brown Vietnamese children—and people are saying there's something wrong with that. I'm just being consistent.

Q. *Are you aware that pulling out of Vietnam is tantamount to surrendering Vietnam and other countries to communism?*

A. I'm not advocating unilateral withdrawal. Realistically, this isn't going to be done. We should take the initiative in creating the atmosphere for negotiations. We need not prove we are the most powerful nation; what we need to prove now is our moral power. We should take the initiative because we took the initiative in building up the war on the ground, the seas, and in the air. Cessation of the bombing could be a good first step. We should be able to negotiate directly with the National Liberation Front because it represents a large segment of South Vietnam. The problem is based on a huge miscalculation about communism—a feeling that communism was some monolithic bloc that had as its basic urge to dominate the world. What is animating the revolutionary movements today is nationalism—not communism.

Dr. Bernard Fall said a few years ago that less than 35 percent of members of the Vietcong were Communists. People must be free to choose the kind of government they want. I would never choose a communist government for myself—but communism is here and we've got to live with it—either peaceful coexistence or violent co-annihilation. So I don't think this is a surrender to communism. Negotiated settlement would be a surrender to truth and justice and some basic facts. I am sorry that America finds itself on the wrong side of the world revolution. Not a single major ally would send a single troop into Vietnam.

We have morally and politically isolated ourselves. If this is an attempt to take over by communism—why is it that the most powerful communist nations are not in the war? Russia doesn't have a single troop in Vietnam—China does not have any troops there. If we keep escalating that war they are going to be there. One of the most hopeful signs was the Sino-Soviet conflict. It proves that communism was not this monolithic bloc but the more we escalate this war, the closer these two forces will draw together. Once that happens, we are headed towards World War III—that nobody can win. That is why I must raise my voice against this mad adventure in Vietnam.

October 27, 1967

George C. Wallace

Former (and Future) Governor of Alabama

A political titan in his home state of Alabama, George Wallace became a national figure as well when he won the race for governor in 1962 and declared "segregation now, segregation tomorrow, segregation forever." The following summer, he made good on his promise to stand "in the schoolhouse door" to block integration of schools: he personally, physically blocked the first two black students attempting to register at the University of Alabama. It took President Kennedy's federalizing of the Alabama National Guard to get Wallace to step aside. Johnson federalized the National Guard in 1965 as well, to enforce the newly passed Voting Rights Act. It had been the action of police outside of Selma, Alabama, in March 1965—greeting marchers with flailing billy clubs—that had helped galvanize support for the Voting Rights Act in the first place. Before The Commonwealth Club audience, Wallace railed against the Act—and took particular pleasure in noting how much support his wife, Lurleen, had received from Selma voters in the 1966 election when she ran for governor. (The state constitution had prohibited George Wallace from serving another term; while Lurleen was governor of Alabama, at least in name, her husband's office was across the hall.)

A week after Richard Nixon announced his candidacy for the 1968 presidential race, Wallace threw his hat into the ring as the candidate of his own American Independent Party. He'd run in several primaries in 1964 and earned surprisingly strong support—surprising to critics, anyway—in states such as Maryland and Wisconsin. Come November 1968, he'd win nearly ten million votes and forty-six electoral votes—and carry five states. He'd also be back on the campaign trail in 1972, this time going for the Democratic Party's nomination, before being hit by a would-be assassin's bullet and paralyzed from the waist down.

When he took to The Commonwealth Club podium at the Hotel St. Francis, though, he was standing on his own two feet and full of piss and vinegar, and he was determined to reclaim the America that he said the Founding Fathers had charted out when they limited the powers accrued by the federal government. Half the audience jumped to their feet repeatedly to applaud Wallace when he spoke; one editor noted that a few looked sick to their stomachs, though he ascribed that to a possible dislike for the squab served for lunch. Wallace would later remark that he couldn't eat the little bird served him, since "I ain't no pigeon eater."

"States' Rights and Constitutional Government"

Alabamans are a fierce and independent people. The people of our state resent being told "We're going to run your life" by pseudo-intellectuals sitting a thousand miles away.

Those of you who may go to a good library will find the debates of the original thirteen states. Those who originated our government brought forth our system of limited powers of the federal government. We get our attitudes from those thirteen colonial states. Two amendments to the Constitution have apparently been forgotten by our present federal judicial system. The Ninth Amendment says: "The enumeration in the Constitution of certain rights shall not be construed to deny or disparage others retained by the people." And the Tenth Amendment says: "The powers not delegated to the United States by the Constitution, nor prohibited by it to the States, are reserved to the States respectively, or to the people." So we in our state are concerned about the trend in our nation that would destroy democratic domestic institutions.

I have never raised the question of race. My wife received 40 to 45 percent of the Negro vote in Alabama. In Selma, half the registered voters are Negro citizens. Over eleven thousand votes were cast for her, as opposed to only two thousand for both of her opponents. One of the top news agencies didn't believe me when I said she received 85 percent of the vote, and sent one of their best men to investigate our "credibility gap." He came back to tell me I was wrong—my wife had received 87.5 percent of the vote. Negro citizens have supported "our" administration.

Many movements today attack our free enterprise system. We have today an elite club in our country unlike anything that has existed prior— something like what exists in Russia and Red China—in which a select few at the top who call themselves intellectuals (but they're really pseudo-intellectuals) look down upon the masses of people in our country and say to the steelworker and businessman, "You aren't able to decide when to get up in the morning or when to go to bed at night, so we're going to have to write you a 'guideline.'"

People in our state and yours can decide these things for themselves. But when the people vote and express themselves in a position in opposition to the intellectuals, they say, "Yes, but you can't do that. You're going to have to change."

It's the pseudo-intellectuals in our country that are always talking about the "people." In Oklahoma the citizens voted to redesign their state government. They were told they couldn't. Why can't the people of Oklahoma decide for themselves? They've told the same thing to the people of California. You voted to decide for yourselves who you'd sell your home to. And you were told that your collective judgment was not as good as theirs. The right to sell is just as important as the right to buy.

Pseudo-intellectuals are more powerful than all the people of your state—this isn't right. A liberal member of the Supreme Court, Justice Cardoza, once wrote that judges have the power, but not the right, to exceed judicial restraints. Our philosophy in Alabama is that we don't advocate disobedience of any law or court order. We must obey the laws whether we like them or not. We can work within constitutional forms if we want to change the laws.

It's the liberals in our country who advocate anarchy—not the people of Alabama. I saw an article in the *Los Angeles Times*, and I suppose we can say it's correct if it's in the *Times*—anyway, I'm going to assume it's correct.

It told about a professor over at UCLA that, because no one turned up to hear his brilliantly conceived lecture on the Vietnam War and disobedience, he says, "When the intellectual and middle class community refuses to even listen to spokesmen from our ghettos, I think that is sufficient grounds to burn our city down and I might even join them." I can tell you this—in Alabama we may be a little crude about it, but the first public college professor that makes that statement in Alabama—he's a fired college professor. Yet he's one of those men who point to Mississippi and Alabama and says, "You obey the law down there, boy"—but then he's the one who advocates disobedience of all laws when his great mind isn't listened to.

Our free enterprise system is under attack and yet it has abolished more poverty than any other system or program the world has known. We need less government restraint on business. As a consequence of our attitude in Alabama, we led all the Southeast in gaining new business last year.

There is a breakdown in law and order. We blame everybody but those who should be blamed. People of all races are increasingly concerned. Now an officer who arrests someone leaving a burglary and who shoots at him must read him a little card. The courts tell that officer, "If you've lost your card, that's too bad!" And then we try the policeman, not the criminal. The man who molests you is out of jail before you can get to the hospital. We who can put a man on the moon should be able to make our streets safe for the citizen.

The U.S. attorney general recently sent my wife a lengthy document on how to get federal troops in case of civil strife. The red tape, wherefores, ifs, ands, and buts are appalling....But Arkansas, Mississippi, and Alabama got troops—and didn't even ask for them.

At colleges I'm often asked, "Shouldn't we put human rights above property rights?" The USSR and Red China have put "human" rights above property rights. And look at the oppression there. Only in those countries where private property rights exist and are protected are people free.

The Voting Rights Act only applies to five states—the five which voted against President Johnson in the election. In my state an illiterate who can't even make an "X" mark—it'll be made for him by a federal official—can register to vote. But if that same illiterate moves to New York State he cannot vote, because it takes the equivalent of an eighth grade education and he must be able to sign his name.

One of the grievances during the American Revolution was that the citizens were deprived of the right to trial by jury. One of the king's judges issued court injunctions and then tried you for violating his rulings. In civil rights and school segregation cases, there is no provision for jury trials.

As to Vietnam, no one has a utopian solution. We *are* involved. We should never become involved in blocking communism unless the efforts are bilateral or multilateral with others who also have something to lose. We should stop foreign aid. Most citizens don't have the pseudo-intellectual outlook of those who trade with the enemy.

Too many, in the name of academic freedom, are giving aid and comfort to the enemy. They talk of free speech, but today I have to have a police escort to get me into those citadels of academic freedom. They're for free speech—"let everybody talk but him." In Alabama we don't understand that type of academic freedom.

A professor at a famous law school was arguing about the "right of dissent" in this "Vietnam War." I told him he admitted it was war, and in war when you aid the enemy who's shooting Alabama boys, that's not dissent, that's treason. We ought to take every bearded professor who advocates victory by the Vietcong, put him before a grand jury, and toss him into the penitentiary.

In 1942 a lot of pro-Communist groups called for war against Hitler's Nazi Germany—but now they call themselves pacifists. We can fight everybody but Communists, according to them. I'm not a supporter of the present president, but I'm for him in Vietnam. It's one thing to sit aside and criticize—it's something else to have to make the decisions.

Our present court system has allowed the bolstering of Hanoi and the death of our boys in Vietnam. FDR and Harry Truman packed the Supreme Court, and folks in Alabama want to unpack it.

I'm the only one who's spoken to the National Press Club and never received their certificate of appreciation. Castro, the Robin Hood of Cuba, received one. Khrushchev received one after he spoke to the group. The group didn't like my "tactics." I wrote the National Press Club and told them they knew what they could do with their certificate. Every cab driver in Alabama knew Castro was a Communist—but some of our best newspapermen writing for the *New York Times* did not.

If the two parties give us a real choice, I won't run. But if they do not, I will. I'll try to get my name on the ballot in this state. If our citizens are given a choice, we'll let the two-party system work for a change. If we get on the ballot in California, it will make both national parties rethink this whole thing.

December 1, 1967

Barry Goldwater

Former (and Future) Member, U.S. Senate (R–AZ); 1964 Republican Presidential Candidate

---

Barry Goldwater's speech to a Commonwealth Club audience at the Sheraton Palace Grand Ballroom was promoted as a talk by "a vigorous speaker who doesn't 'weasel' on important issues." Indeed, Goldwater was once criticized by Eisenhower for speaking "too quick and too loud"; Goldwater had the honesty to admit that Ike was right.

Goldwater had also thumped Eisenhower with his verbal bat. He once called the Eisenhower Administration a "dime-store New Deal," and it was during Eisenhower's tenure that Goldwater emerged as a national leader. When he first spoke at The Commonwealth Club in December 1959, he was already being billed by *Time* as "a rallying point for right-wingers." He laid out the political scene in stark terms: "Today's political conflict is finally narrowing down to conservative vs. radical. I do not say 'conservative vs. liberal,' because there is no group of real liberal-thinking people remaining." His *The Conscience of a Conservative*, published in 1960, solidified his reputation, and without going after the Republican nomination at the 1960 convention, he received ten votes in the first round of balloting. He asked those delegates to vote for Nixon instead.

But he was also gearing up for his 1964 run at the presidency. He won the Republican nomination that year and was then trounced by Lyndon Johnson. Asked, when he spoke at The Commonwealth Club a few years later, about that campaign, Goldwater said, "If I had not known Goldwater and had to depend on press, radio, and TV for my information, I would have voted violently against him. I would have been convinced that we would have war, inflation, and all those terrible things that wouldn't happen under Johnson."

At the Republican convention held in San Francisco in 1964, Goldwater had been introduced by the state party chairman: actor and not-yet-governor Ronald Reagan. In 1967, asked his choice for the Republican ticket in the 1968 presidential election, Goldwater recommended a "Nixon-Reagan combination. With eight years as understudy, Reagan could take over for eight years more—sixteen years of Republican administration. I can't think of anything better." It was Reagan who, nearly two decades later, would carry the conservative revolution that Goldwater began all the way to the White House.

"The United States and the World Today"

As an American who feels that America must, as it always has in the past, stand behind their president in a period of war, I want to congratulate the citizens of this city, who turned down a proposal just a few weeks ago which would have said, in effect, to the president, "We do not go with you," and you would have said to the world that this great and important city had forgotten the great and courageous place it has always held in the hearts and minds of Americans.

Today, in this city which has turned its eyes to the world, never to the wall, I want to speak to you about one of the most dangerous words in the political vocabulary.

That word is isolationism.

It is a word that promises but cannot perform; a word that hides the death of vision and vigor behind a mask of wishful thinking.

If I step on some toes, those toes are not as important to me as the entire body of the nation, which, if it ever becomes infected with the virus of isolationism, will sicken and die.

America is part of the world. We—you and I—are part of the world. We cannot withdraw from the fact or from the future this implies.

There is no Maginot Line long enough or high enough to hide us from the world. There is no ocean broad or deep enough to shelter us from the winds of the world. And we must, as other nations have done before us, when they have worn the mantle of leadership, lead the world toward the goals of peace and freedom and away from the dark goals of slavery and war.

In the time of our own beginning, it was right and proper for George Washington to speak of attending to affairs at home first. Building the nation was the job. The affairs of Europe were, quite literally and correctly, foreign affairs.

Today there are no *foreign* affairs. Neither a sparrow nor a government can fall anywhere on this earth without seismic traces in our own affairs.

We are linked by over forty treaties to the defense of that many nations. War in their areas is instant war. We must face that fact, or abandon the treaties.

Having emerged as the world leader from World War II, it was proper that under Presidents Truman and Eisenhower a basis for our foreign policy was built upon our economic and military strength. As a reaffirmation of this policy, the Senate advised and consented to over forty treaties with other countries, now called Mutual Security Pacts, and these call in specific language for the defense of these countries when defense is required. In light of what we have learned about the difficulties of war in Vietnam, the Senate should reexamine these treaties, not with the specific view of withdrawing our support, for that would be impossible, but so that the American people, through discussion on the Senate floor, might know better the pledges that have been made to other countries. What most of the people who are calling for an immediate withdrawal from Vietnam without regard to victory or honor seem to overlook is that we do have an obligation to that same honor in these forty-odd treaties. The only alternative that I sense in their proposals is the alternative of isolationism plus dishonor.

We are linked by commerce to most nations on Earth. And trade, which should be the most nonideological of pursuits, has become a sharp, cutting weapon of ideology.

We are linked by needs to supplier nations. We are linked by productive surpluses with customer nations. We are linked by research to laboratories everywhere. We are linked by culture to theaters, galleries, libraries, and halls across the oceans and around the earth.

In the face of all of this, we continue to hear the most persistent and highly placed calls for American isolationism since the days of America First and the calls of those who felt that the aggressions of Adolf Hitler were of as little concern then as some say the aggressions of Ho Chi Minh are today.

All those who call for isolationism and dishonor have made common cause around a common complaint. America, they say, must withdraw its interest in the world and substitute for it an obsessive interest only in herself. It was a Republican secretary of state, Mr. Seward, who, just one hundred years ago this year, operating in conjunction with a Republican president, saw the importance of the Pacific to the defense of our own country. In every administration, Republican or Democrat, since that time, the interest of the Pacific has been paramount.

The isolationist will argue that times have changed, and let me say that they have. They have changed to the effect that it should be obvious to all Americans that the historic importance placed by both Republican and Democratic administrations on the maintenance of our strength in the Pacific has become more proper and more needed today.

There have been, as I said, times during which there may have been such reasons for an isolationist America, times when it was not only possible but also proper to be isolationist.

Let me say that it is not today either proper or possible.

The problems of peace are inescapable, for a grim reason which the new advocates of isolation deny but which the realities of our time absolutely verify. That reason is the aggressive nature of communism.

During earlier periods of isolation, it was possible to accurately say that the existence of totalitarian regimes elsewhere in the world did not affect us and could be walled away by the thinking and the diplomacy of a Fortress America.

Mr. Hitler pretty much ended that. Modern, industrially based or industrially aimed tyrannies cannot or at least do not exist in the old-fashioned and static self-containment of oppressing their own people but leaving everybody else alone. Purely agricultural or tribal societies perhaps could exist in perfect isolation—although the tendency of even some modern tribal states in Africa to pillage and invade is a disquieting indication that the virus of aggression is now epidemic.

The Communist tyrannies, however, are clearly involved in expansionist dynamics. The latest adventure in the Middle East, I remind you, is not an exception of Soviet policy but simply an encouragement of it.

Communist China follows, of course, the same path in the world, supporting everywhere it can those who would substitute violence for the peaceful processes of politics.

Stripped of all its many other admittedly controversial features, the war in Vietnam swings upon precisely that conflict—whether violence is to be substituted for peaceful political process. It was the Vietcong, not the Americans, not the South Vietnamese, not the French, who made the first substitution of violence for policy in the current conflict. President Johnson, quoting Hanoi's own figures, reminded the nation that more persons have been killed by Communist terrorists while trying to vote in the South than have been killed in the North by aerial bombardment.

What is happening in Vietnam is nothing but a reflection of the fact that disturbance of the peace today is an ongoing result of the aggressive dynamics of communism. There is *no other operative cause of conflict in the world*. Conditions such as hunger, illiteracy, disease, internal political discontent, even strictly internal tyrannies—such as now dominate most of the newly emerged nations—do not cause, even if they make possible, the highly organized, well-supplied breaches of the peace which call the fate of the entire planet into question.

As proof, you need look no farther than Africa. In some of the new states there, the unbelievably ferocious intertribal slaughters—slaughters with tolls far more vicious than those even of Vietnam—have been the slaughters of intertribal warfare, fed by all the conditions which some are so fond of citing as the absolute causes of war; meaning poverty, ignorance, etc.

Yet the peace of the world is not threatened by these bloodlettings, even though the conscience of the world might be offended. I think, as a matter of fact, it must be.

The reason is that these terrible things are not at all directly comparable to the Communist thrusts which involve the direct interference of a foreign power in the internal affairs of another nation.

Such a Fortress America would better be described as a Garrison America.

Would you wish to live in such a garrison state? Would the isolationists? Have they—Fulbright, Mansfield, and the others—thought their proposals through to this inescapable end? I see no sign of it. I see only the signs of reactions in panic and statements in haste.

So long as the leaders of the two-headed Communist world remain committed to violence as a tool of diplomacy, there is no possibility of hiding. There is no place to hide. There is no immunity. There is no withdrawal. Wherever that violence spreads, though it be thousands of miles from our shores, it is just inches from our future unless we face up to it and face it down.

My other point, that the technologies of modern warfare make isolation impossible, involves facts of life which are so terrible that few have the stomach to face them.

They cannot be avoided, however, by shutting eyes or ears or minds.

As we stand here today, right this moment, it would be possible for the defense establishments of Great Britain, of France, of the Soviet Union, of Red China, or of the United States to kill millions of persons anywhere on Earth. The difficulties are just details. For the Red Chinese those difficulties would involve nothing much more complex than a major job of smuggling. For the French it would be a question of refueling. For the British it might be the same. For us or for the Soviets it might be a question simply of the accuracy of maps, or the state of some maintenance schedule or other.

I know that is a terribly oversimplified way to put it. But modern weapons, for all their technical complexity, do pose starkly simple problems. One, for instance, is the avoidance of their use.

Today the major weapons of mass destruction—which are not limited, mind you, to nuclear weapons—are withheld from use not because there is a so-called balance of terror but because there is, quite to the contrary, an *imbalance* of terror.

The destructive inventory of this country, developed during the Eisenhower Administration, is so great even today that there is good reason to believe it could overpower and make insanely costly any use of such weapons by anyone else.

There is every responsible reason to believe that, given the absolute refusal of this administration to permit the development of new, major strategic weapons systems, this imbalance will end in the decade of the 1970s and that the balance itself will shift to an imbalance on the side of communism thereafter. The Communist states, remember, have *not* been standing still along with us. Research expenditures in both the Soviet

Union and in Red China have been directed toward upsetting, not maintaining, a balance of terror.

How odd it must be for the ghosts of Republicans past to hear the talk which today would tell them that it is Republicans who are leading the fight for a fully involved, fully committed, and fully international American viewpoint—while it is Democrats who lead the chorus for isolationism!

Those who speak for the isolationist view, of course, feel that there is no need or place for American strength because they feel there is no need or place for American presence anywhere beyond the borders of the nation.

They carry that belief as they would a magical umbrella. They carry it precisely like the magical umbrella that Neville Chamberlain carried to and from Munich. And they carry it under just such clouds as hovered over the world then.

Millions died because of the folly of men who wanted to play it safe by playing it blind. Today many millions *more* have their lives and their freedoms on the line. And the forces that would use violence in the world are stronger, more experienced, more entrenched.

There is only the isolation of the graveyard for those who will not live in and be part of the world today. We cannot stop the world and get off. Let it never be America against the world. Let it always be America *with* the world.

It is our, and the world's, very last hope.

January 4, 1968 and May 31, 1968

Robert F. Kennedy

Member, U.S. Senate (D-NY); 1968 Candidate for Democratic
Presidential Nomination

There were nearly half a million Americans in Vietnam when the curtain closed on 1967. Sixteen thousand had died in combat since the beginning of U.S. involvement. Opinion polls showed just under half of America thought involvement in Vietnam was now a mistake; the majority thought the U.S. should "win or get out." Secretary of Defense Robert S. McNamara resigned just after Thanksgiving. The next day, liberal Democrat Eugene McCarthy, citing a "deep crisis of leadership" in the country, announced he would challenge Lyndon Johnson for the Democratic nomination for president.

For Robert F. Kennedy, three years into his term as U.S. senator from New York, 1968 began with a soul-searching speech to The Commonwealth Club. Kennedy titled his talk "What Should We Stand For?" His answer: the liberation of the human spirit. The speech is epic in its sweep, grappling with the impossible tension between mustering the resources to win the War on Poverty and pouring that money into the war in Vietnam. In Kennedy's eyes, the cost of war was not just financial ($75 million a day) but moral as well. The nation was confronting its fundamental identity, and the question was whether a democratic America would survive or, like ancient Athens, surrender its ideals. Head of the Senate Special Subcommittee on Indian Education, Kennedy was holding hearings on West Coast reservations around the New Year. In his January speech he cited unemployment and suicide statistics on reservations. The *Washington Post* took note of the hearings and editorialized that the federal government's failure to provide adequate Indian education was "a failure not in Indian interests alone but in terms of the whole American ethos."

Kennedy was funny as well, and he didn't miss a beat when the questions started with "Senator, what is the secret of your luxuriant hair growth?" followed by "Would you appear on a news conference on KCBS radio, the number-one news information station of the West? If you are unable, I still think you're groovy." He declined to project whether he would run for president in 1972. ("That's too far in the future," he said. No one asked about 1968.) Asked about the investigations and statements by New Orleans District Attorney Jim Garrison about John F. Kennedy's assassination, he said, "I don't discuss that, I'm sorry."

Kennedy had spoken to The Club in 1959, when he was making a name for himself exposing corruption in labor unions. And he was back one more time, on May 31, 1968—this time campaigning for the Democratic nomination for president only days before the California primary. What happened in the five months between RFK's two 1968 speeches at The Commonwealth Club? In Vietnam, on January 21, North Vietnamese army (ARVN) troops laid siege to the American airbase at Khe Sanh. The ARVN troops outnumbered the Marines there four to one, and the media (and Johnson in private) drew comparisons to the French disaster at Dien Bien Phu in 1954. The battle was the biggest in the war up to that point, and it would take seventy-seven days before the siege was lifted. After that the U.S. would abandon the base.

At the end of January, with the coming of the lunar new year, known as Tet, Vietcong guerrillas and ARVN troops launched an offensive against dozens of cities and towns throughout South Vietnam. American television crews captured the bloody fighting, and back home it was shown on the nightly news. An AP photographer and NBC camera crew also captured on film the execution in the street of a suspected Vietcong guerrilla by South Vietnam's police chief. Walter Cronkite returned from Saigon at the end of February and told viewers that the war was certain "to end in a stalemate." The heaviest fighting took place in the city of Hue (mentioned by Kennedy in his May address), where American troops had to retake the city house by house, aided by air and artillery strikes. In Hue alone, in one month of fighting more than two hundred American soldiers were killed and more than thirteen hundred wounded. After bombs leveled another small city near Saigon, an American officer was quoted as saying, "We had to destroy it in order to save it."

Militarily, the Tet offensive was a failure for the North Vietnamese. It was meant to incite a nationwide uprising in South Vietnam. It didn't. Thousands of Vietcong troops died, and they never posed the same combat threat again. William Westmoreland, commander of U.S. forces in Vietnam, asked that more than two hundred thousand additional troops be sent. His wasn't meant to be a public request, but the New York Times made it so on March 10. Two days later, Johnson squeaked past Eugene McCarthy to win the New Hampshire primary. RFK still had not declared his candidacy. Instead, on March 14 he offered Johnson a deal in private: he would stay out of the race if Johnson would appoint a committee—one including Kennedy—to map a new course in Vietnam. Johnson turned him down, and two days later Kennedy announced his candidacy.

Hoping once more to get the North Vietnamese to negotiate, President Johnson at the end of March reined in American ships and planes, restricting them to North Vietnamese targets "where the continuing enemy buildup directly threatens allied forward positions and where the movements of their troops and supplies are clearly related to that threat." In a live televised address, Johnson discussed the massive budget that military expenditures required; and how the U.S. was trying to build up South Vietnam's capacity so that they could "progressively undertake a larger share of combat operations against the Communist invaders." And he stunned supporters and detractors alike when he finished his speech by announcing he would not run for president in 1968. Four days later, Martin Luther King Jr. was shot.

Over the course of the spring, Eugene McCarthy and Robert Kennedy duked it out in the primaries, though it wasn't clear that either one of them was destined to win the Democratic nomination. Kennedy won four out of the five states he competed in, but McCarthy had garnered more delegates. Even so, most states would choose which candidate their delegates would support at state party conventions, not through primaries. There Vice President Hubert Humphrey, who had announced his candidacy at the end of April, was on the inside track. However the chips from the primaries fell, it was clear the Democratic National Convention in Chicago in August would be an interesting one.

Much of Kennedy's May talk at The Commonwealth Club is on Vietnam. On May 5, the Vietcong launched rocket and mortar attacks against more than one hundred cities—an offensive that RFK mentioned in his talk, and that was dubbed "Mini Tet" by others. The following week, the North Vietnamese and the U.S. at last sat down for peace talks in Paris, but the talks quickly stalled. The talks would continue, off and on, for the next five years. Kennedy's speech also came days after an upset victory by McCarthy in the Oregon primary. In California on May 30, the McCarthy for President Committee rolled out a full-page ad in the *San Francisco Chronicle*, *Los Angeles Times*, and a number of other papers, featuring a photo of wounded U.S. soldiers and the headline "How Many More?" One-time Attorney General Kennedy, the ad pointed out, was part of the team behind the Bay of Pigs and initial U.S. involvement in Vietnam. In the middle of his speech at The Club, Kennedy drew attention to the ad with what journalist David Broder described as an off-the-cuff reference, saying that the ad "distorts the truth and demeans politics." He acknowledged that "In 1961, '62, and '63, I was part of an administration that developed some policies for Vietnam. If blame is to be assessed, that administration and I have to take responsibility. But I think we have to learn from the situation, and that is why I spoke out about Vietnam in 1965, earlier than any others...seeking the presidency." Regarding the leadership role the U.S. played, he said, "In all the things that we need to do, I think of what a poet wrote several thousands of years ago: what really we have to dedicate ourselves to in this country is to feel the giant agony of the world, and more like slaves to poor humanity, labor for mortal good."

In addition to his May talk at The Club, Kennedy campaigned around the Bay Area and spoke to crowds in Oakland (where supporters pressed in and for blocks slowed his car to a creep) and in the economically depressed San Francisco neighborhood Hunter's Point. Outside the ramshackle Christian Center there, Los Angeles Rams lineman Deacon Jones helped shield RFK from a surging crowd. The *New York Times* captured the visit in a patronizing piece subtitled "Bobby in the Ghetto." He was reaching out to blacks and other minority voters, and in the question–and–answer session at The Club, when asked a question about closing the budget deficit, he noted, "We cut back on everything except military spending." The welfare system as it existed was a mistake, he said; "jobs are the long-run answer," and job creation and housing should be controlled locally, not from Washington. Jobs were also a short-term answer for problems the country faced at home: "We cannot tolerate lawlessness and violence in the U.S.," he said. "An emergency job program is cheaper than welfare or violence."

The May 31 speech was one of the last Kennedy made. On June 5, he won the California Democratic primary, and after giving a victory speech to a crowd of gleeful supporters at the Ambassador Hotel in Los Angeles, Kennedy was shot and killed, purportedly because of his staunchly pro-Israel policies, by Sirhan Sirhan, a Palestinian immigrant.

"What Do We Stand For? The Liberation of the Human Spirit"

January 4, 1968

As I look out in this audience, I think of the poll that a national business magazine took recently of a group of four hundred businessmen of who their favorite political figure was in the United States and who they would like to see run for president, and I received one vote. I'm the only politician in the United States that can take all his supporters to lunch at one time. As I look at you, I think of the Senate and how much I enjoy the Senate of the United States and all my colleagues there. I was ill a short time ago, and they sent me a message through the majority leader. They said they hoped I would recover, and the vote was forty-three to forty-one. But I'm pleased to be here. I'm out here to hold some hearings on Indian affairs and to ensure that there is no effort to and no success in the "Draft Kennedy" movement taking place here in the state of California. I think my brother, Teddy, is much too young to run for president of the United States.

Recently a young poet was jailed for inciting a demonstration against the verdict of a court which had found another young agitator guilty of various disruptive activities. At his trial, the young poet declared that freedom of speech and of the press is freedom to criticize. Just as the rights of the Communist Party were protected by the United States Supreme Court, he contended, so his rights to demonstrate must also be protected. He's defied the court and he declared his intention to again organize demonstrations as soon as he was free. The defendant was not from Berkeley, or from San Francisco State. He was a young Russian named Vladimir

Bukovsky. The trial took place in Moscow and the record was smuggled to the West by Pavel Litvinov, the grandson of one of the oldest heroes of the Bolshevik Revolution.

This is a remarkable series of events. One American court decision, one small aspect of the freedom that we take for granted here in this country, cut through all the suspicions and all of the lies, all of the propaganda of the Communist state; it inspired these young men to risk years of hard labor in Siberia and to help subvert the vast power of the once unquestionable domination of the Communist government. In another sense, however, it is not so remarkable at all. From the beginning, we have known, as George Washington said, that "the preservation of liberty...[is]...finally staked on the American experiment";[1] we would be, as Jefferson said, the "best hope" of all mankind, and so it has proven. Everywhere I have traveled around this globe, in great world capitals but also in tiny villages, I have seen men looking to the principles, often to the very words of our history, to find inspiration in their own struggles for freedom—even Ho Chi Minh, who began the Vietnamese war against the French, he began by quoting not Marx, not Lenin, but the American Declaration of Independence.

Now we are in a year in which we elect a president of the United States. It is a year of debate and of argument, of political battles and personal clash. The most urgent problems of our own society, from the war in Vietnam to the smoldering discontent in our cities, will be weighed and analyzed and solutions offered. Yet this is a year in which America must examine not only the candidates but also the country, must ask not only who will lead us but also where we wish to be led. We must look not only to immediate crises but also to the nature and the direction of the civilization that we wish to build, that we wish to take part in.

The great national debate must not become a contest of only particular programs. We need discussion, we need understanding for the most basic and far-reaching goals of American civilization.

For we have been told by cabinet officers and commentators, by journalists and citizens, that America is deep in a malaise of spirit: discouraging

1. While this is what Kennedy said, the exact words Washington said in his first inaugural address were "The preservation of the sacred fire of liberty and destiny of the republican model of government are justly considered, perhaps, as deeply, as finally, staked on the experiment entrusted to the hands of the American people."

will and action and dividing Americans from one another by their age, their views, and the color of their skin. We have fought great wars, made unprecedented sacrifices at home and abroad, made prodigious efforts to achieve personal and national wealth; yet we ourselves are uncertain of what we have achieved and whether we like what we have accomplished. Now demonstrators shout down government officials, and the government drafts protestors. Anarchists threaten to burn the country down, and some have begun to try—while tanks have patrolled American cities and machine guns have been fired at American children. A "poet" proclaims that "throat-cutting time is growing nigh and / we're going to be ready"; while a National Guard general speaks calmly of plans to use heavy weapons in the city of New York. Our young people turn from the Peace Corps and public commitment of the early 1960s to lives of disengagement and sometimes despair, turned on with drugs and turning off from America. Truly, we seem to fulfill the vision of Yeats: "Things fall apart, the center cannot hold, mere anarchy is loosed upon the world."

Entangled abroad and embattled at home, America searches for answers: not just to specific programs, but to the great question: What do we stand for?

Where do we want to go? Do we stand for our wealth? Is that what is important about America? Is that what is significant about the United States? Ask better, perhaps: Are we really so wealthy? Half a million American children suffer from serious malnutrition—and I have seen personally some of them starving in the state of Mississippi, their stomachs bloated, their bones and their bodies scarred, many of them retarded for life. Up to 80 percent of some Indian tribes are unemployed; the suicide rate among the high school children is shockingly high, dozens of times the national average. For the black American of the urban ghetto, we really do not know what the unemployment rate is, because from one-fifth to one-third of these adult men in these areas have literally dropped out from sight—uncounted and unknown by all of the agencies of government, drifting about the cities, without hope and without family and without a future. By these standards, we are not so rich a country. Truly, we have a great gross national product, almost $800 billion, but can that be the criterion by which we judge this country? Is it enough? For the gross national product counts air pollution and cigarette advertising and ambulances to clear our highways of carnage. It counts special locks for our doors and jails for the people who break them.

It counts Whitman's rifle and Speck's knife and television programs which glorify violence in order to sell toys to our children.[1]

The gross national product does not allow for the health of our children, the quality of their education, the joy of their play. It is indifferent to the decency of our factories and the safety of our streets alike. It does not include the beauty of our poetry or the strength of our marriages, the intelligence of our public debate or the integrity of our public officials. It measures neither wit nor courage, neither our wisdom nor our learning, neither our compassion nor our duty to our country. It measures everything, in short, except that which makes life worthwhile; and it can tell us everything about America—except why we are proud to be Americans.

Is it then our wealth or is it our military power that we stand for in the United States? Beyond our borders, we have become the greatest force in the world. Some have even spoken of us as the new imperial power. Even if we should desire such a role, it is no longer possible, as the history of the last twenty years has so unmistakably shown. The day has passed when a country can successfully rule distant lands by force. The issue for us is whether we will live as an island in the midst of a hostile world community or whether we will be joined with other independent nations in search of common goals. We must understand this, because so much depends on what is going to happen in the future as to whether this concept is clear to us. For other countries will associate themselves with us not because they will be forced to, but because they find in our acts and in our policies a common interest and an understanding of their own ideals and their own

1. On August 1, 1966, Charles Whitman, an Eagle Scout and Marine Corps vet, barricaded himself in the University of Texas clock tower. Armed with an assortment of weapons, Whitman fired indiscriminately at the passersby below. Before he was shot and killed by Austin police, Whitman had killed fourteen people (including his mother and wife, earlier that same day) and wounded nearly three dozen. On November 12, 2001, Whitman's fifteenth homicide victim, David H. Gunby of Forth Worth, Texas, died of complications from a gunshot wound to his one functioning kidney.

   Two weeks earlier—on July 14, 1966—an alcoholic drifter named Richard Speck had broken into a townhouse shared by several South Chicago Hospital nursing students. Over the next four hours, Speck murdered eight of the women; the only survivor, Corazón Amurao, saved herself by hiding under a bed. Speck was found after a massive manhunt, tried, and sentenced to death; his sentence was later commuted to eight consecutive 50- to 150-year prison terms. He died a day short of his fiftieth birthday in 1991.

aspirations; an understanding of the values that they can respect and admire; an understanding of the values that they can strive to emulate.

Thus, consideration of our wealth and our power brings us full circle to the question with which we began: What do we stand for? Nor should we be surprised; for this is the most powerful and constant lesson of all of history. The wars and the conquests, the politics and the intrigues of state are soon covered by the years. The triumph of Athens, the empire of Rome, the march of armies, the names of governors—all these did leave some imprint, but it is the ideas and the statues, the plays of Sophocles and the philosophy of Plato that endure most vividly, shaping and enriching our lives to this very day. The mastery of transient events, our accomplishments, our victories will ultimately matter far less than what we contribute—all of us in this country—to the liberation of the human spirit.

That is what we have always stood for in the past and it is what we must stand for at the moment. That is what has given us our unique position, our unprecedented strength. That is why, in fact, we are proud to be Americans. For two hundred years, America has meant a vision of national independence and personal freedom and justice between men.

But whether it will continue to mean this will depend on the answers to difficult and complex problems. It will depend on whether we sit content in our storehouses, dieting while others starve, buying eight million new cars a year while most of the world goes without shoes. It will depend on whether we act against crime and its causes and wipe the stain of violence from this land. It will depend on whether we can halt and can reverse the tide of ever greater centralization in Washington and return the power to the American people in their local communities.

It will depend on whether we can turn the private genius of industry to the service of great public ends—using comprehensive tax incentives to help industry create the jobs, train the workers, and build the housing which all of the efforts of the federal government have so far failed to do.

It will depend on whether we still hold, as the framers proclaimed, "a decent respect for the opinions of mankind," or whether we will act as if no other nations existed, flaunting our power and flaunting our wealth against the judgment and desires of neutrals and allies alike. It will depend on whether men still believe, as de Gaulle said at the height of the Cuban missile crisis, that this great nation, the United States, does not act in small ways—or whether, like Athens of old, we forfeit sympathy and support alike and ultimately our own security in the single-minded pursuit of our own goals and our purposes.

These are the questions to debate in this election year. This is the true agenda which faces not just the contenders for office but all of the American people. To meet and master these challenges will take great vision and will take great persistence. To paraphrase Abraham Lincoln just one hundred years ago, we must know where we are and whither we are going before determining how to get there. In this, the most dangerous and yet the most challenging period in our history, this is what it so desperately needed. Vietnam, the crisis of our cities—these matters can and will be resolved. But the larger question of whether we have advanced our civilization and the cause of freedom will depend on our own morality and our philosophy, on our commitment to our ideals and to our principles. These precepts must guide us again as the great debate begins; if we do have the will, the vision, and the courage to create and to hold fast, to be shaping ideals which men follow, not from the enslavement of their bodies, but from the compulsions of their own hearts. If we do this, then we know that men will stand with us at home and abroad among our friends and even in the camp of our adversaries. For it is the shaping impulse of America that neither fate nor nature nor the irresistible tides of history, but the work of our own hands, matched to reason and principle, that will determine our destiny. This is the pride, even the arrogance, of America, but it's the experience and it is the truth. And, in any case, it is the only way that we can live.

May 31, 1968

Speech to The Commonwealth Club of California

Santayana told us that "wisdom comes by disillusionment." If that is true, then we should be the wisest of peoples today. As we have watched the course of the war in Vietnam over the last three years, our days have been filled with disillusion. This winter, in the harsh light of the enemy's Tet offensive, we learned the final truth: behind all the official statements, behind the confident predictions of ever greater victory, there was a failed vision and a bankrupt adventure.

March 31, we thought, was a watershed in our war policy. At last the futile policy of constant military escalation would come to an end. For the first time, there would be a serious effort toward negotiations—an effort whose sincerity was underlined by President Johnson's decision not to seek reelection.

Those, at any rate, were our expectations. But recent developments in Saigon, Washington, and Paris compel us to ask: Has the American government really learned anything from the last three years in Vietnam?

It is right and natural that the administration should not reveal totally, or in public, its position in the Paris talks. But even as the talks in Paris appear to be stalled, there are other and deeply disturbing signs. High officials tell us that the Vietcong can expect only the most minor and ineffective place in the future politics of South Vietnam. There is no insistence that the South Vietnamese government commence its own talks with the National Liberation Front. And meanwhile the war, far from subsiding, heats up. Field commanders are directed to seek victory within the next three months; later we are told that this is only a "pep talk." Only yesterday, the commanding general told us that the enemy is "close to desperation."

But this is what we have heard from generals and officials—French and American—for twenty years and more. For a generation, we have run after a rainbow of victory. Yet some people still think that this is the day we may find the pot of gold.

Clearly, we feel that time is on our side. We seem still to hold to a naïve faith in our military power—that its continuing application will eventually force a favorable settlement from the North Vietnamese negotiators in Paris. From their unyielding position, the North Vietnamese and the Vietcong feel that time is on their side—that they can wait for a settlement.

Judgment is not easy, from a distance of ten thousand miles. But some things are clear.

First, we are still not adequately protecting the cities. American troops are sent on sweep-and-destroy operations into remote jungles, operations described as the largest offensives of the war. Meanwhile, the local-force guerrillas infiltrate the cities with apparent ease. The second wave, or May offensive, was counted a failure by our authorities. Perhaps, in the statistics of the body count, it was. But it is also true that the result is the destruction of whole new areas. These areas housed the families of government and army officials who now have become homeless refugees, like other millions of their countrymen. The greatest actual damage has not been done by the Vietcong. It has been done by our own immense firepower—artillery and gunships and bombers. Just as in the Tet offensive, we seem willing to destroy any part of South Vietnam to save it—even the most loyal of areas. At this very moment, Saigon is being destroyed district by district. It is slowly becoming another Hue.

Second, the countryside is less secure. The latest statistics, those for March 1968, show the percentage of the population under our control is lower. That under the Vietcong is higher. In the last year, over a million people passed from the nominal control of the Saigon government, many of them to direct Vietcong control. Moreover, Vietcong defections were only at one-quarter their 1967 rate, while South Vietnamese army desertions were 30 percent over their 1967 rate. Therefore, despite heavy casualties, the Vietcong have been able to maintain their hold over the countryside—and make up much of their manpower losses through recruiting in their newly controlled areas.

Third, there is still no evidence that we recognize the nature of the war we are fighting. There are ninety thousand North Vietnamese in South Vietnam. But there are over five hundred thousand Vietcong, who are still our main adversary. Thirty years ago, the French controlled all of Indochina with only eleven thousand troops. Now five hundred thousand American troops and seven hundred thousand Vietnamese soldiers cannot control a small portion of that territory. The reason is that in the interval, there has been a revolution waged by the Vietcong and their predecessors, the Viet Minh. It has comprised land reform, effective political and military organization, and its own version of the most powerful political ideal in the world today: nationalism. These elements of success were never used by the South Vietnamese government. To make up for its shortcomings and weakness, we have time and again supplied more American power, resources, and more American lives.

Yet making this an American war was the most terrible error. The more evident the American troops and advisors and AID personnel, the more powerful and effective our presence, the less legitimate the official government of South Vietnam must seem to its people—and the more the Vietcong must seem to be the only legitimate nationalist force in the country.[1]

1. AID, the Agency for International Development, is now generally referred to as USAID.

There is no reason to think that the enemy will lose either the will or the capacity to continue in this way.

We can, of course, continue to wage what our commanding general has told us is a war of attrition. Yet we might ask ourselves to whose advantage such a war really works. Is it to the advantage of the American people—already losing over five hundred of our finest sons every week, our economy weakened and strained, our allies alienated, and our own country divided? Or is it to the advantage of the Vietcong—their forces steadily rising despite casualties, while the government and society of South Vietnam progressively disintegrate under the blows of war? As one of our officials has said, we are fighting the Vietnamese birthrate. It is not a winning battle.

It is clear that the present course of the war is not favorable to the interests of the United States. And we must understand that the longer the negotiations go on—the longer the fighting continues—the worse our position is likely to become, unless the administration has the wisdom and courage to change its course in Vietnam. As long as we continue to seek a settlement which concedes little or no future to the Vietcong, there is unlikely to be a settlement in any case.

All the errors, all the wasted years and opportunities of the past, have at last come down to roost. Today the newspapers reported on how the decision to back negotiations was made. The government's own officials confirmed: that the bombing of the North was not effective; that American bombs and napalm could not win, but would lose, the essential political struggle; that only a South Vietnamese government able to win the loyalty of its own people could use our support effectively—and that only such a government would deserve our support. These were my analyses and predictions about the escalation policy beginning in 1965, when the escalation began, and repeated throughout these three years since. There is no avoiding the need for change—searching and fundamental—along the following lines: First, we must abandon the futile dream of crushing the enemy's forces or his will to continue the struggle. The population centers, the lives and property of those South Vietnamese loyal to the government, must be protected. We cannot allow them to carry out another Tet offensive, or even to repeat the May fighting. Therefore we must effectively concentrate our forces around the cities and population centers—assuming the strategic defensive but maintaining the tactical offensive with our great firepower. American troops should not be sent on more extensive and costly sweep-and-destroy missions.

Second, we must do far more to reinforce the non-Communist nationalist elements within South Vietnam. For many of the long-promised programs, such as land reform or the ending of corruption, it may now be almost too late. But it is not too late for the Saigon government to become representative of the people of South Vietnam. Only a government that is committed to peace—and not a government that seeks endless war—can command the loyalty of the South Vietnamese people, for whom peace is the deepest desire. It is the South Vietnamese themselves who seek greater representation in their own government. They should be actively encouraged to do so; and we should sharply reduce our overidentification with the Thieu-Ky government.

Third, such a South Vietnamese government should enter its own talks with the Vietcong. This should always have been a Vietnamese war; it must be a Vietnamese peace. Any hope of a South Vietnam which is independent of the North in any degree depends on genuine independence in both the Communist and non-Communist elements in South Vietnam. In their accommodation with each other—and not in agreements between North Vietnam and the United States—lies the ultimate hope of their country. And for the mandarins and generals who resist any accommodations with the Vietcong—while allowing Americans to fight the war and swell their pockets with our aid—let them at long last be informed that neither the interests of the United States nor the interests of their own people can be subordinated to their selfish views.

These are some of the things we must do if the talks in Paris are to ripen into serious negotiations or ever lead to peace. None of them, however, will happen unless we are determined to face the facts with truth and candor. None of them will be undertaken by an administration still entranced by the spectacle of its own military power, or so committed to the defense of past error that it cannot recognize the dangers of the present or the needs of the future. Since the errors of our present course are the same that have dogged us in the past, those—like Vice President Humphrey or Mr. Nixon—who have supported and still support this policy cannot hope to bring success, either on the battlefield or at the negotiating table. That demands a new policy and a new administration. It is the policy and the administration I hope to offer the American people.

August 22, 1969

Tom Smothers

Singer; Comedian; Producer

Ten years after Dick and Tommy Smothers made their showbiz debut at the Purple Onion in San Francisco, they became the center of a national controversy over censorship, politics, and the media. CBS execs threw their *Smothers Brothers Comedy Hour* up against *Bonanza* in February 1967, making it the tenth show the network had sent to do ratings battles with the popular western. Clean-cut in appearance, the Smothers brothers dished up satire laced with jokes about marijuana and the Establishment and jibes against U.S. policy in Vietnam that garnered the comic folksinging duo a devoted following among younger, hipper viewers. The Jefferson Airplane and the Doors appeared on the show, as did Jimmy Durante and Kate Smith. But the creative control CBS had granted the Smotherses, seemingly insignificant at the outset, in fact led to censorship battles with the network from the fourth or fifth show, Tommy Smothers recalled. CBS nixed (at least temporarily) an appearance by Pete Seeger, who was going to sing his "Waist Deep in the Big Muddy," a tale of a World War II commander that was really about the U.S. in Vietnam, and Harry Belafonte singing the calypso tune "Don't Stop the Carnival" with images of the 1968 Democratic convention in Chicago showing behind him.

March 1969 brought the showdown: CBS refused to broadcast the show the Smothers brothers had taped for broadcast on Easter Sunday. One executive cited a routine by comedian David Steinberg as being in particularly poor taste on the holiday—and the week of Dwight Eisenhower's funeral. As Steinberg's biblical revisionist sermonette had it, Job wasn't swallowed by a whale—he was tossed overboard by thirty-two gentiles. Singer Joan Baez's dedication of a song to her husband, who had been sentenced to prison for refusing to be inducted into the Army, was also a problem. And the show included Tommy Smothers singing, with Nancy Wilson, a camp duet of "Sweetheart, Sweetheart," poking fun at racial stereotypes. While Americans saw a repeat of a November show, the Easter show was broadcast as scheduled in Canada and soon thereafter screened for the U.S. media. In April, CBS attempted to smother the Smothers problem by canceling the show—after having already opted to renew it for the next season—claiming the brothers had failed to turn in on time a videotape of their upcoming show for vetting by affiliate stations.

Why all the fuss? It wasn't just the material. Just before CBS canned the Smotherses, network president Frank Stanton had been in the room where Senator John O. Pastore (D-RI), head of the subcommittee on commerce, had raked network execs over the coals for the burgeoning of sex and violence on television and for not submitting material to review by local stations before broadcast. Coincidentally, the Smothers show that CBS yanked also included a routine in which Tommy Smothers and Dan Rowan of NBC's *Laugh-In* awarded Pastore the Flying Fickle Finger of Fate Award for having been upset at the sight of a French actress in a low-cut gown on the *Merv Griffin Show*. Following the hearings, NBC and ABC agreed to have their shows vetted by the code authority of the National Association of Broadcasters. CBS said it would keep the previewing in-house.

On the television show, Tommy Smothers played the dumb brother. As publicity materials put it at the time, Tommy "plays guitar haltingly and blinks at the world in seeming confusion...stumbles over words, sings off-key, goes through elaborate double-talk, and in the process renders sacred cows to luncheon meat." When their show was canceled, Dick headed to Florida to race cars, and Tommy went on the warpath over censorship, flying to Washington, D.C., to meet with the FCC, writing an opinion piece for the *New York Times*, and speaking at The Commonwealth Club in San Francisco. Tommy later thanked The Club for the opportunity to speak and wrote, "It was a pleasure to be there before such a warm and enthusiastic audience...and very 'heavy' to join such company as past speakers Charles de Gaulle and Ann Landers." The Smothers brothers filed three lawsuits against CBS for violation of the First and Fifth Amendment, violation of antitrust laws, and breach of contract. In 1973 they were awarded $776,000 by a Los Angeles jury.

Though their show was canceled by CBS, the Smothers brothers continued work with the network as producers, Tommy counting the *Glen Campbell Goodtime Hour* among his credits. The brothers launched a musical show on ABC in the fall of 1969, and they continued to appear on television throughout the 1970s, though without drawing the controversy the *Comedy Hour* had.

"Censorship and the New Freedoms"

Many people have said that as a performer I have no right to I discuss my personal views on national issues. I feel that I have the right not to be a hypocrite. Everyone has a right to express publicly his private views, and on the biggest platform that is available.

I would like to slightly change the topic "Censorship and the New Freedoms" to "New Censorship and the Old Freedoms." The "old freedoms" is the right to say what you believe; the new censorship is you have the right to say what you believe but not to those you want to say it to. The Bill of Rights gives us freedom of speech, but there isn't a clause to say freedom of hearing. The only right of censorship is the right of people not to listen. That is the only kind of censorship I will accept, and I will continue to fight for that right—for people to hear. I believe America wants to know. Eldridge Cleaver has something to say, you might not agree with him. I hear Joe Pyne, I don't agree with him. William F. Buckley, I hear; he's eloquent, but I don't agree with him. And I hear Ronald Reagan. I don't even believe that.

Marshall McLuhan said man lives in an environment of information. Therefore we react to the information that is given to us. And regardless of whether the information is correct, incorrect, valid, invalid, we make decisions on that information.

The older generation was brought up before television. The younger generation was brought up with television and electronic communications.

The problem between the generations is not age—it is attitude. We can see a riot instantly on television, but the news does not tell of the frustrations leading up to it. Everything that this new generation has is instantaneous on television.

Television isn't doing the job. Every columnist, every critic says that here comes another crummy season with no content, nothing. This younger generation, of which I am a part, is a child of change. The solutions to problems are solved in a half hour. It is no wonder that I and they (younger generations) want to have instant justice, instant brotherhood, and instant peace. Why shouldn't we have it? That is the way it is. Why should the process be so slow?

This generation has also had an awareness of hypocrisy. It is aware of the hypocrisy of going to church on Christmas and Easter, then going out and messing with someone's wife. They know of the hypocrisy of fixing traffic tickets, messing with taxes; morality is only for public versing not private belief; or war isn't good but you have to have it.

The news is pretty disgusting: killing, riot—boom—every night. It is a direct result of television not fulfilling its obligation to air views or have dialogue. It is better to see it on the screen, to hear what the other guy is up to, than to go into the street to attract attention and get a platform to speak from.

The networks charge full rate to every politician who is running for office. Whoever has the most money has the most time. It should not cost to share the public's business with the public. Every station in America generally makes a 100-percent profit, and yet they don't even want competition. That isn't the American way either.

What are the most important issues we talk about? The problems in the ghettos, with students, the young, the problems with civil liberties, the problems with war and peace. If we want solutions to the problems, give access to the media to all, then we can make decisions. Where was the ABM discussion? Where was Johnny Carson and those people when it was a hot issue?

I believe that any man that has any power had better use it, because you only go through life once. When you see a wrong being done, or someone in trouble, or a fellow man is in need, and you don't help now, you will never pass that point again.

In colonial America the place for discussion was the town square. They had soapboxes, maybe three soapboxes in the square. Today we have three networks, which own or are affiliated with about 94 percent of all the stations in this country. It is a triopoly. The networks aren't concerned with true dialogue to make people think.

The great breakdown in communication is that people don't take the time to listen, or the networks won't allow us to listen because they are worried about an objectional letter. The Smothers brothers' comedy was intended to be humorous and thought provoking. When should that become an issue?

Thomas Jefferson said, "If I had to choose government without newspapers or newspapers without a government, I would never hesitate to choose the latter."[1] An informed electorate is a free electorate; and we haven't been informed. We haven't been informed about the reasons the blacks are pushing now. What are the reasons the youth are saying, "I don't dig your style anymore"? We don't hear a Black Panther on a national show, and yet they are in the papers all the time.

Profit has become the sole motivating purpose in our country. In Sacramento we just saw a consumer protection bill that, by the time it was ready to be passed, it was a businessman's protection against the public. And it was nearly through before the public knew about it.

Mark Twain said in a piece called "The Czar's Soliloquy," "Our patriotism is medieval, outworn and obsolete....The modern patriotism, the true patriotism, the only rational patriotism, is loyalty to the nation *all* the time and to the government only when it deserves it."

He said in *A Connecticut Yankee in King Arthur's Court*, "My kind of loyalty was loyalty to one's country, not to its institutions or to its officeholders....Institutions are extraneous, they are its mere clothing, and clothing can wear out, become ragged....To be loyal to rags, to shout for rags, to worship rags, to die for rags—that is a loyalty of unreason....The citizen who thinks he sees that the commonwealth's political clothes are worn out, and yet holds his peace and does not agitate for a new suit, is disloyal; he is a traitor. That he may be the only one who sees this decay, does not excuse him; it is his duty to agitate anyway."

Even though a man has been silenced, that does not mean that he has been converted.

---

1. Tommy Smothers was paraphrasing slightly. Jefferson said, "Were it left for me to decide whether we should have a government without newspapers or newspapers without a government, I should not hesitate to prefer the latter."

November 14, 1970

Abba Eban

Minister of Foreign Affairs, Israel

Renowned for his eloquence (a *New Yorker* profile favorably compared his speaking abilities to Winston Churchill's), Abba Eban was a perennial favorite at The Commonwealth Club. With professorial knowledge and a long view of history, he developed a congenial if formal rapport with Club audiences, that of a welcome dinner guest able to broach sticky topics while maintaining a sense of reason and balance. (In 1970, appearing for a "Ladies Night" event, he ribbed The Club for having excluded women from the audiences on each of his previous appearances: "There is, after all," he said, "no need to exclude the more intelligent half of the human race from the opportunity to pass a gentle but objective judgment on a righteous cause.") Despite his reputation for brilliant oratory, Eban was reportedly nervous in public; one leg would twitch when he had to stand before an audience. And despite the warm reception international audiences gave him, he was not popular in Israel.

When he took to the podium in 1970 as Israel's foreign minister, a position he held from 1966 to 1974, it was his fourth appearance at The Commonwealth Club. He had previously been Israel's permanent representative to the UN and ambassador to the U.S., serving as a powerful spokesman for Israel with the West. This Club talk comes nearly midway between the

Six-Day War in 1967 and the Yom Kippur War of 1973. In the face of imminent attack from Egyptian forces in May 1967, Israel had attacked Egyptian air force planes on the ground and, in the war that followed, defeated Egypt, Syria, and Jordan and occupied the West Bank, Gaza Strip, and Sinai Peninsula—a territory three times Israel's original size. When the sirens sounded at noon on October 6, 1973—the Jewish Day of Atonement—it was because Egyptian forces had swept into the Sinai and Syrian troops had stormed the Golan Heights. The war would last three weeks, with Israeli forces eventually driving into Syria and Egypt before a cease-fire was brokered by U.S. Secretary of State Henry Kissinger.

Dubbed the father of Israeli diplomacy, Eban went on to negotiate the return of some territories that Israel had captured in the wars. At home, he argued against holding onto the Gaza Strip. And after Yasser Arafat rejected the 1978 Camp David accords, it was Eban who said Arafat "never misses an opportunity to miss an opportunity." Abba Eban died in November 2002.

"The Middle East: Its Past Agony and Its Future Hope"

It is always for me a source of deep contentment to be in the commonwealth of California. The common features of California and Israel go far beyond the benevolence of our climates. You, of course, are bigger, more numerous, almost as turbulent and restless in the rhythm of your lives. You have a similar nobility, a pioneering spirit, a creative genius, an instinct for freedom. All that I find wrong with you is that you have a disturbing practice of growing your own citrus fruit instead of buying ours. This, however, is not enough to place any barriers between us. Certainly nobody can come to discuss the problems of the Middle East without feeling the warm waves of kinship and understanding that flow to Israel from the United States.

We speak of a region which has had a determining influence on the thought and spirit of mankind. In the heart of that region, at the very center of its history and geography, there lives a small state called Israel. From Israel there have gone forth currents of influence which have flown into the stream of universal culture and have fashioned the lives and the ideas of the Mediterranean and, later, of the Atlantic world.

There is tension, there is peril in the Middle East for one single cause: Israel's right to statehood, sovereignty, nationhood, security, economic development have, for the whole twenty-two years of her existence, been violently assailed. There are many symptoms of the Middle Eastern crisis, but there is only one cause. The tension is not caused by territorial problems, or by a refugee problem, or by problems of navigation. These are the episodic symptoms of the basic disturbance. None of these problems would exist—or, if they existed, all of them would have been solved—were it not for the fundamental challenge to the concept of Israel as an organic part of the Middle East.

The alienation therefore exists, first of all, on the level of thought and emotion. It is an ideological conflict. The political and the military tensions flow from the refusal or the inability of Arab intellectual and political leadership so far to grasp the depth, the passion, the authenticity of Israel's roots in the region in which our nation was born and from which it sent out a radiant influence across the entire range of human history. The crux of the problem is whether, however reluctantly, Arab leadership, intellectual and political, comes to understand the existential character of the Middle East as an area which cannot be exhausted by Arab nationalism alone. Of course, the Arab nation has a large, even a predominant place in Middle Eastern life, but it has no monopoly. Not only must the modern world reach an equitable distribution of its material resources, it must also distribute nationhood and sovereignty with a sense of equity. In the Middle East these cannot be monopolized; they must be shared.

The scales of equity show the protagonists in this dramatic conflict in their true light: the Arab nation, in the era of its triumph, resplendent in fourteen sovereignties over an area of 4.5 million square miles, in which one hundred million Arabs live under their sovereign flags, replete with immeasurable resources of mineral wealth, endowed with a vast power of exercising influence on the scales of world strategy, a multiple representation in international organs. If Arab nationalism had a true understanding of its own achievement, it would be striding toward its future in a mood of confidence and buoyancy. Rarely in all history has any people achieved so large a measure of its ambition in so short a time. But turning its back upon this affirmative promise, Arab nationalism broods these twenty-two years with senseless rancor on the fact that another people has simultaneously achieved its national independence in an area one five-hundredth of their size, with a population one-fiftieth of theirs, with a parsimony of resources which mocks their pretensions to see us as a danger to their existence.

What is at issue now is not the self-determination of the Arab people, which is lavishly assured. Because of their fourteen states and their 4.5 million square miles, and their multiple sovereignty, the Arab states face Israel on the wrong side of the balance of equity. Israel is the only nation which stands or falls in history by the way in which this conflict is resolved, yet the basis of the Middle Eastern tension lies in this refusal to regard Israel as an organic part of the Middle East. We find ourselves the victims of a grotesque paradox and fantasy which regards the Middle East as an area in which Israel's existence is optional, or illegitimate, or inorganic, or external, or alien. Israel inorganic, alien to the Middle East, indeed.

There are 127 members of the organized international community, but there is one state and one alone which speaks the same tongue, upholds the same faith, inhabits the same land as it did three thousand years ago. There is no parallel in all the history of nationhood for the strength and the mystery of this continuity. So much for the Middle Eastern past. The Middle Eastern present is determined by an international structure which endows Israel for the past twenty-two years with a right of sovereign equality on the same level as that of any other state. There must be some axiom, there must be some starting point in any international discussion; and the existence of legitimate sovereignties is axiomatic. It is the starting point, it is not the destination, of any negotiating process.

This then is the posture with which Israel faces the world in the long and unending dialogue between the Jewish people and the rest of mankind. Israel's existence as a sovereign state is for us not something to be defended, or to be explained, or to be apologized for. It is something to be proclaimed as an inexorable part of historic reality, and those who plan the future without it are building their concepts on foundations of sand.

There are some governments which, in a benevolent spirit, offer to secure the consent of the Arab states to the recognition of our right to exist. It is sometimes my duty to say that we do not ask any recognition of our right to exist, because our right to exist is independent of any recognition of it. An international community which can accommodate 127 sovereign states from Afghanistan to Zambia in alphabetical order, from Fiji to Albania in chronological order, with dozens of statehoods, not all of which have such a sharp identity of spiritual and cultural individualism as Israel—such a world community can accommodate a state of Israel within a few thousand square miles and give to the Jewish people, after its long, tormented martyrdom, the opportunity to deploy its energies in creativity and in peace.

What would have happened if, twenty-five years after the new international order was established in this city of San Francisco in the absence of our people—if twenty-five years later we were to see a world community in which every nationhood and culture and political entity was represented, except for the eternal exception. The decision of our people in this generation is no longer to be the exception to the universal rule. We have ceased to be the passive victims of historic process and have become autonomous agents in fashioning our own destiny.

This violent challenge to our existence has erupted at many times in overt war. In 1948 an attempt was made to strangle the state of Israel at its birth. Nearly two decades later, circumstances came together which conspired to bring about a new attempt to cut Israel off from the roots of its security. Through a design mounted by the United Arab Republic with Soviet endorsement and support, we live today in the aftermath of the great traumatic and glorious memories of 1967, the unforgettable summer, the days that will never perish from our recollection.[1]

Nobody in Israel can forget that forty months ago, the prospect of our physical extinction was being seriously discussed across the world—in Arab capitals with wild exaltation of spirit, in other lands with genuine anguish but in total impotence of intervention. It is the sense of having stood upon the brink, of having passed from danger to salvation on a very narrow margin of vigilance; this is the haunting obsession which broods upon all Israel's life today; the knowledge that many things in our history are too strange to be believed, but nothing is too terrible to have happened.

The universal conscience was then aroused across the world, because at issue was not simply the fortunes of any state, but of a state whose name evokes the deepest spiritual memories of mankind—a state which is nothing, after all, but the last station, home, sanctuary of a people that had already lost six million of its sons in the greatest orgy of violence and hatred that had ever swept over any family of the human race. The consciousness that this, the vastest crime of modern history, might be compounded by the

1. The "United Arab Republic" at first designated a political union of Egypt and Syria, its capital in Cairo, from which Syria withdrew in 1961. Egypt continued to use the name until 1971.

murder of that state which was the remnant and the refuge of the most martyred of all peoples. This it was that created that high sense of moral drama which attended Israel's ordeal and Israel's emergence from it.

Now, from these memories, which are still vivid with us, we draw the central themes of our policy. Does anybody expect us to forget those memories? We brood upon them day and night. We live intimately with them. From them, we have taken this resolve: never, never again to put ourselves into a position of danger and fragility such as that from which we narrowly escaped. National suicide cannot be an international obligation. Experience exists in order that men may learn from it. Our task is not to reconstruct the old armistice corroded by hatred and weighed down by war, but rather to embark upon an exercise in innovation, to build a new order of relations in the Middle East, to unfold a story that has never been heard or told before, to be satisfied this time with nothing less than peace.

And it is against that background that, in our dialogue with ourselves and with the world, we try to define in simple terms what Israel will do, what Israel will not do, and what are the central purposes and interests of our national life.

We will not withdraw from the positions necessary for our security, except in the context of permanent peace. No withdrawal without peace. This is not a unilateral Israeli position. This is the law, the precedent, and the tradition of the nations. This is the policy which has the sanction of the main body of enlightened opinion. If we were to withdraw without peace, we should be doing something so irrational and unprecedented that it is extraordinary to hear it ever suggested at all. Even in international organs in which Israel has a permanent and vast numerical disadvantage, we have been able to defeat any idea that there can be withdrawal from the cease-fire lines, except in the context of a permanent peace; and in the context of that permanent peace there must be an attempt for the first time to define Israel's territorial structure.

We shall not renounce our right in the peace negotiation to determine secure boundaries, as distinct from cease-fire lines or armistice lines. There is no reason for us to be apologetic about the concept that there must be an element of territorial negotiation. It is not good enough to say "the old armistice lines," just as we do not say "the present cease-fire lines." The old armistice lines reflected a military situation in 1948. The present cease-fire lines reflect a military situation created in 1967. What must be done is to achieve a negotiated boundary in which the dignity and the interests of all the contiguous states are brought into harmony. This, after all, has always happened after wars.

Mr. Gromyko, in the speech that I had heard three weeks ago, took an attitude of territorial fundamentalism. Ah, but he took that attitude only about the Middle East. When he came to discuss the security system of Europe, he was full of lucid realism. Of course it was necessary after the Second World War not to reproduce the inflammatory situations which had caused the war. The Soviet Union even has its Golan Heights. It was arranged after the Second World War that it was impossible for Leningrad to be within thirty-eight miles of the "ferocious Finns," and therefore the Soviet Union claims secure and recognized boundaries. I suggest to you that our farmers in the Jordan Valley and Upper Galilee are in rather more imminent danger from Syrian guns than is Leningrad from the fury of the modern but pacific descendants of the Vikings.

Nobody suggests in central Europe that the Polish agony be reconstructed by a mutilation of the postwar boundary, or by the introduction into Poland of tens of thousands of Germans who had lived there for centuries, but whose reintroduction would break up the cohesion of the state and open it out to the kind of internal disruption which contributed so mightily to the tragedies of 1939. Therefore every precedent, every law is on our side when we say the boundaries have not yet been decided. They should not be dictated unilaterally, neither by Israel nor by the Arab states. Therefore the only course is to establish them by agreement within the peacemaking process. This concept of a territorial negotiation, upheld by Israel, by the United States, and by a majority of central-international opinion, marks the second of our principles: not to withdraw without peace, not to renounce the opportunity for negotiating secure and recognized boundaries. This does not mean that we have an encyclopedic attitude to all the territory now under our administration. Of course, we would withdraw armed forces from the cease-fire lines, but only to those boundaries which, taking account of our vital security, are determined in the peace negotiation—to boundaries which have not yet been determined, because the negotiation has not yet started.

A third thing that we will not do is to suffer such an inundation of our country as to change its basic vocation as the central expression of the civilization and the culture and the language of the Jewish people. If there can be a Swedish Sweden and a French France and an almost unlimited infinity of Arab states, then there can be an Israeli state in the Middle East—that is to say, a state whose central purpose is to reanimate, preserve the Hebrew culture and the levels which the Jewish people bestow upon our state in respect of its democracy, its parliamentary system, its social originality, its technological, intellectual, and scientific standards.

But no less important is to say what we shall do. We shall be ready to negotiate with each and any Arab state for the establishment of a permanent peace. Negotiation, of course, presupposes the concept of the sanctity of agreements. There is now an obstacle to the dialogue between Israel and the United Arab Republic, because that government, having signed an agreement for a cease-fire standstill, violated it the following day with the full support and endorsement of the Soviet Union. This raises issues more important than the military issue itself; it raises the transcendent question of the credibility to be attached to Egyptian signatures and to Soviet engagements. For Israel, the problem of the credibility of the Egyptian signature is the crucial issue, because if we negotiate, it will be with the object of reaching an agreement. Under that agreement, Israel would have to renounce something concrete and tangible: territory, not all of them, but much of them; there would have to be a heavy measure of territorial renunciation. What shall we get in return? An agreement, a signature, something intangible, something much more easily revocable. Therefore, the degree of trust and confidence to be ascribed to an Egyptian engagement is at the very heart of any negotiation.

On the broader level, the violation by the Soviet Union of a solemn engagement to the United States raises international issues which have an adverse effect across the whole range of international life, because if that engagement could be so easily repudiated, then what value can be attached to other engagements which either exist or are in negotiation concerning arms limitation, concerning the future of Europe, concerning Southeast Asia? It is a very grave event to have a Soviet engagement thus violated. That is why both Israel and the United States, from their respective vantage points—in our case a regional vantage point, in the American case a global vantage point—refuse to pass over in silence and acquiescence this violation. That is why we call for rectification of this violation, not only in order to restore a disturbance of the military balance, but, more fundamentally, in order to create that confidence in the validity of contracts which is the first law of international civility. But there is no such obstacle with Jordan.

We are ready to negotiate; we are ready to reach agreement. It is a central theme of Israel's policy that the Middle Eastern peace must be built by the Middle Eastern peoples and cannot be imposed upon them from outside. The days are past when a small hierarchy of great powers inflicted, or imposed, or bestowed upon smaller nations the conditions of their existence. Agreement and not an imposed solution. Of course the great powers, and especially the two greatest, exercise their influence upon the course and the flow of events, but it is certainly not possible for external jurisdiction to replace internal agreement.

Yes, we shall negotiate; we shall reach agreement. Yes, there will be a withdrawal of troops, but only to those boundaries that are determined in the peace negotiation. There are four or five neuralgic points which, if they are not treated differently from the past, will be the cradle of future wars. There is a difference in the prospect of peace between the situation with Israel in the Valley and Syrian troops on the Heights: that is a recipe, that is a prescription for war. Israel on the Heights and in the Valley: that is a prescription for peace.

Divided cities create wars; the natural condition of a city is unity. But of course the unity of Jerusalem is not incompatible with a special status for the holy places of Christendom and of Islam, in order that that which is truly universal in Jerusalem, beyond its secular jurisdiction, can be the subject of international agreements. We want not only secure boundaries but open boundaries such as those which exist in the European Community, boundaries which define jurisdiction and cultural identity but which are otherwise open to the free and mutual flow of commerce, men, and ideas. That is the modern concept of the boundary—it should be a bridge and not a barrier—and although boundaries must exist to define sovereignty and cultural identity, there should be in the Middle East, beyond a formal peace, a high measure of economic and social integration, especially across the whole of the former Palestine area; that is to say, in the relationship of Israel with its eastern neighbor.

Yes, we will contribute to a solution of the refugee problem. That problem was created by war; therefore it can be solved only by peace. It is the refusal to make peace which perpetuates that problem, which creates a vested and a deliberate interest in its perpetuation. But if there is a mutual desire for peace, this will be accompanied by a mutual desire to contribute, by regional cooperation and with international aid, to the solution of one of the easiest problems in their bulk which have ever existed—smaller than the refugee problems of Europe and of Africa, and of the Indian subcontinent. Those problems were solved because there was a desire by the states concerned to live in peace. This problem has been perpetuated as a consequence of a determination not to live in peace. It is not the case, as some of us used to say (I must say I used to say it), that a solution of the refugee problem will bring about peace. No. Peace will bring about a solution of the refugee problem. It is the context of interstate relations which creates the situation congenial to a solution of all the population problems of the area.

Yes, we are prepared for cooperation in economic development. The Middle Eastern states, Israel, and the Arab states, in twenty-two years have spent $20 billion on war. A small proportion of that sum would have been sufficient to solve all the population problems of the Middle East, and to open out for our area a new horizon of development.

These, then, are the things we will do: cease-fire, negotiation, agreement, the determination of agreed boundaries, withdrawal of forces to the boundaries when agreed, the construction of a community of Middle Eastern states, each secure in its separate sovereignty but united in a common devotion to the region in which both the Arab and the Israeli peoples took their birth, and from which they have written such radiant chapters in the story of civilization.

Now, beyond all of this, we strive to do something other than to survive: to be the working model of a free society. We are sometimes told that we only have one state of Israel against the Arab fourteen. That isn't quite true: there are two Israels. There is the Israel of reality and there is the Israel of the newspaper headlines. Unfortunately, only one of them has a vote in the United Nations. Now the Israel of the newspaper headlines is a very turbulent place in which everybody is preoccupied with hand grenades and bombs. But the Israel of reality, although the cares of security can never be far away, is also a society full of vital energies, pioneering zeal, enterprise, growth—growth of population, growth of industrial product, growth of agricultural profusion, growth in the scope and range of international contacts, growth in the number of technical development agreements that we have with sixty-five other nations with whom Israel is sharing its accumulated pioneering experience, growth in its cultural base, growth in the intensity of its scientific, intellectual, and technological penetration.

Our neighbors would have secured a great victory if they could so paralyze Israel and obsess it with the need for survival that we were doing nothing else. An Israel that was doing nothing except surviving would not be Israel in the deeper moral and historical sense. Israel is not Sparta; for three and a half years we have had to be a fighting nation; we have not become a warrior state. The central vocation of democracy, of freedom, of immigration, of economic development, and of international cooperation have gone forward without any decrease of momentum.

This is the spectacle that we would like to present to the world, of a nation whose impulse for growth triumphs even in conditions of siege. This is still a nation in which it is more important to build than to smash, more important to construct than to destroy. We may perhaps be old-fashioned and out of touch with the nihilistic currents in contemporary culture, perhaps because we are still living the rhapsodical age in our youthful and formative life.

All of this has relevance as well as deep fascination for all other peoples and especially for the people of the United States, which has accompanied the drama of Israel's emergence with fidelity and with constant interest. I do not claim that our policies are identical. There are no two free countries whose policies are identical. If you ever see two countries whose policies are identical, then one of them is in serious trouble. We are not satellites of each other, but there is a parallelism and a general harmony of interests. Americans understand, from their own historic consciousness, those processes of pioneering, immigration, creation of a new culture out of so many diverse and disbursed elements, the sense of enterprise, the affirmative vision of the scientific and the technological age. They also share with us devotion to the same set of moral principles which were first proclaimed on Israel's soil and later became the heritage of the Mediterranean and the Atlantic world.

Never has the harmony between our interests and our policies been as deep and close as it is today. We ask from American policy four things: to maintain the balance of strength, for if Israel is weak there will be no cease-fire and there will be no peace. There would not be a cease-fire today if the United States had not replenished our defenses in the past ninety days. If Cairo had had any impression that its own massive import of arms had been unaccompanied by a parallel reinforcement of Israel, of course they wouldn't have accepted the cease-fire; of course they will not extend it beyond the ninety days if they have any impression that they have achieved military superiority. That is the first objective, the balance of strength.

The second: deter the intervention of the other great power, of the Soviet Union. I believe that if the Soviet Union is aware that its active participation for the expansion of this conflict risks a global confrontation, it will recoil. This idea of preventing confrontation exists in American policy; we think it should be enunciated, illustrated, and developed with the utmost consistency.

Third, we ask that our efforts to maintain a common interest of the free world against such heavy pressures should not be at the price of our economic collapse. Therefore, noting that the United States makes prodigious efforts to enable other small countries to maintain their security without wrecking their economy, we hope for a similar consideration here. Israel makes no claim, actual or contingent, upon American manpower. That is what distinguishes the Middle East from Southeast Asia. Here in the Middle East you can defend a common interest without any risk of that vast involvement of your manpower which has had such poignant results in tragedy and sacrifice, and which has cast and created so heavy a scar across American society. Here, because of Israel's vigor and autonomous spirit, you can achieve the defense of the common interests of the free world with nothing but the supply of some hardware. Surely if that were your position in Southeast Asia and elsewhere, the sigh of relief that would go out across the United States would almost deafen our ears.

And fourthly: to support our right to the negotiation of a secure boundary and to use your influence for a renewal of the peace dialogue in conditions of mutual confidence. These are our four requests: the balance of power, the deterrence of Soviet intervention, the support of economic progress, and the promotion of negotiation in conditions of confidence. I believe that in making these proposals Israel becomes America's most undemanding ally, because all of these requests involve no burden upon the internal cohesion or the external security of the United States.

This, then, is the message that I bring these many thousands of miles from Jerusalem. And the Jerusalem of which I speak is a dual concept. Above the Jerusalem of bricks and mortar, of streets and cities, there is the ideal Jerusalem that lives forever in the hearts and hopes of men, symbol in every land and every age of man's unending quest for individual and social perfection. To the reconstruction of that ideal Jerusalem in our days, let us forever dedicate ourselves.

November 12, 1971

Ronald V. Dellums

Member, U.S. House of Representatives (D-CA)

Running for the U.S. House of Representatives in 1970 on an anti–Vietnam War platform, former Berkeley city councilman and "young radical in bell-bottoms" Ron Dellums was catapulted into the national spotlight when Vice President Spiro Agnew, in a speech at a fundraiser in Arkansas, called Dellums "an out-and-out radical" who should be "purged from the body politic." Dellums went on to win the race as well as spot number six on Richard Nixon's enemies list. Named to the House Armed Services Committee in 1973, he was not made to feel welcome: at his first meeting there were not enough seats, and he literally had to share his chair with Pat Schroeder. The Oakland native would later become chair of the committee and fight to curb defense spending, and he would lead the effort to impose sanctions on South Africa. He served in the House for twenty-seven years, until his retirement in 1998.

"A Radical Perspective on Life"

I told the officers that one way to pack a luncheon is to put the word "radical" in the title of the speech and you'll find that a great deal of people will come. I purposely used the term "radical" in the title of my speech because that's the way I have been labeled for several months. And I think, unfortunately, in this country we've been preoccupied with labeling people without ever placing in juxtaposition what we mean by that label. We rarely translate that label. We rarely define it. So I'd like to think that Ron Dellums is a complex human being who frankly can't be labeled in one term.

I choose to talk about the issue of life because I don't wish to stand before you as a traditional politician and give you a traditional political speech. I really don't define myself as a politician in the classic sense of the term. My speech may seem a little philosophical at some points, it may even seem a little metaphysical at points. But I think that you and I have got to find a way to talk about the serious human questions that confront us in this country and in the world.

There's something that we try not to think about, we try desperately to forget. It's the fact that all of us gathered in this room, at some point, are going to die. It's something we—obviously—fight against. But you and I are going to die, because death is inevitable. And I thought about that: if all of us at some point are going to die and if death is, in fact, inevitable, then perhaps the most courageous act that man can engage in is not the act of dying. But the most courageous act is to engage in the struggle to live, and man's most courageous act, most noble challenge, is the challenge of life and enhancing the quality of life. Well, what are the factors that stand in the way of our ability to come together as human beings? Because I'm unalterably committed to the notion that man's most powerful force is not his ability to build and drop the bomb, but in his total and absolute unity. Anything short of total unity of human beings in this country and on the face of this earth is divisive. Absolute unity is our greatest strength, our greatest power, not our ability to build bombs. But what stands in the way of us coming together as people, what stands in the way of our ability to achieve the glory of life as opposed to the agony of and the preoccupation with death? What stands in the way of our ability to achieve the serenity of peace as opposed to the horror of violence? Or the comfort of plenty, as opposed to the pain of poverty? Or the strength of total unity and freedom and justice as opposed to the divisiveness of racism and discrimination? And these are the human questions that I think you and I have got to deal with. Because if you agree with me that man's most courageous act is his ability to engage in the struggle to live and in the battle of life, then that means that we've got to struggle against those evils that pit us against each other. Black against white, young against old, man against woman, Jew against gentile.

So let's look at some of the factors. Scientists over the past few years have been predicting, with great regularity, that if we continue to destroy our environment at the rate in which we are, that we may not be able to sustain life on the face of this earth ten years, twenty years from now. Well, these are scientists, not demagogues. These are scientists engaged in intellectual discourse and not rhetoric. And if the scientists' predictions are true, and that is that, perhaps the curtain is falling on Act III of the big show, namely human life on the face of the earth, then isn't it absurd for us to continue to engage in the rhetoric of who's a nigger and who's a honkie, who's a Communist, who's non-Communist? Who's the poor and who's the non-poor? Who's the welfare recipient, who's the non-welfare recipient? Who's the responsible and who's the irresponsible? But we've allowed ourselves to be put into that kind of divisiveness.

If, in fact, the world is in desperate shape, if it is true that 40 percent of oxygen-producing organisms in the ocean have already died, if it is in fact true that species are dying, if it is true that we are endangered in this country and in the world because of our exploitation of the environment and the ecology, then it seems to me that it's in the best interest of all of us in this country and in the world to come together as a family of nations to deal with our self-interest, our common self-interest, survival of mankind on the planet Earth. But rather than move aggressively to achieve a sense of peace and cooperation in the world, what have we done? Let's look for a moment at our approach to foreign aid.

It has been suggested many years ago that we commit 1 percent of our gross national product to humanitarian aid in the world. Yet we find politicians in the Congress and the Senate opposed to spending $9 billion to achieve some sense of humanity in those nations who are less fortunate than us. Because maybe it's not expedient to take that position in terms of one's ability to face the electorate and indicate clearly that you've cut back taxes. But we will spend thirty and forty billion dollars a year waging war and death and destruction in Indochina. We can continue to have a Defense Department budget of over $60 billion a year, but we can't afford $9 billion to find some way of coming together as a family of nations in the world. We can't find it within ourselves to project ourselves as a nation preoccupied with the issue of peace, because the common self-interest is survival of the man and we'd better start dealing with the desperate straits that the world is in, in terms of our ability to survive as people.

Some of us rally to the position that we should cut back on all of our foreign aid. We should stop all of our commitments to multilateral agencies. We want now to be advocates of isolationism, which, in my estimation, would be a very dangerous posture if this country chose to pursue that course. Just the other day—while at one level we talk about peace and freedom and justice and humanity, self-determination and democracy as our basis for our commitment in Vietnam—on the floor of the House two days ago, we voted to end the embargo against Rhodesian chrome. We now have joined South Africa and Portugal as the only two nations in the world who have blatantly violated the UN sanctions against Rhodesia, our international obligation. It could not be an issue of need; we have 4.45 million tons of high-grade chrome. The present administration already has a bill on the Senate side that asks that we unload 1.3 million tons of chrome as excess stockpile. So that decision can only be defined as a victory for the forces of racism and reaction in the world.

We can't play it both ways. South Africa, unfortunately, does not see people of color as human beings able to move in freedom and justice across their land. We all live in a nation of democracy committed to peace, committed to freedom, but we have made no statement about the fact that many major corporations are involved in economic support of South Africa. And we see no contradiction in that position, but I do. It stands in the way of our ability to achieve the kind of world that we're all concerned about.

We continue to use military appropriations as our major commitment in foreign aid, as opposed to humanitarian aid to nations who desperately need the help. We continue to be involved as a nation concerned about war and death and destruction. Let's think for just a moment. Why is it that us old folks, for the most part, don't engage in war? You ever thought about that? Because those of us who have been on the face of this earth long enough, most of us, love life so desperately that we choose not to risk it, but we'll send the children. Many of us say, "I can't go fight in Vietnam, but I think it's a just war because I have a job, but send the children. I have a business, but send the children. I have family commitments, but send the children. I have a concern in this community, but send the children." And when the children of America have asked us, "Why should we go fight and die?" we don't answer them with specifics, we answer them in abstractions. We say, "Son, you're fighting for democracy." "What does that mean?" "I don't know, but it's good. Go fight and die."

And when they come back from war, what has changed? Why did they go give up their lives? Some of them with their arms, legs blown away, bodies crippled. Some of them would never return, and we'd never answer those questions. Now that I'm in Washington, I can go to the Arlington cemetery when my family or friends come back, and I have to take them on the tour, you know. You can ride a bus around the Arlington cemetery, and a very attractive young stewardess sitting in the front of the trolley says, "By 1980, all of the graves in Arlington cemetery will be filled." And nobody ever says why. Nobody ever says for what reason. No one ever says for what purpose do we send the children to fight and die in insane adventurisms throughout the world.

Many of us have become pompous in our commitment to death and destruction, but I would suggest something to you that many of you in the room may disagree with. We have not engaged in war as a nation out of compassion; we've done it out of fear. We look back to the Second World War and we say, we stood up in a humanitarian, compassionate effort. But why did six million Jewish people have to die before we became involved in that struggle, if we were so compassionate and so humanitarian? We engaged in that war at the point where we saw the fear to ourselves; engaged in the war in Indochina because of fear, communism—major bugaboo. That is a very simplistic view of the world. We can't continue to shape America's foreign policy on the basis of who the black hats and the white hats are; who the good guys and the bad guys are. The world is much too complex for that.

May 6, 1972

Shirley Chisholm

Member, U.S. House of Representatives (D-NY); 1972 Candidate for Democratic Presidential Nomination

When Shirley Chisholm took the stage at a Baptist church in Bedford-Stuyvesant to announce her bid for the Democratic Party nomination for president, nobody—including Chisholm—thought she had a chance to win. Elected to the House of Representatives in 1968, she became the first black woman to make a bid for a major party candidacy, though she was not officially endorsed by most black politicians or women's rights organizations. Her goal? "Repudiate the ridiculous notion that the American people will not vote for a qualified candidate simply because he is not white or because she is not a male." The media remarked on her fieriness ("only ninety-eight pounds...but no weakling" and "no shrinking Shirley") and noted that she was set on using her campaign to wield influence at the Democratic Party convention. Just before Chisholm spoke at The Club, she had garnered 4 percent of the Democratic primary vote in Florida—an election won by former Alabama Governor George Wallace. Chisholm would serve in the House for another decade.

"Democratic Party Presidential Candidate Speaks"

I want to say to you that we can't do anything about the problems confronting us here at home until we are able to end that atrocious war which takes seventy cents out of every dollar that we pay into the federal treasury. Part of the reason for the disquietude, the anxiety, and the concerns of the American people have to do with the fact that their tax dollars that are being paid into the federal treasury are not being returned to them in terms of what it is that they should get out of this government—which is their government, and which is supposedly government of the people, by the people, and for the people.

We heard much in the 1968 campaign of the Nixon promises of jobs and training for black Americans, and of his firm support for black capitalism. One look at the record and at the ghettos of America's cities shows the utter emptiness of these campaign promises. The only action by the administration to promote black capitalism was the creation of an office of Minority Business Enterprise in the Commerce Department, an office with no authority to make loans or to fund or supervise the programs. One after another, the helpless officials of this program have, not surprisingly, been forced to quit the program. The administration having virtually destroyed any hope for improvement in the miserable economic position of the poor of this country—Congress acted. It passed the law to provide hundreds of thousands of immediate jobs to the unemployed, and the president vetoed it. Congress passed a bill providing day care centers for children whose mothers could then join the workforce and get the kind of training and skills that are necessary to cope in a very highly automated society— because, after all, haven't many Americans been saying, "What are we going to do with the bums and the lazy people on welfare?" Well, we're here to tell you that they don't want welfare, and many of them have been on public assistance because of the presence in this country of an economy, and of a system, that's relegated thousands of poor people to second-class citizenship status, and people who never had the opportunity to really realize that this American dream everybody talks about is really meaningful to them. People don't want welfare, believe it or not, even poor people. They have pride, they have dignity, but if by virtue of a society that has inherent racism they have not had the same kind of equality of opportunity through the years, of course they're caught in a situation. We're in a highly automated society; they need training, they need skills, and they don't have it, because the unions won't even open up to let them in for apprentice and journeyman training programs. So we have to stop scapegoating and generalizing about people and say that the Republic is in trouble. It hasn't always treated everybody well.

The administration then turned around and, showing where its real interest lay, acted to give billions of dollars of tax relief to business via the 10-percent investment credit, on top of its $4 billion-a-year depreciation reform. So this incredible story ends. If the chairman of the board of General Motors, earning a salary of three-quarters of a million dollars in 1971 at the same time that the unemployed in Seattle have so little to eat that Japan feels obligated to ship some food over here to help them survive, gosh....

More and more thoughtful Americans, including a growing number of businessmen, have been shocked to learn of the economic inequality and exploitation which is destroying the very fabric of American society. They have come to realize that this a government of, by, and for big business. The Nixon cabinet and other top officials in the administration represent one of the greatest concentrations of individual wealth in the world. For the past one year I've been studying this—and someday we'll be able to really see what I've come up with—and as such, they predictably resisted for so long the use of the powers of the presidency in curbing the inflationary pressures that have been destroying the value of the American dollar. The economic philosophy of the administration is based on the principle that the business of America is business, and this being the case, the economic reality for the inexperienced and the untrained black man and the Indian and the Chicanos and the poor will have to continue to be the last hired and the first fired. This is an administration which ignored the social and psychological cost of its policies to the common man. It is an empty shell, the tool of slick advertising techniques, the prisoner of narrow political allegiances, and the faithful servant of those privileged and selfish economic interests which systematically blocked every attempt to narrow the gap between the rich and the poor in this country.

Rebuilding and revitalizing this society after four traumatic years depends more than anything else on meaningful changes in our economic priorities, and this the Nixon Administration, by its very nature, can really never accept. A government so heavily dependent on a small fleet of corporate millionaires, industrial polluters, and privileged power brokers can never be seriously expected to concern itself with the day-to-day problems of the poor, the working man, the unemployed, the black, the young, or the elderly pensioner.

I believe that the future of our great society depends upon ending of government by the conservative, repressive, and selfish. It depends upon the ending of economic exploitation of the common man, both black and white, by those privileged powers which now rule in Washington. Of course, for people who have not really known what it is to be poor or for people who do not really understand the significance of the rumblings of the veritable social revolution that is going through this country, it is impossible for you to understand the outrage, the outrage of people who are saying that they're sick and tired of tokenism. They're sick and tired of see-how-far-you've-comeism. But they want their just share of that dream and that pride that everybody talks about.

If you've traveled in this country you've seen how the Indians are living. Do you know that this country belongs to the Indians? And to see how these people are living and to realize that the latest Department of Labor statistics indicate quite clearly that close to 70 percent of these people do not live to see the age of forty—you could never come back here in this room and feel the same when you visit the reservations and see what is happening to these people. You go into the Appalachia region of the country, this most affluent society, and see the numbers, the numbers of poor whites. And I have visited with them. They haven't seen politicians in fifty years, and many of them are a little bit surprised when they see me, because what am I doing, a black woman, coming into a poor white community? And I've said to them, "I'm concerned about your humanity. Of course you're not going to see politicians, haven't you read the message? You're not important, you're poor." You'll see them every four years when it's time for votes. But to go into those areas and to see how those people are living in West Virginia and the hills of Kentucky—no floors, dirt. You walk into their place, it's dirt. No modern sanitary plumbing facilities; you have to go out in the back. America, this land of the free and the home of the brave. And to see how we can send so many care packages abroad. We have a sense, a deep sense of our moral obligation to people who are less fortunate than we are, and thank God that we're able to extend a helping hand. But have you thought recently of sending care packages to America's children in the hinterlands of this country? And so I say that the time has come in America when those of us who by dint of economic security, financial stability, have a responsibility, a gut commitment if you will, to help this country to readdress itself to the priorities of human beings first of all, particularly the human beings who are in need of so much help, particularly the helpless and the powerless. The time has come in America when we must recognize that vacuums in this society are being filled all over America by white extremists and by black extremists, and this should be a clear indication to all of us that you are not assuming your correct role of leadership because you're so contented, perhaps, in your own little world that you don't even recognize that those who have been relatively helpless and/or powerless are taking over completely, because they can't depend on you any longer to give a sense of direction and take them by the hand and say "come along, we will help."

The Republic is in deep trouble. We just put $225 billion the other day into a space program. Where are we going? And in cities of this country—to realize that so many thousands of Americans take two to three hours daily to go to work from their places of residence back home again, the whole day? That money should be utilized for the development of massive transportation facilities. What are we building, going up there for, when right here on Earth our people can't even get transportation to go to work? What madness are we on? And to watch how people have to get up at four o'clock in the morning in many areas of this country to get to work to a job that starts at seven a.m. There's no reason for that. Our priorities are all mixed up, ladies and gentlemen. This is why we need some people now with common sense. We need people who are not merely academicians and theoreticians and bureaucrats, drawing up blueprints for change in this country when these people have absolutely no attunement or sensitivity to the kinds of programs and projects that are necessary to help America. I'm not talking about black people. At least black people are just asking for *in* because they've been left *out*. But a lot of your own folks are saying, "What is wrong that government is not addressing itself to the needs of the American people?" And I just hope that we will begin to realize what is really happening to all of us at this hour in America.

The time has come when we can be no longer the passive recipients of whatever the politics or the morals of a nation may decree for us as a people. But if you have the courage of our convictions and if we believe in the Judeo-Christian doctrine, and if you believe just simply in man's humanity to man, if you believe that it is time to really save America's children, then a lot of us will go home and reassess our own commitments and our own priorities and move in a different sense of direction to help to save our country. The challenge is here for all of us: will we merely continue just to use the powerless and the helpless as scapegoats, or using generalizations against them or about them? Or will we now take the bull by the horns and say that we have failed in certain areas but we will come together and make the American dream, at least in this generation, become some kind of reality for lots of folks?

November 17, 1972

Katharine Graham

President, The Washington Post Company; Publisher,
The Washington Post

On June 18, 1972, the *Washington Post* carried a story by staff writer Alfred E. Lewis under the headline "5 Held in Plot to Bug Democrats' Office Here." Among those listed as contributing writers were Bob Woodward and Carl Bernstein, who wrote a story, published the next day, revealing that James W. McCord Jr., the salaried security coordinator for President Nixon's reelection committee (CREEP), was among those arrested for the break-in. Thus began the *Post*'s coverage of Watergate. In October, the *Post* revealed that FBI agents had "established that the Watergate bugging incident stemmed from a massive campaign of political spying and sabotage conducted on behalf of President Nixon's reelection." That election was achieved by a landslide in November 1972, just a week before Katharine Graham spoke at The Club.

Not long before, under her leadership as the paper's publisher and head of The Washington Post Company, the *Post* had published the Pentagon Papers. Along with the Watergate stories, these established the *Post*'s reputation for hard-hitting investigations—and brought accusations that the *Post* was gunning for the Nixon Administration.

"Fairness and Freedom of the Press"

To be in San Francisco today and to have an opportunity to talk to this very distinguished group about the news business gives me particular pleasure, for two reasons. First, it's always a joy to come to this lovely city, and second, it's also something of a joy at this moment to get out of Washington, if only for a few days.

It's not that I do not love the city and the community that I live and work in, but as some of you may know, a certain tension, which we hope and trust will be short-lived, has developed between the *Washington Post* and the administration over our coverage of the so-called Watergate affair. The *Washington Post* was central to the pursuit and public disclosure of most of what we now know about the story. And although the administration has not chosen to recognize this achievement with a silver trophy or even a parchment scroll, it has offered recognition of sorts, in a spate of public attacks on the *Post* itself and on some of its individual employees. Taking this kind of heat is, by no means, an unprecedented experience for those of us in our profession. Still, it is nice to get out of the kitchen every once in a while.

If it makes me a liberated woman, so be it. A certain degree of heat is, of course, a natural and expected part of our business. Our company publishes a daily newspaper, the *Post*, and a weekly magazine, *Newsweek*, and it operates three television stations and two radio stations. When you're that much exposed to the critical judgments of that many customers with a brand-new product every day, one that is different by definition from yesterday's product, the grievance rate is necessarily going to be high. It may be measured in somewhat the same way as the statistics on the number of babies being born every day in the world. Somewhere, at any given moment, it seems inevitable that somebody or something arising out of the operations of The Washington Post-Newsweek Company is probably giving someone offense. I hope pleasure, too, and information.

The controversy that has grown up out of the Watergate affair, however, is of a different order from the sort of customer complaint that all of us in business receive on a regular basis. What we're now experiencing is something more than an automobile buyer's gripe about a folding catch on the glove compartment. The administration is claiming defects in our coverage of the Watergate case which some of its members seem to believe are grounds for wholesale, and some might say permanent, recall. We do not, for some reason, agree with this judgment. But that's not why I bring the subject up, or why I'd like to discuss it with you today. The performance of the reporters and editors on the Watergate story speaks for itself. And in our judgment it speaks well for American journalism.

That said, what I'd like to talk about today is the Watergate affair, in terms of what it tells us about the state of relations between the news media on the one hand and the reading or viewing public, in the larger sense of the word, on the other. I have in mind those readers who are not in government as well as those who are; in others words, I want to discuss something of fundamental concern for us all. For what it really comes down to is nothing less than the state of the First Amendment; our freedom to gather the news and to publish it, and your freedom to read it.

This is what we believe to be at stake in much of the controversy swirling around the press just now. And we find disturbing confirmation for this concern in a number of actions taken and tendencies shown by government at all levels and in all branches. These include such disparate-seeming activities as efforts to shake confidence in the purveyors of those news reports government does not like, and the singular effort in the case of the Pentagon Papers to restrain in advance the publication of the news. They also include efforts to challenge the claims of the press to the right to protect confidential sources, and to refuse to disclose confidential information, even under court order. This last right is important enough to our profession that reporters are willing to go to jail to uphold it, and, as you all know, have in the recent past.

You may well be asking by now how the Watergate case fits in with all this. And the best way for me to answer that question is to recapitulate the essence of the Watergate affair, both the *Post* coverage of it and the government's response, and to talk a little about the questions both raise concerning the responsibilities as well as the rights of the press.

The charge that's been leveled against the *Washington Post* is that we have written extensively about the Watergate case out of a deep-down desire to damage the Nixon Administration, on the one hand, and to elect Senator McGovern president, on the other. On at least four occasions, surrogates for the administration made this charge in remarkably similar language prior to the election. And just last weekend, still another White House official reopened the argument, alleging that our handling of the Watergate story has been a tragedy and that the net impact was probably to erode public confidence in the institutions of government. He went on to share his worry that it also eroded the confidence of a lot of fair-minded persons in the objective reporting of the *Washington Post*. While the official in question did not say which troubled him the most, his concern over public confidence in the *Post* struck us as not so much perhaps a worry as a hope.

This is not a charge we can afford to take lightly, because it goes straight to the central issue of fairness and objectivity as distinct from bias in the reporting of news. These are familiar words. We were encountering them and dealing with them long before Vice President Agnew began his long campaign against the so-called elitist press. And we were encountering them, let me assure you, from all shades of the political spectrum—from left and right, from establishment and dissenter. I do not myself subscribe to the view held by some in journalism that engaging the wrath of both sides in a dispute means, as the saying goes, that we must be doing some-thing right. On the contrary, it seems to me that one must not discount the possibility that we are doing everything wrong. I introduce the point only as evidence of a general and widespread discontent with the media at this time in history, and to suggest that our acknowledged failings do not begin to account for it entirely. Rather it seems to me to be connected with a larg-er dissatisfaction and restlessness on the part of the public concerning its institutions as a whole. And to some extent I think it also proceeds from our role as the bearer of much bad news, news of the foment and disorder of the sixties, for example, which though not of our making, was ours to report; ours to leave on the doorstep every morning, and ours to bring into the living room at night.

We at the Post Company are aware of a general crisis of confidence within the public concerning the news media. We are, I hope, also aware of the enormous obligations we have in attempting to deal fairly and responsibly with such sensitive if different events as a Watergate burglary or an unruly demonstration or march. We are aware that it is a danger of abusing our large and particular power in our news coverage and display, of overplaying and thus distorting the meaning of any given event. But I would suggest to you that these are much more difficult and potentially dangerous problems than our critics themselves seem to understand. For what our critics of whatever persuasion are often talking about when they speak of bias or lack of objectivity is merely something a newspaper or magazine publishes or a television station airs which does not serve their particular purposes at a given time. Thus, to this administration we are fundamentally liberal and anti-administration. And this supposedly is why we cover the news in the general way we do, and also why we covered the Watergate story in particular the way we did.

There is a much simpler explanation. We covered it in depth because it was major news, an important story from a national standpoint, as well as from the standpoint of our own community. It would've been an equally important story and we would've given it the same treatment regardless of which party was in power or who was running for election.

Now what exactly did happen? We were initially confronted with a highly unusual burglary, a burglary of the headquarters of a national political party, not for money, but for the purposes of bugging and tapping, and stealing documents. It was obviously a police reporter's story, and the editors put two of our best police reporters on it. Despite the strong initial denials of the Democrats' natural antagonists, the Republican Party and the president's reelection committee, that they were in any way connected with the burglary, strong connections were soon demonstrated. One of the arrested men was security coordinator of both the Republican National Committee and the Committee for the Reelection of the President. Another man soon connected with the case, and subsequently indicted, was a White House consultant. Once those links had been established in the face of categorical denials, journalistic professionalism and responsibility dictated that every possible lead be tracked down and checked out. As they went about their checking, our reporters turned up a number of extraordinary and entirely legitimate news stories. They found, for example, that a $25,000 check intended for the president's campaign had wound up in the bank account of one of the men arrested at the Democratic Watergate headquarters. They also learned that an additional $89,000 in the same suspect's bank account had not only been intended for the president's reelection effort, but also been filtered through a Mexican bank to mask its origins. The pursuit of the leads also uncovered a network of political espionage and sabotage efforts directed at the Democrats. Finally, the reporters and other investigators turned up the fact that the sabotage operation was financed from a cash fund kept in the safe of the finance director of the president's campaign committee. I submit to you that these stories uncovered by our reporters and those working for other publications, far from being politically partisan, were in the highest traditions of American journalism. Once on their trail, our reporters had no choice but to pursue them. To have done otherwise would have been gross negligence. In part because this happened in Washington, where we have a large and skilled staff of reporters, the *Post* got out ahead on this story. But we were not alone in the developing interest in it.

Now, as usually happens in an investigative story of this kind, we did have to rely on anonymous sources. Much of what we reported could not be stated categorically as fact, and in a totally conclusive way. Because our informants were people intimately involved on one side or the other of the case, to have revealed their names would've been to risk their jobs and their careers. It would equally have been to eliminate their willingness to provide information, to have dried them up as news sources. However, a responsible paper can and does check one source against another. In all its reporting, the *Post* used three and sometimes four or more checks, and the work of the two main reporters was carefully rechecked by three or four separate editors. Time will tell how accurate our reporting has been.

There are three pending court cases growing out of the Watergate affair, and there will almost certainly be congressional investigations by committees with subpoena power. Sooner or later we confidently expect that the sum and substance of our reporting will be confirmed and expanded upon, if all the facts are allowed to be brought out. It is nonsense to suggest that we could or would have pursued this story with as much intensity as we have done out of some partisan motive and with nothing substantial to go on. To have done that would have been to gamble a reputation and fortunes of the *Washington Post* in an incredibly reckless manner for the essentially elusive and, given the circumstances, forlorn political purpose of electing George McGovern. Yet that is precisely what some members of the administration are contending we did.

Rather than respond on the merits to the disclosures that have appeared in the *Post*, they have by and large given us unambiguous and unsubstantiated denials, and beyond that a continuing effort to discredit not the reports themselves directly, but the bearers of the reports, on the theory presumably that by doing this the reports themselves would be disbelieved. Ironically enough, while accusing the *Washington Post* of reliance on anonymous sources, the administration itself has cited equally anonymous sources in an effort to impute ulterior motives to us. Based on these nameless sources—for instance, the suggestion has been made that out of some personal and, let me add, nonexistent hatred of the president, I personally ordered a campaign against the Nixon Administration in an effort to elect Senator McGovern, with whom I and others on the *Post* are alleged to have a curious, and I quote, "social and cultural and ideological affinity."

There are several things to be said about all this. And the first is that it's untrue. I have to interject that I met Senator Dole on the plane coming out here. I'd never met him before, and he is the one who happened to make that last charge, on *Face the Nation*, and he came bounding across the aisle and said, "Hello, Mrs. Graham, I'm Senator Dole." And I said, "Oh, hello." And then I said, "Hey, I didn't say that. And if I did say it, if I had said anything that foolish, it would have no bearing whatsoever on our editors or reporters, because they don't, it doesn't work like that." And he said, "Well, it was a tough campaign."

But next and almost of equal relevance, it seems to me, is that it suggests an extraordinary innocence about the way a big newspaper or a news magazine functions, and as I told him, about the way news is gathered. And because it ignores so much of the reality of these processes, it also entirely misses the real problem any news operation faces in its efforts each and every day to catch and set down the essence of fast-moving and only really dimly foreseeable events.

By way of explaining how it actually works, let me begin by saying that the *Post* city room numbers close to four hundred. *Newsweek* has a comparable workforce and so, in a lesser way, do the newsrooms of the Post television and radio stations. They deal altogether on a daily basis or a weekly basis with millions of words having to do with literally scores of news stories. In the case of the print media, the problem is one of compressing an enormous body of material into strictly limited space.

In the case of radio and television, it is a problem of compression to meet the limitations of time. There is no way to calculate the number of individual daily judgments that have to be made by reporters in deciding what phrase or sentence to quote from a Supreme Court ruling or an action by a local school board, and by layers of editors and copy readers in deciding what importance to give which story: how much to cut out of this, how much expand that, and how prominently to display each and every one. But it should be self-evident the decision making on this comprehensive and detailed scale is beyond the effective daily control of any one individual, whether owner or publisher or editor. Nor are the people that work on *Post-Newsweek* news operations indoctrinated in a party line. For one thing, we have none. For another, and more importantly, it is our conviction that sound journalism requires a sound professional basis. For when management allows business judgments or personal predispositions to influence the character of the news, it seems to me indisputable that both the public interest and our own professional excellence are substantially undermined.

Finally, even if all this were not true, it has been our experience that good editors and good reporters, the kind of staff on which we insist and on which we depend, are not people who would submit to any such partisan and discreditable dictation. This is not to say that people in the news business are not human beings, subject to their own individual predilections and idiosyncrasies and preconceptions, and yes, obviously, prejudices at times, but it is to say that no common overriding bias determines the end product. As for the notion that some uniform ideological affinity for Senator McGovern explains our handling of the Watergate case, I'd simply call your attention to some of the things we said about the senator's campaign. In one editorial toward the end of the campaign we observed, "It will come as no surprise to those who have been reading our commentary on the candidates in this election so far, that we have our profound misgivings about Senator McGovern's grasp of the essential techniques of political leadership." At another point, "While his emphasis on urgent domestic needs may be admirable, the resultant foreign policy could well involve a considerable element of risk." And on Vietnam we said that Senator McGovern had created a new moral problem, "in the crippling blow he would have this country deal itself and the Vietnamese ally, as it made its way abruptly out of what it had originally proclaimed to be an ennobling enterprise."

And finally, "it can be argued, issue by issue and in a conventionally compelling way, that the burden of proof, in the case for change, is upon the man who would supplant a sitting president—and that George McGovern has failed to meet that burden convincingly." Not much affinity, cultural or otherwise, there. We do not pretend that this answers the question of unfairness or a lack of objectivity. These weaknesses are always a threat. But we try to guard against them in a number of ways. We've expanded reader access to our pages by doubling the space available for letters to the editors. We take pains to publish retractions and corrections. We recently embarked on an effort to give the people in our community a greater opportunity to register their grievances face-to-face with our editors in a series of luncheon meetings in the surrounding counties of Maryland and Virginia and in the District of Columbia itself. We've been publishing, in editorials and in signed columns on our editorial pages, criticism of the news media in general and of the *Post*'s own operations in particular. We have created an official ombudsman with the rank of assistant managing editor to conduct a continuing day-to-day monitoring of our performance, and to deal with specific complaints from readers. Some indication of the seriousness and severity with which this self-criticism has been leveled upon us is to be seen in the fact that we have had to limit this assignment to one year, largely for the protection of the ombudsman.

I should say that both the stations and *Newsweek* are trying to introduce disparate voices and self-criticism, too. It's not only limited to the *Post*, but I'm talking about the *Post* and the specific connection with Watergate. We would not claim perfection, but we would make the case of our own experience that something that might be called "reader bias" often exists and must also be taken into account. By that I mean that unfairness is often in the eyes of the beholder, especially when he feels some particular interest of his own has been adversely affected by what others would term a neutral news report. We are in the business, after all, of describing people and their activities and their causes and conflicts. And it is a simple fact that people do not like to be described by others. The snapshot never looks quite the way you suppose yourself to look to others. It leaves this or that out of focus or out of the picture altogether. It highlights something else that isn't too flattering. It's not, in short, the way you would choose to describe yourself. It can't be. And that's why we so often hear somebody— and I've done it, we've all done it—say, "Well, you know, that can't be fair, because I was there, and that's not the way it was."

Thus we had Vice President Agnew in recent years assailing the press at a time when he thought the press was being unfair to the president. But in 1972, at a time when an overwhelming majority of American newspapers had endorsed President Nixon for reelection and most papers were assiduously reporting imperfections and incompetency in the McGovern campaign, the Agnew crusade against the media suddenly stopped. It is significant in the same sense that when William Safire, White House speechwriter, and Frank Mankiewicz, the political director of the McGovern campaign, were asked on an NBC panel show during a campaign whether news coverage on the election had been fair, it was Mr. Safire who said Yes and Mr. Mankiewicz who said No.

In the eyes of Mr. Agnew, we remained radic-libs. In the eyes of Mr. Mankiewicz, as he wrote on our editorial page a few weeks ago, the *Washington Post* editorial page is "a citadel of Conservative Chic." Bias, one discovers after a time in this business, must be very much in the eye of the beholder.

Nothing may better illustrate this point than a really tough experience we had in reporting the shocking attack on Governor Wallace by a would-be assassin at a political rally in a Maryland shopping center just outside of Washington. The assault was a personal tragedy. It was also an event of great political significance. It took place, by happenstance, in our working territory. Our reporters knew the police and the hospitals and the general lay of the land. Thus, as with the Watergate affair, we were able to report before others did the hard and unhappy news that Governor Wallace had been wounded so severely that he would probably be permanently para-lyzed, a development clearly of enormous political significance to the cam-paign. We took no pleasure in reporting it. The Wallace camp understand-ably took still less pleasure in our having done so. And so our news reports on the governor's medical condition were ascribed to our disagreement with Governor Wallace's political views. Subsequently, however, these reports were borne out. And as we have every reason to believe, our report-ing on the Watergate case will also be confirmed. The common denomina-tor of both cases was that we were reporting something that somebody didn't want to hear. And so the first response on the part of many people was to suspect an ulterior motive on our part for having reported it. This is not a new phenomenon among readers, and the encouragement of such suspicions is not a new phenomenon on the part of government.

Those of us who have been around through many administrations know that the Nixon Administration did not invent governmental impa-tience with the press and does not have a corner on it now. There has been, however, a good deal of evidence of an intensified campaign to undermine public confidence—not just in the *Washington Post*, but in those segments of the news media which are thought to be hostile to the administration—to inhibit the functioning of the press, to sport with something that responsible public officials ought to be the first to uphold: the free flow of communications between the government and the governed.

To this chorus I would add the administration's support of efforts on the part of state and federal attorneys to entangle professional newsmen in the law enforcement process by summoning them before grand juries and asking them to reveal confidential sources and information obtained in confidence. This is a new trend. It started only about two years ago and culminated with the government's successful argument in the so-called *Caldwell* case before the Supreme Court. In that case, a newspaperman's right to respect confidences was judged to be less important than the state's right to information upon which indictments could be brought against accused criminals. While respecting the Supreme Court's judgment, our own view is that confidentiality is the essence of news gathering. We could hardly operate entirely on the basis of information provided by sources who are prepared to have themselves publicly identified. And neither, we would add, could the government, for this business of anonymous attribution is used by both sides. That is to say that it is used in the dissemination as well as the gathering of news.

We resist when the government seeks to put out unattributed information to large gatherings of newsmen, under circumstances which conceal the sources only from the reader, but which enable the government to disclaim responsibility for what is written. This is an ancient government practice known in Washington as the backgrounder. We insist, on the contrary, on judging for ourselves on the validity of information gathered from anonymous sources. And it is our further view that the freedom to do just that is part and parcel of the freedom to publish. We would add above all the case of the Pentagon Papers. Although the Supreme Court ultimately ruled against the government in this case and freed us to publish these documents, the *Times* and ourselves experienced, for a period of two weeks or more, under temporary court orders requested by the administration, the first prior restraint of publication in two hundred years' history of this country. I would suggest that the "we" who experienced this unprecedented restraint is not an exclusive or exclusionary pronoun; it does not refer in my judgment merely to those publications that were engaged in litigation, or even to the media as a whole. It refers to all of us, publishers and public alike. And I believe as well that the growing indifference to the First Amendment it reflects is cause for no less concern on your part—indeed, on the part of every citizen—than on ours. For these are not just our rights and freedoms, and this is just not our business. This is also your business, because these are also your rights and freedoms. When the press is intimidated and circumscribed in its capacity to report and to inform and to enlighten in its own fashion, it is the public that loses in the end, by losing its capacity to participate in a self-governing society. This is not a matter of Republicans against Democrats, or of liberals against conservatives, because sooner or later it will cut all ways. James Madison, in describing why our state constitutions included guarantees of freedom of the press, said this: "In every state probably in the Union, the press has exerted a freedom in canvasing the merits and measures of public men of every description which has not been confined to the strict limits of the common law. On this footing the freedom of the press has stood. On this footing, it yet stands."

Some degree of abuse is inseparable from the proper use of everything. And in no instances is this more true than that of the press. It has accordingly been decided by the practice of the states that it is better to leave a few of its noxious branches to their luxuriant growth than, by pruning them away, to injure the vigor of those yielding the proper fruit. We in the news business would ask of our readers and viewers only that they bear in mind this perception of the importance of the free press, whether they count a particular newspaper, news story, or newscast among its noxious branches or among those yielding the proper fruits.

[from the question-and-answer session]

Q. *Do you see a time for more straight reporting and less editorializing? And second, do you honestly believe the news columns or items of your publication and other media are unbiased and unslanted, giving only the who, what, why, and that only in their editorials do they become opinionated?*

A. Speaking of editorializing....I think that we all agree that the who, what, when, where, why school of reporting, while it looks great, doesn't really tell you what's going on. If you follow that conclusion to its end, you deliver the dictionary. I think that what is going on now, as the world has become more and more complicated and events from all over are more and more difficult to put in perspective—I think that what is called in that question "editorializing" is called by us "news analysis." It's trying to tell the readers what really is going on. Because if you tell them—the example we all use is the way Senator McCarthy, years ago, in '52, used the press. It really is what started the new kind of reporting, the analysis. What he would do is every night at six o'clock release a statement saying there were 356 Communists in the State Department. And every morning he would be quoted—on the night news broadcast and again in the morning. And it took a while before we realized that you also had to say that he had said that before, that it had never been proved right. In fact, nothing he had said had ever been proved right. It just really is not as simple as that question implies to tell people the truth.

March 23, 1973

Bella Abzug

Member, U.S. House of Representatives (D-NY);
Feminist Movement Leader

The words that Bella Abzug claimed others used to describe her were "impatient, impetuous, uppity, rude, profane, brash, and overbearing." Known as "Battling Bella" on Capitol Hill, she was a voice for women in America—and what a voice: raspy, with a heavy Bronx accent and capable, some thought, of shattering glass. She could cuss like a plumber, she worked in a shipyard during World War II, and she earned a degree in law. She also earned a death threat from the Ku Klux Klan for defending a black man accused of raping a white woman. At age fifty she was elected to the House of Representatives and then, with her inimitable charm, got herself redistricted out of her seat; she ran and won again.

When Bella Abzug was embarking on her career, her mother advised her to wear hats so no one would mistake her for a secretary. Her flamboyant cha- peaus became part of her persona, and when she was ordered by the door- keeper of the House of Representatives to remove her hat before taking the floor in 1971, she told him, as the *Washington Post* put it, to "perform an impossible act." Then she removed the hat and introduced a resolution call- ing for withdrawal of all U.S. troops from Indochina. She was permitted to keep her hat on when speaking to The Commonwealth Club in March 1973.

She picked out a bright red one for the occasion, matched with (as one reporter noted) bright red and navy platform shoes, and a navy dress with bright red polka dots. She looked over her reading glasses and, taking note of the number of women in the audience (The Club had opened up membership to women less than two years before), asserted, "You are the largest and the most attractive audience that I've ever spoken to in San Francisco."

Doors were being opened to women that had long been closed. As Abzug notes in her speech, 40 percent of the delegates to the 1972 Democratic convention were women. In 1968, only 13 percent of the Democratic and 17 percent of Republican delegates were women. Meanwhile, National Airlines (now defunct) was running a television commercial in which a stewardess enticed businessmen with "Hi! I'm Debbie. Fly me." During the question-and-answer session, Abzug puffed on a cigarette and fielded a question about what place a family had in the life of a liberated woman—and who was going to stay home to take care of the children. Abzug turned to her husband in the audience and asked, "You want to answer that question, Martin?" Then the mother of "two lovely daughters" stated that "society has a fundamental responsibility to recognize changing conditions and to provide the child care and other services....I think that we have a right to expect that, in a great country like this where we've got billions of dollars to waste on cost overruns...and subsidizing big business even for their mistakes."

In 1975, Abzug introduced the first lesbian-gay civil rights bill in Congress. The next year she ran for the U.S. Senate and lost in the primary to Daniel Patrick Moynihan. Appointed by President Jimmy Carter to a nonpaid position in the Labor Department, Abzug was fired in 1979 for criticizing Carter's plan to cut funding for women's programs. In 1990, she founded the international Women's Environment and Development Organization to make women more visible in government and society. She died in 1998.

"Every Issue Is a Woman's Issue"

If a man were invited to address this forum, would the topic be "Every Issue Is a Man's Issue?" We are, of course, a majority of the population, us women, and there's no escaping us. Naturally, everything that happens in the country affects us, just as it affects men. But to paraphrase George

Orwell, we are all equal, only some of us are a little less equal than the others. By "us" I mean women, and so it happens that, purely as a matter of self-interest, women tend to feel more strongly about, and to act more vigorously on, the issue of discrimination, which has made us an oppressed majority in this nation, and indeed in all nations.

Ever since our country was formed by our founding forefathers, who rather consistently neglected to mention our foremothers—which neglect led ultimately to turning the founding mothers and the sisters and the wives into nonpersons who were really not quite recognized as persons under the Constitution—and ever since then, which means from our beginnings, women have been shut out of the power structure of the United States. We have been almost invisible in government at all levels; in the courts, in the legislatures, on the boards of directors of banks and corporations and the executive councils of organized labor, among the elite of the academic world and the churches and, I suspect, even among the guests of The Commonwealth Club. I note that among the sixty-six distinguished speakers listed in your brochure as having been invited to address you since 1903, only seven are women. So I understand you left a few off.

I hope my presence here indicates that times are changing. And the reason is that women are forcing change to take place. It was women who won the women's vote. It is women who are organizing women's political caucuses that helped to elect 20 percent more women to the state legislatures last November and sent five new women to the House of Representatives. There's women who have formed organizations like NOW and the Women's Equity Action League and Women's Political Caucus and other groups to fight for the adoption of the Equal Rights Amendment, to challenge antiquated marriage, divorce, and abortion laws, to expose inequities in the Social Security system, and to file literally thousands of complaints against employers and business corporations, universities and governments, charging them with denying equal opportunity to women in hiring, pay scales, and promotions. Despite the adoption of the Equal Pay Act, it is a fact of American life that a woman earns sixty cents where a man earns a dollar. And a black woman or a Chicana earns even less.

It is, perhaps, in the field of credit where a woman is really made to feel like a nonperson. However capable and reliable she may be, she is treated, solely because of her sex, as though she was totally dependent and unreliable when she applies for a loan, consumer credit, or a mortgage. If she's married, she receives credit only through her husband. He may be unemployed, unemployable, gone, or even dead. Still, she is often forced to get credit in his name.

Of the more quaint examples of the kind of responses women have received, there's one that is one of my favorites, the Equitable Trust Bank in Virginia. When it refuses credit to a woman, it lends a note of charm by sending a letter of "congratulations on your marriage" to single cardholders, but spoils it by adding that "we must now delete your account number. Please return your card. Enclosed is an application for your husband." This is a situation I hope to change with equal credit opportunity legislation, which I've introduced into Congress, which seems to have gotten some interest aroused.[1]

As women organize around women's issues, we welcome and frequently get the support of men who believe, as I have frequently said, that what is good for women (and as that fellow from General Motors said) is good for the country. But we don't look essentially to men for leadership or self-sacrifice in the cause of equality of sexes. We have 15 women out of 435 members in the House of Representatives. We have a Senate of one hundred members which is now a no-woman's land. I have yet to hear of any incumbent or aspiring male politician who will voluntarily step aside, in his announced professions for equality, to make room in Congress for greater representation of women. Nor do I expect any to do so. "Ladies first" may be the practice in entering revolving doors and elevators, but the revolving doors lead women only into the outer rooms of the political institutions. And the elevators stop before they reach the upper floors of political power.

When men come up against the inevitable arithmetic of the political situation—that more women in the House and Senate means fewer men— idealism moves over for expediency, and we hear talk of a male backlash and audible discontent about so-called quota systems. It never fails to amaze me when men, who all their lives have existed contentedly with unwritten quotas that have effectively kept women and blacks and other minorities out of political institutions and out of jobs, begin protesting when affirmative action programs start letting them in. Then they trot out

1. While Abzug's initiative in the House did not lead to federal reform to guarantee women's access to credit, legislation introduced in the Senate was passed in July 1973 and then by the House. The Equal Credit Opportunity Act (ECOA), prohibiting discrimination on the basis of marital status or gender, became law in October 1974.

the charges of quotas and discrimination. It was even implied that women were taking over when they won 40 percent of the delegate seats for the Democratic convention in Miami and 36 percent to the Republican convention—even though that still left 60 or more percent for men, and even though the 40 percent of women came from a great variety of backgrounds and were supporting a variety of candidates.

Some of the more psychologically oriented feminists will tell you that we are all victims of our sexist society—men and women. Like women, men may be trapped at the stereotyped sex roles that cripple their personalities, suppress their natural talents, imprison them in demeaning relationships, and impose false values upon them. Actually, I think that when we look at our society we see that it is not only sexist, it is also racist. It is still basically militarist. Right now we remain half in and half out of the war in Indochina, with the president even now hinting at bombing reprisals against the Vietnamese. It is a society dominated by a corporate power structure, as some of you here might know, that has a lifelong devoted friend in the White House—not only at Chase Manhattan—and representatives strategically placed throughout the administration. We see a society in which the rich are getting richer, the poor poorer, and the lower middle class is being driven to the wall by inflation and wildly rising food prices. Today, many people accept, without much question, that we live in an affluent society, compared to other nations. The United States has the largest gross national product: more cars, more TVs, more phones than the rest of the world combined, sometimes more audiences. We eat more, spend more, and, if you believe the TV ads, our only real problems are which model of car to buy, or which airline to use to fly off to a glorious vacation. (By the way, we don't encourage women to be pilots. But in one of the more insulting and suggestive TV commercials, women can pretend to be airplanes, and invite men to fly them.)

Those are the so-called happy problems. But millions of Americans have very real problems of just getting along. Among them are working women, who on average are at the bottom of the pay scale; working people, in general; migrant farmworkers; from five to eight million unemployed, especially the ghetto youth; women and children on welfare rolls; and millions of senior citizens—most of whom live on average Social Security benefits of fifty dollars a week. Production workers whose supposedly greedy and insatiable demands for higher wages were blamed for the rising cost of living were in fact earning (before taxes, mind you) just $133.73 a week in 1970, the year before President Nixon ordered the wage freeze. That added up to about $6,800 a year. At the same time, the United States Bureau of Labor Statistics was reporting that a family of four in an average American city needed a yearly income of $10,971 to maintain what was described as a moderately decent and healthy standard of living. That $4,000 gap in income explains why more and more married women are working. Like women who are single or who are heads of families—and those are the poorest families—they work not for self-fulfillment, but just to put food on the table and to pay the rent.

More than 40 percent of our workforce are women. I know the popular myth is that the woman's place is in the home. When I first ran for office in 1970, I said, "This woman's place is in the House—the House of Representatives." The workforce of women are used primarily as a source of cheap labor. One union has estimated that industry saves at least $19 billion a year by discriminating against women, paying them less than men for doing the same work, or shunting them into lower-paying job categories.

Meanwhile, this administration has served their masters well. Profits have been rising sharply since 1971. According to *BusinessWeek*, after-tax profits for 1972 will probably hit a new high of $53 billion—15 percent more than in 1971. In the auto industry, for example, profits were up 42 percent compared with the 7.8 percent increase in wages. Lumber and wood products industry profits around 65.5 percent, while wages were held to 5.5 percent—the precise wage-freeze formula imposed by the Nixon Administration.

The result of such gross inequities is the gross maldistribution of income. Forty-five percent of all American families get 73 percent of the nation's total income. A majority, that is 55 percent, are left to share 27 percent of all income. The economic power of conglomerates rose in all directions. In any industry or product line, no matter how unrelated, the single guideline is profit. In the past twenty-five years we have seen the startling rise to economic supremacy of American-based multinational companies and banks that operate subsidiaries and branches in foreign countries. They control about sixty billion American dollars in Europe and about twenty billion American dollars in Japan. They go abroad in search of cheap labor and untaxed profits, and they don't give a damn if they leave behind in America ghost manufacturing towns, workers without jobs, and ordinary taxpayers carrying the tax load that they avoid.

These giant U.S.-based multinationals, as well as foreign companies and speculators who hold dollars, were responsible for the run on the dollar that occurred in the summer of 1971 and again last month. They began dumping dollars and buying other currencies. In cold fact, U.S. corporations put profits ahead of patriotism, selling their own country's currency in order to make fast profits, and leaving American consumers with the burden of paying higher prices resulting from the dollar devaluation.

Think back over the past four years and recall whether you ever heard President Nixon talk about any of this. Perhaps you'll say, "Thank God he didn't, it's so dull." It's unfortunate that listening to facts about profits, wages, multinational corporations, and the economic exploitation of women can be so tedious. But I would suggest that I have been talking about the reality of American life—while President Nixon is talking insulting drivel when he lectures us about the work ethic at the same time that his policies create unemployment; when he advises self-reliance even as he continues to pamper big business and the Pentagon; when he says the only alternative to his $12-billion slash in social programs is a general tax increase, even though he knows that closing up the tax-privilege loopholes used by big business, the rich, the multinational corporations could bring in billions of dollars.

According to George Meany, if we closed up those tax loopholes, we would have an additional $29 billion, enough to continue social programs and overcome our budget deficit.[1] Philip Stern, in his remarkable book *The Rape of the Taxpayer*, estimates that tax favoritism, or what he calls "welfare for the rich," is costing us $77 billion a year. Because of these loopholes, we ordinary people pay not just our own taxes, but the taxes of someone like John Paul Getty. He almost pays no taxes himself, even though he makes $300,000 a day. The celebrated International Telephone and Telegraph Company, you may have noticed in the headlines, which treats the White House, the State Department, the Justice Department, and the CIA like wholly owned subsidiaries, paid less than $5 million in taxes to the federal government in 1971, compared with nearly $139 million to foreign governments. When they first made their $400,000 contribution to President Nixon's campaign fund, I said, "Well, what would you expect?" I

1. Labor leader George Meany (1894–1980) led the merger of the American Federation of Labor (AFL) and Congress of Industrial Organizations (CIO) and served as president of the merged organization from 1955 to 1979.

mean, I suppose, you know, if I had $400,000, I might run the government for them too.

The current battle of the budget in which we in Congress are engaged is focused around several major issues. The president has proposed a $4-billion increase or more in the military budget. We think it should be cut considerably and this is one of the proposals in the counter-budget being developed by liberals in Congress. The president is unconstitutionally impounding from $12 billion to $18 billion in funds appropriated by Congress for housing, economic development, water pollution, and other social programs. Lawsuits have been filed challenging the constitutionality of this action. We are also pushing legislation that would prevent the president from impounding money.

Finally, there is the president's proposed dismantling of social programs to save about $12 billion. I say "proposed," but in fact, the administration is already shutting down these programs without waiting for congressional action. No milk for school lunches, no more rent subsidies or money for housing, Title I education funds slashed, neighborhood health centers closed down, mental health programs abandoned, basic medical research and postgraduate health training cutbacks, fewer youth jobs this summer, model cities, community action, and poverty programs dumped, more money squeezed out of the elderly for Medicare. Nixon is even cutting back rural electrification, the New Deal program that brought electric power to the poor farmer and washing machines to his overburdened wife. These cuts certainly affect poor people. They affect women, they affect the elderly, the handicapped, and veterans. They also affect millions of other Americans. A sharp cutback in mental health funds and medical research touches all people. The freezing of funds for water and sewer projects will be felt most acutely in suburban communities, particularly in new developments. The freezing of funds for antipollution projects will impair the quality of the air we all breathe and the water we all drink.

Perhaps the cruelest cut of all is aimed at the ten million working mothers, elderly, handicapped, and others who received child care and other social services under Title IV of the Social Security program. This is being done in a rather sneaky way. Last year a $2.5 billion federal ceiling was imposed on these social services expenditures. That in itself created tremendous hardship for many people. Now the Health, Education and Welfare Department, under Caspar Weinberger, is proposing new regulations that would deprive about three million people of these services and slice more than a billion dollars off that already inadequate ceiling. Think of it, a government that gives one tax break after another to the super rich is telling a working woman with a few kids that if she earns more than $5,400 a year, she is too rich, and she can't send her youngsters to a subsidized day care center. Her alternatives are to find a lower paying job, give up her job and go on welfare, or to leave her kids in makeshift arrangements.

The other day I read an article in the *New York Times* about the men around President Nixon—Ehrlichman, Haldeman, Ziegler—their names, views, and faces seem interchangeable. The article describes them as technicians, systems-oriented managers, administrators, and advertising men. The kind of men who regard budgets as holy writ and computer printouts as life guides. They also have, says the article, short hair and are male chauvinists. That, apparently, is a revelation to the *Times*, but certainly not to those of us in Washington who have observed the Nixon Administration in operation on such women's issues as child care, health services, affirmative action programs, and job opportunities. According to the *Times*, the Nixon men see themselves as just like the majority of Americans. Of course, the majority happen to be women. But we'll let that pass. I emphatically reject the claim that these soulless technicians and corporation graduates represent either the needs or the aspirations of a majority of Americans—men or women. Behind the carefully cultivated facade of middle-American values that this administration presents to the public—John Wayne movies, country music, football, and Billy Graham sermons (I don't know where Bebe Rebozo fits into this, but somewhere[1])—exists the philosophy and a power structure that is single-hearted in its devotion to the needs of big business and the military establishment, and that with all the shortsightedness of Calvin Coolidge or a Herbert Hoover neglects the needs of ordinary Americans. And you know what happened when they were around.

1. Charles Gregory "Bebe" Rebozo (1912–1988) was a close friend of Richard Nixon, whose winter White House was on Key Biscayne, Florida, where Rebozo lived. The son of Cuban immigrants, Rebozo made himself a millionaire through real estate investment and founded the Key Biscayne Bank—in which Nixon had been the first depositor. According to Rebozo, he and Nixon were swimming in front of his house when they learned of the Watergate break-in. Rebozo himself was investigated by Congress for accepting, on behalf of the Nixon campaign, $100,000 from industrialist Howard Hughes.

This is the issue that is at the core of what has been variously called the constitutional crisis and the budget crisis. President Nixon is seeking and gathering extraordinary powers—far beyond those authorized by the Constitution—to prevent Congress from interfering with his economic, social, and military policy. He is declaring his entire staff, both past and present, out of reach of congressional inquiry. He is intimidating the press and TV into silence, or at least a more acquiescent position. He is transforming the Supreme Court into his own image. Did you ever stop to think about this? We're almost going to be two hundred years old, and never once in the history of this country has there been a woman on the Supreme Court bench, albeit that bench metes out justice day in and day out to more than a majority of the people who are women. When we raised this issue in the Congress—the women in Congress, both Republicans and Democrats—the president said he couldn't find a woman who was good enough. I have always answered to that, he couldn't find a woman who was bad enough.

He is substituting what he calls "efficiency" for what we call "democracy." I think he is interpreting his reelection as a mandate for reaction. I believe his objective is to bring us 1984 by 1976, to saddle us with a legacy of one-man rule, and possibly, one-party control. Whether he succeeds will be determined by the Congress and the American people. Right now the mood in Congress is very angry. Whether it will maintain that fighting mood right down to the finish and force President Nixon to back down depends ultimately on how angry the people get and on the kind of political leadership we can expect.

I am not going to excuse Congress; of course I wasn't there. Not having had a share of power, it's much easier for women to see what could be done. But the fact is that although Congress for a long time did abdicate its power, it has suddenly turned around and found that it's impotent. And you know what a shock that is to discover that you're impotent. Once they've come over that shock there is a real determination and an anger to restore constitutional government to this country. (Because no matter how you put it, it's not true, and it can't be, that in this great democracy of ours, to take the hard-earned tax dollars of the people in this country and to take the elected representatives, to whom the people of this country have entrusted these hard-earned tax dollars so that they could appropriate the needed programs that they need with that—no matter how you put it, when a president impounds the billions of dollars that he is impounding, he is really saying, "Forget those things, they don't belong to you, they belong to me." In the Constitution of the United States, the president has no such power. His power is merely to faithfully execute the law as we in the Congress enact it. And in so doing, he is saying to the American people, "I don't believe in the constitutional form of government."

More and more, these executive actions of impoundment—the assertion of executive privilege on your right to know and the right of the Congress to know—is a major threat, not a little bit of nicety. If some of you think that the Watergate scandal is a matter of Macy's spying on Gimbel's, you're wrong. It was essentially a very serious political intrusion and invasion, and a subversion of the democratic process. And what is at stake in this country, be you a Democrat or a Republican, is the survival of democratic institutions themselves. And I come all the way out here to The Commonwealth Club, where I may or may not be liked, to make that message and to bring that message.

I bring this message because I believe that the effect of these policies, these budget cuts, these political intrusions upon democracy itself can be changed. It is important that it be changed for all levels of the population, not only poor people and working people and women and minorities, but people in middle income and indeed those interested in the business sector of our life. No one can suggest that this is a healthy economy in which we find ourselves. Not even my husband, Martin, who is sitting over there and who's in the stock market, would tell you that. In any case, I believe that whether you're in the city or in the countryside, in the rural area or the suburbs, that what is at stake—whether you're white or poor or black or Chicano—is the question of fighting for all of the people in this country. Fighting to make democracy work for all of the people. We are the biggest country, the greatest country, we have the largest number of resources, the greatest tradition of democracy. We have to put together a very natural coalition of people, regardless of party and their class and their race, to fight together for this great country. This issue is, indeed, a woman's issue, it is a man's issue. It is an issue for all Americans who believe that our nation should not be the private preserve of the rich, but a country that indeed belongs to all of us.

August 1, 1974

Jesse Jackson

American Civil Rights Leader; Founder, Operation PUSH (People United to Serve Humanity)

When Jesse Jackson spoke to The Commonwealth Club, the nation was in turmoil—and exactly one week away from seeing Richard Nixon resign as president. But one of the points Jackson makes in his impassioned plea for progress in civil rights, with a focus on economic justice in America, is that the "nation's ills will not be cured by simply the negation of [President Nixon]....We are in a civilizational crisis." In his efforts to combat that crisis, in 1971 Jesse Jackson founded Operation PUSH (People United to Serve Humanity), after having worked with the Southern Christian Leadership Conference (SCLC) for half a decade. A Baptist minister, Jackson began his talk to Commonwealth Club members at San Francisco's Hotel St. Francis by quoting Scripture.

During the question-and-answer session, Jackson was asked if there will ever be a black president of the United States. In the 1980s, Jackson himself took up that challenge, campaigning for the Democratic nomination: in 1984, under the Rainbow Coalition banner, and in 1988, more politically savvy, finishing a strong second to Michael Dukakis. The 1980s also saw Jackson emerge as a figure in international affairs. In 1984 he secured the release of a captured U.S. Navy officer from Syria; in 1987 he obtained the freedom of forty-eight Cuban and Cuban American prisoners from Castro; in 1990 he brought hostages out of Iraq and Kuwait. President Clinton named him a special U.S. envoy to Africa in 1997.

"Rebirth of a Nation"

Amongst other things, I am also a country preacher, and I'd like to share with you a few verses of Scripture that give some base from where I am coming. Saint John the third chapter, the first through the seventh verses:

> And there was a man of the Pharisees named Nicodemus, a ruler of the Jews. His son came to Jesus by night and said unto him, Rabbi, we know that thou art a teacher come from God, for no man can do these miracles that thou doest except God be with him.
>
> And Jesus answered and said unto him: "Verily, verily, I say unto thee, except a man be born again, he cannot even see the kingdom of God. And Nicodemus said unto him, How can a man be born when he is old? Can he enter a second time into his mother's womb and be born? And Jesus answered, Verily, verily, I say unto thee, except a man be born of water and of the spirit, he cannot enter the kingdom of God.
>
> "That which is born of the flesh is flesh, and that which is born of the spirit is spirit. And so marvel not that I say you must be born again."

Speaking before a group such as this group, marvel not that I say that fundamentally America needs to be born again. We come at a period approaching the bicentennial of this nation where we assess where we have come from and we assess where we are going, and I argue that the most fundamental need in America today is to be reborn—the rebirth of a nation. Not to deal—just with being two hundred years old and starting all over again: we were once born of the water, a baby in its mother's womb is in water. So all of us have already been born of the water. America's already been born as a nation two hundred years ago, but there's a rebirth of the spirit of the nation that must take place again. There's nothing wrong with our money and our matter and our established institutions theoretically, except there's something terribly wrong with our attitude.

It is not your aptitude, but your attitude that determines your altitude. The set of your mind determines your greatness, it determines the heights that you climb to. This very rich ruler who came to meet with the rabbi, who came to meet with the teacher by night representing the Pharisee tradition, had all the legalism on his side. He had all of the rituals, and our nation has all of the ritualism and all of the legalism.

If one wants to deal with health and this nation from a ritualistic point of view, there is a health department. However, people are sick. There is a housing department. However, people are ill-housed. There is a board of education. However, people are not being educated. There is an unemployment office. However, people are unemployed. There are banks. However, people cannot get money. And so, in some sense likened unto the Pharisee, we have all of the rituals and all of the notions and all of the motions and the institutions, but something more fundamental than that which we see is missing in the nation today.

As we approach the bicentennial, all of us agonize at the state of the nation. We have our various opinions about the guilt and the innocence of persons in high positions in Washington—except one thing that all of us can agree to is that the nation today is in disgrace. And, the nation is in shame. And it's not enough to self-righteously hide behind your set of reasons. The sum total of the matter is, we're trapped in a severe moral-civilizational crisis.

We use very simplistic assessments. We say the nation is in an urban crisis because of what's been happening in major cities. And we are in an urban crisis, but more than that, we say we are in a racial crisis and we are. But it's more than that. We say we are in a crisis of the sexes and we are, but it's more than that. We say there is a generation gap, but that's not the only gap. And when you pull all of these crises together, what one has is a civilizational crisis bigger than any rich man's purse, bigger than any ethnic dominant group's righteousness.

To that extent, we will either deal with the crisis in true perspective or fall prey to the law of general ruination and become one of the great nations that died. We have become preoccupied with Nixon. We must become occupied with him, he is the president, but not preoccupied, inasmuch as the absence of Nixon is not the presence of justice. The absence of

Nixon is not the presence of balance. The nation's ills will not be cured by simply the negation of him and some kind of two-year substitute. We are in a civilizational crisis.

Dr. and Mrs. Charles Beard, some years ago, attempting to size up their studies of the rise and fall of civilizations, reduced all of their writings to four very witty statements—statements often used, but which must be seen in a new light. One, they said that the mills of the gods grind slowly, but they grind exceedingly small. And from the foot of this nation where lies were told and slavery existed and cards were pushed under the table, the mills of the gods grind slowly, but they finally got into the head of the nation and they are grinding exceedingly small.

Secondly, whom the gods would destroy they first make mad, and to be in the White House and its environs; breaking in the office of psychiatrists, violating people's basic liberties is the work of people who have gone mad, and their madness—not the body politics, not the military, not the established business institution, not the hippies, but their madness—is driving them out of office.

Thirdly, the ordinary honeybee feeds the flower that he robs, and when the wealthy of this nation are more willing to invest abroad than to protect the laborers on whose backs they stand, they're not exercising the sense of the ordinary honeybee. When we are willing to overspend the military budget by $27 billion, which would completely wipe out unemployment if applied adequately, and would rebuild most American cities, we're not exercising the judgment of the ordinary honeybee.

And lastly, when it is dark enough, you can see the stars, and it is at that level that even in the darkness—darkness can never be fully declared until we allow our lights to go out, and everybody has a light—as long as there's a light, there's hope. As long as there's hope, there's possibility, and that is the pinhead of optimism on which we stand today, our own light.

The attitude of the nation determines its course. The Constitution is our legal attitude put on paper. The Statue of Liberty and the words inscribed represent our social attitude: Give me your tired, give me your poor, give me your huddled masses, we love people, there are things for people to do, give us the dispossessed; that was a great national attitude. Capital of the free world—not the world police or the military—but the world's savior with an attitude.

But now our attitude has gone wild. People in power project the notion that poor people have a nature that is inferior to rich people—not their circumstance, that their nature is different. The same kind of incentives that are provided for the wealthy are self-righteously and viciously taken away from the have-nots. When Mr. Reagan did not pay taxes and Mr. Nixon did not pay taxes, they said these are basically good men but the tax system is wrong, the tax system has loopholes. Good men, bad system.

But when poor people, trapped in an economy where beans have gone up 256 percent, beef 80 percent, pork 60 percent, who do not even have the allocation in their budget for toiletries, use somehow that money to make ends meet, they say it is a good system but they're bad people. "Good system, bad people" when applied to the poverty-stricken. That is questioning the very nature of poor people, it goes into the nature of God and theology.

The rebirth of a nation, a new attitude. Many people have lost the desire to see black and white people relate in a civilized fashion. Many people have lost the urge for full employment. Many people have lost the urge for a uniform public educational system. As of 1974 you were deprived of the best education, based on class, based on neighborhood. Citizenship—not suburbs or inner city—citizenship should be the basis for getting the best education that the nation has to offer. And unless and until that happens, the poor have a right to march and/or be bused and/or apply to the superior schools. We fight wars together, we pay taxes together, we should be educated together. But we have to be born again to even see that as civilized.

It is not enough to go into 1976 fighting for welfare. We must see welfare as a failure of the economic system, not the people. We don't want and need welfare, we need a full employment economy, we need an alternative to welfare. No people are legitimately striving to be on welfare, people need to work and work needs people. The suburban housewife and the inner city mother, both of them come up awfully empty, one getting a check from her husband, the other getting it from the state, but neither one has the glory and the reward of hope and work. People need to work. There's fulfillment in work, but people need to get paid for the work that they do and need to be respected as they engage in socially useful work.

What is fundamentally bad about the welfare system is that the economists who designed it were not as intelligent as they had been projected to be. But the present welfare system is an endless cycle that does not have built into it the incentive to earn or to learn. If you're on welfare getting two hundred dollars a month and you go out and make two hundred dollars a month, they take the whole two hundred dollars; so you say, "Why work?" The incentive to earn is destroyed; you make a dollar, they take a dollar. If you're on welfare in the tenth grade and you go back to night school to get a degree, which increases your ability to go into the labor market, chances are you'll be put off of welfare and discouraged, so there is no incentive to earn or to learn. The system is bad.

We must be of service without being servile, because service is power, and that's fundamental. We must glory in work and production. Somehow the sense of craftsmanship in America has gone low, because of total alienation between production and the producers. Lastly, there must be some major détentes and summit meetings within the nation between her many ethnic groups. Black people and Jewish people have been together too long to allow their relationship to just disintegrate without having at least a summit meeting. Black people and Arab people need to sit down and have a summit meeting. We need to have a détente between Chicano Americans and black Americans and white Americans. We need to clean up our own house, be born again of the spirit, and have an earnest desire to have a better nation.

Let us earnestly seek a new nation, let us seek a new peace. Let us develop a uniform educational system that will educate all of our children. Let us obliterate hunger and starvation. We have the capacity if we have the will. Let us learn to love and respect each other.

Let us reduce the military budget, stop the killing abroad, start the healing at home. Let us be that great nation that God called us into existence to be, a nation that would advocate starting war no more, beating swords into plowshares, and declaring the glory of the Lord. That's our possibility, that is our hope. We will not be able to accept such a challenge unless we have the courage of our convictions. Let us diagnose the case accurately. Let us prescribe the remedy, however painful, and let us have the discipline to follow through for the nation's sake.

February 3, 1976

Henry A. Kissinger

U.S. Secretary of State

In 1975, two hundred years after Paul Revere's ride, the last American helicopter left Saigon, and the U.S. military withdrawal from Vietnam was complete. That same year, Portugal was extracting itself from its colonial possessions: Angola was given independence, and various factions there struggled for control. The civil war quickly became a proxy war, with Cuban troops sent to support the Popular Movement for the Liberation of Angola (MPLA), which ruled the country, and the U.S. and South Africa backing the Union for the Total Independence of Angola (UNITA). What was really happening, however, said U.S. Secretary of State Henry Kissinger in his February 1976 speech to The Commonwealth Club, was a Soviet-American showdown. Kissinger spoke three months after Castro had committed forces to Angola in response to a South African invasion, and just weeks after the U.S. Congress, wary of CIA involvement in the conflict, had ordered that funding for UNITA be halted. The cutoff took effect February 9—less than a week after Kissinger gave this speech.

It was a difficult time for the man who had been serving both as national security advisor (since 1969) and secretary of state (since 1973). In both 1972 and 1973, a Gallup poll had ranked him as the most admired man in America, and in 1973 he was awarded the Nobel Peace Prize for negotiating an end to U.S. involvement in Vietnam. He'd inaugurated the era of détente with the Soviet Union with the Strategic Arms Limitation Talks (SALT), paved the way for President Nixon's visit to China in 1972, and in 1973 his "shuttle diplomacy" led to a truce in the Yom Kippur War in the Middle East. But in autumn 1975, the man whom journalists had labeled "smartest guy around" had been cited for contempt by a congressional committee investigating the CIA. He also was assaulted from the Right, with retired Admiral Elmo Zumwalt likening his peacemaking efforts to Neville Chamberlain's appeasement of Hitler at Munich. And in the midst of a shake-up of Gerald Ford's cabinet a little over a year after Ford succeeded Nixon as president, Kissinger stepped down as national security advisor.

Kissinger's talk was given on the seventy-third anniversary of the founding of The Commonwealth Club. In San Francisco, his loudest critics were from the Left: some eight hundred demonstrators gathered outside the Fairmont Hotel, where he spoke, carrying placards and hanging him in effigy.

A second speech to The Club was arranged for June 1976, but at the last minute it was canceled—amid accusations that Kissinger was in effect out campaigning for President Ford in the upcoming Republican primary in California, where Ford was being challenged by former Governor Ronald Reagan.

"The Permanent Challenge of Peace: U.S. Policy Toward the Soviet Union"

America enters its third century and its forty-eighth presidential election with unmatched physical strength, a sound foreign policy design, yet scarred by self-doubt. In the past decade and a half we have seen one president assassinated, another driven from office, and a third resign. We have lived through the agony of Vietnam and Watergate. We are still struggling to overcome the bitterness and division that have followed their wake. We face no more urgent task than to restore our national unity and our national resolve.

For we, the strongest free nation, cannot afford the luxury of withdrawing into ourselves to heal our wounds. Too much depends on us—peace or war, prosperity or depression, freedom or tyranny. Too much is at stake for America to paralyze itself tearing up the past, seeking sensational headlines in the present, or offering panaceas for the future, for our own well-being—

American lives and American jobs—will be affected if we permit our domestic disunity and turmoil to cause us to falter in meeting our international responsibilities.

America finds itself, for the first time, permanently and irrevocably involved in international affairs. At the same time, the catastrophic nature of nuclear war imposes upon us a necessity that transcends traditional concepts of diplomacy and balance of power—to shape a world order that finds stability in self-restraint and, ultimately, cooperation.

Since de Tocqueville it has been a cliché that Americans, as a people, are slow to arouse, but that once aroused we are a tremendous and implacable force. Thus, even when we ventured forth in foreign affairs, we identified our exertion as a temporary disruption of our tranquility.

Even in the first twenty-five years after World War II—an era of great creativity and unprecedented American engagement in foreign affairs—we acted as if the world's security and economic development could be conclusively ensured by the commitment of American resources, know-how, and effort. We were encouraged—even impelled—to act as we did by our unprecedented predominance in a world shattered by war and the collapse of the great colonial empires. We considered our deployment of troops in Europe and elsewhere to be temporary. We thought that the policy of containment would transform the Soviet Union and that a changed Soviet society would then evolve inexorably into a compatible member of a harmonious international community.

At the same time, the central character of moral values in American life always made us acutely sensitive to the purity of means—and when we disposed of overwhelming power we had a great luxury of choice. Our moral certainty made compromise difficult; our preponderance often made it seem unnecessary.

Today, while we still have massive strength, we no longer enjoy meaningful nuclear supremacy. We remain the world's most productive and innovative economy, but we must now share leadership with Western Europe, Canada, and Japan; we must deal with the newly wealthy and developing nations; and we must make new choices regarding our economic relations with the Communist countries. Our democratic principles are still far more valued by the world's millions than we realize, but we must also compete with new ideologies which assert progressive goals but pursue them by oppressive methods.

Today, for the first time in our history, we face the stark reality that the challenge is unending; that there is no easy and surely no final answer; that there are no automatic solutions. We must learn to conduct foreign policy as other nations have had to conduct it for so many centuries—without escape and without respite, knowing that what is attainable falls short of the ideal, mindful of the necessities of self-preservation, conscious that the reach of our national purpose has its limits. This is a new experience for Americans. It prompts nostalgia for a simpler past. As before in our history, it generates the search for scapegoats, holding specific policies responsible for objective conditions.

We cannot afford to swing recklessly between confrontation and abdication. We must not equate tough rhetoric with strong action, nor can we wish away tough realities with nostalgic hopes. We can no longer act as if we engage ourselves in foreign affairs only when we choose—or only to overcome specific problems—so that we can then shift our priorities back to our natural concern with ourselves. The reality is that there can be no security without vigilance and no progress without our dedication.

The issue of how to deal with the Soviet Union has been a central feature of American policy for three decades. What is new today is the culmination of thirty years of postwar growth of Soviet industrial, technological, and military power. No American policy caused this; no American policy could have prevented it. But American policy can keep this power from being used to expand Soviet influence to our detriment; we have the capacity to enable allies and friends to live with a sense of security; we possess the assets to advance the process of building an international order of cooperation and progress.

We must do so, however, in unprecedented conditions. In previous periods, rivalry between major powers has almost invariably led to war. In our time, when thermonuclear weapons threaten casualties in the hundreds of millions, such an outcome is unthinkable. We must manage a fundamental clash of ideologies and harness the rivalry of the nuclear superpowers, first into coexistence and then mold coexistence into a more positive and cooperative future. For as President Kennedy once said, "In the final analysis, our most basic common link is that we all inhabit this small planet. We all breathe the same air. We all cherish our children's future. And we are all mortal."

In the period after World War II, our nightmare was that the Soviet Union, after consolidating its occupation of Eastern Europe, might seek to spread its control to other contiguous areas in Europe and Asia. Our policies, therefore, sought to build alliances and positions of military strength from which we could contain and isolate the Soviet Union. These policies served us and our allies well. Soviet expansion was checked. Behind our shield of security and with our assistance, our friends and allies in Western Europe restored their economies and rebuilt their democratic institutions.

Yet the hope that these policies would produce permanent stability, positive evolution of the Soviet system, and greater normality was only partially realized.

In strategic military terms the USSR has achieved a broad equality with the United States, as was inevitable for a large nation whose rulers were prepared to impose great sacrifices on their people and to give military strength the absolute top priority in allocation of resources. With only half our gross national product, Soviet military expenditures exceed those of the United States.

For the first time in history, the Soviet Union can threaten distant places beyond the Eurasian land mass—including the United States. Soviet diplomacy has thrust into the Middle East, Africa, and Asia. This evolution is now rooted in real power.

Coping with the implications of this emerging superpower has been our central security problem. This condition will not go away. And it will, perhaps, never be conclusively "solved." It will have to be faced by every administration for the foreseeable future.

In the nuclear era, when casualties in a general nuclear war will involve hundreds of millions in a matter of days, the use of force threatens utter catastrophe. It is our responsibility to contain Soviet power without global war, to avoid abdication as well as confrontation.

We must strive for an equilibrium of power, but we must move beyond it to promote the habits of mutual restraint, coexistence, and, ultimately, cooperation. We must stabilize a new international order in a vastly dangerous environment, but our ultimate goal must be to transform ideological conflict into constructive participation in building a better world. This is what is meant by the process called "détente"—not the hunger for relaxation of tension, not the striving for agreements at any price, not the mindless search for friendly atmosphere which some critics use as naïve and dangerous caricatures.

It is the great industrial democracies, not the Soviet Union, that are the engine of the world economy and the most promising partners for the poorer nations. The industrial democracies, if they face their challenges with confidence—if they do not mesmerize themselves with the illusion of simple solutions—possess vast strengths to contain Soviet power and to channel that power in constructive directions. Our essential task is to recognize the need for a dual policy that simultaneously and with equal vigor resists expansionist drives and seeks to shape a more constructive relationship. In recent years, the United States has firmly resisted attempts by the Soviet Union to establish a naval base in Cuba, to impede the access routes to Berlin, to exploit the explosive situation in the Middle East. Recently, we have sought to halt blatant intervention in Angola—until prevented from doing so by congressional action.

At the same time, we have an historic obligation to mankind to engage the Soviet Union in settlements of concrete problems and to push back the shadow of nuclear catastrophe. At the very least, we owe it to our people to demonstrate that its government has missed no opportunity to achieve constructive solutions and that crises which occur were unavoidable. This is why the U.S. has set forth principles of responsible relations in the nuclear age: respect for the interests of all, restraint in the uses of power, and abstention from efforts to exploit instability or local conflicts for unilateral advantage.

It has been our belief that, with patience, a pattern of restraints and a network of vested interests can develop which will give coexistence a more hopeful dimension and make both sides conscious of what they would stand to lose by reverting to the politics of pressure, confrontation, and crisis. In the early 1970s, when current U.S.-Soviet relations were shaped, our nation had already passed through traumatic events and was engaged in an anguishing war. There were riots in the streets and on the campuses demanding rapid progress toward peace. Every new defense program was challenged—including the ABM treaty which was approved by only one vote, the development of multiple warheads, the Trident submarine, and the B-1 bomber. Successive Congresses passed resolutions urging the administration to reorder our national priorities away from defense. Only a few short years ago, the pressures in this country and from our allies were overwhelmingly to move rapidly toward better relations with Moscow. We resisted these pressures then, just as we now refuse to let ourselves be stampeded in the opposite direction. The country needs a balanced, long-term policy, combining firmness and conciliation, strong defense and arms control, political principles and economic incentives. And it must be a policy for the long term, that the American people can sustain, offering promise of a constructive future.

It is, therefore, ironic that our national debate seems now in many respects to have come full circle. The conditions in which détente originated are largely forgotten. Those who pressed for concessions and unilateral restraint toward Moscow now accuse the government of being too conciliatory. Those who complain about our failure to respond with sufficient vigor to Soviet moves are often the very ones who incessantly seek to remove this country's leverage for influence or action, through restrictions on trade and credit, through weakening our intelligence capabilities, through preventing aid to friends who seek to resist Soviet aggression. The human rights issue is a matter of deep and legitimate concern to all Americans. But the congressional attempt to link it openly with economic relations, without subtlety or understanding of Soviet politics, both deprived us of economic levers and sharply reduced Soviet emigration. Other industrial countries have stepped in to provide credits and technology, with less concern for the objective of inducing political restraint which we had envisaged.

So let us understand the scope and limits of a realistic policy: We cannot prevent the growth of Soviet power, but we can prevent its use for unilateral advantage and political expansion.

We cannot prevent a buildup of Soviet forces, but we have the capacity, together with our allies, to maintain an equilibrium. We cannot neglect this task and then blame others if the military balance shifts against us.

We have the diplomatic, economic, and military capacity to resist expansionism, but we cannot engage in a rhetoric of confrontation while depriving ourselves of the means to confront.

We must accept that sovereign states, especially of roughly equal power, cannot impose unacceptable conditions on each other and must proceed by compromise.

We must live with the reality of the nuclear threat, but we have it in our power to build a new relationship that transcends the nuclear peril.

So let us end the defeatist rhetoric that implies that Soviet policy is masterful, purposeful, and overwhelming, while American policy is bumbling, uncertain, and weak. Let us stop pretending that somehow tough rhetoric and contrived confrontations show confidence in America. We have a design and the material assets to deal with the Soviet Union. We will succeed if we move forward as a united people.

There is one central fact that distinguishes our era from all previous historical periods—the existence of enormously destructive weapons that can span unlimited distances almost instantaneously. No part of the globe is beyond reach. No part of the globe would be spared from the effects of a general nuclear exchange.

For centuries it was axiomatic that increases in military power could be translated into almost immediate political advantage. It is now clear that new increments of strategic weaponry do not automatically lead to either political or military gains. Yet in the nature of things, if one side expands its strategic arsenal, the other side will inevitably match it. The race is maintained partly because a perceived inequality is considered by each side as politically unacceptable.

We thus face a paradox: at current and foreseeable levels of nuclear arms, it becomes increasingly dangerous to invoke them. In no crisis since 1962 have the strategic weapons of the two sides determined the outcome. Today, these arsenals increasingly find their purpose primarily in matching and deterring the forces of the opponent. For under virtually no foreseeable circumstance could the United States—or the Soviet Union—avoid one hundred million dead in a nuclear exchange. Yet the race goes on because of the difficulty of finding a way to get off the treadmill.

To be sure, there exist scenarios in planning papers which seek to demonstrate how one side could use its strategic forces and how in some presumed circumstance it would prevail. But these confuse what a technician can calculate with what a responsible statesman can decide.

Sustaining the nuclear competition requires endless invocations of theoretical scenarios of imminent or eventual nuclear attack. The attempt to hedge against all conceivable contingencies—no matter how fanciful—fuels political tensions and could well lead to a self-fulfilling prophecy. The fixation on potential strategic arms imbalances that is inherent in an unrestrained arms race diverts resources into strategically unproductive areas—especially away from forces for local defense, where shortfalls and imbalances could be turned rapidly to our disadvantage. If no restraint is developed, the competition in strategic arms can have profound consequences for the future of international relations, and indeed of civilization.

The U.S., therefore, has sought and achieved, since 1963, a series of arms control agreements which build some restraint into nuclear rivalry. There was a significant breakthrough to limit strategic weapons in 1972. If the 1974 Vladivostok accord leads to a new agreement, an even more important advance will have been made.

Yet at this critical juncture, the American people are subjected to an avalanche of charges that SALT is a surrender of American interests. There are assertions that the U.S. is falling behind in the strategic competition and that SALT has contributed to it. There are unsupportable charges that the Soviets have systematically violated the SALT agreements. What are the facts?

First of all, American policy decisions in the 1960s set the level of our strategic forces for the 1970s. We then had the choice between continuing the deployment of large, heavy throw-weight missiles like the Titan or Atlas, or undertaking development and deployment of large numbers of smaller, more flexible ICBMs, or combinations of both types. The administration then in office *chose* to rely on an arsenal of 1,000 small, sophisticated, and highly accurate ICBMs and 656 submarine-launched missiles on 41 boats along with heavy bombers; we deployed them rapidly, and then stopped our buildup of launchers unilaterally when the programs were complete.

The Soviets made the opposite decision; they chose larger, heavier missiles; they continued to build up their forces through the 1960s and 1970s; they passed our numerical levels by 1969/1970 and continued to add an average of two hundred missiles a year until stopped by the first SALT agreement.

Thus, as a consequence of decisions made a decade ago by both sides, Soviet missiles are superior in throw-weight while ours are superior in reliability, accuracy, diversity, and sophistication, and we possess larger numbers of warheads.

The interim SALT agreement of 1972 froze overall numbers of launchers on both sides for five years, thereby limiting the momentum of Soviet programs without affecting any of ours. It stopped the Soviet buildup of heavy missile launchers. It forced the Soviets to agree to dismantle 210 older, land-based missiles, to reach permitted ceilings on missile-carrying submarines. The agreed-upon silo limitations permitted us to increase the throw-weight of our own missiles, if we decided on this avenue of improving our strategic forces. What no negotiation could do is reverse by diplomacy the results of our own long-standing decisions with respect to weapons design and deployment. Moreover, the SALT agreements ended for an indefinite period the prospect of a dangerous and uncertain competition

Film director and producer Cecil B. De Mille (center) with men wearing San Francisco Police Department uniforms. *Courtesy of the San Francisco History Center, San Francisco Public Library*

Above: In September 1951, Senator Joseph McCarthy holds documents that he says demonstrate the Communist affiliations of Philip C. Jessup, President Truman's appointee as roving ambassador. *Courtesy of Robert Mulligan/International News Photo, the San Francisco History Center, San Francisco Public Library*

Right, top: Soviet Premier Nikita Khrushchev waves enthusiastically to the crowd at the Commonwealth Club dinner in his honor held in September 1959. *Commonwealth Club Collection, Hoover Institution Library and Archives*

Right, bottom: A protestor in front of San Francisco's Ferry Building reminds Americans that it was Khrushchev who directed Soviet repression of the Hungarian revolution of 1956. *Courtesy of the San Francisco History Center, San Francisco Public Library*

Left: Speaking at a Commonwealth Club dinner at the Palace Hotel, President Eisenhower tells his audience, "The central need in all international affairs today is to forge a commonwealth of nations." *Courtesy of the San Francisco Chronicle*

Right: Arriving in San Francisco in October 1960, President Eisenhower is greeted by a tickertape parade. *Courtesy of Peter Breinig/San Francisco Chronicle*

Left: Physicist Edward Teller educating television viewers about science. *Courtesy of the San Francisco Chronicle*

Below: Unidentified men examining the components of a nuclear fallout shelter, as shown in this scale model. *Courtesy of the San Francisco History Center, San Francisco Public Library*

Above: William Westmoreland, commander of U.S. forces in Vietnam, meets with Vietnamese women in January 1967. *Bettmann/CORBIS*

Right: In late winter 1967, a pro-war billboard graces the San Francisco skyline. *Courtesy of Joe Rosenthal/San Francisco Chronicle*

Left: In April, on the eve of 1967's "long hot summer," Martin Luther King Jr. spoke to The Commonwealth Club on the future of integration. *Courtesy of the San Francisco History Center, San Francisco Public Library*

"*Get the Facts*"

GUEST SPEAKER

Martin Luther King Jr.

"THE FUTURE OF INTEGRATION"
Subject

"*Get the Facts*"

GUEST SPEAKER

George C. Wallace

"STATES' RIGHTS & CONSTITUTIONAL GOVERNMENT"
Subject

Right: Once and future Alabama Governor George Wallace spoke to The Commonwealth Club in 1967, declaring, "It's the liberals in our country who advocate anarchy." *Courtesy of Joe Rosenthal/San Francisco Chronicle*

Right: Senator Robert F. Kennedy visits an Indian reservation in Sonoma County, California, in conjunction with January 1968 hearings on education on reservations. *Courtesy of Barney Peterson/San Francisco Chronicle*

Below: American soldiers in the battle for Hue during the Tet offensive, in February 1968. *Bettmann/CORBIS*

Above: The Black Panthers in Oakland, California, in July 1968, on the second day of the murder trial of Panther leader Huey Newton. *Courtesy of The Bancroft Library, University of California, Berkeley, Online Archive of California*

Left: Stanford antiwar protestors on University Avenue in Palo Alto during their twenty-block march (May 4, 1970). *Courtesy of Vincent Maggiora/San Francisco Chronicle*

This page:

Top: *Washington Post* editor Benjamin Bradlee and publisher Katharine Graham celebrate the Supreme Court's ruling in June 1971 clearing the way for the *Post* and the *New York Times* to resume publishing the Pentagon Papers. *Courtesy of UPI/San Francisco Chronicle*

Bottom: Operation PUSH founder Jesse Jackson told his Commonwealth Club audience in 1974, "It's not your aptitude, but your attitude that determines your altitude." *Courtesy of Stephanie Maze/San Francisco Chronicle*

Opposite page:

Top left: When Ron Dellums was running for a seat in the House of Representatives, Vice President Spiro Agnew said he should be "purged from the body politic." The remark brought Dellums national attention. *Courtesy of Barney Peterson/San Francisco Chronicle*

Top right: "Battling Bella" Abzug was elected to Congress in 1970 on the slogan "This woman's place is in the House—the House of Representatives." *Commonwealth Club Collection, Hoover Institution Library and Archives*

Bottom: In 1972 Congresswoman Shirley Chisholm ran for president, the first black woman to make a bid for the nomination of a major party. *Courtesy of Dave Randolph/San Francisco Chronicle*

Right: U.S. Secretary of State Henry Kissinger won the Nobel Peace Prize in 1973, but in 1976 he lost the battle to maintain U.S. government aid to UNITA rebels in Angola. *Courtesy of the San Francisco Chronicle*

Below: Soviet-backed Angolan fighters pause to pose for the camera (December 19, 1975). *Bettmann/CORBIS*

in antiballistic missile defense—a competition that promised no strategic advantage but potentially serious instabilities and the expenditure of vast sums of money.

Obviously, no single agreement can solve every problem. This is not a question of loopholes but of evolving technology, with respect to which we intend to remain vigilant. We will negotiate carefully to make certain that the national interest and national security are protected. But if we succeed in turning the Vladivostok accord into a ten-year agreement, we will have crossed the threshold between total, unrestrained competition and the difficult but promising beginning of long-term strategic equilibrium at lower levels of forces.

If the process of negotiation falters, we must consider what new or additional strategic programs we would undertake, their likely cost, and above all, their strategic purpose. An accelerated strategic buildup over the next five years could cost as much as an additional $20 billion.

Tensions are likely to increase; a new, higher baseline will emerge from which future negotiations would eventually have to begin. And in the end, neither side will have gained a strategic advantage. At the least, they will have wasted resources. At worst, they will have increased the risks of nuclear war.

As the United States strives to shape a more hopeful world, it can never forget that global stability and security rest upon an equilibrium between the great powers. If the Soviet Union is permitted to exploit opportunities arising out of local conflicts by military means, the hopes we have for progress toward a more peaceful international order will ultimately be undermined. This is why the Soviet Union's massive and unprecedented intervention in the internal affairs of Africa with nearly $200 million of military equipment, its advisors, and its transport of the large expeditionary force of eleven thousand Cuban combat troops must be a matter of urgent concern.

Angola represents the first time that the Soviets have moved militarily at long distances to impose a regime of their choice. It is the first time that the U.S. has failed to respond to Soviet military moves outside the immediate Soviet orbit. And it is the first time that Congress has halted national action in mid-crisis.

When one great power tips the balance of forces decisively in a local conflict through its military intervention, and meets no resistance, an ominous precedent is set, of grave consequence even if the intervention occurs in a seemingly remote area.

The U.S. seeks no unilateral goals in Angola: we have proposed a cease-fire; withdrawal of all outside forces—Soviet, Cuban, and South African; cessation of foreign military involvement, including the supply of equipment; and negotiations among all three Angolan factions. This approach has the support of half the nations of Africa.

Last summer and fall, to halt a dangerously escalating situation, the United States provided financial support through African friends to those in Angola—the large majority—who sought to resist Soviet and Cuban domination. Using this as leverage, we undertook an active diplomacy to promote an African solution to an African problem. We acted quietly, to avoid provoking a major crisis and raising issues of prestige.

At first it was feared that the Soviet-backed faction, because of massive Soviet aid and Cuban mercenaries, would dominate totally by Independence Day, November 11. Our assistance prevented that. African determination to oppose Soviet and Cuban intervention became more and more evident. On December 9, the president warned Moscow of the consequences of continued meddling and offered to cooperate in encouraging a peaceful outcome that removed foreign influence. The Soviet Union appeared to have second thoughts. It halted its airlift from December 9 until December 24.

At that point, the impact of our domestic debate overwhelmed the possibilities of diplomacy. It was demanded that we explain publicly why our effort was important—and then our effort was cut off. After the Senate vote to block further aid to Angola, Cuba more than doubled its forces and Soviet military aid was resumed on a large scale.

As our public discussion continues, certain facts must be understood. The analogy with Vietnam is totally false; the nation must have the maturity to make elementary distinctions. The president has pledged that no American troops or advisors would be sent to Angola, and we were prepared to accept legislative restrictions to that effect. What was involved was modest assistance to stabilize the local balance of forces and make possible a rapid political settlement.

It is charged that the administration acted covertly, without public acknowledgment. That is correct, for our purpose was to avoid an escalated confrontation that would make it more difficult for the others to back down, as well as to give the greatest possible scope for an African solution. Angola was a case where diplomacy without leverage was likely to be impotent, yet direct military confrontation would involve needless risks. This is precisely one of those gray areas where unpublicized methods would enable us to influence events short of direct conflict.

More than two dozen senators, one hundred and fifty congressmen, over one hundred staff members of both houses, and eight congressional committees were briefed on twenty-four separate occasions. We sought in these briefings to determine the wishes of Congress, and there was little sign of active opposition to our carefully limited operations.

It is said that the Russians will inevitably be eased out by the Africans themselves over a period of time. This may or may not prove true. But such an argument, when carried to its logical conclusion, implies that we can abandon the world to interventionist forces, and hope for the best. And reliance on history is of little solace to those under attack, whose future is being decided now.

It is maintained that we should meet the Soviet threat in Angola through escalated methods of pressure, such as altering our position on SALT or grain sales. But these arrangements benefit us as well as the Soviet Union and are part of the long-term strategy for dealing with the Soviet Union. History has proved time and again that expansion can be checked only when there is a local balance of forces; indirect means can succeed only if rapid local victories are foreclosed. As the president has pointed out, the Soviet Union has survived for nearly sixty years without American grain; it could do so now. Cutting off grain would still lose Angola.

Let us not bemuse ourselves with facile slogans about not becoming the world's policeman. We have no desire to play such a role. But it can never be in our interest to let the Soviet Union act as the world's policeman. There are many crises in the world where the United States cannot and should not intervene. But here we face a blatant Soviet and Cuban challenge, which could have been overcome if we had been allowed to act prudently with limited means at the early stage. By forcing this out onto center stage, our divisions simultaneously escalated the significance of the crisis and guaranteed our impotence.

The government has a duty to make clear to the Soviet Union and Cuba that Angola sets no precedent, that this type of action will not be tolerated again. It must reassure adjacent countries that they will not be left exposed to attack or pressure from the new Soviet-Cuban foothold. Congress and the executive must come together on this proposition—in the national interest and in the interest of world peace. Let no nation believe that Americans will long remain indifferent to the dispatch of expeditionary forces and vast supplies of arms to impose minority governments—especially when that expeditionary force comes from a nation in the Western Hemisphere.

We live in a world without simple answers. We hold our values too dear to relinquish defending them; we hold human life too dear to cease the quest for a secure peace. The first requirement of stability is to maintain our defenses and the balance of power. But the highest aim of policy in the nuclear age must be to create out of the sterile equilibrium of force a more positive relationship of peace.

America has the material assets to do the job. Our military might is unmatched. Our economic and technological strength dwarfs any other. Our democratic heritage is envied by hundreds of millions around the world. Our problems, therefore, are of our own making—self-doubt, division, irresolution. We must once again become a confident, united, and determined people.

Foreign countries must be able to deal with America as an entity, not as a complex of divided institutions. If our divisions paralyze our international efforts, it is America as a whole that will suffer.

Debate is the essence of democracy. But restraint is the cement of national cohesion. It is time to end the self-torment and obsession with our guilt which has threatened to paralyze us for too many years. It is time to stop dismantling our national institutions and undermining our national confidence.

One of the forgotten truths of our history is that our Founding Fathers were men of great sophistication in foreign affairs. They understood the balance of power; they made use of the divisions of Europe for the advantage or our own revolution. They understood the need for a strong executive to conduct the nation's diplomacy. They grasped that America required economic, political, and moral links with other nations. They saw that our ideals were universal, and they understood and welcomed the impact of the American experiment on the destinies of all mankind.

In our age whose challenges are without precedent, we need once again the wisdom of our Founding Fathers. Our ideals must give us strength—

rather than serve as an excuse for abdication. The American people want an effective foreign policy. They want America to continue to help shape the international order of the coming generation according to our ideals. We have done great things as a united people. We have it in our power to make our third century a time of vibrancy and hope and greatness.

July 23, 1976

George H. W. Bush

Director, Central Intelligence Agency

When George H. W. Bush was confirmed as the new director of the Central Intelligence Agency in January 1976, he acknowledged that it was a "very difficult time" for the agency. Bush had served two terms in the House of Representatives, had been chairman of the Republican National Committee, and was then chief of the U.S. Liaison Office in the People's Republic of China. In 1974, the *New York Times* had begun publishing a series of articles detailing the misdeeds of the CIA, including involvement in the Watergate affair. Congressional investigations followed, and President Ford fired Bush's predecessor, William Colby, for cooperating too freely with the investigations. Colby himself blamed the "sensational and hysterical way the CIA investigations" were "handled and trumpeted around the world" as creating the climate in which a terrorist group killed Richard Welch, the CIA station chief in Athens, Greece, just before Christmas 1975. Rather than dismantle the CIA or other intelligence agencies, with Bush's appointment President Ford also undertook what he claimed was the most sweeping reform and reorganization of the United States intelligence agencies since the passage of the National Security Act of 1947. He created the Intelligence Oversight Board, which Bush also headed, and in his Commonwealth Club speech,

Bush underscored the coordinating role he played as the president's number one man on intelligence. The restructuring, the *Times* assessed, "centralized more power in the hands of the Director of Central Intelligence than any had had since the creation of the CIA. The director has always been the nominal head of the intelligence community, but in fact has had little power over the other agencies, particularly the Department of Defense."

Spring 1976 saw the tables turned on Congress, as a scandal that became known as "Koreagate" unraveled. More than one hundred congressmen were reported to have accepted money, trips, and honorary degrees in exchange for support for legislation favorable to South Korean leader Park Chung Hee. Former Watergate Special Prosecutor Leon Jaworski was brought back for the case. Eventually only one congressman was convicted: Richard Hanna (D-CA). But it was within the context of leaks about intelligence and a corruptible Congress—and just weeks after Israeli military forces had staged a daring nighttime raid at the Entebbe airport in Uganda to free passengers of a hijacked plane—that George Bush spoke of intelligence, security, and secrecy in a democracy.

"The CIA and the Intelligence Community"

Let me tell you something of the mechanism that has been created by the U.S. government to gather and produce intelligence. As you know, it was World War II—and specifically Pearl Harbor—which focused American attention on the need not just for information, but for a unified, *national* intelligence service. Before the war, we had what could be called departmental intelligence. The War Department had military intelligence, the Navy Department had naval intelligence, and so on.

But in today's terminology, no one was "getting it together." All of the information that might have led an analyst to conclude that Japan intended to attack Pearl Harbor was available in Washington. But it was not in one place for an analyst to study; it was instead in separate bits and pieces carefully controlled by each department. After the war, it was clear that America required continuing intelligence on developments and trends abroad, and that a central organization was needed to ensure that we had all our facts together and would never again be caught by surprise.

In 1947, President Truman signed into law the National Security Act, which created the Central Intelligence Agency. The Agency was intended to be—and is—the central point for producing *national* intelligence; that is, intelligence produced to serve national policy makers, and intelligence of interest to more than one department or agency. The National Security Act also created the position of director of central intelligence—the DCI. The DCI is the nation's senior foreign intelligence officer and the president's principal advisor on foreign intelligence. It was intended that the DCI wear two hats: one as director of the CIA and the other as head of the intelligence community as a whole.

In 1971, the president instructed the DCI to take a more active role in coordinating the resources and activities of the community. In the past five years, we have made major strides in building a true intelligence community—with a capital *I* and *A* and a capital *C*. The community now consists of the CIA; the Defense Intelligence Agency; the National Security Agency; and the intelligence components of the military services, the Department of State, the FBI, the Treasury Department, and the Energy Research and Development Administration.

In February, as you probably remember, President Ford issued an executive order that strengthened the DCI's role as the leader of the nation's intelligence community. That order also directed new organizational arrangements to strengthen the DCI's management of the community.

These new arrangements have made some very important changes. A Committee on Foreign Intelligence, which I chair, has been created by the president. It controls budget preparation and resource application for the entire national foreign intelligence program. It manages our intelligence activities and establishes policy for the collection and production of national intelligence.

An Operational Advisory Group has been established to make recommendations to the president concerning special intelligence activities in support of national foreign policy objectives—that is, covert action. The group also reviews and approves sensitive intelligence collection operations. The members of this board include the assistant to the president for national security affairs, the secretaries of state and defense, the chairman of the staff, and the director of central intelligence.

In response to the investigations of U.S. intelligence activities conducted by the Rockefeller Commission and by the Senate and House Select

Committees, the president has created an Intelligence Oversight Board of three prominent private citizens. This board receives and considers reports by the inspectors general and general counsels of the intelligence community concerning any activities that raise questions of legality or propriety. It is the board's responsibility to ensure that the attorney general and the president are properly advised.

In order to enable me to devote more attention to formulating and carrying out policies for the community, the president also has directed that I have two deputies. One is responsible to me for the day-to-day operation of the CIA, and the other is responsible to me for accomplishing my role as head of the intelligence community. Legislation to establish these positions will be introduced in the near future.

The CIA is the nation's resource for producing national intelligence. And it is truly a national resource—our trained, skillful, and imaginative analysts are a wealth beyond price.

Science and technology provide us today with means of collecting information that is beyond the wildest imaginings of even a few years ago. Yet despite the mind-boggling advances made in this area, there is still an essential need for information from people. Trained and experienced people are necessary to acquire information that is only available through access to knowledgeable foreign officials and to the intentions of foreign governments that may be adverse to U.S. interests.

I am a comparative newcomer to the intelligence business, but I have been immersed long enough to have no hesitancy in saying to you that the Central Intelligence Agency is an organization of which the entire nation can be proud.

On my way here today, I was reminded of something that was written by John Buchan in 1940, a time of descending darkness on Europe and the free world, when Great Britain stood virtually alone against the seemingly irresistible enemy. John Buchan, as you remember, is the family name of Lord Tweedsmuir, then governor-general of Canada and also author of some now classic tales of espionage and adventure. John Buchan wrote then:

> The United States is the richest, and, both actually and potentially, the most powerful state on the globe. She has much, I believe, to give to the world; indeed, to her hands is chiefly entrusted the shaping of the future. If democracy in the broadest and truest sense is to

survive, it will be mainly because of her guardianship. For, with all her imperfections, she has a clearer view than any other people of the democratic fundamentals.

That was written in 1940, ladies and gentlemen, and surely it is as true today as it was then. To be sure, many things have changed, largely because of the way that we did discharge our responsibilities after World War II. Largely because of our own policies and actions, we are no longer in the position of food supplier to the free world: we are no longer in the position of the rebuilder and supporter of war-shattered economies of the world; and, largely because of the success of our policies, we have relinquished what tolerance we had for being the world's policeman.

But the world is not yet such as we would want it to be. Maybe it never will be. It certainly is not likely to become a utopian world within our life-time or even in the foreseeable future. And while we are striving to make our contribution to a world of peace and security and trust, we find that we still need—quite consistent with this striving—to have national security second to none in the world.

The one element of the profession of intelligence, that essential component of national security and foreign relations, that has troubled us as citizens of a free nation, is the necessary element of secrecy that is inherent in our profession. It is no wonder that even the very fact of secrecy tends to stimulate suspicion and give an aura of sensationalism, and therefore, often an entirely erroneous perspective, to various disclosures and findings—occasionally, if I may say so, without due regard for the amount and quality of evidence.

If secrecy is essential, so too is accountability. No activity of our government may be conducted without being subjected to a reliable and responsible system of checks and balances. But accountability is one thing; recklessness is another. It is not those who disclose the names of our intelligence officers serving abroad that add to the security of a free society. It is not those who believe they can, on their own judgment, disclose information which has been classified in the interests of our security that contribute to the responsiveness of government to the people. And it is not those who determinedly deny the good will and responsibility of people in and out of government by dwelling on abuses of the past that enhance the mechanism of accountability which this free society has created for the control of legitimately secret government responsibilities.

The great majority of us have faith in the strength and effectiveness of our democratic institutions, for while democratic institutions may be used to sow seeds of weakness and distrust, they exist in order to make us strong and self-reliant, and they have proved their effectiveness in the two hundred years of our history.

I wish you could talk to some of our employees whose heads are high after a couple of years of vicious battering. They are as vigorously opposed to the mistakes of the past as our strongest critics, but they have retained a perspective. They know the need for a strong intelligence community, and they are prepared to withstand the battering, if that is necessary, to work for a cause they believe in.

I wish you could have met the son of Richard Welch, who was gunned down following disclosure of his name by people bent on destroying the CIA. This young man knew well that his father had died for a cause in which he deeply believed.

And I hope that increasingly, also, you will draw reassurance and pride from the manner in which the intelligence community not only responds to the direction of the elected chief executive but also is accountable to the elected representatives in Congress.

I believe that America's intelligence service is a great national asset. We are working hard to make it even better. Your understanding, support, and trust are essential for our success.

November 19, 1976

William Westmoreland

Commander of U.S. Forces in Vietnam, 1964–68

The Tet offensive of February 1968 was a military victory for U.S. forces, General William Westmoreland contended at the time—and years later. But it was a psychological defeat for America, he said, thanks to the media.

Commander of U.S. forces in Vietnam from 1964 to 1968—and named Man of the Year by *Time* in 1965—Westmoreland spoke before The Commonwealth Club several years after retiring from the Army. But in fact one of his greatest battles—against the CBS network and the program *60 Minutes*—lay some years ahead of him.

Under Westmoreland, the U.S. strategy in Vietnam was a war of attrition, with the goal of killing Vietnamese Communist forces more quickly than they could be replaced. U.S. forces engaged in search-and-destroy operations in pursuit of large concentrations of the enemy. But just who the enemy was ultimately became central to the controversy surrounding what critics contended were Westmoreland's underestimations of enemy troop strength. The Tet offensive convinced journalists and, as a consequence, much of the American public, that Communist forces were more numerous than the military was contending. The casualty figures Westmoreland cited in his 1980 memoir, *A Soldier Reports*, were that during the Tet offensive the Communists lost over thirty thousand men while the Americans, South Vietnamese, and allies lost some three thousand. Those numbers belie the fact that there had been tussling between the U.S. Army and the CIA the previous year over the "plan of battle"—the numbers of Communist forces. Westmoreland's concern about the numbers was apparently influenced by worry over press coverage of the war, which Westmoreland felt consistently dwelt on the negative—and was carried out by what he called youthful, inexperienced correspondents who succumbed to a "herd instinct." Reporters, in turn, dubbed the daily press conferences held by the U.S. military in Saigon the "Five O'clock Follies," for what journalists saw as unrealistically optimistic accounts of fighting and, as journalist Peter Arnett put it, "sleight of hand" regarding casualties.

The crux of the intelligence debate was over "irregular forces"—perhaps women, old men, children—who either were or were not an effective fighting force. Westmoreland estimated the forces arrayed against U.S. troops at 250,000 or less. If the irregulars were the ones setting booby traps and mines or waving at American troops as they passed through a village—and then shooting at them when they returned—and these irregulars were included, then enemy troop estimates would, according to one CIA officer, have been closer to 430,000. And for the estimate given to the public to suddenly blossom would be a public relations disaster. That disaster came anyway with Tet, when many wondered how the enemy could suddenly appear to be everywhere at once and attacking in so many places, including the U.S. Embassy in Saigon. That embassy at last fell to Communist forces in April 1975, when Saigon was overrun.

Vietnam was the first war that Americans saw televised, and it's widely acknowledged that the media played a powerful role in shaping broad public opinion on the war. Westmoreland's talk raises the question of what responsibility journalists have in a time of war and when a claim to exercise liberties granted by the Constitution crosses the line and becomes a betrayal of the ideals of democracy.

On January 23, 1982, CBS broadcast an episode of *60 Minutes* under the title "The Uncounted Enemy: A Vietnam Deception." The show ranked dead last in ratings for the night, but in this case, ratings weren't everything. Interviewer Mike Wallace put William Westmoreland on the spot about troop estimates. Showing Westmoreland in a close-up shot known as a "choke" that made the square-jawed soldier with the silvery hair look particularly uncomfortable, the program was introduced as having uncovered a "conspiracy at the highest levels of military intelligence to suppress and alter critical intelligence on the enemy in the year leading up to the Tet offensive." Westmoreland felt he'd been ambushed (or "rattlesnaked," as he told Wallace and producer George Crile after the taping). He held a news conference a few days later to challenge what the broadcast purported to show. *TV Guide* published an exposé on the broadcast and CBS initiated its own investigation. Senior Executive Producer Burton Benjamin found the broadcast "seriously flawed" in its execution—but the network stuck by it nevertheless.

Westmoreland filed a $120-million lawsuit in September 1982. The trial opened in October 1984 in New York. Brought onto the witness stand were the likes of former Secretary of Defense Robert S. McNamara and former White House advisor Walt Rostow. The trial revisited not just the particulars of the *60 Minutes* broadcast, but many of the arguments and policies regarding Vietnam itself. Westmoreland and CBS agreed to an out-of-court settlement in February 1985, with both sides declaring victory.

"Vietnam in Perspective"

Recent years have been traumatic for America. Vietnam and Watergate have been center stage. The Watergate episode has been dissected, plummeted, exploited. The blame for that messy affair has been firmly placed. Lessons have been learned and some heeded. But not so for the Vietnam disaster.

South Vietnam no longer exists. It has been gobbled up by North Vietnam following blatant aggression. The flicker of freedom there has been extinguished, probably forever. Our erstwhile honorable country betrayed and deserted the Republic of Vietnam after it had enticed it to our bosom. It was a shabby performance by America, a blemish on our history and a possible blight on our future. Our credibility has been damaged. There are lessons to be learned and vulnerabilities in our system that need examination.

Our interest in South Vietnam was born in the post–World War II period, motivated by a concern for unchecked Communist movement into insecure and unstable areas. In 1947, President Truman enunciated a national policy that pledged us to the unconditional support of "free people who are resisting attempted subjugation by minorities or by outside pressures." The Congress approved this doctrine by a large majority. In 1950, we sent a military mission to Saigon. President Eisenhower's policy of "containment" followed, associated with his massive retaliation strategy. When Mr. Kennedy was elected president, he became interested in the so-called small war concept, became concerned about the size and readiness of the Army that he thought had been neglected under President Eisenhower. He increased the size of the Army, and personally sponsored the Army's Green Berets. He anticipated the advent of nuclear parity between the U.S. and USSR. After his verbal confrontation with Chairman Khrushchev in Vienna in 1961, Mr. Kennedy reportedly told Scotty Reston of the *New York Times*, "We have a problem in making our power credible, and Vietnam looks like the place."

President Kennedy set the tone of his administration in his inaugural address when he pledged our nation to "bear any burden, meet any hardship, support any friend, and oppose any foe to assure the survival and the success of liberty." Hence he greatly increased our military effort in Vietnam with advisors, Green Berets, American-manned helicopters, and tactical aircraft. The president in his zeal made a grievous mistake in approving our involvement in the overthrow of President Diem of South Vietnam. This action morally locked us in Vietnam. Political chaos prevailed for two years. If not for our involvement in the political affairs of South Vietnam, and based on pragmatic considerations, we could have gracefully withdrawn our support in view of a demonstrated lack of unity in South Vietnam. On the other hand, in the wake of Mr. Kennedy's inaugural pronouncements, it is doubtful if his or Mr. Johnson's administration would have risked the political repercussions. Mr. Kennedy's inaugural address was still ringing in the ears of Americans.

President Johnson inherited the problem and retained most of Mr. Kennedy's advisors. He was obsessed with his Great Society program. In the hope that the war would go away, he made some decisions with the endorsement of congressional leaders that were destined to drag the war on indefinitely. He expanded our military effort to avoid inevitable defeat and increased the national debt to do so. His "guns and butter" policy resulted in business as usual—in fact, a booming economy. No one "bore a burden, met a hardship," except those on the battlefield and their loved ones. In fact, if not for the sensational media coverage piped into the homes of America, few would have appreciated that we were at war.

The president announced that we would not broaden the war. This set for us a defensive strategy on the ground and gave to the enemy great latitude for action. A force on the offensive is stronger than one on the defensive, because it possesses the initiative and can mass its strength where and when it chooses, without concern for the security of rear areas.

President Johnson's administration formulated a strategy briefly described as: hold the enemy; defeat him in the South; help build a nation; bomb war-related targets in the North on a gradually escalating basis until the enemy gets the message that he cannot win and thus will negotiate or accept a divided Vietnam.

The trouble was, the bombing was off and on—a thermometer of public pressure at home. Hanoi adjusted itself to every escalatory step. The enemy got a message—not of resolve and strength, but of political insecurity and weakness—not only from official actions, but from the vocal and emotional elements in our society who chose to resist actively national policy. From this syndrome came fallacies and clichés, such as "illegal war" and "immoral war." The leaders in Hanoi foresaw that they could win the war politically in Washington as they had done against the French in Paris in 1954.

The Gulf of Tonkin resolution by the Congress in 1964, passed by a sizable majority, gave the president authority to commit military forces as he deemed necessary to achieve our objectives. As the war was allowed to drag on and on, the mood of Congress, a reflection of public attitudes, in turn influenced profoundly by the media, particularly by daily TV reports, grew further and further away from the policy of the executive branch. As the war became controversial, the president should have asked for affirmation each year of the Gulf of Tonkin resolution—indeed, the congressional leadership should have demanded it. On the other hand, the policy of the Johnson Administration was "low key." Both the president and the congressional leaders were afraid of an open national debate. They were unsure of the political repercussions, and more concerned about the "hawks" than the "doves" on the convenient theory that Red China might be provoked to enter the war. They took counsel of their fears. The relevance of Vietnam to our security was not apparent, and the idealism implicit in President Kennedy's words faded into obscurity.

A decision of the president and the Congress to defer college students from military service was a cardinal mistake which had widespread repercussions. That unwise policy has been injurious to our society, degrading to our academic institutions, and hindered our war effort. It was discriminatory, undemocratic, and resulted in the war being fought mainly by the poor man's son. I attribute the emotional antiwar sentiments on the campus to a guilt complex, and the frustration of possibly having to participate in a war controlled by a no-win policy. ROTC on the campus became the symbolic "whipping boy," and that source of officers was crippled. In other words, the military have logically drawn their officers from the college campuses. During the Vietnam War, the pool of young men with intelligence and leadership qualities was essentially denied the military. Therefore the Army had to lower its standards for officers, and some marginal types were commissioned. That, incidentally, is the tragedy of Lieutenant Calley, who was obviously not of officer caliber.[1]

In the 1970 period, many college deferments ran out, and the Army received thousands of new soldiers in the rank of private with graduate and postgraduate degrees. Many came from emotionally charged campuses. An education inversion was created, with many privates being better educated than their sergeants and many of the lieutenants. A communication problem evolved and had to be solved by unique methods. Underground newspapers and coffeehouses sprang up, a new lexicon emerged: a career man was a "lifer," a volunteer a "paid killer." Leaflets were passed out as men left their military posts, urging them to thwart military discipline. All of this was in the name of dissent.

You all remember the Tet offensive by North Vietnam in 1968, which was the enemy's reaction to his major setbacks in South Vietnam during 1967. The enemy's objective was to inflict a military defeat on the Vietnamese and the Americans, and to generate a public uprising by the people of South Vietnam against the Saigon regime. The enemy's military defeat was so severe that it took him four years to recover. There were no public uprisings. When the people fled from the North Vietnam invaders, it was often described by the media as a movement to avoid our air and

1. On March 16, 1968, U.S. forces under the command of Lt. William Calley killed some five hundred unarmed men, women, and children in the village of My Lai. A subsequent court-martial held Calley responsible for the massacre, and in 1971 he was convicted of premeditated murder and sentenced to life in prison. Owing to concern that Calley had been unjustly singled out for blame in the massacre (five other soldiers were tried and acquitted for their role in the killings), he was paroled in 1974.

artillery. Most ARVN (North Vietnamese army) units fought well, but it was not the "in" thing in media circles to say anything good about the South Vietnamese.

The media misled the American people by their reporting of Tet, and even a number of officials in Washington were taken in. There is an old military axiom that "when the enemy is hurting, don't let up, increase the pressure on him." Despite military advice to the contrary, our political leaders decreased the pressure on the Hanoi regime and enticed the enemy to the conference table. There they sat in Paris for over four years, and decided only one thing—the shape of the conference table. Our official and unofficial actions provided no incentive for Hanoi to do otherwise. To demonstrate this principle, I remind you that in 1972, after Haiphong harbor was mined, and B-52s were used against important military targets in North Vietnam, Le Duc Tho and his colleagues came to the conference table and actually wept, saying that they could not take any more. We could have put that type of pressure on Hanoi after the defeat of the Tet offensive, and the enemy would have been forced to negotiate on our terms, and thousands of lives would have been saved.

But that was not to be. The antiwar groups dedicated themselves to resisting national policy. They wanted to end the war. Who didn't? The sad thing was that those who were loudly dissenting were unwittingly encouraging the enemy to hang on. And hang on they did, because every practical measure designed to encourage them to change their aggression strategy was undercut by expressions and actions reflecting a lack of resolve, a naïve understanding of warfare, or blissful ignorance of the language that Communists understand—demonstrable resolve.

As our soldiers were fighting and dying for the principle of liberty and the right to dissent, what did we see at home? Burning the flag, abusing public officials, destroying ROTC buildings, extolling the Vietcong, lying and cheating by young men to disqualify themselves for military service, burning draft cards, draft resisters fleeing to Canada and Sweden—unconscionable conduct month after month. Some called it democracy at work. A better definition was anarchy. Call it what you will, it encouraged our enemies, prolonged the war, and sadly cost lives.

In 1969, a withdrawal strategy was adopted without any quid pro quo from Hanoi. The North Vietnamese leadership persisted in promoting the fiction that the war was fundamentally a civil war—a people's revolution.

The Tet offensive should have laid to rest that myth. It should have been obvious that, like the Korean War, it was a war of aggression by the Communist North.

Following the pressure that was finally put on North Vietnam by the invasion of their bases in Cambodia, the incursion into Laos, the mining of Haiphong harbor, and the B-52 strikes into North Vietnam, the enemy decided for the first time to negotiate seriously. An agreement was arrived at in early 1973 which, although defective in many respects, was theoretically workable. But soon any hope of success was dashed by the Case-Church amendment to the 1974 Appropriation Act, which prohibited any funds whatsoever "to finance directly or indirectly combat activities by U.S. military forces in or over or from off the shores of North Vietnam, South Vietnam, Laos, or Cambodia." Moscow and Hanoi recognized the Case-Church amendment as our instrument of surrender; they could break the Paris Peace Accord and get by with it. On top of that, the Congress cut military aid to South Vietnam by one-half and threatened to stop it entirely. All this following our president's many assurances by envoy and in writing to President Thieu that we would fully support his military forces after our withdrawal and would react if the enemy broke the Paris agreement. As you know so well, in early 1975, the accord was flagrantly broken; Hanoi's gamble succeeded. The United States had paralyzed itself.

General Van Tien Dung, who commanded Hanoi's invading forces, in his account of his success in conquering South Vietnam, tells the story. He has reported accurately that the reduction in U.S. military aid ordered by Congress seriously impaired the ability of the South Vietnamese army to fight. He estimates that the firepower by the South Vietnamese army was cut by 60 percent because of a shortage of bombs and communication, while its mobility was reduced by half because of inoperative aircraft and vehicles, resulting from a shortage of spare parts and fuel. Thieu, he said, was forced "to fight a poor man's war." On the other hand, the North Vietnamese forces were fully equipped and supported by Russia and China. Dung gave no meaningful credit to the local Vietcong. The leaders in Hanoi were students of our sensitive political system and the vulnerabilities of our open society. It was no accident that most of their initiatives were shrewdly coordinated with our national elections. They wished to encourage our political leaders to make decisions on the basis of political expediency rather than experienced, sound judgment. They achieved considerable success.

Vietnam was both the most reported and the least reported war in history—if one considers both the coverage from Hanoi as well as Saigon. American families at home were able to see on "the tube" the bloodshed inevitably present on any battlefield. War was reported for the first time like crime on the police beat, or a no-holds-barred political campaign. Hanoi was able to cultivate the fiction that there were no North Vietnamese troops in the South, that the war was basically a people's revolution, that it was an illegal and immoral war. It is astonishing that numbers of our citizens and representatives of the news media were taken in by Hanoi's propaganda. President Thieu became a favorite target for the press and was unfairly maligned, while the conduct of the autocratic leaders in the North were not given equal time. They were ignored. Some of the news media suggested by their subjective reporting that the young country of South Vietnam, with no experience in democracy or even self-government, was expected to be as democratic and free of corruption as America, with almost two centuries of experience. They were presumably expected to demonstrate an advanced form of democracy while fighting for their survival. By comparison, the enemy leaders appeared to be the "good guys."

There were no TV cameras behind the enemy lines. All news from North Vietnam was propaganda to serve their purposes. And serve it, it did.

In a situation where our men's lives were put on the line, it is lamentable that so many did all possible to erode support for a policy associated with six presidents and nine Congresses. Such evident disunity kept before the leaders in Hanoi the smell of victory. It is a sad commentary that our open society and our political systems were masterfully manipulated by Hanoi and Moscow to serve their interest.

My analyses would not be complete without mentioning those men in uniform and their civilian associates who tried zealously to make good the commitment our national leaders made to the people of South Vietnam. Those men and women performed admirably under circumstances unique in history. It is not easy to maintain morale on the battlefield if there are doubts about the support of the American people.

My thesis is simple. Our nation blundered in Vietnam, and hence betrayed a chosen ally. One can learn more from failure than success. In our national interest, let us get about determining where we went wrong. I don't propose any more witch hunts, but I do urge that we not sweep the homemade mess under the rug.

I presume to conclude with several broad conclusions of my own. We overextended ourselves in the post–World War II period, economically, militarily, psychologically, and politically. A day of reckoning was inevitable. Our foreign policy should be given a nonpartisan review at least every two years. We must develop a bipartisan foreign policy, free of politics as far as possible. We should select our leaders carefully—broad-gauged statesmen, not slaves to the public opinion polls, wise men who can lead public opinion. When there is a threat of war, our military leaders deserve a stronger voice in policy making. When our political leaders commit us to war, the military voice should be given priority consideration. The military should not acquiesce to unsound military decisions. It is unfair and fatal to send our troops to the battlefield if they are not going to be supported by the nation. When we go to war, the burden and hardship must be shared by a cross section of our society. We should heed an old Oriental saying: "It takes the full strength of a tiger to kill a rabbit," and use appropriate force to bring the war to an end. When our national reputation and men's lives are at stake, the news media must show a more convincing sense of responsibility. We must be leery as a nation of our adversaries manipulating again the vulnerability of our political system and our open society.

The Vietnam episode is a travesty of the way America should function. Our elected officials at the national level and their advisors share the blame for the disaster. But politicians are a mere reflection of the American people and their institutions. They elected them. So perhaps on balance we must admit the comic strip character Pogo was right: "We met the enemy and he was us." This is the profound lesson.

May 6, 1977

Morton Halperin

Director, ACLU Project on National Security and Civil Liberties

In 1977, former government official Morton Halperin took to The Commonwealth Club podium to articulate the abuses he said were being perpetrated by the FBI and CIA in the name of national security. Among the abuses, Halperin said, was the 1973 CIA-backed coup that overthrew Salvador Allende, the democratically elected leader of Chile. At the time of his speech, Halperin had recently taken the helm of the American Civil Liberties Union's Project on National Security and Civil Liberties. He'd previously served in the Johnson and Nixon Administrations, in the Defense Department and National Security Council, and he'd resigned in 1970 after the U.S. invasion of Cambodia. While he was still serving under Nixon, Halperin himself was the subject of a wiretap for nearly two years because he was suspected of leaking Pentagon documents. He sued Henry Kissinger and eventually won an apology. Halperin was back in the news in 1993 when he was nominated by Bill Clinton for the position of assistant secretary of defense, but after rancorous Senate debate, his nomination was withdrawn. He did, however, serve in other capacities in the Clinton Administration, on the National Security Council and in the Department of State. His current responsibilities include serving as director of the Washington office for the Open Society Institute, founded by George Soros.

"The Crimes of the Intelligence Agencies"

The topic of my address today is the crimes of intelligence agencies. I will be talking about some of their activities which are, in my view, in clear violation of the laws of this land and the Constitution. People of the intelligence agencies feel that these subjects should not be discussed. They describe these matters as "state secrets," which if released, they say, would injure the national security of the United States. We have found that the information which is to be kept secret is information which is readily available to foreign governments, to our potential enemies, and in fact being kept only from the American people.

It is important to understand that the U.S. intelligence agencies and the law enforcement agencies which are supposed to be protecting our security in fact engage in deliberate and systematic violations of Constitutional rights. The FBI engaged in a series of illegal and unconstitutional programs. It engaged in wiretaps without warrants against people who were being investigated for criminal activities. It engaged in burglaries called "black-bag jobs." In defending these activities within the bureau, senior officials of the FBI said that these activities were clearly illegal, but they were useful and should have been carried out.

The FBI had a program of infiltration and surveillance of political organizations in the U.S.: for example, Ku Klux Klan, Communist Party, Socialist Workers Party, Southern Christian Leadership Conference, American Civil Liberties Union, and many others. This infiltration and surveillance were not based on the belief that these organizations were breaking the law. It was based on the belief that the FBI had a right and a patriotic duty to investigate people whose politics the bureau disapproved of, or whose political activities might be of interest to the Communist Party in the U.S., or political activity which the bureau thought jeopardized the status quo within the U.S.

One of the groups which came to the attention of the FBI was referred to as the WLM, the Women's Liberation Movement. Mr. [J. Edgar] Hoover sent out a directive saying that the bureau had decided that the Women's Liberation Movement should be infiltrated and put under surveillance. As a result, many memorandums were sent out, including one from the office in New York which said as far as the bureau office could determine, there was no such organization as the WLM. Instead, it seemed to be a group of different organizations of women who were dissatisfied and protested their situation. The New York office and several other offices said that they did not feel this activity justified FBI intervention. With that came a memorandum from Mr. Hoover saying that this activity was subversive and therefore the bureau would place the Women's Liberation Movement under surveillance. Therefore, whenever women gathered in this country, even in groups of five or six, the bureau was there conducting surveillance. Whenever environmentalists gathered, the bureau was there. When the ACLU had its biannual meetings, the bureau was there. In fact, we have not yet discovered any major political organization which has not received the attention of the FBI through infiltration, surveillance, and in many cases, wiretappings and burglaries.

The bureau was not content to gather information. It moved on to a program called COINTELPRO, the manipulation of organizations whose politics the bureau did not like. The bureau had been confronted by the fact that in the late 1950s and early 1960s, the Supreme Court issued a series of opinions which in effect said that individuals could not be prosecuted for engaging in political activity. Only individuals who advocated violence and breaking the law could be prosecuted. The bureau knew of a number of organizations which it considered subversive, and yet there was no point in bringing this information to the attention of the Justice Department. Therefore, the bureau took the law into its own hands and started its COINTELPRO operations. It began with the Communist Party and moved to the Socialist Workers Party. From there it moved to the antiwar movement and the black nationalist movement. Against each of these movements, the bureau engaged in efforts to undermine the lawful activities and to move these organizations in a violent direction so that they would be discredited.

One of these campaigns was directed at Martin Luther King Jr. You will recall that Martin Luther King gave a speech at the Lincoln Monument, in Washington, in which he talked about a dream for America, a peaceful integration of American society. Most Americans were moved and touched by the speech. The FBI was outraged. The bureau held an all-day meeting in which, according to one of the participants, the FBI declared war on Martin Luther King. His hotel rooms were bugged, his telephones were bugged, and his organization was infiltrated.

The bureau also moved against the antiwar movement. It infiltrated people who would propose to move from peaceful protest to violent activity. According to FBI memos, its motive was to destroy the respectability, credibility, and cohesion of the organizations.

The FBI claims that the COINTELPRO operations have come to an end. It admits that it continues to conduct political surveillance of organizations in the U.S. It predicates this surveillance on the assumption that these groups may someday break the law, or if it believes that the organizations are in some way connected with a foreign power.

The CIA was set up by Congress in 1947 to conduct intelligence activities abroad. From the first day of creation, it engaged in two kinds of activities; neither were authorized by the Congress. The first activity was the surveillance of American citizens when they were traveling abroad, or if the CIA thought these citizens posed a threat to its physical facilities or its information. That led the CIA to infiltrate an organization called the Women's Strike for Peace. We also know that reporters have been subjected to surveillance. The CIA also conducts surveillance under the guise that it is going to hire a particular person. (All of these programs are going on right now under the authorization of the executive order issued by President Ford allegedly to control the intelligence agency.) The second activity that the CIA has carried out since its creation is covert operations—operations designed to interfere with foreign governments. Americans were told that the CIA was a tool of the government, supporting U.S. policy of seeking to promote democracy and freedom throughout the world. In fact, the CIA programs were designed to undermine the principles that the U.S. stands for in the world.

Let us focus our attention on what the CIA did in Chile, at the direction of several presidents. The CIA worked for one objective—to prevent Allende from coming to power. When Allende received the most votes in a free election, there was a meeting of the Forty Committee, which runs the CIA covert operations. The meeting began with Mr. Kissinger, who was then the president's national security advisor, stating the policy of the U.S. with regard to Chile. He said, "I do not see why we need to stand by and watch a country go Communist because of the irresponsibility of its own people." The CIA then launched its campaign against Allende. The CIA said that the only way to prevent Allende from coming to power was a military coup. It began plotting with right-wing groups in Chile to kidnap the Chilean chief of staff, in order to justify a military coup. The Chilean military was told that the U.S. was interested only in keeping Allende out of power. The Chilean military was told that as long as Allende was in power, there would be no military aid to Chile from the U.S. and that the country would be economically forced to starvation. The military finally acted, the chief of staff was kidnapped and killed. Later, a coup overthrew that government with the active support of the CIA.

Less attention has been focused on the CIA's activity in the Congo. Its role there is equally revealing of the way in which the CIA has been used by our presidents. In 1960, in the Congo, [Patrice] Lumumba had been the prime minister and was removed by a coup. There was a discussion in the Forty Committee with President Eisenhower about Lumumba. As a result, it was decided that the CIA should assassinate Lumumba. A cable was sent to the CIA station in the Congo explaining why Lumumba had to be assassinated. It said that he was a threat to American policy in the Congo and in all of Africa. The cable went on to say that whenever Lumumba spoke, people listened and tended to follow him. Therefore, the CIA station was instructed to keep him from speaking until he was assassinated, so that he could not regain support. The cable explained that there was grave danger in the Congo that the freely elected parliament of that country would reconvene. According to the cable, if the parliament reconvened, it would reelect Lumumba as prime minister. Since it is messier to assassinate a sitting prime minister than a former prime minister, the CIA was instructed to see to it that the parliament did not reconvene until Lumumba was assassinated. A hired thug was sent by the CIA to the Congo for the purpose of carrying out the assassination.

These activities are in the past, but again I say that none of them have stopped. We learned just a few days ago of the CIA directive from Mr. Kissinger to infiltrate the Micronesian government. Micronesia is a trust territory of the U.S., placed under American control by the United Nations with the responsibility to guide that territory toward independence. After a free election in Micronesia, a government was elected which appointed a committee to negotiate with the U.S. the future status of that territory. The

U.S. government decided that it was not prepared to engage in open and honest negotiations, and so it infiltrated the negotiating team. It also bugged the rooms of the negotiating team. It sought to subvert their policies so that the negotiations would result in favor of the U.S.

We have a clear record that the CIA has been used by our presidents to carry out those activities which go against the American ideals and values—policies which could not be carried out if they were made public. The CIA has been a secret army of the president. It is startling to me that absolutely nothing has been done to rectify this situation. The CIA and the FBI cannot change their perspective on their rights and obligations, and the fact that they operate beyond the Constitution. The new director of the CIA thinks he has a public relations problem and is trying to restore the good name of the CIA instead of trying to eliminate the activities which violate constitutional rights.

The director of the FBI, Mr. [Clarence M.] Kelley, has complained because last month, for the first time, an official of the FBI was indicted for criminal activities.[1] Mr. Kelley was not proclaiming that this individual was innocent; his claim is that to indict an official of the FBI is to undermine the morale of the FBI. In my view, that is an absolutely outrageous statement. Mr. Kelley is suggesting that, unlike other Americans, who are subject to indictment by trial, the FBI should have immunity. The FBI seems to have learned nothing from its experiences and continues to believe that it has a right to operate above the law. This situation cannot be allowed to continue. What is needed is comprehensive legislation to establish the principle that the intelligence agencies are not above the Constitution.

The FBI should limit itself to investigating criminal activity and should not engage in manipulation and infiltration of political organizations. The

1. On April 7, 1977, John J. Kearney, a former supervisor in the Federal Bureau of Investigation, became the first FBI agent in the history of the bureau to be indicted on criminal charges. As part of the five-count indictment, it was charged that sixty agents working under his command had, from 1970 to 1972, illegally tapped telephones and opened mail in search of fugitives who belonged to the Weather Underground. A week after being indicted, Kearney pled not guilty to the charges in court, while three hundred FBI agents protested outside in a show of support for him and the years he had helped, as one of them said, "in the fight against the enemies of our nation, namely anarchy and terrorism." Charges against Kearney were dropped a year later. In 1981, five victims of illegal wiretaps and burglaries—which they had discovered because of documents involved in the Kearney case—were awarded $10,000 each in civil damages.

CIA should be limited to intelligence evaluation and producing the kinds of intelligence analysis that the president and senior officials need. It should not be engaged in the overthrow of governments. We need to strip away much of the secrecy which surrounds the intelligence agencies. Their budgets and functions should be made public. We also need a special prosecutor to deal with the crimes of the intelligence organizations. The attorney general of the U.S., who uses the intelligence agencies to carry out his duties, is simply not in a position to decide to indict officials of the intelligence agencies. We need to put that job in the hands of an independent prosecutor. We need to strengthen the rights of citizens to go into court and to sue in protest of violations of their constitutional rights.

We are all in the position, if we cherish the Bill of Rights, to work for effective controls on the intelligence agencies so they are brought under the Constitution, so that they fulfill the role of protecting us and yet leave us free to engage in the lawful political activity which is the cherished right of all of us in a democratic society.

Section Three

Morning in America
and the New World Order

November 6, 1981

Joan Baez

American Folksinger, Guitarist, and Songwriter; Founder and
President, Humanitas International Human Rights Committee

Twenty years after Joan Baez enchanted listeners at the 1959 Newport Folk Festival with her quivering, crystalline voice, she enraged one-time allies in the decade-long campaign to get the U.S. out of Vietnam with a letter. In a full-page ad that ran in the *San Francisco Chronicle*, *Los Angeles Times*, *Washington Post*, and *New York Times*, under the auspices of her new human rights organization, Humanitas, in May 1979 Baez and eighty-one signatories published an open letter to the Communist government of Vietnam, taking it to task for human rights abuses. (This from the singer whose 1973 album, *Where are You Now, My Son?*, included recordings made in North Vietnam.) Among the signatories shaming the government for torture, holding hundreds of thousands of political prisoners, and creating "a painful nightmare that overshadows significant progress made in many areas of Vietnamese society" were poet Allen Ginsberg and activist Daniel Berrigan. Missing were Jane Fonda and Tom Hayden—along with nearly three hundred others whose support Baez had sought.

By 1979, hundreds of thousands of refugees had fled Vietnam for neighboring countries—ethnic Chinese, it was reported, were being forced out following a brief war between Vietnam and China—and many of the refugees embarked on journeys across the ocean in leaky, unseaworthy craft. Baez published her letter of protest, and she also went to the refugee camps in Indochina. Humanitas asked President Jimmy Carter to have the U.S. Seventh Fleet assist with rescuing "boat people" on the open waters. The U.S. also opened its doors to more refugees from Indochina, and at an international conference in Geneva, joined Vietnam's neighbors in seeking a solution to the flood of refugees—as many as ten thousand people a week.

Two years later, Baez made international headlines not with letters but with her voice and guitar. A concert tour of Latin America focused attention on the human rights abuses of the right-wing governments there, which—correctly—understood that Baez's folk music and the spirit of populist empowerment could undermine their authority. Banned from giving public concerts, she sang in private; she met with families grieving for the "disappeared" in Argentina. As her Commonwealth Club speech makes clear, Baez was worried that with Reagan in the White House and Alexander Haig in charge of the State Department, concern about human rights abuses—particularly by anti-Communist governments—would be moved to the back burner. So after her tour of Latin America, Baez went to the State Department and met with Thomas Enders, assistant secretary for inter-American affairs. She spoke at the State Department Open Forum and sang *Pilgrim of Sorrow*, a song she had often sung with Martin Luther King. She said, "Say hello to Haig for me," and she left.

"Human Rights in the Eighties: Seeing through Both Eyes"

I will speak to you as humanly, as directly, and as intelligently as I can, from my heart, from my brain, and from my personal experiences. I'm here as myself, as a nonviolent activist, as the president of a human rights organization, and as a member of what I like to refer to as the new moral necessity. I'd like to tell you about how I and we at Humanitas perceive the colossal job of human survival which confronts the human race in the 1980s; about how we have tried to gain perspective of what things can be done for the betterment of humankind, and some other things that we have done. In the process I hope, of course, to remind people, without being too obnoxious or too cumbersome, of certain moral necessities that must be taken seriously in the 1980s if we want to see something aside from the current near-total moral breakdown taking place within nations and across national borders.

The foundation for all of our activities comes from an idea which is certainly not new, but an idea to which there's enormous resistance wherever people have opinions and feelings in this world. This idea is a part of the new moral necessity; it is the idea of learning to see world problems through both eyes—not just the right or just the left, but seeing clearly and fairly through both eyes. It was really the importance of seeing through both eyes which gave Humanitas its beginnings in early 1979. I was conducting a study group in my home for the purpose of keeping up on world affairs. And in February, our group was visited by two Vietnamese boat people: one a defrocked monk, the other a writer. Both had been against the U.S. support of two regimes. One had been jailed in the sixties for his beliefs and actions. By February of 1979, both had been so disillusioned by the new Communist regime that they had followed in the historical flow of boat people into the South China Sea. They described to us the Vietnam they had left behind as a gulag of reeducation camps, prisons, enforced labor, tremendous repression.

The question to me was, as a person who had shown such concern for the people of Vietnam during the U.S. involvement in that country, was I still concerned about the people of Vietnam? And were any of the others of the sixties who had been so outspoken on behalf of innocent victims of that war—were they still concerned? At that time, February 1979, Amnesty International claimed two hundred thousand political prisoners in Vietnam, and we began to investigate the situation ourselves. It became clearer and clearer that the question was not whether or not Vietnam had become a totalitarian state or why it had become one, it simply was one. The questions were, to myself and to my friends, could we face up to the fact that though we had tried for ten years to liberate that tiny country, tried to bring self-determination and democracy to Vietnam, perhaps we had failed. I must say that I do not for a second regret my activities during those ten years, that I think during the Vietnam War the only civilized way to behave was to deny that that war should exist, and that's what we did. But I realized that five years after the withdrawal of American troops, Vietnam was being run by seventeen aging Stalinists who were making life a hell for the majority of the population, and that the magnitude of the problem was huge, and that nobody I knew wanted to think about it. And that I was developing a case of visual preference which was excluding a priority problem, the very real pain and sorrow of the Vietnamese people in massive numbers. In fact, I discovered how widespread that eye disease was when I tried to recruit well-known activists of the sixties to sign an open letter to Hanoi decrying the status of their human rights. There were eighty-one signers; there could easily have been five hundred.

What we risk by seeing fairly and justly through both eyes is our attachment to ideology. It's attachment to our country, to our party, to whatever clan in which we feel we have invested our identity, to whatever clan we hold an image of ourselves in, to whatever clan we put our money in, and from whichever clan we derive what we call or feel to be a sense of security. I discovered, once again, through the project of the open letter, how blessed I am to have never been burdened with an ideology. I've now been called both a pinko commie and a CIA rat, and a number of other things, I'm sure. I keep waiting for either of those groups to pay up; neither ever does. And I consider the fact of those varying viewpoints and the outrage with which they are expressed to be a compliment to my sanity. My identity is as a member of the human race, certainly a flawed one like everybody else, but it's that and no more and no less. I believe I'm capable of seeing through both eyes, and I'd like to tell you some of the things that I see before me in 1981.

I see a world of such intense beauty that it's quite incomprehensible to me. I see races of enormously beautiful and handsome people walking the earth, full of inborn pride. I see the magnificence of the human mind at work. I see the glory of art and of music. I see the winged victory carved in marble, as smooth as soap. I see the human potential which literally takes us to the moon. Clearly, the rest of my speech today could be an accounting of the gifts, both man-made and of nature, which surround us daily. But then, of course, I see the dark forces of our weaknesses, our greed, and our myopia gaining momentum at a breakneck speed. I see starving children. I see fifteen million refugees. I see pain and sorrow absolutely beyond our comprehension, from El Salvador and Guatemala, where torture and murder are institutionalized, to [Andrei] Sakharov's miserable exile in Gorki. From Vietnamese prison camps to the thousands of disappeared citizens in Argentina. From the dead Haitians on the Florida shores to South Africa's apartheid. From the daily executions in Iran to our own ghettos. All of these holocausts, from the immense to the moderate, emanate from the fact that power politics—whether right-wing or left-wing—that national interests coming from a right-wing or left-wing government and that ideas and ideologies, right-wing or left-wing, are more important than the people they are supposed to serve. Perhaps this is becoming a trend.

There's no ideological safeguard for misery. Hunger is hunger, torture is torture, and dead is dead. I live in a country which I fear, at this point, is mixed up. I believe much of the population here prefers to be lulled to sleep. This makes me afraid. Lulled to sleep by reassuring advertisements on television which give us a range of options from the fastest acting headache pill to the reassurance that we have a government we can count on for a change. The Americans are known throughout the world, certainly in the places that I've ever traveled, for being a very, very warm people. We're also known for our apathy. I have an English friend who tells me, "With all due respect," she says, "Americans will never understand anything, my dear, until their central heating goes out." Which, of course, may not be that far away.

The danger of this apathy is that it reinforces our sense of powerlessness. And when a general population feels powerless, it is willing to follow the dictates of whomever currently sits in power, no matter how visually impaired that leader might be. I criticize the apathy in this country partly out of a tremendous sense of waste. We have so much freedom to speak out, to act, to move, to care, and to really count in the international picture, in the greater scheme of things. Our privileges cry out to be made use of. I, for one, do not like the imposition of powerlessness put upon me. Nor do I think it necessary for me or for anyone else, certainly in this room.

Humanitas is used partially as a vehicle to follow up on the actions of Joan Baez, the entertainer and public personality. Since anyone in the public eye is bound to be used by any faction of people, at any time, I prefer to have as much control as possible over how I'm used. I would like to be used by Humanitas for the betterment of humankind. Something like Martin Luther King saying, "If I'm going to be a drum major, let me be a drum major for justice. Let me be a drum major for peace."

We've continued to raise money for Somalia, for East Timor. We began to see the necessity for building a bridge between human rights and disarmament, because the right to remain alive is a basic human right. We ran a consultation on human rights and disarmament in Madrid with Nobel Peace Prize–winners Adolfo Pérez Esquivel, from Argentina, and Mairead Corrigan, from Ireland.[1] We have had policy consultations on Latin America, during which time I became very interested in trying to go to Latin America, also at the invitation of Pérez Esquivel. So I attempted to have a concert tour. If the concert tour had come off commercially, half of that money would have gone to support the nonviolent groups that we were meeting and the human rights groups that we were affiliated with in Latin America.

I was prohibited from singing publicly in Argentina and Brazil, and Chile never gave me a work permit. All three of the countries' promoters had originally expressed great interest in putting on my concerts. By the time we left on tour, Brazil had a lineup of five concerts in large venues. Argentina was still a strong possibility, and Chile had not yet issued a work permit, but we were innocent enough to think I might still get one. The other countries included on the tour were Mexico, Nicaragua, and Venezuela. Argentina greeted me with no possibilities for a concert, no promoters available, no halls, tear gas lobbed into the meeting of the Permanent Assembly on Human Rights in which I was speaking. On the second night, we were followed twenty-four hours a day by two cars filled with people who referred to themselves as my security but who, when there was a bomb threat at my press conference, suggested that I go on ahead and they'd keep an eye out. I was kicked out of my hotel, and the bomb threats turned out to be quite real bombs.

The beauty of what happened for me in Argentina was meeting the mothers of the disappeared people, young people, and the families of the detained. Probably there is no stronger group of people I've met anywhere on the face of the earth than these mothers. And we should know, those of us here who are parents, what absolute torture it must be for a parent to go to bed every night for—most of the kidnappings took place between five and seven years ago in Argentina—wondering whether your child is alive or

1. Adolfo Pérez Esquivel, an architect and human rights leader, was awarded the Nobel Peace Prize in 1980. In 1976, Esquivel had initiated a campaign to create a UN Human Rights Commission. At the time of this writing, he heads the Servicio Paz y Justicia, a Latin American human rights organization based in Buenos Aires. Mairead Corrigan shared a 1976 Nobel Peace Prize with Betty Williams. Corrigan, Williams, and Ciaran McKeown cofounded Community of Peace People (formerly the Northern Ireland Peace Movement), which advocates a nonviolent resolution of the conflict in Northern Ireland.

dead, whether your child was violated, whether your child was beaten, raped before they were killed. And most of them—it does not look very rosy that they will return. The women go silently and in a very dignified way every Thursday to the center of town, and they march, and they're requesting of the government only one thing: a list of where the children are—which, of course, presents an enormous problem for the government, but this is their request. And they say that they will do that forever, and they probably will.

In Chile, they were much craftier with me. They did not prohibit me from singing an underground concert at which five thousand people showed up. The sadness for me in Chile was that the entertainers with whom I shared an evening were terribly brave and beautiful musicians and magnificent people, and they were all scared, because they were afraid that if repression tightened again in Chile, they would be vulnerable. They would be put on the spot simply because of the evening spent together as entertainers and with Joan Baez. What I tasted in the three countries was some kind of idea of what it would be like to really be censored: that I couldn't go out and do what I do best—God's gift to me is my voice. I wouldn't be allowed to go out and sing my songs to people. And I had the tiniest taste of that, although I knew that I would leave the country, and I could come home, and I would be able to sing.

In Brazil, it was a little more dramatic and a little more shocking, because Brazil somehow now has a picture of being much more liberalized and open. In Brazil, the police came to the door before one of these unofficial concerts and, with a lot of hemming and hawing, finally made it clear that if I tried to sing in public in Brazil, I'd be arrested. So I went to the microphone and explained to everybody what had happened, and everybody had a good laugh. I guess they're used to it. It was sad; in each case, there would be individuals who'd come up to me on the street, upper middle class, mother or father or family. They'd say, "We're very, very embarrassed at the behavior of our government." And I was saying, "So am I—plus which I'd really like to sing." But in each country, I probably sang more than I would have on a regular concert tour. We went from churches to family groups to mothers of disappeared. In those countries, my gift to them, to the families, was to sing and to let them weep. I'd bring out my guitar, they'd bring out their hankies. I would sing and they would weep. We actually joked about it. But that was all that I had to offer.

We went to Nicaragua and Venezuela before coming home. When we returned, I did a number of talk shows, radio, newspapers, talking about what had happened in Latin America, questioning who the Americans choose as their friends and why. We went to Washington because we felt we owed it to the mothers left behind in Argentina to go everywhere that we could. And in Washington, to our dismay, we discovered that human rights were in even worse shape, as far as national priorities go, than we had imagined.

One State Department comment was to a congressman: "If you want human rights programs, you're going to have to make it each time you want it." A high-ranking member of the State Department with whom I met, who deals specifically with Latin America, told us that he didn't feel El Salvadoran refugees should be given any temporary asylum here, because he didn't feel that El Salvador was a particularly unsafe place to live. Well we kind of staggered out of that meeting wondering really, where to begin, and was there a death of human rights in Washington or what?

It is my opinion that a very basic moral fiber of this country, if it's to exist at all, is dependent upon our treatment of people in need, our willingness as the wealthiest and most powerful nation on Earth to share with people who have nothing, to feel and express compassion. Compassion and caring are a part of a new moral necessity. They may save us from international disgrace.

Speaking of compassion and caring, my last subject and the subject of current great interest to Humanitas is the nuclear freeze. We want desperately to find a way to express that we see the threat of nuclear holocaust as imminent, that we see it through both eyes. We feel that by introducing the freeze as a way of decelerating the arms race, we may make it clear that we see the threat as bilateral or multilateral. The fact is that the real threat to human life is probably not coming from either camp so much as it exists twenty-four hours a day in the form of a possible accident—although I must say that I'm absolutely terrified by the current rhetoric in the U.S. administration. I feel we must not continue the path of such light consideration of Europe. We must somehow include Europe in our own backyard. How would we feel if a major power stronger than ourselves toyed with the idea of a small nuclear explosion in Fresno Valley just to show some other major power, also stronger than us, that they must be taken seriously?

Perhaps, here we have come full circle. We're discussing a million dollars a minute spent on armaments worldwide. And we are discussing underdeveloped countries and hunger, refugees, and the general imbalance of everything. I believe that by opening both eyes, we have half a chance of getting things in perspective, if not in focus.

[from the question-and-answer session]

Q. *Now that the Vietnam War is over, a member asks, have your groups or others forgotten the Vietnam vets? We'd like some attention too.*

A. No, we haven't forgotten the Vietnam vets. Humanitas has not made working with vets part of our program, but I generally do, personally, try to do whatever I can for whatever the program is. Certainly an issue is Agent Orange. And earlier this afternoon, I was very moved because I was approached by a young man who said that he was a pilot over Hanoi when I was trapped in Hanoi in Christmas of 1972.

I was delivering mail to American prisoners of war in Hanoi. The young man said that he felt badly about the position he had then. When I was in the shelter there, I remember arguing about sanctity of life. I was arguing with Marxist press people from the French press corps and I was arguing with Vietnamese. And I refused to toast the fallen B-52s. There was a young, enthusiastic Vietnamese, and every time he heard a B-52 had been shot out of the sky, he would run off and try to get some vodka to toast the situation, and I would leave the room. The more adult of the Vietnamese in the group would shush him, in effect, say, "Listen, there's this woman in the room who doesn't approve of this kind of stuff." When the French press finally said to me, in an absolute out-rage—we'd been heavily bombed, and each time, you really do think that's it, that that's the end of your life, and it's a very frightening thing. I consider it a gift to myself that I was there and that I lived through it, because it was something that gives me a little bit of extra vision, I think. This French press corpsman said, "Aren't you happy? Don't you want to celebrate when you see that B-52 shot out of the sky?" I said, "Only if I know that the pilots are safe." And he was furious with me; he wanted to see them all go up in flames. But my entire meaning in life is the sanctity of everybody's life. And that I think all the people, even if I disagree entirely with them, are salvageable, in my opinion, to doing what I think may eventually be the morally correct thing to do. And maybe I'm wrong. I don't think in that situation I was.

February 10, 1983

Walter Cronkite

Special Correspondent, CBS News

"Shut up for a minute," Walter Cronkite told the audience gathered to celebrate The Commonwealth Club's eightieth anniversary dinner. He was also
speaking to the larger audience out there, the millions of Americans who had
turned to him as the most trusted man in America and, for nearly twenty
years, anchor of the *CBS Evening News*. "Listen carefully and quietly for a
while. You could still make out America singing." The renowned journalist
invoked Whitman and looked at the role journalists play in shaping society;
how, in getting their stories, they sometimes drown out the big story in
progress; and the nation's need to keep its original principles in mind in
order to secure a place for freedom on the planet. During the question-and-
answer session, Cronkite discussed his role in fostering Anwar Sadat's historic
visit to Israel. When Cronkite spoke, Israeli Prime Minister Menachem Begin
still had another six months to serve as prime minister; Sadat had been slain
by an assassin's bullet in October 1981.

"Hear America Singing"

I have something good to say about America. In my long career, I have often resisted demands that I emphasize the positive. I think most journalists resist such good-news demands, which we frequently get from special interests of one type or another, because they implicitly want us to distort the facts and suppress or water down the bad. There are times when pessimism seems to be the shape of all assumptions, and when the positive must be emphasized in the interests of simple balance and accuracy.

More than a century ago, Walt Whitman wrote a poem about his country that began, "I hear America singing." It has been a long while since anyone claimed to hear America singing. There is a noise in the land, but it is made mainly by Americans blaming each other for the mess we are in. We find ourselves divided into increasingly hostile and exclusive groupings: conservatives versus liberals, protectionists versus free traders, developers versus environmentalists, and fundamentalists versus secular humanists, to name a few.

We are, I am afraid, experiencing a new and potentially dangerous fracturing of the American consensus. As the decibel level rises, our confidence in ourselves and our institutions falters. For others, the music of America's promise is somehow lost. What I want to say is: Shut up for a minute, listen carefully and quietly for a while. You could still make out America singing, although the sound may be a little faint. The tune is true, and the spirit and purpose are still there.

This nation, groaning economically with unemployment at post-Depression highs and monstrous, unprecedented deficits, nevertheless puts out an annual product worth almost three trillion dollars. The GNP of the next greatest economy is only 55 percent of that. Though our industrial production has slipped, it remains second to none. Our agriculture feeds much of the world, supplying more than half of the grain moving into international commerce.

For all our social and educational problems, we are still one of the most literate peoples in history. While we seem to be losing our technological edge, we remain the technological superpower without peer. We are the same nation that put men on the moon and sent the genius of man, embodied in robot spacecraft, voyaging beyond the solar system. American science may have lost some of its undisputed leadership it once enjoyed, but American scientists still take the lion's share of Nobel prizes every year.

Our national image has indeed been tarnished in recent years, sometimes by ourselves, as with Vietnam and Watergate, and sometimes by the company we keep, as in El Salvador and Guatemala. We continue to serve as the favorite whipping boy for leaders of many developing countries, as well as for the Soviets and their flock. Still, it is the American image that attracts, like a great transglobal magnet, the most ambitious as well as the most depressed among the nations' people. Nobody is trying to crash the gates of the Third World these days. The barbed wire around the Warsaw Pact is not there to keep immigrants out. America remains the beacon of liberty; the hope and model for most of those able to exercise any choice at all.

Keeping that hope alive, maintaining the American example as a viable option into and beyond the twenty-first century, is our challenge. It is an obligation we have to ourselves and to humanity. This means solving our economic and social problems as well as defending the Republic against a host of present and future dangers. We can do this if we have the nerve, and if we haven't lost faith in this country and in each other. We can do it if we believe in ourselves.

We will not do it in a funk of pessimism, divided by escalating recriminations strung out by hysterical, ideological belligerence between right and left that drains both our resources and our common sense. Reserving a place for freedom in this planet's future is not going to be an easy job; it is going to take our strength and resourcefulness as a people. It will take all of our fabled inventiveness and talent for improvisation. This is not a job for the already defeated or those who wear an inferiority complex, fearing ever meeting with the bad guys. It is not a job for those fixated on the partisan issues of the past.

Freedom's future is something I have been thinking about by force of an assignment. Some of us at CBS News have been putting together a look at the date that George Orwell made famous by his book *1984*. We have been measuring the distance from here to Orwell's grim vision. When Orwell coined "Big Brother" or the "Thought Police," he was satirizing the totalitarian trends of the 1940s. He clearly feared that those trends might one day lead to freedom's extinction. With 1984 virtually upon us, we find that they haven't done that. But they haven't disappeared either. A lot has changed since that novel was published, but a lot stayed the same too. Some of the challenges to free societies are new, some are old and familiar. The revolutions by the unscrupulous and the seemingly inevitable tendency of power to corrupt idealism are hardly strangers, nor is the habit of people and parties in power to reach for total power and to perpetuate that power; to lie, mislead, and manipulate public opinion to do so. Orwell's idea of power as its own reward, needing no other purpose or justification—that kind of total cynicism is also evident in today's world.

If you ask the question of whether Orwell's vision is coming true, the answer has to be yes and no. It is already happening to some degree in some places. Stalinist Russia was the target of satire. Pol Pot's Cambodia, with the complete absence of freedom and total presence of terror and cruelty, has outstripped even Orwell's grim imagination. Khomeini's Iran also comes close to the Orwellian model today, adding the dimension of religious fanaticism. Global totalitarianism, however, has not arrived and obviously won't by 1984, though there is still 1994.

Freedom in the world today ebbs and flows with events. Generally, it seems to be holding its own; about one-third of the world's population lives in fully free countries and that figure includes the border case of India and its six hundred and seventy million people. Without them, freedom's future would account for less than one-fifth of humanity. About 15 percent live in partly free societies, such as Argentina, Chile, and South Korea. About half of the world's people enjoy no freedom at all: no political and civil rights nor economic freedom.

What might tip this into a totalitarian future? Orwell's catalyst was nuclear war. Surely the political aftermath of nuclear war would be at least as bad as George Orwell feared it to be. I am one of those who happen to believe that World War III would not leave anything for Big Brother's real-life counterparts to rule over. However, the challenges to freedom's future are not limited to the prospects of nuclear Armageddon. Change alone, if not mastered, anticipated, and adjusted to, will overwhelm it.

During the lifetime of most of us, we have been swept into four simultaneous eras, any one of which would be enough to reshape our world. We have been present at the birth of the nuclear age, the computer age, the space age, and the petrochemical age. It is a great plunging river of change, unlike anything we have encountered before. We are living today through a technological revolution potentially more profound socially, politically, and economically than the Industrial Revolution. We have scarcely begun to identify its implications and adapt our institutions to cope. As a society, we are finding it as difficult to cope as we as individuals are finding it.

In the novel *1984*, Orwell's totalitarians used every technological device the author could imagine to maintain complete subjugation of the people, wiping out the very idea of freedom. That technology included two-way telescreens. Fantastic at the time, that technology is very nearly on hand today. If knowledge is power and information is knowledge, Americans today are surrendering to others a lot of power over their personal lives. Computer networks linked to home television and alarm systems are capable of storing enormous amounts of highly personal information about each of us: where we shop, what we buy, how promptly we pay our bills, what television programs we watch. Think about the potential for blackmail which this information could place in government's or any other hands. There is a two-way television system in operation today which would turn on the set in your home from a control room elsewhere for the purpose of warnings. Infrared alarm systems can determine the number of people in your home and relay that information to a downtown control center.

Electronic eavesdropping equipment has grown extremely sophisticated and difficult to detect. Laser listening devices can penetrate walls to tune in private conversations. If we participate in "talk-back" television systems which poll viewers on a wide range of subjects, we will supply information on how we feel about political and social issues. Add to this the data stored in computers of banks, hotels, credit card companies, telephone companies, city and county governments, police departments, high schools and universities, hospitals, and various federal agencies, and you soon have almost everything worth knowing about almost everybody, simply by letting those computers talk to each other by linking them together. The National Security Agency has the ability now to suck in vast streams of telephone and telex traffic and record it for monitoring purposes. The agency will soon have the ability to store these communications digitally and retrieve a desired conversation quickly. Present law restricts such monitoring to international traffic, but there is no reason why a maligned government couldn't change that rule.

Technology has fashioned a two-edged sword. New surveillance systems make us feel safer but also easier to watch. Computer video systems may make it possible for people to work, shop, and bank without ever having to leave the home. This could have an enormously liberating influence, putting the world at our fingertips, or it could put us at the fingertips of others.

Which it is to be is, of course, up to us. There is no reason for us to tremble before the advent of this new technology. We merely need to guard against its misuse. We need to recognize that it will create new realities to which the institutions of freedom must adjust. It is the kind of concern that should cut across all party lines and deserves more attention than we have been giving it.

This is a time when science and technology are creating revolutionary changes and flowing into the mainstream of the technological change of our generation's economic and political revolutions. The new technologies give proof of man's intellectual capabilities. Can we really believe that he is incapable of applying that same intelligence to solving the great problems the world faces: population, pollution, atomic proliferation, and depletion of natural resources? Can we believe that the beleaguered peoples of the world will long be tolerant of those who possess the tools but who can't make them work for the good of man? There is going to be social, political, and economic evolution coming with such suddenness as to have the character of revolution.

Revolutionary forces are already at work today, and they have man's dreams on their side. We don't want to be on the other side. It is up to us to get into the leadership of that revolution and to channel it in a direction that will ensure freedom's future. If we do not, it will surely imperil that future.

We live on a shrinking planet of more and more people with less and less to share. Current estimates put the global population at more than six billion people by the year 2000. Eighty percent of all humanity will live in the poor, developing countries of Africa, Asia, and Latin America. By the year 2015, the total will become eight billion people; double the number on this planet just seven years ago. This means that the world will have to produce twice as much food as it produces now, meaning a rapid cutting back of forest lands and a greater depletion of ocean fisheries and other resources. The very weight of human numbers is bound to place a growing burden on freedom's future. Already, the pressures of illegal immigration have led to proposals for a national identification card.

We live on an increasingly dangerous planet with the two superpowers continuing to pile up nuclear megatonnage far beyond what is needed to end all life on Earth. A high level of tension and the continued presence of those nuclear arsenals must prove corrosive to freedom, with people ever more willing to surrender individual rights for security needs whenever the two seem to be in conflict.

In the novel, Orwell saw the world divided into three superstates, at least two of which were always at limited war. We now seem to be looking through that telescope from the other end. We see roughly the same divisions, if we consider China as the third superpower.

Population pressures continue to make nuclear power attractive to Third World countries. That leads to breeder reactors to produce fuel, further leading to the diversion of bomb-grade material. For the present, Iraq may have lost its chance to produce an Islamic bomb, but membership in the nuclear club is bound to grow eventually. Moreover, not only do we have to worry about the prospect of nuclear weapons in the hands of the Khomeinis and the Qaddafis of this world, we also must worry about the prospect of bombs in the hands of terrorists or other criminal groups. The tight internal and international security needed to guard against nuclear blackmail might so restrict our individual freedoms as to make George Orwell a prophet.

It becomes painfully clear that we live on an increasingly interdependent planet. Our own dependence on foreign oil is familiar enough, but not so well known is our dependence on strategic metals with properties essential to our high-tech civilization. Complete independence is indeed a myth. We know that protectionist trade measures, toward which many economically injured Americans are tempted, will only raise the barriers elsewhere and lead to a general worsening of the international economy. The loser in all cases will be freedom in those parts of the world where it has just been holding its own. Poverty, scarcity, and hardship are destructive for freedom; they are the tools of tyrants.

In the straitened conditions this planet faces, it seems unlikely that freedom can endure easily for very long among an affluent 10 percent of the world's population. We are going to need converts to the cause of freedom if it is to endure. Freedom must be a growth industry. Freedom has to be nurtured and can't be taken for granted. A lot of Americans are not taught freedom, conditioned to think independently, or make intelligent, rational choices. They grow up thinking freedom is something synonymous with appetite.

Conservatives tend to spend freedom on national security and measures aimed at fighting street crime. When Cold War tensions increase, restrictions on the right to travel and public access to information seem reasonable to many. When the crime rate soars, pressures to restrict the rights of criminal suspects and increased powers to police also rise.

Liberals tend to spend the same coin on items such as social justice. They lobby for the elimination of risks from society, seldom admitting the price to be paid in lost liberties by someone.

I don't want to suggest that we should not try to make America safer and healthier. I am one who has long argued that we should do more to clean up the environment, and protect Americans' physical heritage. For all the difficulties, the traps, the pitfalls, and the challenges in the path of freedom's future, the odds are nevertheless still on the side of the American example. This is because it works better than any form of social organization with which it can be contrasted. For all our weaknesses, the weaknesses of those against us are far greater.

The Russians are certainly a military threat, but they are of no competition at all. We should stop acting as if they were. I think we are smart enough to negotiate with them anytime. I'd call people un-American who think that we don't have the sense and the intelligence to sit down and negotiate with the Russians. I think we are strong enough to take risks in the interest of peace, just as we can afford to take risks in support of freedom's future elsewhere in the world. Unfortunately, however, our allies are not always freedom's friends. I think Americans should be less timid abroad and less set in our ways at home.

We can get this country moving with a full head of steam again if we can junk the partisan distinctions of the past and look at our problems with a kind of principled pragmatism that this nation's founders had to employ. Some union and management groups have provided us with some good examples of this kind of pragmatism, joining forces to survive and even to prosper. We could use more of that willingness to adapt and pull together in the common interest. We have the wherewithal; all we need is the will. It's been a while since anyone has claimed to hear America singing, but they knew something we seem to have forgotten: to hear the music, you also have to sing along.

An important anniversary is coming up in a few years: the two hundredth anniversary of the writing and ratification of the American Constitution. In fact, now is a good time to start remembering it, as we cope with technological and social forces that cast shadow on our basic rights set forth in that document. Now is the time to refurbish our dedication to the principles of representative democracy that it enshrines. If we could rededicate ourselves to renewing the revolution that produced that Constitution, we could enlist the struggling peoples of the Third World in democracy's truth. If we could do that, we will have reserved a place for freedom in this planet's future.

As one of the messengers who, for many years, brought you the daily diet of bad tidings, let me pass on this advice: Listen and read the news reports carefully. They are the fire alarms of our civilization, identifying the areas for concern and alerting us to dangers that need alleviation. As tough as things have been in our past, the indomitable spirit of this nation always has brought us through. There is no reason that we should be of faint heart today.

[from the question-and-answer session]

Q. *What was your most remarkable interview?*

A. I suppose the most important ones were the twin interviews by satellite with Mr. Begin and President Sadat. They were, in effect, the catalyst that brought them together in Jerusalem a week later. I did not go into those interviews to bring them together. What I expected from Mr. Sadat was that he would say he didn't have any intention of going to Jerusalem. In the first interview he gave after he became president, he said, " I shall go to Jerusalem." I asked, "When?" and he answered, "As soon as there is peace." He said this again on Wednesday before the parliament, but nobody paid much attention to it—because that had always been his answer—until a Canadian delegation asked Mr. Begin if he would invite him to come to Jerusalem. Mr. Begin said that he would invite him and he could come anytime he wants to come. That response started a lot of speculation around the world on whether President Sadat would go to Jerusalem or not. I got President Sadat on the satellite Monday morning and asked him if he intended to go to Jerusalem, expecting him to answer as usual, and that would be the end to it. When I did ask him, he said, "As soon as the Israelis pull back from the captured lands of 1967, as soon as there is a Palestinian state, and as soon as they get out of the West Bank." I responded, "Those are your conditions before you would go to Jerusalem?" He answered, "No, those are my conditions for peace; I'll go to Jerusalem tomorrow." Our producers quickly got to Mr. Begin and told him, "Mr. Begin, I've spoken with President Sadat, and he said he's ready to come to Jerusalem at any time." Mr. Begin responded, "Tell him to come." I said, "He needs an invitation, will you send him an invitation?" He said that he would send a formal invitation, and I said, "How soon can he come? He says he could come this weekend." Mr. Begin answered, "Tell him to come this weekend." I started out expecting the speculation to end and I got one of the great scoops of all time.

March 4, 1983

Ronald Reagan

President of the United States of America

When Ronald Reagan strode onto the stage at the San Francisco Hilton for his Commonwealth Club address, the topic of the day was the economy—at least on one level. On another level, he was talking about rejuvenating the sense of the United States as a great nation with the confidence to lead the world. However, in the question-and-answer session, the concerns were international—the Middle East and Central America—as well as domestic. Israel had invaded Lebanon in summer 1982 in an attempt to wipe out Palestinian guerrillas launching attacks on Israel's northern border. U.S. Marines were sent to Beirut in September 1982, and a few months later, Israeli forces began to withdraw. Six months after Reagan's speech, in October 1983, Marines became the target of a Hezbollah suicide bomber. A truck that exploded at their compound in Beirut killed 241 people. The last Marines were withdrawn in February 1984.

In El Salvador, events were turning toward peace after several bloody years in which the country was led by a military junta that allowed paramilitary groups to terrorize political dissidents. Among thousands of murders by the paramilitary groups were the widely publicized assassination in March 1980 of Archbishop Oscar Romero, who had asked the U.S. government not to provide military support to the El Salvadoran government, and four U.S. nuns that December. In 1982, an assembly was elected which, in 1983, created a constitution that safeguarded civil liberties, at least on paper: the death squads continued to terrorize citizens. A presidential election in 1984 put into office José Napoleon Duarte, the first president to be freely elected in El Salvador in fifty years. This talk also came on the eve of one of the hallmarks of Reagan's Cold War showdown with the Soviet Union: his "Evil Empire" speech four days later.

Address to The Commonwealth Club

I have not come here to echo those faint hearts who have little faith in American enterprise and ingenuity. They plead for retreat and seek refuge in the rusty armor of a failed protectionist past. I believe, and I think you do, too, that the world hungers for leadership and growth, and that America can provide it. My message is that our administration will fight to give you the tools you need, because we know you can get the job done.

Our forefathers did not shed their blood to create this Union so we could become a victim nation. We are not sons and daughters of second-rate stock. We have no mission of mediocrity. We were born to carry liberty's banner, to build the very meaning of progress, and our opportunities have never been greater. We can improve the well-being of our people, and we can enhance the forces for democracy, freedom, peace, and human fulfillment around the world, if we stand up for principles of trade expansion through freer markets and greater competition among nations.

In dealing with our economy, more is in question than prosperity. Ultimately, peace and freedom are at stake. The United States took the lead after World War II in creating an international trading and financial system that limited government's ability to disrupt trade. We did this because history had taught us, the freer the flow of trade across borders, the greater the world economic progress, and the greater the impetus for world peace. But the deterioration of the free world and U.S. economies in the 1970s led to the decline of Western security and the confidence of the people of the free world. Too many otherwise free nations adopted policies of government intervention in the marketplace. Many people began thinking that equity was incompatible with growth. They argued for no-growth societies, for policies that undermined free markets and compromised our collective security.

There can be no security without a strong Western economy. And there can be no freedom unless we preserve the open and competitive international and financial system we created after World War II. Prosperity alone cannot restore confidence or protect our basic values. We must also remember our objectives of peace and freedom. Then we can build a prosperity that will, once again, lift our heads and renew our spirits. I am not going to minimize the problems we face, or the long, tough road we must travel to solve them.

For a quarter of the century after the Second World War, we exported more goods each year to the rest of the world than we imported. We accumulated a surplus of funds which was invested at home and abroad, and which created jobs and increased economic prosperity. But during the past decade, we began importing more than we were exporting. Since 1976, imports have exceeded exports every year, and our trade deficit is expected to rise sharply in 1983.

In the past few years, high real interest rates have inhibited investment, sharply increased the value of the dollar, and made our goods less competitive. High interest rates reflect skepticism by financial markets that our government has the courage to keep inflation down by reducing deficit spending.

Well, if the history of our great nation and the character of this breed called American mean anything at all, it is that when we have believed in ourselves, when we pulled together, putting our wisdom and faith into action, we made the future work for us, and we can do that now.

Wealth is not created inside some think tank on the Potomac; it is born in the hearts and minds of entrepreneurs all across Main Street America. For too long, government has treated the entrepreneur more as an enemy than an ally. Our administration has a better idea. We will give you less bureaucracy, if you give America your audacity. We want you to outplan, outproduce, and outsell the pants off this nation's competitors. You see, I believe in what General Patton once said: Don't tell people how to do things. Tell them what needs doing and then watch them surprise you with their ingenuity.

Every citizen has a role and a stake in helping the United States meet her trade challenge in the eighties. We need jobs, and one of the best job programs we can have is a great national drive to expand exports, and that's part of our program.

We have only to look beyond our own borders. The potential for growth is enormous: a two-trillion-dollar market abroad, a chance to create millions of jobs and more income security for our people. We have barely seen the tip of the iceberg. Four out of five new manufacturing jobs created in the last five years were in export-related industries. Yet 90 percent of American manufacturers do not export at all. We believe tens of thousands of U.S. producers offer products and services which can be competitive abroad. Many of these are small- and medium-sized firms.

Our administration has a positive plan to meet the trade challenge on three key fronts. First, lay a firm foundation for noninflationary growth based on enduring economic principles of fiscal and monetary discipline, competition, incentives, thrift, and reward. Second, enhance the ability of U.S. producers and industries to compete on a fair and equal basis in the international marketplace; work with our trading partners to resolve outstanding problems of market access, and chart new directions for free and fair trade in the products of the future. Third, take the lead in assisting international financial and trade institutions to strengthen world growth and bolster the forces of freedom and democracy. Taken together, these actions give the United States a positive framework for leading our producers and trading partners toward more open markets, greater freedom, and human progress.

But progress begins at home. Our economic reforms are based on time-tested principles: spending and monetary restraint to bring down inflation and interest rates, and to give lenders confidence in long-term price stability; less regulatory interference so as to stimulate greater competition; and growth of enterprise and employment through tax incentives to encourage work, thrift, investment, and productivity.

We have suffered a long, painful recession brought about by more than a decade of overtaxing, spending, and intervention. But recession is giving way to a rainbow of recovery reflecting a renaissance in enterprise. America is on the mend.

Inflation has plunged from 12.4 percent in 1980 to just 3.8 in the last twelve months. We have sought common sense in government and competition, not controls in the marketplace. Two years ago, we accelerated the deregulation of crude oil and heard ourselves denounced for fueling inflation.

The national average for a gallon of gasoline when we took office was $1.27. Now you can buy it in many places for under one dollar.

The prime interest rate was a crippling 21.5 percent; now it's down to 10.5 percent. Tax rates have been cut; real wages are improving; personal savings and productivity are growing again; the stock market has hit a record high; venture capital investments have reached record levels; production in housing, autos, and steel are gaining strength; and new breakthroughs in high technology are busting out all over.

To the pessimists who would cancel our remaining tax incentives, I have one thing to say: Don't lay a hand on the third year of the people's tax cut or the indexing provision. Indexing is our promise to every working man and woman that the future will not be like the past. There will be no more sneaky, midnight tax increases by a government resorting to bracket creep to indulge its thirst for deficit spending. To pretend eliminating indexing is somehow fair to working people reminds me of Samuel Johnson's comment about the fellow who could not see any difference between virtue and vice. Sam Johnson's advice was, "When he leaves our houses, let us count our spoons."

If those who would dismantle the tax cuts get their way, the chilling message to the business community will be, "Don't scrap and struggle to succeed, expand your business, and hire more workers, because we won't thank and reward you for helping your country. We'll punish you."

Maybe I am old-fashioned, but I don't think pitting one group of Americans against another is what the Founding Fathers had in mind. This nation was not built on a foundation of envy and resentment. The dream I have always believed in is: no matter who you are, no matter where you come from, if you work hard, pull yourself up and succeed, then you deserve life's prize, and trying for that prize made America the greatest nation on Earth. Let us encourage achievement and excellence. We want America to be a nation of winners again.

There is a great hue and cry for us to bend to protectionist pressures. I have been around long enough to remember that when we did that once before in this century, it was called Smoot-Hawley, and we lived through a nightmare.[1] World trade fell by 60 percent, contributing to the Great Depression and to the political turmoil leading to World War II. We and our

1. The Smoot-Hawley Tariff Act of June 1930 raised U.S. tariffs to historically high levels and is the high watermark of U.S. protectionism in the twentieth century.

trading partners are in the same boat. If one partner shoots a hole in the boat, does it make sense for the other partner to shoot another hole in the boat? There are those who say yes, and call it getting tough. I call it getting wet all over. We must plug the holes in the boat of open markets and free trade and set sail again in the direction of prosperity. No one should mistake our determination to use our full power and influence to prevent anyone from destroying the boat and sinking us all.

There is a fundamental difference between positive support of legitimate American interests and rights in world trade, and the negative actions of protectionists. Free trade can only survive if all parties play by the same rules. We are determined to ensure equity in our markets. Defending workers and industries from unfair and predatory foreign competition is not protectionism, it's just plain common sense.

One example of protectionist legislation that could quickly sabotage recovery is the local content rule. This legislation proposed in the Congress would force foreign and domestic manufacturers of automobiles sold in the United States to build their cars with an escalating percentage of U.S. parts and domestic labor. The congressional budget office concluded that this would destroy more jobs than it would save. It would also add substantially to the cost of a new car.

What the proponents of this bunker mentality never point out is the costs of protectionism for one group of workers are always passed on to another group down the line. Once such legislation is passed, every other industry would be a target for foreign retaliation. We would buy less from our partners, they would buy less from us, and the world economic pie would shrink. Chances for political turmoil would increase dramatically.

Rather than reacting in fear with beggar-thy-neighbor policies, let us lead from strength and believe in our abilities. Let us work at home and abroad to enhance the ability of the U.S. producers and industries to compete on a fair and equal basis in the international marketplace.

More companies will seek the world of exports when they realize this government is no longer an adversary, it's your partner, and I don't mean a senior partner. We have eased substantially taxation of foreign-earned income and introduced a 25 percent tax credit for research and development. We're also working to reform the Foreign Corrupt Practices Act: not to weaken safeguards against bribery, but to remove disincentives that discourage legitimate business transactions overseas.

Another obstacle is export controls on technology. A backlog of two thousand applications greeted us when we arrived in office. We eliminated those and relaxed export controls on low-technology items that do not jeopardize national security. Still, there are limits. I am confident each of you understands: we must avoid strengthening those who wish us ill by pursuing short-term profits at the expense of free world security. Trade must serve the cause of freedom, not the foes of freedom.

To export more, we must do a better job promoting our products. We're strengthening our export credit programs by increasing the level of the Export-Import Bank's ceiling on export guarantees. We've also designed a tax alternative to the Domestic International Sales Corporation that will fully maintain existing incentives to our exporters. We've begun a Commodity Credit Corporation blended export credit program for our farmers; and that's in addition to the increases this year in the regular loan guarantee program for promoting U.S farm exports.

To retain America's technological edge, of which there is no greater evidence than California's Silicon Valley, and to revive our leadership in manufacturing, we've implemented a research and development policy to enhance the competitiveness of U.S. industry in the world economy. In our 1984 budget, we've asked for significant increases for basic research, and we will seek to improve the teaching of science and mathematics in secondary schools so tomorrow's workforce can better contribute to economic growth. We will also seek to encourage greater and more creative interaction between university and industry scientists and engineers, through programs similar to the one between Hewlett-Packard and Stanford University.

Finally, we're taking steps to encourage more industrial R and D through changes in our tax and antitrust policy. We will also seek to remove legal impediments that prevent inventors of new technology from reaping the rewards of their discoveries.

Supporting American producers also means pressing our trading partners in the direction of more free and open markets. We are challenging the unfair agricultural trade practices of Japan and the European Community. We are seeking to chart a new course for the products of the future. We have agreed to a work program with the government of Japan to eliminate trade and investment barriers to high-technology industries. We have also established a working group with the Japanese to actively explore opportunities for the development of our abundant energy resources.

By restoring strength to our economy and enhancing the ability of our producers to compete, America is leading its trading partners toward renewed growth around the world. The world economy, like ours, has been through a wrenching experience: a decade of inflation, ballooning government spending, and creeping constraints on productive enterprise. Other countries, including many of the developing countries, are for now making major efforts to restrain inflation and restore growth. The United States applauds these efforts, and we are working in the IMF to keep a firm focus on the role of effective domestic policies in the growth and stability of the world economy.

But for all countries, international trade and financial flows are extremely important. Either the free world continues to move forward and sustain the postwar drive toward more open markets, or we risk sliding back to the tragic mistakes of the 1930s, when governments convinced themselves that bureaucrats could do it better than entrepreneurs. The choice we make affects not only our prosperity, but our peace and freedom. If we abandon the principle of limiting government intervention in the world economy, political conflicts will multiply and peace will suffer. That's no choice at all.

In trade, for example, we have practically eliminated the barriers which industrial countries maintain at the border on manufactured products. Today, tariffs among these countries average less than 5 percent. Our problems arise instead from nontariff barriers, which often reflect basic differences in domestic economic policies and structures among countries. These barriers are tougher to remove. We are determined to reduce government intervention as far as possible and, where that is unrealistic, to insist on limits to such intervention.

In trade with developing countries, on the other hand, tariffs and quotas still play a significant role. Here the task is to find a way to integrate the developing countries into the liberal trading order of lower tariffs and dismantled quotas. They must come to experience the full benefits and responsibilities of the system that has produced unprecedented prosperity among the Caribbean Basin Initiative to encourage poor and middle-income countries to trade more, and we proposed a North-South round of trade negotiations to maintain expanding trading opportunities for more advanced developing countries. We seek to build a collective partnership with all developing countries for peace, prosperity, and democracy.

At the GATT ministerial meeting last November, the United States took the lead in resisting protectionism, strengthening existing institutions, and addressing the key trade issues of the future. While we were not totally satisfied with the outcome of that meeting, we will continue in our support of free and equal trade opportunities for all countries.

Expanding trade is also the answer to our most pressing international financial problem, the mounting debt of many developing countries. Without the opportunity to export, debt-troubled countries will have difficulty servicing, and eventually reducing, their large debts. Meanwhile, the United States will support the efforts of the international financial community to provide adequate financing to sustain trade and to encourage developing countries in the efforts they are making to improve the basic elements of their domestic economic programs.

Earlier this week, I forwarded draft legislation to the Congress for additional American support for the IMF. Lending by the IMF has a direct impact on American jobs, and supports continued lending by commercial banks. If such lending were to stop, the consequences for the American economy would be very negative.

This spring, the United States will host the annual economic summit of the major industrial countries in Williamsburg, Virginia. The leaders of the greatest democracies will have a quiet opportunity to discuss the critical issues of domestic and international economic policy and reflect on their individual and collective responsibilities to free peoples throughout the world. It is not a forum for decision making. Each leader is responsible primarily to his or her own electorate. But by exchanging views, these leaders can gain a better understanding of how the future of their own people depends upon that of others.

I began by saying if we believe in our abilities and work together, we can make America the mightiest trading nation on Earth. Not far from here are people and companies with the burning commitment we need to make our country great. One of those companies, the Daisy Systems Corporation, is a computer firm in Sunnyvale, California. It was formed in August 1980 and made $7 million in sales its first shipping year. This year it expects to earn $25 million, and by 1986, $300 million. Daisy Corporation is already selling its products in the markets of France, Norway, Belgium, Great Britain, Germany, Israel, and Japan. Its workforce has nearly quadrupled in the last year.

My dream for America, and I know it's one you share, is to take that kind of success story and multiply it by a million. We can do it. Albert Einstein told us, "Everything that is really great and inspiring is created by the individual who can labor in freedom." With all the wisdom in our minds and all the love in our hearts, let us give of ourselves and make these coming years the greatest America has ever known.

[from the question-and-answer session]

Q. *How far are you willing to go in pursuit of your Middle East peace plan, by applying pressure on Israel to meet your peace plan requirement?*

A. We are doing everything that we can to speed this up, because we believe that the more moderate Arab nations have expressed to us now a willingness to negotiate with Israel, and try to arrive at a long-term peace arrangement of the Middle East. But they have predicated this on Lebanon being allowed now to resume sovereignty over its own nation. This calls for the leaving from Lebanese soil, all foreign troops, the Israelis, the Syrians, and the remnants of the PLO still there. We are disappointed by the length of time it has taken and by the haggling and the negotiations, because no one will leave until all three agree to leave. We do want to get that settled and get to the table on the whole overall matter of international peace. I can tell you we will not retreat from every effort that is open to us to bring that about.

Q. *The recent request for escalation of military aid to El Salvador appears to be the beginning of a replay of the early days of Vietnam. What assurances can you offer that this is not the case?*

A. I can give you assurances, and there is no parallel whatsoever with Vietnam. We have the instance here of a government duly elected. Just a short time ago, the people of El Salvador proved their desire for order in their country and democracy. They had no sympathy whatsoever for the rebels who are armed and trained by countries such as Cuba and others of the Iron Curtain. They are supplied with weapons that come in by way of Nicaragua. The threat is more to the entire Western Hemisphere and the area than it is to one country. If they get a foothold and El Salvador should fall as a result of this armed violence on the part of the guerrillas, I think that Costa Rica, Honduras, and Panama would follow. Fifty percent of everything we have to import comes through the Caribbean and the Panama Canal. It is vital to us that democracy be allowed to succeed in these countries as it did in that last election. Now, El Salvador is considering calling a new election, hopefully before the year is out.

We had a bipartisan team of congressmen who went down and witnessed that election. The stories they came back with converted any who had any doubts. They told of a grandmother standing in line who had been threatened by the guerrillas. She told them, "You can kill me, you can kill my family or my neighbors. You can't kill us all." They had destroyed and bombed over one hundred and fifty buses, so that people had to walk for miles in the hot sun to get to a polling place, but they did and then stood in line, for hours. Another woman stood in line, refusing to leave, after she had been shot and wounded by the guerrillas. She refused treatment until she had been able to mark that ballot. They (the bipartisan team) came back and were convinced that there were things to be corrected down there, but we are working with them.

What we mean by expansion is that we have a limit of fifty-five U.S. military personnel for the sake of training their forces there. They need that training. So far, we have filled, on average, over the last couple of years, thirty-seven of those fifty-five positions. Right now, there are forty-five, but we may want to go beyond that fifty-five. In no sense are we speaking of participation in combat by American forces. We are trying to give economic aid necessary to their economy because of the destruction of power plants and industries, and we believe that the government of El Salvador is on the front line in a battle that is really aimed at the heart of the Western Hemisphere, and eventually at us.

January 20, 1984

Prince Bandar bin Sultan

Ambassador from the Kingdom of Saudi Arabia to the United States

When Prince Bandar bin Sultan spoke at The Commonwealth Club on a Friday in January 1984, the 34-year-old diplomat that *Time* described as a "Saudi prince straight from central casting" had been serving as Saudi Arabia's ambassador to the United States for only six months. But he was no stranger to Washington. He had been serving as defense attaché in the U.S. since 1982. Before that, he had been instrumental in convincing the U.S. Congress to permit the sale of F-15 fighters and AWACS planes to Saudi Arabia.

Prince Bandar's talk at The Commonwealth Club was on the topic of peace in the Middle East. What were the prospects of that at the beginning of 1984? Two years before, Israel had both completed the return of the Sinai to Egypt and invaded Lebanon; the PLO had evacuated Beirut and relocated headquarters to Tunis. In an attempt to keep the peace in Beirut, a multinational force including U.S. Marines had been sent to Beirut in September 1982. In April 1983, a Hezbollah suicide bomber had destroyed the U.S. embassy in Beirut, killing more than sixty people; four months later, Israel had begun withdrawing from Lebanon. Bandar himself had negotiated a cease-fire that was announced in Damascus on September 25. But in October, a Hezbollah suicide bomber had hit the U.S. Marine compound in Beirut, killing 241.

Six months after he spoke at The Club, Prince Bandar was approached by Ronald Reagan's national security advisor, Robert C. "Bud" McFarlane, to help fund the Contras—the armed opponents of Nicaragua's Sandinista government, who established bases in Honduras, Costa Rica, and Nicaragua itself. To Reagan, the Contras were "the moral equivalent of our Founding Fathers," battling a Communist government. But the U.S. Congress had cut off direct military aid to the Contras in 1982. Acting upon McFarlane's request, the Saudis eventually funneled some $30 million to the Contras.

Despite the hopes for peace Bandar expressed in the January 1984 speech, the months that followed saw more mayhem in Lebanon. In February, the last U.S. Marines were withdrawn from Beirut. In March, the CIA station chief in Beirut, William Buckley, was kidnapped and later killed. That fall, twenty-five people were killed when the rebuilt U.S. Embassy in Beirut was hit by another bomb. In June 1985, the Israeli government, led by Shimon Peres, ordered its troops to withdraw from most occupied Lebanese territory.

Ten years after this speech, Prince Bandar continues to serve as Saudi ambassador to the U.S. and is currently dean of the diplomatic corps in Washington. In autumn 2002, he and his wife, Princess Haifa al-Faisal, made U.S. headlines when it was alleged that the princess had indirectly helped finance the September 11, 2001, terrorist attacks on the U.S. through support of a Muslim charity. More recently, in June 2003, Saudi Arabia rolled out in the top twenty-five television markets an ad campaign designed to show U.S. and Saudi solidarity in the fight against terrorism. The *Chicago Sun-Times* quoted Prince Bandar as saying, "The terrorists responsible for the recent tragedies in Riyadh reminded us that there are no distinctions to race, religion, or nationality in such horrific acts. We are in the same boat, and we must work together to destroy them." He prefaced his talk to The Commonwealth Club in 1984 by again expressing hopes for cooperation, noting that San Francisco and Saudi Arabia have a long history together: "The Americans who were granted the first successful concession to explore for oil in the kingdom"—in 1933—"came from San Francisco....From that start has grown up what is now generally recognized as one of the crucial economic and strategic relationships in the present world—that between the United States and Saudi Arabia....Let us hope that the second half-century of this relationship may be even more productive and beneficial."

"Peace in the Middle East"

I would like to suggest several basic points at the heart of the increasingly explosive problem confronting the United States, Saudi Arabia, and the entire world: the need for peace in the Middle East. There is a widespread attitude, especially among some in this country, that such an objective is an impossible dream. I do not at all agree with that tired and self-defeating cynicism. Yes, the region's troubles are deeply rooted and complex. But I do not think either the people of the area or the international community— and particularly the United States—can ignore or play down the increasingly dangerous situation there.

If the seeds of a nuclear war abound anywhere in the world, it is in the Middle East. Anyone who is genuinely concerned about the nuclear peril but does not want to come to grips with the Middle East tinderbox, or thinks it can be treated as a matter of politics-as-usual, is deluding himself. The Middle East is where Asia, Europe, and Africa come together—and now America as well. It is where the history of human civilization began and— far more than Berlin or Poland or anywhere else—is where the beginning of the end of human civilization, as we know it, could be triggered.

The Middle East is where over 60 percent of the world's proven oil reserves is located. Profoundly more important, it is where the three great religions—which look to the same Almighty, the same long line of early prophets, the same basic view of this worldly existence—originated: Judaism, Christianity, and Islam. And it is where, far more than anywhere else, they must now sort out their shared destiny and what justice and dignity, and evenhandedness, they really stand for. Yes, I recognize that the Middle East is beset by not just one major problem—the Arab-Israeli conflict—but others too.

The Lebanese tragedy and the Iraqi-Iranian war are glaring immediate examples. As to Lebanon, Saudi Arabia has taken the initiative again and again to help mediate among the principal factions in Lebanon, and to encourage a constructive dialogue between Syria and the United States. We believe national reconciliation and equitable power sharing are essential for Lebanon. Equally, we support that country in asserting its Arab identity and sovereignty, goals which President [Bashir] Gemayel and all the principal groups there have made clear they are committed to. Most important for America, we want to help speed the earliest possible time when President

Reagan can withdraw the Marines under honorable conditions—with reasonable assurance for the people of the area and the vital interests of the United States and the international community as a whole.

But Lebanon obviously does not exist apart from its larger setting. If Lebanon collapses, the stability and peace of the Middle East, and America's diverse interests there, will also be seriously set back. Even if progress is made in Lebanon, what might be achieved will fall apart very quickly if headway is not also made on solving the Arab-Israeli conflict—and that means solving the Palestinian-Israeli problem. Effective diplomacy concerning the Middle East has to take into account the extent to which the region is a series of closely interlocked relationships in religious, ethnic, cultural, and all other important terms. The overriding need is to reinforce stability in the region as a whole. That requires multi-track diplomacy and getting as quickly as possible to the core of the situation.

Similarly, stepped-up efforts to bring the Iraqi-Iranian war to an end are imperative. Expansion of those hostilities could shred the Free World economy and global stability. Some Americans would like to think that the security of the Persian Gulf can be assured without regard to events in the rest of the Middle East. But nothing could be further from reality.

I cannot emphasize strongly enough that the riveting problem which dominates the peoples from the gulf to the Mediterranean, and almost all of the Arab and Islamic world, is the Arab-Israeli conflict and the injustices which the Palestinian people continue to suffer. Facing up to that problem, and making just and durable headway on it, will not solve all of the tensions in that part of the world. But it will do more than any other action to help bring stability to the region and open up the larger economic and human opportunities for the people there, as well as benefit the vital interests of the United States.

Let me be very clear: differences undeniably exist within the Arab world. But sharp differences also exist within the Free World and in practically every other broadly based group—and usually can be managed fairly well. King Fahd is committed to working within, and to further, a broad Arab consensus. And when that weakens, the kingdom has shown again and again that it will work to reestablish a broadly shared understanding. Attempts to divide the Arab countries into separate camps is an approach which has been tried again and again. But every time, it has ended up making the region much less—not more—stable.

I want to emphasize, too, that the credibility and legitimacy of practically everyone—the Arab countries, the United States, Western Europe—is now deeply caught up in resolving the Palestinian-Israeli problem. The U.S. has asserted again and again that it is indispensable to helping bring about peace in the region—and that it is committed to the cause of peace. We in Saudi Arabia have believed that America is the country most capable of helping to solve the Middle East stalemate. And that is so because of Israel's dependence on the United States economically, militarily, and politically over any marked period of time.

In contrast to our view, however, the overwhelming majority of those in the area and in the international community become more and more skeptical, even cynical, about America's ability and resolve to bring about the peace it declares it wants. They have come to that opinion primarily because of the vast and increasing economic and military aid the U.S. provides the Israelis—aid given even when the Israelis spurn specific and important requests from Washington; even when the Israelis clearly and deliberately put in peril vital U.S. interests in the area; even when, as decided two months ago, jobs and business are to be shifted from American communities and workers to the Israelis. The consequence of that kind of aid is to polarize and radicalize much of the region, reinforce Israeli intransigence, and put at still greater risks America's interests and those of your Arab friends.

Even with all the U.S. economic assistance and weapons, Israeli security has not increased at all. In fact, the more that Israeli aid has been increased during the last decade and a half, the more inflexible and reckless the Israelis have become, the more they have suffered casualties, the worse the Israeli economy and Israeli social cohesiveness have grown.

At a more fundamental level, the contrasting injustice done to the Palestinian people has put in question the basic value system of all the parties with an important stake in the region. That is why we believe that no matter how long the task may take, the Palestinians must be accorded the God-given right of self-determination in a homeland of their own. They are entitled to that as surely as any other people with timelessly rooted ties at the eastern edge of the Mediterranean—and with a proven self-identity such as they have made clear in the face of even the most adverse conditions.

For many decades, the United States has been the world's most outspoken champion of self-determination. What President Wilson expressed so eloquently and President Franklin Roosevelt stood for so firmly had particular impact in the Arab world. And that occurred just as Arab society was reasserting its self-awareness and resolve to work out its own destiny. Unfortunately, America's commitment to this key principle is now undergoing its most searching test in the eyes and hearts of the Arab and Islamic people—and, in fact, throughout much of the international community. The question of what America stands for in the world has come to revolve importantly around American policy and attitudes toward the right of the Palestinian people to self-determination.

Let us all be frank with each other: Autonomy as defined by the Israelis is an insult to the world's intelligence. Even their Camp David partners—Egypt and the United States—could not and did not agree to it, as President Carter reemphasized with me personally several months ago. Those who talk about going back to Camp David ignore or forget that critical disagreement and the humiliating inadequacy of what the Israeli version of autonomy means for the Palestinian people.

Keep in mind that Islam, Judaism, and Christianity all insist on the central importance of seeking justice and correcting basic injustices in this world. The imperative of justice underlies the legitimacy of all our societies and all our varied political institutions. Peace must come to the Middle East for the good of everyone. But there can be no real lasting peace without substantial justice being done for the deeply wronged Palestinians. The diplomacy of the months ahead needs to resolve this core issue. And if the ethic of justice does not guide the steps that are taken, it can hardly be expected that the goal of real peace will be brought closer no matter what diplomacy may try to paper over. Yes, the present situation is difficult and dangerous. But all the major parties involved—above all the United States—must be equal to the task and peril which now confronts us, and which can only grow worse the longer a just, honorable, and durable solution is put off.

[from the question-and-answer session]

Q. *Why is peace in the Middle East so hard to achieve?*

A. Everybody is asking the Arabs to produce a Sadat. No one is asking the Israelis to take the initiative for peace and produce their own Sadat who will make peace overtures to the Arabs. The Palestinians are asked to recognize Israel, but nobody is telling them what happens in return.

Q. *What would happen in Lebanon if the United States pulled out entirely?*

A. If the Americans remain in Lebanon as peacekeepers, that's positive. If American policy changes, that will have negative implications. If America cuts and runs, that's disastrous. If America decides to fight it out, that's also disastrous. If America uses the Israeli military to implement its objectives, that too is disastrous. But those aren't the only options that face us.

Q. *How do you establish a Palestinian homeland?*

A. I really believe a Palestinian homeland is a matter of time. You cannot go against history. History, if it tells us anything, tells us that you cannot dislocate four million people from their home. What is now on the table would allow everybody to coexist with each other. We now see a growing peace movement in Israel. I think Israel's security depends on having friendly neighbors around them.

October 5, 1984

Daniel Ortega Saavedra

Head of State, Nicaragua

It was on the eve of elections in Nicaragua that Daniel Ortega Saavedra, then head of the national reconstruction government ruling the country, traveled to California and spoke to The Commonwealth Club. This was five years after the Sandinistas had taken power in Nicaragua, following a revolution that ousted the ruling Somoza family. The U.S. had suspended aid to the country in 1981 following nationalization of private industries and confiscation of private property, and because the U.S. accused the Sandinistas of supporting Central American guerrilla movements and international terrorism. With congressional authorization, hundreds of millions of dollars had been given to Contra rebels in Honduras who were seeking to overthrow the Sandinista government. By 1984, U.S. attempts to bring down the Sandinista government included mining Nicaraguan harbors and attacking ports and oil installations. In December 1982, however, the Republican-controlled Senate had passed the Boland amendment, suspending U.S. military support "for the purpose of overthrowing the Government of Nicaragua."

Shortly after speaking to The Commonwealth Club, Ortega was elected president in an election that international observers called free and fair; the U.S., however, refused to recognize it as valid. Instead, members of the Reagan

Administration had found a way to circumvent the congressional ban on aid to the Contras: Vice Admiral John M. Poindexter and his deputy, Lieutenant Colonel Oliver North, used funds from the sale of arms to Iran to support them. Iran was in need of weapons for its ongoing war with Iraq; the sale also helped secure release of hostages held in Beirut. But when the deal was revealed to the public by a Lebanese newspaper in November 1986, the details of what became known as the Iran-Contra scandal began to unfold. In Nicaragua, after a decade of civil war, the Sandinistas signed a peace arrangement in 1989 that led to national elections in which a right-centrist coalition led by Violeta Barrios de Chamorro was victorious.

"Peace in Central America"

The need for peace between the Nicaraguan and the American people is what motivates my visit to your country. Thousands of Nicaraguans have already fallen as the result of the current administration's policy. North Americans have also fallen; two North Americans were killed in an aerial attack on Santa Clara. This attack originated in Honduras and was organized by the CIA. Besides the two North Americans, four Nicaraguan girls were also killed. Neither the people of the United States nor the people of Nicaragua condone such acts of violence.

We have taken the opportunity afforded by the invitation to speak at the United Nations to also speak to the North American people. This is a crucial time both for the future of Central America and for the image of the United States in Latin America. We have categorically denounced in the United Nations the plans for aggression that are going to be carried out against Nicaragua on October 15. We have enough information to know that this attack is coming. These plans presuppose a first attack by the counterrevolutionary mercenary forces to take over Nicaraguan territory near the Costa Rican–Nicaraguan border. The purpose of this action would be to create tension between Nicaragua and Costa Rica. Depending upon the success of this offensive, a second phase is contemplated. This would be the call by other Central American governments for the United States to come to their defense against Nicaragua. The third phase would be direct North American military intervention, including ground troops and air forces.

Counterrevolutionary forces are being concentrated in Costa Rican and Honduran territory near the border with Nicaragua. North American aircraft from bases in the Panama Canal Zone have been transporting supplies destined for the counterrevolutionary forces. These arms are unloaded at night at the Llano Grande airport in Costa Rica, near the Nicaraguan border. Though the government of Costa Rica does not condone these activities, it is being imposed on them by the CIA and the Pentagon. The purpose of our call to the international community at the United Nations and our call to the North American people is to prevent this plan by the CIA and the Pentagon from being carried out.

Under these circumstances, a hope for peace has arisen. This is the Contadora peace proposal. Some Central American governments have made positive statements regarding the Contadora proposal. For almost two years, the U.S. government has spoken in favor of the Contadora proposal. Now that there is a concrete proposal which benefits the people and governments of Central America and the people and government of the United States, it is not at all surprising that the proposal should be questioned. It is being questioned by some North American officials and now by some Central American governments. The reason for these doubts is that the government of Nicaragua has announced that it supports this proposal unconditionally.

We must prevent the United States government from making the mistake of continuing to promote bloodshed in Central America or from becoming any more involved through direct military intervention against Nicaragua. This would only repeat old history—the history of mistakes the United States has made in its Central American policy. Nicaragua has been invaded by North American forces since the beginning of this century, when the Soviet Union did not exist and when there were no Communist countries who could be blamed for Nicaragua's attitude. It really surprises us that there has been, after all this time, no change in the North American policy. That is why we say that this administration is trapped in past policies toward Central American governments. We have to struggle so that this chain of interventions against the people of Central America will be broken. We must avoid another U.S. intervention in Central America.

The United States has for a long time had a chance to promote peace and justice in Central America. The Central Americans are not responsible for poor U.S. policy toward them. After Sandino was assassinated, the North

Americans had the opportunity of proposing and promoting some type of democratic government.[1] But what did they create in Nicaragua? They created a brutal dictatorship: Somoza. And what did they create in the rest of the Central American countries? Similar dictatorships, situations of injustice, of terror, of human rights violations, of lack of freedom of the press. They created true authoritarianism. That is why we're saying that the North Americans are only reaping the harvest of their own poor policies in Central America. If there was a revolution in Nicaragua, it was because of the poor U.S. policy toward Nicaragua. If there had been democracy in Nicaragua, we would have never struggled against it.

If there has been a struggle in El Salvador, it has been because of the lack of democracy in El Salvador also. That is a struggle that is older than the revolutionary triumph in Nicaragua. The Salvadoran struggle is as old as the lack of justice and the lack of democracy in that country. In Nicaragua we have made a revolution that wants freedom, that wants justice, that wants democracy, which defends a national populist position, which defends political pluralism. But for the crime of being a revolution, the North American rulers refuse to accept it. And they have proposed to destroy that revolution. For every effort that we in Nicaragua make to promote democracy, we are denounced and condemned by the North American rulers as though we were enemies of the United States, as though we were the aggressors, although we all know what the true situation is.

The North American people are not the enemy of the people of Nicaragua. But the North American rulers have become the enemy of the people of Nicaragua. They have declared war against the Nicaraguan people in the name of liberty. And we insist on the need to force that policy to change. That will only be possible to the degree that the North American people demand that it change, regardless of which party and which people are in power. All that Nicaragua is asking for is the right of its people to live, to work, to build their country in peace. A great opportunity for peace exists right now in the Contadora proposal. It represents the salvation of the Central Americans and the United States.

The other alternative is what we in Nicaragua have already been suffering. It is the alternative of war, terror, and death. This has already cost the

1. In 1927, Augusto César Sandino launched a guerrilla war against U.S. forces in Nicaragua. Seven years and five hundred battles later, U.S. forces withdrew. Sandino was then assassinated on the orders of General Anastasio Somoza García, who went on to establish a hereditary dictatorship.

North American people and has tarnished the image and prestige of the United States in Latin America and in the world. Because of your government's poor policy, the image of the United States is becoming dirty. The North American flag is also becoming dirty, as well as the principles on which your government was founded. This is unfair. The North American people must be the first ones to reclaim justice. Nicaragua wants peace with the United States. It defends its right to good relations with your country despite your government's inflexibility and its war that has caused so much pain in Nicaragua. We hope that the North American people will make their government change its attitude before it is too late.

[from the question-and-answer session]

Q. *What assurances can you give Americans who doubt that Nicaragua will hold open and free elections?*

A. There is more pluralism in Nicaragua than we have observed here. We are concerned that all the political parties participate in the election. Of our eleven parties, four are not participating, solely by their own choice.

Q. *If these elections are open and free, why is the press being censored, and why are opposition parties not embracing these free elections?*

A. Press, radio, and television are not being censored either in the political or ideological arenas. You can read in *La Prensa* every day, and you can see on television, attacks on the Sandinista government. The parties who are not participating are not because they know they will be overwhelmingly defeated.

Q. *Please describe the ways in which the Contra attacks have disrupted the economy and other aspects of Nicaraguan life.*

A. Every day in Nicaragua, agricultural cooperatives, food centers, schools, health centers, and child development centers are being destroyed. These are all benefits the revolution has brought. The most serious situation is that the people who go out to pick coffee become victims of the aggression by the so-called freedom fighters. The CIA is attempting to destroy everything which represents work and growth.

Q. *What can you say to American fears that in a time of crisis Nicaragua will ask the Soviet Union for troops?*

A. This is not the concern of the American government. They want Nicaragua to become radicalized and to create a military alliance so that they can say to the Americas and Western Europe that every revolution is dangerous. Travelers to Nicaragua can clearly see that we have a democratic, nationalist, pluralist regime with a mixed economy. But North America does not want this because they don't want change in Latin America. They prefer dictatorships, as can be seen by the fact that they don't campaign to end dictatorships such as Pinochet's or the Paraguayan government.

Q. *What proof do you have of the supposed October 15 invasion?*

A. Since the Reagan Administration came into power, we have been suffering the North American invasion. Troops and military bases have been moving closer to our border. Sea vessels and mines have violated our waters. The United States has invested more than $50 million in terrorist activities against Nicaragua. When we talk about October 15, we do not mean that planes will begin to bomb on that date. We mean that the CIA and the Pentagon will put into effect a new plan to topple our government, as described before. It would be a repetition of a known policy by the United States.

January 22, 1986

Desmond Tutu

Bishop of Johannesburg, South Africa; Nobel Peace Prize–Winner, 1984

In January 1986, it was clear that the days of apartheid in South Africa were numbered. But it was not clear that the system of separateness would go quietly. Desmond Tutu even speculated that the South African government would use nuclear weapons, in its own scorched-earth domestic retreat. The new constitution of 1984 had failed to win black support, and by the end of that year there were some one thousand people dead—mostly blacks—from political violence. As the world community turned increasing scrutiny on South Africa and the oppressive apartheid system, Desmond Tutu was awarded the 1984 Nobel Peace Prize. He used his heightened global visibility to call for international sanctions against South Africa and, within the country, an end to the spiraling cycle of violence. To quell the violence, the government declared a state of emergency in July 1985. The UN Security Council then voted to impose sanctions—with the U.S. and Britain abstaining. South African President P. W. Botha responded with what became known as the Rubicon speech, essentially telling the world community to go to hell. American companies began pulling out of the country and, more significantly for South Africa, the instability frightened investors; massive capital flight became capital stampede, and international lenders became leery of renewing loans.

As Desmond Tutu mentions in his speech, the holiday season of 1985 was also declared to be a Black Christmas, with blacks boycotting white-owned businesses. It was also a Christmas of violence, with five whites killed—including three children—by a bomb detonated at a shopping center in Amanzimtoti, a seaside resort. In his Christmas sermon, Tutu, who had been named bishop of Johannesburg that year, had lamented, "When we look on all this mess, we might be forgiven for thinking God could have made a better job of it."

"Freedom and Tolerance"

There's a story that is told of a drunk who accosted a pedestrian and said to him, "I say, which is the other side of the street?" And the pedestrian, somewhat nonplussed, said, "That side, of course." And the drunk retorted, "Well, strange—when I was on that side, they said it was this side."

"The other side of the street" depends very much on where you are. What you see, what you perceive, is determined very, very largely by who you are, by your experiences which have helped to form you. And this is very clearly illustrated in South Africa, where, almost as an axiom, you could say that what pleases most whites is almost certainly going to dis-please most blacks; and what pleases most blacks will almost certainly do the opposite for most whites. The perceptions are quite, quite different, as if of people inhabiting different planets, different worlds.

Nineteen eighty-five, Christmas was decreed in our community to be a Black Christmas. When you ask most white South Africans, they will tell you that it was utterly unnecessary that there should have been any trouble at all, because the government is reforming. It has, after all, repealed the law prohibiting marriage between whites and people of other races, and that which makes it a criminal offense for sexual intercourse to take place between whites and people of other races. Have they not now said that they will have a common citizenship for all South Africans, and even universal suffrage? Has the government not already produced a new constitution, which, for the first time in the history of South Africa, makes provision for persons who are not white to participate in the highest assembly of the land, share in the business of legislating? Why, there are now "nonwhites" in coats in the cabinet of the central government. At local government level, many black African townships are now run by their own freely elected black city/town councils, and the government intends, so we're told, to open the President's Council to include black African members. Admittedly, this council is not a legislative body, but it can suggest possible legislation and can adjudicate when there is a dispute between the different chambers of the tricameral parliament.

It should be noted as well that most sport in South Africa, so they will tell you, is now no longer segregated; and many business companies are implementing various codes of conduct, such as the European Economic Community Code and the American Sullivan Principles, which have led to considerable improvements in the work conditions of blacks and an enhancement of their quality of life, shown in their vastly improved housing, in their possession of expensive cars, in their ability to send their children to expensive private schools.[1] Why now, at work, most segregation has disappeared! Blacks share the same toilet and canteen facilities with their white workmates. Their chances of upward mobility have improved considerably, and it is "same pay for the same work" in most companies. So, the foreign companies, you are told ad nauseam are a power for good in their enlightened policies, are important trailblazers, helping to bring about change in South Africa: this is supposed to justify their presence in our land. That is the perception of most whites.

The perception of most blacks is almost the direct opposite of this. It is as if we inhabit different planets. We look at what purports to be the same reality, and our perceptions are quite different. Most blacks will say that many of the so-called reforms which make whites so ecstatic are really cosmetic: they deal only with peripheral issues. The harsh reality of apartheid remains as oppressive, as ruthless, as immoral, as evil, as un-Christian as it ever was. Why is it good for the few who are interested in interracial marriage that the relevant laws prohibiting this have been repealed? This, in the nature of the case, will be only very few people. The legislative pillars of apartheid remain firmly in place. South Africans are still classified according

1. The Sullivan Principles took their name from an American civil rights leader, the Reverend Leon Howard Sullivan. The list of ethical directives, formulated by Sullivan in 1977, called for equal pay and job training opportunities for South African workers, irrespective of race. In 1997, Sullivan expanded the principles into the Global Sullivan Principles of Social Responsibility, which have been endorsed by hundreds of businesses and organizations.

to race as if we're prize animals. According to the Population Registration Act, those who are white remain, as always, the most privileged, at the top of the racial pyramid, and other races are arranged in hierarchical stratification, with diminishing rights, below the all-powerful white oligarchy, until you reach the broad base of the pyramid, representing the vast majority of this land, the black indigenous inhabitants with minimal rights.

South Africans still inhabit their segregated residential areas in terms of the Group Areas Act, which is still very much in place: the whites, again, occupying the most salubrious, well-planned, usually affluent suburbs, with standard recreational and other facilities; whilst the other races live in areas that are decidedly of a lower quality, usually, than those occupied by whites; until you reach the bottom of the pile, in the black ghetto townships that you have grown used to in the TV images—monotonous row after monotonous row of identical, matchbox houses in ill-lit, often dusty, unpaved streets, areas that normally lack the most rudimentary amenities which in the other parts are taken for granted.

In most of these areas, blacks still do not have freehold title, for they have been regarded as only temporary birds of passage in the white man's urban areas—tolerated, as long as they are able-bodied and fit to work. When they could not work anymore, then they were considered to be discards, what a former cabinet minister carelessly described as "superfluous appendages"—referring to our aged mothers and fathers, who used to work for their white employers, now to be discarded as if they were useless chattels, useless *things*, not human beings of infinite value because they were created in the image of God as everybody else.

Even in the time of reform—which, we are told this is the era of reform—over one hundred and fifty thousand blacks have fallen foul of the pass laws in 1984. Blacks still do not have the right of moving freely in the land of their birth. The pass laws were also still firmly in place despite the promise of Dr. Piet Koornhof, at that time a member of the government and now chairman of the President's Council, that the government has declared war on the dompas.[1] This was the same gentleman who, a few years ago, had declared in America that apartheid is dead. No one has yet seen fit to invite us to the funeral, and this corpse was certainly still able to inflict much untold suffering and anguish to many of God's children unnecessarily.

1. Dompas were the documents blacks were required to carry proving their right to work in "white" cities. The *Washington Post* (January 27, 1991) quoted Koornhof as saying, "I detest the dompas, I declared war on the dompas."

You thought of how the Nazis had treated the Jews when you looked at some of the treatment meted out to blacks. This is the only country that I know in the world where it is a crime for a *national* to look for work, if his or her pass is not in order. Blacks were "birds of passage" because they were, after all, to be citizens of spuriously independent bantustan homelands, most of whom had not seen nor known of these homelands until the white man, in his wisdom and greed, had decreed they belonged to. So they were turned into aliens in the land of their birth because an alien cannot claim many rights, least of all political rights. That is why, for a while, I traveled not on a South African passport but on a document that described my nationality.

Now, when you look at me, knowing that I am born in South Africa, you'd say it is obvious that I am a South African. And I have said to some people, "I'm obviously as South African as a Krugerrand." But this document described my nationality in these words: "undeterminable at present."

The initial response to that ought to be laughter, because it is ridiculous in the extreme. But I think that the response, more seriously, ought to be far more somber, because this represents the South African government's final solution—and you know the sinister connotations of "final solution."

Now, I do have a South African passport which says I am a South African citizen, but one with no political rights at all. To satisfy their racist political ideology, the minority government has uprooted three and a half million people and dumped them, as if they were rubbish, in the poverty-stricken, arid bantustan resettlement camps where children starve—not because there's no food in South Africa. Children starve not accidentally; children starve by deliberate government policy, because South Africa is normally a net exporter of food. The father has to leave his family, eking out a miserable existence in those bantustan resettlement camps, whilst, if he is lucky, he goes to be a migrant worker in the white man's town, to live for eleven months of the year separated from his family, and he lives in a single-sex hostel. The migratory labor system, which even the white Dutch Reformed Church, which is not noted for being quick to condemn the present government, condemned long ago as a cancer in our society—that migratory labor system is very firmly in place in this time of reform.

Thus, black family life is undermined not accidentally but by deliberate government policy. It would be a crime if the migrant worker's wife were to join him. This is the only country in the world that I know of where it is a crime for a man to sleep with his wife. This in Christian South Africa, lauded by many as the last bastion, the last bulwark against Soviet expansionism and communism; this in Christian South Africa, which used to have (you won't believe it) a public holiday to attest to the sanctity of family life, a holiday called Family Day; this, in a land that upholds the Christian principle that declares about marriage, "What God has joined together let no man put asunder."

In the time of reform, the government has not let up on its policy of forced population removals, so that it is determined to move the people of Malukazi, which is a black settlement which has been in the news, because a number of people have been killed. The people there have resisted being moved, sliced out of one bantustan to which they had been told they belonged to, and quite arbitrarily, cynically, being told that now they are going to belong to another one. And the people have resisted this, and the people have been killed.

In the time of reform, our black children still receive an inferior education, really a travesty intended by its architect to be an education for perpetual serfdom, and which our children rejected so forcefully in 1976, and which they still reject today.[1] Then, to cap it all, in 1984 the government introduced a new constitution which was hailed in many quarters as a step in the right direction. They said this of a constitution which deliberately excluded 73 percent of the population, the blacks, from *any share* in the decision-making processes of a tricameral parliament; which was meant to hoodwink the international community into believing that South Africa was now reforming. How could this monstrosity be declared a step in the right direction when it was a step *away* from democracy? In that new constitution, 1984 vintage, blacks are mentioned in only one sentence; thereafter we cease to exist.

This constitution represents a co-opting of Indians and so-called coloreds to be junior partners in apartheid, collaborators in their own oppression and that of their black fellow-victims. The ratio in the parliamentary committees was to be four whites to two coloreds to one Indian. Now, even if your math was very bad, you realize that two plus one will never equal, let

1. In 1976, the South African government began requiring that certain subjects in high school be taught in Afrikaans—to blacks, the language of white oppression. Student strikes began in Soweto on June 16, with thousands of students taking part. Rioting and confrontations with the police spread across the country and more than five hundred and seventy-five people were killed.

alone be more than four. And so the constitution perpetuates white minority oppression. It was this constitution which blacks interpreted as meaning that the politics of exclusion had now reached its nadir, and which, as such, they rejected. And that was the start of the unrest in August 1984 and which has gone on until now, and which has claimed over one thousand lives.

Unrest has proved to be endemic. You have seen what happened portrayed on your television screens. Peaceful protest has become virtually impossible. The government at last imposed a state of emergency on most of South Africa, and placed the army in black townships. The security forces have been vicious. You saw how they used a decoy system, hiding in crates to lure people to stone them; and when they did, the soldiers emerged from those boxes with guns blazing.

They have detained thousands. My own son was detained for fourteen days, under the emergency regulations, for swearing at a policeman. Now, how does that constitute a threat to the state? Young children have been arrested and detained, even fourteen-year-olds and younger. Just now, a fourteen-year-old has been in detention for five months, incommunicado. He has not had access to his family; he has not had access to a lawyer. And then the state president has made interesting speeches, and disappointed the world with his "Rubicon" speech, where he was truculent and threatening; instead of being a statesman, he behaved like a cheap party hack. He has made promises which we would have found interesting, indeed dramatic, a few years ago; they have remained interesting remarks, because our government are past masters at playing semantic games. He said "common citizenship," and just as we were getting excited, we discover it will be within the apartheid parameters and it will be citizenship without political power. He said "universal suffrage," and just when we say, "Ah! They're beginning to talk," you discover they don't mean what the rest of the world thinks they mean.

The point, dear friends, is that until South Africa deals with the issue of political power sharing, we are just playing marbles. The EEC code and the other code are *unacceptable*, because they are fundamentally ameliorative. They are designed to effect "improvements." Now, we don't want apartheid *improved*—we want it removed; we want it dismantled. You can't reform apartheid. As Dr. Nthato Motlana put it, "We don't want our chains made more comfortable. We want our chains *removed*." And our last chance for peaceful change, friends, for true reconciliation, which will come with repentance and justice, is if the international community is ready to apply effective political, diplomatic, but above all economic pressure. The foreign companies have, consciously or unconsciously, helped to buttress apartheid by their investments in our land. They did little before the pressure of the dis-investment campaign caused them to find ways of justifying their presence in South Africa.

It is not the height of my ambition to share a toilet with a white person; I want to be recognized for what I am, a human person created in God's image, and a citizen of my land of birth. I mean, it must be odd that I, bishop of an important diocese of our church in South Africa, a Nobel laureate, fifty-four years of age, should not vote in my motherland; and yet the whites, and, more recently, colored and Indian, eighteen years old, can vote. The foreign companies are doing no more than being good employers, and we must not be churlish; there have been extensive improvements that have taken place. But what they have been doing is to extend to their black employees the conditions which for several years they were applying only to their white employees.

I hear people say, "But if sanctions are applied, the first people to suffer are blacks." Blacks have two answers. One is a niceish answer: they say, "Well, you see, we are suffering now; we have been suffering; and if it means that the one way in which we are going to end this system is to take on additional suffering, then so be it." A slightly less nice answer is to say, "When did people become so altruistic? Did they not benefit from black cheap and black migratory labor? Did they ever protest against these and other causes of black suffering?"

Our people have recently in two surveys shown what they want. Both surveys indicate that over 70 percent of the blacks want sanctions of some sort to be applied. It is the last chance for reasonably peaceful change. And let me just say: We're not asking you to make a political decision; we're not asking you, in fact, even to make an economic decision. We're asking you to make a *moral* decision. We're asking you to say, are you on the side of justice or injustice? Are you on the side of oppression or of liberation? For in a situation of injustice and oppression, there can be no neutrality. For if you say you are neutral, you have already made a decision: you have opted to support the status quo.

The year in our country ended with land mines and bomb blasts. We have said ad nauseam, we oppose *all* violence as evil—that of a repressive system, and that of those who want to overthrow it. But you can change a political system only in three ways. You can vote those out of office you don't want. We can't use that method, because we can't vote. You can use violence to overthrow the government. We still say we don't want to do this. We want a South Africa for all its people, black and white, where we will live amicably together as God intended us, as members of one family, the human family, God's family.

And so we ask, will you please help us? Will you please help us so that we can create this new South Africa, where people will count, not because of a biological irrelevance, the color of their skin—where people will count because they are of infinite worth, created in the image of God.

And is this not ultimately doing *good* business? Because, you see, we are going to be free; we have no doubt at all in our minds. We will be free and remain, all of us, because until all of us are free in South Africa, no one will be free, truly free. We are going to be free. And there is no way in which you can say what happens in South Africa does not concern you. The late Senator Church, when he was chairman of the Foreign Relations Committee of the Senate, said to me on Capitol Hill once, "You know, Bishop Tutu, why America must be concerned about what happens in South Africa is not because of our financial involvement in South Africa, for it is piffling in relation to our total foreign investment—it's only something in the region of about 1 percent. Why we must be concerned is that, if a race war were to break out in South Africa, it would have the most horrendous consequences for race relations in this country." He could have gone on to say that it would have the most horrendous repercussions for race relations in most of Western Europe, because there are large constituencies of Third World people there.

We thank you for all your support, in prayer, in love and concern, in money, and in other ways. We *shall* be free, because the God of justice and peace and reconciliation is with us. We would like to be able, when we *are* free, to say that the people of America made the right choice; they backed the right horse.

September 23, 1986

Corazón Aquino

President, Republic of the Philippines

August 1983. Philippine opposition leader Benigno Aquino steps off a plane at the Manila airport, returning to his country after three years of self-exile in the United States. Minutes later he is shot in the back of the head at close range. Soldiers protecting Aquino immediately shoot the gunman. There are some one thousand troops altogether at the airport at the time. The gunman is later identified as a notorious killer for hire. But few believe this isn't an execution by the government headed by dictator Ferdinand Marcos.

Benigno Aquino had been warned by Marcos's wife, Imelda, and other members of the Marcos government, that there were assassination plots against him should he return to the Philippines; he was also still under an official death sentence from 1977. Marcos had declared martial law in 1972, and Aquino was the first political rival he had arrested. Aquino had languished in prison until furloughed for heart surgery in the U.S. in 1980. Marcos denied responsibility for the 1983 assassination and created a panel to investigate the murder. The investigation pointed to a military conspiracy. Marcos's chief of staff for the military, General Fabián Ver, and a number of other members of the military, were put on trial. All were acquitted at the beginning of December 1985. The next day, Corazón Aquino declared her candidacy for president in an election that Ferdinand Marcos called for February 1986.

Largely in the background during her husband's career, Corazón Aquino was a diminutive, bespectacled woman known for serving coffee while her husband met with visitors. When she filled out her official application as a candidate, she wrote under "occupation" that she was a housewife. After her husband's death, when she had been mentioned as a possible candidate, she had reportedly responded, "What do I know about being president?" (In fact, her interest in politics manifested itself as early as her college days in the U.S., when she volunteered for Thomas Dewey's 1948 campaign for president.) In December 1985, when she stepped forward as a unifier of the Philippine opposition movement, she carried an unequaled moral authority, in stark contrast to the bankrupt (morally and economically) Marcos regime. By the time the election was held on February 7, she was expected to win in a landslide.

The election was marked by voter intimidation and rampant fraud that even became too much for the official government ballot counters to bear. Aquino declared herself the winner. Marcos's parliament declared him the winner. American officials expressed dismay at the reports of fraud but were wary of pushing Marcos too hard, particularly given that two major U.S. military bases were located in the Philippines. Aquino called for strikes and an economic boycott, and when two military leaders rebelled against Marcos, she voiced her support for the rebels. The archbishop of Manila, Jaime Cardinal Sin, went on radio to rally people to support Aquino. The People Power Revolution had begun. Opposition forces swore in Aquino as president. The morning of February 26, Marcos was sworn in as president as well, at his palace. But he didn't stay long in his new six-year term. That night at nine o'clock, a helicopter spirited him out of the presidential palace, the beginning of his journey to Hawaii, where he would take an American offer to live in exile.

When Aquino spoke at The Club in September 1986, she had been in office only six months and, in July, had already put down the first of more than half a dozen military coups she would face during her term in office. As president, she released political prisoners, attempted to remove corrupt officials Marcos had put in power, and tried to marginalize the Communist rebels and rebuild the devastated economy of the Philippines. Marcos had ruled the country imperiously, and he and his wife, Imelda, were known for their lavish lifestyles while millions of Filipinos lived in horrendous poverty. Mrs. Marcos in particular was known for global shopping excursions and amassing a collection of hundreds of designer shoes and handbags. After she and her husband fled the Philippines in 1986, an inventory of her closets tallied more than 70 pairs of sunglasses, 888 handbags, and more than 1,000 pairs of shoes: hence Aquino's declaration to her San Francisco audience that she was not there on a shopping expedition. Regarding shopping for U.S. aid, she also understood the fiscal austerity engendered by the Gramm-Rudman-Hollings Act passed the year before with the goal of eliminating the annual U.S. budget deficits by 1990. And regarding American pop culture, she was comfortable trotting out, in her American twang, the Wendy's hamburger chain slogan "Where's the beef?"

Corazón Aquino served one term as president and drove away from the 1992 inauguration of her successor in a plain white Toyota. She became an inspiration and model for a new generation of women leaders, not just in Asia but throughout the world. Ferdinand Marcos died in Honolulu in 1989 of cardiac arrest. Aquino announced she would not allow the body to be returned to the Philippines because of safety concerns. Imelda Marcos has run for president several times and in 2001 opened a museum of shoes in Manila.

"People Power"

How does one judge the success of a trip like this? My staff tell me that by inches and minutes of positive print and TV coverage, by the decibel level of audience response, and by the warmth of welcome from Americans everywhere, I can measure this a runaway success. Indeed, the trip was dubbed, from the day of the Congress speech, "a home run." I think there have been a few more useful hits since then. Thank you, America.

These have been possible because Americans everywhere have shown that, for them, recent events in the Philippines were not an obscure upheaval in some distant land. Rather, the Philippine revolution captured the heart and idealism of Americans. Everywhere, I have come across relief and pride. Relief that an old ally has rescued itself from a shaming dictatorship, and pride that a people that have learned so much from America should have been prepared to risk everything for ideals we both hold dear.

So this week has been like visiting friends. Yet, has it produced results? My predecessor had an easy way of measuring achievement on his trips here. He came with two shopping lists. One was his wife's for New

York's Fifth Avenue shops, and the other was for guns and aid in Washington.

Judged by the first shopping list, his trips were always an astounding success.

However, the second list did not go so well in recent years. The Philippines fell behind in the aid league because of what was happening back home.

The purpose of this trip was not to get the Philippines back in line at the trough of American assistance. That would go against the grain of what has been happening in my country. We are through with shopping lists. Our election and revolution were about pride as well as democracy—about a pride that was reborn on the tarmac of the Manila International Airport in 1983 when my husband, Ninoy, was assassinated, and a nation rose in outrage and pride.

For the dictatorship, the shopping list was everything. It had to be, because the government did not believe in the Filipino people. All it knew was the foreign handout. Now the United States faces a Philippines prickly in independence and bent on its own self-development. That makes us a much maturer friend and, if not always an easy one, certainly a more dependable ally, in that the things that truly matter are in our mutual interest.

The Filipino people freed themselves from one slavery, political repression. Now they are at work rescuing their economy from the accumulated years of mismanagement, enforced poverty, and a massive $26-billion foreign debt. Between August 1983, when my husband was killed, and February 1986, when the dictatorship was thrown out by the liberating virtue of self-help, we did it ourselves and nothing can feel better than that.

Today as we fight the second revolution against economic failure, we look first to ourselves. If we were seeking a socialist-style evolution of our economy, that would be enough. Yet we have put our faith in an open, internationally oriented economy. We want to harness the economic dimension of people power: working together through pooling the individual initiative, courage, and aspirations of each Filipino. We are throwing aside the shackles of a state that imprisoned initiative and stole the people's wealth. We are putting in its place a government that uses its resources not to do business but to help business. Until February, the only people on welfare in the Philippines were Mr. Marcos's friends. And what welfare it was! It emptied the national coffers.

By concentrating on what government should be doing, we will leave business to businessmen. The Philippines used to be second only to Japan in its region. We mean to work our way back there. The league table of economic performance, not aid handouts, is what we are concentrating on.

We have agreed with the International Monetary Fund on a financial package that assumes a growth rate of about 6 percent next year. The Philippines is back in business. However, ours is a devastated economy. We are pulling ourselves up after years of economic warfare waged against the people by their leader. Two-thirds of Filipinos now live beneath the poverty line. We have a high level of unemployment and underemployment. Half our precious export earnings are taken up in interest payments on the foreign debt. Our foreign trade has been badly hit, over recent years, by instability at home and trade restrictions abroad.

We are looking for support from friends, from those who have the faith to put their money where their mouth is, from those who see the political earthquake that hit the Philippines as one that opened a rift of opportunity to our mutual advantage. We have not come here to borrow, except to meet the requirements of short-term budget support and the debt rescheduling.

Our revolution put democracy back on the cheap. Yet without economic support now, these gains are fragile. We need to expand our economy. We must finance basic government services. We need to direct financial assistance to areas of greatest need. For instance, we now have a $200-million rural job creation program. The level of debt payments must be reduced for the coming years to one which allows space for recovery. The bankers cannot be blind to the political upheaval in the Philippines. They are no longer dealing with a culprit government; rather, with one that honors both its people and its international commitments. We are looking for foreign investments to help fuel our recovery. We have $7 billion of underutilized state assets that we wish to privatize. We are seeking to liberate our economy, to free it from the regulation and intervention of years of state capitalism and plunder. We have put our faith in the private sector as you have here in America. If the Philippines' economic miracle is to follow on the heels of February's political miracle, we must have access to markets.

So what is the economic scoreboard of the trip? As you would say, "Where's the beef?" Well, your administration and Congress left no doubt of its intentions to make the Philippines a special case for assistance. Within the climate of Gramm-Rudman, that is not easy. Yet Washington showed where its heart was when the House voted through a $200-million supplemental aid bill after my address.

Revolutions breed doubts, not for participants but for observers. Mixed with the exhilaration that Americans felt at the events in the Philippines was a concern about stability. And if I can sum up the single most important success of this trip in one sentence, it is this: The message has struck home to everyone that the Aquino government is here to stay, and with its success, so is democracy in the Philippines. Both well-wishers and former skeptics now understand that our unique limited revolution, which has allowed democracy to flower in all its untidy glory, is here for keeps. Filipinos are never going to let go of democracy again.

That is the essence of the trip's achievement. It has put the froth and antics of a handful of grudging losers in perspective. Further, it has convinced the United States that we are serious about dealing with the Communist insurgency. And in the lecture I gave at Harvard, I sought to lay out a Filipino Catholic philosophy of nonviolence. I explained how I could not betray the interlocking forces of people, power, and prayer that brought me to the presidency. Others may have guns, but nobody else has the people. Americans now understand that I will defend our democracy against all challenges by whatever means it takes. By reconciliation and peace when the enemies of democracy will listen, by arms when they won't.

Our new stability has many roots in the recent past: Ninoy's martyrdom united a nation, and we organized, and organized, and organized. International mythology has me coming to power on the crest of an incoherent wave of protest. Nonsense! We won by the same way you win in America: good organization. The revolution was not a coup by a minority. It was a people rising as one to defend the verdict they had already delivered at the ballot box. Revolution is the wrong word, perhaps, to describe a people's uprising to defend the sanctity of the ballot.

Let me close by saying that stopping over in San Francisco is like the first step home. There is a commonwealth to the Pacific Basin that embraces more than the booming trade links. It is a shared culture of energy and hope, it is that restless spirit of searching for new frontiers that ranges from one shore to the other of this great ocean. In San Francisco, one is standing on the edge of the New World. And from shore to shining shore of this great ocean, one sees only endless opportunities. The rebirth of democracy at the other end has opened a new frontier.

September 29, 1987

Randy Shilts

Journalist, San Francisco Chronicle; *Author*, And the Band Played On

When Randy Shilts joined the staff of the *San Francisco Chronicle* in 1981, he was one of the first openly gay journalists to be hired by a major newspaper. His first story on AIDS appeared the following year, when AIDS was still known as GRID (gay-related immunodeficiency disorder), and he, more than any other journalist, tried to draw attention to the growing epidemic. To prevent the spread of AIDS early on, Shilts called for closing San Francisco bathhouses. He was consequently mocked as a "gay Uncle Tom" by some in the gay community, and there were reports of his being spat on when he walked through the city's Castro district. At the same time, conservatives criticized his writing for having a pro-gay bias.

As Shilts makes clear at the outset of his Commonwealth Club talk, the story of the AIDS epidemic is very much a story of the intersection of politics and the media. He noted the lack of attention most of the media paid to AIDS, especially compared to other public health stories (such as poisoned Tylenol capsules). And during the question-and-answer session, he pointed out that the U.S. is "the only country in the Western world that does not have a national AIDS education campaign," recalling, "When I was in Denmark doing research in late 1985, the mailman dropped an AIDS education brochure into every mailbox. Germany, a few weeks later, did the same thing. Great Britain did it this year." In the U.S., the Centers for Disease Control and Prevention (CDC) had cosponsored the first international conference on AIDS in 1985, but it wasn't until 1987 that President Ronald Reagan first used the word "AIDS" in public. The next year, the CDC mailed out 107 million copies of "Understanding AIDS" to American households.

While writing his landmark book *And the Band Played On*, Shilts refrained from being tested himself for HIV, lest it bias his writing. After completing the manuscript, he learned that he was infected but did not publicize the fact, since he felt he could contribute more as a journalist than as an AIDS activist. He died in 1994 of complications resulting from AIDS.

"The Politics of AIDS"

In our media age, the press and government are indivisible. The news media sets the agenda for social issues. To a large extent it sets the agenda for what government will deal with. Nothing illustrates this fundamental reality of our day better than the AIDS epidemic.

In late 1980, a few alert doctors in Los Angeles and New York were noticing that gay men were dying of strange diseases—diseases that had never appeared before in the U.S., especially among young men, or were so rare as to be virtually unknown. By June of 1981, those isolated cases—five cases of pneumonia, twenty-six cases of a rare skin cancer—marked the discovery of what we now know to be the AIDS epidemic. June of 1981 turned out to be a very inauspicious time to have a new health crisis in the U.S. The Reagan Administration was doing exactly what it promised to do in the 1980 campaign—cut domestic spending. That meant holding the line on health spending. Nowhere were these cuts felt more than in the AIDS epidemic.

We can't be entirely critical of the government and media in 1981. No one thought AIDS could become what it did. At first AIDS wasn't understood to be an infectious disease; it was thought to be a strange fluke that would go away. By December 1981, however, researchers at the Centers for Disease Control were alarmed. By then there was convincing evidence that AIDS was a new, infectious disease, probably of viral origin. The CDC requested $800,000; they never got it, because AIDS research was viewed as nonessential health spending. By the time they were given money—ten months later—they had scaled back their request three times before it was small enough for the Reagan Administration to accept. Thus began the pattern of funding cuts that was to dominate AIDS research—almost to this day.

By early 1982, more people were dead or dying from AIDS than were killed by the epidemic of Legionnaires' disease and toxic shock syndrome combined. Still, in the media, the idea of this gay disease just never caught on. Finally, in mid-1982, with the discovery of AIDS in some hemophiliacs and among intravenous drug users, the *Wall Street Journal* published its first story. The headline said "Gay Disease Appearing in Heterosexuals."

Because of the lack of media attention, it was difficult to mobilize the federal government into allocating enough resources. There were dedicated people, working largely at the Centers for Disease Control and local public health agencies throughout the U.S., but resources—at least at the federal level—simply did not exist.

The story of AIDS in 1981, 1982, and early 1983 is the story of studies that could not be undertaken—and warnings that went unheeded. You may remember the news story from Chicago in October of 1982. Seven people suddenly fell ill; their illness and subsequent deaths were related to Tylenol capsules poisoned with cyanide. For the next month, the *New York Times* had a story every day on the Tylenol situation; sixteen of these stories made the front page. In the two months that followed, the *Times* ran twenty-four more stories.

The day those poisoned capsules were found, 634 people were already ill with AIDS—260 had already died. The federal government put more effort into those first five weeks of the Tylenol scare than it did in the first five years of the AIDS epidemic. I suggest that the difference in the media coverage was determined by who was being stricken.

Most of us first heard about AIDS in early 1983, with the discovery that the virus had infected America's blood supply. This caused the first media boom, because now it apparently posed a serious threat to mainstream American society. AIDS until then had only been covered as a science story, not as a serious public policy story that required the government to set priorities and develop resources. But there was no new infusion of funds, because the media still avoided tough investigative stories on whether or not government policy was coinciding with needs.

Why did the government refuse to fund AIDS research? In all my investigation, I never heard anyone in the Reagan Administration say, "They're only homosexuals, let them die." But because most of the people who were dying were gay men and intravenous drug users, there was no compelling political necessity to invest the kind of money that the government did with the Tylenol scare. It wasn't the aggressive prejudice that some militant gay leaders would assert, but it was functional, nonetheless. It was functional in the news media as well; AIDS was considered a "gay" story—not something to do manly investigative reporting on.

Money was beginning to flow into research, but what funds existed were voted by Congress and generally through the efforts of congressmen from San Francisco, Los Angeles, and New York—areas with large gay political constituencies. The money finally got to AIDS researchers because no one in the administration wanted to put the president in the position of vetoing AIDS funds.

By the end of 1983—once it was determined there was no pandemic spread from blood transfusions—there was very little pressure for government funding for AIDS research. Behind the scenes, scientists were racing to discover the AIDS virus. In truth, once scientists had the funds to look for it, it wasn't very hard to find. It took the National Cancer Institute about seven months. In early 1984, the government, under pressure to produce something on AIDS because of the upcoming elections, announced with much fanfare that they had discovered the virus that caused AIDS. Actually we hadn't—the French had—but there weren't enough reporters covering AIDS to find that out.

By this time dissatisfaction with funding for AIDS research had reached the highest levels of government health officials. The assistant secretary for health was routinely writing blistering letters to the Office of Management and Budget, trying to get funds; it didn't happen. No request for funds was too small to bypass months of scrutiny by the OMB.

In the 1984 presidential campaign, neither the Republican nor the Democratic candidates ever mentioned the AIDS epidemic. No reporter covering the national elections felt the subject was important enough to raise. President Reagan did not once utter the word "AIDS," or in any way indicate that an epidemic existed. By April 1985, there were ten thousand cases of AIDS in the U.S. I thought the national media might begin to cover AIDS; there was no difference. What changed the media's handling of AIDS was the fact that a movie star with the disease collapsed in the lobby of the Ritz Hotel in Paris.

When it was suspected that Rock Hudson had AIDS, a producer from *Face the Nation* invited Congressman Henry Waxman, the House legislative leader on AIDS, to be on *Face the Nation* with Margaret Heckler. Waxman was ecstatic until the producer mentioned that—by the way—if Rock Hudson didn't have AIDS, he was going to cancel the show. By the time Rock Hudson was diagnosed, twelve thousand Americans were dead or dying of AIDS, and at least five hundred thousand were infected. The course of the epidemic was already set. It was too late—that is the tragedy of AIDS.

April 3, 1991

Richard B. Cheney

U.S. Secretary of Defense

In August 1990, more than one hundred thousand Iraqi troops, backed by hundreds of tanks, invaded oil-rich neighbor Kuwait. The UN Security Council condemned the action and authorized a U.S.-led coalition to implement Operation Desert Shield. With Iraqi leader Saddam Hussein refusing to withdraw from Kuwait, in January 1991, a U.S.-led coalition of forces launched Operation Desert Storm, an offensive operation that included the longest continuous air strike in the history of warfare and which drove Iraqi forces out of Kuwait. The very day U.S. Secretary of Defense Dick Cheney spoke to The Commonwealth Club, the UN Security Council passed Resolution 687, laying out the terms of the cease-fire ending the Gulf War. Cheney shared the lessons the 1991 Gulf War offered. He also shared his prescription for the military in the 1990s.

One question to Cheney noted that "the Iraqi ambassador is less than happy" with Resolution 687. Said Cheney, " I don't think I would want a resolution that he was happy with." The resolution, he explained, "demands that Iraq rid itself of weapons of mass destruction, continues an arms embargo, sets up a system for using oil revenues to compensate those who were damaged as a result of Iraqi aggression....It's a take-it-or-leave-it proposition." Also unhappy were Kurds in Iraq, who, one questioner said, had been "abandoned when the president clearly called on the Iraqis to overthrow Saddam Hussein." President George H. W. Bush had frequently encouraged Iraqis to oust Hussein—but when Shiites in the south and Kurds in the north rebelled, no U.S. assistance was forthcoming. Cheney's explanation: "For us to send U.S. forces into Iraq to determine the outcome of that civil war would be a very serious mistake. We would have to establish some kind of government once we had toppled the existing one. We would probably have to go to Baghdad to achieve our military objectives, and we would, without doubt, suffer far more casualties doing it than we suffered in liberating Kuwait....Once you get mired in the bog of trying to sort out who will govern Iraq—and U.S. forces are actively engaged on the ground—it becomes a whole different proposition." And the U.S. troops, he said, in response to another question, "have earned the right to get back as quickly as possible....There may be a transition period during which we have to leave a few units there for a period of months while the situation stabilizes, but there is no need for a long-term, permanent U.S. presence on the ground in that part of the gulf....That would be a mistake."

"U.S. Defense Policy: The Gulf War and Beyond"

It is extremely important for us not to fall into the trap of assuming that because Operation Desert Storm was successful, there are no lessons to be learned from the exercise. Just as it would be a mistake to look at the war in Southeast Asia twenty-five years ago and conclude that because it ended unhappily that everything we did there was wrong, it would be a mistake for us to look at the Gulf War, see that it was successful, and conclude that there is no way for us to improve our performance in the future.

From the first days of Saddam Hussein's aggression against Kuwait, President Bush made it abundantly clear that he would accept nothing less than total reversal of that aggression, that our objective was to liberate Kuwait and restore the legitimate government of Kuwait, and that there was to be no compromise of that fundamental principle. Having that kind of direction from the president made it possible for us to consistently evaluate the effectiveness of recommended courses of action and decide whether to accept or reject them.

When you are preparing to deploy a huge force halfway around the world with the possibility that that force might engage in combat, there are a number of very difficult decisions with potential political ramifications here at home that must be made. For example, calling up a quarter of a million reservists from every state and community in the nation affects the lives of millions of Americans all across the country. It would have been relatively simple for the president to try to find some way to do the job without calling up the reserves. But our entire strategy for years has been based on the notion that in a major mobilization we will call up the reserves. And when that tough decision had to be made, the president never blinked.

When it was time for the November deployment—which was roundly criticized in many quarters—when we decided to double the force that we had deployed to the gulf, the president could have directed us to try to do the job with a smaller force. But if he had wavered in the face of criticism that he knew he would receive, we probably would have suffered more casualties in January and February. The key to the success of the military operation was sending enough force to do the job, do it quickly, and do it at the lowest possible cost.

Another element that was vital was the correct analysis of what it was that held together the international coalition that the president built. To have some thirty nations, a very disparate group, come together to commit forces to the gulf, to have a majority of the members of the Arab League, the Iranians, the Syrians, the Israelis, the Egyptians, the Saudis, and everybody else pull together in a coalition arrayed against Saddam Hussein, required an act of great international diplomacy and leadership. During the hearings on whether or not to give sanctions a chance last fall, the argument was often made that the coalition would not stand for any more dynamic initiative than the simple application of sanctions. That was dead wrong.

The president understood that the coalition was prepared to stay the course as long as its members believed in the United States of America and in our determination and commitment to the cause. Once they saw the kind of commitment the president prepared to make last November, there was never any doubt about our ability to hold the coalition together.

Under these circumstances, you become supremely aware of what you owe your predecessors. General Colin Powell and I were very aware that we were deploying the force that we had inherited; that we had not done much during our tenure because time had been too short to create that force. It was the force that was created in the 1960s, 1970s, and 1980s. It's important to remember that a lot of those systems were the product of prior administrations, Republican and Democrat alike. The F-111s that functioned with such precision in dropping bombs and laser-guided munitions first flew in 1967. Many of the aircraft carriers that were deployed were more than twenty years old. The F-16, the backbone of the Air Force, was first operational in 1976. The total force concept—a mixture of active forces and reserves—was designed by Mel Laird in the early 1970s, during the Nixon Administration. Harold Brown, Jimmy Carter's defense secretary, had a great deal to do with creating the cruise missiles that performed so capably in the early days of the war.

It takes a very long time to build something as impressive as the capability that we used in the gulf; it's the work of decades. That work can be torn down in a very short time by unwise policy decisions. We ignore that fact at our peril.

Technology is absolutely vital, but it is worthless unless it is part of a total system. The Iraqis had some good technology—MiG-29s, the top-of-the-line Soviet fighter; T-72 tanks, the main battle tank of the Soviet armed forces; and some fairly sophisticated command and control systems. But in their hands those systems simply didn't perform as well as did those deployed by the U.S. and our allies. It is not just a question of having a good airplane; you also need a first-class, highly motivated, well-trained pilot to operate it, a very good ground crew to maintain it, an adequate housing budget—because our capacity to attract and retain first-class people to serve depends on our ability to provide for their families.

It's spending money on things as mundane as operations and maintenance, which is the account in the defense budget that includes money for flying hours for our pilots and operating time for our tankers so that our armored divisions are well-equipped and prepared to function in the way that they did. It's not enough to focus on technology; we have to focus on all aspects of our military system.

In the gulf conflict there were a great many heroes. Some are increasingly well known to the public by virtue of their visibility. But we could look all through that collection of five hundred and forty thousand Americans in the gulf and find people who performed far above anything that we have any reason to expect from how much we paid them. We could talk about the airborne assault units that went deep into Iraq the first night of the attack into Kuwait, or the helicopter crews that went in to rescue downed pilots, or the Navy SEALs that operated to clear mines along the beaches, or the logistics people who performed miracles in the most impressive logistics operations ever. You go down the list of forces and find enough legitimate American heroes to last for a very long time.

The role of the reservists and the National Guard was enormously important. One particular unit comes to mind, a group of Marine reservists, Tank Company B from Yakima, Washington. They were called up in December; December was the first time they ever got their hands on the new M1 Abrams tank. On February 24, they went into action into Kuwait. In a series of clashes over the next four days, approximately ten tanks of Company B destroyed fifty-nine Iraqi tanks, most of them the top-of-the-line T-72 tanks. The point is that it is possible for us to have reservists—citizen soldiers who devote their careers to everyday pursuits like the rest of us—trained, properly equipped, motivated, and ready to serve when called upon.

It's important also to talk about our military leadership. Everybody now knows Norm Schwarzkopf—"Stormin' Norman" of Desert Storm fame—and my colleague in the Pentagon, the chairman of the Joint Chiefs of Staff, General Colin Powell. Without taking anything away from either of them, there are people of that caliber at the upper reaches of the U.S. military. They are the officers who got their early training and combat experience in Southeast Asia twenty or twenty-five years ago. They had the dedication and devotion to stay in the U.S. military through the lean years—through the days of bad race relations and drug problems and the hollow Army of the 1970s— and they learned what it takes to create a first-rate, all-volunteer force.

There is no question that this will be a safer world because we undertook Operation Desert Storm. That doesn't mean it's going to be a perfectly safe world or that there aren't problems. But the warning to would-be aggressors that Desert Storm sends around the world is enormously valuable. I am convinced that there are conflicts that would have occurred except for the use of U.S. and allied military power.

The operation was an enormous source of reassurance to friends and allies of the United States. We have demonstrated conclusively to all our friends, to people who believe as we do, that the United States has the capacity and the will to back up its commitments.

We are now in a position to modify our military posture and strategy to reflect the fact that we no longer have to plan for short-warning, no-notice global conflict with Soviet conventional forces. We still have to be concerned with their strategic capability, but increasingly, as a result either of policy decisions by the Soviet government or as a result of their collapsing economy, they will find it difficult to project military power beyond their borders. That's good news. That allows us to change the strategy and underlying assumptions that our strategy has been built on for forty years and move instead to forces that are built on the need to deal with major regional contingencies such as the one we just fought. That means a smaller military. That means a smaller defense budget. And that means adopting those proposals that the president has developed over the last two years that are now before the Congress, and that are the basic thrust of our long-term defense planning.

The world is still a dangerous and a hostile place. Peace and freedom and U.S. interests in large parts of the world can be challenged by people who wish us ill. It is extremely important that we continue to operate in accordance with some of the basic principles that have governed our strategy since the end of World War II: the notion of a system of alliances with other democracies, the idea of forward-deployed U.S. forces to give meaning and substance to those commitments, the notion of having forces here at home of a sufficient size, flexibility, and capability so they can be rapidly deployed to deal with contingencies around the world.

We will also be faced with the fact of an increasingly sophisticated military threat, in terms of the nature of the systems that we will have to cope with. Technology is having an enormous impact on the nature of warfare, with more rapid changes in that area now than in any other time in history. You only had to watch the exchanges between the Scuds and the Patriots over Tel Aviv or Riyadh to begin to understand the nature of the kind of conflicts we're going to have to deal with in the future. We estimate that within the next decade some fifteen developing nations will have ballistic missile capability. Many will have nuclear weapons, and many will have chemical and biological capability as well. It is absolutely essential that we move aggressively to develop the technological capability to deal not just with the threat that it may constitute to the U.S., but also the threat it represents to our friends and to U.S. forces forward-deployed overseas.

Based on our experience in the gulf, we have to conclude that investment in technology in the military saves lives, American lives and the lives of our adversaries as well. We would not have been able to do what we did in the gulf at the very low cost in terms of American casualties if we had not invested in many of those systems that were so ridiculed and that came so close to cancellation in the 1960s, 1970s, and 1980s. That doesn't mean we will always get it right. There will be times when the Department of Defense will invest in a new system, try to develop a new technology, and it won't work, or won't work at an acceptable price. We'll have some false starts.

The notion that because the Soviet threat is receding we can now not invest in technology for the military is totally fallacious. Some of my friends on Capitol Hill suggest that we ought to invest in the technology but put it on the shelf so it will be there if we ever have to bring it down and use it. Harking back to Desert Storm, it is not enough just to have a piece of equipment that will perform a certain function; it's important that the troops have it in their inventory, that they get to exercise with it, that they know how to use it, and that we've developed a doctrine for the application of those systems and capabilities.

If Congress approves the five-year defense program that is now pending, by the mid-1990s we will be spending less of our GNP on defense than we have spent at any time since before World War II. We'll be back to 1939 levels, with 3.6 or 3.7 percent of GNP going for defense. That is what some people call the peace dividend; I prefer to think of the peace dividend as peace. But the point is that we need to continue to maintain our capacity to stay in front in terms of technology for the military. It is vital. American lives depend on it. A lot of young Americans who were deployed to the gulf, who went to war on our behalf, are alive tonight because our predecessors had the wisdom to make the right decision to make those investments. I only hope that fifteen or twenty years from now, when our successors look back on this administration and Congress, that they will be able to say with the same degree of confidence and gratitude that we made the right decisions in the 1990s.

History will record that Desert Storm was a major test of U.S. military capability—of our systems, our doctrine, and our capacity to use those systems. But more than a test of the courage and professionalism of the men and women who serve in our armed forces—all of them volunteers—it was a test of the wisdom, determination, and leadership of our president. And it was the test of the capacity of the American people to accept the burdens of world leadership. I think history will judge that we did indeed meet the test on all those counts.

October 4, 1991

Maxine Hong Kingston

Author, The Woman Warrior, China Men, *and* Tripmaster Monkey

When writer Maxine Hong Kingston spoke to The Commonwealth Club in October 1991, she had been working for several years on a novel called *The Fourth Book of Peace*. When the U.S. led a coalition in Operation Desert Storm to liberate Kuwait, international support for ousting Saddam Hussein from Kuwait was great: Iraq was clearly the aggressor. In the U.S., however, some opposed U.S. military operations in the Persian Gulf, worried that the media portrayed bombing missions with new "smart" weapons as if the bombing runs were a video game, and they pointed out that the U.S. had backed Saddam Hussein in his war against Iran in the 1980s. In her talk, Maxine Hong Kingston discussed not just the Gulf War but the antiwar movement, including the media's dismissive attitude toward opponents of the Gulf War.

As she noted at the beginning of her speech, Maxine Hong Kingston had just suffered a personal loss: the death of her father the week before. Two weeks later, she would suffer another, very different loss: *The Fourth Book of Peace* would go up in flames, along with Kingston's house, in the Oakland Hills fire. Before the fire was finally controlled, twenty-five people would be killed, one hundred and fifty injured, and over twenty-five hundred homes destroyed as sixteen hundred acres burned. In the 1990s, the homes were rebuilt. In 2003, Maxine Hong Kingston finished a new book, *The Fifth Book of Peace*, and the U.S. invaded Iraq and ousted Saddam Hussein from power.

"Writing in a Time of War"

I dedicate my presentation today to my father, who died last week.

Writing is a way of creating the world. In writing I bring more life force into being. During a time of war—a time of destruction—I write to keep alive, to keep all of us alive.

Desert Storm is strange, wrong, fast. And my writing, which I dedicate to peace, is slow. I have been working on a book of peace, trying to imagine peace and to invent a language of peace. This book may take me a decade to complete.

The war breaks into the book, which is only about one hundred pages long.

I'm hearing the war planes again roaring day and night whenever I think to listen. The nightmares have come back. B-52s covering the sky, wingtip to wingtip, going somewhere to carpet-bomb it. And there are missiles, rockets, giant maces, and other flying weapons of my own imagination, all moving at uniform speed and having to fall sooner or later on populations.

The roaring woke me up this morning. I looked out the window at the actual sky and saw darting between clouds a silver airplane, an equilateral triangle, like a spearhead, definitely a warplane, a bomber. Just as I was about to turn away, I saw another such plane coming through the clouds. They were going west, the direction the planes in my dreams usually go, which must be the route to Saudi Arabia. Then a flock of ducks flapped by, then a single white bird, then a passenger plane, a long white cylinder.

I wonder what a C-6 transport looks like, one of those flying gasoline stations, big as a football field. A young friend tells me he runs laps and rides bikes inside his plane after delivering the tanks.

The fleets of killer planes were hallucinations that first appeared during World War II when I was born. As a child I was afraid of the planes coming to get me, but now my horror is that they belong to my government and they are constantly going from my country to do harm on my behalf. Another war and again I'm on the side with the most weapons, and the most ghastly weapons. And again we're the invader, killing children and chasing an enemy fleeing on bare feet. I am ashamed to be an American. I am ashamed to be a human being.

It was during war that Virginia Woolf wrote her book of peace, *Three Guineas*, then drowned herself. She could not bear the roaring in her mind and the roaring in the air. But she did leave us with a story of the village woman who refused to roll bandages and knit socks for the troops. The thought that there was such a woman heartens me, and I won't kill myself, though I am almost wiped out, timid and estranged. Ninety percent are in favor of this war, and they feel euphoria, according to the president, at the war from the air, and more euphoria at the invasion on the ground. They are primitive. If we're winning, they're for it. And whoever kills the most wins. If they are praying any decent prayers, I cannot hear them through the roaring.

Trying for more direct communication than a novelist can have, I wrote telegrams and letters such as the following.

March 2, 1991
Dear President Bush,
I was appalled to hear you on the radio this morning saying the country is solid, that there is no antiwar movement. Isn't it enough that you have had to sacrifice the lives of so many people? Why are you gloating over the death of the best humanitarian values in us, the dream of peace through peaceful means, the lessons of nonviolence taught through Martin Luther King Jr. and Gandhi? Furthermore, I do not think you are getting the news. The peace movement is very much alive, and I am hereby assuring you we are beginning right now to stop the next war. I wish you would help us. You might begin by meditating on the idea of peaceful means to peaceful ends as the sensible way of doing anything. I just turned down an invitation to tour with the USIA. I am so ashamed of being an American.
Sincerely,
MHK

Still working as fast as I can on my book of peace that I hope will prevent a war ten years from now, I had my secretary write letters to newspapers and newsmagazines. We asked them to do a better job of bearing witness. Couldn't they interview people who have ideas for alternatives to war? We ought to be seeing pictures of the effects of the bombing. It's evil for us to kill perhaps one hundred thousand people and refuse to look at what we have done. Greenpeace is saying now that it's between two hundred thousand and three hundred thousand people.

Benjamin Bradlee, executive editor of the *Washington Post*, wrote this letter in reply: "I have no idea who Maxine Hong Kingston is. I have no idea how she knows whether we are providing balanced or unbalanced journalism. We have quoted Gene LaRocque and Maxine Waters constantly over the years.[1] And I must say I resent whoever Maxine Hong Kingston is telling me that we lack objectivity and balance."

Joseph Lelyveld, managing editor of the *New York Times*, answered: "It may not be altogether apparent in Berkeley, but it's apparent practically everywhere else that those currents of feeling are running strongly with the president at least for now. Your letter is a useful reminder that we should give due weight to those who are in outright opposition. We'll endeavor to do so, but due weight at a stage when they are having scant impact cannot mean equal time." Mr. Lelyveld does invite me to submit articles to the op-ed section, which is outside the precincts of the news department. I am back to where I started.

If I want the kind of writing I have in mind, if I want the peaceful world I envision, I will have to create it myself. And I am slow. And the nature of my art is slow—changing the atmosphere, changing consciousness, one reader at a time. It's not due weight or outright opposition I want, but an entire new pacific reality.

In my progress as a writer, my first important book was *The Woman Warrior*. I feel terrible that I wrote a book with the word war in the title and

1. Gene LaRocque fought during World War II and rose to the rank of rear admiral before retiring from the military, a decision in part precipitated by the Vietnam War. He then founded the Center for Defense Information, which seeks to rein in military spending. Maxine Waters (D-CA) has served in the U.S. House of Representatives since 1991. Now representing South Central Los Angeles, she also served fifteen years in the California State Assembly. She voted against the 1990 resolution authorizing President George H. W. Bush to use force to remove Saddam Hussein from power.

that I helped bring a lot of war energy into the world. I am going to correct that in my next work.

In that work I am going to tell another ending for *The Woman Warrior*. Actually, this was an ending that the ancient people had, but I didn't write it down because I had forgotten it. When I wrote *The Woman Warrior*, it was a time of feminist work, and I didn't want a tale in which the heroine returns and becomes a very feminine person. In my next book I will retell the ending where Fa Mu Lan comes home from battle. She's a general and she returns home, bringing her army with her. She calls the army to attention and tells the soldiers to wait for her. She enters her house, takes off her disguise, puts on a beautiful gown, festoons her hair with flowers, puts on makeup, and then emerges and reveals to the soldiers that it was she who had been their general all along. Of course, they are amazed. Then they disperse and return to their civilian lives, having seen their general turn back into a beautiful woman. When the ancient people wrote that ending, they were hoping that there is a way of coming back from war without being brutalized, a way of becoming a nurturing family person again.

As I evolve as an artist, I am also evolving the stories of war and peace, and finding stories of peace. Thinking today about writing during a time of war, I feel that all I could do was to write peacefully, find the language of peace, and also collect works of peace that have been lost, like Mark Twain's "War Prayer." These are the only tactics that I could think of that made sense for the peace movement—using words and hoping that that makes a difference.

October 22, 1991

George Shultz and Don Oberdorfer

Former U.S. Secretary of State

Diplomatic Correspondent, The Washington Post

According to George Shultz, CIA reports in the 1980s said there was nothing stirring within the walls of the Kremlin. After meeting Mikhail Gorbachev, Secretary of State Shultz said there was. Here the man who served in both Reagan administrations as secretary of state joins veteran journalist Don Oberdorfer to recount the brief history of perestroika and glasnost, as well as the impending collapse of the Soviet command-style economy. (Shultz himself has a Ph.D. in economics from MIT, and he'd previously served as secretary of labor, director of the Office of Management and Budget, and secretary of the treasury.) In addition to its remarkable subject—the end of the Cold War—the October 1991 program with Shultz and Oberdorfer is significant in another respect: it brings together one of the leading figures in world diplomacy with one of the media figures who interpreted his actions for readers.

When Shultz and Oberdorfer sat down to retrace the end of the Cold War, it was clear the Soviet experiment was nearly over. Two months before, a group of Mikhail Gorbachev's advisors had put the Soviet leader under house arrest and announced that a new government had taken charge. The coup crumbled within days, but as an outcome Gorbachev was sidelined by history. Two months after this talk, he would step down as president.

"U.S.–Soviet Relations on the Eve of the Revolution"

Don Oberdorfer:
Only eight years ago, the Soviet Union shot down KAL 007,[1] the United States was preparing to deploy the first medium-range missiles on the soil of Western Europe, the Soviet Union was getting ready to walk out of the Geneva arms talks, and the then-leader of the Soviet Union, Yuri Andropov, was about to issue a statement saying no one should have any illusions that there could be an improvement in the relations between these two nations as long the current administration was in office. In November of that year, the Soviet Union notified its intelligence stations to gather all the information they could on an urgent basis because it believed that the U.S. was about to launch a nuclear attack on the Soviet Union. The Soviet Union then alerted nuclear-capable aircraft in Western Europe as a demonstration of their concern. It was that difficult. George Kennan, perhaps the foremost American commentator on Soviet-American affairs, said a few months earlier that there was no way to describe what was going on between the two nations except as "an inexorable march toward war."

Everything has changed in such mysterious ways that even people who covered the story day to day found it difficult to grasp. Probably never before, outside of war, had the relationships of the leading nations of the world changed so rapidly.

I have mentioned the fall of 1983. Then there was the death of Yuri Andropov; the succession of Konstantin Chernenko, whom most of us have forgotten; then, just six years ago, in the spring of 1985, came Gorbachev, a man almost twenty years younger than his predecessor, a vigorous person.

1. On September 1, 1983, Korean Airlines Flight 007—a 747 bound from the U.S. to Seoul, South Korea, was shot down by Soviet fighters after it strayed into Soviet airspace. All 269 people aboard were presumed killed. The Soviets claimed the aircraft, which flew over Sakhalin Island, was flying without navigation lights and had failed to respond to communications. President Reagan called the downing of the unarmed civilian aircraft a "crime against humanity."

In the fall of 1985, the summits began. First there was President Reagan and Mr. Gorbachev at Geneva. The next year they met at Reykjavik, in what was perhaps the most spectacular meeting of American and Soviet leaders in history. They sat in a small room over a dining room table—the two leaders, Secretary Shultz and Foreign Minister Shevardnadze, two interpreters and, sitting a little behind, two note takers—and bargained about the elimination of all the ballistic missiles in the arsenals of the two nations. They even talked about eliminating all nuclear weapons that either nation held. This was the biggest leap toward an agreement on total disarmament in history.

It all seems so far away, until we think about what has just happened recently, when President Bush, on September 27, announced massive cuts in nuclear weapons, challenged Gorbachev to do the same, and a week later, Gorbachev responded.

Remember, too, 1987—the beginning of the march of the Soviet Union out of Afghanistan and the summit in Washington in the fall of that year. In 1988, there was the announcement of the withdrawal from Afghanistan and President Reagan's visit to the Soviet Union. Of that visit, Tom Shales of the *Washington Post* wrote, "There is nothing new or interesting about two politicians kissing a baby, except when the two politicians are Reagan and Gorbachev and the baby is in Red Square."

In December 1988, Gorbachev came to the UN and announced a cut of a half-million men in the Soviet armed forces, stunning everyone. The total impact of what has happened in the last eight years in the Soviet Union and between the U.S. and the USSR will be as important as World War I, World War II, the Bolshevik Revolution, the development of the atomic bomb and the computer chip.

Historians have long argued whether it is great trends or great men and women that are responsible for the turns of history. The trends were there. There was the overmilitarization of the U.S. and Soviet Union—very heavy military burdens on both societies—and even more important, a pileup of nuclear weapons almost beyond comprehension. There was the trend toward a global market, a global economy, and global means of mass communications. The Soviet Union was not part of this trend and simply had to join or be left behind.

There was the increasing sophistication of the Soviet people, something that we don't often think about. The Soviet Union was changing rapidly.

On the eve of World War II, it was two-thirds rural, and only 10 percent of the population had an eighth-grade education. Today, nearly 80 percent of the population has an eighth-grade education or better, and it is two-thirds urban, about the same proportion as the countries of Western Europe.

All those trends were important, but the people were perhaps more important. We tend to forget that when Mr. Gorbachev became general secretary in 1985, it was the first time since 1972 that there had been a politically strong American president and a physically strong Soviet leader at the same time. President Nixon met with [Leonid] Brezhnev in 1972 in Moscow for his first summit, but shortly thereafter he was weakened by Watergate. Then came Gerald Ford, who was not elected president or even vice president. By the time Carter began to exert himself, Brezhnev was in physical decline, and he was followed by two sick Soviet leaders, Andropov and Chernenko. Finally, in 1985 came Gorbachev, at the time when Ronald Reagan had just been reelected by a huge majority. At last, we had two leaders who were ready and able to deal.

Who gets the credit? It's hard to say. Certainly Mikhail Gorbachev will get a large share of it. With all his shortcomings and failings, with all the difficulties, it is clear that he will be a great historical figure of the twentieth century. People will look back at what he did with wonder.

Mr. Reagan was much more ready than I knew, as a reporter covering these things, to engage with the Soviets, even while condemning them in the harshest terms. And he really hated nuclear weapons. This was something that he said all the time, but few of us took him seriously until Reykjavik.

Secretary Shultz played an extremely important role. Ronald Reagan knew what he wanted, but he didn't know how to get there. Shultz is unusual in many respects, one of them being that he is an economist who came to high political office. He thinks with the long-term view of the economist, not of results today. He believed in steady inputs to get those results.

Mr. [Eduard] Shevardnadze, the Soviet foreign minister, came to office, tapped by his friend Gorbachev, with no experience in diplomacy and virtually no experience in democracy. Yet he became an outstanding diplomat and a democrat.

It is too early to evaluate President Bush and Secretary Baker, but they deserve credit for their determined diplomacy moving toward the reunification of Germany. If they had hesitated, things would have been much more complicated.

These events will change international lives in ways we cannot possibly foresee. The whole framework within which the U.S. engaged the world since the late 1940s—the bipolar world—has been invalidated by the demise of the Soviet Union and the end of the Cold War. As Colin Powell, chairman of the Joint Chiefs of Staff, who despite being a military man seems to be the most articulate man in this administration, said: "Our implacable foe of the last forty years has just been vaporized before our eyes."

George Shultz:
What do we learn from the great turn of events? I think we have learned four lessons. The first is that it is very important to have a strategy. We live in a world of tactics. But to accomplish big things, we have to have a big strategy. The U.S. and its allies had a big strategy that dates back to the period immediately following World War II, when we saw the nature of the Soviet Union, when the idea of containment was put forward by George Kennan, when we saw that to contain the USSR we had to put in place a capacity to deter their aggression—and did so through NATO and our alliances with Japan and Korea. We put together a world economic and political system based on more free and democratic societies and on the rule of law, societies where the broad economic policy was based on the ideas of private property, markets, enterprise, and incentives.

President Reagan bore down on those ideas with greater enthusiasm and conviction than almost any of his predecessors. He really rang the freedom bell. He didn't accept the Brezhnev Doctrine that what's mine is mine and what's yours is up for grabs. We confronted the Soviets in Afghanistan, Cambodia, Angola, Nicaragua, and, in a different way, in Eastern Europe. The long-term strategy was that if we could successfully contain the Soviet Union, sooner or later they would be forced to turn inward, and when they did, they would not like what they saw and they would change. That was the strategy. It worked.

So, as a great nation looking to the future, we need a strategy. We have to ask ourselves where we want to go and how we get there. With a strategy, you can then maneuver tactically; without one, you follow the breeze.

The second lesson is about democracy. We endured a period of forty years under a difficult strategy. We spent a lot of money on defense, and people didn't like that. We had to be willing to confront reality when reality wasn't pleasant. President Reagan received a lot of criticism for saying that the Soviet Union was an evil empire. While we can argue whether he was wise to say that, I have not heard anyone say that it was not an empire, and that evil didn't abound.

NATO had its ups and downs, and stories were forever being written about how these countries couldn't hold together. There was a constant need to shore things up. Nevertheless, the democracies held together. People did in the end support those who stood firm.

The third lesson is that, by and large, we had what couldn't have turned out to be a better experiment had a social scientist set out to design it. That long-running experiment had on both sides societies that had able people with good education and lots of natural resources, but the big difference was that one was run on a centralized, repressive basis, and the other on a more democratic, market-oriented basis. We ran that experiment for decades, and it is clear which side came out the better. Morally and in terms of well-being, we have had a demonstration of what works.

It is important to take that demonstration on board, as seems to be happening around the world. But these are lessons that have to be learned and learned and worked at and worked at. We have to try to put these ideas into practice, and that is not easy. It is much easier to sit back and say, "Let some dictator do it."

In preparation for writing my own memoirs, I have been doing a little reading about the period of the 1930s. It's very sobering to see the extent of support for Hitler and Mussolini. Almost all the British aristocracy lined up behind Hitler, and he had a following in the U.S. A lot of people in the Great Depression felt that we needed a strong man. So don't sell this idea short. Openness, democracy, freedom, markets, incentives, and private property have won a clear victory. But we have to keep fighting the battle forever.

The final lesson is that individuals really do make a difference. Ronald Reagan had immense support. He was a president with an agenda that consisted of deeply felt fundamental ideas. He just kept at them. He stuck to a few things I wish he hadn't stuck to, but his idea about strategic defense turned out to be one of the most important bargaining weapons we had. He rang the freedom bell, stood up for what he believed, and managed to have a very interesting personal interaction with President Gorbachev.

I met Gorbachev before President Reagan did, at the Andropov funeral. And I traveled to Moscow in the fall of 1985 for a kind of presummit meeting and had a knock-down, drag-out session with Gorbachev. I got a good feel for him, and I felt that when he and the president got together it would probably click.

Gorbachev will go down as a great historic figure. He recognized that the reality of the Soviet Union was desperate and that he had to change. How clear a vision he had of where these changes would lead is a question. But he saw that he had to change, and he started this process. He started an avalanche.

Shevardnadze was without diplomatic experience, but he understood the process of dealing with other human beings, of figuring out the power structure and what needed to be done to gain objectives. He naturally picked up the ins and outs of foreign affairs. He had a good instinct for it, and he had a great relationship at the time with his friend Gorbachev.

The spring of 1987, after the Iran-Contra story had broken, was a tortuous period for the Reagan Administration. In addition to Iran-Contra, it was reported that Marines in our Moscow embassy had been subverted in the most ancient way known to mankind and had let the KGB run freely through our embassy. It was very demoralizing. At the same time I saw—and the president supported me—some real openings in the Soviet Union. It was no thanks to the CIA that we saw these things; they were saying there was no change. But when Mr. Gorbachev said he would de-link negotiations about intermediate-range weapons, it was a big breakthrough that showed that the Soviets were ready to move forward.

I was due to go to Moscow in the middle of 1987 to negotiate. In the midst of this intelligence breach craze, seventy senators voted that I shouldn't go. I felt I should, the president supported me, and I went. And I went into what turned out to be the most interesting, exciting, and productive meeting a secretary of state has probably ever had in Moscow. During these negotiations, I was wracking my brains for ways to break the tension and change the atmosphere. The routine for going to Moscow for these negotiations was that I would fly to Helsinki, spend a night there to get acclimated, then fly into Moscow early in the morning, start our meeting in the middle of the morning, then go to a semisocial, semiofficial luncheon. There are always toasts at these luncheons, so I decided that when my time came, I would do something different.

I knew that the Shevardnadzes were from Georgia and that they liked Georgia—once my wife referred to Mrs. Shevardnadze as a Russian and almost got her head knocked off. So I got the tape of one of our torch singers singing "Georgia on My Mind." I got the music, had the lyrics translated into Russian, and got four of our Russian-speaking people ready to sing. When my turn came, I handed the words and music to the Shevardnadzes and I started in. "Georgia, Georgia, the whole day through. Just an old sweet song keeps Georgia on my mind..." At the end, Shevardnadze looked over at me and said, "Thank you, George. That shows respect."

That was one of the little things that come along in relationships between people that don't make all the difference, but they help.

[from the question-and-answer session]

Q. *Gorbachev must have known that he was skating on much thinner ice than what was generally perceived. To what extent did U.S. leaders realize that the Soviet Union and Gorbachev were in such a perilous condition?*

Shultz: I thought the Soviet Union was a lot weaker than portrayed by the CIA, and that Gorbachev was much more dedicated to change than they thought. But I didn't think he foresaw the degree to which the situation would change. Gorbachev put in motion forces that, once started, couldn't be managed. It was like setting off dynamite in the Sierras and starting an avalanche. The rule for starting an avalanche is to stay out of the way. But Gorbachev tried to manage the avalanche. I don't think that avalanche has found the bottom of the valley yet, although it's pretty close. I think intellectually Gorbachev became convinced that democratic forms of government and more market-based forms of economic activity were the way to go, but he couldn't quite bring himself on board an idea like private property, so he hesitated at times when he could have taken the decisive action that might have allowed him to manage this better.

Q. *As secretary of state, did you believe that your strategy would result in a breakup of the Soviet Union?*

Shultz: I didn't believe we would see the breakup of the Soviet Union. I don't know anybody who did. People often ask if I was surprised when the Berlin Wall went down. I say "sort of—but not nearly as surprised as I was when Mexico privatized its telephone system." That's important, because it shows that our ideas have spread. Surprising things don't all have to do with the Soviet Union; they are going on elsewhere, and it's very encouraging.

November 21, 1991

Jacques Yves Cousteau

Explorer and Environmentalist

For decades, Jacques Cousteau enchanted millions worldwide with the mysteries of the sea he revealed through undersea explorations from the *Calypso* as it traveled the globe. The wiry inventor of the Aqua-Lung surfaced in San Francisco in November 1991, clad in his trademark turtleneck (but sans red watch cap) to plead for support for the rights of future generations—not just as a concept, but as a bill of rights officially enshrined in the Charter of the United Nations. Before delivering this impassioned address in his soft French accent, he stood, microphone in hand, and spoke with hundreds of children seated cross-legged on the floor. He appealed to their senses of awe and wonder and tried to prepare them to work to save the planet.

The year after Cousteau spoke at The Club, the French president, François Mitterrand, named him chairman of the newly created Council on the Rights of Future Generations—a position he resigned from when France resumed nuclear testing in the Pacific. As for the Declaration of Rights for Future Generations, it was adopted by UNESCO (United Nations Educational, Scientific and Cultural Organization) in 1997, and was finally presented to the UN a decade after Cousteau's talk, in October 2001, with a petition signed by nine million people in 106 countries. It has not yet been incorporated into the

UN Charter. Cousteau lauded the influence that petitions can have on decision makers, since signers can also vote. But the man known as a "wise guardian of the sea" did not live to see the petition presented to the UN: at dawn on a June day in 1997, word came that Cousteau had gone "to rejoin the silent world."

"The Rights of Future Generations"

The greatest adventure of all time is the adventure of humankind. It is an extraordinary event, unnatural, completely paradoxical. Humans are very much the newcomers on the earth. Life has existed for more than three billion years, but we arrived only about three million years ago. Our presence represents only one one-thousandth of the span of life on this planet.

Nature provides newcomers all the time, through evolution. But nature's nature—the *real* nature—is alien to our concepts. Nature is cruel and violent and does not know what justice is. Nature favors the strong, the most violent, the most cruel. It is because of this set of values, which we reject, that nature was successful in developing and populating the world.

But we are not ordinary newcomers. We arrived as naked apes, and as naked apes we were subject to all the violence of nature. We had to behave like nature did, by being violent and cruel, trying to save our own lives. This continued until very recent times—ten thousand to fifteen thousand years ago, when we stopped being mere gatherers of food and established rules, ways to live together, to farm the land, and to use our brain for other purposes than just escaping danger. Then, unanimously, through our primitive and elaborate religions as well as through deep-rooted desire, we rejected the rules of nature; the law of the jungle was not for us. So human beings have proven to be paradoxical animals that could eventually modify their own environment, their own ways of life, and now maybe even their genetics. The moral values that we have introduced as our rules are radically opposed to nature's.

How can we live in this world with such a divorce of methods of living? The two sets of rules—nature's and human's—have had difficulty cohabitating. But we have cohabitated. With bloody adventures, with ups and downs, we have lived with these two sets of values. We have to adopt this moral side of behavior that we are so proud of. But at the same time, we have to protect the rules of nature if we want to live in harmony—even if we are divorced from nature.

I am proud to be one of these revoltees against nature's laws. But the consequences of that revolt are that we have a very difficult discipline if we want to succeed in our gigantic recent adventure. The most difficult part of this cohabitation is that in nature individuals do not count. Individuals are systematically sacrificed to the future of the species. Human beings, however, reevaluated and reasserted that concept of individuality. The most superb proof of this is two hundred years old. It is the declaration of rights that was contained for the first time in the American Constitution, proclaimed two years later by the French Revolution, and adopted and codified by the United Nations at its conception.

These new rules—human rights—are the rules that we are ready to fight for, that we are pushing all the nations of the earth to respect: in South Africa, for example, or in the various countries where Amnesty International is fighting for human rights. These human rights are now so well established that nobody can argue against them. However, in this declaration of rights there is not one single mention of what will happen after us; future generations are forgotten. This omission may be the result of our long fight with nature. Perhaps we have not yet adapted to our new role on this planet.

Think of all our new concepts. Liberty is only possible in a disciplined society. Human rights can only be adopted and respected if a high dose of discipline is exercised by human beings. Self-discipline is a very difficult thing to implement in our own lives. But self-discipline is the only way we can at the same time be proud of our revolt against nature and protect that nature that we have very recently become masters of. We have a sharp turn to make, 180 degrees, from being victims of nature to being protectors of nature. It has taken us about two hundred years to understand that and to begin to act accordingly.

Now, I would like to look at what we have done with the planet. We started to think about that, really, in 1968, when the astronauts took the first picture of Earth from the moon. In those pictures it was obvious that this planet was a jewel, that it was unique in the solar system, that it was a small spaceship in a gigantic universe with one single team on board. Nations were our temporary divisions, but there was only one crew—the human race. It took some time for us to realize this, and while we hesitated to take that sharp turn, we damaged our heritage severely. I could emphasize each one of those damages, but instead I will name them rapidly.

The fluids of life are air and water. And these two fluids are damaged every day to an unbelievable extent by ignorance, neglect, and greed. The fact that we hesitate even now to replace freon in all the refrigerators of the world with another product that we know is safe is an example of this. We know that such replacement will cost a lot of money and we put off the day. This hesitation will cost thousands and thousands of skin cancers and will also lead to crop damage, since the ozone layer is a barrier against ultraviolet rays. There has been controversy about the ozone layer, but now this controversy is finished. Nobel Prize winners who have worked on the problem at NASA have clearly demonstrated that this ozone loss is a reality.

The fruits of life are also damaged by burning fossil fuels. This happens to such an extent that already we have seen that the level of the sea is rising. It is not rising fast—yet—but it is rising. Only seventeen thousand years ago, the level of the sea was 170 meters below what it is today. So the sea has risen almost 600 feet. The frozen water on Earth, if it melted, would raise the level of the sea by 60 more meters, more than 200 feet. That means the sea would cover entire countries. But even if the sea did not rise that far, two or three meters only would wipe out the Maldives, a great portion of Holland, and vast areas of Florida and other parts of the world. This is what we do with the fluids of life.

In 1933, I landed in Borneo for the first time. I remember trying to penetrate into the jungles from along the rivers with some of my friends. It was impossible to walk into the jungle, it was so tight. And it was so noisy with life that it was almost frightening. I returned to the same area of Borneo two years ago. Not one tree is left. They have been bulldozed by loggers to satisfy the needs of the rich countries. Not only are the forests, especially the rain forests, disappearing, but the coral reefs are disappearing too. Coral reefs absorb at least as much carbon dioxide as all the forests of the world, and they hold it forever by making calcium carbonate out of the carbon of carbon dioxide. Forests absorb and reject carbon, so coral reefs are more efficient in fixing carbon dioxide than forests. But we are destroying the coral reefs at a tremendous speed all around the world.

The energy problem and problems of renewable resources are part of the same problem. We treat nonrenewable resources as if they were renewable. We think we will have oil forever. However appealing nuclear energy can be, it produces tons and tons of plutonium, which is not only radioactive for tens of thousands of years, but is also by itself in minute doses a violent poison. This element, which did not exist in nature but was created by man, is now produced in the hundreds of tons. It will be dangerous for future generations for thousands of years, and we don't care.

The overpopulation problem is also one of the most important dangers that we are facing. This is a recent change, not only because we in the developed world are much better off financially, but also because we understand that having too many children creates problems we cannot solve. During my lifetime of eighty-one years, the population of the world has tripled, from 1.6 billion to 5.6 billion. In the next forty years, all demographic specialists agree that the population will again double. In 2030, there will be ten billion people to feed. After that, nobody knows.

But let's take it there. It is in many ways a formidable danger, but mainly for the quality of life. Technology could probably manage to have these 10 billion people survive. There are ways to increase the production of food, to improve distribution, etc. This is not the problem. The problem is what kind of life will these children live. Will they live in overcrowded cities or in concrete suburbs where they will never see anything alive? This is not the way to live. If I told you that I was proud to belong to the species that defied nature and tried to make better sets of values, it is true only provided that we don't spoil the game by making tremendous mistakes.

We have very little time to change our minds. Henry Kendall, the Nobel Prize winner who leads the Union of Concerned Scientists, has come to exactly the same conclusion as we have. The Club of Rome, a very powerful think tank, has also reached the same conclusion: we have no time to lose, and we have to change our ways of leading the world within ten years. This doesn't mean there will be doomsday in ten years. It means that we have a maximum of ten years to change our methods, radically. How can we do that? I am trying to implement a two-stage effort. The first stage is to have a text on which to lean, a text like the declaration of human rights. We mean to have a Declaration of the Rights of Future Generations declared by the United Nations.

This is the beginning of everything. After all, we inherited a world made mainly by our ancestors. We respect our ancestors. Why, then, would we not show our descendants the same love? The only way to do that is to make it impossible to damage their heritage and to make sure that their rights to a dignified life will be respected. So we launched a worldwide petition—it is the biggest effort I ever made—which we want to present to the United Nations with as many signatures as possible, in September 1993. I began in Europe and in less than two months obtained 1.5 million signatures. From the U.S., I will go to South America, then Africa, then Asia. I have become a traveling salesman for future generations.

This is the first step. The second step is that with this Declaration of the Rights of Future Generations in the United Nations Charter, there will be established an international environmental high authority with power to inspect the regulations admitted universally by all nations. Today inspection and enforcement is catch-as-catch-can. It is chaos. It is anarchy. The United Nations can make recommendations, but they have no power to implement them.

January 24, 1992

Audrey Hepburn

Actress; Goodwill Ambassador for UNICEF

Audrey Hepburn was just a girl, living with her family in the Netherlands, when the country fell to the Nazis. Years later, asked about her experiences during World War II, she recalled fear and suffering and acknowledged, "I was surviving on tulips, but you really don't care as a child—if you have just enough....I was ill at the end of the war without knowing it. I was anemic. I had asthma. I just thought those things were perfectly normal." When Hepburn spoke to The Commonwealth Club in 1992, she was speaking on behalf of children suffering throughout the world. As a special ambassador for UNICEF, she spoke of her personal experience with receiving aid from the emergency fund after the war, recalling "those big boxes with food and blankets."

In 1953, Hepburn won the hearts of American moviegoers (and an Oscar) with her performance in *Roman Holiday*. As critics over the years have noted, her warmth, beauty, and sensitivity in films have drawn her fans by the millions. She set aside her movie career in 1966, however, to raise her children. Assuming the role of UNICEF ambassador twenty years later put her on a new and grueling schedule, with travels that included trips to Sudan, El Salvador, Bangladesh, and Vietnam. One of the hopeful developments she pointed to in this talk, one meant to ease the plight of children globally, was the Convention on the Rights of the Child, which had been introduced to the UN General Assembly in November 1989. During the question-and-answer session, one questioner asked Hepburn if the convention wasn't simply an empty political gesture. "The Convention on the Rights of the Child is the greatest gift to children in history," she said. "For the first time, children's interests have become law. There are the cynics who say the convention is just another piece of paper. Well, so is the Declaration of Independence and the Declaration of Human Rights and the Bible. It's a piece of paper which is a standard, which every country with any pride at all will be ashamed to fall below."

Audrey Hepburn died one year later at her home in Switzerland. The convention has become the most widely ratified human rights treaty in world history. As of this writing, two countries have yet to ratify it: Somalia (which has signed the treaty but does not have an internationally recognized government) and the United States. The U.S. signed it in 1995 but the treaty has not been sent to the Senate for ratification. Why the delay? Amnesty International cites American opponents' concerns that the convention is perceived to threaten parental authority as well as national and state sovereignty. The BBC notes that execution of juveniles, which is permitted in some U.S. states, is expressly forbidden by the convention.

"Children First: Building a Global Agenda"

Until four years ago, when I was given the great privilege of becoming a volunteer for UNICEF, I, like all of you, was overwhelmed by a sense of helplessness when watching television or reading about the indescribable misery of the children and their mothers in the developing world. If I feel less helpless today, it's because I have now seen what can be done, and what is being done by UNICEF, by many marvelous agencies, churches, governments, and most of all, with very little help, by people themselves.

Our world has changed dramatically in a short time, and we must now plot a new course for the future. We have to recognize that children have not been our greatest priority, but they must be. And if we seize the opportunity now before us, they really can be.

I was among the first recipients of UNICEF aid after World War II, which is why I have such a deep, personal appreciation for UNICEF. Mine was the first generation to live in the ominous shadow of the nuclear age, and we were the first children to grow up with the term "Cold War" and all its divisive and paranoid implications. We had survived the bombing of Europe only to find ourselves, in a very real sense, coming of age in another war, the costs of which were very steep indeed. This conflict between East and West soon became a political framework for the entire globe. The superpowers intervened in developing countries in order to gain territorial advantages, and rival factions in these countries were all too willing to choose sides in exchange for support in their internal struggles. The prevailing world order was marked by barricades, real and imaginary, and it fostered a mentality of "us versus them."

The real losers, of course, were the children: the children of Africa, Latin America, Asia, and the Middle East who suffered from daily neglect. The choice between guns and bread had never been more immediate nor lopsided as it was during the height of the Cold War. UNICEF, the world's leading voice for children, tried to protect them, reminding governments time and again that the needs of children were urgent and the most important, but its warnings fell on ears that were either deaf or simply too preoccupied to listen. Then, and it seemed to happen overnight, the world changed dramatically. Like the Berlin Wall and the Soviet Empire, the old order has come tumbling down. We now have something that is so rare in the course of civilization: a second chance.

While the world was busy fortifying the ideological chasm that divided it, the children have been paying for it with their lives: forty thousand a day, forty million a year. No earthquake, no flood ever claimed forty thousand children on a single day. Though these children are the quiet catastrophe and never make headlines, they are just as dead. By any measure this is the greatest tragedy of our times. They've been dying from preventable diseases, including measles and tuberculosis. They've been dying in wars, caught in the crossfire of those who should have been protecting them. They've been dying for lack of proper nutrition when the world has more than enough food. They've been dying from dehydration caused by diarrhea more than from any other single cause—because they don't have clean drinking water.

In September of 1990, when the old world order was showing signs of collapse, UNICEF hosted seventy-one heads of state at the World Summit for Children in New York to address the appalling situation of children. The summit yielded a historic agreement on specific goals to help children by the year 2000. In its 1992 State of the World's Children Report, UNICEF offers ten agenda items for the formation of a new world order. A few of them:

A) That the promises of the World Summit for Children be kept. These include a one-third reduction in child deaths, and a halving of child malnutrition by the year 2000.
B) That demilitarization should begin in the developing world, and that falling military expenditures in the industrialized countries should be linked to increased international aid and the solving of global problems. Developing countries spend about $150 billion on arms each year. Meanwhile, the five permanent members of the UN Security Council sell 90 percent of the world's arms. We are entrenched as a global community in a destructive cycle of weapons proliferation. Achieving all of the summit goals would require some $20 billion a year, an amount equal to two-thirds of the developing world's military spending, and just 1 percent of that in industrialized countries.
C) That the growing consensus around market economies be accompanied by a commitment to a strong investment in people, especially children. Simply put, this means that there are things that a free market alone cannot do. Governments must combine free-market forces with assurances of health and education for all, especially children, even in bad economic times. The importance of this proposition is not limited to developing countries.

The situation of urban and poor children in the United States continues to worsen. Child poverty is on the rise, and the real value of Aid to Families with Dependent Children has dropped 40 percent in the last twenty years. Even here, in the country that is the world's model of a free economy, we are slow to realize that all children do not benefit from that system. We must build what amounts to a safety net to catch these children before it is too late.

Rather than share with you the horrors I've witnessed, I prefer to remind you of how easy it is to reach out and help these children. There has never been a better opportunity to give our children the future they deserve. We have low-cost technologies like immunization and oral rehydration therapy. We have ample resources made available due to the end of the Cold War, and we have the commitment of the world's leaders. What remains is for us to change our attitudes as a society, to build a movement for children, and to ensure that the promises of the World Summit for Children are kept.

Twenty years ago, few people thought about recycling their newspapers, few people worried about the effect of hair spray on the ozone layer, few people questioned the amount of pollution their cars were spewing into the atmosphere. But slowly and effectively, the environmentalists in this country and around the world built a movement that could not be ignored, and they have brought about a fundamental change in the way we live our lives and the way we see our planet. We have taken responsibility for our neglect. So too must we take responsibility for the neglect of our children. So too must we effect a basic change in our priorities and concerns. We must resolve ourselves as a community to put the needs of children first—in war and in peace, in good times and in bad.

So today, I speak for children who can't speak for themselves, children who are going blind from lack of vitamins, children who are slowly being mutilated by polio, children who are wasting away in so many ways from lack of water. I speak for the estimated one hundred million street children in this world who have no choice but to leave home in order to survive, who have absolutely nothing but their courage, their smiles, their wits, and their dreams; for children, who have no enemies yet, are invariably the first tiny victims of war, wars that are being waged through terror, intimidation, and massacre; for children who are therefore growing up surrounded by the horrors of violence; for the hundreds of thousands that are refugees; and for the rapidly increasing number of children suffering from or orphaned by AIDS.

The task that lies ahead is ever great, whether it's repatriating millions of children in Africa or Asia or teaching children how to play who only have learned how to kill. Children are our most vital resource, our hope for the future. Until they can be assured of not only physically surviving the first fragile years of life, but are free of emotional, social, and physical abuse, it's impossible to envisage a world that is free of tension and violence.

April 27, 1992

William Greider

National Editor, Rolling Stone

"It's ironic that the one thing that may unify Americans is that we are all angry about politics," William Greider said to The Commonwealth Club in 1992. "You can go to Republican neighborhoods and hear the same complaints that you hear in poor, black neighborhoods."

The past three decades had made Americans feel increasingly disenfranchised, Greider explained. The question was, what can you do about it? Greider was mostly talking about Washington, D.C., when he discussed the betrayal of American democracy and titled his new book *Who Will Tell the People?* "A jury in Simi Valley" seemed to be the answer to that question two days later—when the verdict was announced for Los Angeles police officers accused of beating motorist Rodney King. One officer was found guilty of using excessive force; the others were acquitted of all charges. In the mayhem that followed, businesses were looted, bystanders assaulted, and fires set throughout the city. Four thousand National Guard troops were called out, and it was three days before the violence subsided.

"The Betrayal of American Democracy"

Beyond the elections—which leave us dispirited candidates, who seem so flawed—and TV advertising—which we know is deceptive and manipulative—there is something deeper that people are angry about. That something is a systemic breakdown in the democratic understandings of this society. That breakdown did not happen overnight. It certainly didn't happen in 1992, in 1988, or in the Reagan years. It came about through a series of interacting changes in our politics that have been developing over twenty-five or thirty years. Pull back and look at our politics from the perspective of what we say we believe when we say we are a democracy. And when I talk about a breakdown in democratic understanding, I mean the principles that most of us learned as small children.

I don't have a utopian view of democracy, nor do I believe that we had it once and have now lost it. Our system has always been imperfect, has always involved powerful special interests and lobbyists; some groups have felt utterly excluded. But that does not excuse us from examining the present condition of our politics. Nor does it prevent us from beginning to take some responsibility for our politics. Democracy means the accountability of those in power to the governed. It means equal protection under the law. It means that ordinary people should feel some semblance of connection to the government, that their views and voices are being represented in the larger debates. These are not liberal ideas or conservative ideas; they are the basic tenets of our social faith. And, when you look at our governing system, in all its complicated parts, it is very hard to say that those basic tenets are being lived out in our politics and in our government.

The modern political culture that everybody—Democrats, Republicans, labor, corporations—lives in has actually debased the meaning of law. I am talking about the classical sense of what is a law: commandments that say thou shalt/thou shalt not, government programs that say we will build this road or that bridge. This is a sense of law that people still share, but it is subverted in actuality by the way our government deals with public problems. There are literally dozens, maybe scores, of laws that are quite hollow. They are hollow either because it is years or even decades before they are enforced, or because they fall so far short of their original intent that they cannot be called laws at all; rather, they are bargains that have been struck with different private interests. This means that over the course of a generation, the government has developed a very successful form of politics which makes grand promises and doesn't keep them. Sooner or later, citizens come along and discover that the laws are meaningless or haven't been enforced; then the political response is to pass another law and make the promise over again, even more vigorously than the first time. And the process begins again.

One small example has to do with the Clean Air Act. The first federal Clean Air Act passed in 1970. Among its provisions was one that said that industrial facilities cannot dispense toxic chemicals into the open air in a way that is harmful to the people who live nearby. Whether it was a reasonable provision or not, it was the law. Twenty years later, only 7 of the more than 275 toxic chemicals that are routinely emitted by industry were being regulated by the federal government. And the EPA, under pressure from a few congressmen like Henry Waxman of California, put out a list of 149 factories, smelters, and refineries where the risk of cancer in the surrounding neighborhood was as high as one in ten thousand—and for several dozen, the risk was actually higher than one in one thousand. These emissions were against the law, yet nothing had been done. Why had nothing been done? The answer takes you into the labyrinth of the federal government. And all the players, from environmental reformers to corporate lobbyists to Democrats in Congress to Republicans in the White House, understand the politics of this labyrinth.

The most obvious part of the federal labyrinth is the visible politics—the legislative debate—which plays out in the news. In these politics, the public expresses a desire, the political system responds, a law is passed, there is a signing ceremony on the White House lawn, and everybody congratulates themselves. At that point, most people turn their minds to other subjects.

But in modern federal government, the politics is only just beginning. The bill then goes into an extraordinarily complex game of push-and-shove within the regulatory agencies, the courts, and ultimately the White House, where the losers get another shot at the apple—not just once or twice or for a few years, but for five, ten, fifteen, or twenty years. In the end they may have only won a delay of twenty years, but that is a real victory, if you're talking about spending the money to stop pollution—or something else, if you're talking about somebody who is breathing poisonous air for twenty years. The effect is that what ordinary people usually think of as politics on a public issue becomes shrouded in economics, science, legal terminology, and many other esoteric discussions which most people can't deal with—first, because they are not experts, and second, because they don't see the political content that lies beneath those arguments. They cannot, therefore, see that this is essentially a struggle of winners and losers about what the government really does and does not intend to do.

The tax code is another example. We have about $87 billion in uncollected taxes. Those uncollected taxes are not, for the most part, the result of criminal behavior on anyone's part. Instead, the malleability of the tax code allows a kind of running argument, which could go on for more than a generation, over exactly what the tax code says and exactly how much various players owe. Beyond that, the tax code is riddled with loopholes, exceptions, and preferences, which allow some taxpayers—mostly corporations like big defense manufacturers—to defer their taxes. None of those loopholes, exceptions, and preferences were concocted out of insanity; someone lobbied for each of them. The cumulative effect, as we now know, is a general contempt/skepticism about the U.S. tax code. The IRS has recorded this contempt not only in public attitudes toward taxation but also in taxpayer voluntary compliance.

You see the same effect when you look at social programs, although the blame in this case lies more with the liberals than the conservatives. The promises made in the 1960s were way beyond the government's capacity and its intentions. The elimination of poverty is the most obvious example. However well-intentioned that policy was, it set up a very seductive and satisfying politics of rhetorical performance that gradually got further and further away from reality. Although people may not put this the way I have, I think they see this, and this is part of what is eating away at the public faith in our system.

Another example is Head Start. We have known for years that Head Start actually works, actually helps prepare poor children for school, so that ten years later there is a real difference in their behavior as students. Everybody—liberals, conservatives, businesspeople, educators—loves the program. But Head Start, this universally acclaimed program, is funded at a level that serves just one in five poor children. This is not serious. If this is a government commitment, and they are funding only 20 percent of eligible children, there is something phony in the declaration.

Welfare has a similar deception. It is a long-standing fact that a majority of people who are officially classified as poor do not get a welfare check.

But if you listen to our political debate, there is endless rhetoric about welfare not only sapping the moral fiber of poor people but also draining our treasury. How can welfare be undermining the moral fiber of poor people when most poor people don't get a welfare check?

OSHA, which is supposed to protect worker safety, is well known as a joke, an area of nonenforcement and bureaucratic snarls. Some scholars have said it was clearly designed in a way so as not to function. There is some truth to that. The political system has figured out methods to have it both ways. And I am indicting both Democrats and Republicans, liberals and conservatives. They all play on the same field.

They have it both ways because they ostensibly respond to public desires but do so within a system that never quite closes the door on the private interests. And those private interests, mostly major corporations, have the power to decide for themselves whether or not the law is worthy. If they decide that it isn't worthy, they can, legally, carry on the political fight year after year, even decade after decade.

The clean air bill passed in 1990 dealt with toxic air pollution. In debating the bill, everybody agreed that it was a scandal that nothing had happened in twenty years to correct the problem. But the new bill gives these same interests another twenty years to deal with this problem. So we now have a public desire stated in 1970 which, even if things work this time, will not be dealt with until the year 2010. And for the steel industry, which has made a special plea that it is in difficulty, it is the year 2020. Whatever else it may be, this bill is not a law in any classical sense. It is not a law when you declare a public problem and then take forty or fifty years to work at it.

Why pass such laws at all? The answer goes back to politics, to incumbency and the pursuit of staying in power. I asked this question of a man who has spent the last twenty years in the Senate—a Republican who has been trying to enact environmental laws that work. He said, "If you didn't pass these laws, you wouldn't get reelected." He's right. The public wants action, so our legislators have figured out a response that doesn't accomplish much but has the right banners in place. Meanwhile, there remains a system with endless opportunities for manipulation—if you've got the resources to play at that level.

Modern politics is not reconciled to the psychological burden of using the government's coercive powers. Here we differ greatly from earlier generations, maybe because we live in the television age, or maybe because this country is more complicated, or maybe because we have a separation of shared interests—we could argue the causes endlessly. But the fact is, the system wants something to happen, but it doesn't want to use the government's awesome power to make it happen.

It's ironic that the one thing that may unify Americans is that we are all angry about politics. This anger cuts across class, regional, and party lines. You can go to Republican neighborhoods and hear the same complaints that you hear in poor, black neighborhoods. The language and examples may be different, but the sense that our system is not producing equitable results is nearly universal. Twenty-five years ago, when the polls asked people about government, about one-third said that the government is controlled by a few big interests and doesn't pay attention to the interests of regular people, which is an expression of alienation. A new Gallup poll shows that expression of alienation is up to 80 percent. Something caused that to happen, and it wasn't just Bill Clinton and the New York primary or George Bush and Jesse Helms.

There are deeper things at work here. We need to step back from our usual arguments and ask questions like: What is it we believe when we talk about democracy? If we still believe those things, why are they not functioning at a believable level in our political system? We have all worked out self-justifying, defensive explanations of most public problems and policies. But if you believe in democracy, you cannot escape from its consequences. Democracy is a two-way mirror; it reflects the virtues and the warts back and forth between elected officials and the people.

I am trying to get people to speak again in the language of democracy. That sounds corny, but it is important to use these words as though they mattered, as though we really do believe in them, and as though they really are plausible.

May 19, 1992

Dan Quayle

Vice President of the United States of America

In May 1992, when Vice President Dan Quayle gave his talk at The Commonwealth Club on preserving family values, the nation was in the run-up to the November presidential election, and Los Angeles had been wracked by riots only three weeks before. Quayle's speech immediately became known as "The Murphy Brown Speech" for its singling out of the television newswoman Murphy Brown, played by actress Candice Bergen, as having set a bad example by having a child out of wedlock. Quayle was ridiculed by those he dubbed the "media elites" for this attack. But in the season opener in autumn 1992, Murphy Brown, the fictional character, gave as good as she got: in an episode of the show featuring footage of Quayle's speech, Brown/Bergen delivered a diatribe against the vice president. (Quayle had played along with the art-meets-life game in another way: as a present for Murphy Brown's fictitious baby, he'd sent a stuffed animal elephant.)

The legendary speech has continued to have a life of its own: in 1993, a cover story in *The Atlantic Monthly* declared, "Dan Quayle Was Right." Quayle has stuck by his guns, too, up through a "Ten Years after Murphy Brown" speech at the National Press Club in May 2002, when he again criticized Murphy Brown but offered praise for rocker Ozzy Osbourne's show on MTV.

As for Bergen, she acknowledged in 2002 that Quayle's Commonwealth Club address was "a perfectly intelligent speech about fathers not being dispensable, and nobody agreed with that more than I did." She added, however, "He certainly never watched *Murphy Brown*, which didn't stop him from talking about it."

When he spoke, Quayle had just returned from a week-long trip to Japan.

"The Vice President Speaks"

From the perspective of many Japanese, the ethnic diversity of our culture is a weakness compared to their homogeneous society. I begged to differ with my host. I explained that our diversity is our strength, and I explained that the immigrants who come to our shores have made and continue to make vast contributions to our culture and to our economy. It is wrong to imply that the Los Angeles riots were an inevitable outcome of our diversified society. But the question that I tried to answer in Japan is one that needs answering here. What happened? Why? And most importantly, how can we prevent it in the future?

One response has been predictable. Instead of denouncing wrongdoing, some have shown tolerance for rioters. Some have enjoyed saying "I told you so." And some have simply made excuses for what happened. All of this has been accompanied by pleas for more money. I'll readily accept that we need to understand what happened, but I reject the idea that we should tolerate or excuse it.

When I have been asked during these last weeks who caused the riots and the killings in LA, my answer has been direct and simple. Who is to blame for the riots? The rioters are to blame. Who is to blame for the killings? The killers are to blame. Yes, I can understand how people were shocked and outraged by the verdict in the Rodney King trial. But, my friends, there is simply no excuse for the mayhem that followed. To apologize or in any way to excuse what happened is wrong. It is a betrayal of all those people equally outraged and equally disadvantaged who did not loot, who did not riot, and who were, in many cases, victims of the rioters. No matter how much you may disagree with the verdict, the riots were wrong. If we as a society don't condemn what is wrong, how can we teach our children what is right? But after condemning the riots, we do need to try to understand the underlying situation.

In a nutshell, I believe the lawless social anarchy that we saw is directly related to the breakdown of the family structure, personal responsibility, and social order in too many areas of our society. For the poor, the situation is compounded by a welfare ethos that impedes individual efforts to move ahead in society and hampers their ability to take advantage of the opportunities America offers. If we don't succeed in addressing these fundamental problems and in restoring basic values, any attempt to fix what's broken will fail.

One reason I believe we won't fail is that we have come so far in the last twenty-five years. There's no question that this country has had a terrible problem with race and racism. The evil of slavery has left a long and ugly legacy. But we have faced racism squarely, and we have made progress in the past quarter of a century. The landmark civil rights bills of the 1960s removed legal barriers to allow full participation by blacks in the economic, social, and political life of the nation. By any measure, the America of 1992 is more egalitarian, more integrated, and offers more opportunities to black Americans and all other minority members than the America of 1964. There is more to be done, but I think that all of us can be proud of our progress. And let's be specific about one aspect of this progress. The country now has a black middle class that barely existed a quarter-century ago. Since 1967, the median income of black two-parent families has risen by 60 percent in real terms. The number of black college graduates has skyrocketed. Black men and women have achieved real political power. Black mayors head forty-eight of our largest cities, including Los Angeles. These are real achievements, but as we all know, there's another side to that bright landscape.

During this period of progress, we have also developed a culture of poverty—some call it the underclass—that is far more violent and harder to escape than it was a generation ago. The poor you always have with you, Scripture tells us, and in America we have always had poor people. But in this dynamic, prosperous nation, poverty has traditionally been a stage through which people pass on their way to joining the great middle class. And if one generation didn't get very far up the ladder, their ambitious, better-educated children would. But the underclass seems to be a new phenomenon. It is a group whose members are dependent on welfare for very long stretches and whose young men are often drawn into lives of crime.

There is far too little upward mobility, because the underclass is disconnected from the rules of American society. And these problems have, unfortunately, been particularly acute for black Americans.

In 1967, 68 percent of black families were headed by married couples. In 1991, only 48 percent of black families were headed by both a husband and a wife. In 1965, the illegitimacy rate among black families was 28 percent. In 1989, 65 percent, two-thirds of all black children, were born with never-married mothers. In 1951, 9 percent of black youths between sixteen and nineteen were unemployed. In 1965, it was 23 percent. In 1980, it was 35 percent. By 1989, the number had declined slightly, but it was still 32 percent. The leading cause of death of young black males today is homicide.

It would be overly simplistic to blame this social breakdown on the programs of the Great Society alone. It would be absolutely wrong to blame it on the growth and success most Americans enjoyed during the 1980s. Rather, we are in large measure reaping the consequences of the decades of changes in social mores.

I was born in 1947, so I'm considered one of those baby boomers that we keep reading about. But let's look at one unfortunate legacy of the so-called boomer generation. When we were young, it was fashionable to declare war against traditional values. Indulgence and self-gratification seemed to have no consequences. Many of our generation glamorized casual sex and drug use, evaded responsibility, and trashed authority. Today, the boomers are middle-aged and middle class. The responsibility of having families has helped many recover traditional values. And of course, the great majority of those in the middle class survived the turbulent legacy of the sixties and seventies. But many of the poor, with less to fall back on, did not. The intergenerational poverty that troubles us so much today is predominantly a poverty of values.

Our inner cities are filled with children having children, with people who have not been able to take advantage of educational opportunities, with people who are dependent on drugs or the narcotic of welfare. To be sure, many people in the ghetto struggle very hard against these tides and sometimes win. But too many people feel they have no hope and nothing to lose. This poverty is, again, fundamentally a poverty of values. Unless we change the basic rules of society in our inner cities, we cannot expect anything else to change. We will simply get more of what we saw three weeks ago. New thinking, new ideas, new strategies are needed. For the government, transforming underclass culture means that our policies and our programs must create a different incentive system. Our policy must be premised on and must reinforce values such as family, hard work, integrity, personal responsibility. I think we can all agree the government's first obligation is to maintain order. We are a nation of laws, not looting. It has become clear that the riots were fueled by the vicious gangs that terrorize the inner cities. We are committed to breaking those gangs and restoring law and order.

As James Q. Wilson has written, programs of economic restructuring will not work so long as gangs control the streets. Some people say law and order are code words. Well, they are code words—code words for safety, getting control of the streets, and freedom from fear. And let's not forget that in 1990, 84 percent of the crimes committed by blacks were committed against blacks. We are for law and order. If a single mother raising her children in the ghetto has to worry about drive-by shootings, drug deals, or whether her children will join gangs and die violently, the difficult task becomes next to impossible. We're for law and order because we can't expect children to learn in dangerous schools. We're for law and order because if property isn't protected, who will build the businesses, who will make the investment? Safety is absolutely necessary, but it's not sufficient. Our urban strategy is to empower the poor by giving them control over their lives. To do that, our urban agenda includes fully funding the Home Ownership and Opportunity for People Everywhere program.

Subsidized housing all too often merely made rich investors richer. Home ownership will give the poor a stake in their neighborhood and a chance to build equity. Creating enterprise zones by slashing taxes in targeted areas, including a zero capital gains tax to spur entrepreneurship, economic development, and job creation in the inner cities; instituting our education strategy, America 2000, to raise academic standards and to give the poor the same choices about how and where to educate their children that the rich people have; promoting welfare reform to remove the penalties for marriage, create incentives for saving, and give communities greater control over how the programs are administered—these programs are empowerment programs.

Empowering the poor will strengthen families, and right now the failure of our families is hurting America deeply. When family fails, society fails. The anarchy and lack of structure in our inner cities are a testament to how quickly civilization falls apart when the family foundation cracks. Children need love and discipline; they need mothers and fathers. A welfare check is not a husband, the state is not a father. It is from parents that children learn how to behave in society. It is from parents, above all, that children come to understand values and themselves as men and women, mothers and fathers. And for those who are concerned about children growing up in poverty, we should know this: marriage is probably the best antipoverty program of all.

Among families headed by married couples today, there is a poverty rate of 5.7 percent. But 33.4 percent of the families headed by a single mother are in poverty. Nature abhors a vacuum. Where there are no mature, responsible men around to teach boys how to be good men, gangs serve in their place. In fact, gangs have become a surrogate family for much of a generation of inner city boys. I recently visited with some former gang members in Albuquerque, New Mexico. In a private meeting, they told me why they had joined gangs. These teenage boys said that gangs gave them a sense of security. They made them feel wanted and useful. They got support from their friends and, they said, it was like having a family.

The system perpetuates itself as these young men father children whom they have no intention of caring for by women whose welfare checks support them. Teenage girls mired in the same hopelessness lack sufficient motive to say no to this trap. Answers to our problems won't be easy, my friends. We can start by dismantling a welfare system that encourages dependency and subsidizes broken families. We can attach conditions such as school attendance or work-to-welfare. We can limit the time a recipient gets benefits. We can stop penalizing marriage for welfare mothers. We can enforce child-support payments. Ultimately, however, marriage is a moral issue that requires cultural consensus and the use of social sanctions.

Bearing babies irresponsibly is simply wrong. Failing to support children one has fathered is wrong, and we must be unequivocal about this. It doesn't help matters when prime-time TV has Murphy Brown, a character who supposedly epitomizes today's intelligent, highly paid professional woman, mocking the importance of fathers by bearing a child alone and calling it just another lifestyle choice. I know it's not fashionable to talk about moral values, but we need to do it! Even though our cultural leaders in Hollywood, network TV, and the national newspapers routinely jeer at them, I think most of us in this room know that some things are good and other things are wrong. And now it's time to make the discussion public. It's time to talk again about the family, hard work, integrity, and personal responsibility. We cannot be embarrassed out of our belief that two parents married to each other are better, in most cases, for children than one; that honest work is better than handouts or crime; that we are our brother's keepers; that it is worth making an effort, even when the rewards aren't immediate.

The time has come to renew our public commitment to our Judeo-Christian values in our churches and synagogues, our civic organizations, and our schools. We are, as our children recite each morning, one nation under God. That's a useful framework for acknowledging a duty and an authority higher than our own pleasures and personal ambition. If we lived more thoroughly by these values, we would live in a better society. For the poor, renewing these values will give the people the strength to help themselves by acquiring the tools to achieve self-sufficiency, a good education, job training, and property. Then they will move from permanent dependence to dignified independence. Shelby Steele, in his great book *The Content of Our Character*, writes, "Personal responsibility is the brick and mortar of power. The responsible person knows that the quality of his life is something that he will have to make inside the limits of his fate....The quality of his life will pretty much reflect the quality of his efforts."

I believe that the Bush Administration's empowerment agenda will help the poor gain that power by creating opportunity and letting people make the choices that free citizens must make.

Though our hearts have been pained by the events in Los Angeles, we should take this tragedy as an opportunity for self-examination and progress. So let the national debate roar on. I, for one, will join it. The president will lead it, the American people will participate in it, and as a result, we will become an even stronger nation.

July 17, 1992

Amory Lovins

Physicist; Cofounder and Director of Research,
Rocky Mountain Institute

Lauded as "Hero for the Planet" by *Time*, pegged by the *Wall Street Journal* as
one of a few dozen people "most likely to change the course of business,"
and recipient of a MacArthur "genius" grant, Amory Lovins brought his
ideas for energy conservation and technological innovation to The
Commonwealth Club a month after the Earth Summit in Rio de Janeiro—
and just over a year after the U.S. liberated Kuwait from Saddam Hussein.
"No blood for oil" was (and is) a mantra of Americans who opposed U.S.
intervention in the Persian Gulf. Lovins asserted that if the U.S. had stuck
by the fuel efficiency standards it had laid out under Jimmy Carter, there
would be no need for Persian Gulf oil.

That bit of verbal bomb-throwing is actually atypical of Lovins. The
bespectacled, mustached, Harvard- and Oxford-educated physicist speaks
with the warmth and friendliness you might associate with a favorite, slightly eccentric, and brilliant uncle who calls 'em as he sees 'em—and who happens to be able to see around corners. When he first got interested in clima-
tology in the late 1960s, Lovins told Club members, he realized "we were
going to need to do something as fundamental as undiscover fire."

Answering questions after his speech, Lovins assessed the much-publicized Earth Summit as helpful because it "institutionalized and legitimized much of the international concern not only about the environment but about the nexus of environment and development," but less helpful than it could have been because the "signal-to-noise ratio was rather unfavorable." He discussed the future of nuclear power, declaring it dead of an "incurable attack of market forces" and "so uneconomical that it is cheaper to write off a newly built nuclear plant than to run it." And he described U.S. energy policy as "a kind of Chinese-restaurant-menu approach...you choose one option from column A, one from column B, and so on until all the major campaign contributors are satisfied." Among his prescriptions: "Abolish the Department of Energy, put the bomb-building, if any, in a separate agency, and start over with mostly new people." What kind of people? "We are going to need fewer narrow specialists," he said, "and more people who can make connections which haven't been made before. We are going to need all of the imagination and creativity we can get."

"Abating Global Warming for Fun and Profit"

Carbon dioxide and the other gases whose release threatens to change the earth's climate are invisible, yet the ways we can put less of these gases into the air and stabilize the earth's climate are perfectly visible. They're all around us. Consider a simple compact fluorescent lightbulb, the kind that one California utility has given away over a million of because it's cheaper to do that than to run their power plants. One lightbulb like this uses about 18 watts of electricity to put out the same light you normally get from a 75-watt lightbulb—and for thirteen times as long. It avoids a dozen replacement lamps. That more than pays for the quadrupled-efficiency lamp, so the electric savings you get from it are better than free.

If the electricity thereby saved was being made in a coal-fired power plant, one such lightbulb, over its life, would keep us from putting about a ton of carbon dioxide into the air, along with about twenty pounds of sulfur oxide and other pollutants. If it were saving electricity from a nuclear power plant, it would avoid making half a curie—which is a lot—of high-level waste. If it were saving oil-fired electricity, as might be the case in

Hawaii or in many developing countries, it would save about 1.25 barrels of oil—enough to run your family car one thousand miles, or enough to run a superefficient prototype car across the country and back.

One lightbulb does all this, and you can screw it in yourself. The lamp, over its life, saves tens of dollars more in replacement lamps, installation labor, and utility fuel than it costs. That is, the lamp generates or creates tens of dollars of net wealth and defers hundreds of dollars of utility investment. That's a simple example of a rather powerful idea: it is generally cheaper today to save fuel than to burn fuel. The global warming, acid rain, urban smog, and other kinds of pollution that you can avoid by not burning the fuel can be avoided not at a cost but at a profit. You can get rid of over half of global warming just by using energy in a way that saves money, and the energy efficiency it takes to do that costs less than burning the fuel. You get rid of another quarter of global warming with sustainable farming and forestry practices that are at least as profitable as today's soil mining, often more so. The rest of the global warming you get rid of when you displace chlorofluorocarbons (CFCs). We have to do that anyway to protect the stratospheric ozone layer—so it doesn't matter what it costs.

If the cost of abating global warming ranges from strongly negative to roughly zero to irrelevant, what are we waiting for? The scientific uncertainties about possible changes in the earth's climate are real and substantial; they also cut both ways. But whether global warming is real or not, we ought to do these things anyway just to save money. To get the energy services we want—comfort, mobility, illumination, hot showers, and cold beer—in the cheapest possible way, we should use fewer kilowatt-hours and more brains. Some noted economists have calculated that just meeting the carbon dioxide stabilization target that many countries have already committed to would cost the U.S. about $200 billion a year. Those economists got the number right but the sign wrong. It would actually save about $200 billion a year.

Where does that kind of difference come from? The economists said we live in a market economy, and markets must be nearly perfect, so if people haven't bought all this energy efficiency already, it must be because it's much too expensive. Therefore, to make it worthwhile for people to buy that much efficiency, we'd have to raise the price of energy with a huge tax. Those economists then crank their economic model to see how much it would hurt the GNP to raise energy prices that high. However, the countries we have the most trouble competing with, Germany and Japan, have very high energy prices and are also twice as efficient as we are. That's part of why they're hard to compete with. Their energy efficiency has driven industrial innovation on a broad front. What economists forget is that energy efficiency is much cheaper than burning fuel in the first place. The reason people haven't bought it already is that they don't know how, they don't have the information, or they want their money back from efficiency investment ten times as fast as energy companies want their money back from supply investments. We're not looking at ways to make and save electricity or other forms of energy on an equal footing, and we're not choosing the best buys first.

Saving energy is nothing new. Over the past dozen years, the United States has gotten four and a half times as much new energy from savings as from all net increases in supply. And a third of the new supply came from renewables. We've already cut $150 billion a year off the nation's energy bill through those savings. We're also still wasting twice that much—the energy we are still using when we could substitute efficiency that is on the market, works better and costs less—about $300 billion a year, slightly more than the entire military budget.

The biggest chunk of that savings not yet captured is in electricity—the costliest form of energy and therefore the most lucrative kind to save. Every unit of electricity you save saves three or four units of fuel, mainly coal, at the power plant, so this form of energy saving has the most climatic benefit. The utilities-owned think tank, the Electric Power Research Institute, now says that up to 55 percent of the electricity we use can be cost-effectively saved. We think we know how to save about three-quarters of U.S. electricity several-fold cheaper than you can run an existing coal or nuclear plant, even if construction costs nothing. The technological revolution comes in many forms: saving 70 to 90 percent of lighting energy; roughly half the motor energy; 80 or 90 percent of the space-cooling and air-handling energy; 90 percent of the office-equipment energy; two-thirds or more in household appliances; two-thirds or more in water heating. It's a long list with a thousand kinds of technologies involved.

The simplest example, perhaps, is that my own household electric bill is about $5 a month, and it took ten months to get back the extra investment required to achieve that. We also had, incidentally, five banana crops the winter before last at 7,100 feet up in the Rockies, where it goes as low as minus 47—and we don't have a furnace. Instead, our house is heated 99 percent with superinsulation and superwindows; it cost less to build that way because of all the money we saved not needing a furnace and duct-work. Just the superwindows that made this possible—windows that insulate as well as six or twelve sheets of glass and gain that heat facing north—represent nationwide the potential to save about two Alaskas' worth of oil and gas, at about three dollars a barrel.

Increasingly, utilities are making "negawatts," or saved electricity, into a commodity subject to competitive bidding, futures and options markets, and all the other mechanisms that work for commodity markets. If all Americans simply saved electricity as quickly as ten million did in Southern California in the early 1980s, we could actually cut the absolute electric use each year, even as the economy grew 7 percent a year. We could cut forty giant plants a year worth off the ten-year forecast of this country's power needs. And the cost, based on what Southern California Edison actually paid, would be about 1 percent of the cost of building new power plants.

Much the same can be done with saving oil. There we're also just scratching the surface. From 1977 to 1986, the U.S. saved oil four-fifths faster than necessary to keep up with both economic growth and declining domestic oil output. We saved oil at an average rate of almost 5 percent a year and thereby cut imports by more than half, and cut imports from the Persian Gulf by more than 90 percent. If we had simply kept saving oil as fast as we did for the previous nine years, we would not have needed a drop of oil from the Persian Gulf. That isn't what happened, however, because in 1986 the Reagan Administration thought it would be a nifty idea to roll back the light vehicle efficiency standards and to cut the print run of the government's gas mileage guide by 70 percent, so two-thirds of new car buyers couldn't get one—the well-known telepathic theory of market information. The result was an immediate doubling of oil imports from the Persian Gulf, and we've been going on like that ever since. So, owing to the White House effect, we recently put our kids in 0.56-mile-per-gallon tanks and seventeen-feet-per-gallon aircraft carriers because we did not put them in thirty-two-mile-per-gallon cars. That is all it would have taken, had we done nothing else, to eliminate oil imports from the Persian Gulf.

Cars are the main users of our oil. Typically, a car on the road now gets about twenty miles a gallon; a new car gets thirty. Yet a dozen automakers in the mid-1980s had already tested concept or prototype cars that got anywhere from sixty-seven to one hundred and thirty-eight miles a gallon.

Many of them were quite comfortable, four- even five-passenger cars; many were safer than what you drive now, and some were peppier. At least two would cost nothing extra to produce. Why aren't they on the market? Because you have no incentive to buy them, so the manufacturers have no incentive to take the risk of making and selling them. And the reason for that is that only an eighth of your cost of driving is fuel. Even if we had doubled or tripled gasoline prices, like Germany and Japan, it would have been a very weak incentive to buy a more efficient car.

However, there is something you could do, something that the California legislature passed by a seven-to-one margin two years ago. Governor Deukmejian vetoed it, and we ought to bring it back. It's called Drive-Plus, or a "feebate": when you buy a new car, you pay a fee or get a rebate. Which and how big would depend on how efficient the car is; the fees would pay for the rebates. It's entirely self-financing. That's why it was so politically attractive. I'd like to add a little kicker that says the rebate for your efficient new car will be based on the difference in efficiency between the new car you buy and the old car you scrap. That would be an incentive to get bad cars off the road and good cars on the road. Detroit loves this idea; they'll sell more cars. And it has some important implications for competitiveness, because we now stand on the verge of a car revolution that is at least as big as the microchip revolution. It may be bigger.

We saw a hint of it last January when General Motors released an ultra-light concept car. This is a four-adult family car with four air bags. Outside, it's only as big as a Miata, but inside, it's a lot bigger. In fact, it has the wheelbase of a Buick Park Avenue because they moved the wheels out to the corners. This car is twice as efficient as today's new cars. It averages sixty-two miles a gallon; at fifty miles an hour, it cruises at one hundred miles a gallon on four horsepower. How does it do that? It only weighs fourteen hundred pounds, because it's made of carbon-fiber composite, and it's about twice as slippery as today's cars. It has very little air drag, yet it looks very safe because carbon fiber is an extraordinarily strong, bouncy material, so much so that if you were in a good carbon-fiber car and got hit by an eighteen-wheeler, the car would go flying—kind of like kicking an empty coffee can—but if you were all suspended inside in your belts and air bags, you'd probably walk away.

When the ultra-light came out—a remarkable achievement, because they did it in one hundred days with over one hundred significant innovations—

the trade press said this is all just a joke economically, because carbon fiber costs one hundred times as much per pound as steel. That's leaving out some rather important facts. What matters is not cost per pound, but cost per car. The material is so strong and can be molded in such big, complex shapes that slot together—you can cut the parts count a hundredfold, cut the assembly labor and time tenfold, and put the color in the mold and not need to paint it. There are so many innovations you can do with these moldable materials—and even more with the hybrid electric drive, making electricity on board as needed—that you end up with a radically simplified car that may even cost less than today's cars and could be sold through the mail and repaired at your house just as we do today with computers.

There are many other ways to save oil in buildings, in industry, in heavy transportation. We have technologies—about half of them on the market—that can save about 80 percent of our oil cheaper than we can drill for more. The cost of saving four-fifths of our oil is about three dollars a barrel. The U.S. oil problem is that we have extracted oil longer and faster than anybody else. A few years ago, something like 90 percent of all oil wells ever drilled were drilled in the U.S., only a few percent of the world's land area. Therefore, our new oil costs more than other countries' new oil.

There are three things we can do about this: protectionism, trade, and substitution. Protectionism means taxing foreign oil to make it look costlier than it is, or resubsidizing domestic oil to make it took cheaper than it is. That is a dumb response, because it suppresses efficient use of the oil by making it look artificially cheap. These approaches don't make a lot of sense, because they say the answer to domestic depletion is to deplete faster.

An alternative is to trade for oil as our major competitors do. Germany and Japan import all their oil, they're just better at paying for it than we are. The ways we get oil, the places we get it, the ways we trade it, are now so enormously diversified —a tribute to the international oil industry—that when there was a full-blown war in the Persian Gulf there were no gas lines at home. Who could have imagined that even a few years ago?

Yet there's an even better solution than trading for oil: substitute natural gas, which we now know is an extremely abundant fuel, renewables, or whatever is cheaper than the oil. A lot of things are cheaper than oil, even at today's prices. Most of the oil we use is uneconomically used. We wouldn't be using it at all if we were taking economics seriously.

If you add up the ways of substituting efficiency for electricity, oil, gas, and coal, you find that you have greatly facilitated the transition already underway to renewable sources, which don't hurt the climate and are very cost effective. Five national labs recently found that if we put a little more R and D into polishing some of the existing technologies, the total cost of that investment being less than the cost of a single nuclear power plant, then by 2010 (which is not that far off in energy terms), we would be able to get at least half as much energy and about as much electricity as the U.S. uses today from highly cost-effective renewable sources. PG&E has already testified in Congress that there is a potential to power California entirely with renewable sources.

You can't spend a dollar on two different things at the same time. If you spend a dollar on something expensive, like nuclear power or solar cells at present prices, you won't get much electricity for your dollar, and you won't be able to displace much fuel burning and global warming for your dollar. That's what expensive means. If, on the other hand, you bought something cheap with your dollar, like efficiency—better lights, motors, and appliances—you'd get a lot of it per dollar. That's what cheap means. Whenever you spend a dollar on something expensive instead of on something cheap, you release a lot of extra carbon into the air that would not have been released if you had chosen the best buys first. That is why the order of economic priority is the order of environmental priority—and it's why nuclear power makes global warming worse. I hasten to add, by the way, that solar cells are indeed cost effective now in many applications; PG&E has already found that they're about the cheapest way to expand or to support a fully loaded substation without having to expand the whole thing at high land prices.

There are a lot of other benefits from the least-cost approach. You get better national security from less reliance on foreign oil and other vulnerable sources and from helping to stop the spread of nuclear bombs. And you get other environmental benefits: fewer oil spills, less land degradation, less urban smog, less acid rain. You also end up with more sustainable development.

If you can't keep the bathtub full because the water keeps running out, do you get a bigger water heater, or do you get a plug? Energy efficiency is a very powerful plug for keeping dollars in our economies, whether on the scale of a village, or a country, or the globe. The World Bank and others project that developing countries which want to electrify will consume almost their entire economic growth to pay for the power plants and grids. They'll have no money left to build the things that were supposed to use all the electricity. That kind of business as usual doesn't work.

A quarter of all global development capital is going to electrification on the supply side. If we spend a small part of that on the demand side, we will free up the capital we need for female literacy, infant immunization, clean water, land reform, all the other development basics. Electric efficiency can also make it affordable to bring solar power to the villages with photovoltaics. It is perhaps the most powerful single lever for sustainable global development, and therefore for equity and justice.

In short, global warming is a problem we don't need to have. It's cheaper not to have it, and if we take economics seriously, we will probably not have climatic problems and we will solve a lot of other problems at the same time.

May 7, 1992

Mikhail Gorbachev

Former President, USSR

In December 1991, Mikhail Gorbachev became the former president of a country that no longer existed. In the years before then, he had captured the imaginations of America, Europe, and the world, and it is impossible to tell the story, without including him as a major figure, of the end of communism in the Soviet Union and Europe. But the image Americans had of Gorbachev in the 1980s and early 1990s—when "Gorbymania" had people across the U.S. rooting for the head of the USSR—was very different from his image at home, where his star was already fading.

"Glasnost" and "perestroika" are terms that Gorbachev gave to the English language, and his outspokenness and liveliness were very different from the gray decrepitude that had characterized Soviet leadership for decades—first under Brezhnev, then the short-lived reigns of Yuri Andropov (1982–1984) and Konstantin Chernenko (1984–1985). Former U.S. Secretary of State George Shultz praised Gorbachev in 1992 as "among the truly influential people who helped to bring about this vast change which is so beneficial for all of us. He was and is a man of action." Shultz also told of the first time he met Gorbachev, at the funeral for Andropov in March 1985.

The U.S. delegation was accorded about an hour and a half of meetings with the new general secretary. When we came out, I said to Vice President Bush and others in our delegation, "This man is different. He has fresh ideas. He has a broader worldview than any of the Soviets I have met with before. He obviously has high intelligence. But more than that, he has a mind of energy that reaches out and works at problems. He will be decisive and he will be a formidable interlocutor with us. So we will have to be on the ball."

Gorbachev had begun calling for openness in Soviet society even before being elected general secretary in 1985. In 1986, he spearheaded the rebuilding of Soviet society, went to Iceland to meet with Ronald Reagan to negotiate nuclear arms reduction, and released from exile physicist and Nobel Peace Prize–winner (and father of the Soviet H-bomb) Andrei Sakharov. He visited Prague in April 1987 and called for the elimination of nuclear weapons from Europe; two months later Ronald Reagan stood at the Brandenburg Gate in Berlin and said, "Mr. Gorbachev, tear down this wall!" Gorbachev didn't tear down the wall, but he did let it be torn down in 1989. That same year, the Red Army completed its withdrawal from Afghanistan. And in 1990, Gorbachev was awarded the Nobel Peace Prize.

Gorbachev's wife, Raisa, also dazzled Americans. Svelte and outspoken, she broke the American stereotype of the dowdy Russian babushka; she even carried an American Express card. But the same qualities Americans loved were resented at home. And while Gorbachev's star was still ascendant abroad, at home many citizens of the Soviet Union, at first enchanted with what glasnost and perestroika offered, now wanted to see the general secretary put his money where his mouth was. Meanwhile, the hardliners fought change at every turn and, in August 1991, led a coup to remove Gorbachev. The coup quickly failed, but the system Gorbachev had tried to mend was clearly broken beyond repair. He dissolved the Communist Party, granted the Baltic republics independence, and presided over the creation of a looser, primarily economic confederation that went under the name Commonwealth of Independent States. With the Soviet Union defunct on December 8, he resigned as its president on December 25.

Gorbachev's May 1992 journey to the U.S. was his first since stepping down as leader of the Soviet Union. In this speech, he is holding forth as a statesman who no longer has a constituency to answer to. (He would, however, run for president in the 1996 Russian elections and receive less than 1 percent of the vote.) Donning the mantle of elder statesman and meeting with Ronald Reagan in Santa Barbara, where the Reagans presented the Gorbachevs with a pair of Stetsons, he went on to tour the U.S. aboard the Forbes-owned jet *Capitalist Tool,* raising funds for the new Gorbachev Foundation. Yet his talk here reflects a broader wisdom at work, because this is a man speaking now to the world, to history, no longer having to watch his back.

A Special Presentation by His Excellency Mikhail Gorbachev

I hope you understand that you have in me a person who has gone through a great deal. I am not a naïve individual.

What has been happening over the past few years should have happened much earlier. During World War II, we were all able to unite in a great coalition against Nazism, and in uniting we overcame the things that separated us, particularly ideological obstacles and barriers. We have to regret that the politicians of that time missed the opportunity that was opened by that common victory over Nazism. We are meeting on the eve of the anniversary of that great victory, and I would like to take this opportunity to express my very special feelings of gratitude to the generation of people that endured that very difficult fight.

We unfortunately missed the opportunity of uniting after the war, of cooperating together to go along a new path. And so we had to go through very difficult decades. That led to the early 1980s, when the world found itself on the edge of a precipice, when people intuitively felt that trouble was knocking at their doors.

I would like to pay tribute to the generation of political leaders who understood the concern and anxiety of their peoples, and who then opted for a new policy that changed that situation. Here I must mention the contributions of President Reagan, Prime Minister Thatcher, President Mitterrand, Chancellor Kohl, Prime Minister Andreotti of Italy, and many others who understood the challenge of the times.

From the very outset it was my view that without a new relationship, a relationship of partnership and eventually of friendship, between the Soviet

Union and the United States, nothing would change in the world. Our partners understood that too. It was very difficult to take the first step. But we did take that step, and today we find ourselves in a totally new situation.

But today I am concerned, because there are many ways that this new situation could be used. We could stop and content ourselves with what has been achieved, or we can continue to work together to unite the efforts of the peoples and governments of all nations to cooperate for a new world. Because of my concern, I have decided to take the opportunity offered by hundreds of invitations from the United States to come to your country. I very much appreciate the efforts of Secretary of State Shultz, my partner and friend, who together with President Reagan, the honorary chairman of the host committee, organized this trip and the itinerary of my American visit. I very much value the fact that my path crossed with George Shultz. We found in ourselves the strength to work for a new world, to pave the way for a new world, and I pay tribute to Secretary Shultz for his contribution.

[from the question-and-answer session]

Q. *You say that you believed that the October Revolution of 1917 was a genuine people's revolution. But many critics argue that it was an antidemocratic movement from the very beginning. How do you respond?*

A. After the February Revolution of 1917, also a great event in our history, developments took a dramatic turn. The situation was probably affected by the fact that the country was in the midst of war and also by the fact that after the Romanov dynasty was removed, we did not have any democratic institutions or traditions in our country. The economic situation in the country was extremely severe. All of these factors played a role to some extent, and as a result, it was inevitable that developments took the turn that they took after the February Revolution. The question then was whether there would be a military dictatorship—and there were people who wished to become military dictators—or whether there would be another attempt for a political and economic revolution that would continue the transformations that began in February. The events of July of 1917 accelerated the process that culminated in the events of October 1917. And as a result, power was transferred to the Bolsheviks. The slogans that the Bolsheviks upheld at that time—"Land to the peasants,"

"Factories to the workers," "Peace for peoples," and "Self-determination to all nations!"—had the support of the people.

What happened next is now history—our history. We are now trying to understand why those slogans and the hopes of the people were not fulfilled. In the final months of his life, Lenin was able to engage in a very critical analysis of what had happened, and he decided that there was a need for a new policy. He developed a new policy, but it was not his fate to be able to implement that policy. So the whole nation was forced into a utopian and unrealistic model, one that had nothing to do with real life and with the vital interests of the people. How it all ended is well known. It was the goal of perestroika to find a way out of the crisis of that system and to implement political reforms, reforms of ownership, and reforms in our multiethnic state which would make it possible to end the crisis. Step by step, we were moving in that direction.

Q. *How do you want to work with the African American community?*

A. I believe in the democratic traditions of your country. And I believe that the institutions that exist within the framework of your Constitution and that the enormous democratic experience you have in this country make you quite capable of addressing any problems that exist here. I'm sure that the current election campaign will be one of the most substantive and lively campaigns. I'm sure that that campaign will make it possible for the American people to address all their urgent problems. I urge you to use the coming months to find the right solutions.

We are perhaps witnessing a revival of nations and ethnic communities. Over the years of perestroika, I have had to address the problems of ethnic diversity, and I have discovered that there is no other way but to recognize the legitimacy of the interests of nations, peoples, ethnic groups: big and small. One thing that I have seen during these years is that the problems related to interethnic relations in multiethnic countries like ours cannot be dealt with by force. The approach to these problems should be based on equality of rights and justice. And here I am referring to human rights, to equal representation of each ethnic group in the bodies of power, and to equal access to education, culture, and science and technology. And to jobs and to being able to live prosperously. I have seen very often how people react to any manifestation of injustice or disrespect for the individual. I was asked in Los Angeles what I thought about the situation in that city, and I said to the mayor and the others in that meeting that if human rights are the highest value for us, if the dignity of the individual is supreme for us, then we must be on the side of that person whose rights were trampled. I think that what happened to that person in the end will be righted and corrected. All of us at that meeting agreed that what had happened to that one man was a signal that we had to understand.

Now let me make a very important point: I believe—and I said so then—that the level of democracy existing in the United States will make it possible to analyze the situation, to draw the lessons from what has happened, and also to change the policies where necessary. I am sure that the people and the government of the United States will work together and will do what is necessary. This problem of diversity is now particularly acute in Russia and the other countries of the Commonwealth of Independent States. When we began perestroika, we wanted to reform the state, which, although it was called a federation, was indeed a unitary state. The bureaucratic, totalitarian government not only suppressed political freedoms and dissidents but also ignored and disregarded the legitimate interests of many peoples and ethnic groups. Democracy and glasnost spotlighted all those problems which had previously been ignored. The process of reform was unfolded in a very acute and dramatic political struggle. It was my view, and I believe it was the view of most of our society, that the old union had to be reformed. But at the same time, I believed that we had to stay together as one state, as one union. On this issue, there were two points of view and those points of view were in conflict: on the one hand, we wanted to preserve a union state, to reshape and refashion it but to continue to exist as one country. On the other hand, there were those who wanted to dismember that state. I believed then and I believe now that whatever we do—even now, when we do not have one single union state but a Commonwealth of Independent States—our number-one priority in any situation has to be human rights, the rights of the individual. Seventy-five million citizens of the former Soviet Union live outside what would be their ethnic or national republics. Now that they live away from what would be their state, they need very firm guarantees of the protection of their rights. We will not be able to solve the problem you have raised here if we do not say openly and firmly that we are against extreme nationalism anywhere.

All these problems, including the problems of frontiers between these new states and of the territory of these new states, urgently need to be addressed if we want to create a real commonwealth. The initial development of this commonwealth has been very difficult, but it is our fate that we have to cooperate, because our country evolved as one country. Even now that it has become a Commonwealth of Independent States, we cannot afford irresponsible policies that would disregard that important, historic reality, that would disregard the way people in our country have lived for centuries. Our people understand that we have to cooperate; it is now time for the politicians to understand it.

Q. *You have long opposed the extension of weapons of mass destruction into space. Are you disturbed by President Yeltsin's recent call for a global SDI, or Star Wars, system?*

A. It would be very strange, something that I could not understand, if having made all those efforts to move toward the abolition of nuclear weapons, we suddenly decided to extend the race into space. I very, very much doubt that anything good could come out of that. If we become involved in such a move, then an arms race is inevitable, and the least that would do would be to create suspicions on the part of other countries. There are other ways of dealing with the problems of assuring security for all nations. The mechanisms exist to address security problems, and we need to strengthen and use those mechanisms: the United Nations and its Security Council, the non-proliferation treaty, and similar mechanisms.

Q. *You have spoken about individual human rights, and under your leadership many political prisoners were released. Why are there still thousands of gay men and lesbians incarcerated in Soviet prisons undergoing forced psychiatric therapy? When will there be basic human rights for sexual minorities in your country?*

A. You are asking a very difficult question. It is difficult for me personally, and therefore I can only tell you my attitude from an ethical standpoint. I am in favor of a healthy way of life. I am in favor of a healthy society. That's all.

Q. *Capitalism is a catastrophic stage. We are dying throughout the world. Forty thousand children die every day. What is happening? What is there for the future? I want to fight for that international revolution that Trotsky and Lenin once spoke of. Is there hope? What about human rights? What about basic needs? Are we going to keep putting profits before human needs?*

A. We have come to a phase in the development of global civilization when the search for a just society must be based on certain indispensable elements, such as human rights, democracy, social justice, acceptance of dissidents, and above all, certain universal values. We stand on the threshold of a new civilization, and we have to avoid any attempt to impose one model on that society. If you were to say that at this threshold of the twenty-first century we stand empty-handed, with nothing to propose, nothing to say to mankind, I would not agree. We have to look at what is actually happening in the world and the changes underway. The prevailing trends in the world today are the internationalization of all developments, the increasingly integrated character of the world, the democratization of nations, and the fact that the last totalitarian regime is leaving the scene of history. So we are not facing a choice of socialism or capitalism; rather, we have to build a new world, a new civilization based on the changes and needs that have accumulated over the past centuries, and particularly over recent years. When I recently visited Japan, they asked me the same question: "Why are you destroying your state, your government? Why are people in your country promoting a kind of wild market, the market of early capitalism?" I am convinced that government has a role, and that that role is to seek to harmonize relations within society. It has to address the problems and contradictions that emerge in the process of the development of society, including problems concerning the role and position of certain groups in society. And I think that there has to be a policy developed by governments that would address the conflicts that you have mentioned. Democratic structures and procedures make it possible for people to elect a government that is capable of developing and pursuing such a policy. We have to bear in mind the actual experience of our country, which shows that policies of equalization are not really just. They remove the mainspring from the society, they remove the incentive for being active, they suppress initiative, they suppress social energy. The result of that is that the mindset of the people also changes. But there is also the experience of other countries, the experience of a totally different policy which results in a social situation that sets nations apart, in which nations have poles of rich and poor and have the kind of gap between rich and poor that cannot be explained in any way and cannot be accepted in any way. That is the other extreme; and that kind of society is doomed to live in a state of social tension and to be unstable. So these are the questions that policies should address.

September 30, 1994

Václav Havel

President of the Czech Republic

Czech President Václav Havel's 1994 talk on human rights is a call to adhere to morals that transcend politics. Havel was, after all, a president who came into office cresting a wave of enthusiasm for democracy that had people in the streets carrying placards demanding "Havel na hrad!" (Havel to the castle!) He was a leader above the partisan fray: the group, Civic Forum, that he headed was a movement, not a political party. It later split into factions that became parties, and Czechoslovakia began to deal with the chore of restructuring a moribund economy. The country itself split on New Year's Eve 1993 in the "Velvet Divorce," and Havel resigned from the presidency rather than preside over the end of the country. Reversing this stance, however, he then agreed to serve as president of the newly created Czech Republic.

Havel's talk here was given less than two years into the ten he would serve as president—an office that is largely ceremonial, with the day-to-day business of running the country in the hands of the prime minister and his cabinet. Nevertheless, to Americans jaded with their political system, Havel offered an image of a president far more hip than anything the Republicans or Democrats could serve up: he was a playwright; he'd been sent to prison for his work in trying to get Communist Czechoslovakia to adhere to international norms for civil rights; instead of searching for PAC money or holding political fund-raising dinners, he hung out with Lou Reed. And Prague itself was the cool place to be for young Americans; it was to the nineties what Paris was to the twenties for American expats. At the time Havel gave this speech, there were some forty thousand Americans living in the Czech capital; every night at least a few dozen of them were staying at a youth hostel that had been a secret police prison where Havel was jailed.

As for his service as president: "Stop talking about all the love you have in your heart," one Czech journalist said, describing how her fellow citizens felt about Havel's highmindedness, "and explain to me instead why oranges are so expensive." In talking about human rights, though, Havel was speaking about something he had personally suffered for. It was for founding Charter 77—which had demanded the Czechoslovak government adhere to the international accords on human rights it had signed—that he had been sent to prison in 1978 and held until 1983. The question of human rights within the Czech Republic would in fact be part of the agenda for the Czechs' accession talks with the European Union—specifically discrimination against the Roma. The most poignant point of conflict began in 1994 in the Czech city of Ustí nad Labem—and on this domestic issue, too, Havel tried to take the high road, ultimately calling for the appointment of a deputy prime minister of human rights.

Havel would serve a second term as president of the Czech Republic and leave office in February 2003, to be succeeded by one of his former prime ministers, the leader of the conservative Civic Democratic Party, Václav Klaus. During his tenure, Havel saw the country successfully integrated into NATO and on track to join the European Union. He has seemed to step easily into his post-presidential role as dissident redux, and in summer 2003 was onstage with the Rolling Stones.

"From Prisoner to President"

In the first half of this century, we have witnessed some of the most terrible abuses of human rights in the history of mankind. It could be said that its second half ushered in an era when the respect for human rights not only reemerged as one of the guiding principles of human conduct but has become a norm in a large part of the globe. Human rights were the reunifying force for the opposition in a number of former Communist countries and for its supporters abroad. Support from organizations such as Amnesty International and several successive administrations was very important in bringing about the ultimate collapse of the antidemocratic and inhuman regimes in the former Soviet bloc. The respect for human rights has also returned to many countries in Latin America. More recently, the cause of human rights was instrumental in bringing about the end to apartheid in South Africa. Never in human history have so many people in so many countries enjoyed fundamental human rights.

In spite of all these achievements, this state of affairs should be a cause for reflection rather than rejoicing. There are several reasons for that.

First of all, there are still many places in the world where human rights are violated. The fact that there are fewer of such places, and that the violations are less frequent or less violent than they used to be, doesn't make them more acceptable. Nor does the fact that, in some cases, they have been justified by other than totalitarian ideologies. There is no such thing as a respectable human rights abuse; it is always motivated by intolerance and a lack of respect for others.

Secondly, the very category of human rights is somehow less clearly defined today than it was twenty years ago, when individual human rights, such as freedom from oppression, freedom from torture, freedom from discrimination, and freedom from censorship constituted an unquestionable conceptual core. Since that time, many new human rights, some individual, others collective, have been claimed without winning universal recognition or clear definition.

When our bill of rights was debated in our parliament, a number of deputies demanded that the right to work be guaranteed under the constitution. But how does one define such a right? Should it mean the right not to be arbitrarily prevented from working, or should it mean the right to a job? If it is the latter, how can the state guarantee this without reverting back to a totalitarian mode of governing? Is there a right to health, and does it mean the right of access to health care opportunities, or the right to a universal and comprehensive health care system? Could it even mean perhaps the right to be healthy? If it is the last, how can the state guarantee it? Without trying to answer all these difficult and much debated questions here, it would seem reasonable that the state should only legislate and guarantee such rights as it is capable of enforcing. Otherwise, it risks not only that some human rights will become empty gestures, but also that the respect for all human rights—including those we all would agree on—will be diminished as a consequence.

In addressing this and other issues, a great deal of open-minded goodness and humility is required. Ideological doctrines rarely work. The recent conference on population in Cairo showed that it is possible to reach a high degree of consensus even on difficult and highly sensitive issues such as family planning. While it is certainly in the interest of us all that population doesn't grow beyond our capacity to support it, and while we would all agree that it is important that women be able to exercise control over their own destinies, we should probably stop short of trying to prescribe specific solutions for every woman in the world.

It is not that I advocate cultural relativism where human rights are concerned. If I believe in certain universal human values, such as life, freedom, truth, justice, and dignity, I also believe in the existence of certain universal human rights stemming from these values. However, these values may be manifested in different ways in different cultures, resulting in a different formulation of specific human rights. From a practical point of view, permanent respect for human rights is only achievable when they are securely internalized by a society and adopted as its own. Attempts to impose such norms from outside are as a rule doomed to failure.

Another new element in the human rights debate is the growing number and perceived importance of collective rights. In some ways, human rights activities have always revolved around ethnic, social, or political groups, although the exercise of those rights always rested with the individual. But there is a new emphasis on rights having to do with group identity, group status, and group objectives. The right to self-determination, national independence or autonomy, or to any specific treatment of any ethnic group as such is often taken to be such a right.

People have always grouped together to achieve certain goals, and people have also often been discriminated against on the basis of their group characteristics. The employment of group strategies to end such discrimination is thus quite understandable and justified. It would be, however, somewhat risky to elevate collective human rights above the level of basic individual human rights. An attempt to subordinate individual human rights to group constraints could in effect threaten the very rights that we have been

Above: In December 1964, Joan Baez sang antiwar songs in front of Sproul Hall at the University of California, Berkeley. *Courtesy of the Oakland Museum of California, Online Archive of California*

Right: As thousands of Vietnamese "boat people" fled their country as political refugees, President Jimmy Carter dispatched the Seventh Fleet to assist with rescuing them on the open sea. *Bettmann/CORBIS*

Right: Walter Cronkite standing before St. Basil's Cathedral on Moscow's Red Square in 1981.
Courtesy of CBS

Below: Devastation in Beirut on June 11, 1982, less than a week after Israeli troops invaded Lebanon. The country had been wracked by civil war since 1975.
Bettmann/CORBIS

Above: President Ronald Reagan called Contra rebels fighting to overthrow Daniel Ortega Saavedra's Sandinista government in Nicaragua "freedom fighters." But the U.S. Congress cut off aid to the Contras in 1982, and members of the Reagan Administration turned to other sources for funding. *Bill Gentile/CORBIS*

Left: Nicaraguan head of state Daniel Ortega Saavedra. *Courtesy of John O'Hara/San Francisco Chronicle*

"Get the Facts"

GUEST SPEAKER

THE RIGHT REVEREND DESMOND MPILO TUTU
ANGLICAN BISHOP OF JOHANNESBURG

"THE TOLL OF APARTHEID"
Subject

Above: President of the Philippines Corazón Aquino on a triumphant tour of America following the People Power Revolution of February 1986. *Courtesy of Steve Ringman/San Francisco Chronicle*

Opposite page, top: In calling for an end to apartheid in South Africa, in January 1986 Bishop Desmond Tutu pleaded with Americans to "make a moral decision," asking, "Are you on the side of justice or injustice?" Shirley Cohelan Burton, *Commonwealth Club Office Archives*

Opposite page, bottom: Anti-apartheid protests in Berkeley in April 1986 are put down by police. *Courtesy of Roger J. Wyan/San Francisco Chronicle*

Right: As secretary of state, George Shultz would ask new ambassadors to turn the globe to "your country." When they would point to the country they were assigned to, Shultz would spin the globe back to the United States and say, "No, let me explain something…" *Courtesy of Scott Sommerdorf/ San Francisco Chronicle*

Below: President Ronald Reagan meets with Soviet leader Mikhail Gorbachev in the Oval Office in December 1987 to sign an arms reduction treaty. To Reagan's immediate right are a translator, Secretary of State George Shultz, and Vice President George H. W. Bush. *Courtesy of the George Shultz Collection, Hoover Institution Library and Archives*

Above: Assembling pieces of the AIDS quilt—including a square for actor Rock Hudson, who went public with the fact that he had AIDS. His death in 1985 awakened many Americans to the magnitude of the crisis. *Courtesy of Liz Hafalia/San Francisco Chronicle*

Left: Nurses and health-care workers at San Francisco General Hospital crowd the doorway at a press conference held to announce that an unidentified colleague had been infected with AIDS. *Courtesy of Brant Ward/San Francisco Chronicle*

Above: After the Iraqi invasion of
Kuwait in August 1990, the U.S.
assembled a coalition of thirty-four
countries and itself sent nearly half a
million troops to the region as part of
Operation Desert Shield. Operation
Desert Storm, launched in January
1991, drove Iraqi forces out of Kuwait.
*Courtesy of Vincent Maggiora/San
Francisco Chronicle*

Right: A CNN reporter dons his gas
mask as Iraqi SCUD missiles hit
Jerusalem during the 1991 Persian
Gulf War. *Courtesy of the
San Francisco Chronicle*

Left: In April 1991, U.S. Secretary of Defense Richard Cheney recounted the victory the U.S. had just achieved in the Persian Gulf and discussed the future of the U.S. military. *Shirley Cohelan Burton, Commonwealth Club Office Archives*

Below: Marches protesting U.S. involvement in the Persian Gulf were the largest antiwar demonstrations in the U.S. since the Vietnam War. One year after the beginning of Operation Desert Storm, a protestor marks the anniversary at the Concord Naval Weapons Station. *Courtesy of Michael Maloney/San Francisco Chronicle*

Right: Actress Audrey Hepburn emerged from private life in 1988 to travel the globe as a UNICEF ambassador, drawing attention to child immunization efforts and other programs worldwide. *Paul Eric Felder, Commonwealth Club Office Archives*

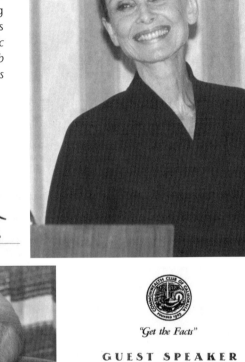

"Get the Facts"

GUEST SPEAKER

"CHILDREN FIRST: BUILDING A GLOBAL AGENDA"
Subject

"Get the Facts"

GUEST SPEAKER

"THE RIGHTS OF FUTURE GENERATIONS"
Subject

Left: Jacques Cousteau meets with a child before arguing the case for the UN to enshrine in its Charter a "Declaration of the Rights of Future Generations." *Paul Eric Felder, Commonwealth Club Office Archives*

Left, top: Vice President Dan Quayle told a Commonwealth Club audience in 1992, "It doesn't help matters when prime-time TV has Murphy Brown, a character who supposedly epitomizes today's intelligent, highly paid professional woman, mocking the importance of fathers by bearing a child alone and calling it just another lifestyle choice." *Paul Eric Felder, Commonwealth Club Office Archives*

Left, bottom: Tabloids played up Dan Quayle's slam of Murphy Brown, while those whom Quayle had dubbed the "media elites" ridiculed him. *Courtesy of Associated Press/San Francisco Chronicle*

Below: In the wake of riots in Los Angeles in 1992, a billboard offered a message of hope, quoting the man whose beating by police officers had ultimately led to the violence. *Courtesy of Liz Hafalia/San Francisco Chronicle*

Above: Physicist Amory Lovins argued in 1992 that photovoltaic cells and electric efficiency offer "the most powerful single lever for sustainable global development, and therefore for equity and justice." Shown are solar panels in California's Mojave Desert. *Courtesy of Kendra Luck/ San Francisco Chronicle*

Right: Triumphant Civic Forum leader Václav Havel raises his hand in a victory salute while Alexander Dubcek, a prominent figure in the 1968 "Prague Spring," stands behind him, on November 24, 1989, the day the Czechoslovak Communist leadership resigned. *Courtesy of Jan Sibik*

trying to protect and promote for so long. The exercise of collective human rights, unlike that of individual rights, can also have a far-reaching effect on other groups, effects which cannot always be predicted. Let's not forget that the widespread and massive abuses of individual human rights in the former Yugoslavia have been all too often justified in the name of a collective human right, such as the right to self-determination. Finally, should human rights rest with groups of people rather than individuals, the fragmentation of society into a number of isolated groups as guardians of their respective and specific rights, and the fragmentation of the world into isolated and competing spheres of civilization, would seem to be unavoidable.

There is, on the other hand, a degree of universality above the elementary individual human rights of something that brings people together, rather than setting them apart. But all this is not the main reason why I think that the human rights paradigm is as important as it has been in recent history. For me, it is not the final word in the eternal struggle of man for a better and happier life. The respect for human rights not only helps to eliminate inequalities and injustice which are centuries old, but it also removes the constraints on individual activity, enterprise, and creativity. While it liberates the human potential of every individual, it does not automatically fulfill that potential. It is a promise of a reward, not the reward itself. There is a price to be paid for it.

The freer we are and the more rights we enjoy, the greater is our own responsibility for our acts as well as those of others. The freer we are to decide our own future, the more responsible we should feel for it. Our new-found freedom should enable us to start searching for total universal human values on which a global civilization could be founded and its future secured. It is my belief that such values are hidden in our collective human experience, in our sad memories, and in our half-forgotten awareness of the universal order of being. We need to discover these values and transcend the horizons of our day-to-day existence. We can only do that if we are free. Among the fundamental human rights that Thomas Jefferson wrote about in the Declaration of Independence was the right to the pursuit of happiness. It is not a right to happiness, but a right to pursue it. Let us undertake the journey.

Q. *You are a creative artist. How do you balance this with your duties as president of the Czech Republic?*

A. How can an artist be in office as a politician? It can be done, but it is certainly not easy for an artist to do. It needs a certain kind of discipline which artists usually don't find to be much fun. Having done two years of military service and five years in prison, I have had some training.

Q. *You were president of Czechoslovakia before the country was divided into separate republics. What was the reason for this split? How have relations between the two countries been since then?*

A. The reason Czechoslovakia split up was not due to the whims of politicians who thought there were too few states in Europe and that it should have more. The real reason was that Slovak party representatives, who were elected in democratic elections, wanted to build a statehood of their own. The Slovak people had never had one before, and it was something for which they obviously had been longing. As president of the Czech and Slovak Federation, I exerted a great deal of effort to maintain the federation and adjust it to the development of all the population. The Slovak desire for independence proved to be stronger and, naturally, I respected that. What I have found to be most important is the fact that the split proved to be one of the rare examples of dividing a state, without conflict and in a peaceful manner, on the basis of an accord. The relations with the two republics are good and close. A common border unites and links the two nations. Nobody intends to cut these natural ties among the citizens of the nations. I would admit that it was not easy for me to accept the candidacy for the Czech presidency and to come to terms with the fact that I may be the only person in the world who was the last president of one state and the first president of another. Eventually, I have come to terms with that, because what is more important than the size of a nation is the values underlying it.

Q. *How has the conflict in nearby Bosnia and the rest of the former Yugoslavia affected your country? What should be done to reduce the violence and suffering there? What role should the U.S. play?*

A. I have not come to the U.S. in order to advise the American government on what to do. In my opinion, Bosnia-Herzegovina was a country where people belonged to different ethnic groups and adhered to different religions. They were living together and set an example of a created civil coexistence, cooperation, and mutual enrichment. What was an issue in Bosnia-Herzegovina was not so much a conflict among the individual groups, but rather a conflict between the principle of civil coexistence and the principle of ethnic superiority, ethnic purity, and pure nationalism. Three groups are fighting each other there, and the world has been negotiating with them. However, there is a fourth group. This is the one consisting of people who do not want any war; they just want to live together as citizens. Nobody has been negotiating with them. Nobody has been talking with them, because they don't have guns. It is depressing to see the behavior of the democratic world; there is a tendency to agree to the division of Bosnia-Herzegovina. This amounts to a denial of the very values underlying the democratic world. This is particularly true of Europe, where it means a denial of the very principle on which European integration is based. Precise and perfect ethnic group border lines in that country would have to go across every village, every family, and every person.

Q. *Is assigning a high priority to environmental protection consistent with the urgent economic development needs of your country?*

A. One should not rely on the market's ability to provide for a sound environment on its own. The state is duty bound to create a wide variety of instruments that will make the economy behave in accordance with environmental needs.

Q. *Does the U.S. position as a world power bring with it a moral obligation to enforce human rights—militarily, if necessary—even if it is not in our national interest?*

A. I come from a country that had the experience of Munich. A capitulation before evil ultimately led to an evil of a much greater magnitude. Evil must be combated; that is a principle of fundamental human solidarity. Unfortunately, there are situations when there is no other way to combat evil but by using force.

America Y2K and the Jihad

April 2, 1993

Madeleine Albright

U.S. Permanent Representative to the United Nations

"The strongest military in the world cannot protect you from global warming," Madeleine Albright answered to a question following her speech at The Commonwealth Club in 1993. "You can have all kinds of missile systems, but they cannot protect our way of life, make our children healthy, or prevent disease from spreading. Star Wars cannot protect us from the problems of the twenty-first century." Albright had been appointed in January 1993 by Bill Clinton to serve as U.S. representative to the United Nations, and she was engaged in a public diplomacy tour back home in April—some ten weeks after Clinton had taken office, and only a month after terrorists had attempted to topple the World Trade Center by detonating a bomb in a parking garage beneath the towers.

Albright also fielded a question about Somalia, where "there was some lack of clarity in the initial plan when [President] Bush committed himself and America to Somalia," she said. "He had said that the troops would go in and come out quickly." The UN had authorized a peacekeeping force to intervene in the failed state, where thousands of people were dying each day of starvation while military warlords looted food aid arriving on the docks. President Bush had sent thirty thousand U.S. troops as part of Operation Restore Hope, and the media had been there to record the Marines landing in Mogadishu.

The media would also be there in October 1993, when Somali fighters downed two U.S. Blackhawk helicopters that were part of an operation to apprehend a Somali warlord—and Americans at home watched in horror while the bodies of American soldiers were dragged through the streets.

In her Commonwealth Club appearance, Albright singled out the conflict in Bosnia as a UN concern. Although the United Nations had authorized a peacekeeping force in February 1992, the conflict in Bosnia raged on. Two weeks before Albright spoke, a UN humanitarian relief convoy finally got through to the besieged city of Srebenica. And ten days after her talk, NATO warplanes—with UN authorization—began enforcing a no-fly zone over Bosnia. Two of the three forces in conflict had signed the Vance-Owen peace plan, which would divide Bosnia into three mini-states: Muslim, Serb, and Croat. The holdouts—Bosnian Serb leaders—would sign the plan on May 2, but their parliament refused to ratify it. The UN established "safe areas" within Bosnia, and shelling of Sarajevo resumed in June. After another attempt at peacemaking, the parties in conflict signed the Dayton Accords, negotiated at an Air Force base in Ohio. With more than twenty-two thousand troops in Bosnia under UN command, still fighting continued. Before U.S. forces finally arrived in 1995, some two hundred thousand civilians had been killed and two million people were homeless.

A few weeks before Albright spoke, North Korea put itself back in the international spotlight by announcing that it would withdraw from the Nuclear Non-Proliferation Treaty and that inspectors would no longer be allowed access to nuclear sites. During the question-and-answer session, Albright noted that the North Koreans had started a three-month countdown by announcing the intention to withdraw, and it was now time for diplomacy to get them to change their minds. As it turned out, open conflict with North Korea was averted, at least for the duration of the Clinton Administration. But there was more trouble elsewhere: less than two weeks after Albright spoke, an assassination plot against former President George Bush was discovered while he was visiting Kuwait. Clinton would order air strikes on Iraq that summer in retaliation.

Cambodia is the one UN project that Albright mentioned where the organization was clearly succeeding in the effort to help a once war-torn nation make the transition to democracy. The UN had assumed administrative functions for the government in 1992. UN peacekeepers would supervise the country's first-ever democratic elections in May 1993.

After Clinton was reelected in 1996, Madeleine Albright was appointed to succeed Warren Christopher as secretary of state. The first woman ever appointed to the position, Albright, alluding to her footwear, told the departing Christopher, "I hope my heels will fill your shoes."

"What You Need to Know about the UN and Foreign Policy Today"

The reason I am here today and the reason I will be traveling throughout America in the months ahead is that I do not believe I can fulfill my mission to the UN unless I am also able to persuade the American people of the importance of that mission. For the United Nations can't succeed without our leadership, and we cannot lead at the UN—at least not for long—without your support and that of the public at large. So I decided the first day on the job that an important part of my role would be to get out into the country for the purpose of explaining and conducting a dialogue about the UN.

I approach that dialogue with a personal interest, because my family never would have come to America if not for the UN. My father, a Czechoslovak diplomat, was a member of the first UN Commission for India and Pakistan. Shortly after he was chosen for that post, in February 1948, there was a Communist coup in Czechoslovakia—and my father went from government representative to political dissident. My family did then what so many others from so many lands have done in search of liberty: we came to the United States, and thanks to the generosity of the American people, I had the opportunity to live and grow up in freedom. So I am a child of the Cold War, acutely conscious of its costs, and anxious that we make the best of the historic opportunities now before us.

We have reached a point in history that is reminiscent of the periods after the First and Second World Wars. On both occasions we were summoned to lead the world in building a stable peace out of the shattered fragments of international conflict. In the first case, we shunned the leader's role and sought, instead, to retreat from international responsibility. We rejected the League of Nations. We chose a course that we thought would shield us from entanglement in foreign conflict and wound up inviting a second world war.

In 1945, we chose a harder, wiser path. Having won the war, our leaders set out to create a lasting peace. The Marshall Plan helped rebuild the world's prosperity; NATO defended our interests; and the United Nations was established, in the words of its Charter, "to save succeeding generations from the scourge of war...to reaffirm faith in fundamental human rights...to establish...respect for the obligations...of international law...and to promote social progress and better standards of life."

For almost as long as I have been alive, the work of the UN was frustrated by the rivalry of the two superpowers. Although much was accomplished, the need for consensus among Cold War antagonists prevented the UN from becoming the institution envisioned by its founders. Today we have reached the point where that dream can finally be realized—but it will not happen without strong leadership from the United States. It will not happen unless our generation, too, chooses the harder but wiser path, unless we work step by step to build the United Nations into an effective and broadly respected force for human development and peace.

What does that require of us? First, that we be honest about the problems that exist. It is said that you can search all the public parks without finding a monument to a committee, and there is no question that the UN is the ultimate committee. Imagine a bargaining table at which sit representatives of every race, culture, religion, and ethnic group on the face of the globe. Under the circumstances, although we would not call it acceptable, we cannot consider it surprising that inefficiencies and frustrations occur. It would be a miracle if they did not. Despite the secretary-general's commitment to reform, the UN remains at times slow and wasteful; some officials are paid too much for doing too little, while others are paid too little while forced to do far too much. There are problems of accountability, and plans that often seem sensible on the drawing board have a habit of going awry in the field.

An independent inspector general would help. The personnel system should do more to reward merit and less to reward personal or political connections. UN offices need to be introduced to 1990s technology. The entire structure needs to be streamlined and refocused to take into account the new security threats of the post–Cold War world. And, I can't resist adding, it wouldn't hurt if the UN and its delegations had a few more women in positions of responsibility.

Critics of the UN are right to stress the need for reform. But bear in mind, the total UN budget is $5.2 billion. America's total share of that is less than two-tenths of 1 percent of our budget. And improvements in efficiency alone will not be enough to meet the challenges we now face. In short, American leadership at the UN will require us to do more than take the accountant's view.

Never before have we expected so much of the United Nations. Within the past five years, the UN has moved from the margins of international affairs to absolute dead center. Not a month goes by without some nation or group dialing the equivalent of global 911, asking the UN to help cope with a new human conflict or natural disaster. More UN peacekeeping operations have been initiated in the past five years than in the previous forty-three. And for the first time, UN forces are being sent into countries where there is no peace to keep—as peacemakers and peace enforcers and even as a precaution against the outbreak of war. It is the philosophy of the new UN, from the secretary-general down, that without peacekeeping, nations will not have the security needed to develop; without development, people will fight endlessly over limited resources or become rootless and disruptive; and without democracy, neither long-term economic development nor long-term peace and stability will be possible.

After almost a half-century of gridlock, the UN agenda now bears a striking resemblance to America's agenda. The Clinton Administration, building in part on the work of the last, wants to capitalize on this sharing of interests—to forge a partnership between the U.S. and the UN that will create, if not a new world order, then at least a stronger, broader commitment to international law, freedom, and human dignity than we have ever known. That partnership has already begun.

Consider, for example, the range and scope of what has occurred at the UN, with U.S. leadership and support, in the past two months: First, we have followed up strongly on last summer's Earth Summit in Rio by establishing a new UN Commission for Sustainable Development and by beginning a review of options to strengthen both international and domestic commitments on controlling global climate change. This administration believes that environmental threats must be treated as seriously as any other threats to our security. Logic demands it, our children deserve it, and the scope of the environmental crisis facing our planet compels it.

Second, we have taken steps to strengthen ambitious but troubled peacekeeping efforts in Cambodia and Angola, and to launch a new effort in Mozambique. In each case we seek to heal wounds inflicted or gravely exacerbated by the Cold War. In each case we face considerable odds. In each case the fate of hundreds of thousands of people—the survivors, in some cases, of decades of struggle—hangs in the balance.

Third, the UN-sponsored Truth Commission has released a shattering report about violations of human rights in El Salvador over the past decade. Only the authority provided by the UN could have empowered the authors of this report to find the truth and report it.

Fourth, we are on the verge of completing the U.S.-led phase of one of the largest humanitarian assistance operations in history—Operation Restore Hope. The goal of creating a secure environment for the delivery of food and medicine to the people of Somalia is being met. Last Friday, the Security Council adopted a resolution that sets in train the transfer of principal responsibility for this operation from the U.S. to the UN. Although a lot of hard work remains, lives have been saved, discussions about the future government of Somalia have begun, and the partnership between the UN and the U.S., despite disagreements about timing and tactics, has been strengthened.

Finally, the UN is at the center of efforts to resolve the crisis in the former Yugoslavia. It authorized the humanitarian relief effort recently bolstered by the American airdrop of supplies to villages isolated by blockades and violence. It is cosponsoring efforts to negotiate a settlement designed to end the killing without rewarding aggression. It imposed the economic sanctions which we are tightening every day against Serbia and Montenegro. And the UN Security Council authorized the creation of a tribunal to sit in judgment of those who have committed war crimes and other violations of international humanitarian law. This is the first time since Nuremberg that such a tribunal has been authorized—a testament to the revulsion around the globe at the policies of ethnic cleansing and mass rape perpetrated during this conflict.

The UN is trying to do things that no one has ever attempted to do before. There is no manual for Bosnia. There is no easy way to deal with opponents of such ferocity and proven brutality as the Khmer Rouge. There is no simple remedy for the chaos of a Somalia. But history warns us that the challenges posed by these conflicts do not diminish when ignored, when aggression is appeased, atrocities rationalized, or disorder allowed to spill across national borders. These warnings of history have special meaning for those of us in the United States. For they remind us—looking back to the errors made after World War I—that America cannot turn its back on the world.

President Clinton has assumed office at a time when America is, in many ways, more inward looking than at any time in my memory. There is a mood that says, "Let's take care of our own; let's get our own house in order; let's leave the role of global Samaritan, global risk taker, global heavy lifter to someone else." The principal reason for all this is no secret. California's economic crisis exemplifies the first priority of the Clinton Administration: jobs and economic growth. There is far too much uncertainty about jobs, about our schools, about our ability to give our kids the same optimism for the future that we and generations before us had growing up in America. We know we have to give first priority to the problems we face at home. But the administration also knows that neither our history nor our character nor our self-interest will allow us to withdraw from the center stage of global political and economic life. It is the responsibility of leaders not simply to parrot public opinion, but also to shape it. And we have a responsibility to convey the fact that in today's world, domestic and foreign policy are no longer separable things.

Yes, it costs money to help keep peace around the world. But by any measure the most expensive peacekeeping mission is a bargain compared to the least expensive war—not just because it costs fewer dollars, but because it costs fewer lives, creates fewer refugees and orphans, and plants the seeds of future reconciliation, not future revenge. But for every $1,000 the world spends making or preparing for war, we still spend only $1.40 keeping the peace.

The UN will always have its skeptics—and that is healthy. But it seems to me that among the things most worth striving for in this world is the UN and what it represents. Because the UN reflects us—all of us. It is not perfect. It will make mistakes. But because it reflects what is best in us, we cannot allow it to fail. The diversity of the UN should not daunt or frustrate us; rather, our nation, more than any other, is a testament to what diversity united in a common cause can accomplish, and sadly, what diversity untended can do to the neighborhoods of our great cities. Either we confront head-on the racial problems at home and the ethnic divisions abroad, or we will slide further into crises that will have no end. We need to start finding endpoints to these crises, not excuses.

America was established in the name of freedom by those who had suffered persecution. The UN was established in the name of peace in San

Francisco by those who had just emerged from the most terrible war in history. Even when the path seems hard, great dreams are worth striving for. The aspirations represented by the UN reflect one of the great, shared dreams of humankind. The opportunity to make progress toward that dream has never been greater than it is today. With your help, we can build a partnership with the UN to promote peace, law, and respect for human dignity, and in so doing, we can forge a world which we will be proud to bequeath to our children and to theirs.

April 20, 1998

Kofi Annan

Secretary-General of the United Nations

In February 1998, UN Secretary-General Kofi Annan borrowed French President Jacques Chirac's jet and flew to Baghdad to stave off an escalating military confrontation in the Persian Gulf. Iraq had ejected UN weapons inspectors in autumn 1997, and the U.S. was beefing up military forces in the region in preparation for a showdown. At The Commonwealth Club two months later, Annan told the crowd in his low, even voice that before he had left to meet with Saddam Hussein, "the press made lots of comments about my being soft-spoken" and wanted to know: "'Are you ruthless enough to take on Saddam?' 'Do you have the stomach?'" Indeed, the day before he left, the last question after a talk Annan gave to the press was, "Mr. Secretary-General, are you tough enough for Saddam Hussein?" Annan's answer: "What a silly question, have a good day."

Annan's brief visit to Baghdad did produce immediate results: Iraq pledged to allow inspection of presidential palaces. Questioners at The Commonwealth Club wanted to know how Annan had convinced Saddam Hussein "to do something that he had sworn he would never do." "I reasoned with him," Annan said, "and we smoked a couple of cigars." Annan also shook hands with Saddam Hussein and drank orange juice with him, and came back declaring that the Iraqi leader was "a man I can do business with." Chirac (who had asked Annan to pass along his personal greetings to Saddam Hussein) welcomed Annan back with a state dinner and praised him for averting a world war. Access would be granted to the palaces, but inspectors would be accompanied by diplomats to ensure the sites received the "sensitive treatment" the Iraqis demanded. American critics howled appeasement. And chief UN weapons inspector Richard Butler said Annan had tried to "destroy" the UNSCOM (United Nations Special Commission) inspection process. The inspection process resumed two weeks before Annan spoke to The Club and, with the crisis averted, Annan's speech could focus on the bigger picture of transforming the United Nations and the world. It met with a warm reception.

After the U.S. had blocked reelection of his predecessor, Boutros Boutros-Ghali, Annan took office as secretary-general in January 1997. The first black African and first career UN official to hold the position, he had served most recently as head of UN peacekeeping operations—during which time peacekeepers had withdrawn in ignominy from Somalia; UN safe areas were overrun and civilians massacred during the conflict in Bosnia; and genocide in Rwanda went unchecked. In husky, measured tones, Annan hoped aloud before the San Francisco audience that "by the time I leave, the UN is considered as an organization that has renewed itself, and is responsive to the needs of the world, and it is seen as an organization that is doing what it was established to do. In other words, a United Nations that is focused, that is effective, and that is responsive." He had already succeeded in convincing perhaps the most vociferous UN critic of them all, U.S. Senator Jesse Helms, that the UN was streamlining its bureaucracy, with the result that Helms released nearly a billion dollars in unpaid American dues owed to the United Nations.

Four months after Annan's speech, in August, the Iraqis declared they would cease cooperation with UN inspectors, and inspectors were ordered out in October. U.S. and British bombers were airborne and within an hour of their targets when Annan received a letter from Saddam Hussein pledging cooperation. The inspectors' minuet with the Iraqi government resumed, but only for a few weeks. Inspectors were withdrawn in December, and U.S. bombing began on the sixteenth of that month. A year later, the UN introduced a new inspection body to take on the situation in Iraq; however, the Iraqis did not agree to the new inspections. Still, Annan's accomplishments did not go unrecognized: he flew to Oslo in December 2001 to receive the

Nobel Peace Prize, which had been awarded to him and the United Nations. (In the same month, he also appeared on Sesame Street to help resolve a conflict among Elmo and some of his friends.)

"The United Nations in Our Daily Lives"

I know that the San Francisco of song is a city of the heart, but for me it is also the city—the progressive, worldly city—where the soul of the United Nations was forged and made real. At this crucial juncture in world affairs, I am pleased to have this opportunity to hear what Californians have to say about the state of the world: where we've been, and more importantly, where we are going.

What is this crucial juncture to which I have just referred? It is a moment of promise and peril, an era of complexities and contradictions. Peace spreads in one region as hatred rages in another. Unprecedented wealth coexists with terrible deprivation. Globalization presents new opportunities and knits us closer together while intolerance keeps us apart.

The United Nations itself is also, to paraphrase Dickens, experiencing both the best and worst of times. The recent agreement with Baghdad on access by UN weapons inspectors shows what four united and determined international communities can achieve through the United Nations. This was neither a "victory" nor a "defeat" for any one person, nation, or group of nations; it was a victory for peace, for reason, for the resolution of conflict by diplomacy.

As we implement the agreement and seek full compliance with the Security Council's resolutions, my mind cannot help but turn to other challenges as well. For what we achieved in Iraq, we must also achieve across our entire agenda: the fight against drug trafficking, for example, or the struggle to uphold human rights, or the negotiations to establish an International Criminal Court. We need only summon the political will. I say "only" because I believe that political will is not finite, as some would argue; like the California sun, it is a renewable resource. So today I am emboldened to think ambitiously for our United Nations. At the same time, I am constrained and disturbed by the organization's precarious and perpetual financial instability. It is no exaggeration to say that the United Nations is on the edge: on the edge of scaling back its operations, on the edge of being unable to meet the most basic expectations of the world's people.

The United States is the biggest debtor, as is well known. Less publicized is the extent of other nations' arrears, which account for some 40 percent of the whole. Overall, only fifty-six nations have paid their current assessments. The lack of commitment runs wide and deep, despite the successful diplomacy with Baghdad; despite my "quiet revolution" of UN reform and renewal; and despite a long list of UN achievements spanning more than half a century. This problem hasn't gone away; it may be getting worse.

So this seems an appropriate time, and certainly the right place, to dwell on the meaning and presence of the United Nations in our daily lives. I would like to begin by dispelling a few myths.

First, we are not a bloated bureaucracy. Five times as many people work for McDonald's. UN staff size has been cut by 25 percent in the past decade, and last year's annual budget for our worldwide operations, including peacekeeping, was less than that of the city of San Francisco. Second, we are not a paper factory. The amount of paper we use for documents in a year is equivalent to that used by the *New York Times* for a single Sunday edition. Third, we have no designs on America's or any other country's property and land. Those UNESCO "World Heritage List" or "Biosphere Reserve" designations you may have heard about for places such as Yosemite, Yellowstone, or the Grand Canyon merely state the obvious: these are glorious places of rare natural beauty or distinction, worthy of touring, preservation, or both. Finally, as for those notorious black helicopters, the idea would be laughable were it not also so tragic.[1] We have no helicopters of our own. The ones governments give us for peacekeeping are painted white. When crisis erupts, as it did in Rwanda four years ago, the ability to respond quickly can mean the difference between life and death. But without any troops or

1. Sightings of the "notorious" black helicopters began to be covered in the U.S. media in the early 1990s and, fueled by right-wing talk radio and militia publications, peaked in the middle of the decade. Reputedly spotted across the United States (some Arizona residents claimed they witnessed the helicopters following UFOs into clandestine mountain hideaways), the helicopters were alleged to be property of "multijurisdictional task forces" of the UN and officials at the U.S. Federal Emergency Management Agency bent on overthrowing the country by coup. In 1995, Idaho Congresswoman Helen Chenoweth convened a hearing on the mysterious aircraft to address her constituents' concerns. The black helicopters were found to belong to state wildlife officers patrolling for poachers.

equipment of its own, the United Nations is put in the position of needing to build a firehouse from scratch every time a fire breaks out.

This is a prescription for ineffective action. I am in no way calling for a standing army, but there is a gap to be filled. Dozens of nations have earmarked troops that could stand on the ready in their home countries and be available for rapid deployment, and it is my hope that this will help and not just be a quicker way to hear "no" for an answer when a crisis erupts and we go scavenging for troops.

But if these are all the things the United Nations is not, what are we? What does the United Nations mean to you? Is its day-to-day work present in your lives? Here in San Francisco and around the world, the big picture is familiar: the UN as an advocate of universal values such as equality and tolerance, justice and progress, democracy and peace, harmony among peoples and nations. Most people also know a fair amount about our work on the ground: our blue-helmeted peacekeepers; our programs of disaster relief, refugee protection, and electoral monitoring; our immunization of children against deadly diseases—efforts which have brought the UN system seven Nobel Peace Prizes. As familiar as we are, however, I know that sometimes the United Nations can seem very remote, especially in the developed world. Our activities take place in conflict zones you will rarely if ever visit; in impoverished areas far from major tourist sites; or behind the scenes, in clinics and classrooms where progress occurs without bells and whistles and is measured steadily but slowly.

Media reports can bring you closer. Sometimes they generate concern and prompt people to get involved. But they also do the opposite, accentuating the distance between your lives, in one of the world's richest nations, and their lives somewhere else, somewhere poorer and less secure. A sense of common humanity is our saving grace; it is why the United Nations was created and why polls show such strong American support for the organization at the grassroots level, regardless of what is said and done on Capitol Hill. But I would also like to suggest that even here, in the United States, Americans need look no further than your own lives to experience the United Nations system at work.

Consider the last twenty-four hours of my own life. I flew to San Francisco yesterday afternoon, enjoying a smooth flight while reading and watching an in-flight movie, *As Good As It Gets*—an appropriate title! After settling into my hotel, I made a few telephone calls. Dinner last night featured some fine California wine and seafood. Before going to sleep I watched the news on television. And prior to joining you here today, I ate a light California breakfast of fresh fruit and whole grain bread.

Where is the UN family to be found in such ordinary scenes of day-to-day life? Let's examine this picture again, this time in slow motion. I said that I'd had a smooth flight. Thanks to the International Civil Aviation Organization, there are global standards for airplane and airport safety; a common language, English, for aviation communications; and standards for the performance of pilots, flight crews, air traffic controllers, and ground and maintenance crews. I should also mention the World Meteorological Organization and its World Meteorological Vigil System, which enables planes to pick safe routes through stormy skies. And let us not forget the in-flight entertainment, and the fact that the World Intellectual Property Organization helps protect copyrights for one of California's major exports: movies.

Next, I said I made a few telephone calls. Since taking office, I've rarely been more than a few feet from a telephone. This is sometimes an intrusion on my privacy, but more often it is quite convenient: I can enjoy a walk in the woods while doing business. So I am grateful for the International Telecommunication Union, which helps connect national communications infrastructures into global networks, and which manages the sharing of radio frequencies and satellite orbital positions. The news I watched last night, including reports from abroad, also owes no small debt to the ITU.

As for my meals, Californians need no lessons from anyone about growing high-quality produce; your Central Valley is one of the wonders of the world. Even here the United Nations plays a part. The Food and Agricultural Organization and the World Health Organization set international norms for food additives and limits for pesticide residues. The International Labour Organization promotes safe working conditions for migrant farmworkers. The United Nations Convention on the Law of the Sea, meanwhile, stipulates that coastal states have sovereign rights over natural resources and certain other economic activities in a two-hundred-nautical-mile exclusive economic zone, meaning that California's waters are protected from fishing armadas from other countries.

This is not world government; it is sovereign nations such as the United States coming together in common use. Nor is this intrusive; it is pragmatic problem-solving. The United Nations is your tool, your vehicle, your instrument; it exists to help nations navigate the new landscapes of international life. So let us not think in terms of your lives and their lives, but of our lives. If you thought that the United Nations was something of a charity, existing only for the poor and less fortunate on Earth, think again—for Americans are not only giving to the United Nations, you are living the United Nations.

Friends, I took office pledging to bring this organization closer to the people it exists to serve. We are getting there: sometimes in massive operations; sometimes in small actions; in all cases guided by the Charter. We are making direct and vital connections with your daily lives and aspirations. But I need your help. I need your ideas, your energies, your voices. I especially need you to make sure your elected officials know how much you care about the United Nations. Let us, together, build and protect the fragile edifices of peace in the fullest sense of that word.

February 26, 1999

William Jefferson Clinton

President of the United States of America

The speech that President Clinton delivered at San Francisco's Grand Hyatt Hotel in February 1999 was the first foreign policy address he had made in a year. The tone was somber; there weren't many applause lines. Underscoring the importance of the talk, Secretary of State Madeleine Albright and National Security Adviser Sandy Berger joined the president onstage. Behind them hung a backdrop declaring, "American Leadership for Peace, Prosperity and Freedom." Clinton staked out the foreign policy agenda for his last two years in office—and for the United States in the twenty-first century.

Clinton had already achieved some success in the capacity of peacemaker in Haiti, Northern Ireland, and even in the Middle East, where he would push hardest for a peace agreement between Israeli leaders and Palestinian leader Yasser Arafat in 2000. The record of American leadership in Rwanda and Bosnia was less exemplary; and critics claimed Clinton's hopes that China, if further engaged through trade, might be forced to alter its repressive human rights policies were naïvely optimistic. Indeed, the very day that Clinton spoke to The Commonwealth Club, the U.S. State Department issued its annual human rights report: running to more than five thousand pages and covering 194 countries, the report noted China's human rights record had "deteriorated sharply" in the past year. (The report also noted that Afghanistan under the Taliban was the site of "perhaps the most severe abuse of women's human rights in the world.") With Mexico, Clinton advocated working more closely to combat illicit drug trafficking, and he certified that Mexico was "cooperating fully" with the U.S. in this effort. Some, including California Senator Dianne Feinstein, saw this as a charade. A *San Francisco Chronicle* editorial called it a "contradiction of record and rhetoric."

Clinton reserved his own harshest rhetoric for Yugoslav President Slobodan Milosevic, whose record from the previous year included a military campaign against guerrilla insurgents in Kosovo. The Kosovo Liberation Army (KLA) was fighting for the independence of Kosovo from Yugoslavia. Populated largely by ethnic Albanians, Kosovo had enjoyed greater autonomy before Milosevic became president of Yugoslavia and assumed direct control over the region. In February 1999, Kosovar Albanians and Serb leaders spent nine days in the first round of peace talks in Rambouillet, France. The Kosovar Albanians said they would sign an agreement when talks resumed in March. But on the same day that Clinton issued warnings to Milosevic from The Commonwealth Club podium, Serbian forces massed tanks and armored vehicles on ridges for an attack on KLA rebels, and elsewhere Serbian forces were cutting branches and saplings to camouflage their armor—activities Yugoslav military leaders described as a "winter training exercise."

Fighting continued in Kosovo, and on March 15 Kosovar Albanians accepted the peace agreement. The Serb delegation refused to sign it. So on March 24, following a failed last-ditch peace effort by U.S. negotiator Richard Holbrooke, NATO launched air strikes on Belgrade, attacking a sovereign European capital for the first time in the alliance's history. Serb forces responded with a brutal campaign of ethnic cleansing in Kosovo, which only ended in June, when Yugoslavia began withdrawing its forces in Kosovo and the province became a UN-administered region.

"A State of the Union for Foreign Policy"

For the first time since before the rise of fascism early in this century, there is no overriding threat to our survival or our freedom. Perhaps for the first time in history, the world's leading nations are not engaged in a struggle with each other for security or territory. The world clearly is coming together.

Since 1945, global trade has grown fifteen-fold, raising living standards on every continent. Freedom is expanding; for the first time in history, more than half the world's people elect their own leaders. Access to information by ordinary people the world over is literally exploding. Because of these developments, and the dramatic increase in our own prosperity and confidence in this, the longest peacetime economic expansion in our history, the United States has the opportunity and, I would argue, the solemn responsibility to shape a more peaceful, prosperous, democratic world in the twenty-first century.

We must, however, begin this discussion with a little history and a little humility. Listen to this quote by another American leader, at the dawn of a new century: "The world's products are exchanged as never before, and with increasing transportation comes increasing knowledge and larger trade. We travel greater distances in a shorter space of time, and with more ease, than was ever dreamed of. The same important news is read, though in different languages, the same day, in all the world. Isolation is no longer possible. No nation can longer be indifferent to any other."

That was said by President William McKinley one hundred years ago. What we now call globalization was well underway even then. We, in fact, had more diplomatic posts in the world than we have today, and foreign investment actually played a larger role in our own economy then than it does today. The optimism being expressed about the twentieth century by President McKinley and others at that time was not all that much different from the hopes commonly expressed today about the twenty-first. The rise in global trade and communications did lift countless lives then, just as it does today. But it did not stop the world's wealthiest nations from waging World War I and World War II. It did not stop the Depression, or the Holocaust, or communism. Had leading nations acted decisively then, perhaps these disasters might have been prevented. But the League of Nations failed, and America—well, our principal involvement in the world was commercial and cultural, unless and until we were attacked.

After World War II, our leaders took a different course. Harry Truman came to this city and said that to change the world away from a world in which might makes right, "words are not enough. We must once and for all prove by our acts conclusively that right has might." He and his allies and their successors built a network of security alliances to preserve the peace, and a global financial system to preserve prosperity.

Over the last six years, we have been striving to renew those arrangements and to create new ones for the challenges of the next fifty years. We have made progress, but there is so very much more to do. We cannot assume today that globalization alone will wash away the forces of destruction at the dawn of the twenty-first century, any more than it did at the dawn of the twentieth century. We cannot assume it will bring freedom and prosperity to ordinary citizens around the world who long for them. We cannot assume it will avoid environmental and public health disasters. We cannot assume that because we are now secure, we Americans do not need military strength or alliances, or that because we are prosperous, we are not vulnerable to financial turmoil half a world away.

The world we want to leave our children and grandchildren requires us to make the right choices, and some of them will be difficult. America has always risen to great causes, yet we have a tendency, still, to believe that we can go back to minding our own business when we're done. Today we must embrace the inexorable logic of globalization—that everything, from the strength of our economy to the safety of our cities, to the health of our people, depends on events not only within our borders, but half a world away. We must see the opportunities and the dangers of the interdependent world in which we are clearly fated to live. There is still the potential for major regional wars that would threaten our security. The arms race between India and Pakistan reminds us that the next big war could still be nuclear.[1] There is a risk that our former adversaries will not succeed in their transitions to freedom and free markets. There is a danger that deadly weapons will fall into the hands of a terrorist group or an outlaw nation, and that those weapons could be chemical or biological. There is a danger of deadly alliances among terrorists, narco-traffickers, and organized criminal groups. There is a danger of global environmental crises and the spread of deadly diseases. There is a danger that global financial turmoil will undermine open markets, overwhelm open societies, and undercut our own prosperity.

1. India announced its possession of nuclear weapons with five nuclear tests in May 1998. After expressing alarm, Pakistan detonated its first nuclear weapon. The U.S. imposed sanctions on both countries. In May 1999, India launched air strikes against Pakistani-backed forces in Kashmir. The conflict did not go nuclear.

We must avoid both the temptation to minimize these dangers, and the illusion that the proper response to them is to batten down the hatches and protect America against the world. The promise of our future lies in the world. Therefore, we must work hard with the world—to defeat the dangers we face together and to build this hopeful moment together, into a generation of peace, prosperity, and freedom. Because of our unique position, America must lead with confidence in our strengths and with a clear vision of what we seek to avoid and what we seek to advance.

Our first challenge is to build a more peaceful twenty-first century world. To that end, we're renewing alliances that extend the area where wars do not happen, and working to stop the conflicts that are claiming lives and threatening our interests right now. The century's bloodiest wars began in Europe. That's why I've worked hard to build a Europe that finally is undivided, democratic, and at peace. We want all of Europe to have what America helped build in Western Europe—a community that upholds common standards of human rights, where people have the confidence and security to invest in the future, where nations cooperate to make war unthinkable. That is why I have pushed hard for NATO's enlargement and why we must keep NATO's doors open to new democratic members, so that other nations will have an incentive to deepen their democracies. We are building a stronger alliance with Japan, and renewing our commitment to deter aggression in Korea, and intensifying our efforts for a genuine peace there. We also create a more peaceful world by building new partnerships in Asia, Africa, and Latin America.

Ten years ago we were shouting at each other across a North-South chasm defined by our differences. Today, we are engaged in a new dialogue that speaks the language of common interests—of trade and investment; of education and health; of democracies that deliver not corruption and despair, but progress and hope; of a common desire that children in all our countries will be free of the scourge of drugs. Through these efforts to strengthen old alliances and build new partnerships, we advance the prospects for peace. However, the work of actually making peace is harder and often far more contentious.

It's easy, for example, to say that we really have no interest in who lives in this or that valley in Bosnia, or who owns a strip of brushland in the Horn of Africa, or some piece of parched earth by the Jordan River. But the true measure of our interests lies not in how small or distant these places are, or in whether we have trouble pronouncing their names. The question we must ask is, what are the consequences to our security of letting conflicts fester and spread? We cannot, indeed, we should not, do everything or be everywhere. But where our values and our interests are at stake, and where we can make a difference, we must be prepared to do so. And we must remember that the real challenge of foreign policy is to deal with problems before they harm our national interests.

It's also easy to say that peacemaking is simply doomed, where people are embittered by generations of hate, where the old animosities of race and religion and ethnic difference raise their hoary heads. But I will never forget the day that the leaders of Israel and the Palestinian Authority came to the White House, in September of 1993, to sign their peace accord. At that moment, the question arose—and indeed, based on the pictures afterward, it seemed to be the main question—whether if, in front of the entire world, Prime Minister Rabin and Chairman Arafat would actually shake hands for the first time.

It was an interesting and occasionally humorous discussion. But it ended when Yitzhak Rabin, a soldier for a lifetime, said to me, "Mr. President, I have been fighting this man for a lifetime, thirty years. I have buried a lot of my own people in the process. But you do not make peace with your friends."

It is in our interest to be a peacemaker, not because we think we can make all these differences go away, but because, in over two hundred years of hard effort here at home, and with bitter and good experiences around the world, we have learned that the world works better when differences are resolved by the force of argument rather than the force of arms.

That is why I am proud of the work we have done to support peace in Northern Ireland, and why we will keep pressing the leaders there to observe not just the letter, but the spirit of the Good Friday Accord.

It is also why I intend to use the time I have remaining in this office to push for a comprehensive peace in the Middle East, to encourage Israelis and Palestinians to reach a just and final settlement, and to stand by our friends for peace, such as Jordan. The people of the Middle East can do it, but time is precious, and they can't afford to waste any more of it. In their hearts, they know there can be no security or justice for any who live in that small and sacred land until there is security and justice for all who live there. If they do their part, we must do ours.

We will also keep working with our allies to build peace in the Balkans. Three years ago, we helped to end the war in Bosnia. A lot of doubters then thought it would soon start again. But Bosnia is on a steady path toward renewal and democracy. We've been able to reduce our troops there by 75 percent as peace has taken hold, and we will continue to bring them home.

The biggest remaining danger to this progress has been the fighting and the repression in Kosovo. Kosovo is, after all, where the violence in the former Yugoslavia began, over a decade ago, when they lost the autonomy guaranteed under Yugoslav law. We have a clear national interest in ensuring that Kosovo is where this trouble ends. If it continues, it almost certainly will draw in Albania and Macedonia, which share borders with Kosovo, and on which clashes have already occurred.

Potentially, it could affect our allies, Greece and Turkey. It could spark tensions in Bosnia itself, jeopardizing the gains made there. If the conflict continues, there will certainly be more atrocities, more refugees, more victims crying out for justice and seeking out revenge.

Last fall, a quarter of a million displaced people in Bosnia were facing cold and hunger in the hills. Using diplomacy backed by force, we brought them home and slowed the fighting.

For seventeen days this month, outside Paris, we sought with our European partners an agreement that would end the fighting for good. Progress was made toward a common understanding of Kosovo's autonomy—progress that would not have happened, I want to say, but for the unity of our allies and the tireless leadership of our Secretary of State, Madeleine Albright.

Here's where we are. Kosovar Albanian leaders have agreed in principle to a plan that would protect the rights of their people and give them substantial self-government. Serbia has agreed to much, but not all, of the conditions of autonomy, and has so far not agreed to the necessity of a NATO-led international force to maintain the peace there.

Serbia's leaders must now accept that only by allowing people in Kosovo control over their day-to-day lives—as, after all, they have been promised under Yugoslav law —it is only by doing that can they keep their country intact. Both sides must return to the negotiations on March 15 with a clear mandate for peace. In the meantime, President Milosevic should understand that this is a time for restraint, not repression. And if he does not, NATO is prepared to act.

Now, if there is a peace agreement that is effective, NATO must also be ready to deploy to Kosovo, to give both sides the confidence to lay down their arms. Europeans would provide the great bulk of such a force, roughly 85 percent. But if there is a real peace, America must do its part as well.

Kosovo is not an easy problem. But if we don't stop the conflict now, it clearly will spread. And then we will not be able to stop it, except at far greater cost and risk.

A second challenge we face is to bring our former adversaries, Russia and China, into the international system as open, prosperous, stable nations. The way both countries develop in the coming century will have a lot to do with the future of our planet.

For fifty years, we confronted the challenge of Russia's strength. Today, we must confront the risk of a Russia weakened by the legacy of communism and also by its inability at the moment to maintain prosperity at home or control the flow of its money, weapons, and technology across its borders.

The dimensions of this problem are truly enormous. Eight years after the Soviet collapse, the Russian people are hurting. The economy is shrinking, making the future uncertain. Yet we have as much of a stake today in Russia overcoming these challenges as we did in checking its expansion during the Cold War. This is not a time for complacency or self-fulfilling pessimism. Let's not forget that Russia's people have overcome enormous obstacles before. And just this decade, with no living memory of democracy or freedom to guide them, they have built a country more open to the world than ever; a country with a free press and a robust, even raucous debate; a country that should see in the first year of the new millennium the first peaceful democratic transfer of power in its thousand-year history.

The Russian people will decide their own future. But we must work with them for the best possible outcome, with realism and with patience. If Russia does what it must to make its economy work, I am ready to do everything I can to mobilize adequate international support for them. With the right framework, we will also encourage foreign investment in its factories, its energy fields, its people. We will increase our support for small business and for the independent media. We will work to continue cutting our two nations' nuclear arsenals and help Russia prevent both its weapons and its expertise from falling into the wrong hands.

The question China faces is how best to assure its stability and progress. Will it choose openness and engagement? Or will it choose to limit the aspirations of its people without fully embracing the global rules of the road? In my judgment, only the first path can really answer the challenges China faces.

We cannot minimize them. China has made incredible progress in lifting people out of poverty and building a new economy. But now its rate of economic growth is declining—just as it is needed to create jobs for a growing, and increasingly more mobile, population. Most of China's economy is still stifled by state control. We can see in China the kinds of problems a society faces when it is moving away from the rule of fear but is not yet rooted in the rule of law.

China's leaders know more economic reform is needed, and they know reform will cause more unemployment, and they know that can cause unrest. At the same time, and perhaps for those reasons, they remain unwilling to open up their political system, to give people a peaceful outlet for dissent.

Now, we Americans know that dissent is not always comfortable, not always easy, and often raucous. But I believe that the fact that we have peaceful, orderly outlets for dissent is one of the principal reasons we're still around here as the longest lasting freely elected government in the world. And I believe, sooner or later, China will have to come to understand that a society, in the world we're living in—particularly a country as great and old and rich and full of potential as China—simply cannot purchase stability at the expense of freedom.

On the other hand, we have to ask ourselves: What is the best thing to do to try to maximize the chance that China will take the right course, and that, because of that, the world will be freer, more peaceful, more prosperous in the twenty-first century? I do not believe we can hope to bring change to China if we isolate China from the forces of change. Of course, we have our differences, and we must press them. But we can do that, and expand our cooperation, through principled and purposeful engagement with China, its government, and its people.

Our third great challenge is to build a future in which our people are safe from the dangers that arise, perhaps halfway around the world—dangers from nuclear proliferation, from terrorism, from drugs, from the multiple catastrophes that could arise from climate change.

Each generation faces the challenges of not trying to fight the last war. In our case, that means recognizing that the more likely future threat to our existence is not a strategic nuclear strike from Russia or China, but the use of weapons of mass destruction by an outlaw nation or a terrorist group.

In the last six years, fighting that threat has become a central priority of American foreign policy. Here, too, there is much more to be done. We are working to stop weapons from spreading at the source, as with Russia. We are working to keep Iraq in check so that it does not threaten the rest of the world or its region with weapons of mass destruction. We are using all the means at our disposal to deny terrorists safe havens, weapons, and funds. Even if it takes years, terrorists must know there is no place to hide.

Recently, we tracked down the gunman who killed two of our people outside the CIA six years ago.[1] We are training and equipping our local fire, police, and medical personnel to deal with chemical, biological, and nuclear emergencies, and improving our public health surveillance system, so that if a biological weapon is released, we can detect it and save lives. We are working to protect our critical computer systems from sabotage.

Many of these subjects are new and unfamiliar, and may be frightening. As I said when I gave an address in Washington not very long ago about what we were doing on biological and computer security and criminal threats, it is important that we have the right attitude about this. It is important that we understand that the risks are real and they require, therefore, neither denial nor panic. As long as people organize themselves in human societies, there will be organized forces of destruction who seek to take advantage of new means of destroying other people.

And the whole history of conflict can be seen in part as the race of defensive measures to catch up with offensive capabilities. That is what we're doing in dealing with the computer challenges today; that is what we are doing in dealing with the biological challenges today. It is very important that the American people, without panic, be serious and deliberate about them, because it is the kind of challenge that we have faced repeatedly. And as long as our country and the world is around, unless there is some completely unforeseen change in human nature, our successors will have to do the same.

1. Mir Aimal Kasi, a Pakistani native, shot five people outside CIA headquarters in January 1993 to protest U.S. treatment of Muslim countries. He used a Chinese-made AK-47-style assault rifle and ammunition purchased at a gun store in the U.S. He was captured in Pakistan in June 1997 and taken back to the U.S. by FBI agents, to whom he said he had wanted to kill CIA head James Woolsey. He was convicted of murder in November 1997 and sentenced to death.

We are working to develop a national missile defense system which could, if we decide to deploy it, be deployed against emerging ballistic missile threats from rogue nations. We are bolstering the global agreements that curb proliferation. That's the most important thing we can be doing right now. This year, we hope to achieve an accord to strengthen compliance with the Convention against Biological Weapons.[1] It's a perfectly good convention, but, frankly, it has no teeth. We have to give it some. And we will ask our Senate to ratify the Comprehensive Test Ban Treaty[2] to stop nations from testing nuclear weapons, so they're constrained from developing new ones.

Again, I say: I implore the United States Senate to ratify the Comprehensive Test Ban Treaty this year. It is very important for the United States and the world.

Our security and our safety also depend upon doing more to protect our people from the scourge of drugs. To win this fight, we must work with others, including and especially Mexico. Mexico has a serious drug problem, increasingly affecting more of its own young people. No one understands this better than President Ernesto Zedillo. He described it as the number one threat to his country's security, its people, its democracy. He is working hard to establish clean government, true democracy, and the rule of law. He is working hard to tackle the corruption traffickers have wrought.

He cannot win this battle alone, and neither can we. In any given year, the narco-traffickers may spend hundreds of millions of dollars to try to suborn Mexican law enforcement officials, most of whom work for under ten thousand dollars a year.

1. Signed in 1975, the Biological Weapons Convention is meant to prevent countries from developing, producing, stockpiling, or obtaining means to employ biological weapons. President Clinton was concerned that, while more than 140 countries had signed on, the convention still lacked provisions for enforcing commitments through mandatory declarations and inspections.
2. President Clinton became the first world leader to sign the Comprehensive Test Ban Treaty (CTBT) when he did so in September 1996. By the following November, when Clinton sent the treaty to the U.S. Senate for ratification, nearly one hundred and fifty countries had signed, and eight had ratified the treaty. But the U.S. Senate did not allow the treaty to go to a vote until October 1999, when it was defeated 51 to 48. Americans who oppose the treaty have cited among their reasons that it is not verifiable and not enforceable; that in ending nuclear testing it undercuts U.S. security; and that it puts the U.S. on the path toward nuclear disarmament. As of this writing, one hundred and twelve countries have ratified the treaty.

As I certified to Congress today, Mexico is cooperating with us in the battle for our lives. And I believe the American people will be safer in this, as in so many other ways, if we fight drugs with Mexico, rather than walk away.

Another global danger we face is climate change. As far as we can tell, with all the scientific evidence available, the hottest years our planet has ever experienced were 1997 and 1998. Nine of the ten hottest years recorded in the last several centuries occurred in the last decade.

Now, we can wait and hope and do nothing, and try to ignore what the vast majority of scientists tell us is a pattern that is fixed and continuing. We could ignore the record-breaking temperatures, the floods, the storms, the droughts that have caused such misery. Or we can accept that preventing the disease and destruction climate change can bring will be infinitely cheaper than letting future generations try to clean up the mess, especially when you consider that greenhouse gases, once emitted into the atmosphere, last and have a destructive environmental effect for at least one hundred years.

We took a giant step forward in 1997 when we helped to forge the Kyoto agreement. Now we're working to persuade developing countries that they, too, can and must participate meaningfully in this effort without forgoing growth. We are also trying to persuade a majority in the United States Congress that we can do the same thing.

The approach I have taken in America is not to rely on a whole raft of new regulations, and not to propose big energy taxes, but instead to offer tax incentives and dramatic increases in investment in new technologies, because we know now that we have the technological capacity to break the iron link between Industrial Age energy-use patterns and economic growth. You're proving it in California every day, with stiffer environmental standards than other states have.

We know that the technology is just beginning to emerge to allow us to have clean cars and other clean forms of transportation; to dramatically increase the capacity of all of our buildings to keep out heat and cold, and to let in more light. We know that the conservation potential of what we have right now available has only just been scratched. And we must convince the world, and critical decision makers in the United States, to change their minds about a big idea—namely, that the only way a country can grow is to consume more energy resources in a way that does more to increase global warming.

One of the most interesting conversations I had when I was in China was with the environmental minister there, who thanked me for going there to do an environmental event, because he was having trouble convincing the government that they could continue to lift the Chinese people out of poverty and still improve the environment. This is a central, big idea that people all over the world will have to change their minds about before we will be open and free to embrace the technological advances that are lying evident all around us. And all of you that can have any impact on that, I implore you to do it.

Our fourth challenge is to create a world trading and financial system that will lift the lives of ordinary people on every continent around the world. Or, as it has been stated in other places, to put a human face on the global economy. Over the last six years, we've taken giant steps in opening the global trading system. The United States alone has concluded over two hundred and seventy different trade agreements. Once again, we are the world's largest exporting nation. There is a lot more to be done.

In the first five years of my presidency, about 30 percent of our growth came from expanding trade. Last year, we had a good year, but we didn't have much growth from expanding trade because of the terrible difficulties of the people in Asia, in Russia, and because of the slowdown in growth in Latin America, and because we did not reach out to seize new possibilities in Africa. Those people are suffering more, and our future prospects are being constrained.

The question is what to do about it. Some of the folks outside who were protesting when I drove up were saying by their signs that they believe globalization is inherently bad and there's no way in the wide world to put a human face on the global economy. But if you look at the facts of the last thirty years, hundreds of millions of people have had their economic prospects advanced on every continent because they have finally been able to find a way to express their creativity in positive terms, and produce goods and services that could be purchased around the borders of their nation.

Now, the question is, how do we deal with the evident challenges and problems that we face in high relief today, and seize the benefit that we know comes from expanding trade? I've asked for a new round of global trade negotiations to expand exports of services, foreign products, and manufacturers. I am still determined to reach agreement on a free trade area of the Americas. If it hadn't been for our expansion in Latin America, from

Mexico all the way to the southern tip of South America, we would have been in much worse shape this last year.

But trade is not an end in itself. It has to work for ordinary people; it has to contribute to the wealth and fairness of societies. It has to reinforce the values that give meaning to life, not simply in the United States, but in the poorest countries, struggling to lift their people to their dreams. That's why we're working to build a trading system that upholds the rights of workers and consumers, and helps us and them, in other countries, to protect the environment, so that competition among nations is a race to the top, not the bottom. This year we will lead the international community to conclude a treaty to ban abusive child labor everywhere in the world.[1]

The gains of global economic exchange have been real and dramatic. But when the tides of capital first flood emerging markets, and then abruptly recede; when bank failures and bankruptcies grip entire economies; when millions who have worked their way into the middle class are plunged suddenly into poverty; the need for reform of the international financial system is clear.

I don't want to minimize the complexity of this challenge. As nations began to trade more, and as investment rules began to permit people to invest in countries other than their own more, it became more and more necessary to facilitate the conversion of currencies. Whenever you do that, you will create a market against risk, just in the transfer of currencies. Whenever you do that, you will have people that are moving money around because they think the value of the money itself will change, and profit might be gained in an independent market of currency exchange.

It is now true that on any given day there is $1.5 trillion of currency exchange in the world—many, many, many times more than the actual value of the exchange of goods and services. And we have got to find a way to facilitate the movement of money—without which trade and investment cannot occur—in a way that avoids these dramatic cycles of boom and then bust which have led to the collapse of economic activity in so many countries around the world.

1. At a special ceremony at the World Trade Organization meeting in Seattle in December 1999, President Clinton signed the International Labor Organization's Convention 182, "the Convention Concerning the Prohibition and Immediate Action for Elimination of the Worst Forms of Child Labor." The protocols were adopted by the UN, prohibiting forceful recruitment of children for use in armed conflict and protecting children from slavery, prostitution, and pornography. Clinton signed them in July 2000.

We found a way to do it in the United States after the Great Depression. And thank goodness we have never again had a Great Depression, even though we've had good times and bad times. That is the challenge facing the world financial system today.

The leading economies have got a lot of work to do. We have to do everything we can—not just the United States, but Europe and Japan—to spur economic growth. Unless there is a restoration of growth, all the changes in the financial rules we make will not get Asia, Latin America, or Russia out of their difficulties.

We have to be ready to provide quick and decisive help to nations committed to sound policies. We have to help nations build social safety nets so that, when they have inevitable changes in their economic conditions, people at least have the basic security they need to continue to embrace change and advance the overall welfare of society.

We have to encourage nations to maintain open, properly regulated financial systems so that decisions are shaped by informed market decisions and not distorted by corruption. We also have to take responsible steps to reform the global financial architecture for the twenty-first century.

In the meanwhile, we have to recognize that the United States has made a great contribution to keeping this crisis from being worse than it would have been by helping to get money to Brazil, to Russia, to other countries, and by keeping our own markets open. If you compare, for example, our import patterns with those of Europe or those of Japan, you will see that we have far, far more open markets. It has worked to make us competitive and productive. We also have the lowest unemployment rate in the entire world among all advanced countries now, something that many people thought would never happen again.

On the other hand, we cannot let other countries' difficulties in our open markets become an excuse for them to violate international trade rules and dump products illegally on our markets. We've had enough problems in America this year and last year—in agriculture and aerospace, especially—from countries that could no longer afford to buy products, many of which they had already offered. Then, in the last several months, we've seen an enormous problem in this country in our steel industry because of evident dumping of products in the American market that violated the law. So I want you to know what while I will do everything to keep our markets open, I intend while this crisis persists to do everything I can to enforce our trade laws.

Our fifth challenge is to keep freedom as a top goal for the world of the twenty-first century. Countries like South Korea and Thailand have proven in this financial crisis that open societies are more resilient, that elected governments have a legitimacy to make hard choices in hard times. But if democracies over the long run aren't able to deliver for their people, to take them out of economic turmoil, the pendulum that swung so decisively toward freedom over the last few years could swing back, and the next century could begin as badly as this one began in that regard. Therefore, beyond economics, beyond the transformation of the great countries to economic security—Russia and China—beyond many of our security concerns, we also have to recognize that we can have no greater purpose than to support the right of other people to live in freedom and shape their own destiny. If that right could be universally exercised, virtually every goal I have outlined today would be advanced.

We have to keep standing by those who risk their own freedom to win it for others. Today we're releasing our annual Human Rights Report. The message of the Human Rights Report is often resented, but always respected for its candor, its consistency for what it says about our country and our values. We need to deepen democracy where it's already taking root by helping our partners narrow their income gaps, strengthen their legal institutions, and build well-educated, healthy societies.

This year, we will see profoundly important developments in the potential transition to democracy in two critical countries—Indonesia and Nigeria. Both have the capacity to lift their entire regions if they succeed, and to swamp them in a sea of disorder if they fail. In the coming year and beyond, we must make a concentrated effort to help them achieve what will be the world's biggest victories for freedom since 1989.

Nigeria is the most populous country in Africa. Tomorrow, it holds its first free presidential election, after a dictatorship that made it the poorest oil-rich country in the world.[1] We are providing support for the transition, and if it succeeds, we have to be prepared to do more. Because we count on further progress, today we are also waiving the sanctions we imposed when its government did not cooperate in the fight against drugs.

1. Nigeria's elections on February 27, 1999, ushered in, as the BBC put it, the " most important political transition in Africa since the end of apartheid." General Olusegun Obasanjo, backed by the People's Democratic Party, won more than 60 percent of the vote in an election that, while marked by cheating, was deemed to be valid by most international observers.

Indonesia is the fourth-largest nation and the largest Islamic country in the entire world. In June, it will hold what we hope will be its first truly democratic election in more than forty years.[1] Indonesia desperately needs a government that can help it overcome its economic crisis while maintaining the support of its people. We are helping to strengthen the social safety net for its people in providing the largest contribution of any nation to support the coming elections.

Whether these struggles are far or near, their outcome will profoundly affect us. Whether a child in Africa or Southeast Asia or Russia or China can grow up educated, healthy, safe, free from violence, free of hate, full of hope, and free to decide his or her own destiny, this will have a lot to do with the life our children have as they grow up. It will help to determine if our children go to war, have jobs, have clean air, have safe streets.

For our nation to be strong, we must maintain a consensus that seemingly distant problems can come home if they are not addressed, and addressed promptly. We must recognize we cannot lift ourselves to the heights to which we aspire if the world is not rising with us. I say again, the inexorable logic of globalization is the genuine recognition of interdependence. We cannot wish into being the world we seek. Talk is cheap; decisions are not. That is why I have asked Congress to reverse the decline in defense spending that began in 1985, and I am hopeful and confident that we can get bipartisan majorities in both houses to agree. I hope it will also agree to give more support to our diplomats, and to programs that keep our soldiers out of war; to fund assistance programs to keep nations on a stable path to democracy and growth; and to finally pay both our dues and our debts to the United Nations. In an interdependent world, we cannot lead if we expect to lead only on our own terms, and never on our own nickel. We can't be a first-class power if we're only prepared to pay for steerage.

I hope all of you, as citizens, believe that we have to seize the responsibilities that we have today with confidence—to keep taking risks for peace; to keep forging opportunities for our people, and seeking them for others as well; to seek to put a genuinely human face on the global economy; to keep

1. In June 1999, the long-awaited free elections in Indonesia led to the victory of Megawati Sukarnoputri's Indonesian Democratic Party-Struggle (PDI-P) and ultimately to her selection has president. For four decades, the country had been led by authoritarian rulers Sukarno (1955–1965) and Suharto (1965–1998). Suharto had allowed for six elections during his reign, but only under tightly controlled conditions that ensured his Golkar Party always won.

faith with all those around the world who struggle for human rights, the rule of law, a better life; to look on our leadership not as a burden, but as a welcome opportunity; to build the future we dream for our children in these, the final days of the twentieth century, and the coming dawn of the next. The story of the twenty-first century can be quite a wonderful story. But we have to write the first chapter.

April 6, 1999

Mavis Leno

Chair, Feminist Majority's Campaign to Stop Gender Apartheid

It had been just over ten years since the Soviet withdrawal from Afghanistan when Mavis Leno spoke to The Commonwealth Club on behalf of the Feminist Majority Foundation, which represents over one hundred women's organizations. It had been not even five years since a band of fighters calling themselves Taliban, or student, emerged in Afghanistan. They established themselves as a force to be reckoned with—and, to many, a moral anchor in a brutal power struggle—when they freed a thirty-truck convoy that had been waylaid in Kandahar by forces under the command of two Afghan warlords. Two years later, the Taliban captured the capital, Kabul, though fighting in the civil war continued. Where they ruled, the Taliban imposed a harsh interpretation of Islamic law which included among its effects the removal of women from any public role. By 1997, U.S. Secretary of State Madeleine Albright was calling the Taliban's record on human rights "despicable," and in March 1998, International Women's Day was celebrated to honor Afghan women worldwide. Mavis Leno, wife of *Tonight Show* host Jay Leno, gave $100,000 to the Feminist Majority campaign. She also devoted time to trying to garner public support in the U.S. and internationally to pressure the Taliban to cease oppression of Afghan women. As she discovered, despite a critical State Department fact sheet on Taliban treatment of women and girls that had been issued in 1998, it was difficult to gain traction in Washington for meaningful actions against the Taliban.

First Lady Hillary Clinton also spoke out against the Taliban's treatment of women in spring 1999. But it wasn't the Taliban's treatment of women that earned them significant space in the American media. It was Al Qaeda. After the terrorist network bombed two U.S. embassies in Africa in 1998, President Clinton authorized cruise missile strikes on two Al Qaeda training camps in Afghanistan. The Taliban condemned the U.S. attacks and vowed to protect Osama bin Laden, who had been the target of the unsuccessful strikes. The Taliban's treatment of women would, however, come back as a moral justification for U.S. forces to overthrow the regime in the fall of 2001.

In 2002, the Feminist Majority Foundation renamed its campaign. The Campaign to Help Afghan Women and Girls is meant to "win the full and permanent restoration of women's rights, promote the leadership of women in the planning and governing of post-Taliban Afghanistan, increase and monitor the provision of emergency and reconstruction assistance to women and girls, urge the expansion of peacekeeping forces, and support the Afghan Ministry for Women's Affairs and Afghan women–led nongovernmental organizations (NGOs)." In post-Taliban Afghanistan, education for women and girls is no longer banned, and once again women can work as doctors and teachers. However, in 2003, Human Rights Watch reported that in many parts of the country women are not always free to seek education and health care or, "in some cases, even to leave the walls of their family compound." Is the problem less with the Taliban and more with the West's inability to accept some cultures' rejection of liberal attitudes toward women? At least one member of the audience at Leno's speech thought so and interrupted the talk from the floor.

"Buried Alive"

Everybody recently has said, "You have so much courage to do this." This is funny to me, because you cannot imagine the courage of the Afghan women I have met in the course of pursuing this. My perception of myself is that I was born in paradise and upgraded to heaven. So the least I can do is pay some attention to people who didn't win the lottery, and these women sure as hell didn't win the lottery.

Back in college when I was taking an art appreciation class, I remember learning that during the Middle Ages there was a repellent religious theme often depicted in paintings. Hieronymus Bosch was particularly fond of this theme. People would be going down a thoroughfare where there would be rich people, poor people, tradesmen selling their goods, wealthy people off to a party in their finery, poor people in the streets begging—everybody going about their business on an ordinary day in their lives. That would be a first panel. Second panel, the ground would suddenly open with no warning, and all of these people would be swallowed into the fires of hell. Particularly in the Bosch paintings, you'd see little tiny people plummeting into the mouths of grotesque beasts and limbs being severed. Violence didn't originate with American films. The worst part of these paintings, and the theme that they depicted, was not actually shown. After these people fell into the gaping jaws of hell with no warning, in the middle of their lives, the earth would close and they would be forgotten. No one would know what happened to them, and they would be lost.

This is what happened to the women of Afghanistan. When I first heard what was going on there, fairly early in the situation—it was about three months old—I found myself, in my mind, in the same position as a person who happens to be walking by a lake when someone's going down for the third time, and you know that you can swim. I couldn't know this and not do something about it.

Afghanistan has been decimated by a twenty-year-old civil war. It is either the first or second most land-mined country in the world. It is mainly an agrarian society, and this is particularly hard, because it's difficult for people to farm countryside that is thickly sown over with land mines. Most of the infrastructure of the country has been destroyed. There is great poverty, great hardship, and all of these things were true before the Taliban took over.

Nevertheless, women were contributing members of that society at every level. As is true in almost every country in the world, in the urban areas women were living modernized lives. Some of them wore Western dress, some more traditional dress, but it was entirely their choice, and they had had equal rights under the law since the sixties. They held down an enormous quantity of all the important positions in the government, and in the professions. In the countryside, women did live more conservative lives, but they had a rich support system among the other women of their community, and although some of them did wear the burqa—the garment that all women have to wear if they leave their houses, according to the Taliban edict—they wore the burqa mainly for visits to the town.

The burqa is a very expensive garment. One of the great hardships that has been visited upon women in Afghanistan since the Taliban took over falls heavily on the rural areas where women cannot afford a burqa, and therefore as many as twelve or fourteen women share in the use of one garment. Should you have an emergency, should your child fall ill, break a leg—you need to take this kid to the hospital or any available medical care right now—if it's not your turn for the burqa, too bad.

One of the many Afghan women that I have come to know told me that it is ridiculous to suggest that the women in rural areas wore the burqa as a common thing. Not only is it too expensive for most of them to have owned, but in most farming areas, most women worked in the fields alongside their husbands, which you cannot do in a burqa. In fact, there is almost nothing you can do in a burqa. One of the singular qualities of this garment is that it renders you incapable of almost any independent action. It is the case under the Taliban edicts that you must go out of your house not only wearing the burqa but accompanied by a close male relative. But in truth, it would be very difficult for somebody to navigate and manage their tasks while wearing the burqa if they did not go out accompanied by someone.

You have no peripheral vision in this garment. In fact, the only vision provided to you is through an approximately two-and-a-half by two-inch square of mesh which sits over your eyes. This little square of dense mesh, which is hard to see through, provides no peripheral vision and also does not allow for breathing. You breathe through the solid cloth of the burqa itself. It's the only view of the outside world that is left to these women anymore, since their windows have to be painted an opaque color; they cannot look out of them. If a woman rides in a car, all the windows except for the front window must also be either curtained or painted opaque.

These are the kinds of egregious, excessive restrictions which have prompted us to call this "gender apartheid." In reality, the people who suffered under apartheid in South Africa had fewer restrictions, by far, than these women do. They can no longer work in any capacity, even if their families have no other means of support, which is a serious issue in a country where so many men have been killed in war, and where women far outnumber men. There are many widows. Many women are the sole support of their families. Now that they can no longer work, they are sometimes allowed to beg, but there is almost no other form of self-support left open to them, even though these women were once lawyers, doctors, professors, midwives, nurses, teachers.

When we made the film, we had to go to the Afghan American community to get enough pictures of how the women lived before the Taliban took over. We asked people to give us home movies, family photographs, anything that showed the good times that they had enjoyed prior to the takeover. We had to do this because the Taliban insists that many of these situations never occurred.

This desire to erase history has plagued people for a long time. It was a feature of the Nazis in the concentration camps that they would often tell the Jews that when the war was over and they had won, they would destroy the concentration camps, they would hide all the evidence of what had happened there, and they would tell the populace at large that the Jewish population had gone to live in other nonfascist countries, so that no one would ever know what had happened to them.

Many people that were interned in those camps have said that one of their main motives for surviving in such a terrible environment was that they were determined to live to tell their story and call the Nazis liars. These films and photographs that we got from the Afghan American community do the same thing on a smaller scale. The Taliban would like to say that their country was always a conservative Islamic culture, that women never enjoyed the freedoms that in fact they enjoyed. But that is not the case, and we are here to put the lie to it.

The Taliban is essentially a tribal group; they are predominantly Pashtun. There are three major ethnic groups that live in Afghanistan: Pashtun, Tajik, and Hazara. The Hazara have always been subjected to a certain amount of prejudice. They have some Mongolian ancestry. The Pashtun occupy not only Afghanistan but a great deal of Pakistan. When the lines of demarcation were drawn to create the state of Pakistan, the Pashtun population was essentially divided in half between the two countries. So it is not so odd that Pakistan has helped promulgate the Taliban and recognized them as the legal government of Afghanistan. Pakistan is one of only three countries that makes that recognition, and they give them fiscal support. One of the things that the Feminist Majority would like the United States to do is to address this issue with Pakistan. Pakistan has a long, strong relationship with America. We give them money, we help them out and have a lot of interaction with them. We need to say to them, "You have to speak to these people."

The fact is that there is no fabulous alternative government for Afghanistan at the moment. I can't say, "If only the Taliban weren't there, the such-and-such could take over." There is no really rich, wonderful, democratic alternative. And even if there were, that's none of my business. That's not America's business. I am strictly concerned with the human rights of the women and girls there. I do not want to displace the Taliban. I want them to understand how enormously wrong their treatment of women is to the rest of the world, and to moderate it. Give these women back the lives and the freedoms that they enjoyed before.

Recently, some people have been suggesting that the Taliban has in fact moderated. They have yet to rescind their edicts, and it is from these edicts that we get the information that I have just given you about how the women are treated. In other words, this is not word of mouth from people who witnessed it. This is from the Taliban themselves. If they wish to be seen as moderating their position, they must rescind these edicts. They must allow observers into the country to confirm that they are, in fact, treating the women in a fair, humane, and equal way. That's all we ask. We don't want any sort of revolution there. We simply want these people to listen to reason.

There are a lot of things that everybody can do to help this cause along. The Taliban does not have a lot of money. The country is destroyed. It will take a lot of money and effort to rebuild it. One of the things that gives me hope about moderation of the Taliban stance is that I see no possible way that it or any other government can rebuild this country while it keeps better than half of its population under what essentially amounts to house arrest.

One of the things that I believe has made the West so strong and powerful and successful is that we use all our human resources. Who knows how many ideas, how inventions and innovations, are lost to countries that will not give equal rights to women, certain racial groups, and whatever these particular people decide is a group that should be singled out to have no opportunity in their society? Afghanistan needs every single citizen to rebuild the country. The people that I speak to from the Afghan community say, "Do not imagine that this is a monolithic group. They have lots of factions, some of whom are much more moderate. It happens that the extremists are in power now." It is my hope that the more moderate, more reasonable people will realize that not only will they never gain acceptance in the world community while they treat women like this, but they'll never fix their country unless they want to spend the rest of their natural lives walking up and down the streets of the country with shotguns and chains, hitting people because they're not conforming with some tiny minutiae come up with by the Taliban developers. They're not going to be able to reconstruct the society that will live on its own.

We need to increase immigration to this country from Afghanistan so that people who have fled or are able at some point in the future to leave can come to this country. You would imagine that we would be inundated by Afghan immigrants, but when the Feminist Majority checked the statistics, we found that thousands of Afghans were let into this country and welcomed during the war with the Soviets. But since the Taliban takeover two and a half years ago, guess how many Afghan people have been admitted to this country? Zero.

No one is a political refugee if these people aren't political refugees. And if you don't think that this is a human rights violation, then I don't know what you mean by human, or I don't know what you mean by rights.

That is the first step that we can take: pressuring the government to take this action. Then we can ask America to speak to three nations in the Middle East who are alone in recognizing the legal government of Afghanistan, and alone in giving them money: Saudi Arabia, Pakistan, and the United Arab Emirates. We have strong influence with Saudi Arabia and Pakistan; we should use it. We should speak to them in the name of decency and reason and say, "This is your family. There's one in every family. You go talk to them. Tell them it won't fly."

Another thing that we need to do is to be concerned about United States companies setting up in Afghanistan and financing—not perhaps as a direct result of their business being set up there, but as an indirect result—the Taliban. If the Taliban had a lot of financial support, it would have no need to listen to the world community. They could take the ball and go home. We don't want that to happen. The problem is that Afghanistan is, by far, the most viable country through which to run a gas pipeline from Turkmenistan, which has no coast, to Pakistan. Some people have suggested that the gas deposit there is so large it might last as long as five hundred years. It is this pipeline which brought me into direct contact with Unocal. I spoke at a stockholders' meeting, and I participated in a number of actions to try to persuade them not to build a pipeline and fund this terrible regime.

Let me be very clear about this. Somebody's going to get this gas. I would like it to be the United States. We're a decent and humane country; we stand for human rights as much as anybody in the world. The business of business is to make money; there's nothing wrong with wanting to put the pipeline through there. But you don't have to become a fiscal giant at the expense of being a moral dwarf. Go to the Taliban and say, "You can have hundreds of millions of dollars right now. Let the women out of their houses. Knock it off." Is that so hard? Is that such a big deal? I think a company could say that.

Furthermore, the Feminist Majority has made it their business to look into which other countries might want to put the gas pipeline through there. Some of you may be aware that there are feminist organizations even in some very unlikely places, including almost all the Middle Eastern countries. We intend to speak to our sisters in Japan, which is trying to involve themselves with the Taliban on the basis of this pipeline, and we intend to speak to our sisters in Great Britain, which also has an interest in putting a pipeline through there. In both of these countries, the gender gap in voting is similar to what it is in the United States. In other words, it behooves the government of both these countries, as it behooves the government of this country, to listen up when women say, "We're really bothered by this. You could find yourself out of office if you don't listen up."

We are going to speak to these women and make sure that no one can do business in Afghanistan comfortably and with the sanction of their population. Eventually, we will make it clear to the Taliban, which is a very young, inexperienced group of people, that women are significant in the cultures of all other countries in the world, that they are a force to be reckoned with, and they do not want—and nor do men who have mothers whom they love, and daughters whom they have great hopes for—the next thousand years to be like the last thousand years for women. The work that the Feminist Majority has done to try to help the women of Afghanistan is beginning to yield some results. We have some profoundly conservative people on board with us, as well as some renowned liberals. This is human rights, human decency; it has nothing to do with political attitudes whatsoever, except the political attitude that the world, if it cannot get better, should at least not get worse.

I was privileged to make a tape for Voice of America, which they promised me they would take into Afghanistan, so that the women there would know that women in the rest of the world know what has happened to them and were not going to rest until something was done. These women were like people buried in a mine cave who had no idea if somebody was searching for them. They had no idea if anybody even knew what happened to them. That's how fast and overwhelming the takeover was.

While making the short tape, they taught me how to say *"Maba shuma hasteem,"* which in Pashtun means, "We are with you." I got a lot of response. What I wanted to tell those women, and what I want to make a reality, is that they're not going to be like those pathetic people in those medieval paintings; that the ground will not close over them; that they will not be forgotten; that it will not be as if they never lived.

April 6, 2000

David Broder

Political Correspondent, The Washington Post

Though he's based in Washington, for his April 2000 talk to The Commonwealth Club, *Washington Post* political writer David Broder turned his sights on California's "derailed democracy"—derailed care of the ballot initiative process. A Progressive reform from 1911 in California, ballot initiatives were meant to take power away from corruptible politicians when it came to crucial issues, and to return this power directly to the people. The cure for democracy, the wisdom went, was more democracy. (Commonwealth Club member John Randolph Haynes was the driving force behind the process; The Club debated the issue at length at the time, and Club member Hiram Johnson was elected governor of California on a platform that included the ballot initiative, as well as a process for recalling state officials.) But if money corrupts elected officials, Broder noted, it also corrupts the initiative process, which has grown into an industry where, in order to get an initiative on the ballot, you have to answer the million-dollar question: "Do you have a million dollars?"

"Democracy Derailed"

I grew up in the Chicago area, and my view of politics was undoubtedly shaped by the Daley organization that existed then. The best definition of the way in which Chicago politics operated was given when a young man from Wisconsin went down to his ward committee headquarters and said, "My name is so-and-so; I'm here because I'd like to volunteer." The ward committeemen said, "Who sent you?" He said, "Nobody sent me; I just came to volunteer in the campaign." And the committeemen said, "We don't want nobody that nobody sent." That became the title of a very good book about Chicago politics, and that is the tradition from which I view the initiative process. So let me put my bias right out there in front of everybody: we don't want the people messing around too much in Chicago.

The text for my sermon today was provided by a noted scholar, Dear Abby. In her column this Monday, she was asked by A.P. in Spartanburg, South Carolina, to repeat a column that she had run seven years before, where she came up with her own definitions of various forms of government. For example, communism: you have two cows, the government takes both of them and gives you part of the milk. Bureaucracy: you have two cows, the government takes both of them, shoots one, milks the other, then pours the milk down the drain. And the final one, democracy: in a democracy everyone has two cows, then a vote is taken, and whatever the majority decides to do, you do, and that's no bull.

I was in Oregon in the fall of 1997, on an assignment for the *Washington Post*. I found myself talking to people who were on opposing sides of a ballot initiative on the issue of physician-assisted suicide. The first time Oregon voted on that issue, it passed by the overwhelming majority of 51 percent to 49 percent, and the losing side had sufficient influence in the legislature in Salem to persuade them to put the same issue back on the ballot for a second vote. Talking to the people involved in that battle, I came to understand how profound and deep the emotions and the intellectual debate about that question ran. It raised the most profound ethical, moral, religious questions in people's minds: the meaning of life itself, whether any human being had the right to interfere with God's design for our life span, or alternatively, whether any individual or the state had the right to deny an individual with a painful, lingering, fatal illness the expression of freedom about determining when they should let themselves go to another world. All of these issues were being debated and with great passion on both sides of the question.

I found myself wondering whether this was a good issue to put to a vote of the people, particularly now that in Oregon the public is almost evenly divided, and whichever way it is decided, there will be a very large number of individuals who feel deeply that the wrong thing has happened. The people I asked looked at me as if that was the dumbest question they had ever heard in their lives. They said to me in quite blunt terms, "Who better than the people to decide the question? You certainly wouldn't want to leave it to the politicians."

I went back to my editors and said, "I think we ought to take a look at this initiative process. It's being used increasingly in half the states of the country, and in my mind, it's a different form of government from that old form that we were accustomed to back in the East, where if you want to write a law, you've got to get somebody to introduce a bill. It's got to go through two houses of the legislature, then get past the governor or the president before it can become law. This is a different form of government." And they said, "Go ahead, if you think there are some stories to be done about that."

I spent much of the 1998 election cycle going from state to state where there were initiative battles on the ballot and learning what I could about that process. Much of my time was spent here in California. Actually, Oregon has more initiatives on the ballot per cycle than California. But many battles are fought here—the headline battles—and I discovered many things I did not know existed until I got into this reporting. There is an initiative industry that is largely headquartered in this state: firms that make a pretty good living out of collecting the signatures that qualify initiatives for the ballot; lawyers who make a specialty out of writing initiative language and then fighting it all the way through the process and generally ending up in a court suit about the initiative if it has been successful; and most of all, the campaign consultants, the pollsters, the media advisors, the advertising people who conduct these campaigns in which initiatives are fought over on the ballot every primary and every general election.

The high-tech people in this state have become major players in the initiative process or the initiative industry. The first one that I know of came when the late David Packard supported an effort by Rep. Tom Campbell to create what people call the "blanket primary" that we all became familiar with this past March, when the controversy came up about whether only Republican votes should count when choosing Republican delegates, whether it was right or wrong for people who were not registered as Republicans or Democrats to have a voice in choosing the nominees of the Republican and Democratic primary.

Then came Ron Unz, who passed Proposition 227, the bilingual education initiative, and who tried this past March to change the campaign finance laws of California but had less success. Reed Hastings, another Silicon Valley millionaire, collected the signatures for a big charter school initiative. When the legislature in Sacramento saw he was going to succeed in putting it on the ballot, they shortcut the process and gave him the kind of bill that he wanted to greatly expand the number of charter schools in California. This November, there will be two more Silicon Valley–sponsored education initiatives competing on the ballot. One will be a second try for the one that failed narrowly, at 50 percent, in March to reduce the required majority on passage of school bonds from two-thirds down to 55 percent. Another will be the second try to get the state of California to allow taxpayer money to be spent for school vouchers for private and parochial schools.

All of these come out, essentially, of the personal political agendas of a number of your fellow citizens who have made their fortunes in the high-tech world of Silicon Valley. The great allure of the initiative process for people like that, and for people generally who decide that they want to use this device, is its decisiveness. People look at Sacramento or at Washington, D.C., and they see a legislature or Congress that seems constantly to be spinning its wheels, not getting anywhere, mired in partisanship and all the phrases that people use about legislatures and congresses these days who don't make the decision, or at least the decision that that person or group would like to have made. They look at the initiative system, which came into California about one hundred years ago with a group of reformers who called themselves the Progressives; it was Hiram Johnson in this state. It came to California and other western states as a device to combat and overcome the power that the interest groups of those days had fastened on the legislature in Sacramento and other state capitals. Railroads, banks, and others had literally gone out and bought off legislatures, sometimes for as little as a season pass on the railroad, and sometimes for cash on the barrelhead. They purchased control not just of state policy, but also of the United States Senate, because in those days senators were elected not by the people of the states but by the legislatures of the states. Reformers found in Switzerland this other device of letting people vote directly on the ballot on legislation and they brought it to this country, now in twenty-four states plus the District of Columbia, and it's being used with increasing frequency.

This is not an ideological phenomenon, one by groups and individuals who we would classify as people on the liberal or Left persuasion, or by conservatives, the Right, or by people in the middle who have no identifiable ideology, or by the animal rights people. (I don't know where you would put them on the political spectrum, but they have made very good use of the initiative process of the states where it's available.) The common ingredient for almost all of these groups, and for the individuals, like some of the Silicon Valley millionaires, who use it to carry out their own personal political agendas, is access to or possession of a good deal of money.

This was brought home to me most vividly when I was interviewing a lawyer here in San Francisco whose firm makes a specialty out of writing initiative language and then trying to protect the initiative as it goes through every stage of the process. I said, "Suppose for a moment that I come in to see you not as a reporter from the *Washington Post* but as an average California citizen. I want to put on the ballot an initiative because I think it's a terrific idea and ought to be the law of California. Just walk me through the steps I would have to go through to make that happen." He said, "The first thing that would happen is that I would ask you the million-dollar question." I said, "What's the million-dollar question?" He said, "Do you have a million dollars? Because if you don't, you are not going to get your initiative on the ballot in California." That is just the opening bid, because after that come the lawyers' fees, and after that come the campaign expenses and the consultants, and so on. Money is one thing that I find is a cause of concern in this process.

The second thing that gave me some concern was the rigidity of the effects of an initiative process. There have been a number of occasions where an initiative passed by a majority of Californians voting in that particular election has installed in the state constitution a requirement that from that point on, any change in that policy would require a two-thirds majority of the legislature or of the citizens: a majority of the moment mandating that no future majority could change its policy unless that majority was large enough to constitute two-thirds of those involved in the decision.

The second example is that term limits have been a rigid requirement in the sense that they decree that whether you have been a conscientious legislator who has made a real contribution to the work of the legislature in Sacramento; or whether you've been a time killer, somebody who makes no real effort to help shape the outcome of policy; or somebody who goes to Sacramento for a few years to find out ways to line her or his pocket: whatever your merits or demerits, the term-limits initiative decreed that you are out the door the same day everybody else is out the door, and you may never come back again for the rest of your lifetime.

The real question that's raised by the initiative system is the question that the founders debated at the Constitutional Convention in Philadelphia a long time ago. In their view, direct democracy—simple majority rule—had two serious flaws. One: it was at any given moment a threat to individual freedom, because the majority of the moment might at any time be intolerant of that individual in the society who had a different view, a different perspective—a different lifestyle, if you will—and could by simple majority say your behavior or your ideas are anathema to us and will be proscribed in our society. The second thing they believed was that pure democracy could be a threat to the legitimate interests and aspirations of groups in the society which were smaller than a majority but nonetheless, as fellow citizens, had a legitimate claim for consideration before law was written. So they gave us the system of government that we all learned about in our civics classes, with checks and balances built in at every step of the way, so that it became very difficult for something to move from an idea to a law. They were conservative in the classic sense of the word. They understood that government enactments—laws—almost inherently represented some infringement on someone's freedom of action. They were not eager to facilitate the writing of law; quite the contrary, they wanted to do everything they could to find governmental devices which ensured everyone's viewpoint was taken into consideration before something became a matter of law, before we criminalized some behavior. And they did a pretty good job of it—maybe some people would say too good a job of it.

But I am much more comfortable living in a country where you have to take into consideration the views of people who have opposing ideas to your own. Particularly as it operates now, with the high cost of entry for people paying in that process, if you write an initiative, you do not have to spend five minutes thinking about people who have a different view on that subject than you do yourself. You get your lawyer to write the initiative exactly the way you want it written, and if you can get 51 percent of the people to agree to that proposition, then it's in law or it's in the constitution exactly the way that you want to have it done. My hope is that as the initiative process expands to other states, and very likely at some point in the coming presidential campaigns when a proposal comes for a national initiative process that we will think about the trade-offs that are involved in the initiative process, so that we make a right decision about moving to that form of government rather than the one that for the most part we have enjoyed in this country for the last two hundred and thirty years.

March 12, 2001

John McCain and Russ Feingold

*U.S. Senator (R-AZ); 2000 Candidate for Republican Presidential
Nomination*

U.S. Senator (D-WI)

When Arizona Senator John McCain and Wisconsin Senator Russ Feingold
took to the stage before a Commonwealth Club audience at the Fairmont
Hotel, it was only one week before their campaign finance reform bill was up
for debate in the U.S. Senate. Republican McCain referred to Democrat
Feingold as "my partner in crime and strange bedfellow and member of 'the
odd couple'" in the effort to stem the torrent of money flowing into American
politics. (This was the "third or fourth or fifth" time they had tried to present
such a bill, Feingold said, "depending on how you figure out the numbers.")
In addition to their common views on campaign finance reform, McCain
joked about other similarities the senators shared: Feingold "was a Rhodes
Scholar, and I stood fifth from the bottom of my class in the Naval Academy."

Before their talk, the senators met with young journalists for a special
press conference, underscoring that their larger motive was to reinvigorate
young Americans' faith in the political process. During the question-and-
answer session, they cited a study showing that the 1998 elections had the
lowest turnout among eighteen- to thirty-four-year-olds in history.

In 2000, McCain had campaigned for the Republican nomination for president and won seven primaries. He drew unprecedented attention to campaign finance, aided in part by a growing revulsion among Americans to shameless fund-raising, symbolized for many by the fees people paid to sleep in the Lincoln Bedroom during the Clinton years in the White House. "It used to cost $10,000 to spend the night in the Lincoln Bedroom," McCain told The Commonwealth Club. "I wanted to pay $25 and take a nap."

The senators explained that staggering amounts of cash are necessary for political campaigns in order to pay for television ads; the question of the media's shaping of politics with money is at the heart of this dilemma in American democracy. The problem had to be fixed one step at a time, a painstaking and sometimes tedious process, and yet as the senators spoke, there was a feeling that, after years of work, the moment had come for campaign finance reform.

The senators were on a barnstorming tour to drum up grassroots support for their bill, and they got it. The Bipartisan Campaign Reform Act, banning "soft money" (unlimited donations to national political parties for "party-building" activities), passed both the Senate and House and was signed by President Bush in March 2002, who declared in signing that he expected the courts to iron out some of the components of the law he found wanting. Indeed, the U.S. Supreme Court heard arguments in September 2003. Dozens of plaintiffs attacked the bill. Among those gunning for the law in court were the ACLU and the National Rifle Association, with former independent counsel and Clinton nemesis Kenneth Starr arguing that the law violates the First Amendment. In December 2003, the court issued a decision upholding the law.

"Campaign Finance Reform"

Russ Feingold:
Now, what is the problem here? Well, as I like to say, I assume that money and politics were interrelated and intermingled and were a problem even in ancient Rome. These two things will always go together. But what has happened in the last five to seven years is unprecedented. It has never been allowed for corporations in this country, since 1907 and the Tillman

Act, to give contributions to political parties and the candidates. Since 1947, the Taft-Hartley Act, labor unions were also prohibited from giving unlimited contributions to the political parties or the candidates. So how did this happen?

A loophole was created and then exploited in the 1996 election by my candidate, President Clinton, and by Senator McCain's candidate, Bob Dole, who realized they could use unlimited soft-money contributions to pay for political ads. It should have never been allowed. I don't think it's even legal now, but the system has exploded. And now you have standard procedure—politicians calling up people and asking them for $100,000 contributions, $250,000, $500,000, or a million-dollar contribution. This has corrupted our political process.

When John and I started, we weren't even focused on soft money in 1995. But what this has become is a system of legalized bribery and legalized extortion. And we have the opportunity to get rid of it.

In 1992, the total amount of soft-money contributions was $83 million—already a lot. But it was just getting started. In the 1996 election, the figure became $231 million. In the last election, they're still counting, the figure is now $457 million in soft-money contributions in the federal elections. John and I want to remove that half-billion dollars' worth of money from the process.

Why do we want to do that? We want to do it because it is affecting the outcome of public policy. It is preventing us from passing something all Americans want: a patients' bill of rights. It is behind the fact that the bankruptcy bill that will pass this week is a gift to the credit card companies of this country. When Senator Dianne Feinstein and I desperately tried to have a little fairness for AIDS victims in Africa last year, when we got through the Senate a bill that would make sure South Africa could provide medicines to their people at a lower cost, it was big money that quietly took that out of the bill and made sure that the pharmaceutical companies got a good deal.

It is infecting every part of our political process. You've seen it with the Lincoln Bedroom, the raising of money in the halls of Congress. You saw it at the Democratic National Convention in Los Angeles and the Republican convention in Philadelphia. We even saw it in one of the most sacred institutions—the pardon power. When you have that kind of money swimming around, all institutions are threatened, and all institutions can be destroyed.

When I was seventeen, eighteen years old, I wanted to go into politics. Nobody ever said that I'd have to be a multimillionaire or have the ability to raise soft-money contributions to sit at the table of American politics. I got to become a United States senator. But I cannot look young people in the eye now and honestly tell them, in the average community in Wisconsin, that they're welcome to participate, unless we do something about this travesty.

John McCain:
In Russ's last reelection campaign, three million dollars' worth of soft-money attack ads were run against him. His own party said, "We'll raise a bunch of soft money and respond to these ads." Russ Feingold refused.

March nineteenth, my friends, is when this bill will be on the floor of the Senate. This will be the first time in the United States Senate since 1993 when a debate and amendments were allowed. It will be the first time that legislation can be passed since 1974. The reason for that, frankly, is because Russ and I now have the votes which we didn't have before, and our opponents were able to filibuster or block debate or votes on amendments. It's not because anyone found themselves on the road to Damascus.

It's important to keep in mind two fundamental facts. We are asking incumbents to vote to change a system that keeps incumbents in office. In the last election, there were approximately twenty to thirty House races, out of 435, that were competitive, and about seven or eight Senate races. Second, every single special interest that gains access and influence by use of these big-money donations are opposed to us. (Those organizations such as the AARP and others that rely on their membership are those who support us.) We're taking on every special interest group that comes in with a $100,000, $500,000, million-dollar check that buys access and buys influence in Washington, D.C. What's wrong with that? The people with money are sitting in the front of the room in Congress with a megaphone, and those average Americans who do not have the big money are sitting in the back, whispering. That's not what our Founding Fathers had in mind.

In the newspaper entitled *The Hill*, on Wednesday, January 24, 2001, the day after the Inauguration: "'Gentlemen, start your engines,' said Tom Hammond, a prominent Republican fund-raiser. 'The Inauguration period has ended. It's time to start raising some money.'" Today's *USA Today*: "Both Parties Continue to Reap Donors' Cash Crop after Election. WASHINGTON: At a time when donors are usually tapped out from presidential campaigns and begging for a break, both parties are raking in money at a record-setting pace....Both parties may be benefiting from a rush by donors to give soft money, unlimited contributions to parties, before a possible overhaul of fundraising rules."

David Boren, former senator, former governor, former state legislator, now the president of the University of Oklahoma, said that in 1961, when he first ran for the state legislature, *Time* magazine asked a question that they've been asking every year since then: "Do you trust your government to do the right thing for the American people?" In 1961, 76 percent of the American people answered in the affirmative. This year, 19 percent of the American people answered in the affirmative.

Young Americans will not partake in the political process and seek public office, much less vote. My friends, we have to turn that around. I know from my own campaign that young Americans want to serve this country. They want to serve their community, their state, their neighbors, and their families in ways which my generation did not. Young Americans fully appreciate the ennobling aspect of serving a cause greater than one's self-interest. But young Americans understandably will not take part in a system that they believe is corrupt and does not reflect their hopes and dreams and aspirations.

This is one of these seminal events in American political history. It's not the end of the fight, but it is the beginning of the fight. And we have the first glimmer of hope that we can truly change this system which has so badly corrupted American politics.

I ran for president of the United States because I wanted to reform the institutions of government. We need to reform an HMO patients' bill of rights. We need to reform the tax code, which is forty-four thousand pages long. We need to reform the military, which is not equipped to meet the challenges of the post–Cold War era. We need to reform Social Security and Medicare. But the gateway to all of those is reform of the campaign finance system. We cannot reform those institutions of government unless we reform the way that campaigns are financed. Why do you think it is that we don't have an HMO patients' bill of rights? Five people in this room could sit down and write an HMO patients' bill of rights. We don't have it because the Democrats are gridlocked by the trial lawyers, who want anybody to sue anybody for anything, including class action suits; and the Republicans are gridlocked by the insurance company money. Meanwhile, millions of Americans are not receiving the basic fundamental rights that we felt we should guarantee to all Americans. This is a much larger issue than reform of the campaign finance system. This is a reform of the institutions of government so that we can carry out our obligations to all Americans, and not repay debts to a privileged few.

[from the question-and-answer session]

Q. *Explain why restricting my ability to give my money to any politician or cause is not a violation of my First Amendment rights.*

McCain: One reason is because the United States Supreme Court, about a year ago in a case involving the state of Missouri, clearly upheld the constitutionality of a restriction of a $1,000 contribution limit of an individual. The United States Supreme Court went on to say that too much money in politics creates either the appearance of or actuality of corruption in American politics. We're not trying to restrict anyone's First Amendment rights, but we also believe that it is reasonable to uphold a ban on corporate and union contributions. We believe it's constitutional to uphold a $1,000 contribution limit. Why was that law enacted? Because in the 1972 campaign, the chairman of the Committee to Re-elect the President, then known as CREEP, Mr. Maurice Stans, was walking around the streets of Washington with a valise with over a million dollars in cash in it.

Feingold: Under our bill, people are free to express themselves as much as they wish. They can spend as much of their money as they want on political expression. But throughout the whole history of free speech, alongside that history has been laws relating to bribery and the fear that in government, the elected officials' and judges' independence will be compromised by benefiting excessively from getting money from somebody. That's what we call bribery.

McCain: In 1996, a fellow whose name was Roger Tamraz had an idea to build a pipeline across Central Asia. He wanted to talk to the president of the United States about it. He called the White House and said, "I'd like to talk to the president of the United States about building a pipeline across Central Asia." They did a background check on him and found out that he only had a couple of problems, like being wanted by Interpol, so they said no. So Mr. Tamraz wrote out a check for $300,000 to the Democratic National Committee. Mr. Tamraz then went to a number of events in the White House, but he never got a chance to talk directly to the president of the United States about his pipeline.

At the Thompson Committee hearings, Joe Lieberman is questioning Mr. Tamraz, and he says, "Mr. Tamraz, aren't you disappointed in what you got for your $300,000? You gave $300,000, and you never even got to talk to the president of the United States about your pipeline." This was Mr. Tamraz's answer: "No, next time I'm giving $600,000."

Q. *Even if your campaign finance reform bill were to pass, won't the money just find another route to the politicians? Won't we need another campaign finance reform bill in another twenty years?*

Feingold: The reason that we elect legislators every couple of years is that we're supposed to have something to do. Every twenty years or so, yes, you do have to clean up the system. Thomas Jefferson said there ought to be a revolution every twenty years. I don't think there's a problem, then, with having campaign finance reform. It's sort of like tax reform. Loopholes find their way. But I disagree with the notion that all of this party soft money will necessarily flow out to independent groups, because, as John and I have found, a lot of the big corporate and union interests are giving this money to the political parties directly, because it's a transactional kind of deal. It is a situation where if they gave it to an independent group, if they gave it to somebody else—National Right to Life or Sierra Club—it would not have the same character, which is you can actually hand the check to somebody and the next day say, "We want our bill up tomorrow." It's very direct, and this is the thing that has always been prohibited in our democracy.

In 1992, 52 donors gave over $200,000 directly to the parties. In the year 2000, it was 443. In 1992, only 9 people gave over $500,000. In the year 2000, it's 143 people. These people are not just going to give money to independent groups. They're expecting something for these checks to political parties, and I guarantee you, they're getting it.

Q. *Is it politically feasible to require TV broadcasters who are licensed to use the public airways to provide substantial free time to major candidates?*

McCain: The most powerful lobby in Washington is the National Association of Broadcasters. Who else would get $70 billion worth of the American taxpayers' property for free? They got $70 billion worth of spectrum for free on the false promise that they would then have free over-the-air digital television for the American people, and by the year 2002 they would give back their analog spectrum. There's not a snowball's chance in Gila Bend, Arizona, my friends, that they're going to give that analog spectrum to anyone. I hope that sometime you have the chance to listen to Walter Cronkite on this subject. Walter Cronkite, for ten years in a row, was voted the most respected man in America. He is committed and dedicated to the proposition that the public interest portion of the license that a broadcaster receives in return for use of this spectrum obligates them to give free television time to candidates.

You might have also noticed that the coverage of the political campaigns on the part of the networks and the broadcasters of local stations is in a steady decline. You may have also seen, in the last week, the profits of the broadcasters and the individual stations from the purchase of television by candidates and interests, etc., is at an all-time high.

Feingold: I don't even know if campaign finance reform would be much of an issue if it were not for the cost of television. That can change with technological change, but that really is the thing that drives the issue.

October 17, 2001

Bill O'Reilly

Host, The O'Reilly Factor

A journalist with two Emmys under his belt and plenty of hours logged with news teams at CBS and ABC, Bill O'Reilly, with his self-professed "built-in bull detector," has earned a formidable following since the emergence of *The O'Reilly Factor* on Fox News in the 1990s. It's not hard news, but opinion and analysis, that O'Reilly offers, and his brand of infotainment has made the show, as O'Reilly's website declared in 2003, "the most-watched program in cable news." The trade journal *Publishers Weekly*, in announcing in 2001 the rollout of his book *The No Spin Zone: Confrontations with the Powerful and Famous in America* (which shot to the top of the *New York Times* bestseller list), pronounced O'Reilly's approach "articulate, bombastic, scornful, witty, icon-oclastic, passionate, persuasive, and sarcastic." His confrontational style either endears or appalls.

When stepping onto O'Reilly's set, guests are supposed to check "spin" at the door. The terrorist attacks on the U.S. in September 2001 generated a renewed American patriotism and a sense that we couldn't afford spin; it was a time for facing cold, hard truths. And it was in October 2001 that O'Reilly took the stage before an enthusiastic Commonwealth Club audience and took stock of what he saw happening in California and the rest of the country. He shared one incident from his stop in the "little gingerbread town of Cambria, California."

> I decided to go into the exotic oil shop. There are the beads and incense. They had the sitar guy. Behind the counter is a child of Woodstock, a woman of about thirty-eight or forty. She had a little headband and a long, flowing dress. She had the long hair peppered with gray. I could tell that she was a counterculture person. So I grabbed a couple of little ointments. I think they're against the law in New York, but I'm not sure. Then I went up and paid. I said, "Can I ask you a question about the terrorist act?" She had big eyes and looked up. I said, "What do you think the United States should do to Osama bin Laden?" She said, "Kill him." I knew then that everybody was on the same page here.

"No Spin Zone"

There's a pattern in American history: We get the right guy at the right time. We had George Washington, an aristocrat and not a real personable fellow, an accomplished soldier in the French and Indian War; he was respected but was not a firebrand. Against all odds—because more than 50 percent of the colonists didn't want to break away from Britain—he defeated the most powerful army in the world.

Thomas Jefferson encountered the same kind of situation that we are in now. He's got a bunch of pirates over in Libya—that Libya's been a pain in the butt for two centuries—who are attacking American ships, taking American seamen and selling them into slavery. Britain says that they intend to pay the Barbary pirates to ransom back their own men. Jefferson says, "Hell, I'm going to send my guys the Marines over, and we're going to kick some butt." Which he did.

Abe Lincoln—a funny looking guy, not a great presence—came to Washington. People mocked him, saying, "Go on, get out of here, go back to Illinois. Who are you?" He had a wife who was out of control, shrieking in the street. People thought, "How can he run the country when he can't control his own wife?" Then all of a sudden the Civil War came, and he became our greatest president, emerging out of nowhere.

Here comes Franklin Delano Roosevelt, another dandy, another guy with a long cigarette holder. Then Japan and Hitler attack us. All of a sudden he emerges as a strong war leader.

Now people are mocking the presumed smallness of the intellectual capacity of the guy in the White House. He can't get a sentence out straight. Everybody thinks, "What is going on? How did he get to be president?" All of a sudden we are attacked. Now he's got a 90-percent approval rating. Do you know why? He sees things in almost the same way I do, in black and white. "Who did it, Mr. President?" "The evildoers!"

I'm down with that. The evildoers did it. Do I need to understand them? No. Does Bush want to understand evildoers? No. Does he want to know what happened in 1912, and how they lost sixteen camels? He doesn't care. I don't either.

This guy is probably the right guy at the right time. He sees it in black and white: this is a personal attack, like someone coming to your house tonight while you're watching television with your wife or your husband and your three kids. They kick in that door. They have a gun. Well, what are you going to do? If you have a gun, you're going to shoot them. You're not going to try to understand them. You're not going to say, "Hold it. I want to call my neighbor to get a coalition to deal with you." You're going to protect your family and yourself. You're going to do whatever you can to stop those people. There's no negotiation. There's no need to understand. If we have a coalition, fine. If we don't, that's fine too. We take care of these people, because the federal government is mandated to protect the citizens of the United States from outside aggression. That is why we have the government.

Now, the government has let us down, big time, in failing to protect us from people who want to hurt us, and in failing to provide for the common welfare. They won't patrol the borders. They won't do what they have to do in order to regulate immigration. It has to change. They're going to have to put the military on the border. They're going to have to expand the INS in order to know who's in here and who's not.

Why aren't they doing their duty? Because it is politically correct not to do it. One of the most damaging effects of the political correctness of the past twenty years is that we can't have troops on the Mexican border to stop the massive inflow of drugs, because the presence of troops might offend some Mexican Americans. Mexican president Vicente Fox doesn't want them there. "No, you can't do that," he says. "The Treaty of Guadalupe Hidalgo prohibits you having troops on the border." This is a treaty made in the nineteenth century.

If you go to Mexico, guess who's on the border when you cross over? Mexican troops lined up from Brownsville to Imperial Beach. You know why they are there? Believe me, it's not because we are going to invade Mexico. They are there to help the heroin dealers come across, saying, "Come on across, José." So much for the Treaty of Guadalupe Hidalgo.

There are thirty-five hundred miles of border between Canada and the United States. There are three hundred and sixty border-patrol guys, two hundred of whom are on vacation at any one time, as it's a federal job. "Four o'clock?" they say. "See ya later." So Abdullah and his guys can bring down anything they want from Manitoba. "Hey, just bring it through. There's nobody here."

The other seriously damaging product of political correctness during this time was the Torricelli Principle of 1995. Senator Robert Torricelli of New Jersey went to the White House. He told President Clinton that this evil general in Guatemala, despite shooting peasants and being a human rights violator, was on the CIA payroll. Clinton said, "We've got to stop that." So, they called up CIA Director John Deutch. They told him, "Look. The CIA can't be paying anybody who has a criminal record, or who has any kind of human rights baggage, unless you approve it. So, all the station chiefs all over the world have got to wire you to tell you beforehand that they want to give Mohammed ten thousand dollars because he's going to tell you where Osama bin Laden is." However, Mohammed has got five felonies on his record in Oman. The station chiefs told me that as soon as the diktat went out, they said, "I'm not going to cable Washington to say that I want to pay somebody, because it's probably going to be held against me later." So, because of the Torricelli Principle, all of our intelligence dried up.

I'm saying to myself, "Who hangs around Osama bin Laden?" I don't. Do any of you hang around with him? Do any of you know him? He's not going to hang around with me. He's going to hang with a guy who has killed eighteen people. So if we want to know what he's doing, we've got to get one of those guys. But, no, we can't, because of the Torricelli Principle.

I had Torricelli on my program and just beat him with this thing like crazy. He's trying to defend it. He can't. Now there is no more Torricelli

Principle. The CIA is standing on a street corner in Islamabad with arms full of money saying, "Anybody know anything? We don't care who you are." All that political correctness is now gone, because we are in a war and we need information, and all this crazy stuff that led to us being fat, happy, and insecure is gone with it. Thank God.

That brings me to my last point, which is that this is a war. It's going to be painful for us. That's the way war is. But at the end of the war—and there will be an end to it—we're going to emerge as a stronger nation.

The spinners and the politically correct morons are all on the run. You saw what happened in Rocklin, California, where they had a "God bless America" sign outside the grammar school. Out of six hundred and thirty-five kids, the mother of one child objected. She, of course, runs the ACLU. They didn't take the sign down. This parent has been ostracized from the community of Rocklin. Two months ago that wouldn't have happened. People would have said then that it was annoying. Now they are furious.

Children in the United States suddenly know that they have a country. They didn't know that before. They figured that the Fourth of July was about flag-waving. They never really got what the country was, because that wasn't really important to them. Now every kid in America knows about patriotism, what the country is, and what we stand for. It's a tremendous civics lesson that hits even the dimmest of these children. They learned that you have a family, a religion, friends, and a country—and that the country is important. It means something. It's not just a place in which to go to the mall or to the ballgame. You have a responsibility to that country to be a good citizen and not to commit crimes or take dope or do something irresponsible. You have a responsibility to the country to be a good person and to help other Americans. That is a tremendous lesson that never could have been taught except for this terrible war. It bodes well for all of us that those kids finally realize that there's a lot more to life than what they want to do tomorrow and what's on television tonight.

Obviously, we all know what has to be done. It's not pleasant. We don't want civilians killed. We have to defend our country. We have to do the right thing. There is a right and a wrong. Good and evil have to be defined and dealt with. We have got to get back to that if we want to be a country that can protect its citizens, is compassionate, and solves problems so that everyone in the United States can have an equal opportunity to have a nice life.

[from the question-and-answer session]

Q. *Black and white are not the colors of world politics. How do you determine which countries are evil and deserve destruction? Saudi Arabia has funded all the Muslim fundamentalist groups in the world, including the Taliban. When do we bomb Saudi Arabia?*

A. There is black and white in politics; you just don't hear about it. The Saudis are not friends of the United States. We want them to be our friends, and our government praises them. Why? We need their oil, that's why. If we didn't need their oil, we wouldn't ever deal with them. As the questioner rightly points out, their country is the main conduit of funds to Osama bin Laden. They bought protection from him. They said, "We'll let you have all the money you want. You keep those Islamic fundamentalists under control here. You don't hurt us here." They made a deal with the devil. It came back to hurt the United States.

Now, the United States knows that, but what's the alternative? The government has sold out to the oil companies. They haven't developed alternative fuels. They haven't insisted that Detroit make fifty-miles-to-the-gallon automobiles. They could have easily done that. They haven't, because the oil companies don't want that. They want to sell oil. Where do we get the oil? From OPEC, because we won't drill where we can. Why? Because the caribou will get upset. That's black and white.

What I'm telling you is absolutely the gospel truth. There's no refuting what I've just said. We're not going to drill in Alaska because there are caribou up there. John Kerry and guys like that don't want to upset the caribou. We put the pipeline from Prudhoe Bay on down. The caribou liked it, because the pipeline warmed them. They were mating like crazy. There were even more caribou. The caribou want you to drill. They're saying, "Come on up here." It's insane, politically correct nonsense.

Q. *Realizing some of your guests don't deserve ten seconds of airtime, I find that many times the debate isn't close to being over, due to time constraints. How about more time and fewer guests?*

A. We structure the program to move quickly, because 72 percent of people watch television with the remote control in their hand, especially if they're guys. I'm the kind of guy who gets right to the point. There are no delicacies. Then, if the guests start to dance, I cut them off and am rude. If I can't get the answer out of them in six minutes—which is the average length of a segment—then I'm never going to get the answer out of them. That's the philosophy. Why bore you?

November 5, 2001

Hanan Mikhail-Ashrawi

Arab League Commissioner of Information; Secretary General,
Palestinian Initiative for the Promotion of Global Dialogue and
Democracy; Member, Palestinian Legislative Council

On September 28, 2000, Ariel Sharon led a delegation of Likud Party legislators and armed Israeli police to Jerusalem's holiest and most contested site.
Before a gathering Palestinian crowd, he declared, "It's the right of any Jew
in Israel to visit in the Temple Mount." He added that the visit was also "a
message of peace, to see if we Palestinians and Israelis can live together."
Sharon may have offered those words as a genuine entreaty for peace, but
coming as they did from the man loathed by Palestinians for presiding over
Israel's 1982 invasion of Lebanon and tacitly permitting the massacre of
Palestinian refugees at the hands of Christian Lebanese forces in Beirut, the
words incited hostility, not reconciliation. Armed clashes between
Palestinians and Israeli Defense Forces began almost immediately, and within days, dozens of Palestinians would be dead. In this context, the tragic first
act in what is now referred to as the second intifada, Hanan Mikhail-Ashrawi
addressed The Commonwealth Club in November 2001.

A Christian woman fluent in English, Ashrawi may be, next to President
Yasser Arafat, the most recognizable and influential Palestinian voice in Europe

and the United States—owing in part to her appearances on *Nightline*, the BBC, and CNN. A scholar and an educator (she earned her Ph.D. in Medieval and Comparative Literature from the University of Virginia before returning home to found and later chair the English department at Birzeit University in the West Bank), Ashrawi has for the past two decades lived a second life as a diplomat and politician. A participant at every major Middle East peace negotiation since the early 1990s—from Madrid in 1991 to Taba in 2001—Ashrawi has frequently been the voice and face of Palestinian diplomacy.

But Ashrawi's role as a prominent advocate for the Palestinian cause has engendered opprobrium along with international renown. In late 2003, she unwittingly became entangled in a Middle East peace proxy fight nine thousand miles from Jerusalem. In August 2003, the Sydney Peace Foundation in Australia announced that Ashrawi was the unanimous choice for that year's Sydney Peace Prize. Foundation director Stuart Rees extolled Ashrawi's "commitment to human rights, to the peace process in the Middle East and...courage in speaking against oppression, against corruption, and for justice." The announcement was immediately denounced by Sydney's Jewish community, which campaigned to scuttle the Ashrawi selection. Commentary from Ashrawi defenders and detractors filled Australia's major newspapers during the weeks leading up to the award ceremony in November. Piers Akerman of the *Sydney Daily Telegraph* said Ashrawi's selection "makes a mockery of the award." Ashrawi's final rebuke came at the award ceremony itself, in the form of a boycott by Sydney's mayor, Lucy Turnbull, and Australian Prime Minister John Howard.

Among those coming to Ashrawi's defense, however, were two previous winners of the Sydney Peace Prize. Mary Robinson, the former UN high commissioner for human rights, said of Ashrawi, "I admire her courage, integrity, and commitment to seeking a peaceful and just solution to the Israeli-Palestinian conflict," adding, "She has the respect of the international human rights community for her condemnation of violence on all sides and her work to achieve a just peace." Archbishop Desmond Tutu, the 1984 Nobel Peace laureate, said, "No one could be more deserving of this prestigious award. Against daunting odds she has remained committed to finding a peaceful solution to what seems an intractable problem." Ashrawi, for her part, expressed surprise at the bitterness of the award controversy: "I was amazed at the degree of not just negative response, but a certain degree of hatred, which I don't find even with my discussion with Israelis."

Ashrawi's personal controversy may have passed, but as of this writing, the second intifada rages on, now well into its third year. In March 2002, responding to a frightening escalation in the number and lethality of suicide bombings, Israel launched Operation Defensive Shield, and with it Israeli Defense Forces entered and occupied Palestinian cities and refugee camps. Hope for peace returned, fleetingly, in summer 2003 with the release of the U.S.-backed road map and a cease-fire by the Palestinian militant groups Hamas, Islamic Jihad, and Fatah. But the cease-fire did not hold, aggressive U.S. support for peace talks disappeared as focus shifted to the war in Iraq, and Israeli forces remained in Gaza and the West Bank. The collapse of peace efforts has left even longtime peace advocates such as Hanan Ashrawi less than optimistic. In January 2004, Ashrawi told Britain's *Guardian*, "The intifada has been very costly and has distorted the nature of our struggle." And it had taken 950 Israeli and 2,800 Palestinian lives.

"Peacemaking in the Middle East"

We are not isolated, separate nation-states or ethnic groups or religions. On the contrary, we are part of a global human community, and whatever happens anywhere in the world has an impact throughout the world. We do have a responsibility to ensure that injustice, lawlessness, violence, and terrorism in one place do not go uncontrolled without accountability and do not form a pattern of behavior that could spread throughout the world.

In Palestine, we have had ongoing violence, brutality, and the most pervasive and comprehensive form of violations of human rights and liberties. It is a persistent occupation that has been allowed to continue and, as a wound within our region, allowed to fester. It has contributed to ongoing destabilization, to suspension of democracy and human rights, to behavior that can be described mildly as a behavior outside the law—and power politics, militarization, and loss of resources.

Each town, city, and village is still being strangled by a siege that has totally disrupted every aspect of life—not just freedom of movement and the economy, where we have over 60 percent unemployment and almost that percentage of people living under the poverty line. We have seen systematic destruction of our infrastructure, of our institutions; every aspect of our lives has been disrupted, including education, schools, universities, medical care, hospitals, and health services. Every single Palestinian feels personally targeted with the ongoing shelling and the military incursions by tanks into the hearts of our cities and towns, shelling from the air with Apache gunships and F-16s, destruction of homes, crops, uprooting of trees, and the tragic loss of over eight hundred Palestinian lives and the wounding of over thirty thousand Palestinian lives.

Israel continues to behave as a country above the law with total immunity and impunity. The problem is that this kind of reality and mentality are not conducive to trust, confidence, or to the launching of a genuine peace process. In 1991, we launched a peace process in Madrid, which we entered with tremendous hope. It was after the Gulf War when the U.S. administration sponsored this regional and global peace process, saying, "Now is the time to set the record straight, to rectify historical errors, to do justice in the region." There were tremendous promises, hopes, and expectations. Unfortunately, the peace process turned into a punitive process for the Palestinians. The mentality of occupation was brought to bear and superimposed on the peace process. It became an end in itself, rather than a means to an end—which is genuine peace with justice, to end the occupation, and to bring about the Palestinian sovereign and independent state with Jerusalem as its capital.

As the mentality of occupation continued, there was an ongoing policy of unilateralism—a euphemism for actions by the powerful against the weak, negating the essence of the partnership of peace. The start of unilateralism was expressed in ongoing settlement activities, land confiscation, building bypass roads, and fragmenting territorially Palestinian realities. The ongoing mentality of control—economic control, territorial control, the crossing points, the borders—everything was subject to the occupation. Unilateralism was in terms of the imposition of closures, blockades, and states of siege. Instead of getting dividends from the peace process, we ended up paying the price of an ongoing and escalating occupation. That undermined, again, people's confidence. Not a single agreement was fully implemented, not a single timetable complied with or fully honored. Every single agreement was reopened for negotiations.

Unilateralism was also seen in the Israeli positions presented at Camp David—the myth of the generous offer, with a typical patronizing mentality of the occupier against the occupied: You have to be grateful for whatever we dish out, including an Israeli view that was never written; it was an oral statement that they had to maintain settlements. We were asked to bestow retroactive legitimacy on free settlement clusters in the West Bank that would continue the fragmentation and division and destroy any territorial contiguity for the West Bank or any viability of a future Palestinian state. They insisted on more land confiscation—up to 20 percent of the West Bank. They took Jerusalem and its environs as taken for granted as belonging under Israeli's illegal sovereignty. They maintained control over the Jordan Valley. They wanted to keep control over our airspace and borders. Finally, they wanted us to relinquish refugees. They were calling this the end of the conflict and stating that there were no further Palestinian claims. To us, this was very clearly a sure recipe for future conflict and for perpetuating injustice that is liable to provoke further violence and conflict throughout the region and to continue destabilization.

Unfortunately, President Clinton wanted an instant legacy and insisted that we fall into line with the Israeli view; at the same time, the Palestinian side was blamed for the breakdown in the talks. There was the pressure of elections within Israel, where [Ehud] Barak had lost his coalition—and not for anything having to do with the peace process. He wanted to use the peace process to gain another term in office, and that failed. Negotiations continued in Taba, and there was progress and a change in position, which meant that the "take it or leave it" attitude of Camp David suddenly was not productive and not maintained. There was no time left, and the Israelis decided that they didn't want to sign any agreement because it wouldn't save careers.

With that and the ongoing Palestinian victimization, the intifada that broke out in September wasn't planned, and it wasn't gratuitous violence. Sharon succeeded in provoking Palestinian public opinion, entering Al Haram Sharif with military troops and sending a clear message that legality and justice had nothing to do with facts on the ground. With pent-up emotions and erosion of confidence, that led to massive Palestinian protests. It was okay to protest an injustice. However, the immediate Israeli response was use of lethal force and the killing of eight Palestinians the first day and seven Palestinians the second day. This escalated, leading to use of firearms on the part of some individual Palestinians. Barak clamped down with a brutal siege and started shelling and destruction across the board. This was picked up by Sharon.

The government that we see is definitely anti-peace. It wants, as Sharon said, to continue Israel's war of independence, which to the Palestinians means more ethnic cleansing, taking our land to complete the occupation of all of Palestine. We offered the two-state solution, and we are committed to the two-state solution. We've accepted, as part of our historic compromise, 22 percent of historical Palestine, provided we have it clean as the minimal requirement for a viable Palestinian state, with territorial contiguity and without settlements and Israeli incursions, without an apartheid system, and without Israeli control.

Sharon's policy is a combination of extreme right-wing ideological components with extreme fundamentalist religious components, the most strident military components within Israeli society, and with some participation of labor as a thin veneer of civilized behavior, as the public apologist for the most uncivilized policy on the ground. The policies continue with the erroneous assumption that escalation, punitive measures, cruelty, and military subjugation can produce security for the Israelis. The fact is that the more you threaten, undermine, and attack the Palestinians and undermine their security, the less security there is for anybody. The occupation itself is the source of insecurity for everybody, including the Israelis. Sharon still thinks that massacres, gratuitous cruelty, and killing can produce results. He has not learned that armies may defeat other armies, but armies can never defeat a nation or a people's will to be free and independent on their own land and to live in dignity equal to other nations.

The new American administration's approach was in the beginning hands-off—interpreted by the Israeli government as a green light to do whatever they wanted and to persist in these policies without accountability and intervention. We asked for protection. We went to the UN Security Council and were vetoed repeatedly. The Mitchell report involved a period of calm and resumption of negotiations, but said clearly that no security arrangements can succeed outside a political context. Still, we don't have a political context.

The issue of security and violence remains separate from any type of political commitment or process, and Israel hijacked that agenda and decided that it has to be conditional and sequential, and set itself up as the one party to decide. We asked the U.S. to intervene again. The Tenet report came out as a means of implementation. So far, what we've seen is lip service. Actions on the ground continued to have no relationship to any type of agreement, proposal, or political process. The Palestinians have accepted every initiative—from the Egyptian-Jordanian initiative to the Mitchell report to the Tenet plan—and yet we haven't seen any motion. It seems that the definition of "quieting down" is to give Israel a free hand to continue using military violence, provoking the Palestinians beyond endurance, and at the same time, holding the victims accountable and responsible, not just for quieting down, but for the safety of their occupiers.

Now there has been a change. With the September 11 tragedy, it became clear that there is a relationship of interdependence. Israel's behavior of utter lawlessness has become a serious liability to the U.S. in the short term, in terms of its efforts to maintain a coalition against terrorism, with Israel inflaming Arab and Islamic public opinion and creating havoc in the region. At the same time, it is also important, in terms of a long-term strategy in the region, to reassess what went wrong and to be able to formulate a new policy that is not based on the adoption of Israeli interests as the determining factor for American policy throughout the Arab world and the region. Israel has to be treated as a country subject to the global rule of law and not as a country above the law.

President Bush articulated a clear message: that it has always been part of the American foreign policy vision that a Palestinian state will emerge. We are trying very hard now to translate this vision into a policy and a concrete reality. It's not going to happen by default, and it certainly won't happen if Israel continues with its plans and policies to undermine our very existence. President Arafat has expressed a willingness to start negotiations unconditionally and immediately. He has invited Sharon to do that, with no response. Our message to the American administration is: How do we move beyond the pain of the moment? How do we translate this vision into an American policy that is constructive in terms of rectifying a historical injustice and one of the major causes of instability and extremism throughout the world? If we want an end to terrorism and lawlessness, we have to solve long-standing grievances, injustices, and unsolved conflicts.

January 14, 2002

Patrick J. Buchanan

2000 Reform Party Presidential Candidate

In a speech at the Republican convention in 1992, Pat Buchanan declared, "There is a religious war going on in our country for the soul of America." Fresh off his defeat by George H. W. Bush for the party's nomination for president, Buchanan would then go on to battle Robert Dole for the nomination in 1996 before campaigning in 2000 to take back the country as the Reform Party candidate. A columnist and a fixture on CNN's *Crossfire* since 1987, Buchanan had, prior to occupying the pundit's chair, served as an advisor to Richard Nixon and Gerald Ford, and as communications director for Ronald Reagan. Buchanan's transitions between politics and journalism raise the question of the changing, perhaps blurring, relationship between the two. But his 2000 campaign for the presidency was about painting things in black and white. Buchanan's campaign drew support from hard-core Republicans, as well as opponents of interventionist foreign policy and the North American Free Trade Agreement.

When Buchanan spoke at The Commonwealth Club in 2002, he had taken the message to a global scale. Wearing a journalist's hat once again (in this case much resembling a doomsayer's hat), he had recently completed his book *The Death of the West: How Mass Immigration, Depopulation and A Dying*

Faith Are Killing Our Culture and Country. He'd appeared on NBC quoting T. S. Eliot's "The Hollow Men": "This is the way the world ends / not with a bang but a whimper." And during the question-and-answer session at The Commonwealth Club, he cited his own frightening prediction from a few years before:

> ...an act of cataclysmic terrorism on American soil. I said that after the act of terrorism, a man named bin Laden will be killed by U.S. Special Forces. Then, a few years later, some of his cells will get hold of a nuclear weapon and will detonate it—I use Seattle Harbor as an example. These things will happen unless we get out of conflicts and wars and adopt a policy like the Nixon Doctrine of 1969, where other countries have the soldiers to fight their own wars, and we are the arsenal of democracy that provides the weapons, but we are not a front-line, fighting state all over the world. I'm not a globalist. I don't believe in empire. We are Americans. We are not imperialists.

"Death of the West"

It was a tough thing to leave the Republican Party, but I wanted to try and build a new party that would represent my views and values, because I thought the Republican Party was moving away from them. However, late in the campaign of 2000, I realized I wasn't going to succeed. As the campaign went on, I thought, "I'm not doing very well, but I am getting some votes. My tombstone could well read, 'Here lies Pat Buchanan. He elected Al Gore.'" So I started saying to myself a little prayer: "Lord, don't let that one be on my tombstone." And you know what? A voice came through the clouds and said, "Patrick, since you've led a relatively good life, I'm going to do you a favor, just this once. I'm going to help you defeat Al Gore and help you elect George W. Bush....You know all those Jewish folks down in Palm Beach County that love you so much? At the polls they think they're going to vote for Al Gore, who they want, but they're going to vote for you, and as a consequence of that, George Bush is going to be elected president." Then he said, "But Patrick, if you ever try something like this again, I won't be there to help you." So that's how it all ended up in the year 2000.

At that point I decided it was time to tell the straight, unvarnished truth about the condition of our country and Western civilization. The West is dying. There is not a single Western country, not a single European country, except Muslim Albania, where the birthrate is sufficient to keep the country alive. Between now and the middle of this century, Europe's population will decline by the exact amount as if all the people of Belgium, Holland, Sweden, Denmark, Norway, and Germany completely disappeared. Europe's population will shrink by 128 million people. The median age in Europe in 2050 will be fifty years old. One-tenth of Europe will be over eighty years of age. As this population ages, shrinks, and dies, the place set aside for their children is going to be filled by mass migration from North Africa, the Middle East, and southern Africa. For Europe to maintain fifty years from now the same ratio of workers to retirees, about five to one, they will have to bring in over one billion immigrants—as much as the population of China.

Russia had 147 million people two years ago; it now has 145 million. By mid-century, it will be 114 million. I got my statistics from the United Nations—Joe Chamie.[1] I told him to take the present birthrate and simply run it out to the end of this century. He gets Russia down to 80 million. Asian Russia is equal to the U.S. in size but has a population of 10 million. They are aging and dying off. Those lands were stolen from China when China was weak. When I was in the Nixon White House, in 1969, there were clashes between Russian and Chinese troops along the Ussuri River and the Amur River. The area where Vladivostok is right now was taken from China in 1860. These older Russians will die out, and the Chinese will take it back. How will they do it? Not necessarily militarily. They're going to do it the way we took Texas.

In 1821, the Mexican government said they had an empty province up north, so let's invite in the Americans. They've only got to do two things: convert to Catholicism and swear allegiance to Mexico. In 1835, there were three thousand Mexicans in Texas and thirty thousand Americans. So when General Santa Anna took power in Mexico City, the Americans kicked the Mexican army out and declared independence. That's how we got Texas.

1. Joseph Chamie is director of the UN Population Division.

And that's how China will get back Russia in the Far East. In the middle of this century, the people of Alaska are going to look across the Bering Strait, not at old, friendly Russian folks, but at tough, young, Chinese pioneers.

We have thirty-five million Hispanics in the U.S.—13 percent of a huge population. In 1950, 1960, it was 1 percent of a population half the size of ours. What is the difference between the current immigration into America as compared to the immigration when our parents came here? One, almost all our parents came here legally. Half a million Mexicans get into the U.S. illegally every single year. Two, when our parents and grandparents came here, they came to be Americans, to learn the language, know the history, adopt the heroes. The Mexicans who come here are hardworking folks, but they are proud Mexicans. They don't want to become Americans. They retain their Spanish language, watch Spanish television, listen to Spanish-speaking radio, and go back and forth between the U.S. and Mexico. They want dual citizenship. Culturally and socially, they want to be part of Mexico, and economically, they prefer to be part of the U.S. because of our standard of living. In that way lies balkanization. You have two cultures, two languages, as you have on the West Bank between Israel and the Palestinians. You're going to end up with two nations. The new immigrants are coming to a country where multiculturalism is preached, telling you to keep your separate identity and to demand racial entitlements and ethnic preferences.

A growing and expanding population is the sign of a species that is healthy, just like a dying population is an endangered species. People of European descent have fallen to 16 percent from 25 percent of the world's population, and in every Western country, the native-born population is dying out. I've traced it back to the mid-1960s, when the baby boom that had run from 1946 to 1964 started to trail off. What happened back in the 1960s? The counterculture. A generation came onto the campuses in 1964. That was the year you had Mario Savio. It was the beginning of a counterculture that was anti-American, anti-Christian, and anti-Western. The famous intellectual Susan Sontag said in 1967, "The white race is the cancer of human history." The idea was that the West was not only a flawed civilization, but responsible for slavery, imperialism, colonialism, patriarchy— all the evils of the world, sanctioned by the Christian Church. A tremendously hostile counterculture arose in antithesis to Western culture and civilization. It captured the intellectuals, but it did not succeed politically.

Politically, there was success in the conservative movement. After 1964, Richard Nixon won the election and we converted that into a forty-nine-state landslide in '72. After that broke apart, in 1980 Ronald Reagan rode out of the west and won forty-four states. Then we won forty-nine states again. With Reagan's victory, we defeated communism in the Soviet Union. But while we were winning the Cold War, we were losing the cultural war at home. What was represented by McGovern—acid, amnesty, abortion—was prevailing among the young. This counterculture is now dominant in the American media, Hollywood, and television. We have all this blasphemous art. In high schools and grammar schools, they hand out condoms to children. If something like that had happened in the fifties, they would have been lynched or indicted and sent to jail.

This cultural revolution which went to war against the traditional culture in America has triumphed among the elite. Neither Ronald Reagan nor Richard Nixon could win forty-nine states today. With that culture, the counterculture that I believe is carcinogenic, the nations and peoples began to die. T. S. Eliot said that when a religion dies, the people soon discover they no longer have anything to live for. Hilaire Belloc wrote, "Europe is the Faith, and the Faith is Europe." Christianity, which is fundamentally the religion of the West, is basically dormant and dying in Europe. In the U.S. there are strong pockets of religious faith: Orthodox Judaism, Mormonism; and the Southern Baptists, evangelicals, fundamentalists, and Catholic traditionalists are strong. But overall, the faith has died among a huge segment of the population, and that's the part of the population that has begun to die.

As a result of this, more and more women are having zero, one, or at most, two children. You have an average birthrate of 1.1 children in many European countries. That's only half the rate needed to keep them alive. For the salvation of the West, to preserve the West as a separate, unique civilization, it is going to need a massive conversion of the heart. That is beyond politics.

In the next fifty years, the Third World will grow by the equivalent of thirty to forty new Mexicos. If you go to the end of the century, the white and European population is down to about 3 percent. This is what I call the death of the West. I see the nations dying when the populations die. I see the civilization dying. It is under attack in our own countries, from our own people. The descendants of Mario Savio are attacking it, and also the folks coming into this country from China and Mexico. What is the "Greatest Generation" to them? Iwo Jima, Valley Forge, the Gettysburg Address: what does it mean to them? In our colleges and universities, the history of America is not being taught. In a study, they gave five hundred and fifty college seniors from the finest schools in America—Harvard, Dartmouth, Penn—a basic history test: one-fourth of these seniors knew who the American general at Yorktown was; one-third knew that "of the people, by the people, for the people" was associated with the Gettysburg Address; however, 99 percent were able to identify Beavis and Butthead, and 98 percent Snoop Doggy Dogg. No one has yet challenged my numbers in all the interviews I've done. I didn't invent them. Ninety percent of them come from the UN and the other 10 percent come from the *New York Times*, which is not a strong Buchanan paper.

If necessary, you've got to declare a moratorium on all immigration into the U.S. You have to, if necessary, put American troops on the border to protect our borders. What are we doing, defending the borders of Kosovo, Kuwait, and South Korea when the borders of the U.S. are bleeding and hemorrhaging? History ought to be taught to children from kindergarten through first grade all the way through every year of high school, as it was taught to me when I was growing up. These ideas are necessary if we want to maintain the unique nation we are. Solzhenitsyn said that God has made every nation with a unique face. A nation should be preserved. The great battle we all face is to preserve the great character, identity, independence, and sovereignty of the United States of America.

January 24, 2002

Ralph Nader

Consumer Advocate; 2000 Green Party Presidential Candidate

Two weeks before the 2000 presidential election, Green Party candidate Ralph Nader was asked whether he was worried about drawing votes away from Democrat Al Gore that would allow Republican George W. Bush to win in California. "If I was worried about that," Nader told the *San Francisco Chronicle*, "I wouldn't have run."

Nader's critics during the campaign were legion—but that was nothing new to the lawyer who took on the American automobile industry in his seminal 1965 exposé, *Unsafe at Any Speed*. Looking to discredit Nader, General Motors even hired private detectives to follow him. But his three decades of work as a crusader for consumer rights were not enough to keep one-time supporters from publicly urging voters not to "waste" their vote in 2000 by throwing it to a candidate who couldn't win. Acknowledging the danger of a Bush victory, some Nader supporters encouraged voters only in non-battleground states (including Gore strongholds New York and Massachusetts, as well as Colorado, which was destined to be Bush turf) to vote Green. Via the Internet, some attempted to engineer vote-swapping schemes that would maintain national support for the Greens without jeopardizing a Democratic victory in states where the election would be close. For his part, Nader embarked on a "Don't Waste Your Vote" tour of Bush's home state of Texas. Attempting to reinvigorate what he saw as a moribund political system—one that he said was trying to shut him out—Nader declared he was running in part to build a base for Greens in 2004 and to establish enough support to qualify the party for matching federal campaign funds.

As it turned out, California wasn't in play in 2000. But Florida was. There the election was so close that, as Pat Buchanan joked, votes somehow miscast in Palm Beach County would have been enough to sway the election. Americans were introduced to new vocabulary: "overvote," "undervote," "butterfly ballot," and the infamous "hanging chad" (the square of cardboard not fully punched out of a punch-card ballot). There were suits and counter-suits, allegations of African American voters illegally turned away from the polls, and finally, more than a month after election day, a decision rendered by the U.S. Supreme Court declared Bush the winner.

The votes Nader received in Florida earned him the label of "spoiler" from many disgruntled Democrats. Just over a year after the fateful election, Nader took to The Commonwealth Club podium to recount the Greens' Y2K attempt to crash the two-party party—where, he said, the media was as complicit as the Democrats and Republicans in perpetuating the system.

"Crashing the Party"

I wonder why there aren't more Commonwealth Clubs in other cities to develop civic forums the way your club has done. I like the word "commonwealth" because it involves what we own in common in the United States. The greatest wealth of this country is held in common; however concentrated private wealth might be in a few hands, the greatest wealth is in the public lands, the public airwaves, the five trillion dollars of public pension funds, the public works of our country, and all of the government-funded research and development that has led to the emergence of so many industries, from aerospace to biotechnology. I think that word is going to come back into vogue. In the eighty or ninety years since it was in vogue, we tend to have individuated our society to an extreme degree, which is another way of saying the powers that be like to divide and rule by overindividuating societies rather than emphasize what we own together. If we knew and grew up learning about what we own together, in terms of public resources and knowledge, we might want to control more of what we own and let less of it be controlled by private vested interests like the broadcasting and natural resource industries and their increasing concentration in fewer hands.

The political economy in our country is lathered with self-censorship, evasive inattention, and an extraordinary and studied ability to submerge the reality to myth, symbols, slogans, and jingles which reflect too much of presidential politics. Why I ran for president seems to be the obsessive focus of some Democrats in the country. The most important reason I ran is that civil society is being shut out of Washington, D.C., by two parties that increasingly look alike and whose similarities tower over the dwindling real differences that they are willing to contend over. If we focus on one or two of the real differences as the be-all and end-all of our allegiance to one or the other party, we won't recognize the magnitude of the similarities.

When citizen groups who try to improve things are excluded, shut out, can't get through the doors, can't get congressional hearings or get agencies to respond because there are dollar signs on all these doors, citizen groups have three options: one, indulge their illusion and work harder and harder for less and less; two, close down; or three, close down and go to Monterey and watch the whales. Another option is to go into the political arena, stop thinking that politics is sleazy, dirty, ineffective, and listen to what Thomas Jefferson told us a couple of centuries ago: When essentially vested interests take over our government, use it for their parochial services, and/or turn it against its own people, we have to go into the political arena for fresh new political effort, orientation, and movement.

I and many others who worked hard to help coal miners get occupational safety standards, advance the research in areas of disease and trauma prevention, open up freedom of information in government, and improve the safety of motor vehicles and food safety in the 1960s and 1970s find we cannot accomplish these things today. Most of what we accomplished in the 1960s and 1970s would not even be introduced as legislation today. It would not be the subject of a hearing. I could not have gotten through, today, the auto safety law which has saved over a million lives (although it's irregularly enforced) since 1966. Reporters don't cover it as a regular beat. The media have changed in that respect. You don't have the stalwart people commanding the committees in Congress, you don't have any receptivity in the White House, and you don't have the levels of outrage by people around the country who supported the psychological infrastructure for members of Congress to do the right thing.

We live in a country that has far more solutions than it applies and far more problems than it deserves. That is represented by the democracy gap. Corporations produce a lot of wealth, and democracy distributes and produces a lot of justice. When the two are out of sync and the corporate government dominates the opportunity for popular sovereignty and a deliberative democracy, then we have more and more solutions piling up and more and more needs and injustices unaddressed. It's inconceivable that a society of our plentitude can be stuck in traffic the way it has been, especially over the last two decades—because we allow the highway lobby to devastate the prospects for modern mass transit.

We are increasingly being disenfranchised, though the symbols of democracy remain. What influence do the American people have over foreign and military policy, federal reserve policy? Corporations, ever fewer and ever larger, with no allegiance to countries or communities other than to control them, are strategically planning our future. They are planning our economic, political, and educational future, our military policy future, our foreign policy future, our genetically engineered future, our privacy future. The modern corporation is an artificial entity that was the subject of great skepticism in the early nineteenth century. It receives its existence from state and federal charters without which corporations cannot exist, with all their privileges and immunities and abilities to transcend into unfair contests interactions with ordinary human beings who cannot accumulate power and wealth and presence in thousands of places at once the way corporations can. Corporations are getting away with things today that the corporations of fifty years ago would never even dream of at the height of their avarice. And corporations of fifty years ago were getting away with things that corporations of 1850 would never have conceived of.

The mass media expose corporate crime, defrauding of consumers on a systemic scale, poisoning of the environment, looting government resources, the conditions in our inner cities, and nothing happens. Months later, there are still no investigations, no prosecutions and hearings. You know that the democracy is weakening seriously because these corporate abuses are impervious to exposé. That violates a very important principle: that the focus of sunlight is the greatest disinfectant, as Justice Louis

Brandeis once said. In one decision in the 1930s, he also warned the states of allowing corporations to turn into Frankensteins in our midst. Remember, Brandeis was a prominent corporate lawyer before he became a justice of the Supreme Court.

Lots of good people who would ordinarily run for elections are not running because politics is so groveling and distasteful. Politics came out of ancient Greece as an antidote to autocracy, as a purveyor of democracy. It's turned into a dirty word. Even politicians turn it into a dirty word when they dismiss an opponent's position by saying it's just politics.

People's expectation levels toward politics and government have reached perilously low levels. The difference between a cynic and a skeptic is that a cynic makes a diagnosis of society's abuses and withdraws, regaling in their intellectual sophistication. In withdrawing they create a vacuum, and the vacuum is filled with rascals. A skeptic makes a similar diagnosis but roars back to change the conditions that fostered these abuses.

Examples of superior performance are not considered news. It is true Enron is very worthy of news. It is a supermarket of corporate crime, fraud, and abuse. It is symptomatic of what conservative George Will recently called a systemic problem in today's capitalism. In fact, if it is allowed to continue it will etch a chapter in American economic history that can be called "The Corporate Destruction of Capitalism," because capitalism is not supposed to be bailed out, it's not supposed to have a government guarantee. Capitalism is supposed to have competition. It's supposed to be challenged by new and established firms, and increasingly we have more monopolistic or oligopolistic control in one industry after another, and more merging of corporate interests with government services, such as corporate welfare in all of its manifestations.

I announced my candidacy on February 21, 2000, in Washington. Every major television network was there. That evening there was no reporting of the announcement on any of the television networks except CNN. Although the subjects that we had dealt with for thirty-five years were subjects of considerable press attention and the subjects of our agenda, and although I campaigned before the largest audiences of any presidential candidate, and although I had very good contacts with members of the press, they refused to cover the campaign in a regular way. They covered it in feature way. The *Los Angeles Times* would say, "Gee, I wonder what the Nader campaign's doing? We haven't covered it for a couple of months. Let's send

Right: American representative to the UN Madeleine Albright warned her Commonwealth Club audience in 1993, "You can have all kinds of missile systems, but they cannot protect our way of life, make our children healthy, or prevent disease from spreading." *Paul Eric Felder, Commonwealth Club Office Archives*

Below: In June 1996, a truck loaded with five thousand pounds of plastic explosives was detonated outside the U.S. military complex at Khobar Towers in Saudi Arabia, killing nineteen Americans and wounding hundreds more. The bomb was estimated to be more than twice as powerful as the one used at the Marine barracks in Beirut in 1983. *Courtesy of the U.S. Department of Defense*

Above: In December 1995, a father kneels at his son's grave in Sarajevo. *David Turnley/CORBIS*

Opposite page, top: Coffins containing the remains of nearly three hundred identified victims of the 1995 Srebrenica slaughter of up to eight thousand Muslim men and boys by Bosnian Serb forces await burial in a former battery factory in July 2003. *Reuters/CORBIS*

Opposite page, bottom: On April 1, 1999, a convoy of Kosovar Albanian refugees arrives in Albania. *J. B. Russell/CORBIS SYGMA*

Right: In 1998, UN Secretary-General Kofi Annan persuaded Iraqi leader Saddam Hussein to cooperate with UN weapons inspectors. He was lauded by some as a peacemaker, while others accused him of appeasement. *Courtesy of Chris Stewart/San Francisco Chronicle*

Below: On Kids' Day at Camp Demi in Bosnia-Herzegovina in November 1999, a translator explains to children the hazards of antipersonnel mines. *Courtesy of the U.S. Department of Defense*

On September 11, 2001, terrorists hijacked and crashed planes into the World Trade Center in New York, the Pentagon (pictured), and a Pennsylvania field. When journalist and producer Lowell Bergman spoke to The Commonwealth Club on "The Media and the War on Terrorism," he noted that people overseas perceived this as an attempt to overthrow the U.S. government. *Courtesy of the U.S. Department of Defense*

Two Orthodox Jews watch Israeli security forces as they begin to gather at the Western Wall in Jerusalem's Old City on December 31, 1999. *Courtesy of Susanna Frohman/San Francisco Chronicle*

Above: In November 2001, one year after the beginning of the second intifada, Palestinian advocate Hanan Mikhail-Ashrawi expressed hope that multilateral diplomacy would help to bring peace to the Middle East. *Paul Eric Felder, Commonwealth Club Office Archives*

Left: A Palestinian boy shows off his toy machine gun in Gaza City (April 2002). *Courtesy of Justin Sullivan/San Francisco Chronicle*

Right: Bill O'Reilly logged hours as a journalist with CBS and ABC before moving to host *The O'Reilly Factor* on Fox News, where he uses his "built-in bull detector" on guests and offers opinion and analysis. *Courtesy of Gino Domenico/Fox News*

Below: Dubbed a "spoiler" in the 2000 presidential election for drawing support from voters who otherwise might have supported Democrat Al Gore, consumer advocate Ralph Nader was unapologetic about his crusade to crack open the two-party political system in the U.S. *Courtesy of Julia Ann Plasencia/ San Francisco Chronicle*

In March 2001, U.S. Senators Russ Feingold (left) and John McCain traveled to The Commonwealth Club to win public support for the Bipartisan Campaign Finance Reform Act. *Courtesy of Lacy Atkins/San Francisco Chronicle*

Right: Afghan border crossing (December 2003). *Courtesy of Asad R. Ahmed/San Francisco Chronicle*

Below: By March 2002, women were returning to teach and girls were openly attending school in Afghanistan. Depicted: the Rukshana School in Kabul. *Courtesy of the U.S. Department of Defense*

Iraqi children watch American soldiers search cars after a mortar attack on their compound (January 2004). *Courtesy of Matthew Stannard/San Francisco Chronicle*

In *Jihad vs. McWorld,* Benjamin Barber warned that tribalism and global capitalism were undermining democracy. Before The Commonwealth Club, he asked whether, in the post–9/11 world, "smart bombs" or "smart concepts" would prove more valuable in confronting terrorism. *Courtesy of the San Francisco Chronicle*

out a reporter." I met with editorial boards and they were very curious and very kind, and sometimes a reporter was actually there to write an article.

The other two major candidates were running in a two-party society where the assumption was that the country belongs to two parties and no other party, and if you wanted to challenge one or other of the two parties, you would have to learn how to climb a cliff with a slippery rope. There are so many obstacles, beyond any obstacles that face small parties in other Western democracies. A political system that is not congenial to small parties is a political system that cannot regenerate itself any more than nature can regenerate itself if it doesn't allow seeds to sprout, or a business can regenerate itself if it doesn't allow innovators, entrepreneurs, and small business to sprout. Yet this kind of two-party, duopoly thinking has been ingrained in the minds of millions of Americans who are willing to be told, year after year, that you either stay home if you don't like the two parties or you trundle to the polls in a less-than-enthusiastic selection of the least worst. The least-worst approach guarantees both parties get worse every four years.

The lesser of two evils—or the evil of two lessers—is not the direction that should guide American politics. I have criticized Democrats on Capitol Hill—which we now call "Withering Heights"—and the answer is almost always the same. When you criticize the Democrats on issue after issue, they lean forward and say, "Do you know how bad the Republicans are?" Here is a party that defines itself by the worst instead of defining itself by the best it can become. That's when you know that the corporate Democrats have taken over and marginalized the progressive Democrats, who represent a legacy that is the soul of the party.

In early summer of 2000, the headline in the "A" section of the *Washington Post* was "Gore, Family Relax in North Carolina." I decided I'd better head to Vermont and flamboyantly relax, and then maybe I'd get an article. The Nader/LaDuke candidacy received less than 1 percent of the money, less than 1 percent of media coverage, and about 3 percent of the vote. We tried to campaign in a model way, called for by many editorials of many newspapers, who over the years have criticized the Republicans and Democrats for not campaigning forthrightly, honestly, or interactively with the citizenry. We refused to take PAC money, soft money, business money. We mostly raised money by small contributions and some $2,000-maximum contributions. We raised money by filling the largest arenas of the country with ten-dollar, fifteen-dollar, twenty-dollar contributions, and we achieved some matching funds under federal law. We campaigned with the people instead of parading in front of them. We didn't go into the inner city for a photo opportunity. In inner city Hartford, up to 40 percent of children suffer from asthma. There are incinerators not far away. In South Central Los Angeles is a public housing project built on former oil refinery land soaked with carcinogens. In the middle of this square, the children, mostly Hispanic, were running around and breathing the flares that came from a pile of dirt that was an unfinished remediation project from the city's attempt to do something about the contaminated soil. So many people died from cancer that they had a little memorial where they would lay some roses as every cancer death was carted away to the cemetery.

We campaigned with people trying to save the Everglades, trying to stop the coal barons from blowing off the tops of mountains, rumbling the rocks and debris and blocking the streams and scaring the dickens out of the villages in the hollows of Appalachia. We stood by the neighborhood groups in Boston, next to Fenway Park, who were protesting a proposed $400-million tax subsidy for a new ballpark. The neighborhood had other ideas where that kind of money could be used, for the benefit of people other than sports megamillionaires. We marched with workers striving for a livable wage in Madison, Wisconsin, who are working for subcontractors at the university for six or seven dollars an hour before deductions and the cost of getting to work.

We campaigned in front of the New York Stock Exchange, denouncing city and state politicians who surrendered to the New York Stock Exchange demand that it receive over a billion dollars to buy land and build a new stock exchange about a block away. Here is this bastion of global capitalism demanding corporate welfare. They told New York City that they would not go across the river with the stock exchange and establish the Hoboken stock exchange if they received a billion dollars in taxpayer money.

We cannot go to the polls in America and vote no. There is no binding "none of the above." If there was, I think sometimes it would win, and it would cancel the candidates on that party line and order new candidates and new elections in thirty days. We only have the option to vote yes. We cannot vote in a proportional representation system so that more votes can count. We do not have the kind of mechanisms where new parties can have a chance to reach critical mass and become players on the political scene. If the German Greens can get more than 5 percent of the votes, they get 5 percent or more of the parliament.

The democracy is weakening. The standard of living for most people is declining, according to the Department of Labor, after ten years of boom. In our country, the majority of workers are making less in inflation-adjusted wages than they made in 1973 or 1968. We have six million families without affordable housing. We have expanding homelessness, especially with more and more layoffs and the recession. We still have widespread hunger and malnutrition in our country. We have devastated our environment. We have exported a lot of jobs through twenty-seven years of growing trade deficits. We have $7.5 trillion of consumer debt, indicating that people certainly can't live on what they're making, and they're going deeper and deeper into debt. Yet these are not the indicators that we hear from Alan Greenspan, George W. Bush, or others who use corporate indicators, not people indicators, to measure economic progress or regress.

America is sliding backward, even compared with Western European countries, in motor vehicle fuel efficiency, in our public works, repair, and modification. We're sliding backward in our greater energy dependence and greater energy scarring of the environment, in spending more and more money on health care without spending it on disease and trauma prevention. It's hard to face up to these things, to the 20-percent child poverty rate in the U.S. compared to the 3-percent in the Netherlands, where they think there's too much and they're trying do something about it. There's a 2-percent rate in Scandinavia. Why is it that forty years ago, after the rubble of World War II, these countries were able to give their people by law universal health care, full paid maternity leave and family sick leave, four weeks of paid vacation, 41 percent higher real wages for the lower one-third of the workers compared to the U.S., decent public transit, adequate benefits, and rather nice facilities, like libraries that don't close because of municipal budget restrictions while stadiums are built in spite of municipal budget restrictions? Why did they achieve these things many years ago, and yet we can't? Maybe we're not organized enough. Maybe we're too stratified. Maybe the people in this country who get their calls returned are too comfortable, and the people who aren't comfortable don't get their calls returned—and they're the majority. Maybe we've lost a sense of realizable futures. Maybe we're buying a lot of propaganda that is peddled through the mass media in all kinds of ways.

Whatever it is, we can forget about it if we resolve to engage in a new political direction, new civic institutions, and do what we can do if we simply spend more time doing it. The amount of time people spend watching the Super Bowl amounts to five hundred million citizen hours. That amount of time in 1993 would have given us universal health care. It's much more efficient, humane, inclusive, and universal health care does not cost more money. We are already spending $4,200 per capita on health care, almost double what some European countries are spending—and much more than what Canada is spending, where it covers everybody from cradle through nursing home. It's a matter of taking that $4,200 and developing a system that is not so administratively expensive and cumbersome and does not relegate so much of its assets to bureaucratic HMOs who really don't deliver medical care as much as they deliver customers.

Key to public imagination is the conscious refusal to grow up corporate and the conscious need to grow up civic. When did we grow up corporate? We might be surprised at how thoroughly it has permeated our vision and our horizons. Have you ever seen a new car ad on television showing congested traffic? Have you ever seen a new mass transit ad on television with people relaxing, reading the newspaper, chatting with one another on their way to work, parallel to a highway clogged bumper to bumper with trucks, vans, and cars? After forty years of this disparity, we can understand why modern public mass transit is not seen as a glamorous way to get around on the ground. It's true in our growing up not knowing what we own together as a commonwealth so that we can understand how we can better use it for the commonweal. It's the way we allow commercial standards of beauty to disrupt communal standards of beauty and our own interactions personally with one another. It is corporate thinking that gets us to passively sign all our contracts without asking, "Don't we have freedom of contract in this country?" Growing up civic is the liberation of the human mind and the facilitation of the greatest instrument ever devised to solve human problems, prevent injustices, foresee and forestall future perils, and accentuate future benefits: a deliberative, working, daily democracy.

January 9, 2002

Lowell Bergman

Producer/Correspondent, Frontline

The front pages of the newspapers of September 12, 2001, bore enormous photos of the destruction wrought by terrorist attacks in the U.S. the day before. The editions from that day, and the day that followed, became collector's items. Some media observers remarked, however, that the newspapers from the day before the attack would also be remembered as significant, for they were chronicling an era that had ended. With the beginning of the war on terror, everything would be different. Among the effects those attacks and the U.S. invasion of Afghanistan wrought were changes in the relationship between the American media and government. And as journalist Lowell Bergman remarked in his January 2002 talk at The Commonwealth Club, there was a new sense of responsibility among those who shape the news. Reflecting on the horrors, Bergman's talk was also filled with hope that the renewal of international news coverage was part of a renewed engagement on the part of Americans and would be part of the ongoing crucial effort to understand the world around us.

In addition to bringing his experience as producer of documentaries for PBS's *Frontline* (including stories on Saddam Hussein and, prior to September 11, 2001, Osama bin Laden) and as a *New York Times* correspondent, Bergman is a veteran of CBS's *60 Minutes*. His work on an exposé of tobacco giant Brown & Williamson became the stuff of legend when CBS refused to air the program for fear of a lawsuit. The episode eventually became the stuff of film, with Al Pacino playing Bergman in *The Insider*.

"*The Media and the War on Terrorism*"

When I got the request to come here and speak, I, like many other people in the media business, was in the middle of the frenzy that followed September 11. *Frontline*, the weekly public broadcasting program, went into high gear, and we did about four documentaries in the space of time that you would normally do fewer than one. They ranged from a report on Saudi Arabia to a report on the evidence and lobby in Washington that wants to take on Saddam Hussein, and to a piece called "Looking For Answers." I wanted to call it "Why?" Why did this happen? How could this happen? Just before that, PBS and *Frontline* had begun running the documentary we had done two and a half years earlier, "Hunting bin Laden."

One of the positive developments since September 11 has been most of the coverage. Media organizations based in the U.S.—now global organizations—do one thing better than anyone else in the world: cover catastrophes, disasters, car crashes, and emergencies of any kind. It's been true in terms of live events and live television since its beginning, whether it was atomic bombs in the Nevada desert, or an assassination here in the U.S., or the Iranian hostage crisis in 1979, which also resulted in positive changes in the media. That coverage hasn't only been superficial on the networks and cable; it's gotten relative depth compared to most of the coverage that we're used to on commercial television. There have been documentaries and people have done groundbreaking reporting about things considered to be very arcane in the past.

September 11 has been called our Pearl Harbor in the twenty-first century. As a result, you will not hear what you had been hearing for years from network television executives: that foreign news means low ratings and no one cares.

Just before September 11, I was in New York and Washington at meetings between PBS and the *New York Times*, trying to work out how to do better television reporting, particularly in the international area. ABC News, which had its glory days in the late 1970s, moved into international news with "America Held Hostage," which became *Nightline*. Most of the networks were proud of their international news-gathering operations. But in 2001, up until September 11, all the networks, including CNN, were laying people off, closing foreign bureaus, moving to entertainment-style programming, trying to compete with Fox News and what I call "food-fight television," and pushing off the screen more serious, in-depth reporting. The rationale behind it was ratings and money.

After September 11, ABC started to bring back some of the people it laid off, because they didn't have enough people to do the work, especially to go overseas. We now know that foreign news and what is going on in other countries, and the impact of what we call globalization—all of which we were insulated from by a moat of great oceans until September 11—is going to come back to haunt us.

The question "Why?" cannot be answered until we have more information about what's going on. There were some network television people who refused to rerun a documentary about the India-Pakistan fight over Kashmir, saying it was "low ratings." Who would have believed, before September 11, that we would now be focused on Kashmir, that we even know where Uzbekistan may be, that we are beginning to talk about in public the plight of the 1.4 billion Muslims in the world and what their grievances might be towards us, others, or their own rulers?

Reporting on international events and the status of what's going on in the Third and Fourth Worlds is clearly becoming at least as important as reporting on bad hamburgers or other things that may be a threat to your children or your daily life, because now American civilians are dying, and more of us may die in the future because of the consequences of some of our policies and some policies overseas for which we are not responsible. The reaction to that, both in print and television, is a positive thing. In the past, I had a hard time explaining to students why they should learn how to do quality television when there was nowhere to work. There will be more jobs, because even public television, which also has a tendency towards cooking shows and other things more entertainment-oriented, is now investing more money in *Frontline*. You'll see a new series this spring, *Frontline/World*, produced out of San Francisco's KQED and UC Berkeley, which will be a magazine program focusing on international stories, using younger people and the new digital kinds of equipment, presenting stories that you haven't seen before. The Corporation for Public Broadcasting has also put more money into PBS, into *Frontline* itself, to help it continue doing coverage on the war on terrorism. They have put additional funding into an organization in New York headed by Bill Moyers which will be doing a weekly program on Fridays with National Public Radio, also focusing on international events and general subjects in depth.

I'm hopeful that something that Walter Cronkite said not so long ago—that a bonfire in the capital of a small country whose name we can't pronounce could turn into a mushroom-shaped cloud unless we pay attention—is a warning that may, in fact, be felt by our population in general and by the people who control the media. Maybe the next time something like this happens, people at least will have a clue as to why. Why is it that people don't like us? What is it in our policies that link us to people on the other side of the world who may be doing things that we wouldn't like? Is a policy of being allied with people who we would not find palatable here at home something that in the end will work? What is happening right now, when the U.S. government is making alliances in Central Asia or with the government of Russia? What are the implications of those alliances? If there are consequences from them, at least we'll have an informed public. There are those who believe that an informed public is not necessary. There is a serious group of people involved in the media business that believes this.

Look at the change that's taken place, particularly in broadcasting, about requirements for someone who owns a broadcasting license. Those requirements, while they still appear in principle in law, no longer apply in fact to the regulation of the media industry in general and broadcasting in particular. That's one of the reasons why there hasn't been more quality reporting and broadcasting until now. If you have any influence, call the stations, write letters. I'm not trying to be a Pollyanna about the possibilities here. In the end, it's a matter of national security. Because this is where most people get their information, the broadcast industry in particular will begin to regularly provide people with in-depth reporting.

Do you know how much it costs for a broadcast license? If you wanted to drill for oil, you'd have to make various lease arrangements with the state and the federal government and pay a percentage of the gross. You don't have to do that if you're a broadcaster. If it's a new license, it costs you $230 to use the public's airwaves. If it's a renewal, it's $135. No licenses of any major broadcaster have ever been yanked. Because the National Association of Broadcasters is one of the most effective lobbies in Washington, they've been living in that atmosphere for quite a while. Hopefully, in terms of what's happened most recently, that will change. The idea that there is a responsibility to the audience will become something more accepted.

In doing stories over the last part of the year, one thing I found people agreeing on in interviews on camera was—and I'll quote Prince Bandar, who doesn't agree with the Saudi royal dissidents, because he wouldn't be alive very long if they took power: "Nobody [in the United States] spends enough time to understand the culture of other countries. What makes them tick?" This is Prince Bandar, friend of the Bush family. He is quite wealthy himself, from his role in various arms deals between Saudi Arabia and the U.S. He has a large estate in Aspen, as well as one right next to CIA headquarters in Virginia. "What is the reality? What is the falseness? Because you don't do that, you don't want to know what other people need, it's a weakness. It's definitely a weakness." He smiled and went on and said, "It's a weakness we exploit, so maybe you shouldn't." I believe that just out of sheer necessity, the nature of what we do, especially on commercial television, and how we provide information—and to a certain extent in print—is going to change.

We are capable as a country of avoiding reality. But the fact of what happened isn't going to go away. People overseas I've interviewed since September 11 look at the U.S. and say, "Do you people realize that this was a coup attempt?" An attack on the financial center and the military head-quarters and apparently an aircraft that was headed for the political capi-tal—Congress or the White House—looked to them as an attempt to basi-cally overthrow our government. That's how serious it was.

We shouldn't be surprised that the wealth that we have accumulated has also accumulated major enemies. People look at the regimes that are our friends—for example, the moderate Arabs in the Middle East—and the nature of those regimes and their history. In those countries, when you talk to people on the street, you understand that they look at the U.S and see the only way to get rid of that regime would be to go through the U.S. That's what we represent.

One striking thing we ran into two and a half years ago after the Nairobi bombings was the official U.S. government explanation: that a small group of terrorists from outside Kenya and Tanzania had infiltrated the country and carried out these two bombings simultaneously in both capitals. We discovered when we spent some time on the ground that the large minority in both countries was Muslim. They were, in their minds, generally oppressed. They didn't have social services. You hear about Saudi and other Muslim charities that funnel money to bin Laden—that's the story we hear. Some of that is true; it does get to these other organizations. But in Islamic communities in Mombasa or Dar es Salaam, those charities are the only source of social welfare. They are not all run by terrorists or fundamentalists. Some money may get siphoned off. But these are separate communities dependent on international Islamic support. There's no foreign aid getting to these communities from the U.S. In the "Saudi Time Bomb" documentary, we went to the Comoros Islands in the Indian Ocean. They're Muslim. There is no foreign aid to these communities. The only educational aid for people to go into higher education is provided by fundamentalist Islamic schools in Egypt and Pakistan. They're funded by Saudi money. Some people who were involved in Al Qaeda went through that system. That's the reality in that part of the world.

One great danger in all of this—and many of the FBI officials that we interviewed said this—is that we abandon exactly those freedoms that we have here in our pursuit of wiping out the terrorists. For that, the broadcast industry has not done a great job, starting with the phone call that Condoleezza Rice, the national security advisor, made to the network news executives back in October. President Bush wasn't happy that his speech announcing the bombing of Afghanistan was followed by a videotape from Osama bin Laden. That resulted in a call from Ms. Rice in which she got the network executives to agree to "prescreen" all tapes from bin Laden or his organization before they put them on the air, and to watch what you put on the air, because there may be secret signals: he may be wearing something, or there may be a rifle. The network executives responded by saying, "We're going to do something about this, think twice about this," and so on. The silliness and seriousness of this is that Al Jazeera and all the Islamic broadcasting companies in the world were not affected by this. There were no restrictions on putting his messages on the Internet and broadband. It was available worldwide, and there were no restrictions on newspapers or anyone else on providing the text of what he said in any of his messages. That immediate cave-in, without asking any serious, direct questions was a bad sign.

That said, in most other cases the networks have performed relatively admirably, and when the Pentagon made available a live feed of a videotape of Osama bin Laden making off-the-cuff remarks about how it was a great operation on September 11, they put it right on the air and didn't edit it or look at it first. Nor did the White House ask them to do that. So, it is part of succumbing to propaganda or pressure that the message might not be getting across.

In 1950, the FCC put out an order concerning who was qualified to hold a license to broadcast and said that a commercial station itself "must be operated as if owned by the public....It is as if people of a community should own a station and turn it over to the best man in sight with this injunction: 'Manage this station in our interest.'" The standing of every station that is a licensee at the time is determined by that conception, and the Supreme Court, in one decision, said that it's the right of the viewers, not the right of the broadcasters, which is paramount. Hopefully, in reaction to what happened on September 11, those rules will have more effect and we will have better in-depth coverage in the future, and we won't have to ask "Why?" so much.

[from the question-and-answer session]

Q. *Will terrorism increase in the United States?*

A. There are people we have classified as terrorists in the past who become political leaders whom we then deal with. Menachem Begin started out his political career blowing up British barracks, organizing the destruction of the King David Hotel in Israel, which was filled with British troops. He was definitely classified, even by some of his colleagues in Israel, as a leader of a terrorist organization. He later became a political leader, a prime minister, and one of the people at Camp David. The indiscriminate use of the word "terrorist" on our side isn't that helpful. It doesn't help to explain whether there are going to be more terrorist attacks or who is a terrorist. We have to start looking at people and situations where people have no hope, where people have no alternative; there we'll find potential areas of danger.

An example would be Argentina, which is becoming a failed state and which has, by the way, a large Muslim population. It had two of the biggest terrorist attacks in the Western Hemisphere prior to 9/11, which most people in this country don't know. That case has actually never been solved, but it appears it's linked in some way to the Hezbollah. There are many potential places where things could come from. How we use our language is a very important thing that we have to start talking about.

Q. *Comment on the impact the media has on the public's opinion of current events. Can network news twist a story into what it wants it to be, not necessarily what is really happening?*

A. I would come back to the whole issue of criticizing Al Jazeera, because they called suicide bombers in Palestine and Israel "martyrs" but bin Laden a "terrorist." Why is someone a martyr here and a terrorist there? We call all of them terrorists. It's the use of language that's the biggest problem that we're up against, in terms of the "evildoers" versus "the good guys." The latest polls the Pew Center has done overseas show we're not such good guys in the views of leaders around the world.

Q. *The U.S. media admitted that they were self-censoring in post–9/11 Afghanistan. Are we getting the whole story, and does it matter?*

A. Lots of self-censorship goes on in the media about a lot of things. In a wartime situation, you're not going to reveal things that would put troops or operations in danger. Are we getting the whole story? No. News coverage is, as they say, "the first draft of history." We'll learn more as time goes on. We'll learn more about how many people died in that prison in Mazar-e Sharif. We'll learn more once we hear John Walker talk about what it was like to be in the Taliban, if they let him talk.[1]

---

1. John Walker Lindh was labeled the "American Taliban" in December 2001, after he was taken into custody in Afghanistan by U.S. forces suppressing a revolt of Taliban and Al Qaeda fighters at Mazar-e Sharif fortress-turned-prison. Twenty years old when captured, he had been raised in affluent Marin County, California; had converted to Islam in his mid-teens; and had traveled to Yemen and then Pakistan before joining the Taliban. In January 2002, Lindh was charged with conspiracy to kill U.S. forces in Afghanistan. He pleaded guilty to two lesser charges—serving in the Taliban army and carrying explosive weapons during the commission of a felony—and was sentenced to twenty years in prison. The plea agreement precluded Lindh from making money off his life story, and he was required to share with U.S. intelligence officials his knowledge of the Taliban and Osama bin Laden (whom Lindh had met several times).

One of our problems in the past: after the Nairobi bombings, a number of people were arrested and indicted and held in New York. There were special, pretrial rules. They were all found guilty in the end, and none of those defendants or anyone else, like Ramzi Yousef, who did the original World Trade Center bombing, were allowed to talk, even before they were convicted. They were held for twenty-three and a half hours a day in solitary confinement and not allowed to talk to anyone except their attorneys and members of their family, who were then under a restriction from the court not to repeat anything they said to anyone else. That gets in the way of finding out who these people are and why they're doing what they're doing.

Q. *Where was the media regarding terrorism during the Clinton Administration?*

A. The news media in many ways is responsible for the fact that many people in the federal government who thought that a Pearl Harbor was going to happen didn't have enough "media clout" or coverage to get the political momentum to do something about it. Senator [Warren] Rudman's report, along with Paul Bremer's report, predicted this. They talked about how nobody in the intelligence community speaks Arabic, and how we have all these problems of jurisdiction and we can't keep track of this stuff. But nobody read it. The media didn't report on it.

When we did the original documentary, "Hunting bin Laden," for PBS, no one noticed. It got a couple of reviews. We had people on camera in Muslim communities saying bin Laden is great and Sheik Rahman's people talking about all this, but no one cared.

April 25, 2002

Benjamin Barber

Kekst Professor of Civil Society, University of Maryland

Benjamin Barber did not intend his 1995 book, *Jihad vs. McWorld,* to prophesy terrorist attacks on U.S. soil. But he did set out to map where the battle lines were being drawn between global consumerism and a tribalist religious fundamentalism. While the forces of both jihad and McWorld were battling one another, together they were undermining democracy throughout the world. Even in the U.S., citizens were reduced to mere consumers as democratic voting was being philosophically reduced to voting with the pocketbook. Barber's solution: build a sturdy, global civil society.

In the aftermath of the toppling of the twin towers of the World Trade Center, creating that transnational civil society becomes more urgent than ever. (The urgency to understand what was happening was felt throughout the U.S., too, and in the days and weeks after the terrorist attacks of September 2001, *Jihad vs. McWorld* was snapped up in bookstores around the country.) In the battle to win hearts and minds, it's not simply a matter of teaching the virtues of Pepsi and Coke but of accountable government and of organizations that allow citizens to aggregate and draw attention to issues society needs to address: women's rights, the environment, education. What role does the media play in all this? Can media channels that are part of conglomerates that are very much part of transglobal capitalism offer a fair and balanced presentation of what the conglomerates are up to?

"Confronting Terrorism: Smart Bombs or Smart Concepts?"

I am not pleased that *Jihad vs. McWorld* had a prophetic eeriness on September 11. No one wants Osama bin Laden as their publicity agent. But to some degree, what I wrote about several years ago—a confrontation between the forces of global market modernization and commercialization, and a tribal, religious, and ethnic reaction against them—has proven to be one of the key thematics played out in recent years. I'd like to talk about what 9/11 means for this confrontation between the forces of global society and those who seem so fearful of it—in some cases so fearful they have resorted to the most despicable forms of terroristic violence—and possible remedies that move beyond the military and intelligence strategies that have been the primary instruments of this administration.

For the first two hundred years, this nation was wound up in a great, powerful, and in many ways overweening myth: the myth of American independence, isolated by two great oceans, blessed with a continental bounty and a political system that in time opened membership to all and provided a model of democracy for the world. That myth inscribed in the Declaration of Independence has not only been a founding credo for this nation but a continuing presence that has made citizens and politicians alike believe that when threats come to these shores, we deal with them by exporting our soldiers, defeating our enemies, and raising the walls around America even higher.

Wrapped up in the myth was also a myth of American innocence, that this was a "new-found land," as Thomas Paine said, "as at the beginning of the world." America was where the human race was to have a second chance, outside religious turbulence, prejudices, wars, and intolerance. The myth was laced with hypocrisy, because the nation was also founded on slavery and extermination of the indigenous population. But it brought forth a credo that allowed even those excluded from the initial contract—

African Americans in slavery, women, and many others—to gradually fight for inclusion.

This wonderful mythology has made us think we can solve our problems alone, and when evil comes our way, the Lone Ranger climbs on his horse, straps on his guns, and fights the good fight. We've heard a lot of this rhetoric since September 11; it's powerful, and much of the country responds to it. On September 11, America was not just dealt the blow of a savage attack, but it was also treated to an unsolicited yet powerful lesson in the new realities of the world—the ineluctability, the inevitability, of interdependence; the fact that independent nations can no longer survive with their own destiny in their own hands.

It's frightening when our worst adversaries—men with hearts set on annihilation—understand the world better than we understand it, because that means we are in an uneven combat. Though we are far more powerful militarily, economically, culturally, and even in values, it may be that we deploy solutions based on a misunderstanding of the world: a belief that we can solve our problems by ourselves, that unilateralism, though maybe unsentimental and not terribly moralistic, is useful and pragmatically efficient. September 11 taught us that the old realism has become a new kind of utopianism. The belief that America by dint of its own military power ignoring multilateral treaties, new legal conventions, international organizations can overcome terrorism is now a new myth.

Before September 11, people who talked about global democracy, multilateralism, the need to create an interdependent foreign policy to try and deal with problems from AIDS to global warming to global markets looked like a romantic utopia of softheaded liberals. But now the multilateralists are the new realists, because they understand the lessons of September 11. Those lessons have been evident to the Europeans at least since World War II, when it was clear that no single European nation was in a position to protect itself by itself. The evolving economic, ecological, and technological environment was one in which no nation could exercise sovereign independence and control outcomes without being deeply engaged with other nations. AIDS carries no passport. The West Nile virus does not stop for customs inspections. Global warming is no respecter of national boundaries. Terrorism doesn't check in before it moves into a country and register with the police.

Our world is a globalized, in Manuel Castells' phrase, networked society in which the networks and systems are in many ways more important than the individual players. President Bush has, in a desk in the Oval Office, a large sheet of paper with twenty-two photographs of Al Qaeda leaders on it. Each time one is captured or killed, he puts an X through it. That is a deeply insufficient way to take on terrorism, not because there is anything wrong with trying to get the leadership, but because terrorism is about people who operate in the interstices of national systems. To try to find a national state address for terrorism, as this administration has done and continues to do, is a deep categorical mistake. I am not soft about the need to take military action against terrorism, but to think that terrorism can be understood in terms of nation-states that protect or harbor it is to misunderstand the nature of terrorism. Terrorism is a denial of the nation-state system, a denial that territorial states are any longer the chief actors. If President Bush was serious when he said "We will punish, destroy states that harbor terrorism," he would have first of all had to bomb New Jersey and Florida, which had been harboring the terrorists for at least two years prior to the act.

Afghanistan played a lead role in harboring terrorists, but destruction of the Taliban regime has done little to eliminate the Al Qaeda network that reappears now in Pakistan, Indonesia, and in Yemen. Terrorism is like the human brain; it's about the synapses that connect the cells. Terrorists operated here effectively by manipulating and leveraging the American transportation system, the international financial and banking system, and the credit card system. An approach that draws pictures of terrorists, puts Xs through them, or writes down the addresses of the countries where some of them can be found and then makes war on those countries makes no sense. Even if we took out Iraq, Iran, and North Korea tomorrow, the centers of the "axis of evil," terrorism would continue. What's extraordinary is that we use today's smart bombs and smart weaponry to take on our enemies, but we link them with really dumb ideas taken from the nineteenth century.

What terrorism and the global market system share first of all is anarchism—a world without law, without archons. The so-called global order is a global disorder which permits global markets to function in the absence of democratic regulation, legal oversight, and democratic will. That may be useful in the short term, but in the long term, it creates global anarchy—which may sometimes benefit markets, but more often benefits criminals and terrorists.

On the whole, we have globalized our vices rather than our virtues—the weapons trade, crime, prostitution, pollution, and diseases that now move around the world. We have globalized exploitation of women and particularly exploitation of children, who are laborers of many Third World economic systems. Children are the soldiers and victims in many of the tribal wars around the world. In Palestine, I don't want to call them martyrs or suicide bombers, but they are the victims of an adult system, a global system, which makes children the primary ones to pay the cost. On the streets of Brazil are homeless children whose choice is reduced to whether to become prostitutes or organ farms. In Thailand and in other parts of East Asia, children are used as the seductive objects of the global pornography tourist trade that you can sign up for on the Internet.

This is not a critique of capitalism; the great strength of capitalism in the West, with all of its contradictions and raw Darwinist tendencies, is that it works well when it's inside an envelope of democratic oversight and Tocquevillian civic institutions—church, family, philanthropies—which soften some of its worst side effects. They control some of its self-destructive tendencies, because left to its own devices, capitalism undermines and corrodes the very premise on which it operates. Capitalism's strength is that it works off competition, but its tendency is to destroy competition and create monopoly. It avoids that with the help of the rule of law, antitrust legislation and regulation. That doesn't just save capitalism from some of its harsher costs socially, it saves capitalism as a competitive economic system as well.

I'm not an opponent of globalization, I'm an opponent of asymmetrical globalization, in which you globalize the economics without the civics, politics, and democracy. Most people I know in the "antiglobalization movement"—a term dubbed by the media—are not antiglobal. Their question is: globalization for whom, of what, and in the name of which values and interests? Our project is not to stuff the genie of global markets back inside nation-state boxes, that's impossible. Our only hope is to extend the civic, political, and regulatory features of nation-states to the global arena.

It's not so different from nineteenth-century America after the Civil War, when the great new behemoths of American capitalism—oil, steel, railways, and eventually the automobile—operated largely without oversight. Government was still relatively minuscule and impotent compared to the new monopolies. But by the end of the nineteenth century, it became apparent to all Americans that these new robber barons would not just destroy American democracy, but American capitalism, if the state didn't intervene. Teddy Roosevelt, a Republican, was first to understand the need to regulate capitalism so its productive and entrepreneurial energies could be used for the good of all America but its contradictions and excesses contained.

We need a Rooseveltian solution at the global level. But that's hardly on the agenda. Protesters too often talk as if you are somehow going to stop these large global conglomerates. That's not going to happen. Capitalism as a business proposition has acknowledged and recognized interdependence and gone global. Democracy has stayed locked within the nation-state. That discrepancy creates the tensions that we see today between powerful and yet impotent nation-states that can neither control global capitalism nor global terrorism, much for the same reasons.

We see the irony of the U.S. looking for ways to bring global criminals under control and at the same time refusing to ratify and sign on to the new International Criminal Court; of the U.S. looking for a coalition to overcome the "axis of evil" yet refusing to sign on to multilateral treaties which manifest the new spirit of interdependence and cooperation. The conference in South Africa last year on racism turned out to be an anti-Israeli, anti-American operation, but every time we don't win we can't say, "I'm going home, I'm not playing anymore." As a powerful, mature nation, we have to stay and fight. It's not others we damage when we come home, but ourselves. The global warming protocols developed at Kyoto might put extra pressures on the U.S., but we put extra pressures on the world because we are 4 to 5 percent of the population that uses 25 to 30 percent of the world's fossil energy reserves, so maybe that suggests special responsibilities. If we have special claims to make, we have to be there making the arguments. That's democracy. We do it very well internally.

The reality is, if others around the world are impoverished, America will not be permitted to stay wealthy. If others around the world are at risk and generations of their children seem to have no future, then our children may also have no future. There are no walls high enough, no oceans wide enough to separate America's fate from the fate of the world, which means we have to be engaged in shaping that world.

The anarchic world of global markets has to be made governable if the world of terrorism and criminality is to be made governable. You can't have the rule of law for some and not for others. While military campaigns against individuals and regimes will help a little to slow things down, in the long term, terrorism has to be attacked systemically through extension of rule of law, multilateral cooperation through development of institutions of social and economic justice, as well as criminal prosecution. We have to create a world in which there are not fourteen-year-olds who think to be a martyr is a better fate than to be educated, get a job, and have a family.

The problem with Sharon's war in Palestine is that it won't work. The problem with America's war in Afghanistan is that by itself it won't work. This isn't an argument against the use of military force, but against the use of force unaccompanied by the other things that have to be done to give children hope. There is an evil out there, and there is an axis of evil, but mirroring them is an axis of injustice, despair, resentment, and rage. That doesn't justify terrorism, but it helps explain it. It helps explain what the U.S. has to do in order to overcome it.

Terrorism is almost always a symbol of disempowerment. On the whole, you and I pay our taxes, obey the laws—even though we might not agree—because we have pretty good lives. If we don't agree, we know how to change them. If terrorism is the last resort for men and women without power, the only ultimate remedy is empowerment. Democracy is about empowering people to control their own destiny. The Palestinians are without a homeland largely out of their own mistakes and the mistakes of the Arab world. But Sharon will never end terrorism by capturing the man in the act of terror today, because there are generations of children coming up. Sharon has dismantled and destroyed what little civic, health, and educational infrastructures had been created. Without schools, hope, jobs, dignity—why not terrorism? If we want to combat the illusions and dangerous myths of the powerless, we have to find ways to empower them—not the terrorists themselves, but the wider sea of people from whom they come and who feel sympathy for them.

Americans have been saying since 9/11, "Why do they hate us?" It's not that they hate us, but they fear the future. They see the globalization that we represent as an encroachment on their futures. To the degree they feel that way, they become our enemies, hate our regime, and they will engage in a violence far more destructive to them than to us, but that in an interdependent world will bring us all down. Democratic empowerment, the extension of civil society, the globalization of our democratic and governing institutions to encompass and overcome the anarchy of global markets, crime, and terrorism is the only realistic strategy open to us. I don't see administrations in Jerusalem or Washington even contemplating this part of the campaign. America has to take its own democracy seriously and think about creating a democratic global society in which neither rogue corporations nor rogue terrorists are permitted to govern the future.

Afterword: On Context

Gloria C. Duffy, Ph.D.
President and CEO, The Commonwealth Club of California

Why collect and publish major public speeches? In the age of continuous communication, of course it's important to study models of oratory, examples of the "science of speech," to slightly misuse Professor Henry Higgins' term. Whether we are awed by Václav Havel's idealism or guffaw at Dan Quayle's diatribe about Murphy Brown, the words in this book are both notable and quotable.

Another reason to be attentive to the speeches of these individuals is that their words mattered in the course of events. People around the world observed Nikita Khrushchev's trip to the U.S. in 1959, listened to his words in San Francisco and at other stops along his route, and wondered how the course of the Cold War and their own opportunities in life might shift as a result. Those days when relations between the U.S. and the Soviet Union thawed enough to allow Khrushchev's visit were also a time when the idea of greater freedom was planted in the minds of people behind the Iron Curtain, and that idea thirty years later brought some of them to tear down the Berlin Wall.

But the most important purpose of this book is to create context for the issues of today and the events of the past. Context is important to *Each a Mighty Voice* in several ways. Every one of the speeches in this volume was delivered to an audience at a particular time and in a specific place. The motivation of each individual who spoke was different, but they all had one; whether to sway Congress to ratify U.S. membership in the League of Nations (President Woodrow Wilson), or to decry social liberalism in America (Vice President Dan Quayle), or to move beyond an impeachment inquiry to larger issues of foreign policy (President Bill Clinton), all of these speakers sought the ears of the media, the public, and policymakers for their agendas.

And this is heartening. One is tempted to say "only in America" can we find a record of leaders who, over the span of a century, so consistently felt the need to address the people directly. In most societies, it is still rare for leaders to meet with the citizenry and seek their ear on particular questions. We can learn by weighing the words, in the context of what they were trying to accomplish, of those who sought to persuade during the past century.

We can also learn from reading the texts of these speeches at length, as opposed to settling for the short sound bites followed by commentators' discussion that today characterize our impression of what public figures are saying. Nothing substitutes for reading the original words of an historical figure in full. So much of what is said in the public arena is a matter of context, and by considering their presentations at length, we learn what these individuals emphasized, what incidents or stories shaped their views, what moved them.

The physical aspect of context, the place in which the speeches were given—the San Francisco Bay Area—is also important, because it was often an intentional choice by the speaker. Teddy Roosevelt's defining 1911 statement about conservation was specifically addressed to listeners in the American West. Where else would he have spoken of farmers' thirst for water and the importance of preserving the West's natural assets? It's not accidental that we include a number of speeches debating the Vietnam War, representing views as widely separated as those of William Westmoreland and Joan Baez. Nowhere in the country was this war so hotly debated as in the Bay Area, and Commonwealth Club meetings on the subject were not only numerous but, sometimes, surrounded by protest in the streets.

It is also notable that the institutional context for all the speeches was the same. The Commonwealth Club held thousands of meetings in its first century, and The Club continues to meet over four hundred times each year to consider topics of public concern. We can get a sense of this continuity from the photos in this volume. Woodrow Wilson, Franklin Roosevelt, Nikita Khrushchev, and Dwight Eisenhower all stood next to the same marble pillar in the Garden Court of the Sheraton Palace Hotel in San Francisco, and over a span of scores of years, they addressed some of the most controversial issues in the nation's history. This gives a rather remarkable sense of an ongoing national town hall meeting. And the continuity of this public forum endures; the modern glass-walled rooms where The Club meets today are just a block from the elegant site of many of these historic speeches.

Of course, each of these speeches has generated personal and behind-the-scenes stories that render the speakers alive and very human. Leaders of The Club's board, who have traditionally introduced the speakers, conducted the question-and-answer sessions, and sat next to the distinguished guests over the years, are a font of stories about what was said and done privately in the context of major speeches at The Club. Many of our leaders from earlier years maintained their discretion to the end of their lives, and now their tales are lost. But some of the stories have been passed down. We do know that after complaining about the difficulty of growing azaleas at his home in southern France, Charles de Gaulle took notes when a Club member explained a new technique called "dormant fertilization."

One board member tells a story shared with him by former Vermont governor and 2004 presidential candidate Howard Dean when he was at The Club in the mid-1990s. As lieutenant governor of Vermont, Dean was still practicing medicine. He actually had a patient on the examining table when his nurse interrupted him to inform him that the governor had died suddenly and he had to fly to Burlington immediately. Dean finished the exam, drove to Burlington, and was sworn in as governor.

For the past century, The Club has kept thorough files on each major speech, often including the note cards used by speakers, sometimes with their handwritten corrections. It seems quaint, but The Club also collected the autographs of its speakers for many years, and it is impressive and nostalgic to turn the pages past the signatures of Abba Eban, Nelson Rockefeller, and Anatoly Dobrynin, of recently departed friends like Senator Alan Cranston, a participant in Club activities for decades. How extraordinary it is that the records of The Club's speeches and the ensuing discussions have been preserved over such a long period of time. This was made possible because one organization was the host, persevered over a century, and kept often-meticulous records. The Club also maintained audio recordings of the speeches and subsequent discussion with the audience from the 1940s onward.

My own experience with The Club reaches back to the mid-1990s. In 1972 Katharine Graham delivered her powerful speech at The Club on the Watergate controversy. In 1999, when her arthritis had so advanced that she could not fly to the Bay Area, The Club moved its program with the redoubtable publisher to Washington, D.C. There, at a lunch cohosted with the Carnegie Endowment for International Peace, an audience almost entirely made up of professional women heard her reminisce about her long and interesting life. Then we broadcast The Club's radio program from the nation's capital for the first time.

I can also tell you that former Vice President Al Gore intentionally chose to give his September 23, 2002, speech inveighing against going to war in Iraq on the seventieth anniversary to the day of FDR's 1932 speech at The Club. And when my friend Condoleezza Rice was provost at Stanford University, she and I discussed many times the work that The Commonwealth Club was doing in Silicon Valley. When the White House was looking for a Silicon Valley venue for President Bush's "compassionate conservatism" speech in 2002, she was able to point them in our direction.

Guided by its Progressive philosophy, The Club has invited, and often demanded, that leaders from all fields come to its venue to exchange ideas with members and the public. It is remarkable that an organization exists specifically to demand public dialogue from societal leaders, on a daily basis. And although we have not been able to reproduce it in this book, these speeches were generally followed by extensive debate and discussion with members of the audience.

I should note that, in the later years represented in this volume, practicing the principle of free and open discussion has become more challenging in the United States. At this writing, an institution wishing to host a presidential debate in the U.S. must pony up $750,000 in event costs to even be considered by the Commission on Presidential Debates, which closely controls the process. We have a less open system today, and greater needs for systemic reform, than at any time since the Progressives first organized a century ago. But representing this Progressive tradition, The Commonwealth Club and many other organizations continue to conduct public dialogue in the face of these odds. With eighteen thousand members, The Club is by far the largest of these organizations, but smaller groups with a similar mission make important contributions to public debate throughout the United States.

In celebration of its Centennial, and harking back to its founding principles, in 2003 the Commonwealth Club launched the "Voices of Reform" project. From 2003 to 2005, we are examining the issues in California—campaign financing, low voter participation, a less than functional budget process, reapportionment, term limits, limits on public financing for education and infrastructure through Proposition 13, the initiative process—that demand improvements in our system of governance, to make it more responsive to the citizenry and better able to confront the serious problems the state faces. If

California provides leadership on these reform issues, as it did with the leadership of The Commonwealth Club in the early 1900s, then California may again become a model, on a national scale, for dealing with governance issues.

Returning to the question of context, perhaps the most valuable thing this book can offer is a sense of continuity of efforts to improve our society. By reminding ourselves of the concerns of our predecessors, we can measure how well we are addressing those problems they pointed out which are as yet unsolved. Over the span of a century, we are able to see the ebb and flow of attention to certain issues—the environment, civil rights, freedom of the press—and we can see signs of the social progress that has taken place over decades. And we can see where work still needs to be done to move forward the objectives that great leaders have set out for us.

Having this sense of how men and women of extraordinary intelligence and experience have defined the issues in the past and what remains to be done is essential for continued societal progress. And having a historical record like this, and hopefully other volumes to come, helps us to be better long-term thinkers. We're pleased that the original material on which this book is based is now housed at the Hoover Institution Library and Archives at Stanford University, where the records are being cataloged and organized, and the audio material will be digitized and made available to scholars. Some of the audio material is already available on The Club's website. It is through The Club's leaders, a group of volunteers led by its board of governors, with an enduring sense of The Club's importance as a venue in history, that these records exist today.

Because we have these records, we can look to the past for ideas and inspiration today. As I reread Teddy Roosevelt's 1911 speech, thinking of objectives that leaders have set, I was struck by one thought he expressed near the conclusion of his remarks:

> I wish to save the very wealthy men of this country, and their advocates and upholders, from the ruin they would bring upon themselves if they were permitted to have their way.

Roosevelt was speaking of the need to manage resources for long-term productivity, rather than deplete them through consumption. This is a great example of long-term thinking. And we at The Commonwealth Club hope that this compendium will add to the reader's long-range perspective, and perhaps to an ability to change things for the better.

Sources of Speeches

Section One: The Progressive Era and the New Deal

Theodore Roosevelt (1911): Full transcript as it appeared in *The Commonwealth* (edited)
Woodrow Wilson (1919): Full transcript as it appeared in *The Commonwealth* (edited)
Franklin Roosevelt (1932): Prepared remarks
Chaim Weizmann (1941): Abridged version as it appeared in *The Commonwealth* (edited)

Section Two: The Cold War and Vietnam

Cecil B. De Mille (1947): Full transcript made from restored digital archives (edited)
Joseph R. McCarthy (1951): Abridged version as it appeared in *The Commonwealth* (edited)
Nikita Khrushchev (1959): Full transcript (edited)
Dwight D. Eisenhower (1960): Full transcript made from restored digital archives (edited)
Edward Teller (1961): Full transcript made from restored digital archives (edited)
Martin Luther King Jr. (1967): Abridged version as it appeared in *The Commonwealth* (edited)
George C. Wallace (1967): Abridged version as it appeared in *The Commonwealth* (edited)
Barry Goldwater (1967): Prepared remarks and abridged version as it appeared in *The Commonwealth* (edited)
Robert F. Kennedy (January 1968): Full transcript made from restored digital archives (edited)
Robert F. Kennedy (May 1968): Prepared remarks and abridged version as it appeared in *The Commonwealth* (edited)
Tom Smothers (1969): Abridged version as it appeared in *The Commonwealth* (edited)
Abba Eban (1970): Full transcript made from restored digital archives (edited)
Ronald V. Dellums (1971): Full transcript made from restored digital archives (edited)
Shirley Chisholm (1972): Full transcript made from restored digital archives (edited)

Katharine Graham (1972): Full transcript made from restored digital archives (edited)

Bella Abzug (1973): Full transcript made from restored digital archives (edited)

Jesse Jackson (1974): Full transcript made from restored digital archives (edited)

Henry A. Kissinger (1976): Prepared remarks and abridged version as it appeared in *The Commonwealth* (edited)

George H. W. Bush (1976): Prepared remarks and abridged version as it appeared in *The Commonwealth* (edited)

William Westmoreland (1976): Prepared remarks and abridged version as it appeared in *The Commonwealth* (edited)

Morton Halperin (1977): Abridged version as it appeared in *The Commonwealth* (edited)

Section Three: Morning in America and the New World Order

Joan Baez (1981): Full transcript made from restored digital archives (edited)

Walter Cronkite (1983): Prepared remarks and abridged version as it appeared in *The Commonwealth* (edited)

Ronald Reagan (1983): Prepared remarks and abridged version as it appeared in *The Commonwealth* (edited)

Prince Bandar bin Sultan (1984): Prepared remarks and abridged version as it appeared in *The Commonwealth* (edited)

Daniel Ortega Saavedra (1984): Abridged version as it appeared in *The Commonwealth* (edited)

Desmond Tutu (1986): Full transcript made from restored digital archives (edited)

Corazón Aquino (1986): Prepared remarks and abridged version as it appeared in *The Commonwealth* (edited)

Randy Shilts (1987): Abridged version as it appeared in *The Commonwealth* (edited)

Richard B. Cheney (1991): Abridged version as it appeared in *The Commonwealth* (edited)

Maxine Hong Kingston (1991): Abridged version as it appeared in *The Commonwealth* (edited)

George Shultz and Don Oberdorfer (1991): Abridged version as it appeared in *The Commonwealth* (edited)

Jacques Yves Cousteau (1991): Abridged version as it appeared in *The Commonwealth* (edited)

Audrey Hepburn (1992): Abridged version as it appeared in *The Commonwealth* (edited)

William Greider (1992): Abridged version as it appeared in *The Commonwealth* (edited)

Dan Quayle (1992): Full transcript made from restored digital archives (edited)

Amory Lovins (1992): Abridged version as it appeared in *The Commonwealth* (edited)

Mikhail Gorbachev (1992): Abridged version as it appeared in *The Commonwealth* (edited)

Václav Havel (1994): Abridged version as it appeared in *The Commonwealth* (edited)

Section Four: America Y2K and the Jihad

Madeleine Albright (1993): Abridged version as it appeared in *The Commonwealth* (edited)

Kofi Annan (1998): Abridged version as it appeared in *The Commonwealth* (edited)

William Jefferson Clinton (1999): Abridged version as it appeared in *The Commonwealth* (edited)

Mavis Leno (1999): Abridged version as it appeared in *The Commonwealth* (edited)

David Broder (2000): Abridged version as it appeared in *The Commonwealth* (edited)

John McCain and Russ Feingold (2001): Full transcript (edited)

Bill O'Reilly (2001): Full transcript (edited)

Hanan Mikhail-Ashrawi (2001): Full transcript (edited)

Pat Buchanan (2002): Full transcript (edited)

Ralph Nader (2002): Full transcript (edited)

Lowell Bergman (2002): Full transcript (edited)

Benjamin Barber (2002): Full transcript (edited)

Index

AARP, 411
ABC/ABC News, 127-128, 416, 447
Abzug, Bella, "Every Issue Is a Woman's Issue," 167-177; also, xxii, xxvi
Acheson, Dean, 55, 60-61, 63
Adams, Edward F., xii-xiii, xxiii-xxv, xxvii, 4
Afghanistan, 61, 134, 300, 302, 341, 375, 392-400, 445, 450, 452, 457, 460
Africa/African, 38, 81, 92, 108-109, 140, 143, 146, 179, 184, 188, 193-195, 218, 226, 237, 255, 266-274, 309, 312, 315, 317, 351, 368, 378, 386, 389-390, 393, 395, 410, 432, 459
African Americans, 94, 344, 437, 456
Afrika Korps, 38
Afrikaans, 271
Agent Orange, 231
Agnew, Spiro, 143, 157, 162-163
Agora, xxiii-xxiv
Aid to Families with Dependent Children, 316
AIDS, 281-285, 317, 410, 456; HIV, 282
Al Jazeera, 450, 452
Al Qaeda, 393, 450, 452, 457
Alabama, 101
Alabama National Guard, 100
Alaska, 9, 335, 421, 433
Albania, 134, 380, 432
Albany, New York, 26
Albright, Madeleine, "What You Need to Know about the UN and Foreign Policy Today," 359-366; also, 374, 380, 392
Al Haram Sharif, 427
Allegheny Mountains, 10
Allende, Salvador, 214, 217-218

Amanzimtoti, South Africa, 267
Amerasia, 56, 59
America, 17, 21-22, 24-26, 37, 39, 47-48, 50-53, 57-59, 63, 74-76, 79-80, 83, 95, 97-98, 101, 106-109, 111-112, 117-121, 128-129, 142, 147, 149-153, 167, 172, 178-179, 183-186, 190, 196-197, 199, 203-204, 206-207, 212-213, 216, 232-234, 239, 243-246, 248-251, 255-259, 269, 274, 277, 279-280, 283, 288, 326, 328, 340, 359, 361-363, 365, 370, 376-378, 381, 385, 388, 397-398, 415, 420, 430, 433-434, 435, 442-443, 455-456, 458-461, 463-464; Americans, 39, 49-50, 63, 65-67, 73, 76, 106, 108-109, 112, 118-120, 125, 127, 141, 149-150, 152, 171, 174-175, 177, 183, 186-187, 190, 196, 205, 207, 209, 216-217, 219, 227, 230, 232-233, 236, 238-239, 246, 256, 259, 264, 277, 280, 285, 288-289, 292, 318, 323, 327, 331, 335, 340-341, 349-350, 360, 371, 373, 377, 382, 384, 408-413, 420, 431-433, 437, 441, 445, 458, 460; see also "United States"
America First, 108
American Civil Liberties Union, 214-216, 409, 420
American Express, 341
American Federation of Labor, 173
American Federation of Radio Artists, 46
American Independent Party, 101
American Revolution, 28, 103
Americas, 265, 386

Amnesty International, 225, 309, 314, 351
Amur River, 432
Amurao, Corazon, 119
Anarchists, 118
And the Band Played On, 281-282
Andreotti, Giulio, 342
Andropov, Yuri, 299, 301, 303, 340
Angel Island, xix
Angola, 184, 189, 193-195, 302, 363
Annan, Kofi, "The United Nations in Our Daily Lives," 367-373
Apartheid, 227, 266, 268-269, 271-273, 351, 389, 392, 395, 428
Appalachia, 10, 95, 151, 442
Aquino, Benigno, 275
Aquino, Corazón, "People Power," 275-280; also, xxii, xxix
Arab/Arabs, 38, 79, 133-135, 137-138, 140, 183, 251, 255-259, 288, 398, 423, 429, 449, 460
Arab League, 288, 423
Arab-Israeli conflict, 255-256
Arabic, 453
Arafat, Yasser, 132, 374, 379, 423, 429
Argentina, 224, 226, 228, 230, 235, 451
Arizona, 4, 8, 11-12, 370, 408, 415
Arkansas, 103, 143
Arlington National Cemetery, 147
Armageddon, 77, 235
Ashrawi, Hanan, "Peacemaking in the Middle East," 423-429

Asia, 86, 92, 187-188, 237, 255, 277, 312, 315, 317, 378, 386, 388, 413, 448, 458
Associated Press, 61, 113
Athens, 112, 120, 198
Atlantic Ocean, 132, 141
The Atlantic Monthly, 324
Austin, Mary, xv
Austin, Texas, 119
Australia, 47, 424
Austria, 22
Austria-Hungary, 22
AWACS, 253
Azerbaijan, 21
Baez, Joan, "Human Rights in the Eighties: Seeing Through Both Eyes," 223-231; also, xxii, 127, 464
Baghdad, Iraq, 287, 367, 369-370
Baker, James, 301
Balfour Declaration, 38
Balkans, 380
Baltic republics, 341
Bangladesh, 313
Barak, Ehud, 427
Barber, Benjamin, "Confronting Terrorism: Smart Bombs or Smart Concepts?" 454-461; also, xxx
Bay of Pigs, 115
BBC, 6, 314, 389, 424
Beard, Charles, 181
Begin, Menachem, 232, 240-241, 451
Beirut, Lebanon, 242, 253-254, 261, 423
Belafonte, Harry, 126
Belgium, 22, 47, 250, 432
Belgrade, Serbia and Montenegro, 375
Bellamy, Edward, xvii
Belloc, Hilaire, 434
Bergen, Candice, 324-325
Bergman, Lowell, "The Media and the War on Terrorism," 445-453; also, xxii
Bering Strait, 433

Berkeley, California, 116, 143, 296
Berlin, 55-56, 65, 68, 81, 86, 189, 255, 341; Berlin Wall, 86, 305, 315, 464; East Berlin, 86
Bernstein, Carl, 154
Berrigan, Daniel, 223
Bias, 157, 161-163, 281-282
Bierce, Ambrose, xv
Big Brother, 234-235
Biological Weapons, 384; Biological Weapons Convention, 384
Bipartisan Campaign Reform Act, 409
Birzeit University, 424
Black/Blacks, 4, 50, 66, 73, 77, 94-97, 100, 115, 118, 130, 145, 147-152, 167, 169-170, 177-178, 182-183, 216, 266-274, 318, 323, 326-328, 368, 370, 418, 421, 430
Black Christmas, 267
Black Panthers, 130
Black Power, 94
Bliss, Walter, xiv
Boland Amendment, 260
Bolshevik Revolution, 117, 300; Bolsheviks, 343
Boren, David, 412
Borneo, 310
Bosch, Hieronymus, 394
Bosnia, 354, 360, 364, 368, 374, 378, 380; Bosnia-Herzegovina, 355; Bosnian Serbs, 360
Botha, P. W., 266
Boutros-Ghali, Boutros, 368
Bradbury, Ray, xxix
Bradlee, Benjamin, 296
Bradley, Omar, 62
Brain(s) Trust, 25
Brandeis, Justice Louis, 440
Brandenburg Gate, 341
Brazil, 228-229, 388, 458
Bremer, L. Paul, 453
Brezhnev, Leonid, 301-302, 340; Brezhnev Doctrine, 302

Broder, David, "Democracy Derailed,"401-407; also, xxv, 115
Brown & Williamson, 446
Brown, Charlotte Amanda Blake, xiii
Brown, Harold, 289
Bryan, William Jennings, xxvi
Buchanan, J. Patrick, "Death of the West," 430-435; also, xxvi, 437
Buckley, William, 254
Buckley, William F. Jr., 56, 65, 128
Buenos Aires, Argentina, 228
Bulgaria, 22, 70-71
Bull Moose Party, 5
Bunche, Ralph, xviii
Burbank, Luther, xv
Burnham, Daniel Hudson, xiv
Burk, Frederic, xxiii
Bush, George H. W., "The CIA and the Intelligence Community," 198-203; also, 287, 295-296, 300-301, 323, 330, 341, 359-360, 430
Bush, George W., 409, 418, 429, 431, 436-437, 443, 449-450, 457
BusinessWeek, 172
Butler, Richard, 368
Cabrillo, Juan Rodríguez, 67
Cairo, Egypt, 135, 141, 352
Caldwell case, 164
Caldwell, Erskine, 48
California, 3-6, 9-10, 12, 15, 24, 26, 45-46, 66-67, 78, 80, 86, 102, 104, 113, 115-116, 121, 132, 185, 248, 250, 260, 296, 320, 332, 335-336, 338, 365, 369, 372, 375, 385, 401, 403-405, 416-417, 420, 436-437, 452
California Book Awards, xxix
California Farm Bureau, xxvii
California State Assembly, 296
Calley, Lt. William, 209
Calypso, 307
Cambodia, 211, 214, 235, 302, 360, 363

Camp David, 66, 76, 132, 258, 426-427, 451
Campaign Finance Reform, 409
Campaign to Stop Gender Apartheid, 392
Campbell, Tom, 403
Canada, 12, 32, 127, 186, 201, 210, 240, 419, 444
Capitalism, 48, 50-51, 65, 82-83, 149, 279, 346-347, 440, 442, 455, 458-459
Capitol Hill, 167, 274, 292, 371, 441
Cardoza, Justice Benjamin, 102
Caribbean, 81, 249, 252; Caribbean Basin Initiative, 249
Carmichael, Stokely, 94
Carnegie, Andrew, 4
Carson, Johnny, 129
Carter, Finley, 70
Carter, Jimmy, 168, 224, 258, 289, 301, 331
Castells, Manuel, 456
Castro, Fidel, 104, 179, 184
Catholic/ Catholicism, 280, 432, 434
CBS, 126-128, 204-206, 232, 234, 416, 446
Censorship, 48-49, 126-128, 351
Center for Defense Information, 296
Centers for Disease Control (CDC), 282
Central America, 242, 260-263
Central Asia, 86, 413, 448
Central Intelligence Agency (CIA), 173, 184-185, 198-201, 203, 205, 214, 217-220, 226, 254, 261-262, 264-265, 298, 304-305, 383, 419-420, 449; Director of Central Intelligence (DCI), 199-200
Central Valley, California, 372
Chlorofluorocarbons (CFCs), 333
Chabon, Michael, xxix
Chiang Kai-shek, 55, 62, 81

Chamberlain, Neville, 111, 185
Chambers, Whittaker, 56
Chamie, Joseph, 432
Chase Manhattan, 171
Cheney, Richard B., "U.S. Defense Policy: The Gulf War and Beyond,"286-292; also, xii, xxii, xviii
Chenoweth, Helen, 370
Chernenko, Konstantin, 299, 201, 340
Chicago, 6, 39, 94, 114, 119, 126, 283, 402
Chicanos, 150, 177, 183
Chile, 214, 217-218, 228-229, 235
China, 4, 52, 55-56, 58-62, 81, 99, 102-103, 109-111, 185, 198, 208, 211, 223, 225, 238, 293, 374, 381-383, 386, 389-390, 432-433, 435; Chinese, 47, 55, 58, 110, 223, 386, 432-433; Communist China, 109; Nationalists, 55, 81; People's Republic of China, 81, 198; Red China, 58, 102-103, 110-111, 208
Chinatown, 3
Chirac, Jacques, 367-368
Chisholm, Shirley, "Democratic Party Presidential Candidate Speaks," 148-153
Choate, Rufus, 7
Christendom, 139
Christian, 40, 74, 115, 178, 215, 270-271, 423, 433; Christianity, 66, 255, 258, 434
Christopher, George, 66, 72, 74-75
Christopher, Warren, 361
Church, Senator Frank, 274; Case-Church Amendment, 211
Churchill, Winston, 131
Citizenship, 149, 182, 267, 272, 433
Civil Defense, 85-88, 90-91

Civil Rights, 5, 93-98, 104, 168, 178, 235, 268, 326, 350
Civil War, 27, 55, 72, 184, 210, 261, 287, 392, 394, 418, 458
Clean Air Act, 320
Cleaver, Eldridge, 128
Clinton, William Jefferson, "A State of the Union for Foreign Policy," 374-391; 179, 214, 323, 359-361, 363, 365, 374-375, 377, 379, 381, 383-385, 387, 389, 391, 393, 409-410, 419, 427, 453
Clinton, Hillary, 393
CNN, 424, 430, 440, 447
COINTELPRO, 216-217
Colby, William, 198
Cold War, 57, 65-66, 86, 238, 243, 298, 302, 315-316, 361-362, 364, 381, 412, 434
Colorado, 6, 9-10, 12, 16, 436
Colorado River, 6, 9, 12
Columbia River, 11
Columbus, Christopher, 79
Committee to Re-elect the President (CREEP), 115, 154, 246, 413
Commodity Credit Corporation, 248
Commonwealth Club of California, 4-5, 15, 24-26, 38, 45-46, 54-56, 63, 65-66, 76-78, 86, 93-94, 100-102, 104-106, 112-113, 115, 121, 127, 130-132, 148, 154, 167-169, 177-178, 184-185, 198, 204, 214, 224, 232, 238, 242-243, 253-254, 260, 276, 281, 286, 293, 307, 311, 313, 318, 324-325, 331, 345-346, 359-360, 367-368, 374-375, 392, 401, 408-409, 414, 416, 423, 430-431, 437, 445; *The Commonwealth*, xxvii, 63; Friday Flashes, xxvii; Inforum, xxviii; Ladies Day, xxvi
Commonwealth of Independent States, 341, 345-346

Communism, 47, 49-50, 53, 55, 57-58, 60-62, 64-66, 72, 98-99, 104, 108-110, 147, 271, 340, 376, 381, 402, 434; Communist, 48-50, 52, 54-56, 58-59, 61-64, 69, 71, 83, 98-99, 104, 109-110, 114, 116-117, 125, 145, 186, 204-206, 211, 215-216, 218, 223, 225, 254, 262, 276, 280, 341, 349, 351, 361; Communist Party, 50, 54, 58-59, 61, 64, 116, 215-216, 341

Community of Peace People, 228

Comoros Islands, 450

Comprehensive Test Ban Treaty, 384

Congo, 218

Congress of Industrial Organizations, 173

The Conscience of a Conservative, 105

Conservative politics, 58, 105-106, 151, 163, 319, 350, 394, 399, 406, 434, 440; Conservatives, 4-5, 165, 233, 238, 281, 321-322, 405

Constitution (U.S.), 5-7, 9, 27, 100-101, 169, 176-177, 181, 205, 215, 219-220, 239-240, 243, 266-267, 271-272, 309, 344, 351, 405, 407; Bill of Rights, 128, 220; First Amendment, 49, 156, 164, 409, 413; Fifth Amendment, 57, 128; Ninth Amendment, 101; Tenth Amendment, 101

Constitutional government, 101, 176

Contadora peace proposal, 262-263

The Content of Our Character, 330

Contras, 254, 260-261, 264

Coolidge, Calvin, 175

Cooper, Gary, 45

The Corporate Destruction of Capitalism, 440

Corrigan, Mairead, 228

Costa Rica, 252, 254, 261-262

Coulter, Ann, 58

Cousteau, Jacques Yves, "The Rights of Future Generations," 307-312

Cranston, Alan, 465

Crile, George, 206

Croatia, 360

Cronkite, Walter, "Hear America Singing,"232-241; also, xxx, 113, 415, 448

Cross, Frank, xxviii

Cuba, 6, 77, 79, 104, 189, 194-195, 251; Cuban, 120, 175, 179, 184, 193-195; Cuban American, 179

Czech Republic, 349-350, 354

Czechoslovakia, 55, 349-350, 354, 361; Charter 77, 350; Civic Democratic Party, 350; Civic Forum, 349

Damascus, Syria, 253, 411

Dar es Salaam, Tanzania, 450

Darrow, Clarence, xxvii

Dartmouth College, 435

Darwinist, 458

Dayton Accords, 360

De Chamorro, Violeta Barrios, 261

De Gaulle, Charles, 120, 128

De Mille, Cecil B., "The Motion Pictures and International Relations," 45-53; also, xxx

Declaration of Human Rights, 311, 314

Declaration of Independence, 28, 34, 97, 117, 314, 353, 455

Dellums, Ronald V., "A Radical Perspective on Life," 143-147; also, xxx

Democracy, 7, 12-13, 15, 27, 83, 141, 146-147, 176-177, 196, 199, 201, 205, 210, 212, 217, 225, 240, 243, 245, 249, 251-252, 263, 271, 278-280, 301-303, 318-319, 323, 345, 347, 349, 360, 363, 371, 380-381, 384, 389-390, 401-402, 406, 409, 414, 423, 425, 431, 439-440, 443-444, 454-456, 458-461

Democratic National Committee, 77, 414

Democratic National Convention, Chicago (1968), 114, 126; Miami (1972), 168, 171; Los Angeles (2000), 410

Democratic Party, 25, 29, 58, 101, 108, 148, 158, 284, 404, 435; Democrats, 16, 24, 63, 77, 111, 154, 158, 165, 176, 319-320, 322, 349, 404, 412, 437-438, 441

Denmark, 281, 432

Denver, Colorado, 9-10

Detroit, Michigan, 93-94, 336, 421

Deukmejian, George, 336

Deutch, John, 419

Dewey, Admiral George, xxiii

Dewey, Thomas, 276

Diem, Ngo Dinh, 207

Disney, Walt, 45

Disneyland, 73

Dobrynin, Anatoly, 465

Doctor Strangelove, 85

Dogg, Snoop Doggy, 435

Dole, Robert, 160, 410, 430

Dompas, 269

Dooley, Martin, 6

Douglas, Justice William O., xxvii

Duarte, Jose Napoleon, 243

Dukakis, Michael, 178

Dumbarton Oaks, 60

Dung, Van Tien, 211

Dunne, Finley Peter, 6

Durante, Jimmy, 126

Dutch Reformed Church, 270

Earth Summit, 331-332, 363

East Asia, 458

East Coast (U.S.), 5, 8-11, 29, 315, 403

East Timor, 227

Eastern Europe, 187, 302

Eban, Abba, "The Middle East: Its Past Agony and Its Future Hope," 131-142; also, 464

Egypt, 47, 52, 132, 135, 253, 258, 450; Egyptians, 132, 138, 288
Ehrlichman, John, 175
Einstein, Albert, 251
Eisenhower, Dwight D., "Presidential Reflections," 76-84; also, xix, 57, 65-66, 68, 75, 105, 107, 110, 127, 207, 218, 464
El Salvador, 226, 230, 234, 242-243, 251-252, 263, 313, 364
Electric Power Research Institute, 334
Eliot, T. S., 431, 434
Emergency Broadcast System, 85
Enders, Thomas, 224
Energy, 25, 248, 310, 331-334, 338, 385, 443, 459
Enewetak Atoll, 85
Enron, 25, 440
Entebbe rescue operation, 199
Environment/Environmental protection, 3-4, 145, 239, 308, 312, 317, 320-322, 332, 338, 355, 363, 377, 385-387, 439, 443, 454, 467
Environmental Protection Agency (EPA), 320
Equal Credit Opportunity Act, 170
Equal Pay Act, 169
Equal Rights Amendment, 169
Equitable Trust Bank, 170
Esquivel, Adolfo Perez, 228
Europe, 19, 27, 29, 32, 39-40, 49, 52, 58, 62, 107, 137-138, 140, 172, 186-187, 196, 201, 230, 255, 312, 315, 340-341, 354-355, 378, 388, 423, 432, 434; Europeans, 381, 456
European, 20, 32, 51, 55, 67, 355, 375, 380, 432-434, 443-444, 456
European Community, 139, 248
European Economic Community Code, 268

European Union, 350
Everett, Edward, 7
Everglades, 442
Evil Empire, 243, 303
Export-Import Bank, 248
Fahd, King, 256
Al-Faisal, Princess Haifa, 254
Fall, Bernard, 98
Far East, 59, 67, 433
Far West, xiv
Fatah, 425
Faville, William, xiv
February Revolution, 343
Federal Bureau of Investigation (FBI), 59, 154, 200, 214-217, 219, 383, 450
Federal Communications Commission (FCC), 127, 451
Feingold, Russ, "Campaign Finance Reform," 408-415
Feinstein, Dianne, 375, 410
Feminist Majority Foundation, 392-393
Fenway Park, 442
The Fifth Book of Peace, 294
Fiji, 134
Filipinos, 276, 278-280
Finns, 137
Florida, 127, 148, 175, 226, 310, 437, 457
Flying Fickle Finger of Fate, 127
The Folly of Appeasement, 56
Fonda, Jane, 223
Ford Motor Company, xxiii
Ford, Gerald, 185, 198, 200, 217, 301, 430
Foreign Corrupt Practices Act, 247
Foreign Relations Committee, 274
Forests, 4, 6-7, 10, 12, 310
Formosa, 55, 62, 81
Forrestal, James, 55, 60
Fortress America, 108-109
Forty Committee, 217-218
Founding Fathers, 101, 196, 246, 254, 411
Fourteen Points, 15
The Fourth Book of Peace, 293

Fourth of July, 420
Fox News, 416, 447
Fox, Vicente, 419
France, 22, 38, 40, 110, 138, 250, 307, 375; French, 40, 66, 109-110, 113, 117, 122-123, 127, 138, 208, 231, 284, 307, 309, 367, 417; French Army, 40; French Revolution, 309
Franklin, Benjamin, 52
Freedom, 28, 31, 48-49, 51-53, 56, 84, 87, 95, 97, 104, 107, 116-117, 120-121, 128, 132, 141, 145-146, 156, 164-165, 185, 206, 217, 227, 232, 234-239, 243-245, 248-249, 263-264, 291, 302-303, 351-353, 361, 363, 365, 375-378, 381-382, 389, 406, 463
Frontline, 445-448
Fuchs, Klaus, 54
Fulbright, J. William, 109
Gallup poll, 184, 323
Gandhi, Mahatma, 295
Garner, John Nance, 25
Garrison America, 109
Garrison, Jim, 113
Gartz, Kate Crane, xiv
Gay-Related Immunodeficiency Disorder (GRID), 281
Gaza, 132, 425
Gemayel, Bashir, 255
General Agreement on Tariffs and Trade (GATT), 250
General Motors, 150, 170, 336, 436
Geneva, 224, 299-300
Georgia (U.S. state), 12, 48
Georgia (former Soviet republic), 304
Gerdes, Justin, xi, xxxi
Germany, 16, 18-20, 22, 39-40, 52, 62, 68, 85-86, 104, 137, 250, 282, 301, 333, 336-337, 432, 443
Getty, John Paul, 173
Gettysburg, Pennsylvania, 66
Gettysburg Address, 435

Ghetto, 95, 115, 118, 171, 269, 327-328
Giannini, Amadeo Peter, xiv
Ginsberg, Allen, 93, 223
Glasnost, 298, 340-341, 345
Global warming/climate change, 333, 338-339, 359, 363, 382, 385, 456, 459
Globalization, 369, 376-377, 386, 390, 447, 458, 460
Gross National Product (GNP), 233, 292, 333
God, 22, 53, 73, 152, 173, 179, 182-183, 229, 267, 269, 271, 273-274, 330, 402, 420, 435
Golan Heights, 132, 137
Golden Gate Bridge, 26, 67
Goldwater, Barry, "The United States and the World Today," 105-111; also, xxii
Golkar Party, 390
Gompers, Samuel, xxvi
Good Friday Accord, 379
Gorbachev, Mikhail, "A Special Presentation by His Excellency Mikhail Gorbachev," 340-348; also, 298-301, 303-305; Gorbachev Foundation, 342
Gore, Al, 431, 436, 441, 466
Graham, Billy, 175
Graham, Katharine, "Fairness & Freedom of the Press," 154-166; also, xxi-xxii, 465
Gramm-Rudman-Hollings Act, 277, 279
Grand Canyon, 370
Grateful Dead, xxii
Great Britain, 22, 40-41, 77, 110, 201, 250, 266, 282, 340, 372, 399, 417, 423, 425; British, 38, 40, 57, 66, 110, 303, 368, 451
Great Depression, 26, 29, 37, 246, 303, 376, 388
Great Society, 207, 327
Greece, 38, 71, 198, 380, 440
Green Berets, 207
Green Party, 436-437, 443
Greenpeace, 296

Greenspan, Alan, 443
Greider, William, "Betrayal of American Democracy," 318-323; also, xxviii
Grew, Joseph, 56, 59
Gromyko, Andrei, 137
Group Areas Act, 269
Guatemala, 226, 234, 419
Guggenheim syndicate, 9
Gulf of Tonkin, 208
Gulf War, 286-287, 293, 426; Operation Desert Storm, 286-287, 290, 292-294; Operation Desert Shield, 286
Gunby, David H., 119
H-bomb, 85, 341
Haig, Alexander, 224
Haiphong harbor, Vietnam, 210-211
Haiti, 226, 374
Haldeman, H. R., 175
Hale, R. B., 15
Halperin, Morton, "The Crimes of the Intelligence Agencies," 214-220
Hamas, 425
Hamilton, Alexander, 28-29
Hammond, Tom, 411
Hanna, Richard, 199
Hanoi, Vietnam, 104, 109, 208, 210-212, 226, 231
Ul-Haq Zia, Mohammed, xxviii
Harding, Warren G., 16
Harriman, Averell, xix
Hart, Mickey, xxii
Harvard University, 280, 435
Hastings, Reed, 404
Havel, Václav, "From Prisoner to President," 349-355; also, xxii
Hawaii, 276, 333
Hayden, Tom, 223
Haynes, John Randolph, xiv, xxv, 401
Hazara, 396
Head Start, 321
Hearst, Phoebe Apperson, xiv
Hearst, William Randolph Jr., xix
Hebrew, 38, 40-41, 138

Heckler, Margaret, 285
Hellman, Lillian, 48
Helms, Jesse, 323, 368
Helsinki, Finland, 304
Hepburn, Audrey, "Children First: Building a Global Agenda," 313-317; also, xxii, xxx
Hetch Hetchy, 3, 5
Hewlett-Packard, 248
Hezbollah, 242, 253, 452
Hispanics, 433, 442
Hiss, Alger, 54-55, 57, 63
Hitler, Adolf, 39-40, 85, 104, 108, 185, 303, 418
HMOs, 412, 444
Ho Chi Minh, 108, 117
Holland, 310, 432
Hollywood, 45-52, 329, 434; Hollywood Ten, 46
Holocaust, 376
Homestead Act, 7-8
Honduras, 252, 254, 260-262
Hoover, Herbert, 24-25, 47, 175
Hoover, J. Edgar, 59, 215-216
Hoover Institution Library and Archives, xii, xxx, 467
Hotels: Ambassador Hotel, 116; Fairmont, 4, 185, 408; Mark Hopkins, xix; Palace Hotel, 15, 24, 55; San Francisco Hilton, 242; Sheraton Palace Grand Ballroom, 105; St. Francis, 93, 101, 178
Howard, John, 424
Hudson River, 65
Hudson, Rock, 285
Hue, South Vietnam, 113-114, 123
Hughes, Howard, 175
Human Rights, 103, 190, 223-224, 226-228, 230, 263, 309, 311, 314, 344-347, 349-353, 355, 362, 364, 369, 374-375, 378, 389, 391-393, 397-399, 419, 424-425; Human Rights Report (U. S. State Dept.),

374, 389; Human Rights
  Watch, 393
Humanitas International
  Human Rights Committee,
  223-225, 227, 230-231
Humphrey, Hubert, 114, 125
Hungary, 48, 65, 85
Hurley, Patrick, 55, 59
Hussein, Saddam, 286-288,
  293-294, 296, 331, 367-368,
  445-446
I Saw Poland Betrayed, 58
IBM, 66, 69
ICBMs, 192
Iceland, 341
Illinois, 93, 417
Immigration and
  Naturalization Service, 418
Imperial Valley, xxv
India, 81, 140, 235, 271, 273,
  361, 377, 447
Indian Ocean, 450
Indochina, 81, 123, 146-147,
  167, 171, 224
Indonesia, 389-390, 457
Industrial Revolution, 29, 92,
  235
Insull, 25, 36
Intelligence Oversight Board,
  198, 201
Internal Revenue Service (IRS),
  321
International Criminal Court,
  369, 459
International Labor
  Organization, 372, 387
International Monetary Fund
  (IMF), 249-250, 279
International Telegraph and
  Telephone Company, 173
Internet, 436, 450, 458
Interpol, 414
Iowa, 24, 66
Iran, 227, 235, 261, 288, 293,
  446, 457
Iran-Contra Affair, 261, 304
Iraq, 179, 238, 261, 286-287,
  289-290, 293-294, 360, 367-
  369, 383, 425, 457
Ireland, 228

Iron Curtain, 60, 88, 251
Irrigation, 4, 6-8, 11-12
Islam, 139, 255, 258, 452
Islamabad, Pakistan, 420
Islamic, 238, 256, 258, 390,
  392, 396, 421, 425, 429, 450
Islamic Jihad, 425
Israel, 39, 79, 131-142, 232,
  242, 250-251, 253, 257, 259,
  379, 423, 425-429, 433, 451-
  452; Israeli, 132, 136, 138,
  140, 199, 232, 240, 242, 251,
  254, 257-259, 288, 374, 379,
  423-429
Italy, 22, 342
Iwo Jima, 435
Jackson, Jesse, "Rebirth of a
  Nation," 178-183; also, xxvi-
  ii
Jackson State College, 94
Jacksonville, 94
Jaffe, Philip, 56, 59
Japan, 22, 150, 172, 186, 199,
  248, 250, 279, 302, 325, 333,
  336-337, 347, 378, 388, 399,
  418; Japanese, 39, 59, 248,
  325
Jaworski, Leon, 199
Jefferson Airplane, 126
Jefferson, Thomas, 6, 28-29,
  31, 37, 52, 117, 130, 353,
  414, 417, 438
Jerusalem, 139, 142, 240-241,
  423-424, 426-427, 461
Jessup, Philip C., 56, 61, 63-64
Jesus, 179
Jews, 38-40, 85, 145, 179, 270,
  396, 423; Jewish, 38, 40,
  132, 134-135, 137-138, 147,
  183, 396, 424, 431
Jihad vs. McWorld, 454-455
Johannesburg, South Africa,
  266-267
Johns Hopkins University, 56
Johnson, Hiram, 5, 25, 401,
  404
Johnson, Lyndon, 5, 25, 93-95,
  100, 103, 106, 109, 112-114,
  122, 207-208, 214, 246, 401,
  404

Johnson, Samuel, 246
Joint Chiefs of Staff, 290, 302
Jones, Deacon, 115
Jordan, 132, 139, 379
Jordan River, 378
Jordan Valley, 137, 427
Jordan, David Starr, xiv
Judaism, 255, 258, 434
Judeo-Christian, 153, 330
Kabul, Afghanistan, 392
Kai-shek, Chiang, 55, 62, 81
Kandahar, Afghanistan, 392
Kansas, 12
Kashmir, 377, 447
Kelley, Clarence M., 219
Kendall, Henry, 311
Kennan, George, 299, 302
Kennedy, John F., 77, 81, 86,
  100, 113, 187, 207-208
Kennedy, Robert F., "What Do
  We Stand For? The
  Liberation of the Human
  Spirit", "Speech to The
  Commonwealth Club," 112-
  125, also, xxii, xxx
Kentucky, 151
Kenya, 450
Kerry, John, 421
KGB, 304
Khe Sanh, Vietnam, 113
Khmer Rouge, 364
Khomeini, Ayatollah, 235
Khrushchev, Nikita, "The San
  Francisco Speech," 65-76;
  also, xix, xx, 77, 86, 104,
  207; Butcher of Budapest,
  xx, 65
Kieran, James, 25
King, Rev. Martin Luther Jr.,
  "The Future of Integration,"
  93-99; also, xxi-xxii, 114,
  216-217, 224, 227
King, Rodney, 318, 325
Kingston, Maxine Hong,
  "Writing in a Time of War,"
  293-297; also, xxii
Kissinger, Henry, "The
  Permanent Challenge of
  Peace: U.S. Policy Toward
  the Soviet Union," 184-197;

also, xxiii, xxviii, 132, 214, 217-218
Klaus, Václav, 350
Klehr, Harvey, 56, 58
Knowland, William, 61
Kohl, Helmut, 342
Koornhof, Piet, 269
Korea, 55, 60-62, 81, 302, 360, 378, 457; Koreagate, 199; Korean War, 55, 61, 211; North Korea, 55, 61, 211, 360, 457; South Korea, 55, 60-62, 199, 235, 299, 389, 435
Kosovo, 375, 380-381, 435; Kosovar Albanian, 375, 380; Kosovo Liberation Army, 375
Krakow, Poland, 39
Kremlin, 60, 298
Ku Klux Klan, 167, 215
Kurds, 286-287
Kuwait, 179, 286-287, 290, 293, 331, 360, 435
Kuz, 70
Kyoto Protocol, 385, 459
La Prensa, 264
Labor, 20, 28-29, 35, 40, 45, 52, 67, 113, 115, 117, 169, 172-173, 183, 225, 247, 251, 270, 273, 298, 319, 333, 337, 387, 410, 428
bin Laden, Osama, 393, 417, 419, 421, 445, 450-452, 455
LaDuke, Winona, 441
Laird, Mel, 289
Landers, Ann, 128
Lane, Arthur Bliss, 55, 58
Laos, 211
Lardner, Ring, 46
LaRocque, Gene, 296
Latin America, 224, 228, 230, 237, 261, 264-265, 315, 351, 378, 386, 388
Latin American, 32, 228
Lattimore, Owen, 56-57, 60-61
Laugh-In, 127
Lawlor, Justice William P., 0
Lawrence Livermore National Laboratory, 85
Le Duc Tho, 210

League of Nations, 15-16, 18-19, 361, 376; League of Nations Covenant, 16, 18-20; Article X, 15, 18
Leary, Timothy, 93
Lebanon, 242, 251, 253-256, 259, 423; Lebanese, 251, 254-255, 261, 423
Left (politics), 185, 405
Lelyveld, Joseph, 296
LeMay, Curtis, 76
Lend-Lease Act, 39
Lenin, Vladimir Ilyich 52, 58, 76, 117, 344, 347
Leningrad, 137
Leno, Jay, 392
Leno, Mavis, "Buried Alive," 392-400
Lewis, Alfred E., 154
Liberals, 49, 102, 165, 174, 233, 239, 321-322, 399, 456
Liberty Bell, 52
Libya, 417
Lieberman, Joe, 414
Likud Party, 423
Lincoln, Abraham, 52, 72, 121, 421
Lincoln Bedroom scandal, 409-410
Lincoln Monument, 216
Lincoln-Roosevelt League, xiii
Lindh, John Walker, 452
Literary Digest, 25
Little Foxes, 48
Litvinov, Pavel, 117
Lodge, Henry Cabot, 15-16
Lodge, Henry Cabot Jr., 66, 69
Lodz, Poland, 39
Lomax, Louis E., xxviii
London, Jack, xv
Lone Ranger, 456
Los Angeles, 3, 65-66, 73-74, 94, 116, 128, 282, 284, 296, 318, 324-326, 330, 344, 410, 440, 442
Los Angeles Times, 102, 115, 223, 440
Lovins, Amory, "Abating Global Warming for Fun and Profit," 331-339

Loyalty Board, 59
Luce, Clare Booth, xxvii
Luce, Henry, xxvii
Lumumba, Patrice, 218
MacArthur, Douglas, 55, 60-62
MacArthur Foundation, 331
Macedonia, 380
MacLaine, Shirley, 66
Madison, James, 165
Madrid, Spain, 228, 424, 426
Maginot Line, 40, 107
Maldives, 310
Manchuria, 59
Manhattan Project, 85
Manila, Philippines, 275-277
Manila Bay Monument, xxiii
Manitoba, 419
Mankiewicz, Frank, 162-163
Mao Tse-tung, 55
Marchand's Restaurant, xxiii
Marcos, Ferdinand, 275, 277
Marcos, Imelda, 275-277
Marin County, 452
Markham, Edwin, xv
Marshall, George C., 55, 58; Marshall Plan, 45, 362
Marshall, (Chief Justice) John, 7
Marshall, Thurgood, 94
Marx, Karl, 52, 117; Marxist, 231
Maryland, 101, 162-163, 454
Massachusetts, 436
Matsu, 81
Maybeck, Bernard, xiv
Mazar-e Sharif, 452
McCain, John, "Campaign Finance Reform," 408-415
McCarthy, Eugene, 112, 114-115
McCarthy, Joseph R., "Communism in Our Government," 54-64; also, xxii, xxix, 166; McCarthyism, 54, 59
McCord, James W. Jr., 154
McDonald's, 370
McFarlane, Robert C. "Bud", 254

McGovern, George, 156, 159-162, 434
McKeown, Ciaran, 228
McLuhan, Marshall, 128
McNamara, Robert S., 77, 112, 206
Meany, George, 173
Medicare, 174, 412
Mediterranean, 132, 141, 256-257
Mein Kampf, 40, 58
Mexican Americans, 95, 419
Mexico, 12, 228, 305, 375, 384-385, 387, 419, 432-433, 435; Mexicans, 95, 158, 384, 418-419, 432-433
Mexico City, Mexico, 432
Micronesia, 218
Middle East, 81, 109, 132-134, 136-140, 142, 185, 188-189, 242, 251, 253, 255-258, 315, 374, 379, 398, 424-425, 432, 449; Middle Eastern, 133-134, 139-140, 399
Mikhail-Ashrawi, Hanan, "Peacemaking in the Middle East," 423-429
Milk River, Montana, 12
Mills College, xxvi
Milosz, Czeslaw, xxix
Minh, Ho Chi, 108, 117
Mississippi, 24, 94, 103, 118
Mississippi River, 11-12, 24
Missouri, 413
Mitterrand, François, 307, 342
Mombasa, Kenya, 450
Mongolian, 396
Monroe, Marilyn, 66
Montenegro, 364
Moore, Michael, xxix
Morgan, J.P., 9
Mormonism, 434
Moscow, Russia, 56, 65, 74, 76, 117, 189-190, 194, 211-212, 301, 303-304
Motion pictures, 46-48
Motlana, Nthato, 272
Moyers, Bill, 448
Moynihan, Daniel Patrick, 168
Mozambique, 363

MTV, 324
Muir, John, 3-4
Munich agreement, 40, 111, 185, 355
Murphy Brown, 324-325, 329;
Muslim, 254, 360, 383, 421, 432, 450-451, 453; Muslims, 254, 360, 383, 421, 432, 447, 450-451, 453
Mussolini, Benito, 303
Mutual Security Pacts, 107
My Lai massacre, 209
NAACP, xxviii
Nader, Ralph, "Crashing the Party," 436-444; also, xxii, xxvi
Nairobi, Kenya, 449, 453
National Aeronautics and Space Administration (NASA), 310
The Nation, xxvii
National Advisory Commission on Civil Disorders (Kerner Commission), 94
National Association of Broadcasters, 127, 415, 449
National Cancer Institute, 284
National Guard, 94-95, 100, 118, 290, 318
National Press Club, 65, 104, 324
National Public Radio, 448
National Right to Life, 414
National Security Act, 198, 200
National Security Agency, 200, 236
National Security Council, 214
Native Americans (Indians), 95, 113, 116, 118, 150-151; Indian education, 113
NATO, 302-303, 350, 360, 362, 375, 378, 380-381
Nazi Germany, 38-39, 104; Nazis, 38-39, 270, 313, 396; Nazism, 342
NBC, 113, 127, 162, 431
The Negro, 96-97, 102
Negroes, 96
Netherlands, 313, 443

Nevada, 446
New Deal, 105, 174; New Dealer, 58
New Hampshire, 12, 114
New Jersey, 9, 419, 457
New Mexico, 12, 329
New Orleans, Louisiana, 39, 113
New York (state), 10, 24, 103, 112, 323, 417, 436; New York (city), 9-11, 24, 35, 39, 56, 60, 65, 77, 79, 94, 103, 112, 118, 206, 216, 282, 284, 315, 323, 417, 436, 442, 446, 448, 453
New York Stock Exchange, 442
The New York Times, 25, 104, 114-115, 127, 164, 175, 198-199, 207, 223, 283, 296, 370, 416, 435, 445-446
Newark, New Jersey, 93-94
Newsweek, 155, 160, 162
Ngo Dinh Diem, 207
Nguyen Van Thieu, 211-212
Nhu, Madame, xxviii
Nicaragua, 260-264
Nicholson, Meredith, 27
Nigeria, 389
Nightline, 424, 447
Nixon, Richard M., 65, 77, 81, 94, 101, 105, 125, 143, 149-151, 154, 156, 160, 162-163, 172-176, 178, 180-182, 185, 214, 289, 301, 431-432; Nixon Doctrine, 430-431, 434
The No Spin Zone, 416
Nobel Peace Prize, 16, 184, 228, 266, 341, 369
Norris, Frank, xv
North (U. S.), 5, 8-9, 96
North Africa, 38, 432
North America, 265; North Americans, 261, 263
North American Free Trade Agreement (NAFTA), 430
North Carolina, 12, 441
North, Oliver, 261
North Vietnam, 95, 125, 206, 209-212, 223; Army of the

Republic of North Vietnam (ARVN), 113, 210
Northern Ireland, 228, 374, 379
Northern Ireland Peace Movement, 228
Norway, 38, 250, 432
Nuclear Non-Proliferation Treaty, 360
Nuremberg, Germany, 364
Oakland, California, 115, 143, 293
Oakland Hills, 293
Oberdorfer, Don, "U.S.-Soviet Relations on the Eve of the Revolution," 298-306
Occupational Safety and Health Administration (OSHA), 322
October Revolution, 343
Ohio, 10-11, 360
Oklahoma, 102, 412
Omaha, Nebraska, 94
Oman, 419
Office of Management and Budget (OMB), 284
Organization of the Petroleum Exporting Countries (OPEC), 421
Open Skies, 77
Open Society Institute, 214-215
Operation Barbarossa, 39
Operation Defensive Shield, 425
Operation PUSH (People United to Serve Humanity), 178
Operation Restore Hope, 359, 364
Oregon, 11, 115, 402-403
O'Reilly, Bill, "No Spin Zone," 416-422
O'Reilly Factor, 416
Ortega Saavedra, Daniel, "Peace in Central America," 260-265; also, xxx
Orwell, George, 169, 234-236, 238
Orwellian, 235

Osama bin Laden, 393, 417, 419, 421, 445, 450-452, 455
Osbourne, Ozzy, 324
Oslo Accords, 368
Owens Valley, California, 3
Political Action Committee (PAC), 350, 441
Pacino, Al, 446
Packard, David, 403
Paderewski, Ignace, xxvii
Paine, Thomas, 455
Pakistan, 76, 361, 377, 383, 396-398, 450, 452, 457
Palestine, 38, 40-41, 139, 425, 428, 452, 458, 460
Palestinian, 240, 242, 256-259, 423-429; Palestinians, 257-259, 379, 423, 426-429, 433, 460; Palestine Liberation Organization (PLO), 251, 253; Palestinian Authority, 379
Palm Beach County, Florida, 431, 437
Panama, 252; Panama Canal, 4, 252, 262
Paraguayan, 265
Paramount Studios, 45-46
Paris, France, 16-17, 66, 76-77, 115, 122, 125, 208, 210-211, 285, 350, 380
Paris Peace Accord, 211
Park, Chung Hee, 199
Pashtun, 396, 400
Pastore, John O., 127
Patients Bill of Rights, 412
Patton, George S., 244
PBS, 445-446, 448, 453
Pearl Harbor, 39, 199, 446, 453
Peary, Admiral Robert E., xxvii
Pentagon, 173, 214, 262, 265, 290, 451
Pentagon Papers, 154, 156, 164
People Power Revolution, 276-278, 280
Peres, Shimon, 254
Perkins, Frances, xxvii
Persian Gulf, 256, 293, 331, 335, 337, 367
Peshawar, Pakistan, 76

Phelan, James Duval, xiv
Philippines, 275-280
Piel, Gerard, 86-88, 90
Pinochet, Augusto, 265
Pissis, Albert, xiv
Poindexter, John M., 261
Poland, 38, 55-56, 58, 137, 255; Polish, 137
Polk, Willis, xiv
Polls, public opinion, 24-25, 112, 213, 323, 371, 452
Popular Movement for the Liberation of Angola (MPLA), 184
Population Registration Act, 269
Portugal, 146, 184
Poster, William Z., 58
Pot, Pol, 235
Potomac River, 244
Poulson, Norris, 66
Poverty, 84, 94-95, 97, 103, 109, 112, 145, 174, 238, 276, 278-279, 316, 321, 326-327, 329, 382, 386-387, 394, 425, 443
Powell, Colin, 288, 290, 302
Powers, Francis Gary, 76
Prague, Czech Republic, 341, 350
Press, 52, 56, 60-61, 63, 86, 106, 116, 155-157, 162-163, 165-166, 176, 205, 212, 228, 231, 263-264, 282, 337, 367, 381-382, 408, 440
Princeton University, xxvi
Progressive, 5, 31, 186, 401, 441, 466; Progressives, 25, 404, 466; Progressive Party, 5 (AKA Bull Moose Party)
Prohibition, 387
Protectionism, 246-247, 250, 337
Prudhoe Bay, 421
Prutkov, Kozma, 70
Puerto Ricans, 95
Purple Onion, 126
Pushkin, Alexander, 66, 73
Pyne, Joe, 128

Quayle, Dan, "The Vice President Speaks," 324-330; also, xxii, xxviii, 463
Quemoy, 81
Quezon, Manuel, xxvii
Radosh, Ronald, 56
Rahman, Sheik Omar Abdel, 453
Railroads, xxiv-xxv, xxxi, 25, 30, 404
Rainbow Coalition, 178
Raker Act, 5
Rambouillet, France, 375
Reagan, Ronald, "Address to The Commonwealth Club," 242-252; also, 45, 86, 106, 128, 182, 185, 224, 254, 256, 260, 265, 282-284, 298-304, 319, 335, 341-343, 430, 434
Rebozo, Bebe, 175
Reclamation Act, 4
Reclamation Service, 8
Reconstruction Finance Corporation, 31
Red Menace, 46-48, 50, 55, 58, 60, 87
Reed, Lou, 350
Rees, Stuart, 424
Reform Party, 430
The Republic, 14, 28, 35, 150, 152, 234
Republican National Committee, 158, 198
Republican National Convention, Chicago (1960), 105; San Francisco (1964), 106; Miami (1972), 171; Houston (1992), 430; Philadelphia (2000), 410
Republican Party, 5, 15, 24-25, 29-31, 49, 54, 58, 105-106, 108, 158, 168, 177, 185, 284, 289, 318, 323, 404, 409, 431; Republicans, 65, 111, 165, 176, 319-320, 322, 349, 404, 412, 430, 437, 441
Reston, Scotty, 207
Revere, Paul, 184
Reykjavik summit, 300-301
Rhodesia, 146

Rice, Condoleezza, 450
Right (politics), 185, 405
Rights of Future Generations, 307-308, 311-312
Rio de Janeiro, Brazil, 331, 363
Rio Grande River, 12
Riots, 93-94, 96, 189, 324-326, 328
Riyadh, Saudi Arabia, 254, 291
Robeson, Paul, xxvii
Robinson, Mary, 424
Rockefeller Commission, 200
Rockefeller, Nelson, 465
Rockies, 334
Rocky Mountain Institute, 331
Rodriguez, Richard, xxix
Rolling Stone, 318
Rolling Stones, 350
Roma, 350
Roman Holiday, 313
Romania, 49
Romanov Dynasty, 343
Rome, Italy, 120, 311, 409
Romero, Archbishop Oscar, 242
Rommel, Erwin, 38
Roosevelt Dam, 4
Roosevelt, Franklin Delano, "Present Public Problems," 24-37; also, xi, xvii-xviii, xxii, xxxi 39, 55, 59, 104, 258, 418, 464, 466
Roosevelt, Theodore, "The Doubtful Zone of Authority Between State and Federal Authority," 3-14; also, xviii, xxiii, xxx, 31, 37, 459, 464, 467
Rosenberg, Caroline, xxvi
Rosenberg, Julius, 57
Rossi, Angelo J., 24
Rostow, Walt, 206
ROTC, 209-210
Rough Riders, 6
Rowan, Dan, 127
Rowell, Chester, xv
Rubicon speech, 266, 272
Rudman, Warren, 453
Russia, 22, 48, 59-60, 62-63, 71, 73-74, 88-89, 91, 99,

102, 211, 235, 345, 381, 383, 386, 388-390, 432-433, 448
Russian, 62, 67, 70, 88-89, 91, 304-305, 341-342, 381, 433; Russian Army, 62, 70, 432; Russians, 70, 88, 91-92, 195, 239, 432
Rwanda, 368, 370, 374
Saavedra, Daniel Ortega, "Peace in Central America," 260-265; also, xxx
Sacramento, California, 130, 404, 406
Sacramento River, 11-12
Sadat, Anwar, 232, 240-241, 258
Saddam Hussein, 286-288, 293-294, 296, 331, 367-368, 445-446
Sakhalin Island, 299
Sakharov, Andrei, 226, 341
Salt River, 8, 11
Salt River Valley, Arizona, 4
Salton Sea, California, 9
Salvadoran, 263
San Francisco, 3, 5, 11, 15, 24, 49-50, 52, 66-67, 69-71, 73-74, 79, 89, 93-94, 106, 115, 126-127, 135, 155, 185, 254, 277, 280, 284, 307, 368-371, 405, 463; Ferry Building, xvii; Golden Gate Park, 93; Union Square, xx, xxiii; Neighborhoods: Castro, 281, Hunter's Point, 115; Nob Hill, 4; Streets: California, xix, Geary Street, xxiii, Market Street, 24
San Francisco Bay Area, 115, 464
San Francisco Chronicle, 4, 115, 223, 281, 375, 436
San Francisco State (Normal School) University, 116
Sandinistas, 254, 260-261, 264
Sandino, Augusto Cèsar, 262-263
Santayana, George, 121
Sarajevo, Bosnia and Herzegovina, 360

Saroyan, William, xxix
Saudi Arabia, 253-255, 257, 294, 398, 421, 446, 449; Saudis, 254, 288, 421
Savio, Mario, 433-434
Scandinavia, 443
Schroeder, Pat, 143
Schwarzenegger, Arnold, xxv
Schwarzkopf, Norm, 290
Screen Actors Guild, 45
Scripture, 178-179, 326
Scud missiles, 291
Seattle, Washington, 150, 387, 431; Seattle Harbor, 431
Seeger, Pete, 126
Selma, Alabama, 100, 102
Seoul, South Korea, 299
Serbia, 364, 380; Serbs. 360, 375; Serbian army, 375;
Service, John Stewart, 56, 59-60
Sesame Street, 369
Seward, William, 108
Shales, Tom, 300
Sharon, Ariel, 423, 427-429, 460
Shevardnadze, Eduard, 300-301, 304-305
Shiites, 287
Shilts, Randy, "The Politics of AIDS," 281-285; also, xxx
Short, Frank, 5-6
Shultz, George, "U.S.-Soviet Relations on the Eve of the Revolution," 298-306; also, 340, 343
Siberia, 22, 117
Sierra Club, 4, 414
Silicon Valley, California, 248, 404-405
Simi Valley, California, 318
Sin, Jaime Cardinal, 276
Sinai Peninsula, 132, 253
Sinatra, Frank, 66
Sinclair, Upton, xxvii
Sirhan, Sirhan, 116
Six-Day War, 132
Skilling, Jeffrey, xxix
Slovak Federation, 354
Smith, Kate, 126

Smoot-Hawley Tariff Act, 246
Smothers Brothers Comedy Hour, 126
Smothers, Tom, "Censorship and the New Freedoms," 126-130; *Smothers Brothers Comedy Hour,* 126
Social Security, 169, 171, 174, 412
Socialist Workers Party, 215-216
A Soldier Reports, 204
Solzhenitsyn, Alexander, 435
Somalia, 227, 314, 359-360, 364, 368
Somoza, Anastasio, 260, 263
Sontag, Susan, 433
Soros, George, 215
South (U. S.), 5, 8-10, 48, 95-96,
South Africa, 143, 146, 184, 226, 266-268, 270-274, 309, 351, 395, 410, 459; South African, 184, 194, 266, 268, 270-271
South America, 92, 312, 387
South Carolina, 12, 402
Southeast Asia, 138, 142, 287, 290, 390
Southern Baptists, 434
Southern California, 3, 9
Southern California Edison, 335
Southern Christian Leadership Conference, 178, 215
Soweto, 271
Spain, 62, 79
Sparta, 141
Special Forces, 431
Speck, Richard, 119
Spock, Benjamin, 94
Sproul, Robert Gordon, xxvii
St. Mary River, Montana, 12
Stalin, Josef, 63; Stalinists, 225
Stanford University, 70, 248
Stans, Maurice, 413
Stanton, Frank, 127
Starr, Kenneth, 409
Statue of Liberty, 181
Steele, Shelby, 330

Steffens, Lincoln, xxvii
Stegner, Wallace, xxix
Steinbeck, John, xxix
Steinberg, David, 127
Stephens, Henry Morse, xv
Stern, Philip, 173
Strategic Air Command, 76
Strategic Arms Limitation Talks (SALT), 185, 192, 195
Strategic Defense Initiative (SDI), (AKA "Star Wars"), 86, 346, 359
Sudan, 313
Suez Canal, 81
Sullivan, Leon Howard, 268
Sullivan Principles, 268
bin Sultan, Prince Bandar, "Peace in the Middle East", 253-259; also, 449
Sustainable development, 338, 363
Sweden, 138, 210, 432
Switzerland, 314, 405
Sydney Peace Prize, 424
Syria, 132, 135, 179, 255; Syrian, 132, 137, 139
Taba, 424, 427
Taft, William Howard, 5
Taft-Hartley Act, 410
Taiwan, 81
Tajik, 396
Takaki, Ron, xxviii
Taliban, 375, 392-399, 421, 452, 457
Tamraz, Roger, 413-414
Tan, Amy, xxix
Tanzania, 450
Tel Aviv, 291
Television, 106, 171, 176, 206, 208, 212, 269, 277, 319, 329, 414
Teller, Edward, "Peace Through Civil Defense," 85-92; also, xxii, xxx
Temple Mount, 423
Ten Commandments, 40, 45
Tenet Report 428-429
Tennessee, 12
Terrorism, 5, 58, 219, 254, 260, 382, 425, 429, 431, 446, 448,

451, 453, 455-457, 459-460;
Terrorists, 109, 238, 254,
359, 377, 383, 450-452, 457,
460-461
Texas, 52, 94, 119, 432, 437
Thailand, 389, 458
Thatcher, Margaret, 342
Thieu, President Nguyen Van,
211-212
Third World, 234, 238, 240,
274, 434, 458
Tho, Le Duc, 210
Thomas, Norman, xxvi
Thought police, 234
Three Gorges Dam, 4
Tillman Act, 409
Time, 25, 105, 204, 253, 331,
412
Title I, 174
Title IV, 174
Tobacco Road, 48
Tobruk, 38
De Tocqueville, Alexis, 186;
Tocquevillian, 458
Tolstoy, Aleksei, 70
Tonight Show, 392
Torricelli, Senator Robert, 419;
Torricelli Principle, 419
Treason, 58, 104
Treaty of Guadalupe Hidalgo,
419
Truman, Harry S., 55-57, 60,
64, 104, 107, 200, 206, 376
Trumbo, Dalton, 46
Tse-tung, Mao, 55
Tunis, Tunisia, 253
Tuolumne River, California,
xiv
Turkey, 18, 22, 380; Turks, 70;
Turkish, 71
Turkmenistan, 398
Tutu, Desmond, "Freedom
and Tolerance," 266-274;
also, xxii, xxix, 424
TV Guide, 206
Twain, Mark, 3, 130, 297
Twentieth Century Fox, 65
Tydings committee, 54, 59, 64
U-2 spy plane, 66, 76
UFOs, 370

Uganda, 199
Ul-Haq, Mohammed Zia, xxviii
Uncle Sam, 5, 8, 10
The Uncounted Enemy, 205
Unilateralism, 426, 456
The Union, 7, 11, 165, 243
Union for the Total
Independence of Angola
(UNITA), 184
Union of Concerned Scientists,
311
Union of Soviet Socialist
Republics (Soviet Union), 39,
45, 48, 53, 55, 57, 59, 63,
65-69, 71, 74-77, 81, 86, 99,
103, 110, 137-138, 142, 185-
195, 207, 243, 262, 265, 271,
289, 291, 298-306, 315, 340-
342, 345-346, 351, 381, 381,
463; Soviet Army (Red
Army), 55, 86, 341; Soviet
Empire, 53, 315; Soviets, 55,
66, 77, 82, 84, 86, 110, 192-
193, 234, 298, 302, 304, 341,
398
United Arab Emirates, 398
United Arab Republic, 135,
138
United Nations (UN), 6, 56, 60
63, 65-66, 68, 77, 80, 84,
131, 140, 146, 218, 228,
261-262, 266, 300, 307-309,
311-312, 314, 316, 346, 359-
373, 387, 390, 424, 428, 432,
435, 442; UN Charter, 80,
307-308, 312, 362, 373; UN
General Assembly, 77, 314;
UN Security Council, 266,
286, 316, 346, 364, 369, 428;
UN Children's Fund
(UNICEF), 313-316; UN
Commission for Sustainable
Development, 363; UN
Educational, Scientific, and
Cultural Organization
(UNESCO), 307, 370; UN
Human Rights Commission,
228; UN Population
Division, 432; UN Special

Commission (UNSCOM),
368
United States, 5, 7, 10, 15, 17,
20, 22, 30-31, 33, 46, 65, 67,
71, 74-78, 82, 84, 86, 88, 91,
101, 110, 116, 118-120, 124-
125, 132, 137-138, 141-142,
169, 171, 176, 178, 188-189,
191, 193-194, 198, 201, 211,
215, 242-245, 247, 249-250,
253-259, 261-265, 275, 278,
280, 288, 290, 299, 314, 316,
334, 343, 345, 361-362, 364,
370-372, 374, 376, 384-388,
397-399, 413, 418-421, 424,
435, 437, 451, 466
United States Agency for
International Development
(USAID), 123-124
United States Air Force, 76
United States Army, 47, 57,
127, 204-205, 207, 209, 290,
297, 371, 375, 417, 432, 452
United States Bureau of Labor
Statistics, 172
United States Congress, 5-6,
15, 20, 46, 57, 61-63, 85-86,
145, 149, 168, 170, 173-177,
184, 193, 195-196, 199, 203,
207-208, 211, 217, 247, 250,
253-254, 277, 279, 284, 291-
292, 320, 338, 385, 390, 404,
410-411, 438-439, 449
United States Department of:
Commerce, 149; Defense,
55, 146, 199, 214, 292, War
Department, 199; Energy,
332; Health, Education, and
Welfare, 174; Justice, 173,
216; Labor, 151, 168, 443;
State, 54, 56, 58-61, 63, 166,
173, 200, 214, 224, 230, 374,
393; Treasury, 200
United States House of
Representatives, 6, 45, 97,
143, 146, 148, 167, 169-170,
172, 198, 200, 280, 285, 296,
409, 411; House Armed
Services Committee, 143;
House Un-American

Activities Committee
(HUAC), 45-46
United States Information
Agency (USIA), 295
United States Marine Corps,
113, 119, 242, 253-254, 256,
290, 304, 359, 417
United States Navy, 62,179;
Naval Academy 408; Naval
Radiological Defense pro-
gram, 89
United States Peace Corps, 118
United States Senate, 15-16,
54, 57, 59, 62-63, 107, 116,
145-146, 168, 170, 194, 200,
214, 260, 274, 314, 322, 384,
404, 408-411
United States Seventh Fleet,
61-62, 81, 224
United States Supreme Court,
5-7, 13, 31, 94, 102, 104,
116, 160, 164, 176, 216, 409,
413, 437, 440, 451
University of: Alabama, 100;
California, Berkeley, 447;
California, Los Angeles, 103;
Maryland, 454; Oklahoma,
412; Texas, 119; Virginia,
424
Unocal, 398
Unsafe at Any Speed, 436
Unz, Ron, 404
UPI, 93
USA Today, 411
Ussuri River, 432
Ustí nad Labem, Czech
Republic, 350
Uzbekistan, 447
Valley Forge, Pennsylvania,
435
Vance-Owen Peace Plan, 360
Venezuela, 228, 230
VENONA, 57-58
Ver, General Fabian, 275
Vermont, 441
Vienna, Austria, 207
Viet Minh, 123
Vietcong, 98, 104, 109, 113-
115, 122-125, 210-211

Vietnam, 313; Refugees (boat
people), 223-225;
Vietnamese, 117, 124, 161,
204, 209, 223, 225-226, 231
Vietnam War, 94-95, 97-99,
103-104, 107, 109, 112-115,
117, 121-126, 143, 146-147,
161, 184-185, 194, 204-213,
223, 225, 231, 234, 251, 296,
464; National Liberation
Front, 98, 122
Virginia, 162, 170, 250, 295,
424, 449
Vladivostok, Russia, 192-193,
432
Voice of America, 47, 57, 400
Voting Rights Act, 94, 100, 103
Vyshinsky, Andrew, 63
Wadleigh, Henry Julian, 56, 60
Walcott, Earle Ashley, xxv
Wall Street, 5, 50
Wall Street Journal, 283, 331
Wallace, George C., "States'
Rights and Constitutional
Government," 100-104; also,
xxii, xxx, 148, 163
Wallace, Lurleen, 100
Wallace, Mike, 205
Ward, Stuart, 63
War on Poverty, 94, 112
War on terror, 445
Warren, Earl, xxvii
Warsaw, Poland, 39
Warsaw Pact, 234
Washington, D.C., 16, 30, 45,
49, 60, 115, 120, 122, 127,
147, 151, 155, 159, 162-164,
175, 180, 199, 208, 210, 216,
230, 253-254, 257, 278, 290,
300, 318, 383, 393, 401,
404-405, 411, 413, 415, 417,
419, 438, 440, 446, 449, 461,
465
Washington, George, 107, 117,
417
The Washington Post, 113, 154-
157, 159, 163, 167, 223, 269,
296, 298, 300, 401-402, 405,
441

The Washington Post-
Newsweek Company, 154-
155
Water, 3-9, 11-13, 40, 86, 174,
179, 233, 310, 315, 317, 334,
338-339
Watergate, 154-159, 161-163,
175, 177, 185, 198-199, 206,
234, 301
Waters, Maxine, 296
Watts riots, 94, 332
Waxman, Henry, 285, 320
Wayne, John, 175
Webster, Daniel, 7
Weinberger, Caspar, 174
Weinstock, Colonel Harris,
xxiv
Weizmann, Chaim, "The Jew
and the World Today," 38-
41; also, xxvii
Welch, Joseph, 57
Welch, Richard, 198, 203
Welfare, 27, 36, 71, 73, 115-
116, 145, 149, 171, 173-175,
182-183, 278, 321-322, 326-
329, 388, 418, 440, 442, 450
West (U. S.), 3, 5, 8-10, 24, 26,
29, 67, 113, 464
West Bank, 132, 240, 424-425,
427, 433
West Coast (U.S.), 49, 61, 113
West Nile virus, 456
West Virginia, 54, 151
Western civilization, 60, 432-
433
Western democracies, 68, 117,
131, 243-244, 281, 315, 393-
394, 430, 432-434, 441, 458
Western Europe, 62, 186, 188,
257, 265, 274, 299, 301, 378,
443
Western Hemisphere, 196,
251-252, 452
Westmoreland, General
William, "Vietnam in
Perspective," 204-213; also,
114
Wheeler, Benjamin Ide, xxiii-iv
White House, 4, 57, 65, 106,
156, 158, 162, 171, 173, 175,

181, 206, 224, 320, 335, 379, 409, 413-414, 418-419, 439, 449, 451
White Mountains, 10
White Paper, 38
White, Walter, xxvii
Whitman, Charles, 119
Whitman, Walt, 232-233
Why I Spied for the Communists, 56
Wickson, Edward, xv
Will, George, 440
Williams, Betty, 228
Wilshire, H. Gaylord, xiv
Wilson, James Q., 328
Wilson, Nancy, 127
Wilson, Woodrow, "The Peace Treaty and the Covenant of the League of Nations," 15-23; also, xviii, xxix, 5, 31, 37, 257
Wisconsin, 54, 101, 402, 408, 411, 442
Wolfowitz, Paul, xxviii
The Woman Warrior, 293, 296-297
Women's Environment and Development Organization, 168
Women's Equity Action League, 169
Women's Liberation Movement, 215-216
Woodstock, New York, 417
Woodward, Bob, 154
Woolf, Virginia, 295
Wordsworth, William, xxix
World Bank, 4, 338
World Health Organization (WHO), 372
World Heritage List, 370
World Intellectual Property Organization, 372
World Meteorological Organization, 372
World Meteorological Vigil System, 372
World Summit for Children, 315-317

World Trade Center, 359, 453-454
World Trade Organization (WTO), 387
World War I (First World War),(Great War), 15, 22, 32, 296, 300, 361, 365, 376; Allies, 15; Central Powers, 15, 22
World War II (Second World War), 47, 60, 68, 70, 85, 107, 126, 137, 147, 167, 186-187, 199, 202, 206, 213, 243-244, 246, 291-292, 294, 296, 300-302, 313-314, 342, 361, 376, 443, 456
World War III, 99, 235
Wright brothers, 79
Wyler, William, 48
Yale University, xxvi
Yalta summit, 55, 63
Yellowstone National Park, 370
Yeltsin, Boris, 346
Yemen, 452, 457
Yenan, 59
Yom Kippur War, 132, 185
Yosemite National Park, 3-4, 370
Young, C. C., xxvi
Young, John P., xxiii
Yousef, Ramzi, 453
Yugoslavia, 38, 353-354, 364, 375, 380
Zambia, 134
Ziegler, Ron, 175
Zion, 40; Zionist, 38
Zumwalt, Elmo, 185